LANDMARKS OF
MODERN BRITISH DRAMA

The Plays of
the Seventies

ALAN AYCKBOURN: JUST BETWEEN OURSELVES

HOWARD BRENTON: WEAPONS OF HAPPINESS

TOM STOPPARD: EVERY GOOD BOY DESERVES FAVOUR

PETER SHAFFER: AMADEUS

PETER NICHOLS: PASSION PLAY

SIMON GRAY: QUARTERMAINE'S TERMS

CARYL CHURCHILL: TOP GIRLS

in the same series

Landmarks of Modern British Drama
The Plays of the Sixties

LANDMARKS OF
MODERN BRITISH DRAMA

The Plays of
the Seventies

Alan Ayckbourn: Just Between Ourselves
Howard Brenton: Weapons of Happiness
Tom Stoppard: Every Good Boy Deserves Favour
Peter Shaffer: Amadeus
Peter Nichols: Passion Play
Simon Gray: Quartermaine's Terms
Caryl Churchill: Top Girls

with introductions by
Roger Cornish *and* Violet Ketels
Rutgers University   Temple University

METHUEN · LONDON and NEW YORK

This collection first published in 1986 simultaneously
in hardback and as a Methuen Paperback
in Great Britain by Methuen London Ltd,
11 New Fetter Lane, London EC4P 4EE,
and in the United States of America by Methuen Inc.,
29 West 35th Street, New York, NY 10001.

Printed in Great Britain
by
Hazell Watson & Viney Ltd
Member of the BPCC Group
Aylesbury, Bucks

British Library and Library of Congress Cataloging-in-Publication Data
Main entry under title:

Landmarks of modern British drama. Vol. 2.
The plays of the seventies.
1. English drama—20th century. I. Cornish, Roger, 1934- . II. Ketels, Violet.
PR1272.L35 1985   822'.914'08   85-18856
ISBN 0 413 59090 9 (Hbk)
ISBN 0 413 57270 6 (pbk)

Contents

General Introduction

The contemporary English drama, which everyone dates from 1956 and *Look Back in Anger*, established itself with a first rush of important dramatists – Osborne, Pinter, Wesker, Arden, Bond and Barnes, among others. At the end of the sixties, it gathered fresh momentum, producing what John Russell Taylor called 'the second wave' of new dramatists and a variety of fresh theatrical phenomena – including a new political drama, an alternative or 'Fringe' theatre, and the women's theatre movement.

In *Stages of the Revolution*, Catherine Itzin sums up the events that politicized a new generation of writers and strengthened the leftist tendencies of the 'first wave'. An eruption of global troubles makes 1968 a turning point, Itzin explains, citing the Soviet invasion of Czechoslovakia, the 'Prague Spring,' the student riots in Paris that spread to other countries, the riots at the Democratic Convention in Chicago, the peak of the Vietnam war protest, the assassinations of Martin Luther King and Robert Kennedy, the Six Day War in Israel, the dispatch of troops to northern Ireland, among other disquieting events.

Itzin singles out the radicalization of students as the most significant event for the theatre. For, by 1968, the war-baby generation was coming to political awareness 'of environmental plundering and pollution, cold-war imperialism, conspicuous consumption,' and the struggles of the third world. Social and economic disappointments at home exploded the materialist myth for the middle-class young. The response was 'disillusion, despair, pessimism – and anger' that turned into a movement of the political left, with Marx 'a symbol of the revolutionary transformation of society'. In the theatre all this was reflected in the subject matter of the new plays and in the proliferation of new theatre groups and forms. The Theatres Act of 1968, that ended censorship, was a historical footnote.

The Theatres and Theatre Organizations

Writing in 1985, we can say that vital English playwriting draws much of its energy from the vital English theatre, a theatre that many American theatre-lovers regard with envy. We don't propose here to decry American theatre, which is, in many ways, healthier than it has ever been. The one hundred and fifty or so non-profit professional theatres that now dot the American map dwarf in number and quality what any American would have envisioned two decades ago. But when Americans regard theatre at its highest reaches – always excepting the musical theatre – they see in England a glory they seek in vain at home.

In the West End, London's Broadway, theatre producers never cry anything but poor. Costs continually rise and the subsidised theatres skim off so many good new scripts that the commercial producer feels hard put to find worthy new plays. Nevertheless, an American looks at the West End theatre guide and sees a choice of eighteen straight plays. He turns to the Broadway guide and finds twelve. Worse, five of the twelve are English (one Shakespeare, the rest modern) and of the native American plays two have been premiered in London! The West End's major advantage over Broadway, of course, is its relatively modest costs. By general estimate it costs three to five times as much to mount a play on Broadway as in the West End. (This can't be marked down simply to national wage differentials. The average American worker earns about 50% more than his English counterpart, but in the theatre, American scales range from 100% to 400% above English standards.) So the West End producer, hard put though he may be, faces less economic discouragement than his Broadway counterpart. He also faces a less daunting critical atmosphere. It is commonly assumed that if the *New York Times* dislikes a Broadway play, it dies. London has ten dailies (to New York's four) and no single bad review presents such a threat. As a result, there are always more plays on view in the West End than on Broadway.

A major force behind the upsurge of English playwrights in the seventies was the rise of the Fringe or alternative theatre, London's answer to New York's Off- and Off-Off Broadway. The Fringe includes theatre in pubs, in cellars, in tents, in churches, and at lunch-time. Its productions are rough, not smooth, inexpensively mounted, of course, and frequently aimed at offending average sensibilities (though, ironically, people of average sensibilities tend to avoid the Fringe as they have always avoided the avant-guarde).

Every historian of the Fringe acknowledges that it is an American offspring. The Fringe was born in 1968 when Jim Haynes, the American who had founded Edinburgh's Traverse Theatre Club five years before, opened the Arts Lab, a model for anti-establishment theatre, in London. In 1968 another American, Charles Marowitz, who had worked with Haynes in Edinburgh and with Peter Brook on the 1974 Theatre of Cruelty season, started the Open Space in a London cellar. And, also in 1968, American Ed Berman founded Inter-Action, a community arts and with Peter Brook on the 1964 Theatre of Cruelty season, Ambience Lunch Hour Theatre Club, the Almost Free Theatre, and Dogg's Troupe.

Inspired by these American expatriate innovations, young English artists started a host of venturesome companies, such as the Pip Simmons Theatre Group (1968), John McGrath's 7:84 Theatre Company (1971), and the Black Theatre Cooperative (1979). The Fringe had become a self-renewing main force in English theatre.

Among the central tendencies of the Fringe may be cited experimental physicality (for which the English theatre also owes a debt to such American influences as the Living Theatre and Cafe La Mama); performance art as an alternative to literary, narrative theatre; anti-establishment politics; and, most important to us, the development of new plays and playwrights. (John Elson in his book, *Post-War British Theatre*, points out that Fringe theatres often choose new scripts as a way to attract Arts Council grants.) Thus, the Portable Theatre produced new plays by David Hare (its founder with Tony Bicât), Howard Brenton, and Snoo Wilson. Joint Stock Company premiered plays by Hare, Howard Barker, Caryl Churchill, and Barrie Keeffe. By finding a home on the Fringe, a young playwright could produce a body of work and could mature as an artist, despite (or because of) being unwelcome in the establishment theatre.

In addition to the Fringe, three organizations have been critical to the current and future health of the new drama – the English Stage Company at the Royal Court, the Royal Shakespeare Company, and the National Theatre. Of the English Stage Company, we do not add much beyond what we have said in the Introduction to the companion volume of plays from the sixties, except to say that in the seventies and eighties it remained the lodestar for aspiring young playwrights. Not ony did the Royal

Court premiere major plays by such as David Storey, Christopher Hampton, David Hare, Howard Brenton, Edward Bond and Caryl Churchill, but it continued to do the equally important job of premiering minor, even apprentice, plays be emerging playwrights.

During the period covered by this volume the theatrical flagships, the Royal Shakespeare Company and the National Theatre, each achieved the added stability, even majesty, of splendid new quarters, and each began to make greater impact as a producer of new drama.

In 1973, Peter Hall, having stepped down at the RSC, replaced Director Laurence Olivier at the helm of the National Theatre. Under Hall, the National finally moved to its permanent home in 1976. Although John Osborne has called the National's spectacular South Bank complex 'Colditz on Thames,' such aesthetic carping did not keep audiences from crowding its three theatres, the Olivier, the Lyttleton, and the Cottesloe. In an average month, nine different plays were performed on National stages, while numerous lectures, script readings, and short plays were presented in lobbies and on forestages before the main production curtain times. No wonder the National became the tourist's first stop and the commercial theatre managers' most dreaded competition.

For a time, led by Hall's former protégé, Trevor Nunn, the Royal Shakespeare Company continued to stage its main London work at the Aldwych, a West End fixture since 1905. In 1977, the company leased a 200-seat theatre, the Warehouse, where it could present new scripts, including those transferred from the Other Place, its experimental stage in Stratford. In 1982 the RSC finally moved into London's Barbican Centre, Western Europe's biggest arts complex, where the company now stages Shakespeare and the occasional modern play in the 1,100 seat Barbican Theatre – and a repertoire of new plays and revivals in a 180-seat studio, the Pit. The RSC had become, in the words of Nunn's co-director, Terry Hands, 'the biggest theatre organization in the world', its four auditoria – two in London, two in Stratford – liable to hold 'on any given night more than 5,000 people'. And in 1984 the RSC announced plans to add yet a third Stratford stage, the Swan.

Between them, the two national companies were receiving about ten million pounds annually from the British Arts Council (a subsidy greater than the total allocated for all theatre in the United

States in the 1986-7 National Endowment budget proposed by the White House). Even so, both companies feared funding cuts that might undermine their lavish production standards. In early 1985 Peter Hall was forced to close the Cottesloe, the smallest of the National's three theatres but the one most associated with new work, because of reductions in the Arts Council's support.

Without substantial subsidies, the two national theatres could not have made a major impact as producers of new plays. But both could point to many premieres of major plays by established authors, which, on the trickle-down theory, probably encouraged other theatres to premiere lesser known playwrights. The National premiered Bond, Gray, Brenton, Pinter and Shaffer among others. The RSC premiered Peter Nichols, David Edgar, Caryl Churchill, Pam Gems, and Stephen Poliakoff, in the course of staging about five new plays a year, not a negligible record for a theatre dedicated to Shakespeare.

The two national companies also supported dramatists by commissioning them to prepare new versions of classics and foreign language plays, an activity that, in the United States, is more likely to be assigned to professional translators, poets, and scholars (when new versions are commissioned at all). Michael Frayn, Christopher Hampton, Bond, Stoppard, and Brenton are among the major playwrights who received such commissions. The practice lends to the playwright's craft an aura of professionalism and intellectuality not often felt in America.

Perhaps more important than the number of new plays the prestigious subsidized companies produced was the encouragement their very existence offered to the creation of large plays that demand big casts and epic staging, plays like *Amadeus*, Edgar's adaptation of *Nicholas Nickleby*, or Peter Barnes' *Bewitched*. In the United States the playwright learns early to cut his cloth to suit the circumstances of modest theatres or watch his plays go undone. In professional journals, American theatres frequently advertise that they are willing to examine new scripts only if they fall within certain limits – one set, cast of eight or less. But the RSC and the National Theatre were able to allow English playwrights to dream beyond the kitchen sink. And beyond the sink and its domestic detritus stands the great subject of the contemporary English drama, politics.

The Politics

A major difference between English and American dramatists is the amount of time the former devote to political issues. Benedict Nightingale, an English critic on loan to the *New York Times* in 1984, saw the difference in terms of pathology – English writers investigating socio-political pathologies, and Americans digging still into family pathology, the Freudian pit.

Such judgments must always be taken in relative terms, of course. According to Marxist analysis, distinctions between political and non-political drama are illogical. Every play is political, if only by its tacit support of the status quo when it ignores politics. (Or, as Ionesco put it in *Un homme en question*, to claim to be apolitical is an act of politics.) Some major English dramatists do steer resolutely clear of overt political references in their work, Ayckbourn and Pinter, for example. (Pinter finally entered politics with *One for the Road* in 1984, but he approached the subject of state oppression so obliquely that one cannot tell if his brutish political policeman comes from the right or the left, Chile or the GDR.)

Even if we assume that only those plays are political which overtly confront political issues, contemporary English dramatists do, indeed, politicize many of their plays. Government officials, declared radicals, and identifiable party partisans abound as characters. Electioneering, government repression, and revolutionary plotting provide many of the story lines. And a significant number of the playwrights publicly espouse specific political positions, usually on the left. One strong demonstration of the perceived superiority of the British dramatist in the political realm was the 1984 commissioning of an English dramatist (Trevor Griffiths) by an American organization (the Williamstown Theatre Festival) to write a play about violent left-wing American youth in the Vietnam era (*Real Dreams*).

Since Osborne, Arden, and Wesker, of course, the critique of England's socio-political system has been a strong element in the drama. But the end of the 1960s saw a sharpening of the political emphasis, due partly to the arrival of a generation of playwrights too young to share the patriotic afterglow of World War II, and partly to the growth of a new kind of theatre, the Fringe. Fringe theatres like 7:84 Theatre Company and Welfare State, founded on partisan principles, were naturally more receptive to radical political plays than commercial producers likely to regard anti-establishment political drama as a double threat – to their own stations and values, and to box-office revenues.

At any rate, from 1968 to 1973, a number of politically-minded, talented playwrights emerged – Howard Brenton, Howard Barker, David Edgar, Trevor Griffiths, and Caryl Churchill especially prominent among them – and continued to spearhead political drama into the eighties. And they tended to be leftist.

English theatre people joke that there are no political dramatists of the right. William Gaskill, artistic director at the Royal Court during the late sixties, is reputed to have said that he would produce a good right-wing play if someone would write one. In 1984, Ian McKellen took the position that Tom Stoppard had finally done that with *The Real Thing*, in which Stoppard demolishes the pretences of a self-proclaimed anti-missile demonstrator and victim of the English class system by showing him to be totally deficient in both acumen and intellectual honesty. Stoppard is probably the outstanding dramatic partisan of conservative politics. Even before *The Real Thing*, in *Every Good Boy Deserves Favour* and his teleplay, *Professional Foul* (1977), Stoppard attacked repression behind the Iron Curtain. In other plays, Stoppard attacks targets which the English left would defend, such as trade unions and third world governments. Thus, in *Night and Day* he depicts the staunch trade unionist as a dishonest careerist and he makes the black ruler of a newly emerged African state a murderous tyrant.

Like Stoppard, other playwrights, including David Mercer with *The Monster of Karlovy Vary* (1979), David Pownall with *Master Class* (1983), and Howard Brenton with *Weapons of Happiness*, have depicted the failures of socialism in the Soviet Union and its satellites. In *Master Class*, for example, Pownall demonstrates the tendency of Communism to enslave the spirit by showing Stalin bully Prokofiev and Shostakovich into composing their music to suit the purposes of the state. But when the same writers deal with British political life, they usually swing back to the left by making the class system, colonialism, or some other right-wing failure the target. Thus, in *Motocar* (1977), Pownall's play about the last days of English rule in an African country, all the English characters, now mere souvenirs of imperialism, are bigoted or blind; only the African, Motocar, who may be mad, earns our sympathy.

So it holds that, for the most part, political drama is left-wing drama. In that field, the unquestioned leader is Edward Bond. Starting with *The Pope's Wedding* (1962) and *Saved* (1965), Bond has always expressed contempt for capitalism. But those early realistic plays focus on the empty domestic lives of poor young people, emphasizing their limited powers of understanding and communication so that numerous critics considered Bond a disciple of Pinter. With *Early Morning* and *Narrow Road to the Deep North* (both 1968), however, Bond widened his canvas to include every stratum of society, especially the power structure. He also broke forcefully out of the boundaries of realism into satiric or cruel theatricalism which, in every major play, dramatizes the need to overthrow the status quo and, in some, like *The Bundle* (1978) shows the way to do it – violent revolution.

Bond's genius is clearest in his ability to make his political point with striking theatrical metaphors. In *The Bundle*, Bond's hero, Wang, faced with the choice between caring for an abandoned baby and pursuing his revolutionary duty, chooses duty and throws the baby into a river. Bond makes the baby a bundle wrapped in a white sheet which unfurls as Wang hurls the infant. For a split second the stage is totally dominated by the bright strip of cloth, and the climatic decision becomes a visual image fixed firmly in the mind of the audience.

Bond augments his published scripts with polemical poetry or prose in support of his socialist vision. So serious and fervent are these non-dramatic writings that some critics believe his politics undermine his dramatic talent. Whether this is so or not, Bond's commitment to using the theatre in the service of a socialist revolution is uncompromising.

The highly political work of Howard Brenton and Caryl Churchill is discussed elsewhere in this volume. But a word should be devoted here to several other left-leaning playwrights who make political statements in their plays.

David Hare is closely associated with Howard Brenton, having collaborated with him both as co-writer and director. *Brassneck*, their first major collaboration, is Brentonian in effect — a turbulent canvas in which the corruption of British politics and business overflows the picture frame. But Hare's own plays like *Knuckle* (1974), *A Map of the World* (1983), and *Plenty* (1978), depend on a much more austere style that is literate and witty. In those plays, sophisticated and privileged young men and women embody the decay of English might and morals and cry out for a higher set of goals than their society offers. In *Fanshen* (1975), Hare attempted something very different. Working from William Hinton's study of a Chinese village during the first two years after the Communist revolution and using a semi-Brechtian theatricality, Hare did what few of his contemporaries have tried: he pictured a post-revolutionary socialist society moving forward in a positive, humane way. *Pravda*, also co-written with Brenton, is a comic-grotesque critique of the capitalist press, where journals and journalists are bought and sold at the whim of monstrous tycoons. When it opened at the National Theatre in 1985, it was said, incidentally, to be the last large-scale play the National could afford to mount – because of cuts in subsidy.

Trevor Griffiths is as well known for his television and film writing (*Reds*, 1981) as for his stage writing. Griffiths claims that all his work 'is political in one way or another', and he is considered solidly Marxist. In two of his plays, *Occupations* (1970) and *The Party* (1975), Griffiths dramatized the intellectual debate about the ways and means that the left must choose if it is to triumph. In *Occupations*, the Italian Communist intellectual Gramsci and the Comintern agent Kabak argue the proper strategy to pursue in an auto strike. Gramsci seeks to protect the workers from unnecessary hardship, and Kabak demands the subordination of immediate human considerations to the long term – largely theoretical – interests of the international Communist movement. In *The Party*, a professor and a Trotskyite organizer (the latter played by Sir Laurence Olivier in his farewell stage performance) engage in a theoretical debate of a size and complexity that would be likelier at a real party gathering than in a theatre. By probing intellectual and ethical questions at the heart of Marxist action so fully, Griffiths challenges his audience to regard the theatre as a forum for ideas rather than a haven for relaxation and distraction.

David Edgar is best known as the adaptor of the RSC's *Nicholas Nickleby* (1980), perhaps the outstanding theatre event of the eighties. *Nicholas Nickleby* is a graphic display of laissez-faire capitalism at its most cruel, especially in the Yorkshire school exploitation of Smike and other abandoned boys, and in the machinations of the steely financier, Ralph Nickleby. It is ironic that a production of such clearly anti-capitalist insinuations (however balanced by sunny moments) should have sold out on Broadway at one hundred dollars a ticket. There were few abandoned boys in the audience.

Even before *Nicholas Nickleby*, Edgar had established himself as the most prolific of the left-leaning dramatists in the second wave. From 1970 to 1977, taking advantage of the new opportunities offered by the proliferation of Fringe theatres, Edgar managed to secure productions of about five new plays each year. Some were quickly forgotten, but *Destiny*, which the RSC premiered at the Aldwych in 1977, established his reputation. In it Edgar anatomizes England's neo-fascist potential – a recurrent nightmare of the left – and shows the monied classes manipulating the ordinary people of England by racist and nationalist appeals. In 1983, Edgar won the London Theatre Critics' Best New Play Award for *Maydays*, a massive epic examining the failure of an English leftist to remain true to his beliefs and contrasting him with a Russian dissident who refuses to be co-opted by the English right even though he has been a victim of Stalinist persecutions.

Like Edgar, Howard Barker makes much of the criminal capacities of the establishment. In *That Good Between Us* (1977) he puts England in the grip of right-wing death squads of the sort most of his audience would associate with Argentina or El Salvador. In *Victory* (1983) he attacks the capitalist mentality by painting seventeenth-century English society as greedy and treacherous. Like Brenton and Bond, Barker ignores the limits of ordinary realism, manipulating time, space, and characters freely in order to suggest the complexity of an entire social order.

One approach to expressing distaste for the social order has been called by Richard Grenier, in the American conservative journal, *Commentary*, 'treason chic'. Grenier refers to a number of English plays and films of the eighties which take a sympathetic, even affectionate view of Englishmen who became Soviet agents during the early years of the cold war. Alan Bennett's BBC-TV play, *An Englishman Abroad*, presents traitor Guy Burgess as a good-humoured, charming, quintessential Englishman, content to live in exile as long as he can replace his Moscow drab with suits from Savile Row.

Hugh Whitemore's West End and Broadway success *Pack of Lies* (1983) deals with the Lonsdale spy case of the sixties. However, the drama focuses not on treason but on the dishonesty which an ordinary English family must practise in order to help MI5 catch spies. Espionage against England is merely a circumstance allowing Whitemore to explore the questionable morality of deceiving spies in order to catch them. In Julian Mitchell's *Another Country* (1981), also a 'treason chic' play, Guy Burgess is thinly disguised as public school boy Guy Bennet. Homosexual, careless, self-indulgent, Guy doesn't have a political thought in his head. But when the system of privilege and power that dominates public school life persecutes him, in part for his homosexuality, in part for his individuality, Guy recognizes the system as his mortal enemy and pledges his life to its destruction. As the light fades on the last scene, Guy picks up *Das Kapital* and begins his political training. By the logic of *Another Country*, treason is the natural response to the realities of an English education.

English political drama of the seventies and eighties is overlaid with pessimism. In *The Seventies: The Decade that Shaped the Future* (New York: Stein and Day, 1981), Christopher Booker describe the decade as the 'death throes' of English optimism, the time in which the belief in progress that had informed British life in the years since World War II seemed no longer tenable. By and large, these political plays reflect such a loss of optimism. While they certainly express antipathy towards the enemies of the left and sympathy for its goals, they show little faith that these goals will ever be achieved in England. Indeed, many of them suggest that England will regress into neo-fascist repression rather than progress toward socialist enlightenment.

In Stephen Poliakoff's *Strawberry Fields* (1977), right-wing terrorists seek a nationalist revival that will free England from such perceived enemies as blacks and leftists. In Act One, the terrorist leader, a woman, kills a policeman who gets in her way. At the play's climax, she shoots young Nick, a hitchiker unwillingly involved in her plans. She leaves Nick to die on the site of former English glories, a Wars of the Roses battlefield; the crypto-fascists are victorious in a mini-war of succession. So are the fascists in Howard Brenton's *The Churchill Play* (1974), which predicts an England where workers and their allies languish and die in right-wing concentration camps. David Edgar's *Destiny* climaxes with the election success of the rightist-racist Nation Forward Party.

When the plays don't warn of the threat of fascism, they bemoan the fecklessness of the left. In the Hare/Brenton collaboration *Brassneck*, the Labourite union leader sells out his political faith and enters the House of Lords. In Brenton's version of *Macbeth*, *Thirteenth Night* (1981), a radical socialist becomes Prime Minster of England only to turn into as bloody a tyrant as any Hitler or Stalin. In Griffiths' *The Party*, England's revolutionary intellectuals are co-opted by the bourgeois establishment, which dulls the edge of a rebellion with prestigious jobs and material bonuses. In David Mercer's *Then and Now* (1979), a miner's son comes out of World War II full of high hopes for a better, fairer England. Thirty years later, he is a wealthy physician who has replaced his interests in politics and society with a sex obsession. Mercer pictures a middle-aged England too tired to carry a political banner.

Edward Bond, of course, has tried to keep his faith in the triumph of socialism. In such works as *The Bundle* and *Restoration* (1981), Bond finds it possible to finish on an optimistic note. In *The Bundle* a new society is born in Asia, and in *Restoration* a new social consciousness is born in eighteenth-century England. In *The Worlds* (1979), however, the first Bond play since *Saved* to be set in contemporary England, revolution is a total failure. A group of radical activists stage a kidnapping that, like the kidnapping in Brenton's *Magnificence*, serves only to weaken their position and strengthen that of the monied establishment. It is as if a confrontation with the English condition of his own time robs Bond of his confidence in the possibility of growth and change. He seems to imply what Wesker had implied in *Chips with Everything* twenty years before: *they* will always find a way to win.

So it is with many contemporary English dramatists; they cherish within themselves a vision of a new society – socialist, classless, benign, peaceful. But they can't find within themselves the faith that it will happen in their England, which seems to them to have outlived its capacity for growth and achievement. As Itzin quotes Howard Barker, '. . . it is very difficult to be an optimistic socialist in England'.

Yet there *is* political optimism in the English drama today. It is in the politics of feminism.

Women's Theatre

In the judgment of Michelene Wandor, who probably deserves the title of chief theoretician of women's theatre in England, the contemporary feminist movement in England began about 1969 or 1970 with a squadron of women playwrights unparalleled in English (or American) theatre history.

Of course, the vital women dramatists of the English seventies and eighties wouldn't claim to tread where no women have gone before. There is no Margaret Thatcher of dramatists. There are precursors, important among them Ann Jellicoe and Shelagh Delaney. In her first play, *A Taste of Honey* (1958), Delaney created a model for the scruffy teenagers who would become so prominent in the dramatic population of the sixties and seventies. And by pairing young Jo with a black sailor, Delaney pointed to a looming problem – the changing nature of England's racial make-up – which few Britons were talking about in 1958. *A Taste of Honey* was a hit in London and New York, but Delaney drifted away from writing for the stage. So she may be best considered as part of the Osborne-inspired revolution of the late fifties rather than as a force in a rising tide of women dramatists.

Instrumental in the extraordinary success of Delaney's play was the pre-eminent English theatre woman of the fifties, Joan Littlewood. By her leadership of Theatre Workshop (discussed at length in the companion volume on the sixties), she set an example of the group identity, improvisational method, and free theatricality that characterize much of women's theatre today.

Though she never matched her great success of 1961, *The Knack*, Ann Jelicoe has remained productive as writer, director, and teacher. Jellicoe's *The Sport of My Mad Mother* (1958) was the first play by an English woman to reach the main stage of the Royal Court. And by co-directing with George Devine, Jellicoe also became the first female director at the Royal Court, where she thereafter staged a number of plays, including her own *The Knack* and *Shelley* (1965). Lately Jellicoe has exemplified a quality often found in feminist theatre, the incorporation of performing group contributions into the emerging play text. In 1984, for example, as playwright and director of *The Western Women*, an historical pageant of the Civil War in the West Country, she directed a hundred and seventy-two residents of Lyme Regis, working their improvised scenes into the final script.

To the extent that it is a movement, women's theatre can be analyzed in political terms. Wandor, who is both a playwright and an anthologizer of *Plays by Women* as well as a theorist, believes that feminist theatre converts what men see as private or domestic subject matter into political drama. Thus, women's political theatre (private) runs opposite to men's political theatre (public): '. . . in the early seventies, feminism, in the name of a new "politics" was drawing attention to personal life, while the socialist theatre of that time, also in the name of a new "politics" was taking attention away from personal life'.

Wandor identifies three political viewpoints in the plays of women writers: radical feminism, which regards males as the enemy, all of whose values are suspect; bourgeois feminism, which simply seeks to put women on an equal footing in the world men have made; and socialist feminism, which transcends a narrow focus on women by taking aim at the economic and political system under which both men and women live. Such a scheme offers a handy glass for examining plays by women playwrights, but, needless to say, few plays fit perfectly into such categories. For example, *Top Girls* dramatizes all three feminist positions. Marlene is a bourgeois feminist who, playing by male rules, has aimed at men's prizes and won them. Her sister, the socialist-feminist, sees the system Marlene embraces as totally rotten and regards their father as one of its victims while Marlene remembers him as a wife-exploiter. The radical feminists from history in Act One present women as the victims of men who were eager to subjugate them under any and all circumstances.

To note the progress of the women's theatre movement is not to say that women have overcome in the English theatre. In 1983, the Conference of Women Directors and Administrators surveyed English theatres to clarify the status of women in the field. For women dramatists, the situation was far from rosy. In the 1982-83 production year, only 11% of the plays produced by publicly-funded theatres were written by women. Figures were brighter for women administrators and directors, especially the former, who, as in the United States, find men more willing to share the daily grind of organizing, cajoling, fund raising, and paper pushing than the glamour jobs of 'doing art'.

The Royal Court has taken important initiatives in developing women playwrights through its Young Writers Festival and a 'Woman Live' festival, as well as by its regular encouragement of new work. Sarah Daniels, whose *Masterpieces* (1983) is a controversial play of the radical feminist caste (the play's heroine pushes a man to his death under the wheels of a train), echoed the male writers of the fifties and sixties when she said that the Royal Court's rejection of her first play was none the less so humane that it gave her the courage to become a playwright.

However, the first port for women's plays has been women's

theatres. Of the more than a dozen women's theatres operating in 1984, two were pre-eminent: Monstrous Regiment and the Women's Theatre Group.

Women's Theatre Group made its name touring London schools and youth clubs with *My Mother Says I Never Should* (1974), a group-created piece dealing with teenagers and birth control. In the next years the company mounted group-created works on such topics as a women's strike for equal pay (*Out! On the Costa del Trico*) and images of female appearance (*Pretty Ugly*). In 1979 the group began working with texts by outside writers such as Elizabeth Bond and Jacqui Shapiro. But the WTG retains its identity as a touring collective.

Monstrous Regiment, born in 1975, is not devoted to female work exclusively. Not only does it include a minority of male actors, but it has turned to men for scripts. With Susan Todd, David Edgar took part in group explorations and then wrote *Teendreams* (1979), which traces the twenty-year odyssey of an upperclass innocent to feminist awareness. The company's desire to work with men can be attributed to the fact that Monstrous Regiment is socialist as well as feminist. This also accounts for the strong historical thread in their work, which has approached such topics as the women of the 1870 Paris Commune (*SCUM*, Claire Luckham and Chris Bond, 1975) and witchcraft in the seventeenth century (*Vinegar Tom* from workshop by Caryl Churchill, 1976).

A salient characteristic of women's groups is the co-operative effort that cuts across job specializations. All sorts of people contribute to decisions that in the theatre of the old male stamp would be made by designated authorities – directors, designers, especially writers. Much of the credit for this development belongs to Joan Littlewood, who inveighed against the authority of individual genius and encouraged her actors to contribute to the text. The conservative student of the drama will say such a tendency undermines the writer, who always works best as a solitary creator. Playwrights Churchill and Luckham would argue that the support of the collaborative process outweighs the loss of autonomy. (Such autonomy is a chimera anyway, as any dramatist who has worked with a wilful director can testify.)

Doubtless affected by the women's theatre movement, plays written by men project a changed image of women, their powers, their potential for growth and change. Often in David Hare's work a woman dominates, sometimes in her neurosis, as in the television play *Dreams of Leaving*, but more often in her greater insight into social truth, as in *Plenty* or *Knuckle*. Recently, Edward Bond has made women the political visionaries in worlds controlled by blind men. Rose alone understands the events in *Restoration* as they occur. In Ted Whitehead's *Old Flames* (1975) three female characters sum up the case against men: mother, first wife, and second wife invite an exploitative male to dinner and make him the main course, which they voraciously devour. The leading feminist play by a male playwright is probably Willy Russell's *Educating Rita*, in which a young blue-collar wife sheds both her ignorance and the husband who lacks the wit to let her grow. Her dauntless, venturesome spirit is clearly preferable to the cheerless erudition of the professor who educates her.

Among the many English women playwrights, the unquestioned leader is Caryl Churchill, who is discussed in more detail in the introduction to *Top Girls*. She easily transcends the patronizing praise, first among women. No contemporary English male playwright, nor American, aside from Neil Simon, has had three plays running simultaneously in New York, for example, as did Churchill in 1983 with *Fen*, *Top Girls*, and *Cloud Nine*.

Pam Gems encapsulates in her career the pattern of gradual awakening often depicted in feminist drama. Born in 1925, the generation of Osborne, Shaffer, and Nichols, she lived the traditional life of wife and mother before beginning to write for television in the sixties and the stage in the seventies. She turned out a flood of plays, twenty in ten years, and she is still writing. Some critics question her feminist commitment. In *Dusa, Fish, Stas and Vi* (1976), Fish commits suicide over failed love. In *Queen Christina* (1977), although the title character fights hard against men for her throne, she finally begs a man to get her with child. Like Churchill, Gems is not a polemical feminist, but a playwright who happens to be a woman. A member of the Women's Playhouse Trust, she believes, however, that the success of women in theatre requires theatres dominated by women.

Louise Page is the new generation. Deciding to be a writer at five, she was only twenty-six when *Salonika* (1982) won her the George Devine Award at the Royal Court. By 1984 she was moving fast with *Golden Girls*, a play for the RSC about female Olympians, and *Real Estate*, which, after its London opening in May 1984, crossed the Atlantic to the Arena Stage, Washington. In *Real Estate*, the men bake the cakes and worry about the children; the women – mother and daughter – hustle real estate sales with a drive that threatens their marriages and relationships. Like Churchill, Page seems to say that succeeding like a man means failing like a man, too.

Like Page, Catherine Hayes digs into the minefields between mother and daughter (as well as sister and sister) in *Skirmishes* (1982). Following its successful British premiere at the Hampstead theatre, the play's well-received Manhatten Theatre Club production helped to make 1983 the year New Yorkers began to register the rise of English women dramatists. In *Not Waving* (1983) Hayes presents a middle-aged comedienne who, having failed as both mother and lover, defies life to do her any more damage. Her eighteen-page comedy monologue is a striking theatre metaphor for the dying animal joking through the flames.

The Qualities of the Plays

The outstanding plays of the seventies and eighties defy common labels, but they share a number of characteristics important to note. First among them is violence expressed in obscene language and shocking images as well as in physical action.

While most English playwrights still observe a certain gentility and restraint, a good number have jettisoned what once seemed necessary to stage decorum. Their language is tough and direct. They seem to have declared war on euphemism. In *Cloud Nine* characters soliloquize about homosexual intercourse and female masturbation. Such sexually explicit dialogue in plays by a Churchill or a Brenton no longer appears to shock audiences, a sign of how difficult it is for an artist to keep ahead of the times. If language shock is still possible, perhaps it is only when a polished writer like Simon Gray, who seems to be working in a familiar tradition such as comedy of manners, suddenly has one of his sophisticated characters break decorum. In *Otherwise Engaged*, when Simon Hench describes fidelity as 'more than a suck and a fuck with the likes of you,' audiences are likely to gasp.

On the other hand, explicit physical violence, which has become equally common, retains its shock value. Howard Brenton's plays always turn on violent action. In *Sleeping Policemen* (1983), written in collaboration with native English black dramatist Tunde Ikoli, an upwardly mobile young Englishman responds to the vandalizing of his flat by slitting the throat of a half-mad street innocent with a razor. Were he arraigned for this stage violence as he was for the homosexual rape in *The Romans in Britain*, Brenton would surely offer the same defence Bond offered for the baby stoning in *Saved*: the madness of contemporary life is the greater obscenity, the greater crime, and it is that madness the play indicts.

Outstripping even Brenton and Bond in the violence of his imagery is David Rudkin. Having already introduced a ritual beheading into his powerful first play, *Afore Night Come* (1962), Rudkin went on, in *The Sons of Light* (1976) and *The Triumph of Death* (1981), to use anal impalement as a symbol of power, lust, and self-abasement – and incidentally provoke the question as to whether it is the ugly physical life of these two remarkable plays or their complex staging requirements that have kept them from major productions.

The temptation to reject the violence of these neo-Jacobean playwrights as gratuitous sensationalism, a sign of creative poverty, should not be indulged too quickly. The writers themselves make a good case for the violence in their plays as simply reflecting the accelerating violence in our society. And they argue its shock value as an essential strategem to awaken audiences increasingly hard to shock. The cruelty endemic in their plays indicts Western civilization for its unblinking acceptance of global violence. In *The Second Wave*, John Russell Taylor calls these manifestations of cruelty 'an anarchism of despair', a judgment which should certainly acquit the accused of mere sensationalism.

This modernist despair also appears in plays that look like straightforward comedies. The gradual darkening of Alan Ayckbourn's comic vision is noted in the introduction to *Just Between Ourselves*. The abuse of the corpse in Orton's *Loot* reproves us for sentimentalizing the dead we are so likely to punish in life.

In their departure from realism conceived as literal stage verisimilitude, most of these playwrights also left behind the compact three-act, one-locale structure that had become standard for realistic drama. The wide-ranging purposes, and the free-wheeling style, of these new writers led them to prefer the flexibility of an episodic structure, variously called Shakespearian, epic, and cinematic.

Brenton divides *The Romans in Britain* into fifteen scenes

covering more than two thousand years of British history. David Edgar uses twenty scenes in *Destiny* and twenty-three in *Teendreams*. Peter Nichols delivers *The National Health* in nineteen scenes and adds a television show. The last suggests one of the reasons English dramatists range so freely in time and space. Many of them write for film, radio and television, as well as for the stage. Hare, Griffiths, Brenton, and Stoppard all write for television and film. John Arden, Pinter and Stoppard all had early work premiered on radio and have gone on writing original radio plays. Nichols began as a television writer. Pinter may be the greatest screenwriter alive. For most American playwrights, television and screen commissions are hard to come by; they tend to be on the wrong coast.

An important factor in this liberation from time and space is the redefinition of realism in the modern theatre. On the one hand, *real* in the English theatre has come to mean an attention to the minutiae of everyday life – real worries, real talk, real obsessions, real social and economic problems. On the other hand, the idea of *real* has divorced itself from mere scenic verisimilitude – the box set, the complete bedroom suite, the functioning light fixtures – because such externals are too limiting. Brecht, Littlewood, and their sympathisers have triumphed by shifting the focus of realism from the object to the subject. Unchained from the object, the writer can o'erleap time and space in pursuit of the subject.

The shift of attention to contemporary social and political issues also pushed the drama in a cinematic direction. When the play focuses on the family or intimate relations, the writer can easily bring the key parties together in a moment of crisis played out on one home ground. But dramatists who seek to illumine the socio-political world must present both private and public scenes. And if they wish to show the impact of social or political forces on individual lives, they must dramatize whole processes, not only pivotal moments. A quintessential Bond play – say *The Fool* (1975) – can make its point only by showing not only the youthful decision of John Clare to withdraw from society in favour of love and poetry but also the results of his decision, his destruction by a system he should not have failed to take note of. So it is that the action of *The Fool* ranges over a lifetime.

The Language of the Drama

The language of the drama itself is the standard against which English drama has always been measured. Although the Shakespearian heights may not be threatened, a great deal of wonderful language has emerged in the contemporary English drama. Americans in particular admire the striking ability of English playwrights to travel linguistically beyond the boundaries of routine realism. This is not to say that Americans never do. Sam Shepard's jazz songs and the mythic images and broken rhythms of his dialogue are supra-realistic. David Mamet makes the vocabulary of the street hustler – a patois of obscenity and empty hype – into a true poetry of the theatre. But there are more English playwrights who explode the limits of ordinary language and transmute it into poetry in highly original ways.

At one end of the spectrum are the minimalists, led by Pinter, who strip away rhetoric and ornament, leaving a language that, in its very spareness, implies worlds not articulated. It signals darkly of threatening depths beneath the words. In *One for the Road*, Pinter's one-act about political repression, an interrogator generates immense terror without raising his voice:

NICOLAS: When did you meet your husband?
GILA: When I was eighteen.
NICOLAS: Why?
GILA: Why?
NICOLAS: Why?
GILA: I just met him.
NICOLAS: Why?

The unhinging effects of brainwashing are implicit in the laconic repetition of that inappropriate, insistent '*why?*'.

Pinter's influence on the language of the drama can hardly be exaggerated. Some of the current playwrights, notably Bond and Gray, seem to have negotiated Pinter periods before finding their personal voices. For others a minimalist style like Pinter's, though not slavishly so, seems comfortable. In Louise Page's *Real Estate*, a mother and daughter meet after a twenty-year separation:

JENNY: I have a car.
GWEN: Oh.
JENNY: And a flat. Two bedrooms. Second floor.

GWEN: Where?
JENNY: London. Hammersmith.
GWEN: Oh.
JENNY: There's a view of the river from the balcony.
GWEN: I see.

Absent are the routine sentiments or pleasantries that might be expected at such a meeting, the 'how are you's, the 'you know's, by which ordinary people and ordinary realistic characters grease the wheels of social contact. In the context of the play, the missing pleasantries are an ominous declaration of war between the characters.

And because neither Jenny nor Gwen uses a name or title of address for the other, their relationship is not disclosed at once, at least not through their verbal language. The actresses playing the roles may let audiences guess by their wary body language. A virtue of minimalist dialogue is the emphasis it throws onto the theatre poetry of intonation, gesture, and movement.

Minimalism is supra-realistic in that it so often withholds the expository information normally doled out in the opening scene of a play. A traditional playwright would make the point that Gwen is Jenny's mother. In real life, however, anyone might eavesdrop on such a meeting without ever discovering the relationship. In real life, exposition comes, if it comes, when it comes. That being so, Pinter and the other minimalists are the more realistic in telling less.

At the other end of the spectrum are the maximalists who so flood the stage with words that the play's subtext almost disappears. Some theatre artists prefer this style, which forces actors to concentrate on simply communicating the immediate meanings of the words they speak. John Dexter, a leading theatre and opera director, says, 'I hate that bloody word – subtext!' Other directors, trained up on Stanislavski-oriented theatre practice, are discomfited by the maximal torrent. James Christy, who directed the American premiere of Brenton's *Magnificence* at Villanova University, confessed that twenty years of approaching modern plays through subtext had left him unready for Brenton's flow of words that mean exactly what they say and say it with a rich fullness that American actors expect to encounter only in the classics.

A way to appreciate the stylistic gap between the minimalists and the maximalists is to turn the pages of a script, not bothering to read. A typical Pinter page is a series of short exchanges, each character speaking only a word or two. (Pinter can write the long monologue, but it is not what makes him Pinter.) A page from a play by John Arden and Margaretta D'Arcy is likely to contain solid blocks of print, long speeches by one character after another. The playwrights are not carelessly verbose, of course. Their expansive language is necessary to their intentions and the scope of their subject matter. In *The Little Gray Home in the West* (1978), Baker-Fortesque, a 1959 absentee landlord, uses words to transform himself, in effect, into Lloyd George in order to threaten his Irish tenants. 'Across the whole of Ireland, nothing you've known so far/From torturing Tans or hangmen shall compare/With that huge avalanche of horror I can rear . . .' Arden and D'Arcy pack the language of their characters with references and allusions; they fill the mind with more images and ideas than ordinary realistic language can.

Peter Barnes is the most effusive maximalist of all. In intentional emulation of Ben Jonson, he overwhelms the stage with a huge fantastical vocabulary – standard words, made-up words, and sounds that are not words at all. Out of them he creates images that an audience can absorb only by intense concentration. Barnes makes a virtue of plenty, piling word upon extravagant word, image on image. In *Tsar* (1978) Ivan and the Tsarevitch reminisce about women:

IVAN: . . . what strumpets, whores, two-roubled hacksters.
TSAREVITCH: What lickerous-eyed plovers, what wagtails tripping 't soft.
IVAN: What trugs bearing their bellies out magestical.

By such linguistic profusion, Barnes and the other maximalists celebrate the rich past of the English drama in its present.

Between the austere and the opulent lies a third language of the English drama – the polished wit of the drawing-room, the heritage of Wilde, Coward, and Rattigan revitalized by Stoppard, Orton, and Christopher Hampton. Orton and Stoppard actually parody Wilde. Stoppard speaks for all the writers whose scrupulous zeal to set the right words in the right place approaches reverence. Playwright Henry speaks for Stoppard when he answers Annie's question in *The Real Thing*, 'What's so good about putting words together?' with a cricketing analogy:

> This thing here, which looks like a cricket bat, is actually several pieces
> of particular wood cunningly put together in a certain way so that the
> whole thing is sprung, like a dance floor. It's for hitting balls with. If
> you set it right, the cricket ball will travel two hundred yards in four
> seconds. . . . What we're trying to do is to write cricket bats so that
> when we throw up an idea and give it a little knock, it might . . . travel
> . . .

In their several ways, English dramatists create language that
travels very well.

They use the language of physical and aural theatricality equally
well. In *Equus* Shaffer achieves a moment of religious epiphany
when Alan Strang mounts a human actor become horse. In
Restoration, Bond recreates a society when Lord Are arranges
himself against a tree to look like a lord surveying his lands. In
Good (1982) C. P. Taylor underscores John Halder's gradual
descent into Nazi barbarism with a running tapestry of music –
sentimental, bombastic, kitschy, all ironic – that is understood to
emanate from Halder's mind. The music expresses Halder's
corruption as powerfully as verbal language might. David
Rudkin's use of sound as an expressive element is so complex that
in productions of his recent plays, he has acted as his own sound
designer. The visual and aural are well combined in David
Pownall's *Master Class* when, at the climax of Act I, Stalin
terrorizes Prokofiev by breaking a collection of the composer's
recordings, one by one. Each crack echoing through the theatre is
a harsh metaphor for the brutality of power.

The Image of America in British Plays

Because these volumes are edited by Americans and will be read
by many Americans, it seems worthwhile to make a small point
about the image of America in contemporary English plays.
Whether because they don't regard England as crucial to American
life, or because they are the products of a more parochial
education, American playwrights seldom depict contemporary
England or the English. Many practising English dramatists have
a go at America and Americans. And despite rumblings of
discontent about American foreign policy, American deficits, and,

of course, the vulgarity of American style, the treatment of their American cousins by British playwrights tends to be even-handed, occasionally even affectionate.

There are, of course, those plays that paint America in standard garish colors. Snoo Wilson's *The Grass Widow* (1983) is set in a California agricultural community whose leading cash crop is marijuana. The world depicted is dominated by macho-madness and violence, and the only reasonably sane character is the visiting Englishman. In *Sufficient Carbohydrate* (1983), Dennis Potter's American businessman seems at first a healthy-minded pragmatist stuck with a drunken, neurotic English junior partner. But the play gradually shows the American as a man whose profit fixation blinds him to the needs of the spirit, to which the more civilized Englishman is more sensitive. Christopher Hampton's *Tales from Hollywood* (1982) satirizes America through the views of European intellectuals – Mann, Brecht, and others – exiled to Hollywood by Hitler. In their eyes, America is soulless and crude. Hollywood, of course, is an easy target: the crassness of its film magnates is exemplified when a producer tries to commission a famous Austrian dramatist to script *Bonzo Goes to College*.

However, Americans are not generally ugly in English plays. The American journalist visiting Cuba in Michael Frayn's *Clouds* (1976) turns out to be not a CIA tool, but a sympathetic observer. The title character in Brenton's *The Genius* is an American scientist who tries to keep his latest invention from hastening the world's march toward Armageddon. In the last scene he is mounting the barricades with anti-missile marchers. In David Edgar's brilliant *Mary Barnes*, it is a young American radical shrink who leads the title character out of madness to health.

Occasionally, America is celebrated. Stoppard's *New-Found-Land* is a ten-minute monologue in which an English diplomat sings a coast-to-coast American travelling song filled with warm images of American silliness and sublimity from 'New York! New York! It's a wonderful town!' to 'past the crude wooden crosses of Boot Hill' to 'where picture palaces rise from the plain'. That the matter is myth detracts not a whit from the tone, which is loving.

Charles Wood celebrated the American bicentennial in his *Has 'Washington' Legs?* (1978). The play depicts an American film director become Prince Hal on the eve of Agincourt as he prepares his crew to film the Battle of Bunker Hill on an Irish hillside. Though many of the unflattering clichés about American film people appear – especially the fast talk of the smoke pedlars – the point of this huge satire seems to be the American capacity to dream big and somehow to make the big dream come true.

English plays show a certain fascination with Americans, a need to deal with them as with obstreperous children, some regret for their often limited grasp on the world, and a persistent wonder at their often surprising power to do what an older culture seems too tired to do.

Apologia

Anyone reasonably acquainted with the English drama could name the accomplished playwrights included here. And for any of these dramatists, other title selections could be argued. Is *Close of Play* less worthy to represent the gifts of Simon Gray than *Quartermaine's Terms*? Hardly. Each of the writers has produced a number of plays worth seeing and reading. The choices, then, depend not so much on their individual merits as on availability, representativeness, or relation to the whole. (Gray's *The Rear Column*, for example, is a wonderful play, but does not catch the central tone of Gray's work.)

The omission of certain dramatists implies no lack of deserving in them. The premise of this anthology is that contemporary English drama is rich, so rich indeed that there is no room for all the plays worthy of inclusion. In this volume alone there is good reason to include such authors as Howard Barker, Stephen Poliakoff, Michael Frayn, C. P. Taylor, Christopher Hampton, Pam Gems, and at least five Davids – Hare, Rudkin, Storey, Edgar, and Pownall. Space, not lack of appreciation, is the dictator.

Selected Bibliography

Beauman, Sally. *The Royal Shakespeare Company: A History of Ten Decades*. London and New York: Oxford University Press, 1982.

Bigsby, C. W. E. 'The Politics of Anxiety: Contemporary Socialist Theatre in England.' *Modern Drama* 24 (December 1981) pp. 393–403.

Craig, Sandy, ed. *Dreams and Deconstructions: Alternative Theatre in Britain*. Ambergate: Amber Lane Press, 1980.

Drama: The Quarterly Theatre Review. No. 150 (4th Quarter 1983): Special Issue on the National Theatre and the RSC. No. 152 (2nd Quarter 1984): Special Issue on Women in Theatre.

Elsom, John. *Post-War British Theatre*. London: Routledge & Kegan Paul, 1976.

— and Nicholas Tomalin. *The History of the National Theatre*. London: Jonathan Cape, 1978

Findlater, Richard, ed. *At the Royal Court*. Ambergate: Amber Lane Press; New York: Grove Press, 1981.

Hall, Peter. *Diaries*, ed. John Goodwin. London: Hamish Hamilton; New York: Harper & Row, 1984.

Itzin, Catherine. *Stages in the Revolution: Political Theatre in Britain since 1968*. London and New York: Methuen, 1980.

Kerensky, Oleg. *The New British Drama: Fourteen Playwrights Since Osborne and Pinter*. London: Hamish Hamilton; New York: Taplinger, 1977.

Sunday Times Magazine, 26 November 1978. Special Issue: 'The State of British Theatre.'

Taylor, John Russell. *The Second Wave*. London: Eyre Methuen, 2nd ed., 1978. New York: Hill and Wang, 1971.

Todd, Susan, ed. *Women and Theatre: Calling the Shots*. London: Faber and Faber, 1984.

Trussler, Simon, ed. *New Theatre Voices of the Seventies*. London and New York: Methuen, 1981.

Wandor, Michelene. *Understudies: Theatre and Sexual Politics*. London and New York: Methuen, 1981.

– (ed.). *Plays by Women*, volumes one to four. London and New York: Methuen, 1982–5.

Weintraub, Stanley, ed. *British Dramatists Since World War II*, two vols. (*Dictionary of Literary Biography*, V 13.) Detroit: Gale Research Co., 1982.

Alan Ayckbourn

Scarborough is a middle-sized, solidly middle-class town on the coast of north-east Yorkshire. It was there, as Ian Watson records, that Stephen Joseph 'found the right mix of circumstances and individuals to base a revolution in British theatre that was precisely contemporaneous with the revolution that George Devine was fostering with his stable of writers in Sloane Square'. Like Devine, Joseph was founding a writers' theatre. However, he based his revolution, not on the subject matter of plays, but on an obsession for opening up the proscenium arch into a theatre-in-the-round for greater immediacy between actors and audiences. When the teenaged Alan Ayckbourn turned up in 1957 to ask for a job, Joseph took him on as assistant stage manager and occasional actor. When Ayckbourn complained about his role in *Bell, Book and Candle*, Joseph dared him to write himself a better one. The result was Alan Ayckbourn as a guitar-toting pop singer in *The Square-Cat*, a farce so successful at the box office that Joseph encouraged Ayckbourn to continue writing.

Ayckbourn did continue to write, gradually setting a pattern he still follows of premiering each new play, at least one a year, at Scarborough before its transfer to London. In 1970 Ayckbourn took on the running of the theatre. In 1976 he and the Scarborough Company moved to their own year-round permanent theatre, renamed after Joseph's death, the Stephen Joseph Theatre-in-the-Round.

Some of Ayckbourn's distinctive qualities as a playwright doubtless developed out of the requisites of the Scarborough theatre: the arena configuration with only two doors for entrances and exits challenged Ayckbourn to the adroit manipulation of stage space that is his trademark; the more or less permanent acting company of six or eight actors controlled cast size and meant writing team plays rather than star vehicles; the unsophisticated tastes of local audiences who wanted to be entertained inclined Ayckbourn to comedy rather than tragedy.

Yet his underlying theme is inherently tragic. As Benedict Nightingale pointed out, human desperation keeps breaking out in his plays, its cause everywhere the same: the everyday inhumanity of people to each other, especially in ordinary marriage and family life. In his meticulously observed pictures of the English middle-class, Ayckbourn shows more sharply and consistently than many feminist playwrights the unequal status of women in marriage, their appalling plight in the bourgeois world.

Ayckbourn is not the Neil Simon of London, as some critics too readily convinced by surface likenesses would have it. Both are prolific writers and successful at making audiences laugh. Both focus on middle-class characters who are bound by conventional values and prejudices, and inadequate even to the trivial demands their mundane material aspirations lay on them. Worse, they are heedless of their effect on others. They fail at everything from getting successfully through doorways to relationships. In Simon such bungling impotence is made to seem lovable and harmless. Audiences leave a Simon play bolstered in their habit of evading the implications of their own failures and personal insensitivity. In Ayckbourn, however, the consequences of one person's actions in the lives of others are all too clear. Ayckbourn characters provoke nervous laughter that disturbs rather than confirms audience complacencies.

The sensibilities at work in the two writers are profoundly dissimilar. As John Lahr shrewdly observed, Simon colludes with his audiences in their self-congratulatory desire to feel good about themselves. He ignores the consequences of the pathology his characters exhibit in their relationships. Insensitivity, unkindness, deception, infidelity, even flagrant cruelty among his characters are made to seem laughable tics that do no lasting harm. As American critic John Simon (no relation) noted of Neil Simon's plays, 'The ring of truth is regularly sacrificed for the ring of laughter.'

In Ayckbourn, by contrast, the ring of laughter barely covers over the real pain the characters feel. They busy themselves with fixing appliances when what needs mending are hearts and minds. Caught in the inevitable change and decay of time, they are not restored even to temporary harmony at the end of the play. Instead their plights are more desperate and they themselves more damaged as human beings by the ravages of their struggles. The men struggle at avoidance, the women for redemption. And unlike Simon's characters they are seen to suffer. But when they cry out for rescue they are unheeded. In *Just Between Ourselves* Vera, on the verge of despair, tries to tell her husband she needs help. His reply is obtusely inattentive to the substance of her plea.

> Yes, well, look, tell you what. When you've got a moment, why don't you sit down, get a piece of paper and just make a list of all the things you'd like me to help you with. Things you'd like me to do. Things that need mending or fixing and then we can talk about them and see what I can do to help. All right?

Like Simon, Ayckbourn uses stock comedic devices. The characters spill wine, make embarrassing mistakes of identity, sing off key, and lock themselves out of their own homes. The women forget to put petrol in the car and the men have bad backs and end up on the floor, unable to reach the telephone: typical situations in farce comedy. And they are comic in Ayckbourn. But there is also a latent sadness in them because they are shown to be symptoms of desperation. That sadness, not a virtue in itself, becomes one in Ayckbourn because it is true to life. As in Chekhov, hearts are heard to break among the clatter of the crockery. The pain the characters suffer rings as true as their silliness and connects us to our own. They are real people, confounded by the intractability of their own natures and demoralized by a social context that routinely invites, only to defeat, their aspirations.

To make matters worse, the world they live in doesn't work. There is a malice in the things that clutter their lives. Their kitchen appliances burn out; their overhead garage doors don't open; their cars need repair; their do-it-yourself projects collapse; their family festivities – Christmas, birthdays, reunions – and even their philanderings are inevitably disastrous. It rains a lot in Ayckbourn plays, so their picnics and parades are often spoiled. They get crumbs in their beds, and are trapped without clothes on when the guests come to deposit their coats in the bedroom. The air freshener turns out to be fly spray. These comic mishaps move us to hilarity, yet we brood on them. The multiplication of such ordinary, familiar daily defeats creates a nightmarish world inimical to the floundering efforts of human beings to survive. We see ourselves ridiculous, spending our powers on absurd objects, powerless to change.

Ayckbourn tracks his characters upstairs, downstairs and all through the house, inside and outside their spirit-crushing domains. His plots work off the activities likeliest in particular domestic settings.

Absurd Person Singular, which won the *Evening Standard* Award for the best comedy of 1973, is set in the kitchens of three unhappily married couples during three successive Christmas Eve parties. The furnishings and degree of order or disorder are visual clues to the status and tastes of their owners, and to the unequal status in marriage of the women (who are always more miserable than men in Ayckbourn plays). In Act I, when Jane, the insecure wife of a crassly ambitious store manager, runs out of tonic water, she sneaks off in the rain to get some, wearing her husband's galoshes and old raincoat. Her insecurity is so extreme that she is traumatized when she can't get back in without being seen by her guests. Eva, married to a congenital philanderer, refers to herself as 'an embarrassing smudge on a marriage licence' and neurotically pops pills. When the men converge on the kitchen, their talk disparages their wives and lecherously assesses the putative charms of other women.

Act II is set in Eva's untidy homespun kitchen, where she writes suicide notes and makes several attempts to kill herself during the party. Her husband misconstrues her actions as routine neurotic symptoms and the guests utterly fail to grasp her pain. The obsessively tidy Jane finds Eva with her head in the oven, assumes the oven wants cleaning, and promptly sets to work. Marion, the wife of the bank manager, whom Jane's husband wants to impress by the Act I party, moves among the guests scattering noblesse oblige and swallowing unseemly amounts of gin.

In Act III, wearing only a negligee, Marion wanders into her own high-ceilinged Victorian kitchen late in the party in search of a drink. Her husband has just finished regaling the guests with the tale of his first wife's flight from their marriage. 'Quite amazing,' he says. 'I mean I had literally no idea she was going to. . . . Some time later again, I took up tennis and married Marion.' He sums up the male incomprehension that annihilates the women in Ayckbourn plays:

Well – this whole women business, really, I mean, this may sound ridiculous, but I've never to this day really known what most women think about anything. Completely closed book to me. I mean, God bless them, what would we do without them? But I've never understood them. I mean, damn it all, one minute you're having a perfectly good time and the next, you suddenly see them there like – some old sports jacket or something – literally beginning to come apart at the seams.

At the end of the play, the suicidal Eva and her husband are incessantly wrangling, Marion is a tragic alcoholic, and the vulgar store manager has outstripped the other two husbands professionally, a triumph visually displayed in all its crassness when he forces them into a ludicrous game of forfeits in which he calls the tune and names the degrading penalties. The situations are funny on the stage. We laugh, feeling superior. But they are familiar enough to cut cruelly near the bone. The heartache under them is unmistakable and true to life. We see ourselves; and the tragic fuses with the comic.

Ayckbourn's technical inventiveness, which his punning titles abet, is more complicated in *The Norman Conquests*. A trilogy, the plays are about the amorous adventurings of Norman, an assistant librarian whose main pursuit is the conquest of more or less willing ladies, women who are starved enough for affection to welcome the abortive weekend gropings that are all he offers. A bunglingly cheerful seducer he lays siege to the sexual favours of his spinster sister-in-law Annie, his own angry wife, and another sister-in-law, a super-housewife who henpecks her husband – all in a single summer weekend in an appallingly awful middle-class Victorian manse.

Three inter-related comedies originally performed on three successive evenings, the plays offer three separate but simultaneous views of Norman on the make. *Table Manners* is set in the dining-room; in *Living Together*, we are shown what was going on at the same time in the living-room; in *Round and Round the Garden*, we see the simultaneous goings-on in the garden. There are crossovers from one play to the next; each is funnier and means more in relation to the others. Beneath the high-jinks of a sex farce, however, is an intelligent, troubled comment on the insufficiencies of social rituals and the sterile lovelessness of ordinary marriage and family life.

In *Sisterly Feelings*, which questions the role of chance and choice in human destiny, the writer supplies alternative scenes. The actresses playing the two sisters can choose which scenes to play by tossing a coin on stage at the end of the first scene. The play, however, always begins with this scene, entitled 'A Funeral,' and always ends with 'A Wedding'. No matter which of the variable scenes are enacted, therefore, the ending is always the same. By neither strategem nor choice can either sister win the man she longs to wed. In addition, as always, the malice of things trips up the characters, who must struggle in the rain with sand, paper plates, bikes, camp gear, midges, collapsing tents, and damp matches.

The bleakness of Ayckbourn's view of life is disclosed in *Just Between Ourselves*, which he called the 'first of my winter plays'. A young wife, Vera, who can't penetrate her husband's cheerful oblivion, is going insane from loneliness and insecurity. A maddeningly amiable tinkerer with little mechanical aptitude, Dennis spends his time pottering in the garage, abandoning Vera to the incessant carping of her mother-in-law. He ignores her pleas for help because he is pathologically incapable of understanding what her problem is. Vera, suffering from the inhibitions of a conventional upbringing with its assumptions about the superiority of men, lacks the ability or self-confidence to express herself clearly. She is the butt of her husband's put-down humour, especially in the presence of a third party. The first act barrage is typical:

DENNIS: A little tip when you're next using an electric kettle. They work far better when you don't keep slinging them on the floor.

VERA: I couldn't help it. I just caught it with my elbow.

DENNIS (*to* NEIL, *laughing*): Caught it with her elbow . . . If I told you, Mr. Andrews, the things my wife had caught with her elbow. . . .

VERA (*shy and embarrassed*): All right.

DENNIS: You would not believe it, Mr. Andrews, cups, saucers, dinner plates, radio sets . . .

NEIL: Really.

DENNIS: Whole tray of glasses.

VERA: Dennis . . .

DENNIS: And that's just for this month. You ever want a demolition job doing, Mr. Andrews, she's your woman . . . Elbow's going like pistons.

NEIL: Well, I suppose we all tend to . . . occasionally.

DENNIS: Yes, quite. (*Hugging* VERA.) I was only joking, love, only joking. I'm always pulling her leg, aren't I love? Eh?

Neil and Pam, engaged in the skirmishes of an equally bad marriage constantly in the crisis stage, are as oblivious as Dennis to Vera's horrifying plight. They add to the dismal household their own unpleasant bickering. They hardly respond, except to jolly her along, as Vera slowly slips into catatonia.

Each of the four scenes of the play marks the birthday of one of the characters. Their reactions to the passing of time expose the bleak states of their souls. Dennis laughs it off as usual, while Vera retreats into silence; Neil accepts it with false bravado, while his wife fights with her terror of losing her attractiveness; the mother-in-law watches like a basilisk, ready to triumph over Vera's routing.

In the final scene the group celebrates Vera's birthday on a cold January morning, outdoors, where Vera sits huddled in a large rug. The others lamely josh her along, unable even in the face of her complete physical and emotional catatonia, to acknowledge the gravity of her condition. In the supreme moment of irony, the mother-in-law appears bearing a very small birthday cake with a single candle on it. 'It's only a little token,' she says. Dennis, uncomprehending to the end, adds, 'No point in doing anymore. She wouldn't really appreciate it.'

Born in 1939 Ayckbourn came by his theatrical inclinations early and naturally. His maternal grandparents were music-hall performers, his father a violinist with the London Symphony Orchestra. His mother was a writer. Like Stoppard, Ayckbourn left school without a university degree. Determined to be an actor, he worked in Sir Donald Wolfit's company in Edinburgh. He was nineteen, married, and already a father, when he went to work for Stephen Joseph.

Ayckbourn acknowledges that his primary aim is to give his audiences a good time. But he sees to it that the stage tricks that make his plays visually amusing do not deny his characters 'their true destinies', and he hopes they don't say things they would not normally say to get easy laughs. They don't. His funny lines arise out of the predicaments his characters find themselves in and place them precisely in time, status, and state of soul.

Critics have begun to regard Ayckbourn as a social critic who wants a better world, a goal he professes himself. However, he is unsympathetic to the impulses of his leftist peers to be politically instructive in the theatre, preferring enlightenment that comes as a by-product of entertainment. 'I don't know much about Marxist rallies and neither do theatre-goers,' he insists. 'They worry about their leaking roof, their central heating.'

The dream of a working-class theatre, so earnestly propounded by Wesker, Bond, and Joan Littlewood, seems unrealistic to Ayckbourn, who points out that the working class thinks of the theatre as elitist culture. They want to dress up when they go out and enjoy a glimpse of high life. They are not lured by the scruffy settings favored by working-class dramatists.

Such public pronouncements, as well as his plays, have evoked mixed responses from critics. Writing in *The Second Wave* in 1971, John Russell Taylor summed up Ayckbourn as a farceur 'with no trace of social or political indoctrination . . . let alone of cosmic anguish'. Ronald Bryden's review of *Absurd Person Singular* in 1974 declared that Ayckbourn is a political propagandist 'who works on people's minds without letting them know he's doing it . . .'. Bryden added more explicitly, 'No one's written more sharply about the way class-politics express themselves as sexuality in Britain . . .' and he concluded, 'I think [the play] may make many of its audiences think twice before voting again for the free market economy, individual enterprise and the competitive principle.'

The temptation to dismiss Ayckbourn because he is prolific, commercially successful, and always hilariously funny may at last be put to rest by Michael Billington's new appreciative study of his work. It prompted the *Plays and Players* reviewer to thank the publisher 'for having the wit to see that Ayckbourn has earned a place in a pantheon like Modern Dramatists – alongside Pinter, Arden, Stoppard and earlier classics'.

Major Plays

How the Other Half Loves, Library Theatre, Scarborough, 1968.
Absurd Person Singular, Library Theatre, Scarborough, 1972.
The Norman Conquests, Library Theatre, Scarborough, 1973.
Absent Friends, Library Theatre, Scarborough, 1974.
Bedroom Farce, Library Theatre, Scarborough, 1975.
Just Between Ourselves, Library Theatre, Scarborough, 1976.
Ten Times Table, Stephen Joseph Theatre-in-the-Round, Scarborough, 1977.

Joking Apart, Stephen Joseph Theatre-in-the-Round, Scarborough, 1979.

Sisterly Feelings, Stephen Joseph Theatre-in-the-Round, Scarborough, 1979.

It Could Be Any One of Us, Stephen Joseph Theatre-in-the-Round, Scarborough, 1984.

Intimate Feelings, Greenwich Theatre, 1984.

Selected Bibliography

Billington, Michael. *Alan Ayckbourn*. London and New York: Macmillan, 1984.

Bryden, Ronald. Review of *Absurd Person Singular*, *Plays and Players*, August, 1973, pp. 39–41.

Lahr, John. *Astonish Me*. N.Y.: Viking Press, 1973.

Page, Malcolm. 'The Serious Side of Alan Ayckbourn,' *Modern Drama* March 1983, pp. 36–46.

Simon, John. *Singularities*. N.Y.: Random House, 1975.

Watson, Ian, ed. *Conversations with Ayckbourn*. London: MacDonald, 1981.

ALAN AYCKBOURN

Just Between Ourselves

Just Between Ourselves was first produced at the Library Theatre, Scarborough, on 28 January 1976 and subsequently by Michael Codron at the Queen's Theatre, London, on 20 April 1977 with the following cast:

DENNIS	Colin Blakely
VERA	Rosemary Leach
NEIL	Michael Gambon
MARJORIE	Constance Chapman
PAM	Stephanie Turner

Directed by Alan Strachan
Settings by Patrick Robertson

ACT ONE	Scene 1:	February, Saturday morning
	Scene 2:	May, Saturday morning
ACT TWO	Scene 1:	October, Saturday evening
	Scene 2:	January, Saturday morning

ACT ONE

Scene One

February. A garage attached to a medium price executive house on a private estate belonging to DENNIS *and* VERA. *Our view is from the side of the house looking into the garage through its side wall. Its 'up and over door', furthest from us remains closed throughout the action. Down one wall of the garage a workbench littered untidily with tools etc. In fact the whole place is filled with the usual garage junk, boxes, coils of rope, garden chairs etc. In the midst of this, sideways on, a small popular car, at least seven years old, stands neglected. Over the work bench a grimy window which looks out over a small paved or semi-paved 'sitting area'. On the other side wall a door, opening outwards leading across a small dustbin yard to the backdoor of the house. There is also a paved walkway round the side of the garage, nearest us, leading to the 'sitting area'. A wrought iron or similar ornamental gate leads off the 'sitting area' and round to the front of the house and garage proper.*

 DENNIS, *in his forties, is busy at his workbench. He is prodding at an electric kettle with a screwdriver, muttering to himself. After a moment,* VERA, *his wife, a few years younger, emerges from the backdoor of the house. She is followed by* NEIL, *in his late thirties and smartly dressed in contrast to* DENNIS *who has on his weekend clothes.*

DENNIS (*frowning at the kettle*). That goes in there . . . and then that one goes . . . through there to that one . . . which should join up with the other one. In which case . . .

VERA (*knocking gently on the garage door*). Dennis . . . Dennis.

DENNIS (*still absorbed*). But in that case, that one . . . should be joined to that one . . . (*Calling.*) Hallo . . . (*Returning to the kettle*.) . . . unless that's the earth. In which case, it's that one.

VERA (*struggling with the door trying to open it*). Dennis.

DENNIS. Come in. (*Back to the kettle.*) On the other hand, if that's the earth, which one is the live one . . .?

VERA. Dennis dear, can you open the door for me, please? It's stuck again.

DENNIS. Hang on, hang on, hang on. Live . . . earth . . . neutral.

VERA (*apologetically to* NEIL). It's always sticking.

NEIL. Ah.

DENNIS. Earth, neutral, live.

VERA. My husband's going to fix it as soon as he has a moment but . . . Dennis dear.

DENNIS (*backing towards the door keeping his eyes fixed on the kettle*). Right. In which case, if that's the earth it goes in there . . . Hang on . . . not in there . . . right. Stand back.

VERA (*to* NEIL). Stand back.

> DENNIS *heaves against the door.*
> *It flies open.*

DENNIS. I'll tell you one thing,the fellow who invented the electric kettle . . . (*Seeing* NEIL.) Ah. Afternoon.

NEIL. Good afternoon.

VERA. Dennis dear, this gentleman's come to look at the car.

DENNIS. At the car?

VERA. Mr. . . . sorry, I've forgotten your name.

NEIL. Mr. Andrews.

DENNIS. Pleased to meet you, Mr. Andrews, come in, come in.

NEIL. Thank you.

VERA. This is my husband, Mr. Crowthorne.

DENNIS. Excuse the jumble. The place is due for a spring clean. Amazing what you collect.

NEIL. Yes, yes.

DENNIS. Amazing. I mean, where does it all come from? Just look at it. I mean, where does it all come from?

NEIL. Yes, yes. Accumulates.

DENNIS. Accumulates. That's the word, accumulates.

VERA. How's my kettle?

DENNIS. Coming along, coming along.

VERA. It just wasn't heating up at all. Your mother's making tea in a saucepan.

DENNIS. Well, I'll tell you, my love, I'll give you a little tip shall I? A little tip when you're next using an electric kettle. They work far better when you don't keep slinging them on the floor.

VERA. I couldn't help it. I just caught it with my elbow.

DENNIS (*to* NEIL, *laughing*). Caught it with her elbow.

NEIL *smiles*.

If I told you, Mr. Andrews, the things my wife had caught with her elbow . . .

VERA (*shy and embarrassed*). All right.

DENNIS. You would not believe it, Mr. Andrews, cups, saucers, dinner plates, radio sets . . .

NEIL. Really.

DENNIS. Whole tray of glasses.

VERA. Dennis . . .

DENNIS. And that's just for this month. You ever want a demolition job doing, Mr. Andrews, she's your woman. (*He laughs.*)

NEIL *joins in halfheartedly*.

VERA *less so still*.

Elbows going away like pistons . . .

NEIL. Well, I suppose we all tend to . . . occasionally.

DENNIS. Yes, quite. (*Hugging* VERA.) I was only joking, love, only joking. I'm always pulling her leg, aren't I, love? Eh? I'll have it fixed in a jiffy. I'll bring it in.

VERA. Right. I'll make you both some tea when the saucepan's boiled. Do you take sugar, Mr. . . .

NEIL. No, thank you. Unfortunately. I'm afraid I'm unable to take it.

VERA. Right then.

As VERA *turns to leave,* MARJORIE, *a woman in her sixties, comes out of the backdoor.*

MARJORIE. Vera dear, there's a terrible smell of gas . . .

VERA. All right, mother, I'm coming. Excuse me.

MARJORIE. I'm sure this stove still isn't right.

DENNIS. Check the pilot light, Vee. Check it hasn't blown out.

MARJORIE. It hasn't been right since I gave it that thorough clean.

VERA. All right, mother, all right.

DENNIS. Vee'll see to it mother.

VERA *and* MARJORIE *go back into the house.*

My mother, you met my mother?

NEIL. Yes, I met her on the way through to . . .

DENNIS. Sixty-six.

NEIL. What?

DENNIS. Sixty-six years old.

NEIL. Really?

DENNIS. Not bad for sixty-six.

NEIL. No, No.

DENNIS. It's the pilot light, you see. It's in a cross draught. It's very badly sited that stove. They should never have put it there. I'm planning to move it. Right, now. You've come about the car, haven't you?

NEIL. That's right.

DENNIS. Well there she is. Have a look for yourself. That's the one.

NEIL. Ah.

DENNIS. Now, I'll tell you a little bit about it, shall I? Bit of history. Number One, it's not my car. It's the wife's. However, now before you say — ah-ah, woman driver — she's been very careful with it. Never had a single accident in it, touch wood. Well I mean, look, you can see hardly a scratch on it. Considering the age. To be perfectly honest, just between ourselves, she's a better driver than me — when she puts her mind to it. I mean, look — considering it's what now — seven — nearly eight years old. Just look for yourself at that bodywork.

NEIL. Yes, yes.

DENNIS. I bought it four years ago for her. It was then as good as new — virtually. Three years old and as good as new it was.

NEIL. It looks very good.

DENNIS. It is really, amazingly good.

NEIL. I suppose being under cover . . .

DENNIS. Ah yes, well, quite. As I was just about to say, being under cover as it is.

NEIL. Important.

DENNIS. Vital. Vital to keep a car under cover. I mean, frankly that's why we want to get rid of it. I want to get my own car under cover. I don't know if you saw it when you were coming in, parked just out there, on the road there.

NEIL. Yes, I think I . . .

DENNIS. It's doing it no good at all. It's an urgent priority to get that car under cover. You've got a garage, I take it?

NEIL. No.

DENNIS. Ah. Well, when I say that, with a car like this one, it's not as vital as with some cars. I mean, this one (*He slaps the bonnet.*) this is a very, very sturdy vehicle indeed. As a matter of fact, they're not even making them any more. Not this particular model. They took up too much raw material.

They're not economic to make. There's a lot of raw material in this. Mind you, there's no problem with parts. They're still making the parts, they're just not making the cars. Not that you'll ever need a part. We've never needed a part not in four years. No, as a matter of fact, I'll let you into a little secret. This car has barely been out of this garage in six months.

NEIL. Really?

DENNIS. Barely been out. As a matter of fact, frankly, just between ourselves, the wife's had a few, what shall I say, health worries and she hasn't really been up to driving.

NEIL. Oh, I'm sorry to . . .

DENNIS. Oh, she's better now. She's very much better now. But she's gone off driving altogether. You can see, look — look at that clock there — I'll be surprised if it's done fifty thousand. (*Peering in.*) Here we are. Fifty-five thousand two hundred and fifty-two miles . . . well, fifty-five, fifty thousand, round about that figure.

NEIL. Amazing.

DENNIS. Peanuts for a car like this. It's hardly run in.

NEIL. Right.

DENNIS. Have a look for yourself anyway. Feel free.

NEIL. Thanks.

NEIL *wanders round the car aimlessly.*

DENNIS. I'd let you have a test drive in it now but — actually it's a bit embarrassing — the up and over door there, you see it's gone and jammed itself somehow, can't get it open at all. Still, that's my next job.

NEIL. Oh. Well, it'll be important, won't it to . . .

DENNIS. Oh, surely, surely. Wouldn't expect you to consider it without a run around. Still, you can have a preliminary look. See if it's the sort of thing you're looking for.

NEIL. Oh yes.

DENNIS. Here. We can have a butcher's at the business end. Just a tick. (*He releases the bonnet.*) There she is.

NEIL. Oh yes.

DENNIS. Not bad, eh?

NEIL. No.

DENNIS. Economic.

NEIL. Really.

DENNIS. Very smooth runner.

NEIL. Ah.

DENNIS. I'll tell you what I can do for you, I can turn it over for you. Then you can hear the sound.

NEIL. Oh well, that's . . .

DENNIS. Keys are in it, I think . . . yes, right. (*Sliding into the driver's seat.*) I can't run it for too long, not in an enclosed space, you understand but . . . bit of choke . . . right, stand by for blast off.

Engine turns over but fails to start.

She'll be a little bit cold.

Engine fails to start again.

Come along, my beauty. She's been standing, you see . . .

He tries again. It fails to start.

Come on. Come on, you bastard.

Engine turns and starts to fire.

There we are. (*Climbing out of the car to join* NEIL *by the bonnet.*) Listen to that. Purring like a kitten.

NEIL. Beg your pardon?

DENNIS (*yelling above the din*). That's with the bonnet open, of course.

NEIL. Yes.

They stand and survey the turning engine. After a moment, it starts to misfire and peters out. Silence.

DENNIS. Battery'll be a little flat, I expect.

NEIL. Probably.

DENNIS. Once it's had a bit of a run round. Desperately needs a good run. Do you do a lot of driving?

NEIL. No. As a matter of fact, I don't drive at all.

DENNIS. Eh?

NEIL. No, I never got round to learning. My wife drives.

DENNIS. Oh, it's for your wife then, is it?

NEIL. That's right.

DENNIS. Oh I see, I see. Surprise, is it?

NEIL. That sort of thing, yes.

DENNIS. Surprise. That's nice. Does she suspect? Does she know where you are today then?

NEIL. Yes.

DENNIS. Ah.

NEIL. She's here as well.

DENNIS. Here?

NEIL. I left her in your front room, talking to your mother.

DENNIS. Well, doesn't she want to come and have a look? Since she's here.

NEIL. No, I don't think so.

DENNIS. Well, of course it's an ideal woman's car. Not too big, you see. And it's got the radio. That comes with it, of course. It's a good radio.

DENNIS *turns it on. A buzzing noise. He turns it off swiftly.*

It won't work of course, not while it's in the garage. And then you've got your mirrors behind the sun visors here.

NEIL. Oh yes.

DENNIS. Little touches like that. Sort of thing a woman looks for.

NEIL. Handy.

DENNIS. Oh yes. Funny her coming all this way with you and

then not wanting to see it herself.

NEIL. We hadn't far to come.

DENNIS. She prefers to leave it to the expert, does she?

NEIL. Oh, I'm not an expert. No, I was going to have this car delivered for her this morning from another man.

DENNIS. Ah.

NEIL. Only he let me down at the last minute.

DENNIS. It's undersealed, you see. Have a look underneath, see.

NEIL (*bending down to look*). He sold this car of his to somebody else. Phoned me late last night. I didn't want to let her down. Oh yes, very nice.

DENNIS. Important to underseal.

NEIL. So I had to phone round in a hurry this morning. (*He suffers a mild spasm of indigestion.*) Excuse me.

DENNIS. You all right?

NEIL. Oh yes. Just a touch of indigestion.

DENNIS. Oh dear. Been living it up, have you?

NEIL. No, no. I only get it when I bend down. Nothing serious.

DENNIS. That's odd. Sure it's indigestion?

NEIL. I think it is.

DENNIS. Could be something else.

NEIL. Could it?

DENNIS. Possibly. I'd get it looked at, if I were you.

NEIL. Think so?

DENNIS. No harm. I mean, nine times out of ten you're probably right it's indigestion, but the stomach's a peculiar thing.

NEIL. Is it?

DENNIS. Yes. I've had experience with stomachs.

NEIL. Have you?

DENNIS. Better safe than sorry.

NEIL. Anyway this chap let me down, you see, at the last minute.

DENNIS. I see, yes.

NEIL. I didn't want to disappoint her. Birthday, you see.

DENNIS. Birthday? It's your wife's birthday then?

NEIL. Yes.

DENNIS. Today?

NEIL. Yes.

DENNIS. Good heavens above. Pisces, eh?

NEIL. What?

DENNIS. Her star sign. Pisces.

NEIL. Oh yes.

DENNIS. You better keep an eye on her, mate.

NEIL. How do you mean?

DENNIS. They can get very moody, can Pisces. Very moody, brooding people. Unless you keep a very close watch on them. What sign are you as a matter of interest?

NEIL. Er well, Scorpio I think.

DENNIS (*with a yell*). Scorpio.

NEIL. Yes.

DENNIS. Living with a Pisces.

NEIL. Yes.

DENNIS. Good grief.

NEIL. Is that bad?

DENNIS. Perfect, perfect. Made for each other. Couldn't be better.

NEIL. Oh good.

DENNIS. You don't look like a Scorpio. My mother's a Scorpio. She's a typical Scorpio. I mean, she's got the Scorpio bone structure. But you don't look a bit like a Scorpio. What date are you?

NEIL. 28th of October.

DENNIS (*with another wild yell*). 28th of October! I don't believe it. I do not believe it.

NEIL. Eh?

DENNIS. You won't believe this. You will not believe this. You were born on exactly the same day as my mother.

NEIL. Oh.

DENNIS. Exactly the same day. Exactly the same day.

NEIL. Coincidence.

DENNIS. This was meant. I'm sure it was meant. It's extraordinary.

NEIL. Yes, yes it is.

DENNIS. Ah, well Scorpio, eh? I'll have to keep an eye on you.

NEIL. Really?

DENNIS. Oh yes. Very deep waters, Scorpio. Very deep, secretive, scheming and occasionally, I regret to say, devious.

NEIL. Oh, well. I'll watch it then.

DENNIS. What a coincidence. Incredible. You don't have to worry about me though. I'm a Taurus.

NEIL. Oh good.

VERA *comes out from the kitchen with two cups of tea.*

VERA. Dennis.

DENNIS. Ah ha. That sounds like Aquarius. The water bearer bringing the tea. (*He wrenches open the door.*)

VERA. Here's your tea.

DENNIS. Vee, now you won't believe this, Vee, we have just discovered that Mr. Andrews here has exactly the same birth date as mother. Isn't that extraordinary?

VERA. Oh, coincidence.

DENNIS. To the day. Both Scorpios. Exactly the same date.

VERA. Not the same year though.

DENNIS. Same year? Oh yes, rather. Exactly the same year. Mr. Andrews here will be sixty-seven next birthday, won't you,

Mr. Andrews?

VERA. No, I said not the same . . .

DENNIS. Same year. Get on with you. Same year. (*He hugs her.*)

VERA. Careful. I'll drop them.

DENNIS. Well, it won't be the first time.

VERA. Dennis . . .

DENNIS. Aquarius. You can tell, can't you? Typical bloody dopey Aquarius. Aren't you, my love?

VERA. Sugar's in it, Mr. Andrews.

NEIL. Oh. Is it? Thank you.

DENNIS. You given Mrs. Andrews some tea?

VERA. Yes, she's talking to mother.

DENNIS. Well, I don't know about talking to Mother. I think she ought to be out with me and Mr. — look, can I call you by your Christian name, all this Mr. this and Mr. that.

NEIL. Neil.

DENNIS. Neil. Right, I'm Dennis. This is Vera. Vee she prefers.

NEIL. How do you do.

DENNIS. Well, don't you think we ought to ask er — your wife . . .

NEIL. Pam.

DENNIS. Pam — Brian's wife's called Pam, isn't she?

VERA. Yes.

DENNIS. Ask Pam out here. After all it's her present. I mean, assuming you're still interested.

NEIL. Yes. It's just that I don't think she's . . .

VERA. Oh, is the car for your wife?

NEIL. Yes.

VERA. Oh I see. It's very good. It's a nice little car. I've had very little trouble with it.

DENNIS. Very little? Now be truthful, Vee, you've had no

trouble. Be truthful.

VERA. I did break down that once on the ring road.

DENNIS. Petrol. That was petrol.

VERA. Oh yes.

DENNIS. It's not the car's fault if you don't put petrol in it, is it? Not the car's fault. Whose fault is it if there's no petrol in it?

VERA. Yes, all right.

DENNIS. Whose fault?

VERA. Yes all right, Dennis.

DENNIS. It's little Vee's fault. Vee's fault, that's whose it is. I tell you, Neil, I don't know if your wife's the same but if you do give her a car, watch her like a hawk. She'll never put petrol in it. She'll never put water in it. She'll never do the tyres and as for oil . . . well, they've never heard of oil except on salads. Eh?

NEIL *laughs. A token laugh.*

Except on salads, eh?

VERA. Shall I fetch Pam in here?

DENNIS. Yes, fetch her in, Vee, fetch her in. Let her have a look at it.

NEIL. I don't think she's that bothered actually.

DENNIS. Of course, she's bothered. What is it, her first car is it?

NEIL. No, she had one a long time ago before we were married.

DENNIS. Well, nearly her first car. Her first car for some time. She'll want to see what she's getting. My God, if I was getting my first car, I'd be —

VERA. Yes all right, I'll fetch her. Drink your tea, Mr. — Neil.

NEIL. Thank you.

VERA. Mother burnt herself on that saucepan, Dennis.

DENNIS. First Aid tin, top shelf over the boiler.

VERA. I know, I have already. She says it's the wrong stuff.

VERA *goes into the house.*

DENNIS. Now, listen. We must do this thing properly. When Pam comes through the door everything must be right. She comes in the door, what does she see? She sees the car . . . You all right?

NEIL. Yes, fine. I seem to have got the tea with the sugar in.

DENNIS. What? (*He takes a swig of his own.*) Here have this one. That's hardly got any sugar in at all.

They exchange cups, DENNIS *stands appraising the situation.* NEIL *takes a sip of* DENNIS's *tea and reacts unfavourably. He puts the cup down.*

She comes in, she sees the car and, how about if you were sitting behind the wheel, no, in the passenger seat, that's it, in the passenger seat and as soon as she sees you, you say to her — happy birthday, my darling Pam or whatever you usually call her, dearest, dear, now would you like this for your birthday?

NEIL. Well, I don't think she's the sort of person who goes for . . .

DENNIS. Look, Neil, there is not a woman who has yet been born who does not respond to a romantic gesture. Come on, man, where's your romance?

NEIL. Do you mind if I leave this tea?

DENNIS. Is that too sweet as well?

NEIL. It's even sweeter.

DENNIS. It's all right, I'll drink them both. I'll drink them both.

VERA *comes out of the house with* PAM, *a woman in her mid to late thirties.*

VERA. They're just out here.

DENNIS. Here they come. Here they come. Quick, get in the car. quick, quick, quick.

NEIL *does so without much enthusiasm.* DENNIS *leans against the door, till* NEIL *is in position.*

VERA (*tugging the door handle*). Dennis. Dennis. Can you let us in?

DENNIS. Just a minute. Just a minute. (*Flinging open the door.*)

VERA. Stand back.

They stand back just in time.

DENNIS. Come in. Come in.

He steps aside as PAM *enters, followed by* VERA, PAM *sees* NEIL *sitting in the car and stares at him.*

NEIL. Hallo.

PAM. Hallo.

DENNIS (*gesticulating wildly to* NEIL). Go on.

PAM. What are you doing?

NEIL. Er — just looking at the car.

PAM. Oh.

NEIL (*getting out*). What do you think?

PAM. I said, it's up to you.

NEIL. Yes, I know but — I mean you're going to be driving it.

PAM. As long as it goes.

VERA. Oh it goes. It did go anyway.

DENNIS. Still goes.

NEIL. What do you think?

PAM. Well.

NEIL. Yes?

DENNIS (*in another of his fierce undertones*). Show her the radio. And the — (*He gesticulates.*) the mirror.

PAM *opens and shuts a door listlessly.*

NEIL (*in an undertone*). What do you think?

PAM (*likewise*). What's he asking?

NEIL. Four hundred.

DENNIS. Four hundred.

PAM (*moving further away from* DENNIS). It's not worth four hundred.

NEIL. I don't know.

PAM. It's never worth four hundred. Offer him three fifty.

NEIL. Oh, you know I can't . . .

PAM. Three fifty. Settle for three seventy five. He'd still be doing us.

NEIL. Oh, you know I can't do that sort of thing. You know I —

PAM. Yes, I know you. (*To* DENNIS.) How long have you had it?

DENNIS. Three and a ha—

VERA. Four years.

DENNIS. Nearly four years.

VERA. Served me very well. Nice little car.

DENNIS (*bounding forward unable to restrain himself*). Look, you see. It's got the mirror here.

PAM. Oh yes, so it has.

　　NEIL *and* PAM *move away.*

NEIL. Well, do you want it?

PAM. It's nothing to do with me, love, it's your money.

NEIL. No, it's our money.

PAM. Yours. You wanted to get a car. I didn't ask for one.

NEIL. But you did say you'd like one, didn't you? You said —

PAM. I said nothing of the sort.

NEIL. You said —

PAM. I have not said a single word on the subject. Not a word. It's entirely up to you.

NEIL. I just thought you'd . . . that you could get out occasionally.

PAM. When am I going to get out occasionally?

NEIL. I just thought . . .

PAM. Where the hell am I supposed to be going?

NEIL. I simply thought you'd . . .

PAM. It's your money, love. If you want a car, you buy one.

DENNIS. Oh, by the way, just a point of interest. It is taxed for another three months. I forgot to mention that.

NEIL. Yes, well . . . I think we'll leave it for now if you don't mind.

DENNIS. Leave it?

NEIL. Just for the time being. It's a bit difficult deciding in a rush, you know. Till we've had a chance of a run out in it. You know.

DENNIS. Ah. Now, I'll have that garage door fixed in the next twenty-four hours.

VERA. Oh do please. It's been like that for months.

NEIL. It's a bit difficult to decide just on the spur of the moment. It may be just a bit more than we were prepared to . . .

DENNIS. Well, I said four hundred. Because that's the fair price, but I'll take a near offer. Three seventy five?

NEIL. No, not just at the . . .

DENNIS. Three sixty five. There you are. Now I'm giving it away. Three sixty five.

NEIL. No. Perhaps I could pop back sometime.

DENNIS. Yes, you're welcome to do that. But I must warn you I have one or two interested people.

PAM. Yes, I'm sure.

DENNIS. Yes. Well. Feel free to pop back.

NEIL. Thank you. (*He has another spasm of indigestion.*) Excuse me.

PAM. Don't do that.

NEIL. I can't help it.

PAM. Take one of your tablets.

NEIL. I left them at home.

PAM. Oh God.

VERA. Anything the matter?

PAM. Heaven knows.

NEIL. No, no. Just a touch of indigestion I suffer occasionally.

VERA. Oh dear. Would you like some bicarb?

NEIL. No, no, that's . . .

VERA. No, we've got some milk of magnesia somewhere.

NEIL. No, no thank you. I have my own special tablets.

VERA. Oh I see.

DENNIS. I'd have a check up if I were you.

VERA. Can be nasty, indigestion.

DENNIS. Supposing it is indigestion.

VERA. Oh yes, supposing it is.

NEIL. Yes, well, thank you very much.

DENNIS. Not at all. We're always open.

NEIL. Leave you to get on with your kettle.

DENNIS. Yes, yes.

VERA. Have you far to go?

PAM. No, not far.

NEIL. Easterly Road.

VERA. Oh, Easterly Road. We used to live just off Easterly Road didn't we Dennis?

DENNIS. That's right.

VERA. One of the new houses, is it?

PAM. No, the old ones.

NEIL. On the left just at the top.

VERA. Oh, I know them, yes. In that little block on its own. Didn't Mrs. — er — whatever's her name — didn't she live up there, Dennis?

DENNIS. I didn't know they were still there, those places.

PAM. Just about.

VERA. What was her name, Dennis? She used to live there with her son who was a bit funny. You know, peculiar.

DENNIS. I thought those places were scheduled to come down.

NEIL. I hope not. We're still paying for ours.

DENNIS. I thought I read that somewhere.

VERA. Mrs. — er . . .

DENNIS. For road widening.

NEIL. We've never heard anything about it, have we?

PAM. That's hardly surprising.

VERA. Mrs. — um . . .

DENNIS. Yes, road widening. I'm sure it was that end of Easterly Road.

NEIL. Just be our luck, wouldn't it?

PAM. Well, we must get on.

VERA. Mrs. Mandelsham. That was her name, Mrs. Mandelsham.

NEIL. Mrs. Mandelsham?

VERA. Do you know her?

PAM. She's my mother.

NEIL. Pam's mother. Living with us now.

VERA. Good gracious. Did you hear that, Dennis?

DENNIS. Yes, yes.

VERA. Then you must be Pamela Mandelsham.

PAM. I was.

VERA. Well. Isn't that extraordinary? We used to know Mrs. Mandelsham ever so well. Do you remember, Dennis? The nice woman with the cakes.

DENNIS. With the cakes, that's right.

VERA. Of course, you weren't there when we were.

PAM. No, I was working away. I came back when I married Neil.

VERA. Of course we knew you brother. Graham, wasn't it?

PAM. Adam.

VERA. Adam. That's right. How is he?

PAM. Still a bit peculiar. He got married and moved to Liverpool. Haven't seen him for ages. Got masses of kids.

VERA. Oh well, fancy that. And your mother? How is she? Keeping well?

PAM. Fine.

NEIL. Yes.

PAM. She's babysitting for us.

NEIL. She's well. She's very well indeed.

VERA. Well, just fancy that. You must come round again. Bring your mother.

PAM. Yes. We must.

VERA. She made those wonderful cakes, didn't she, Dennis? She was always trying to teach me. I'd like to see her again.

PAM. Yes.

DENNIS. Yes.

NEIL. Yes

    A pause.

PAM. Well. We better get on with it. Get Darren his tea.

VERA. Oh yes. Let me . . . (*She leads the way out.*)

NEIL (*to* DENNIS). Well, goodbye. Thanks very much again.

DENNIS. Not at all, Neil. As I say, look in any time. If you want a second look at this thing — just barge in. You're always welcome.

NEIL. Thanks.

DENNIS. Goodbye Pam.

PAM. Bye.

DENNIS. Happy birthday.

VERA. Oh yes, happy birthday. Whose birthday is it?

DENNIS. Hers. Pam's. It's Pam's birthday.

VERA. Oh, happy birthday.

MARJORIE *emerges from the house.*

MARJORIE. I'm going to have to leave the potatoes to you, Vera.

VERA. Oh, mother. You shouldn't have started on that yet. It's far too early.

MARJORIE. I've been struggling with that little knife of yours.

VERA. We're not having dinner for hours.

DENNIS. Go on, mother, you clear off out of it. Let the Queen back in her kitchen.

MARJORIE. It's all very well. We've been having our meals later and later.

DENNIS. Bye.

NEIL. Bye.

They go into the house, leaving DENNIS *alone in the garage.*

DENNIS. Now then. Where were we? This little one comes up here and joins up with this one. Now which did we say was the earth?

MARJORIE *comes from the house and into the garage.*

MARJORIE. Come on then. Let's have your cups.

DENNIS. Help yourself.

MARJORIE. That's if I can carry them.

DENNIS. Your hands bad again?

MARJORIE. Not so good today.

DENNIS. Oh dear. Must be the weather.

MARJORIE. No, it's not the weather. I'm afraid it's age, Dennis. It's what happens when you get old, I'm afraid. Everything just stops working bit by bit. I'm afraid you'll soon find that out for yourself.

DENNIS (*unperturbed*). Probably will, mother, yes.

MARJORIE. Someone hasn't drunk his tea.

DENNIS. He didn't take sugar.

MARJORIE. Oh. That was Vera. Did you sell the car?

DENNIS. No.

MARJORIE. No, I was talking to the woman. She didn't seem very keen. I don't think she wanted a car anyway. It was him. I told her. I said you don't want a car. They're more trouble than they're worth.

DENNIS. You told her that, did you?

MARJORIE. Well, I mean, look at Vera. She's had this car for years. She never drives it. I doubt if she's driven it once this year.

DENNIS. Ah well, in Vera's case . . . you know.

MARJORIE. You want to keep more of an eye on her, Dennis.

DENNIS. How do you mean?

MARJORIE. She's a sick girl. She's not well, if you ask me.

DENNIS. No, she's better now, mother. She's much better.

MARJORIE. Now, don't let her fool you, Dennis. She's not a bit better. You don't get better. Not from that. When it's up here, in your head, it's there for good.

DENNIS. She seems all right to me.

MARJORIE. I've got a feeling she's got what our Joan had. God rest her soul.

DENNIS. Oh come on, mother, Auntie Joan went right round the bloody bend.

MARJORIE. Yes, I know. I nursed her. And she started just like Vera.

DENNIS. The doctor said she was better.

MARJORIE. Did he? Well.

DENNIS. Well, nearly better anyway. That was months ago.

MARJORIE. When she dropped that kettle, I was watching her closely. She just burst into tears, you know.

DENNIS. Not surprised. So did I. Nearly brand new this is. No, mother, if there's anything wrong with Vera it's because she's in a rut. She needs cheering up. Taking out of herself. She takes life too seriously. For that matter, both of you do.

MARJORIE. Well, Dennis, that might be your solution but I can tell you from my experience it is not the solution for Vera. Nor for me, I'm afraid. Nor was it for Auntie Joan, God rest her soul. I know they say laughter's a great tonic but there are some things it can't heal. You can't laugh everything off, Dennis.

DENNIS. I know that. I . . .

MARJORIE. I've certainly never been able to, and nor was your father able to. I sometimes wish you took after your father, Dennis, I really do. Not in all ways but in some things. You could do well to follow him.

DENNIS. How do you mean?

MARJORIE. Well, for one thing he didn't try and laugh every-thing off. He had a deep and wonderful understanding of suffering. In fact, on occasions one could have said too much so. I think by the end, he had taken on everyone's suffering.

DENNIS. He was a miserable old sod when he died.

MARJORIE. And another thing your father always did. He always kept his garage tidy. He wouldn't have left it in this state. How do you ever find anything?

DENNIS. I can find things, mother, don't go on.

MARJORIE. Look at his tools, Dennis. Look at your father's tools. They're all over the place. It would have broken his heart to see them. Why don't you do what he did? Make your-self a proper rack for your tools screwed in the wall. He had little clips, you see. He had his chisels and his screwdrivers and all his hammers.

DENNIS. I know. I know.

MARJORIE. And then on his bench itself, up one end he had all his little tins with his screws and nails and so forth. And he had them all labelled, you see. So whenever he wanted a little nail or a screw, he could just put his hand straight on it.

DENNIS. Yes, I know, mother, I was there.

MARJORIE. Now, I remember saving you some tins, Dennis. The ones I had my cough sweets in. What did you do with those?

DENNIS. I don't know. They're under that lot somewhere. I haven't got time, mother, to start putting things in tins. If I want a nail, there's a nail. I bang it in and that's that. If I can't find a nail, I use a screw. And if I can't find a screw, I don't bother.

MARJORIE. It'd break his heart in two to see it. Do you remember him working out there in his garage till all hours? Hammering away, making little things. Always beautifully finished. Do you remember his pipe rack?

DENNIS. Yes. Tremendous. It was a classic among pipe racks.

He applies himself with fresh fury to the kettle.

MARJORIE. He cut that with such care. Do you remember, Dennis? In fretwork, wasn't it? and he cut the letters out in fretwork as well. Pipes. PIPES across the top.

DENNIS (*muttering*). In case he forgot what it was for.

MARJORIE. That gave him more pleasure than anything. Till his eyesight went. Then he could hardly find his way to the garage at all, poor soul. Let alone his fretwork. Ah well, that's age, Dennis, that's age.

DENNIS. True. True. There's your kettle.

MARJORIE. It's not going to blow up, is it?

DENNIS. I've arranged it so it does.

MARJORIE. You're not very good at electrics. I'm still having trouble with that bedside light.

DENNIS. I've told you it's perfectly safe. The switch may be slightly faulty but it's perfectly safe.

MARJORIE. It's not the switch I'm worried about. The whole thing keeps falling out of its bottle. I had a lighted bulb in bed with me the other night.

DENNIS. I'll have another look at it.

MARJORIE. I daren't turn it on at all.

VERA *comes out from the house.*

VERA. Mother, you left the saucepan on with no water in it.

MARJORIE. No, that wasn't me, Vera. It wasn't me.

VERA. You made the tea. I haven't been near it.

MARJORIE. I may be getting old, Vera, but I wouldn't be stupid enough to put an empty saucepan back on a lighted gas. I'm not that old, Vera.

DENNIS. Now then, girls.

VERA. Well, it doesn't matter.

MARJORIE. I thank God that my mind is still perfectly clear.

VERA. What do you mean?

DENNIS. Yes, well as soon as it starts to go I'll send for the van, mother, don't worry.

MARJORIE. No, don't joke about it, Dennis, don't joke. It's only too true. Vera, could you carry these for me? I'm frightened I'll drop them. (*She gives* VERA *the kettle and both cups.*)

DENNIS. Well, don't give them to Vee.

MARJORIE. Can you manage?

VERA. Yes, I can manage.

DENNIS. I suppose I'll be mending that again in a minute.

VERA. Don't keep on, Dennis love.

DENNIS. Sorry. Sorry . . .

MARJORIE. Now don't tease her, Dennis. You're always teasing the girl. No wonder she's in a state.

VERA. I'm not in a state. I'm perfectly all right.

DENNIS. She's all right now, mother, don't keep on.

VERA. Will you be out here much longer, dear?

DENNIS. Why?

VERA. Oh, no reason. I've had the fire on in the front room. It's very cosy.

DENNIS. Lovely. Right.

VERA. Fancy that woman being Mrs. Mandelsham's daughter.

MARJORIE. Was that Mrs. Mandelsham's daugher?

VERA. Yes.

MARJORIE. Well, I never. Yes, she does. She looks like her.

VERA. Well, slightly.

MARJORIE. She will do when she's older.

VERA (*going to the door and pushing it open with her knee*). Anyway apparently her brother, you know, the one we all thought was a bit peculiar, well — it's all right, mother, I can manage — well, he went to Liverpool and — (*A cup falls from its saucer. She attempts to catch it and succeeds in dropping everything.*) Oh God in heaven, this door.

DENNIS (*roaring with laughter*). There she goes again. What did I tell you.

VERA *stands surveying the wreckage. On the brink of tears, unable to cope, she rushes into the house.*

MARJORIE. There you are, Dennis, what did I say? What did I say?

DENNIS. She's all right, mother.

MARJORIE *follows* VERA *into the house.*

Oh, good grief . . .

He starts whistling to himself cheerfully and tidying up his tool-bench.

Scene Two

The same. It is now May and sunny. NEIL *is setting up a small garden table round the side of the garage in the 'sitting area'.*

After a moment, PAM *enters from the house carrying a tray of teatime preliminaries.*

NEIL. Can you manage?

PAM. I can manage.

NEIL (*testing the table*). I think this is secure.

PAM. Any chairs?

NEIL. I don't know. I couldn't find any.

PAM. Are we all supposed to stand?

NEIL. You can't find anything in that place. Oh God, are these cucumber?

PAM. You don't have to eat them.

NEIL. Why cucumber?

PAM. These are paste. Have the paste.

NEIL. We could have brought Darren, you know.

PAM. Oh no.

NEIL. He'd have been happy enough, playing out here. He couldn't have come to any harm.

PAM. I'd have been up and down all through tea. If there's something that child can get his hands on that he shouldn't do, he does.

NEIL. I don't know. He's —

PAM. You don't know. That's just the point. You're out all day. aren't you.

NEIL. No, what I'm saying —

PAM. I'm with him, remember. All day. Every day.

   NEIL *mooches about. After a moment:*

NEIL. If you'd let me buy you that car, you could've —

PAM. What was I supposed to do with it? Stick Darren in the boot and just drive off.

NEIL. No. Your mother would have looked after him. You could've gone off for the odd day.

PAM. He's getting too much for her now. I can't keep asking her. I trust him more than her.

NEIL. Well, in the evenings. You could've got to your night classes.

PAM. Night classes?

NEIL. Yes.

PAM. I think that was just a lovely dream. Neil. I'm getting too old for that.

NEIL. Too old? You're only . . .

PAM. I know how old I am, thank you. I don't need reminding.

NEIL. I thought you said you wanted to go to night classes.

PAM. There's lots of things I want, Neil. But they're not to be, are they? If you follow me . . .

NEIL. How do you mean?

PAM. You know.

NEIL. No, what?

PAM. You know perfectly well.

NEIL. What?

PAM. I'm not spelling it out, Neil.

NEIL. Oh.

PAM. Yes. That.

NEIL. Well.

PAM. That's what I'm talking about.

NEIL. Well, I . . . (*He picks up a sandwich, embarrassed, and chews it.*) It's not that I . . . well . . .

PAM. You're eating cucumber.

NEIL. Oh God.

VERA *has come out of the house.*

VERA. Thank you so much, Pam. If I'd carried it, I'd've probably . . . oh, chairs. Have we got no chairs, Neil?

NEIL. I could only find this table.

VERA. Oh, Dennis put them away at the end of last year. First time we've brought them out this year. I hope we're doing the right thing today. Still, it's very mild.

PAM. It's lovely.

VERA. Considering it's May.

NEIL. Yes.

VERA. It shouldn't hurt mother's cold. She's over the worst. Neil, I wonder if you'd be very kind and ask Dennis if he would look out the chairs for us. They're probably tucked away at the back there somewhere. Only he's the only one who'll know where he put them.

NEIL. Right. (*A spasm of indigestion.*) Excuse me.

PAM. Neil.

NEIL. Sorry.

VERA. He was in the sitting room a moment ago watching the telly.

NEIL *goes in.*

PAM. Your mother-in-law's better then?

VERA. Oh yes. Over the worst. It's something that's going round, I think. She got up at lunchtime. She wouldn't miss Dennis's birthday tea, that's for sure. She thinks the world of Dennis.

PAM. Yes, I gathered.

VERA. Won't hear a word against him.

PAM. I think Neil's of the same opinion.

VERA. Yes, you're right. They're very thick these days, aren't they?

PAM. Almost inseparable. Every other evening. I'm just going to have another look at that car, he says, and off he goes.

VERA. Well, he's no trouble. Hardly see them. Both shut away in that garage. He keeps Dennis out of mischief.

PAM. Yes. (*Pause.*) I hope you don't mind me saying so, you don't look at all well.

VERA. Really? Oh . . .

PAM. Sorry, I don't mean to . . .

VERA. No, no. I've probably had a bit of a bug as well.

PAM. Oh.

Pause.

VERA. Yes. It's a bit of a bug. Been going around.

Pause.

PAM. Was it your idea to sell the car?

VERA. Er — yes. I think it was, yes. I mean, after all it's my car. Dennis bought it for me but it is mine.

PAM. Didn't you use it then?

VERA. No, not very much. I — well, if we're going anywhere I go with Dennis. So I go in his car.

PAM. But you go out on your own occasionally?

VERA. Not to speak of.

PAM. Still, I'd have thought it would have been very useful. Shopping, things like that.

VERA. Oh no. It's quicker to walk really. And then there's the parking and all that. It's very bad these days trying to park. Dreadful. (*Slight pause*.) And then, well really I found I didn't really enjoy driving really. I used to get so tense, you know. All the other traffic and, er, I couldn't seem . . . well, I'm not a very good driver. Dennis always said I couldn't concentrate. He used to hate driving with me. I mean, he didn't show it. He used to laugh about it but I know he hated it really. And I just seemed to get worse and worse at it. So I gave up eventually. I think I'm a born pedestrian. That's what Dennis said. All thumbs, you know. (*Pause.*) Would you like the car? I mean, supposing you wanted to buy it, would you like it?

PAM. Yes. Yes, I would.

VERA. Well, why don't you? I mean, if it's the price I'm sure I can get Dennis to . . . I'm sure I could. It's better than having it stuck in the garage there.

PAM. I don't think I could even afford to pay for the petrol.

VERA. I expect Neil could though.

PAM. Oh yes, Neil could.

VERA. Well . . .

PAM. But then if Neil bought it, it wouldn't be mine would it?
It would be Neil's.

VERA. Well, I suppose so. Technically.

PAM. Really it would. When I get a car, I'll buy it.

VERA. I can't say I can really see the difference. Still. Did you
work before you were married?

PAM. Yes. I was a secretary. Then a supervisor.

VERA. Oh really.

PAM. I was in charge of twenty-five girls at one time.

VERA. Twenty-five. Goodness.

PAM. I was the youngest supervisor they ever appointed. Then I
was expecting Darren. I planned to go straight back to work as
soon as I'd had him but it didn't work out like that.

VERA. No, well, your priorities change, don't they?

PAM. Yes.

VERA. You could probably go back now though, couldn't you?
If only part time.

PAM. I'm not sure that going back to supervise a typing pool is
really worth the effort. Even supposing they'd have me.

VERA. Well, no. I expect it's very hard work too, isn't it? And
as you get older, you . . .

PAM. Yes.

VERA. Not that you're old.

PAM. No.

VERA. Still.

PAM. What I'd really like to do is take a degree course.

VERA. A degree? You mean at a university?

PAM. And then teach perhaps. I'd like to teach.

VERA. Oh, that'd be nice. Teaching would be nice. Younger ones.

PAM. No. Older ones.

VERA. Oh. Well. I worked in Safeways. We had a really nice lot there. When I was there. Really nice. I don't see them much now. Most of them have got married.

PAM. You ought to get a job.

VERA. Me? Heavens above.

PAM. Do you good.

VERA. At my age? You must be joking. Anyway I'm far too busy for that. And I'm not qualified. You need qualifications these days. I mean, there was a time when I thought it would be nice to work with old folk, you know, but you need to have qualifications for that. To do it properly. Otherwise you can handle them wrong. I wouldn't want to handle them wrong.

PAM. There's nothing to stop you. If you really want to.

VERA. No, I suppose not. No more than you, really.

PAM. No.

DENNIS *comes from the house followed by* NEIL.

DENNIS. Here I am then, here I am. Who wants me?

VERA. Oh, there you are.

DENNIS. Here I am. Here comes Taurus the Bull. (*To* PAM.) Well?

PAM. Hallo.

DENNIS. No, not hallo. Happy birthday. Say happy birthday, Dennis.

PAM. Happy birthday, Dennis.

DENNIS. Thank you.

VERA. What about some chairs then, Mr. Taurus? We're both standing around here like sore thumbs.

DENNIS. They're in the garage.

VERA. Well, can you get them please?

DENNIS. Oh dear me, they're not that heavy. (*To* NEIL.) Dearie me.

VERA. Get on with you. I'm glad it's not your birthday every day.

DENNIS. Ah now, be careful what you say to me. We are two nil down at half time. You're looking at an anxious man.

VERA. Oh, sport, sport, sport.

DENNIS. Two nil down.

NEIL. Really.

VERA. Every Saturday afternoon, running, kicking, shooting, jumping. All afternoon.

DENNIS. You like the wrestling.

VERA. I don't like it at all. Great flabby things.

DENNIS (*bounding at her ape-like*). Grrr.

VERA. Oh, get off, Dennis, get off.

DENNIS *laughing goes off round to the garage.*

DENNIS. Can you give us a hand, Neil, there's a good lad?

NEIL. Right.

VERA. I'll just see how mother's managing, then I'll make the tea.

PAM. Can I help?

VERA. No, no. You stay out here. You might get a chair in a month if you're lucky.

DENNIS (*struggling vainly with the garage door*). Oh, this damn door.

VERA (*passing them on her way to the kitchen*). Why don't you fix it?

DENNIS. I'm going to when I've got a minute.

VERA. The up and under's still jammed as well. The electricity man got trapped in there the other day. He had to crawl through the window.

DENNIS. That'll teach him to read other people's meters. (*Succesfully opening the door.*) Ah, that's it.

The men go into the garage. VERA *goes into the house.*

During the next, PAM *wanders out through the ornamental gate to the front of the house.*

I'm really glad you came round today, Neil. I appreciate it very much.

NEIL. Oh, that's . . .

DENNIS (*moving to the back of the garage and rummaging*). Now where the hell did I put them last year? No, I really appreciate it. And Pam as well. I don't know what it is about birthdays. Some people, you know, they get to our age they start to forget about them but I've always — ever since I was a kid this is — I've always had this special thing about birthdays. (*Finding a chair.*) Ah ha. Here's one — here, cop hold of that. I suppose one of the reasons is that I always had these marvellous birthdays when I was a kid. Marvellous. My Dad, you know. My father, he always made me something. Didn't just buy it. He made it. He'd go into the garage two or three days before my birthday — (*Finding more chairs.*) here's a few more — before my birthday and I wasn't allowed near. I used to hear him sawing away, hammering and that, every evening when he was home while I was lying in bed and I'd think — what's he making this year? What's he going to make for me this year? And then. On the morning he'd produce something I'd never dreamt of like a — well, one year it was a roundabout, you know. Little wooden horses going up and down. All painted. All wood. Beautiful work. Right, that's it. One, two, three, four, five. Five chairs, five of us. Oy, before you go. Don't forget to have another look at your car. Two hundred and fifty quid, it's yours.

NEIL. Well . . .

DENNIS. Nobody else wants it. You won't get it any cheaper. In fact, if you leave it much longer, it'll become a vintage car and start going up again.

NEIL. Well, I'd buy it, yes. It's Pam, you see. I don't think she — well, she doesn't like the idea of me buying it for some reason.

DENNIS. Why not? You can afford it, can't you?

NEIL. Yes, I can afford it. She just doesn't want me to buy it. She wants to buy it.

DENNIS. Well then, give her the money as a present and let her buy it. What's the difference?

NEIL. No, it's not that. She's — odd like that. (*Suddenly wincing.*) Ah . . .

DENNIS. What's the matter?

NEIL. Nothing. Just this slight shoulder pain. I don't know what it is.

DENNIS. Oh.

NEIL. No, it's almost as if she resents accepting things from me. See what I mean?

DENNIS. Lucky fellow. Save yourself some money.

NEIL. It's as if she's trying to prove something. Only I don't know what it is. That she can do without me or something. But then again sometimes she's . . . she's . . .

DENNIS. What?

NEIL. Well, very amorous.

DENNIS. Really?

NEIL. At night time. I wake up and she's grabbing onto me. Digging in with her fingernails, you know . . .

DENNIS. That's probably what's wrong with your shoulder.

NEIL. And scratching — I've got a terrible scratch mark.

DENNIS. Well, fancy that. She doesn't look the sort.

NEIL. No.

DENNIS. What do you do?

NEIL. Well, I say like — lay off will you. I'm trying to get to sleep. I mean, it's about four in the morning she starts this.

DENNIS. You need your sleep.

NEIL. I do. I need eight hours. By the way I think the rumour you heard — about our house being scheduled for demolition — I think it was right. The bloke next door heard it too.

DENNIS. Oh. (*He ruminates for a second.*) Look, Neil, I've been meaning to ask you — if you're — if you were at some time considering buying this, it occurred to me you must have a bit of spare capital.

NEIL. Well, a bit, yes.

DENNIS. I was just curious. I hope you don't mind.

NEIL. No. It was a legacy. Got left it.

DENNIS. Oh really. Somebody die then?

NEIL. Yes. My father.

DENNIS. Ah. What's it doing at the moment?

NEIL. Well, it's in the bank.

DENNIS. Ah. Well. Now. It's just that I heard something the other day. Just between ourselves, there's this bloke who's working for this decorating firm and he's decided to set up on his own. And he's looking for capital. Just to get him started.

NEIL. Ah well . . .

DENNIS. No, he's a good man. I've known him for years. And he's as sharp as they come. He's been slogging his guts out for this lot and finally decided he'd be better on his own. And you know the way these fellows work — I mean, if he leaves, you can bet your bottom dollar he'll take a lot of the best customers with him. But he needs premises, equipment, transport. It all costs money. Now you can say, it'll be a gamble, but to my way of thinking I wouldn't even call it that.

NEIL. Well, I don't know. I'm not much . . .

DENNIS. No. Quite. What I'm saying is, if you've got, say, for the sake of argument, a thousand pounds to spare . . .

NEIL. Oh, it's more than that.

DENNIS. More than that, fair enough. But for the sake of this discussion let's say a thousand pounds — now you can put that thousand pounds of yours in the bank and you can literally watch it depreciating even with the interest. By the time you're sixty-five or seventy, you've got the equivalent of thirty pence. Now this way, looking at it long term, he expands, you expand. His profit's your profit, see what I mean? When you come to sell out, you're laughing.

NEIL. Well, I suppose it's possible.

DENNIS. Look, I'm not trying to talk you into anything. Believe me. It's your money but — tell you what, I'll try and arrange for you to meet this fellow. Then you can make up your own mind about him. His name's George Spooner and, as I say, he's a good man. Just see what you think.

NEIL. O.K.

DENNIS. See what you think. He's a first class workman. Wonderful. Did you happen to notice our lounge? That lounge in there.

NEIL. Oh yes, very nice.

DENNIS. Not the hall. That was somebody else. But he did the lounge. Beautiful work. You just have a look at the way that paper hangs when you next go in there.

NEIL. I will.

DENNIS. He's got terrific pride, that's what I like about him. Right, are you fit? You take those. I'll take these.

NEIL. Right.

They make their way round with the chairs. They meet PAM *wandering back.*

PAM. About time too.

DENNIS. Patience. Patience. Seldom found in woman. This looks good. Is mother coming down?

PAM. Vee went to fetch her.

DENNIS. I didn't think she'd miss out. (*Presenting* PAM *with a chair.*) Madame.

PAM (*sitting*). Thank you.

DENNIS. There you are Cecil.

NEIL. Thanks.

DENNIS. Oh by the way, while we're alone, just a quick word
. . . Er — how shall I put it? Vee is a bit — well I think looking
after mother and me and all that — she's tended to get a bit —
what shall I say? — tensed up. A bit tensed up. Nothing serious
but if she — you know — drops anything or spills her tea or
slips on her arse — anything like that — er — best to pretend
not to notice. Don't laugh or anything.

PAM. Why should we laugh?

DENNIS. I don't know. I mean, if you felt like laughing.

PAM. I won't laugh. If somebody falls over, I don't laugh.

DENNIS. Well, that's fair enough. Fine. No problem. All I'm
saying is if you did feel like laughing.

PAM. I won't.

DENNIS. Good. Then you're all right. Neil then?

NEIL. I wouldn't laugh.

DENNIS. Great. That just leaves me.

PAM. Just leaves you.

DENNIS. Good. Well. Fine.

> MARJORIE *comes out of the house in her coat. She carries a
> rug, a hot water bottle and her handbag.*

MARJORIE. I don't know why we're eating out here, I'm sure.
We'll all be in bed tomorrow.

> DENNIS *springs up and goes to her assistance, helping her to
> the table.* NEIL *rises and offers her his chair.*

DENNIS. Here she is. Welcome back to the land of the living.

MARJORIE. We'll all be in bed with pneumonia tomorrow.

DENNIS. For tomorrow we die.

> DENNIS *passes* MARJORIE *to* NEIL *who supports her*.
> DENNIS *opens a chair.*

MARJORIE. You'll be laughing at my funeral you will. I still haven't forgiven you for that kettle. Blowing up in my face.

DENNIS *laughs.*

DENNIS *(looking round).* Which way's the wind . . .

NEIL. From over there.

DENNIS. Right.

DENNIS *takes* MARJORIE *from* NEIL *and moves her round the table. He is about to help her into a chair. He hands* NEIL MARJORIE's *handbag which is encumbering the operation.*

PAM. No, it's not. The wind's coming from here. From round here.

DENNIS. Right.

He moves MARJORIE *again, forcing* PAM *to rise.* DENNIS *hands* PAM MARJORIE's *rug which is getting in the way. He is now hauling* MARJORIE *round the table like a stuffed dummy.* VERA *comes out with the teapot.*

VERA. All right, everyone. Sit down now. *(Taking in the scene.)* No Dennis, put her round there. She'll be out of the wind. She'll be out of the wind.

MARJORIE. I can't sit in the wind, I'm sorry.

VERA. You're not going to, mother. Dennis is putting you there. Put her there, Dennis.

DENNIS. I am putting her there.

VERA. Yes, put her there . . . All right then. Sit down, Neil. Help yourself.

NEIL. Right.

DENNIS *has sat* MARJORIE *at some considerable distance from the table, still in view of everyone but tucked round the corner.*

VERA. We'll put the birthday boy here.

DENNIS. Fine.

VERA. Oh it's really nice, isn't it? I never thought we'd be able to.

NEIL (*who has been displaying signs of the cold*). Very mild.

MARJORIE *coughs.* VERA *reacts.*

VERA. Could you pass me the cups, dear.

DENNIS. Coming up.

VERA (*starting to pour* PAM's *tea*). Just as it comes for you, Pam?

PAM. Please.

MARJORIE. I'll have to have mine weak.

VERA. Yes, you'll get it weak, mother. Just a minute.

DENNIS. Well, this is a nice spread. Very nice. This you, Vee, or mother?

VERA (*handing* PAM *her tea*). I did this. (*Proffering plate of cucumber sandwiches.*) Have a sandwich, Neil.

NEIL. Er, yes. I'll stick to those if you don't mind.

VERA *puts down the plate of cucumber, rather over-anxious.* NEIL, *with a swift reflex gesture, prevents the plate sliding into his lap.* VERA *offers the paste sandwiches.* NEIL *takes one. Meanwhile,* DENNIS *helps himself to cucumber. Both men help themselves to side plates and napkins.* VERA *offers a paste sandwich to* PAM. PAM *takes one.* VERA *puts down the sandwiches and gives* PAM *a plate and napkin.* VERA *resumes pouring tea, this time* NEIL's *cup. As she starts this.*

MARJORIE (*suddenly*). Where's his cake.

VERA. What?

MARJORIE. Where's Dennis's cake?

DENNIS. Ah — (*He rises expectantly.*)

PAM *and* NEIL *also look more or less expectant.*

VERA. We didn't make one this year, mother, did we?

MARJORIE. Dennis always has a cake.

VERA. Yes, but you've been ill, mother, remember.

MARJORIE. You could have made him a cake, Vera.

VERA gives NEIL his tea.

DENNIS (*mouthing, sotto, across to MARJORIE*). It doesn't matter, mother.

MARJORIE (*mouthing likewise*). She could have made you a cake.

VERA becomes aware of this silent conversation. DENNIS and MARJORIE continue mouthing and gesturing till DENNIS becomes aware of VERA's gaze.

VERA (*pouring DENNIS's tea*). You know what I'm like with cakes. And I can't do all that icing like you do. I just get it all over everything. We should have asked Mrs. Mandlesham . . .

MARJORIE. You don't need to ask anyone how to ice a cake.

VERA. Well, I can't do it.

PAM. Nor can I.

DENNIS. It's all right, mother, it's all right.

VERA gives DENNIS his tea. She offers DENNIS a cucumber sandwich. He takes one. She offers NEIL who declines. She offers PAM.

PAM. What about your mother?

She takes the plate from VERA and offers the sandwiches to MARJORIE. VERA pours her own tea.

MARJORIE (*unaware of PAM*). Ever since he was a little boy, he's always had his cake. Even when your father was dying, Dennis, I still made you your cake.

PAM gives up proffering the plate, waves it at MARJORIE somewhat 'V' signlike and replaces it on the table.

DENNIS. Yes, marvellous they were too, mother. Marvellous.

A long silence. VERA reaches for the hot water jug. She catches the sugar spoon with her wrist, sending sugar high in the air. VERA attempts to ignore this. The others concentrate their attention elsewhere. Shakily, VERA replenishes the teapot with hot water. The others find this, despite themselves, compulsory viewing. She returns hot water jug to the table, as it happens close to NEIL's *place.* NEIL, *nervous, shifts his legs. Having safely negotiated this,* VERA *smiles round. Everyone looks away.* VERA *reaches for the remaining empty cup and saucer. She rattles it dangerously but places it in front of her. She puts milk in the cup. She starts pouring tea.* MARJORIE's *voice suddenly breaks the silence.*

MARJORIE. Remember when you were in the army. (VERA's *tea-pouring experiences a hiccup.*) I parcelled them up and I sent them to you overseas.

VERA. Yes, well, I'm very sorry. (*She rises with the cup, preparing to take it across to* MARJORIE.)

MARJORIE. I think the least you could have done, Vera, is to make him a cake. It was really very thoughtless to forget . . .

The teacup begins to vibrate uncontrollably in VERA's *hand.*

VERA (*through gritted teeth*). Will someone take this cup, please? Will someone take this cup from me?

PAM (*taking the cup from her*). Here. Here, all right.

PAM *takes cup to* MARJORIE. NEIL *rises, takes a couple of sandwiches, puts them on a sideplate and takes them over to* MARJORIE.

NEIL. Would you like a sandwich, Mrs. —

PAM *returns and sits.*

MARJORIE. Yes, I might as well have a sandwich.

NEIL *returns and sits. Pause.*

Seeing as she hasn't made a cake.

VERA (*spills a cup and saucer*). Oh.

Tea pours all over the table, running down between the slats. NEIL *and* PAM *rise hastily.* DENNIS, *still seated, suppresses his mirth.*

DENNIS. Oh God.

PAM. It's all right. I'll do it. Don't you move, Vee, you'll have it all over everything.

VERA. I'm sorry, I —

PAM. No damage.

NEIL. Can I?

PAM. No, please don't.

NEIL. But if I held this, you could . . .

PAM (*sharp*). Please, Neil, leave it to me.

NEIL (*angrily*). All right. All right. I was only trying to . . . I'll keep my mouth shut in future. (*He takes a sandwich and jams it into his mouth.*) Oh.

DENNIS. Eh?

NEIL. Cucumber.

VERA (*in an undertone*). If she says one more word about that bloody cake.

PAM. There we are. All mopped up.

VERA. Thank you, Pam.

A silence.

DENNIS *continues his struggle to contain his laughter.* NEIL *has an indigestion spasm.* PAM *glares at him.* DENNIS's *laughter erupts. He moves away from the table. At length recovers. Wipes his eyes. Stands surveying the miserable group, smiling.*

DENNIS. Well.

Pause.

(*Softly.*) Happy birthday to me.
Happy birthday to me.
Happy birthday, dear Dennis,
Happy birth —

He catches NEIL's *eye.* NEIL *gently incidates* VERA. DENNIS *darts a look at* VERA. *He tails off into silence. They sit.*

Curtain.

ACT TWO

Scene One

The same. October. The lights are on in the garage. Outside it is dark. DENNIS has looped a string of coloured electric light bulbs high up round the inside walls of the garage. Some of the bulbs are missing from the sockets. He is at present working on his present for his mother. It is a needlework box he has made. He is sanding it with an electric drill with sander attachment. NEIL is perched on the bench, a glass of wine in his hand, the bottle nearby. DENNIS's glass stands untouched. He is absorbed and hardly listens to NEIL's conversation which, anyway, is intermittently drowned by the sound of the drill.

    DENNIS drills. He stops.

NEIL. . . . . you see, my trouble — Pam's trouble is this. I think we —

    DENNIS starts drilling, the next is inaudible.

    — both expect things from each other. Things that the other one is not prepared to give —

    DENNIS stops drilling.

    — to the other one. Do you get me?

DENNIS. Uh — huh.

NEIL. I suppose it's nature really, isn't it?

DENNIS. Ah.

NEIL. You have your opposites — like this. (*He holds up his hands to demonstrate.*)

    DENNIS starts drilling.

    This is me — that's her. And they attract —

    DENNIS stops drilling.

— like a magnet.

DENNIS *starts again.*

Only with people as opposed to magnets, the trouble is with people —

DENNIS *stops drilling.*

they get — demagnetised after a bit. I honestly think Pam and me have reached the end of the road. (*He looks to* DENNIS *for a reaction to this.*)

DENNIS *drills.* NEIL *waits.* DENNIS *stops.*

I'm saying I think we've reached the end of the road. Pam and me.

DENNIS. Ah.

NEIL. It's a terrible thing to say. She's drinking as well, you know. I'm the cause of that.

DENNIS. Oh, I shouldn't think so. (*Holding up his work.*) Does that look level to you?

NEIL. Looks it. I've reached a crossroads, you see, Dennis.

DENNIS. I've mislaid the spirit level.

NEIL. Suddenly I've got to decide. I've got to make decisions. That's not something that comes very easily to me. Frankly, I find it difficult to make decisions and that truly is what gets Pam. Decide, she says. You decide. She admires strength, Dennis. I think she admires you, actually.

DENNIS. Oh, does she? That's nice.

NEIL. Women need a rock, you see. A rock. Trouble is, I'm a bloody marshmallow.

DENNIS *drills,* NEIL *drones on.*

Weakness in a man. That's something a woman can never respect. Even today with all this equality, she still expects to find in a man someone she can rely on in a crisis. And if that man doesn't stand up to the test, God help him.

DENNIS *stops drilling.*

DENNIS. True. True.

NEIL. Well, you can't say I haven't tried. Anyway, she's given up clawing me to death in the night. (*Pause.*) You can't say I haven't tried.

DENNIS. No.

NEIL. I mean, this business with George Spooner. That's a start isn't it? I decided that myself. I said, right, if Dennis says he's O.K., he's O.K.

DENNIS. He's O.K. is George Spooner.

NEIL. So. I didn't even ask her. I just did it. I drew out the money, handed it to him and said there you are, George, there's three thousand, five hundred quid. Get on with it. Do your worst.

DENNIS. You won't be sorry.

NEIL. I know that. I know that. I liked him. I liked old George.

DENNIS. The only way you'll lose your money with him is, if he drops dead from overwork.

NEIL. That's what I told Pam.

DENNIS. What did she say?

NEIL. She said — she said I was an idiot. You idiot, she said.

DENNIS. We'll see, won't we?

NEIL. We will. We'll see about that. Did I tell you she's drinking? I can always tell when she's drinking. She gets very — abusive.

DENNIS. Ah well. Blows over.

NEIL. Vera's looking better.

DENNIS. Oh, she is. She's a lot better.She's getting better every day. Once she and mother can bury the hatchet, we'll be laughing.

NEIL. Are they still . . .?

DENNIS. Not talking at all.

NEIL. Really.

DENNIS. Well actually, it's Vera who's not talking to mother.

Mother comes in one door, Vera goes out the other. Ridiculous. Been going on for weeks. I said to them — look, girls, just sit down have a laugh about it. There's only one life, you know. That's all you've got. One life. Laugh and enjoy it while you can. We'll probably all be dead tomorrow so what's the difference? Do they listen to me? Do they hell. (*Admiring his handiwork.*) That's not bad. Not bad at all.

NEIL. I took your advice by the way. Went to the doctor.

DENNIS. Oh yes?

NEIL. Yes.

DENNIS. And?

NEIL. He said there was nothing wrong with me.

DENNIS. Oh good. That must be a relief.

NEIL. The trouble is, can I believe him? Is he saying that genuinely or is he saying there is something wrong with me but it's so wrong that there's no point in telling me?

DENNIS. Oh, I don't think they do that sort of thing.

NEIL. They do. I have that on very good authority. They do just that.

DENNIS. Well, I'd look on the bright side.

NEIL. Yes, quite right. I had confirmation about our house this morning.

DENNIS. Oh really.

NEIL. It's definitely listed for demolition. They reckon in about a year.

DENNIS. Well, they'll rehouse you.

NEIL. Oh yes. We'll get rehoused. If we're still together.

DENNIS. Well, there you are then. Nice new house. Nothing wrong with that.

NEIL. No. No. True. (*Slight pause.*) God, I sometimes feel like jumping off a bridge, Den.

DENNIS. Oh, come on. Cheer up. It's your birthday.

NEIL. If I wasn't able to come along and talk to you like this, I think —

DENNIS *picks up a hammer and bangs a loose joint into place.*

— I think I'd have gone and done away with myself —

DENNIS *stops hammering.*

— long before this.

DENNIS. There we are.

NEIL. Very good.

DENNIS. Now we'll see who's the joiner in this family. I'll show her.

NEIL. That your mother's birthday present, is it?

DENNIS. Yes. Needlework box.

NEIL. Thanks for the tie, by the way. Very nice.

DENNIS. Oh, glad you liked it. Mother chose it actually.

NEIL. Ah. Very nice. Good taste.

DENNIS. Yes, she has. Now then, what's next. Happy birthday, by the way.

NEIL. Oh, thank you.

DENNIS. No, you see, just between ourselves, I'm rigging up a little surprise for mother. Father always used to do that. He always had some little surprise for her on her birthday. I try to keep up the tradition.

NEIL. Is that what those are for?

DENNIS. The lights. Yes. Just a little touch. Had them left over from a barbecue. Look. (*He switches them on by the door. They fail to go on.*) Ah. Something wrong. I'll check those. Yes, look, some of the bulbs are missing. Steps? Stepladder . . .

NEIL. 'Course one of the problems is what to do with Darren.

DENNIS. When's that?

NEIL. When Pam and I separate.

DENNIS. Ah. What did she give you by the way?

NEIL. What?

DENNIS. For your birthday. What did Pam give you?

NEIL. Oh, I don't think she really had time. She's got her hands full with Darren at the moment.

DENNIS. There's a square box here somewhere with some coloured bulbs. Can you see if you can see them?

NEIL. — er . . . (*He starts to search.*)

> PAM *comes out from the house. She rattles the doorknob of the garage.*

PAM. Hey, you two. Open up.

DENNIS. Just a minute. Just a minute. (*To* NEIL.) Quick, sling us that cloth.

NEIL. Eh?

DENNIS. To cover this up, quick.

PAM. Open up.

DENNIS. Right. Open up.

> NEIL *struggles with the door.*

> Give it a shove. I must fix that. And the other one, come to that.

> NEIL *manages to open the door.*

PAM (*entering*). What are you doing out here, for heaven's sake?

DENNIS. Hallo, hallo, here's trouble. Aha, a box of bulbs. These are they.

> *He erects the stepladder, takes out a bulb and starts to climb.*

PAM. Just what do you think you're doing?

NEIL. How do you mean?

PAM. We're all sat in there twiddling our thumbs waiting for you. What's going on.

DENNIS. Surprises, surprises.

NEIL. Just getting things ready, that's all.

PAM. And what are we supposed to do in the meanwhile? I mean, there's Vee and me in the kitchen, and Marjorie sitting on her own in the sitting room because Vee won't go in there if she's in there, and we're all having a marvellous time. I thought this was supposed to be a birthday party.

NEIL. Well, don't look at me.

PAM. I am looking at you. I want you to come in there and socialise.

NEIL. All right, all right.

DENNIS. Could you pass me one of those bulbs, please, from the box?

NEIL (*doing so*). I'll be in in a minute.

PAM. No, Neil, I mean now. Right now.

DENNIS. Ta.

NEIL. Look, I can't at the moment, Pam. I'm —

PAM. I don't care what you're doing, I'm not sitting in there for another half hour.

NEIL. Look, don't keep on Pam, for God's sake. Don't keep on. I've had it up to here.

DENNIS. And another one, please.

PAM. Oh, don't you start that one. You know what happens if you start that one.

NEIL. I know. I know.

DENNIS. Bulb, bulb, bulb.

PAM. Well, just you remember. You have absolutely no right to complain about anything ever. You've handed over total responsibility to me. You have forfeited any right to say anything ever again.

NEIL. What the hell are you going on about?

DENNIS. Another bulb, *s'il vous plaît*.

PAM. You have left me to deal with the running of the house

entirely. You have left me to bring up your child and you have left me to nurse mother on my own.

NEIL. I don't know how you can say that.

PAM. Because it is true, my love. That is why I can say it.

NEIL. It isn't true.

DENNIS. Could somebody steady the steps, please.

NEIL (*placing a hand on the steps*). It just isn't true at all.

PAM. Of course it's bloody true.

NEIL. Look, don't swear Pam. Every time you get angry, you start swearing.

PAM. I'll do more than bloody swear in a minute if you don't come straight back in there with me this instance.

As she speaks, she grips the side of the steps in fury.

DENNIS. Look, steady, steady. I'll fall off in a minute.

NEIL. Look, don't do that with the steps, Pam, he'll fall off them.

PAM. Serve him right if he did. (*She shakes the steps.*)

DENNIS. Oy. Oy. Do you mind?

NEIL. Pam, he'll fall off them.

VERA *comes in from the house.*

VERA. Dennis. Dennis.

DENNIS. Hallo there.

VERA. Dennis, will you please come down at once. Come into the house, go into the sitting room and ask your mother, ever so nicely, if she would mind turning down the television.

DENNIS. Can't you ask her yourself, love, I'm a bit . . .

VERA. I have asked her. Twice I have asked her. She has taken not a blind bit of notice. In fact, I think she's actually turned it up. Do I have to remind you there is a small baby next door.

DENNIS. Yes, all right. All right.

VERA. Who is very probably asleep.

DENNIS. Would somebody go and turn the television down, please?

PAM. I'll go.

VERA. No, I want Dennis to go. It's his mother. He can cope with her. I want him to see what she's like.

DENNIS. How can I go? I'm up a ladder.

PAM. It's all right, I'll go. (*She does so.*)

VERA (*calmer*). What are you doing, Dennis? Will you please tell me what you're doing out here?

DENNIS. I'm just fixing up a little surprise, that's all. Like I always do.

VERA. Surprise?

DENNIS. For mother's birthday, love. It's her birthday.

VERA. Oh God, don't remind me. Sixty-seven today. I don't look sixty-seven do I, Dennis? Everyone was amazed when they heard I was sixty-seven.

DENNIS (*descending the ladder*). Look, Vee, Vee, come on. Calm down, love, calm down.

VERA. And the butcher, he said — oh are you sixty-seven, Mrs. Crowthorne, I'd never have guessed.

DENNIS. Vee, Listen, it's her birthday. It's only once a year. Now go on. Go in there and give her a smile. That's all she wants. Just a smile. Say — happy birthday, mother and give her a little drink.

VERA. She doesn't need a little drink. She's already downed half a bottle.

DENNIS. Vera. Now, Vera, for me. Come on, love, for me.

VERA. Oh God, Dennis, you just don't . . . you don't . . .

DENNIS. Now what is it? What don't I do.

VERA. You don't . . . look, would you mind very much, Neil?

NEIL. Eh?

VERA. Could you find somewhere else to go just for a minute?

NEIL. Oh, right.

DENNIS. He's all right. He's all right.

VERA. He's not all right.

NEIL. It's all right. I'm going.

DENNIS. Thanks, Neil. Thanks.

NEIL *goes out of the door.*

Now, Vee. What's the trouble?

VERA. It's just —

NEIL. I'll shut the door, shall I?

DENNIS. Thank you, Neil.

NEIL *closes the door, contemplates whether or not to go into the house and finally opts to sit on a dustbin.*

VERA. It's just — I think I need help, Dennis.

DENNIS. How do you mean, help?

VERA. From you. I don't think I can manage much longer unless I get your help.

DENNIS. Help. What way? With mother? Do you mean with mother?

VERA. Partly. No, not just her. You never seem to be here, Dennis.

DENNIS. What do you mean? I'm here. I'm home as much as most men. Probably more than most men.

VERA. Yes, but then you're out here, aren't you?

DENNIS. Not all the time.

VERA. Most of the time.

DENNIS. Well I'm doing things. For the house. I mean, you're welcome to come out here too. There's nothing to stop you if you want to talk. Talk things over.

VERA. But we've got a home, Dennis. I spend all day trying to make it nice. I don't want to spend the evening sitting in a garage.

DENNIS. Oh, come on.

VERA. I mean, what's the point of my . . . doing everything? I mean, what's the point? I need help, Dennis.

DENNIS. Yes, but don't you see, you're not being clear. Vee. You say help but what sort of help do you mean?

VERA. Just help. From you.

DENNIS. Yes. Well, look, tell you what. When you've got a moment, why don't you sit down, get a bit of paper and just make a little list of all the things you'd like me to help you with. Things you'd like me to do, things that need mending or fixing and then we can talk about them and see what I can do to help. All right?

VERA *does not reply.*

How about that, Vee? All right? Does that suit you?

VERA *moves to the door.*

Vee?

VERA *goes slowly out and into the house.*

Vee. Vee.

NEIL *sticks his head round the door.*

NEIL. She's gone inside.

DENNIS. Oh well. All this house needs, Neil, is a little bit of understanding and a little bit more of people being able to laugh at themselves. (*He starts to ascend the steps.*) That's all it needs. Sounds simple enough, doesn't it? But when I think of the times I've said it and the times it's . . . (*Suddenly, loudly.*) Steady the ladder.

NEIL (*diving for the steps and steadying them*). Sorry.

DENNIS. Blimey, I nearly went that time. One more bulb.

NEIL. One more bulb.

DENNIS. Now, I'm going to need you for the cake, Neil.

NEIL. Cake?

DENNIS. This is what happens. I want you, if you would, to wait in the kitchen. I've hidden mother's cake on the top of the shelf over the fridge. It's in a big maroon tin. Now. I'll call mother out here. As soon as she's through the kitchen, out with the cake and light the candles. She walks in here — (*Demonstrating.*) you see, like this — I'll be hiding behind here, you see. Now as soon as she's through the door, I'll give you your signal. That'll be one long blast on the horn. O.K.? At the same moment, I jump up — happy birthday, mother — and uncover the present. Meanwhile, you have come in behind her with the cake — if you like, singing happy birthday, dear Marjorie or something — and if you can manage it, switching on these lights from here, you see? And at the same moment, Vee and Pam also come out of hiding. And you just watch mother's face. It'll be a picture. A real study.

NEIL. You're very fond of your mother, aren't you?

DENNIS. Yes, well, I suppose I am. I have to admit it. She's got her faults. She's like Vee, you know. She gets a bee in her bonnet about things but you can soon joke her out of it. Easy as that.

PAM *enters from the house with a broken glass in a dustpan.*

PAM. Where do you keep your dustbins in this place?

DENNIS. Round the side there. Just behind you.

PAM. Oh yes.

DENNIS. Been a mishap?

PAM. Just a little one. Only one or two glasses. Nothing serious. (*To* NEIL.) Hallo, dearest.

NEIL. You all right?

PAM. Fine, dearest, fine.

NEIL. Right.

PAM. I'm getting very hungry. Is there any chance of eating soon?

DENNIS. Yes, we're nearly all set.

PAM. What have you been doing?

DENNIS. Never mind. You'll see. Eh, Neil?

PAM. As long as you haven't persuaded him to give away any more money.

NEIL. Look, it was my money.

PAM. Oh quite, quite.

DENNIS. Not unless he still wants to buy the car.

PAM. He can't afford it now anyway.

NEIL. Oh look, Pam, please.

PAM. Go to hell.

NEIL *goes out into the house.*

DENNIS (*at the back of the garage*). Neil, would you mind . . . oh, has he gone?

PAM. 'Fraid so.

DENNIS. Oh well, perhaps you wouldn't mind, Pam. I just want to clear a bit of space in here. Could you pass me that box?

PAM. This one?

DENNIS. Ta.

PAM (*handing him the box*). You'll really have to do something about those two, you know.

DENNIS. Who do you mean?

PAM. Your wife and your mother.

DENNIS. Ah well. It's a traditional problem really, isn't it? Nothing much you can do. They rub along.

PAM. They do not rub along.

DENNIS. Oh well, not just at present. No. But these rows happen. You haven't seen us normally, Pam. I can tell you, there were times in the past when we three, we've sat round in there and we've laughed and pulled each other's legs about things. You'd be amazed.

PAM. I would. (*Indicating another box.*) You want this one?

DENNIS. If you would, thank you.

PAM *bends to pick up the box. She becomes giddy. She*

stands up and steadies herself.

You all right?

PAM. Wah. Yes, fine. You ever going to sell this thing?

DENNIS. Well, frankly, nobody seems really interested. And then I thought, well, it could be that in a few months Vee might get it into her head to want to start driving again. I mean, the way things are going she might. I mean, in general terms, she's getting better every day.

PAM. What exactly was wrong with her?

DENNIS. Oh well, she got these very gloomy depressions. You know. Nothing was right. She got very jittery so she went to see this doctor, psychiatrist, and he said primarily she was just to take it easier. She wasn't to rush at things. And she went on seeing him for a couple of months, and then she seemed to be feeling better and she just stopped going. I mean, I think we got the message. All Vee needs is a happy family atmosphere. To feel she has a home around her.

PAM. Could be. Good old Dennis.

DENNIS. Beg your pardon?

PAM (*holding up the bottle of wine*). May I?

DENNIS. Help yourself. Help yourself.

PAM. I must say, you're very resilient. I think I'd have given up years ago.

DENNIS. Given up what?

PAM. Trying to spread jolly cheer.

DENNIS. Well. Smile costs nothing, does it?

PAM. True. True. Could you jolly me up, please, Dennis.

DENNIS. You? You're all right, aren't you?

PAM. Amazingly enough, no.

DENNIS. All right. You tell me your problem. I'll sort it out.

PAM. Well. Here am I, constantly being reminded by this avalanche of birthdays we all seem to be having, that I'm no longer as young as I'd like to be.

DENNIS. What does that mean, eh? For a start, what's that supposed to mean?

PAM. I feel old, Dennis — old, unfulfilled, frustrated, unattractive, dull, washed out, undesirable — you name it. And I've got absolutely nothing to look forward to. How about that to be getting on with?

DENNIS. Well, for a start you've got your kid. What about your little boy?

PAM. He'll soon go. As soon as he's strong enough to walk, he'll be gone.

DENNIS. Well, there's Neil,

PAM. Next.

DENNIS. Er — no wait. You can't just say that. What about Neil?

PAM. I don't really look forward to Neil as much as I used to Dennis.

DENNIS. Really?

PAM. Really and truly.

DENNIS. Well then. I don't know.

PAM. Do you know what it's like, Dennis? To feel undesirable?

DENNIS. No. No. Can't say I do.

PAM. That's what he's done to me.

DENNIS. Sorry? Who's this? We're still talking about Neil, are we?

PAM. He's made me feel ashamed. Why should I be made to feel ashamed?

DENNIS. Depends what you've been up to, eh? (*He laughs.*)

PAM. He hasn't even paid me the compliment of going after another woman. I could accept that, just about. But to be frozen out, as if I was unnatural, some sort of freak. It isn't me, is it? It's him.

DENNIS. Neil?

PAM. There's something wrong with him.

DENNIS. Health worries, you mean;

PAM. That man is destroying me. He is systematically destroying me. I was the youngest supervisor they'd ever had. I had prospects. They told me. Prospects. They were grooming me for something bigger. That's what they told me when I left.

DENNIS. That a fact?

PAM. They had their eye on me. They said so.

DENNIS. Very good. You must have made an impression. Good.

PAM. You don't find me undesirable, Dennis, do you?

DENNIS. Ah well. Now remember, I'm a married man.

PAM. Presumably you've still got feelings.

DENNIS. Not if I can help them, I haven't. (*He laughs.*) No, you're very attractive. I mean, I'm perfectly sure, in another life, assuming such a thing existed, that you'd very probably attract me. I'd go so far as to say, I'd probably fancy you.

PAM. Then why the hell doesn't Neil?

DENNIS. What?

PAM. Fancy me, or whatever you call it.

DENNIS. Well, he possibly does. In fact, I'm sure he possibly does. But listen, Pam, when you get to our age, you have to slow down. We all do. I mean, I would do things ten years ago I can't do now. I used to be able to play forty-five minutes each way. Football. Down the road there. Couldn't do it now to save my life. Same with you, same with Neil. You need to adjust.

PAM. It is age then? You think?

DENNIS. Probably nothing more than that. (*Pause.*) That any help at all?

PAM. No, I'm sorry, Dennis, you're not doing a very good job . . . . . . I'm still very depressed.

DENNIS. Well, I don't know. I mean, what do you want? Want

me to do a funny dance for you or something?

PAM. Oh yes, please. Do a funny dance.

DENNIS. No, I mean seriously. Seriously I can't cheer you up unless you're serious about it.

PAM. Perhaps I should have said yes to the car.

DENNIS. Well, the offer's still open. Two hundred quid.

PAM. I can't afford two hundred pence, Dennis. I used to have some money. Quite a lot of money actually. That I'd saved. But now I'm a housewife so I'm not allowed to have any. And I spent all my money on curtains and pillow cases and lavatory brushes —

(*She sits behind the wheel of the car.*) Brrm brrm.

DENNIS. Runs well.

PAM. Fasten your seat belts. Start her up, Dennis.

DENNIS. Haven't got the keys.

PAM. Start her up and let's slip away.

DENNIS. No, that door's still stuck, you see. I really must fix that.

PAM. Come on, Dennis, start her up.

DENNIS. You can't. Not in the garage. Not with the door shut.

PAM. Brrm brrm.

DENNIS. You all right?

PAM. Brrm.

DENNIS. Pam, Pam.

PAM (*loudly*). BRRM.

DENNIS. Now come on, Pam. Pam.

PAM. Brrm — oh. Oh, Dennis.

DENNIS. What is it?

PAM. I think I'm going to be car sick.

DENNIS (*alarmed*). Now hold on, hold on. Not on the upholstery.

I'll help you out. Hang on.

PAM. Oh God.

DENNIS (*struggling with her*). Come on, you're all right. Come on.

He tries to tug her clear.

She appears to be tangled with everything, especially the seat belts and the steering wheel. DENNIS *tugs at her sweater sleeve. Her arm comes out of it.*

Oh blimey o'reilly. Come on Pam.

MARJORIE *comes out of the house in her party frock.*

MARJORIE. Now, you can say what you like, Dennis, I am not sitting in there any longer. I want my surprise. Dennis? (*She enters the garage.*)

DENNIS. Oh mother, look, could you give me a hand?

MARJORIE. Oh, Dennis, you naughty boy.

DENNIS. Mother, please.

MARJORIE. It's all right, Dennis. It's all right. I've seen nothing. You needn't worry.

DENNIS. Mother. (*He continues to struggle.*)

MARJORIE *goes out and is closing the door when she is confronted by* VERA.

MARJORIE. It's all right, Vera, there's no one in there.

VERA. What do you mean? Dennis is in there.

MARJORIE. No, Dennis is not in there, Vera. And I would prefer you didn't go in.

VERA. Oh, get out of the way. (*She pushes* MARJORIE *aside.*)

MARJORIE. I will not have my son being unjustly accused.

VERA. I said, get out of the way.

She opens the door and goes in.

MARJORIE. All right. On your own head be it.

VERA. Dennis I — (*Seeing them.*) Oh, I'm sorry I . . .

DENNIS. Vee, will you give me a hand.

MARJORIE. I told you not to come in. Serve you right. There are certain things it is best a wife doesn't know about.

VERA. You poisonous old woman. You're loving this, aren't you? It's what you've really wanted all along, wasn't it? For Dennis to go off with somebody. To break up my home.

MARJORIE. I don't know what you're talking about, Vera, you're being most offensive.

VERA. You nasty old toad. You've always hated me. You've always wanted my home.

DENNIS. Now, Vera.

MARJORIE. I don't know what's come over you.

VERA. Oh, I'd love to — I'd love to sandpaper your rotten face.

She picks up the electric drill.

MARJORIE (*screaming and running up to one corner of the garage*). Vera. Vera.

DENNIS. Now, girls, steady. Girls.

VERA (*screaming above the drill whose cable is too short to allow her to reach* MARJORIE.) You sneaky, rotten, deceitful sly, old toad.

MARJORIE. Now, you stop that. You stop that. Dennis, help me.

DENNIS (*releasing* PAM *and cautiously approaching* VERA *and the whirling drill*). Now, Vee . . .

PAM, *released, slumps forward on to the steering wheel. The horn blasts loudly and continuously.*

Now, Vee. I want you to stop that. I want you to put that down.

VERA. Bitch, bitch, bitch.

MARJORIE. Stop her, Dennis, stop her. Tell her to stop it.

NEIL *enters from the kitchen bearing the illuminated cake. As he enters the garage, he switches on the lights, bathing the scene in a glorious technicolour.*

NEIL. Happy birthday to you
  Happy birthday to you
  Happy birth —

  He tails off.

Scene Two

The same. January. A cold clear morning. VERA sits in the garden in the 'sitting area'. She is enveloped in a large rug, with just her face showing. After a moment DENNIS comes in through the gate. He carries two large supermarket carrier bags. He has on his coat, scarf and gloves.

DENNIS. There. That didn't take long, did it? I think I've got everything we need. Except the soup. I couldn't get your soup, Vee. Had to get another sort. But the man said it was just as good. Just as good. Now, are you sure you're warm enough out here?

Vera (*in a whisper*). Yes.

DENNIS. Well, as long as you don't die of exposure on us. I'm not having that. See? I could get Mother to bring you out a hot water bottle. I mean, if you insist on sitting out here . . . Very crowded in town today. Saturday morning, I suppose. Oh Vee, now this'll interest you. Listen to this. I heard something today. You remember old Spooner? George Spooner, you remember? The man who did our sitting room. Well, guess what happened? He's run off. With his secretary from his office. Drawn out all the money and done a bunk. Left his wife, his business, everything. What about that, eh? Would you credit it. Nobody knows where they've gone. All those poor people with half their wallpaper hanging off. Eh? Poor old Neil though. There goes his money. Well, we live and learn. Old George Spooner. I'd have laid my life on the line for George Spooner.

  MARJORIE *comes out of the house.*

MARJORIE. Oh, Dennis, you're back. Did you get on all right?

DENNIS. I think so, mother. I can cope with a bit of shopping without falling down, you know.

MARJORIE. Well, knowing you. How is she?

DENNIS. She seems all right.

MARJORIE. As long as she's warm enough. If only she'd stay in the house, I'd feel happier. I could keep more of an eye on her. She won't have it. She doesn't like it. She gets so fidgety and restless.

DENNIS. Well, maybe the fresh air'll help her along.

MARJORIE. Did you get her soup?

DENNIS. Yes, we're well stocked up now.

MARJORIE. I'll try her with some at lunchtime. She had her rice krispies this morning so she's not doing so badly, are you, dear? Would you like to take those through to the kitchen, Dennis.

DENNIS. Will do. Will do.

MARJORIE. You must be nearly ready for your lunch.

DENNIS. I wouldn't say no to that, mother.

MARJORIE. I've got you a nice chop.

DENNIS. Lovely. Yum yum.

He goes into the house.

MARJORIE. Now, you're positive you're warm enough, Vera? (*Tucking her in more securely.*) That's it. That's better. Now you just sit there quietly. You've no need to worry, do you hear? Dennis is being taken good care of. I'll see to him. You just look after yourself. We just want to see you get better. You know what Dennis has made for me? He's made me a little table. Little bedside table. You know, I've always needed one. And he mended my lamp. Wasn't that kind? Are you going to have a little soup for your lunch? Eh? Vera? A little soup? Would you like a little bowl of soup? Oh well, I expect you'll tell us if you want anything. I'll be back in a minute, dear. (*Calling.*) Dennis dear, put the kettle on, will you?

DENNIS (*distant*). Just a sec. Front door.

MARJORIE. Oh. Front door. Front door, Vera. I wonder who that can be?

MARJORIE *heads towards the house.* DENNIS *emerges with* PAM *and* NEIL.

DENNIS. Guess who? Guess who then?

MARJORIE. Well, fancy that. Hallo there.

NEIL. Hallo.

PAM. 'llo.

MARJORIE. We haven't seen you for ages, have we?

NEIL. No, no.

MARJORIE. Haven't been avoiding us, have you?

NEIL. No, no. Not really. We just — er . . .

MARJORIE. How's your mother?

NEIL. Much the same.

MARJORIE. That's good. Have you come to see the patient?

PAM. If we could.

MARJORIE. She's just round there in the sun. I'll make us a cup of coffee, shall I, Dennis?

DENNIS. Lovely. Lovely, mother.

MARJORIE. Won't be a moment.

MARJORIE *goes into the house.*

DENNIS. Well, this is nice. Nice surprise.

NEIL. Well, we were . . . we though we'd —

PAM. How's Vee?

DENNIS. Well, in point of fact, she's a lot better. She's making giant strides. The doctor's delighted. He's over the moon about her. Here we are, Vee. Vee love, look who's come to see you. Pam and Neil, Vee. Come to see you.

PAM. Hallo, Vee.

NEIL. Hallo.

VERA *looks at them blankly. They stand round her.*

DENNIS. Say hallo, Vee. Say hallo. Hallo.

VERA (*faintly*). 'llo.

DENNIS. There you are, you see. There you are.

NEIL. Well, that is progress.

DENNIS. Certainly is. I mean, last time you saw her, I don't honestly, to be absolutely frank, think she knew who you were. So you see, she's coming along.

NEIL. Oh yes.

DENNIS. I mean, yesterday was a breakthrough. An absolute breakthrough. She had, what — two good full bowls of soup. Now, that means her appetite is returning which is a very good sign. Two good bowls she had.

PAM. Is she all right out here? It's quite cold.

DENNIS. Ah well. Quite. But when she's in the house, she only frets.

NEIL. She what?

DENNIS. Frets. Starts fretting. She seems to be happier out here. I mean, we'd sooner she was in. Than sitting out here exposed to all the elements. I'd be happier. I think we'd all be happier if she was under cover.

NEIL. I'd have thought she ought to have been under cover.

DENNIS. Right.

PAM. What's the doctor say?

DENNIS. Well. Go along with her wishes. That's what it boiled down to. Good old rest, that's all she needs. I mean, we talked round the possibility of her, you know, going into a hospital but — er — on balance we decided that the home environment would probably do more for her in the long run. She always hated going away. Hated it. Never enjoyed hotels. That sort of thing. Always at her happiest at home. Home's where she belongs.

NEIL. Yes, I'd have thought so.

DENNIS. Of course, at the moment, she's still very much in herself.

NEIL. Yes. Yes.

DENNIS. The doctor was explaining. A mental injury, which is what Vee's got, is not unlike in many ways a normal physical injury. Like, say, cutting your hand. It takes time to heal. Knit together again, you see. It's the same with her mind. That's what it's doing now. It's knitting together.

NEIL. Amazing.

DENNIS. Yes it is. It's amazing.

NEIL. It's a miracle of engineering, the mind.

DENNIS. True. True. Mind you, to her advantage she's always been a very fit woman. Physically very strong. She had a good home background, you see. Paid off.

NEIL. Ah.

DENNIS. Here, I'll let you into a secret, shall I? You know how old she is today? I know she wouldn't mind me telling you.

PAM. Oh, is it her birthday?

DENNIS. Yes, yes. But have a guess how old. You'll never guess. She's forty-two.

PAM. Really?

NEIL. Good gracious.

DENNIS. Now, you would have never guessed that, would you?

NEIL. No.

PAM. She's lucky. She's got a very good bone structure.

DENNIS. She was a lovely girl.

NEIL. Must have been.

PAM. Vera? Vee . . . Vee . . .

NEIL. Does she say much then?

DENNIS. Er, no, not really no. She says yes occasionally, and no. That sort of thing. And you get her to say hallo if you work at it. I mean, she can understand you. She'll understand what we're saying now.

PAM. Vee . . .

DENNIS. I wouldn't bother, Pam. I really wouldn't.

Pause.

Neil. I've just heard about George Spooner.

NEIL. Oh yes.

DENNIS. Yes, I'm sorry.

NEIL. Yes.

DENNIS. I'm still absolutely amazed, I don't mind saying. I mean, he just didn't look the type, did he? Rushing off like that. With his secretary, was it?

NEIL. I understand so, yes.

DENNIS. Well. They're bound to catch up with him.

NEIL. Yes.

DENNIS. Bound to in the end. I suppose you'll have dropped a bit then?

NEIL. No. I dropped the lot actually.

DENNIS. Ah. Well, it seems like Pam was right for once. Eh, Pam?

PAM. Nothing to do with me.

DENNIS. No, you could really have knocked me down with a . . . George Spooner. But you know the most unbelievable thing of all — what I really can't understand. He was a Capricorn.

NEIL. Ah.

DENNIS. Capricorns just don't do that sort of thing. It's not in their nature.

Pause.

(*Laughing.*) As a matter of fact — er — talking of rumours, I'd heard that you'd both separated. Shows how much you can rely on rumours. Don't know where I heard that.

PAM. From your mother probably.

DENNIS. Oh?

PAM. Who got it from mine.

DENNIS. Ah.

PAM. We did separate for about a week.

DENNIS. Oh, I see.

PAM. Yes.

NEIL. But we're sort of together again now. Temporarily anyway. You see, we felt that Pam needed to get qualified. Before she could really start out on her own. What with Darren and that. So she'll probably be working on her qualifications for a bit.

DENNIS. You'll need qualifications.

NEIL. She will.

DENNIS. What are you planning to do, then?

PAM. Well, I was considering public relations.

DENNIS. Ah.

NEIL. I thought you said you were going into the prison service.

PAM. That was a joke.

NEIL. Oh.

  DENNIS *laughs. Pause.*

DENNIS (*drawing them aside*). Look — er — just between ourselves, I'm glad you came round actually. I was going to give you a ring. That car of Vee's. You know, the one you were interested in . . .

NEIL. Oh yes?

DENNIS. Well, Vee obviously won't be up to driving it for quite some time — and, er, well, it's just lying there going to waste really. So I wondered if you'd care to have it. I know Vee would like you to have it.

NEIL (*exchanging a glance with* PAM). Well . . .

PAM. I don't think so, thank you.

DENNIS. I mean, as a gift, you know.

PAM. I don't think we'll be needing a car.

DENNIS. Oh.

NEIL. Thanks anyway.

DENNIS. Well, if you do change your minds . . .

NEIL. Thanks. (*Pause.*)

DENNIS. Hey, guess what I did last Saturday.

NEIL. What?

DENNIS. I fixed those garage doors. What about that?

NEIL. I don't believe it.

DENNIS. I didn't have much choice. I had mother after me.

NEIL. Oh, I see.

MARJORIE (*distant*). Woo-hoo.

DENNIS. Oh, there she goes. (*Calling.*) All right, mother.

NEIL. She's looking well these days.

DENNIS. Oh, she's on top form at the moment. Wonderful. Sixty-seven, you know.

NEIL. Very good.

> MARJORIE *emerges from the house with a tray of coffee.*

MARJORIE. Coffee up.

DENNIS (*hurrying to her*). All right, mother, I'll take them. Are we going to have it out here then? It's a bit chilly.

MARJORIE. Well, yet it is. But what about the . . .

DENNIS. Oh, my word yet. I nearly forgot. It's a good job you did come round today, you two. Bearing in mind who's twenty-one today, eh? Old Aquarius here. (*Drawing them aside.*) Look, look, mother's made her a little cake, see? (*He displays a very small iced cake with a single candle on it.*)

NEIL. Ah.

MARJORIE. It's only a little one. Just a token.

DENNIS. No point in doing any more. She wouldn't really appreciate it. It's a good job you remembered, mother.

MARJORIE. Somebody's got to remember your wife's birthday.

DENNIS. Vee. Can you see? Mother's made you a little cake, see? Just to prove we haven't forgotten you.

VERA stares blankly.

I think she knows. I think she does.

MAJORIE. I don't know how she can sit out in this wind.

DENNIS. We can't keep her in the house, can we? Wouldn't you like to come back in the warm, Vee? Be tucked up at home, eh? Wouldn't that be nicer?

VERA (*after a pause, softly*). No.

DENNIS looks at MARJORIE.

MARJORIE. No?

DENNIS. No. (*To the others.*) She's still disorientated, you see.

MARJORIE (*handing out the coffee*). Pam.

PAM. Thanks.

MARJORIE. Neil. That's yours. No sugar, is that right?

NEIL. Ah, thank you.

MARJORIE. And Dennis. That's sugared, Dennis.

DENNIS. Thank you, mum. Well, happy birthday to Vee, eh?

PAM. Vee.

MARJORIE }
NEIL.   } Happy birthday, Vee.

Slight pause.

DENNIS (*singing softly*). Happy birthday to you
Happy birthday to you

MARJORIE joins in. She motions to NEIL and PAM who join in too. VERA's lips move silently with them.

Happy birthday, dear Vera.
Happy birthday to you.

The lights fade.

Curtain.

Howard Brenton

In Howard Brenton's *Magnificence*, a band of hapless would-be revolutionaries seize an abandoned London house; they mean it to be a 'base camp' for their ascent to a socialist revolution. But they make no impression at all on a society impervious to youthful anger. The police throw them out; one of their members suffers an accidental abortion; another is accidentally blown to bits by his own bomb. The play's last word, 'waste', encompasses nicely the results of revolution by the ignorant. Almost the only thing left behind by the foolish children is a scrawled slogan they painted on a wall of the seized flat: 'weapons of happiness.'

That 'weapons of happiness' should reappear in 1976 as title of Brenton's play commissioned by the National Theatre may be taken both as an echo of and as a motto for Brenton's work. Each of his plays is, in some sense, a weapon of happiness, a tool designed by Brenton to move society toward the socialism which he sees as the only truly human possibility. According to Brenton, a play should be a 'petrol bomb through the proscenium arch', blowing up bourgeois self-satisfaction and lighting the fire of change.

Howard Brenton was born in Portsmouth in 1942. His father was an enthusiastic theatre amateur, a policeman by profession, and a Methodist minister (a second career that he began when his son was nineteen). Brenton's work speaks of paternal influence in several ways. Brenton tells us that at the age of nine he began to emulate his father's love of theatre by writing plays. In 1970 he wrote for a Methodist church the short play, *Wesley*, a Brechtian salute to the founder of Methodism. But the most notable evidence of his father's influence is the fact that every Brenton play features among its characters a policeman, sometimes vicious, sometimes humane, always on the side of the rulers keeping a lid on the ruled.

Brenton claims to have hated Cambridge, but his first play, *Ladder of Fools*, was produced there during his final year, 1965. After graduating with honours in English, Brenton worked as a stage manager in regional companies and saw his early plays done by fringe groups. Then, as with so many others of his generation, he got his big boost in 1969, when the English Stage Company produced *Revenge* at the Royal Court Theatre Upstairs. At the Royal Court, Brenton met David Hare, who encouraged him to write the brilliant one-acter, *Christie in Love* (1969), a play which presents England's most famous post-war murderer and rapist, Reginald Christie, as a prototypical product of middle-class banality and sexual repression. Hare directed the play for his touring Portable Theatre, thus beginning an important working partnership with Brenton.

Hare and Brenton collaborated on *Brassneck*, a thirty character chronicle of thirty years of decay and deceit in the managerial class. With Snoo Wilson and Howard Barker, Hare and Brenton soon became known as 'the wild bunch', playwrights who were, in the words of John Peter, 'political moralists united in disillusion'. Then, in 1976, Hare directed *Weapons of Happiness* at the National Theatre, and the play won the Evening Standard Award.

A clear set of common elements appears in one Brenton play after another. First, the depiction of the English economic/political system, both left and right, as decadent, corrupt, and ineffectual. Lord Rack of *Epsom Downs* is an ex-Labourite fallen from power because of a sex scandal. His memory of achievement is summed up by, 'I was kissed by Aneurin Bevan.' In *The Churchill Play*, a parliamentary sub-committee consists of a drunken Labourite, a woman who advocates lobotomizing dissidents, and a Conservative whose party has turned Orwell's *1984* on its head by turning England into a gulag archipelago filled with left-wing instead of right-wing prisoners. In the play within the play, Churchill himself is a homosexual ('Give us a kiss, Jolly Jack Tar'), who lives in terror of his 'Black Dog,' the memory of his father's syphilis, and creates the myth of his own heroic wartime leadership by fictionalizing history.

The language by which Brenton actualizes these characters is richly overripe. It's full of images of decay and physical corruption, the poetry of a plague journal. In *Sore Throats*, Judy inventories among her lover's charms the 'little sausages of dirt in the cleft between his toes'. In *Thirteenth Night*, Beaty, a modern Macbeth, describes America as the place 'where pigs can grow fat, snort, and churn in the mud'. In *The Churchill Play*, M.P. Morn paints the neo-fascist rule of England in unbridled Brentonian style: 'So the blood flows, eh? And you tear the skin back, eh? Rip the flesh. And you go on, through the epidermic wall, deep into the body, to put your hand on an internal organ, liver, kidney, heart . . . To squeeze. I speak of the body politic.'

Brenton reinforces the shock of his language by physical theatricality, an element of his drama that attracts both attention and abuse. In *Christie in Love*, the numerous women who were Christie's victims become a single dummy which, as Christie belabours it, takes on the emotive presence of a monster puppet. In *Scott of the Antarctic* (1971), which Brenton wrote for ice-rink production, Jesus and King George V play for the great globe by kicking a soccer ball. And in *Epsom Downs*, the most cheerful of Brenton plays, nine actors recreate the entire Derby, horses and all, on a bare stage.

Brenton's physicality reached its peak (and drew the most fire) with *The Romans in Britain*, his epic treatment of imperialism in 54 B.C., 515 A.D., and the present. Critics and *Times* letter writers debated the legitimacy of stage spectacle that includes male nudity, simulated homosexual rape, and dog strangling, not to mention a double-figure body count. Brenton ought to have been pleased by the hullabaloo over *Romans*. He freely acknowledges his wish to agitate the audiences; aggro (for aggression) is his pet term for the shock technique he uses to unsettle them.

But the feature of Brenton's work most evident to even a casual observer is his fascination with 'Coppers. Rozzers. Fuzzywuzz. Bottle boys. The men in blue. Old Bill. Police', to repeat Alf's lexicon from *Weapons of Happiness*. Brenton's ubiquitous men of the law are reactionary ('The country's gone to the devil,' says Commissioner Macleish in *Revenge*), ignorant (the Constable of *Magnificence* failed English), brutal (Chief Inspector Jack kicks his wife in the belly in *Sore Throats*), and willing to do anything to serve the establishment (to achieve an old lady's eviction, the bailiff of *Magnificence* steals her cat and pushes human waste into her letter box).

Brenton's obsession with the police is merely a concrete expression of his desire to overturn the system of protected property and privilege in favour of the socialism which he sees as the true state of happiness for man.

Weapons of Happiness bears all the Brenton hallmarks. In it the establishment is a messy, totally inept alliance of Britain's worst: a drunken, sentimental chip factory owner; a policeman to whom the adhesive of society is hate; a labour organizer who has sold out to the status quo; and a factory foreman who colludes with management to close the plant and eliminate jobs.

Against these practitioners of exploitation is ranged a gallery of workers pathetically incapable of wise action. Like another socialist playwright, Edward Bond, Brenton sees ignorance as the greatest bar between the working man and effective political action. In Bond plays, illiteracy is the common symbol of crippling ignorance. But in *Weapons of Happiness*, Brenton's proletarians exhibit a dozen kinds of ignorance. Like a Bond hero, Ken is illiterate. But Stacky is deaf and dumb, a kind of ignorance so debilitating that he is hired by the plant owner, who makes a point of hiring the handicapped. The handicapped work well but rebel poorly. A third worker, Billy, can both read and talk, but his mind recoils from complex thought. 'He hurts my brain', says Billy when Hicks lectures him on industrial relations. Old Alf represents a generation of workers too old to learn, and young Liz represents a generation whose taste for the telly and the hair drier has turned their brains to soft plastic.

Most interesting in her ignorance is Janice, a self-taught Trotskyite whose voracious reading into socialism has filled her head with names and dates but no revolutionary logic. 'And I read and read. Shiny books you get from Moscow. And plastic covers, red, from Peking, you know? All printed faint. Couldn't understand a word. But I believed in it.'

With such a roster of unpromising proletarians, Brenton might easily repeat the picture of doomed revolution he painted in such plays as *Magnificence* and *The Churchill Play*. Instead, in *Weapons of Happiness* he sets out to solve two problems that confront all western socialist playwrights: how to deal with the ugly truth of neo-Stalinism and how to write optimistic drama about socialist progress in an England where the system seems unbudgeable.

The heritage of neo-Stalinist evils that still besets the socialist states of the Soviet bloc has proven a daunting problem for many left-wing dramatists. Like Brecht before him, Edward Bond has avoided confronting in a play the question of communist repression and rigidity. Instead, Bond contents himself with exposing the flaws of capitalist exploitation or, in a play like *The Bundle*, presenting an optimistic picture of an innocent utopia that might come to exist after the overthrow of capitalism in a third world nation. In *Summer*, his one play actually set in a present-day communist nation, Bond ignores the politics of contemporary communist rule. Instead, he focuses *Summer* on the memories of two elderly women who grew up in the pre-socialist world and experienced the Nazi occupation of their country. *Summer* avoids questions about the socialist present by concentrating on the evils of the capitalist past.

Brenton, however, takes a hard look at the worst kind of socialist failure in *Weapons of Happiness*. His leading character, Joseph Frank, is a refugee from Czechoslovakia. Through Frank's memory, Brenton depicts the dark side of a socialist nation gone wrong. In flashback Frank relives the Soviet suppression of the Prague uprising, his own false arrest, and torture. Thus Brenton confronts head-on the question any non-believer is bound to ask a socialist playwright: 'Why should we rebel against the crimes of capitalism when contemporary history tells us the crimes of socialism will be worse?' Brenton depicts the Soviet corruption in as bleak a light as could the most right-wing dramatist.

Having acknowledged dramatically that socialism can go wrong, did go wrong in Eastern Europe, Brenton must now show that the best ideals of socialism can still take hold in England. It is his responsibility as a socialist playwright to express plausible faith in the triumph of the socialist vision. For, as George Steiner, whose Cambridge lectures on Marxism Brenton admired, points out in *The Death of Tragedy*, an essential feature of Marxist drama is optimism – it must not express tragic despair but must, even when it depicts defeat, demonstrate that the march to the future is inexorable and victory for the historical imperative certain. Only happy endings are allowed.

So, in *Weapons* Brenton counterpoints socialist failure in Czechoslovakia with a socialist victory in England. It is the victory of Joseph Frank, whose ideals take root among the ignorant young English workers he meets in the potato chip factory. At the beginning of the play, Frank has no thought of political activity in England, his new home. He still suffers from the injuries of his imprisonment by the Soviets and wishes only to slip quietly into the oblivion of simple creature comforts and forgetfulness. But Janice, the naive fledgling communist, won't let him. Eager to learn from his revolutionary experience and wisdom, and touched as well by his sufferings ('poor body'), Janice determines to involve Frank in her strike action against the factory owners. Although he resists her at first ('Don't ask me to play with you, little girl'), his determination to stand aside is undercut by two things; Janice's refusal to be rebuffed, either politically or sexually, and the irrepressible life of Frank's own inner faith. When the factory uprising starts, Frank can't resist the old activist instinct, and he dashes through a hailstorm of potatoes thrown by the strikers to join the rebels inside the plant. Such a moment occurs in a score of socialist plays: the reluctant intellectual finally casts off his doubts and mounts the barricades. It is one expression of the necessary optimism of which Steiner speaks. The return to the fold of the strayed member of the faith implies inevitable victory.

Having joined the rebels, Frank gradually assumes the mantle of leadership. He tutors the young workers, especially Janice, in revolutionary principles. He outlines the basic strategy by which to live revolutionary lives: purge (gently) the useless Liz; squash Billy's 'utopian tendencies'; 'don't get pregnant'. Then, having passed on the word, Frank succumbs to his old injuries and dies as the young workers escape from the factory. Such is optimistic Marxist tragedy. From Frank's death, only a momentary stumble on the march to the future, springs the play's final vision, the five young people camped in a snowy orchard, English Maoists at the start of their long march, Janice providing firm leadership by the light of Frank's wisdom.

By that same light, Brenton has achieved the logic of a complete socialist drama for a contemporary English audience. He has combined an honest treatment of socialist revolution gone awry with the stubborn insistence that the ideals of socialism can still prompt a new generation to more successful revolution.

Major Plays

Magnificence, Royal Court Theatre, 1969.

Brassneck (with David Hare), Nottingham Playhouse, Nottingham, 1973.

The Churchill Play, Nottingham Playhouse, Nottingham, 1974.

Weapons of Happiness, Lyttelton Theatre (National Theatre), 1976.

Epsom Downs, Joint Stock at the Round House, 1977, then on tour.

Sore Throats, Royal Shakespeare Company at the Warehouse, 1979.

The Romans in Britain, Olivier Theatre (National Theatre), 1980.

The Genius, Royal Court Theatre, 1984.

Bloody Poetry, Foco Novo at Haymarket, Leicester, then on tour, including Hampstead Theatre, 1984.

Pravda (with David Hare), Olivier Theatre (National Theatre), 1985.

Selected Bibliography

Beacham, Richard. 'Brenton Invades Britain: The *Romans in Britain* Controversy.' *Theatre*, XII, 2 (Spring 1981) pp. 34–37.

Brenton, Howard. 'Petrol Bombs Through the Proscenium Arch,' interview with Catherine Itzin and Simon Trussler. *Theatre Quarterly*, V, 17 (March 1975) pp. 4–20. Condensed version in: Simon Trussler, ed. *New Theatre Voices of the Seventies*. London and New York: Methuen, 1981.

Bull, John. *New British Political Dramatists*. London: Macmillan; New York: Grove Press, 1984.

Cameron, Ben. 'Howard Brenton: The Privilege of Revolt.' *Theatre*, XII, 2 (Spring 1981), pp. 28–33.

Merchant, Paul. 'The Theatre Poems of Bertolt Brecht, Edward Bond, and Howard Brenton.' *Theatre Quarterly*, 9 (Summer 1979), pp. 49–51.

Morley, Sheridan. 'The Man Behind the Lyttelton's First New Play.' *Times*, 10 July 1976, p. 9.

Peter, John. 'Meet the Wild Bunch,' *Sunday Times*, 11 July 1976, p. 31.

HOWARD BRENTON

Weapons of Happiness

To Sam

WEAPONS OF HAPPINESS was commissioned by the National Theatre, London, and first performed there, in the Lyttleton Theatre, on 14th July 1976. The cast was as follows:

JOSEF FRANK	Frank Finlay
RALPH MAKEPEACE	Michael Medwin
BILLY	Derek Thompson
KEN	Billy Colvill
STACKY	Nick Brimble
JANICE	Julie Covington
LIZ	Annie Hayes
ALF	Frederick Radley
SYLVIA MAKEPEACE	Thelma Whiteley
MR STANLEY	Bernard Gallagher
INSPECTOR MILLER	Maurice O'Connell
HICKS	Matthew Guiness
DOUBEK Interrogators	Maurice O'Connell
KOHOUTEK	Matthew Guiness
RUSSIAN ADVISER	Michael Medwin
CLEMENTIS	William Russell
NKVD MEN	Pat Connell
	Martin Friend
	Shaun Scott
	Jeremy Truelove
STALIN	Geoffrey Bateman
WAITER	Chris Hunter
COMMENTATOR	Geoffrey Bateman
GUARDS	Martin Friend
	Chris Hunter
CONSTABLES	Pat Connell
	Martin Friend
	Jeremy Truelove

Director: David Hare
Designer: Hayden Griffin
Lighting: Rory Dempster

A Note

The real Josef Frank was hanged in Prague on the 3rd of December 1952

Act One

SCENE ONE

By the factory wall at night. JOSEF FRANK *alone.*

FRANK. I don't sleep. I walk about London. So many people, sleeping. Around you. For miles. After so many years, it is better to be tired. Not to think or remember. Ten million, asleep, around you, is warm. The ignorant English, like a warm overcoat. About me. It is better. While in the nightmare of the dark all the dogs of Europe bark.

A shaft of light from an opened door shines across the stage at the back. The light goes off. RALPH MAKEPEACE *comes on. He is dressed in a fine coat and carries a briefcase. He has been drinking alone.*

RALPH. Who's that there?

JOSEF FRANK turns away.

Mr Frank?

RALPH MAKEPEACE walks towards him.

It is you, Frank.

FRANK. Walking . . .

RALPH. What are you doing by the factory, this hour?

A pause.

FRANK. Sleepless.

RALPH. Ah.

FRANK. I . . .

RALPH MAKEPEACE waves his briefcase.

RALPH. Working late. On the books. Not a very good cook with numbers, eh?

He tries to laugh and fails. A pause.

How long have you been with us?

FRANK. A week. One week.

RALPH. Week isn't it? Yes. You don't find the work too heavy?

FRANK. I . . .

RALPH. Manual work. Man of your age, intelligence? Perhaps some clerking, filing in the office . . .

FRANK. No . . .

RALPH. We like to . . .

FRANK. I prefer . . .

RALPH. Prefer it?

FRANK. I . . . Yes.

RALPH. Funny thing to make really. Crisps.

> *A pause.*

> My father always made a point of sprinkling the workforce with foreigners, foreign people. And disabled . . . Disabled people. We get by, don't you think?

> JOSEF FRANK *hesitates.*

> The secret's in the crunch.

FRANK. Work is work.

RALPH. What? Ah, yes.

> JOSEF FRANK *stumbles.*

RALPH. Are you . . . Not well?

FRANK. No.

RALPH. Cold night. Been threatening snow . . .

FRANK. I am well.

RALPH. Will you ever go back to Hungary?

FRANK. Czechoslovakia. The Czechoslovak Socialist Republic.

> *A pause.*

RALPH. Goodnight then.

FRANK. Goodnight.

> RALPH MAKEPEACE *walks away, jangling his car keys.*

RALPH. Tuck yourself up. Good book, hot drink and a packet of crisps. Ha!

YOUNG MAN'S VOICE (*off*). Mr Makepeace!

> *Three figures, dressed as* YOUNG MEN, *although one of them is a* YOUNG WOMAN, *with balaclavas pulled to the bridges of*

their noses, run on. They knock RALPH MAKEPEACE *over and kick him.*

YOUNG WOMAN. Tossing cunt.

FIRST YOUNG MAN. Get his keys.

RALPH. What are you?

SECOND YOUNG MAN. Here's the case. What I tell you? No chain.

The FIRST YOUNG MAN *picks up* RALPH MAKEPEACE'S *car keys.*

FIRST YOUNG MAN. Flash away in his flashy car!

SECOND YOUNG MAN. Case we want, idiot.

FIRST YOUNG MAN. Fucking Rolls, though.

YOUNG WOMAN. Split let's split.

The SECOND YOUNG MAN *points at* JOSEF FRANK.

SECOND YOUNG MAN. What about him?

YOUNG WOMAN. Foreign git.

The three figures run off. RALPH MAKEPEACE *crawls on the ground in pain.*

RALPH. Contact lens.

FRANK. I plead.

RALPH. If it comes on to snow I'll never find it. Frank!

FRANK. I plead.

RALPH. Help me, man!

JOSEF FRANK *shakes his head.*

FRANK. I plead.

RALPH. For godsake, what's the matter with you?

FRANK. I plead guilty of being a war criminal. And of committing a whole number of grave crimes for the benefit of the U.S. imperialists. To the detriment of the working people of Czechoslovakia and the whole peace camp. All the dogs of Europe.

SCENE TWO

Factory yard. Lunch break.
JOSEF FRANK takes a pack of sandwiches out of his pocket.
There is a wall at the back. Cricket stumps are chalked upon it.
Two young women, JANICE and LIZ, lean against the wall.
They are in working clothes. They wear plastic coats and their
hair is bound up in muslin cloth.
An old man, ALF, sits on a cooking oil drum. He has a plastic
lunch box and a thermos flask.
Three young men, BILLY, KEN and STACKY, are playing cricket.
BILLY is batting. He has a guitar strung around his back. KEN is
bowling. STACKY, who is deaf and dumb and six and a half feet
tall, fields.
JANICE translates STACKY's sign language as a matter of course,
even when there is a large space between them.
KEN bowls to BILLY who strikes the ball. The ball runs off stage.

BILLY. Six!

KEN. What do you mean, six?

BILLY. Poetry poetry.

KEN. What do you mean, six?

BILLY. Went in the bog door, didn't it. Ball in the bog door's six.

KEN. But the bog door's open! Only six if it goes in under.

BILLY. You can't just change the rules.

KEN. I'm not changing rules.

　　STACKY makes signals.

JANICE. Stacky says can he bowl now?

LIZ. Just like school. Work? Never know you'd left the bloody
　　playground.

　　KEN, looking off.

KEN. Oh no. Who's gone and gone in the bog? Oy! You got our
　　ball in there!

　　KEN runs off. BILLY swings the guitar to his front and fiddles
　　with it. STACKY watches him.

JANICE. Like we're still running around in nappies. Wondering
　　where the smell's come from.

　　STACKY is picking his nose. A pause.

LIZ. Ooh I know he's deaf and dumb, but I wish he wouldn't pick his nose and eat it. Oy Stacky!

STACKY has his back to her. He turns. JANICE *catches his eye. They signal.*

What's he say?

JANICE. He says one nostril is salt and vinegar and the other is cheese and onion, which do you prefer?

STACKY smiles.

LIZ. Sad.

ALF. Playing with a hard ball in the yard. Trying a prove something Billy?

BILLY: What do you know of it? Old man. Old old man.

LIZ. How old you then, Billy darling?

JANICE. Pretty ancient actually. Do you know he remembers Bob Dylan?

LIZ. Coo, bring out your dead.

JANICE and LIZ laugh.

BILLY. He could have changed the world, Dylan. Still could if we'd let him.

BILLY hits the guitar. A horrible chord.

JANICE. Sad.

LIZ. Make you weep.

A pause.

Age. I saw my Mum in the bath last night. You know, nude. Like curried chicken.

JANICE: Funny how their bodies fall apart when they're over thirty.

LIZ. Sad.

JANICE. It gets 'em.

ALF. Joey.

FRANK. Alfred

A slight pause.

Would . . . You like a sandwich?

ALF. Special are they?

ALF *lifts the bread, suspiciously.*

What's that white stuff in there?

FRANK. Cream . . . Cream cheese.

ALF. No thank you. You want a build yourself up. Look less of a dog's dinner. Give you a bit a my beef, if it weren't mine.

FRANK. I cannot . . . Take flesh.

ALF. Oh yeah?

ALF *eats and speaks with his mouth full.*

Rolled young Mr Ralph last night. Hear that?

FRANK: Rolled?

ALF. Knocked over. Bashed. Leant upon. Hit. Right outside the gate here.

FRANK. Who was responsible?

ALF. Hot heads. The wild ones, I ask you.

ALF *laughs.*

C.I.D.'s up the office right now.

BILLY *and* JANICE *start.*

FRANK. C.I.D.?

ALF. Coppers. Rozzers. Fuzzy wuzz. Bottle boys. The men in blue. Old Bill. Police.

FRANK. Police?

BILLY. Oh fuck.

JANICE. Shut up. What did you say, Alf?

ALF. Up the office with Mr Ralph. Right now.

BILLY. Why do they think it was us, eh? Why do they make that assumption?

JANICE *signals to* STACKY. *He goes off.*

FRANK. Police?

ALF. Back in the thirties I was in a dole queue. Bloke in front a me, took out a gun and shot the pay clerk dead. Just like that. Did no good though. Another one popped up in his place.

ALF *laughs and spits.* STACKY *comes on with* RALPH MAKEPEACE's *briefcase. He gives it to* JANICE. JANICE *makes a signal to* BILLY *then she runs to him, he gives her a stirrup jump and she drops the briefcase over the wall.* ALF *and* JOSEF FRANK *see this. They stare.*

LIZ. I hope you know what you're doing, Jan.

KEN (*off*). Catch!

The ball bounces back onto the stage. STACKY *fields it.* KEN *comes on.*

What's going on?

JANICE (*to* KEN, *unheard*). Police up the office. We dumped the case over the wall.

A pause.

KEN. Right. What we want's a bit a intimidation round here. (*To* JANICE.) Tell Stacky a give him a bouncer.

BILLY. No bouncers.

JANICE *is signalling to* STACKY.

We not got pads on and it's a real ball.

KEN. Right little Mike Denness in't we.

STACKY *signals to* JANICE.

BILLY. It's the rules!

KEN. Change the rules!

JANICE. Stacky says he'll take a long run up.

STACKY *goes off, purposefully.*

BILLY. Bad light stops play.

KEN. Blinding sunlight. Look, blinding Australian sun.

BILLY. You change the rules, I'll change the weather.

KEN. Thousands a Aussies in their shirt sleeves. Stoned out a their minds and baying for your blood.

SYLVIA MAKEPEACE *walks on. All except* JOSEF FRANK *stare at her. She is well and sharply dressed with a knee-length hemline, sheer nylons and high heel shoes.*

KEN. Uh uh. Boss pussy.

LIZ. Look at the skirt. It lilts.

JANICE. Cow.

LIZ. Yeah.

KEN *bars* SYLVIA's *way. She stops.*

KEN. Morning Mrs Makepeace. Come for lunchies?

SYLVIA MAKEPEACE *stares at him.*

LIZ. They do say she cuts her hairs. You know . . .

JANICE. What, her pubes?

LIZ. Yeah you know. In the shape of a heart.

JANICE. What for?

LIZ *shrugs.*

LIZ. Romance?

LIZ *and* JANICE *laugh.* SYLVIA *walks round* KEN.

KEN. Kiss kiss.

SYLVIA *goes off.*

Sometimes I think a all the places I'll never go. (*To* STACKY *off.*) Come on then Stacky. Thump your bollocks down the pitch.

STACKY *powers on to the stage. At that moment* JOSEF FRANK, *wandering across the stage, gets between batsman and bowler.* STACKY *restrains himself from bowling at the last moment.* BILLY *ducks instinctively.*

KEN. Joey! You stupid Ruskie!

BILLY. What happened?

KEN. Get out the way.

FRANK. I . . .

JANICE. Don't think he's Russian, Ken.

STACKY *has hurt his leg.*

BILLY. You all right, Stacky?

KEN. Now look what you gone and done. Stacky's going a miss the next Test.

KEN *laughs.*

FRANK. I do not understand cricket. What is short leg?

MR STANLEY *comes on.*

STANLEY. Frank?

BILLY. Here comes Big Brother.

KEN. Thought I heard his iron balls clanging together.

STANLEY. Alf. How's the window box?

ALF. The locusts are massing.

> MR STANLEY *stares at* ALF. ALF *smiles.*

STANLEY. Oh Joey, they want a see you up the office.

> KEN *and* BILLY *look at each other quickly.* JANICE *walks a few steps from the wall towards* KEN. *She looks at* BILLY, BILLY *looks at her.* BILLY *puts the bat down on the ground, carefully.*

FRANK. No. I would . . . Not. Prefer not.

STANLEY. Playing with a hard ball in the yard again, Ken?

KEN. Oh yeah, the real thing, Stanley.

STANLEY. Mr Stanley to you.

KEN. Since when?

STANLEY. Since now.

KEN. You're just the foreman here. Stan, old man.

STANLEY. Na, come on Kenneth.

> MR STANLEY *ruffles* KEN'S *hair. He is about to turn away when* KEN *hits his hand away.*

STANLEY. What's all that for?

KEN. Chummy.

STANLEY. Come on, Ken. You were a kid when your first came in here to work. Saturday mornings cleaning?

KEN. Chummy, that's all.

> MR STANLEY *makes a placating gesture.* BILLY, *choosing his moment, bumps goodnaturedly into* FRANK.

BILLY. Give us the ball then, Joey.

> BILLY *drops the ball between himself and* JOSEF FRANK.

FRANK. What . . .

> BILLY *stoops and picks up the ball. He shows it to* JOSEF FRANK, *smiling and standing near to him.*

STANLEY. All piss in't it Kenneth?

KEN. Yeah but management, in't you, Mr Stanley. Mr Ralph's finger, in't you. Winkling in there. Touching us up. Keeping us giggly.

STANLEY. Don't talk to me about fingers, lad.

KEN. We know, we know . . .

MR STANLEY holds up a mutilated hand.

STANLEY. Two fingers . . .

KEN
STANLEY   *(together).* Half a thumb.

KEN. Yeah, yeah.

STANLEY. In the cutters. Thirty . . .

KEN. Yeah thirty years. Bits a Mr Stanley turning up in packets a crisps, Lands End a John A' Groats. Yeah, yeah. Should a started a new line. Specially enriched protein crisps, scab foreman flavour.

A pause.

STANLEY *(to FRANK).* Get up those stairs, Joey. Mr Ralph's wanting a few words with you.

JANICE goes to BILLY and puts her arm across his shoulder as she says to JOSEF FRANK, suddenly . . .

JANCE. And keep your mouth shut.

JANICE walks away.

FRANK. What . . .

BILLY. Sh.

STANLEY *(to FRANK).* Go on then. *(To KEN.)* Bugger, are you not, Ken?

KEN. Why that's what I must be then, Mr Stanley.

MR STANLEY takes out a Daily Mirror.

STANLEY. Want a read a the football?

KEN takes a step back.

KEN. Na . . .

STANLEY. West Ham did very well last night.

KEN. Na . . .

STANLEY. Racing page?

KEN. Bastard!

STANLEY. Garth?

KEN. You know I can't read!

STANLEY. Why, so you cannot, Kenneth.

KEN. All right!

 A pause.

 All right.

STANLEY. That's you in your place.

KEN. Oh yeah?

 A pause.

 Yeah that's me in my place.

 FRANK *walks away.* KEN, BILLY *and* JANICE *watch him going.* STANLEY *folds up the* Daily Mirror.

STANLEY. Just have to take the world on trust then, don't you.

 KEN *looks at* STANLEY.

KEN. You what?

SCENE THREE

Factory office.
The light is that of strip lighting, one strip on the blink.
RALPH MAKEPEACE, *who has a hand bandaged,* INSPECTOR MILLER *and* BOB HICKS *stand round about* JOSEF FRANK *who has just risen from a plain wooden chair.*

FRANK. The light, please . . .

RALPH. What are you thinking of, Frank?

FRANK. The light. A headache. It flickers.

MILLER. If you would sit down again, Mr Frank . . .

FRANK. The flicker . . .

RALPH. For godsake man, no need to be so nervy. You were not well last night. As for my eye thing, got a good pair of glasses.

 RALPH MAKEPEACE *takes out a pair of glasses and puts them on.*

 See? No harm done. And this is a policeman, only doing his job.

HICKS. Ralph, I don't think I really should be here for this.

RALPH. Do hang on, Bob. Lunch I said, lunch it will be.

MILLER (*to* JOSEF FRANK). All I need is a simple statement. Tell me what happened, I will write it down. You can read it through, in your own good time, and make any amendments . . . Changes . . . You wish, and sign it.

FRANK. No no, it is impossible. The light, my vision. Blinded . . .

JOSEF FRANK *stumbles*.

I have a pressure. A hairline fracture. The bone thickened when it healed.

A pause.

RALPH. Here, sit down Frank.

JOSEF FRANK *sits*.

FRANK. A blow healed with time.

HICKS. Ralph I am here as the Labour Party . . .

RALPH. Don't go all ratty on me Bob . . .

HICKS. Your workforce has approached me with a view to advice about Union Representation here . . .

RALPH. All tight on me Bob . . .

HICKS. If you should take action against this employee here, Mr Frank here . . .

RALPH. There is no question of Mr Frank having action taken against him . . . Tight arsed on me, Bob . . .

HICKS. Don't want to be unseemly. Seen . . .

MILLER. Mr Makepeace, sir, I would like to complete this statement.

RALPH. Need you, Inspector?

MILLER. This man did see your briefcase stolen?

RALPH. There was nothing in it.

MILLER. No sir?

RALPH. Apple cores.

MILLER. What I really want to do . . . Set up a trestle table in your canteen. Have a Detective Sergeant and four DC's down here, going through every one of your employees.

FRANK. Flick flick.

HICKS *looks at* JOSEF FRANK.

RALPH. None of my workers knocked me over. That's flat. That's final.

MILLER. Not really your workers, are they. In this day and age. More the workers' workers. I get the impression you want to be a nice person, sir.

RALPH. I hope I am 'A nice person.'

MILLER. Oh we can all hope.

HICKS. Industrial relations your pitch is it, Inspector?

MILLER. I know I know I'm just a jack. But you take the word of a jack.

HICKS (*to* FRANK). You, er, all right, brother?

MILLER. You got a group of human beings here. And no group of human beings, in a big city, hangs together by niceness. Hate yes, love no.

RALPH. A thinking policeman.

MILLER. Yes yes. Just a public servant with his thumb in the dyke. Can I get on with my job Sir?

JOSEF FRANK *stands, knocking the chair over. Suddenly the light . . .*

SCENE FOUR

Suddenly the light changes to a fierce, overhead square, the rest of the stage in darkness. The beam of a film projector shines in JOSEF FRANK'S *face. The shadows of the actors loom large at the back of the stage in the beam, which projects a photograph of a bare, dirty room with a naked light bulb.* JOSEF FRANK *holds his hands behind his back, in the manner of a handcuffed man.*

MILLER *as* DOUBEK. HICKS *as* KOHOUTEK. RALPH MAKEPEACE *as* BESHCHASNOV.

FRANK. I appeal to the Secretary General of the Czech Communist Party Klement Gottwald . . .

DOUBEK. You are a criminal.

KOHOUTEK. Confess.

DOUBEK. You were a fascist collaborator.

KOHOUTEK. You are an American spy.

DOUBEK. You are a Trotskyist.

KOHOUTEK. Confess.

FRANK. I am a Communist.

KOHOUTEK. You are filth.

DOUBEK. What were your relations with the American Saboteur Noel Field?

FRANK. Just tell me what I've done, that's all . . .

KOHOUTEK. Do you think the Party would arrest you if you had done nothing? Confess.

FRANK. What? What?

KOHOUTEK. Confess.

DOUBEK. Confess.

KOHOUTEK. Confess.

FRANK (*aside*). Never allowed to sit.

KOHOUTEK. Now. Confess.

FRANK (*aside*). Walk, walk all the time. They give you little leather slippers . . .

KOHOUTEK. All the time you were a Government Minister you were an American spy. Your fellow conspirator, Clementis, has already confessed. Why do you not? Confess. Now.

FRANK. Eighteen, twenty hours a day they question you. You are cold. You are hungry. You sleep a few hours on a plank. They wake you every ten minutes you must stand and report. Detention prisoner 1274. Number in cell one. All in order. You are handcuffed. You drink the thin soup with your handcuffs on, on the floor. You are kicked blindfolded cell to cell. You walk for three days and nights in a cellar filthy mud to your ankles. Your feet are infected, the toenails bulge with pus. You are offered a sandwich they tear it from your mouth before you can swallow. And you are lied to. All your life is made a lie. Your head is beaten against the wall. You try to kill yourself. To starve yourself to death. They find out what you're up to, they force feed you. It goes on for a year.

KOHOUTEK. President Truman has ordered the attack upon the U.S.S.R.

A pause.

FRANK. What . . . Did you say?

KOHOUTEK. The war with America has begun.

FRANK. War?

KOHOUTEK. The war with America.

FRANK. W . . . When?

KOHOUTEK. It has begun.

FRANK. The . . . Third World War?

KOHOUTEK. Anyway, has not the socialist world been at war for decades?

FRANK. Are you telling the truth?

KOHOUTEK. You doubt that the socialist world is surrounded by enemies?

FRANK. No of course I don't . . .

KOHOUTEK. All we have struggled for, Joseph, since we were boys, they wish to wipe off the surface of the planet. And with such enemies, in such a crisis, is it not logical that they have penetrated the Party? At every level? We must preserve the Party, root out the enemy. Help the Party Joseph. Confess you are the enemy.

BESHCHASNOV, *in Russian, to* DOUBEK.

BESHCHASNOV. Shto tam vozítsya s étoi sobákoy? Pristrelítch yevó, i vsyo.

DOUBEK. The Soviet Comrade wishes to know . . .

He screams and spits at JOSEF FRANK.

Why we waste time with this filthy little Jew.

Suddenly the light . . .

SCENE FIVE

Suddenly the light reverts to that of the factory office. JOSEF FRANK *has just stood, knocking the chair over. They stare at him. A pause.*

FRANK. I wish to relieve myself. It is unreasonable that a man not be allowed to relieve himself. An inalienable human right, for all that's sacred, to let a man have a common piss.

JOSEF FRANK *weeps. A silence.* SYLVIA MAKEPEACE *comes on.*

SYLVIA (*to* RALPH): Are we going for lunch, or are we not?

FRANK. Don't you understand? A . . . A man could stand naked in such a room as this, his bowels open, the poor thin stinking stuff of his gut running down his leg.

A silence.

HICKS. Er . . .

RALPH. I . . .

SYLVIA. Ralph, what is this?

RALPH. Not now, my sweet.

MILLER. Why don't you sit down again, Mr Frank?

FRANK. Forgive me.

RALPH. No problem.

FRANK. A faintness.

RALPH. Of course.

FRANK. Forgive me.

JOSEF FRANK *sucks back a sob.*

SYLVIA. Is this the man who saw you attacked?

RALPH. Not now, my sweet.

SYLVIA. Want my lunch, that's all.

RALPH. All right? Darling? All right?

SYLVIA. I am an intelligent form of life. I too receive tax demands.

RALPH. Christsake. More than flesh and blood can stand.

RALPH MAKEPEACE *takes out a drinking flask.*

MILLER. Could we . . .

RALPH. Tot?

MILLER. Get on?

RALPH. Frank?

FRANK. No . . .

RALPH. Malt. Blend it myself. Bit of a hobby.

SYLVIA (*to* HICKS). It's true, he does all his own blending. All alone, up in his room.

HICKS. Really?

RALPH. Shut up Sylvia.

SYLVIA. I am a director of this firm. I mean I was put on the board.

RALPH. by your father, not mine.

A pause.

Yes. Yes or . . . Go home? Taxi? Or, Inspector Miller, you could run Mr Frank home?

MILLER. All things are possible. (*To* FRANK.) Are you a registered alien, sir, or do you hold a British passport?

FRANK. No no, I will work . . .

RALPH. He's ill and in another country . . . .

MILLER. Just tell me, just quickly, who attacked Mr Makepeace here?

FRANK. I was out walking. At night. In London. There was nothing.

INSPECTOR MILLER *sighs.*

SYLVIA. Just don't let him . . . (*To* JOSEF FRANK.) You're in this country on sufferance, know that?

FRANK. All I want . . . To work. In a place of reasonable height. And silence, in silence. Not speaking.

RALPH. Pointless . . .

HICKS. Where you come from, Party Member were you?

FRANK. Can I go now?

RALPH. If you're sure you're all right . . .

FRANK. Thank you.

FRANK *walks away. He stops as he hears* INSPECTOR MILLER *say . . .*

MILLER. The last man I saw frightened as that had just killed his wife and two little babies.

SCENE SIX

Street. Early evening. JOSEF FRANK *alone.*

FRANK. Too much lost.

A pause.

Too much blood.

JANICE *rides onto the stage on a motorcycle.* BILLY *is riding pillion.*

JANICE. Hello Joey.

BILLY. Walking home?

FRANK. Walking.

BILLY. Violence on the buses eh? Don't like to come out, do they. Stay in their nests. Seeing a bus round here's like seeing the abominable snowman.

JANICE. What did you say to them, Joey?

A pause.

To the Police.

FRANK. Nothing.

JANICE. Oh yeah?

FRANK. I was taken ill. In the room. The office. An oppressive air. I am a claustrophobe.

BILLY. Like going down the tube, eh?

JANICE. So what did you say?

FRANK. I'm deaf. I'm blind. I don't see anything. I don't hear. I'm a . . . Hole in the air. I'm dead to you. You're dead to me. I'm nothing. You want to beat up the owner of the pathetic little, grubby little capitalistic concern that hires you, do so. Why should I see or hear? I'm more mute than . . . Your fellow dumb workers in that place. I'm . . .

A slight pause.

A vacuum.

A pause.

BILLY. Tell you what you are, Joey. Spooky.

JANICE. Don't you want a know what's going down, back there at the factory?

FRANK. I do not.

JANICE. You work in the place. Look, we're having a meeting.

BILLY. Don't tell him that!

JANICE. Worker like the rest of us, isn't he?

BILLY. Can't trust him. He's old and all fucked. In't you Joey.

JANICE. Tonight. Half seven. Out the Rock Wharf Site. Know where that is? Going on out to Greenwich.

FRANK. Think of me as ill.

BILLY. Fucked inside.

FRANK. I'm going now.

> JOSEF FRANK *turns away.*

JANICE. Come from a communist country, don't you?

FRANK. Forgive me.

BILLY. Said he's sick, Janice . . .

JANICE. Sick or ashamed. Workers' state over there. Stalinist, but a workers' state. What you do? Run away?

BILLY. Let him alone.

JANICE. I asked you a question! What you do, run away? I asked you a question!

> JOSEF FRANK *turns on her.*

FRANK. Little girl. I have spoken to Stalin. In Moscow. At three in the morning, in 1947. He was as close to me as you.

> *A slight pause.*

And you do not know the half of it.

BILLY. Stalin?

JANICE. Aren't you just full a shit.

BILLY. Funny how they do badges a all the others but not Stalin.

FRANK. Therefore I asked you, in all decency, do not ask me to play with you, little girl. In your games. I am going home.

> JOSEF FRANK *walks away.* BILLY *shouts after him.*

BILLY. Spook.

> JANICE *guns the motorcycle and drives off.* JOSEF FRANK *is left alone on the stage.*

SCENE SEVEN

JOSEF FRANK *alone. Night.*

FRANK. Spooky.

> *A pause.*

> Ghostly.

> *A pause.*

> Nineteen forty-seven.

> *A pause.*

> Moscow.

> VICTOR CLEMENTIS *comes on quickly at the back of the stage.*

CLEMENTIS. Joseph?

> JOSEF FRANK *turns to him. They embrace.*

> Joseph.

FRANK. Victor. The relief at seeing you!

CLEMENTIS. Yes?

FRANK. The flood of relief, Comrade Foreign Minister. Now that you will lead the delegation in my place.

> *A slight pause.*

> You will lead our trade delegation now?

CLEMENTIS. Not exactly.

FRANK. Victor, you must. Wasn't my report clear?

> *A slight pause.*

> My report on the deadlock?

CLEMENTIS. It was clear . . .

FRANK. Good Czech steel for Russian food. That should be a simple bargain. But the harshness of their demands . . . If they persist we will have to break off the negotiations all together . . .

CLEMENTIS (*interrupting*). Joseph I . . . I asked for you at the hotel. They said you walked this way.

> CLEMENTIS *shivers.*

> Moscow nights. I'd forgotten the cold.

FRANK. Trade negotiations with the Soviet Comrades fast become nocturnal. But why wasn't I told the time of your arrival? I'd have been at the airport to meet you . . .

CLEMENTIS. We travelled from Prague by train. They feared the fuel would freeze in the plane's tanks. The Russian heartland, Joseph! Mile after mile. The devastation. One could hardly bear it, even from a train window.

A pause.

FRANK. You do agree with my report.

CLEMENTIS. Yes, I said. It is clear.

FRANK. As your junior I am not empowered to break off the trade talks with the Soviet Government. I had to ask for you to come from Prague. Surely that is understood, Comrade Minister.

CLEMENTIS. No, I agree absolutely. Joseph, a hundred yards away. There is a car parked.

A pause.

Why are you being watched by their security police?

FRANK. The Soviet comrades have a certain paranoid style. Night-time limousines?

CLEMENTIS. Yes?

FRANK. I meant . . .

CLEMENTIS. Did you? Joseph, I do feel sometimes you are a little . . . Overweening.

FRANK. For Godsake, Victor. I have bargained for the Czech Government. As I expected them to bargain for the Russian Government. It is my duty to argue in the interests of the Czechoslovak working class.

CLEMENTIS. Absolutely.

FRANK. But?

CLEMENTIS. Sorry?

FRANK. You were going to say 'But?'

CLEMENTIS. So I was.

CLEMENTIS *laughs.*

Absolutely. But. Joseph, you know the configuration of that 'But.'

FRANK. Yes.

CLEMENTIS. We are in Russia. We are not mere National

Governments, bargaining our national interests. We share a deeper responsibility . . .

FRANK. The communist nation is world wide.

CLEMENTIS. The communist nation is world wide. Yes.

FRANK. Yes!

A pause.

And that is why I saw the Soviet Minister of Trade last night at Party Level. Not as a mere trade delegate with a begging bowl. But as a fellow communist.

CLEMENTIS. You asked for a meeting with Mikoyan at Party Level?

FRANK. A young man came to my hotel room, just past midnight. He took me to a back street. A car was waiting. Mikoyan was in the back. We drove through Moscow slowly. The chains on the wheels slipped in the snow at street corners. We spoke for three hours. In a big black car, skulking through the streets of the socialist capital of the world, at dead of night. He shouted and scoffed at me. He was Soviet Minister of Trade. It was his duty to get the most advantageous terms possible. I told him of our Party's position. That we communists do not yet control the Czech government. That I am the official spokesman of a non-communist government. That it is vital that the trade agreement be seen as a generous act by Russia. Our harvest is a disaster. The foodstuff and grain we wish to purchase by exchange of kind, with rolled steel and iron, is desperately needed. Our people will starve within months if the food is not delivered. We must have the food, the grain, now. If the food and grain is not delivered now the Czech Communist Party will be blamed. The Czech Revolution will be threatened. As I spoke, Mikoyan scraped a face in the condensation of the car window. I thought then it was Winston Churchill. Later I thought was it the face of some old enemy, in the frost? (*A pause.*) This brutality. Brutal no. Don't they know we love this country? That it is an honour for us to stand here on the socialist earth of Soviet Russia? That the allegiance is to what happened here, always? A thousand miles that way, a thousand miles that way . . .

A pause.

Deadlock.

CLEMENTIS. Comrade Mikoyan met me at the Moscow

Station tonight.

A pause.

FRANK. He met you . . .

CLEMENTIS. An official reception. He has agreed to all the
terms you asked for.

FRANK. Agreed?

CLEMENTIS. There was a band. And they gave me red roses. In
midwinter!

FRANK. Agreed?

CLEMENTIS. Everything. And two hundred thousand tons of
grain more than we asked for.

A pause.

FRANK. Stalin.

CLEMENTIS. Absolutely.

FRANK. Yes.

CLEMENTIS. Stalin intervened personally.

FRANK. I can see that is what happened.

CLEMENTIS. Yes.

FRANK. An enormous relief. Stalin.

CLEMENTIS. A very great man.

FRANK. Just like that.

> JOSEF FRANK *laughs.*

> I feel . . . Shaky!

CLEMENTIS. The relief is enormous.

> CLEMENTIS *laughs. A pause.*

CLEMENTIS. We have done right. The right thing for the working
class. It cannot be wrong. Not if Stalin has agreed.

A pause.

Can it.

*The sound of a car's doors opening and slamming. Three
YOUNG MEN dressed in heavy black overcoats and black fur
hats and gloves come on at the back.*

YOUNG MAN. Comrade Clementis! Comrade Frank! Comrade
Stalin says . . . Why walk in the street, in the cold, at so late

an hour? We are to take you to him.

He spreads his hands.

For a drink.

A choir sings. The portrait of STALIN, huge, glows through the snow. STALIN advances, smiling, smoking a pipe. A WAITER walks at his side, a step behind, carrying a tray set with glasses and a vodka bottle. Behind STALIN a crowd of men in a long line, all in dark suits and smiling and carrying vodka glasses, advances. STALIN stops. The entourage stops. The snow ceases to fall. A silence. STALIN takes a glass from the WAITER'S tray. He knocks the drink back in one. The entourage knock their drinks back in one. A silence.

STALIN. The Union of Soviet Socialist Republics.

A pause.

Has a very great.

A pause.

Ice-hockey team.

STALIN laughs. Everyone laughs. A silence. STALIN and his entourage as a tableau. It fades as JOSEF FRANK speaks aside.

FRANK. What do you expect me to see when I look in that mirror? The empty world. Like a room from which all human beings have fled. Leaving filth upon the walls, a few torn newspapers upon the floor. Oh we had the world to remake. The universe in our hands, history was water in a cup, we had only to drink. Who could have, then, imagined this dereliction. This filthy empty room, the broken doors, the exasperation. Too much lost, too much blood. Now, I do not even want revenge on all that I once believed in. I wish only to lie in the sludge of the debris, of what once was a fine building. Miles deep, stirring only for a little warmth.

The tableau has faded. JOSEF FRANK is alone. He stares out into the auditorium.

SCENE EIGHT

Early evening. JOSEF FRANK alone. JANICE drives the cycle back on stage, BILLY riding pillion.

JANICE. Off you get, Billy.

BILLY. You what?

JANICE. I'm taking him out the Rock.

BILLY. You don't fancy him Janice.

JANICE. Get off.

BILLY. You can't fancy him. Look at him. He's all mangle-worsy.

JANICE. You heard what I said.

BILLY *sighs then gets off the pillion.*

BILLY. You in't half a flashy chick sometimes, Jan. Whose bloody bike is it anyway?

JANICE. Mr Never Never, I thought. Anyway disqualified from driving it in't you.

BILLY. Yeah. I just love red wine.

JANICE. Give Joey the helmet.

BILLY. Here you are then, old chap.

BILLY *takes off the helmet and puts it on* JOSEF FRANK'S *head.*

FRANK. What . . .

JANICE. Help him with the strap.

JOSEF FRANK *stands, slightly stooped, hands loose by his sides while* BILLY *does up the straps.*

BILLY. Why were you born so gormless Joey? Ugh, you in't half got bad breath. What you got at the back a your throat? Dog that died?

The helmet fixed, BILLY *knocks on it.*

Wake up Joey. Your big chance. You want a climb out a your wank pit for a touch a the real thing.

JOSEF FRANK *hesitates.*

Now don't say no to a lady.

FRANK. Do I . . . Put my turns-ups in my socks?

BILLY. That is really up to you, my friend.

JANICE. Get on Joey.

BILLY *helps* JOSEF FRANK *on to the pillion.*

BILLY. Lift up your leg. The throb a do you good.

FRANK. I protest! I am not involved!

JANICE *guns the motorcycle.*

SCENE NINE

Dockland. A derelict site. JANICE *and* JOSEF FRANK *on the motorcycle.*

FRANK. What is this place?

JANICE *gets off the motorcycle.*

JANICE. Wharf. Before they knocked it down.

She shouts into the dark.

Ken! Liz!

A pause.

Played here when we were kids. Mothers and fathers.
Vietcong meet the Daleks. First boy I fucked was here.

JANICE *laughs.*

That's the River over there. Low tide. Tell by the smell. Sh!

A slight pause.

Hear the rats?

A slight pause.

Smashing London apart, you see. Ruins and holes.

A pause.

I'm a Communist too.

FRANK. You are a baby.

JANICE. I follow Trotsky.

JOSEF FRANK *laughs.*

FRANK. You do *what?*

JANICE. Don't you believe me?

FRANK. Dear child.

JANICE. I'm dead serious.

FRANK. Dear little baby.

JANICE. That why they throw you out a Czechoslovakia?

FRANK. What do you mean?

JANICE. Trotsky.

JOSEF FRANK *laughs.*

Don't laugh at me!

FRANK. Is that why you stuck me upon this machine? Because you thought I was a fellow Trotskyite?

JANICE. Lot a you, wan't there? Slansky? Clementis?

A silence.

FRANK. How did you get hold of those names?

JANICE. You one a them?

FRANK. How did a silly little girl in South London, get hold of those names?

JANICE. Prague Treason Trails. 1952. Conspiratorial Centre they called you, didn't they?

FRANK. A stupid adolescent, get those names in her mouth?

JANICE. Can read, can't I?

FRANK. You have no right to have those names in your mouth.

JANICE. What you been doing with yourself for twenty-five years? Been in prison?

FRANK. No right!

JANICE. First book I read 'bout Communism was called *The Evil That Was Lenin.* Think it was meant to put me off. 'Stead it put me on.

FRANK. No right!

JANICE. And I read and read. Shiny books you get from Moscow. And plastic covers, red, from Peking you know? All printed faint. Couldn't understand a word. But I believed in it.

JOSEF FRANK *laughs.*

I knew it was right!

FRANK (*to himself*). Filth on the walls. All torn.

JANICE. Then I got in with this crowd. Big flashy flats. Lots a cushions and booze. That's how I met Trotsky.

FRANK. The little girl met Trotsky. Oh God.

JANICE. I was their pet, in a way. Real, wan't I. The real stuff. Proletarian. Na, they were all right I s'pose. Kept on wanting a poke me rigid though, some of 'em. So I gave that lot up. And I gave school up. Wanted me to do 'A' levels.

She laughs.

One teacher, woman, Mrs Banks . . . You know thirty and raddled with groovy afro hair . . . Said I'd got a go a University. Said if I didn't I'd ruin myself.

She laughs.

I mean, I may as well a been a hundred. And I left.

FRANK. Juvenile.

JANICE. Yeah I'm juvenile! But I'm working on it. See . . . They're not going a get me.

FRANK. There is too much lost, too much blood. Can't you understand?

JANICE. No I don't. Less you're saying you're a clapped out old man.

FRANK. Yes, yes, say that. I am a clapped out old man.

JANICE. Well we're going a change this fucking country.

FRANK. Nothing will change in England. Decay, yes. Change, no.

JANICE. We're going a have a revolution in England.

FRANK. There will never be a revolution in England.

JANICE. Who are you to say? You're a clapped out old man.

FRANK. Painful for me, I do not wish to continue the discussion . . .

JANICE. No one's discussing mate, I'll telling you. Be bad for you, eh? Run away to soft old, squidgy old England. And then it breaks out here. What you ran away from. Be nowhere for you to hide. Be a nothing.

FRANK. There was a violinist. A Jew. At the time of Hitler he hid his race. One day he had to play, it was Beethoven's Violin Concerto, at a concert with Hitler present. At the entrance of the violin, after the orchestral introduction, the violinist found he could not play. In the awful silence he left the platform. After the war, after surviving the camps and many sufferings, he lived obscurely in retirement. It was the violinist's birthday when a friend gave him a gramophone and a record. It was Beethoven's Violin Concerto. The violinist put it on the gramophone. The orchestra played the introduction. The moment for the violin to play came . . . And went. No violin. It was a practice record. The music continued, a mockery. The violinist looked at his hands and killed himself.

A pause.

JANICE. Oh Joey, aren't you still a Communist?

FRANK. Cannot you understand? Will you not understand?

JANICE: Mum's the word.

> KEN *and* LIZ, *unseen, set up whistles and catcalls.* JANICE *puts two fingers to her mouth and lets out a piercing whistle.*

JANICE (*to* JOSEF FRANK). Don't let on.

FRANK. About what?

JANICE. Tell 'em what I told you. 'Bout Trotsky.

FRANK. When I was fourteen I was already in prison. The police had found Young Communist leaflets under my bed.

JANICE. Don't you.

FRANK. Mum is the word?

JANICE. That's right!

> JANICE *kisses* JOSEF FRANK *quickly.*

What's the smell?

FRANK. Garlic.

JANICE. Not your teeth?

FRANK. No, I . . .

JANICE. Great. I'm really happy.

> JANICE *shouts into the dark.*

Over here Ken!

FRANK (*to himself*). Kindergarten.

> KEN, STACKY, LIZ *and* ALF *come out of the dark.*

KEN. Where's Billy?

JANICE. Walking.

KEN. Well he ought a be here!

JANICE. He will be here!

KEN. We got a be all . . . All in on this!

> STACKY *makes signs.*

> Oh shut up Stacky.

> KEN *turns away.*

JANICE. What's a matter, Ken?

> KEN *kicks at the ground.*

ALF. Joey.

FRANK. Alfred.

ALF. Fun and games, eh?

FRANK. What are these children doing here?

ALF. Tearways. Bloody hoodlums. I'm all for it myself.

> ALF *laughs and wanders away, rolling a cigarette.* KEN
> *shouts into the dark.*

KEN. Com on come on! Where are you?

LIZ. What you up to, Jan? (*She nods at* JOSEF FRANK.)
Nibbling old men?

JANICE. So?

LIZ. Ooh Jan, how could you. The boys say . . . You know in
the washroom . . . You could have his skin for breakfast
'stead a cornflakes.

JANICE. So?

LIZ. So don't be disgusting.

JANICE. Maybe I like being disgusting.

LIZ. Jan, you not . . .

JANICE. It's a meeting a minds.

LIZ. How horrible.

> BILLY *runs on, breathless.*

BILLY (*to* KEN). The man's got his car. Over by the boilers.

> *A slight pause.*

> Stanley's with him.

KEN. Stanley?

JANICE. Oh no.

KEN. What's he want with Stanley?

ALF. Stir, stir, nice and stinking.

*ALF laughs. BOB HICKS and MR STANLEY walk on.
A pause.*

STANLEY. Now you boys and girls. What's all this, dragging Mr Hicks out here?

KEN. Piss off, Stanley.

STANLEY. I resent that, Kenneth.

HICKS. Now let's all have a calm, here.

JANICE. We want a talk with you.

BILLY. That's right . . .

LIZ. You're a Union man. You're meant a be on our side.
(*To* JANICE.) Or have I got it wrong?

BILLY. We talk to you.

KEN. Not the boss's bum boy.

STANLEY. Have you across my knee lad . . .

STACKY makes signs to JANICE. JANICE replies by signs.

KEN (*to* MR STANLEY). Yeah? Let me tell you something, Mr Foreman. Mr come on boys and girls be good. It should not a been your fingers got cut off in the machines, it should a been your neck.

A silence.

HICKS. Now we are all working people here . . .

BILLY. You're not.

HICKS. Shush shush.

STANLEY. Personal abuse all you got to hand . . . ?

JANICE. Stacky says when are we going a have a strike then?

A silence.

STANLEY. Strike?

KEN. You heard what the dumb man said.

STANLEY. You kids . . . You want a get back in the pages a the *Beano* where you belong.

HICKS. Shush shush Ted, no.

A slight pause.

But you . . . Young people . . . You had better get a bit of hard, real thinking done. Now.

HICKS *flexes his shoulders.*

I take it you represent the workforce at Makepeace's.

A silence.

All right I take it you are a representation. Now you want to unionise yourselves. And before we all go up in the air 'bout strikes that means discipline. That means all agreements you have evolved over the years with the Makepeace family, with the management, not only rates of pay but conditions, over-time practice, safety, sickness . . . All that will have to be put down. On paper.

BILLY. We don't want any of that shit . . .

HICKS. Everything. Think about it. Because you may not like it.

ALF. Here we go. Shoot one of 'em, another pops up in his place.

ALF *laughs.*

BILLY. What's he trying a say?

HICKS (*to* BILLY). It may not be worth your while.

STANLEY. Now listen, listen a Mr Hicks.

HICKS. I mean, I'll help you. Any time you want advice, always talk it over. Over a pint. Just give me a ring.

STANLEY. Now just listen a Mr Hicks. Someone older for a change.

HICKS. See, the best you can hope for in this world is to nudge.

Give it a bit of a nudge.

HICKS *flexes his shoulders.*

Industrial relations, that's a mighty animal. Bit of a dinosaur. Or, to look at it another way, bit of a giant oil tanker . . .

BILLY. What the fuck is he talking about?

STANLEY. Billy Mason . . .

BILLY. I can't help it. He hurts my brain.

STANLEY. Why won't you listen, why won't you learn? Mr

Hicks is a respected man. Spent many years keeping the
wolf from the door a working men and women.

HICKS, *low.*

HICKS. 'Nough said, Ted.

STANLEY. And you do not know it, but Mr Hicks may one day
be your Union-sponsored MP.

BILLY. Wow. Let's all have a good wank.

STANLEY. Right. That's it. That's the remark I been waiting for.
All go home now. Strike? You're wet behind the ears, or
gaga. Yes I'm talking about you, Alfred Mallings.

ALF. Nice.

STANLEY. Silly old man. Go and warm your hands up 'front a
your telly set, 'fore you catch your death. Weed your window
box. And the rest a you. Go on. Get home to your Mums and
Dads.

A pause. No one moves.

ALF. If I kick the telly in and pour Harpic over the window box,
will things get any better? On the whole I'd say . . . Yes.

JANICE. Mr Hicks, the Makepeaces are going to sell the factory . . .

MR STANLEY *and* HICKS *look at each other. A slight pause.*

You do know that?

BILLY. Course he knows that.

HICKS. Look love, don't think I don't realise, but . . .

KEN. They're going a sell off the machines! Strip the whole place
out!

JANICE. You do know that?

A pause.

STANLEY. You got the wrong end a the stick.

KEN *goes into the dark.*

HICKS. Does look like it.

STANLEY. All along the line.

BILLY. Jan, do they know or don't they?

JANICE. Don't know . . .

BILLY. I look at 'em and I can't tell. (*At* HICKS.) He standing there, taking up air, lying to me?

HICKS. Now, now.

STANLEY. Way above your heads anyway. You're no better than kids out on the street. How you know what's going on? I mean in the head of a man like Mr Ralph.

KEN runs out of the dark whirling RALPH MAKEPEACE's briefcase round his head. He throws the briefcase on the ground. A pause.

Why, Mr Ralph's briefcase.

A pause.

Oh Kenneth.

KEN. Look inside.

STANLEY (*to* HICKS). I think we better leave, Bob.

HICKS. Sadly.

KEN. Take a look!

STANLEY. Criminal, Kenneth.

KEN. You can read. I can't. Go on. It's stuffed full of it.

JANICE. It's all there. Letters . . .

BILLY. Yeah. He writes poems too. All sex and death.

JANICE. He's going a screw us. Throw us away. Like we were nothing, you understand? That's why we got a, we got a . . .

A pause.

STANLEY. You got a what, girl?

KEN. Take hold. Got a take hold.

JANICE. Else, what is there for us?

STANLEY. I'm not going a argue another word. Ken, you go straight to Mr Makepeace first thing tomorrow morning. I'll put a word in for you, the bugger knows why.

KEN runs to the briefcase. He takes out a fistful of papers.

KEN. Words. Scribble. All over us. Lies and money. Why am I pig ignorant? Why can't I even read the name a the station on the fucking Underground?

STANLEY. Cos you want the whole world. Plop.

KEN clicks a flick knife open.

You will put yourself beyond the pale, Kenneth. For life.
Tomorrow morning.

He points at the briefcase.

With that. Bob . . .

JANICE. Dead end, in't we. The . . . Dead end. Grotty little
factory in a grotty hole. And working there . . . Few women,
few old age pensioners, yobbos and the deaf and dumb.
Don't want a know us, do you? No threat, are we?

HICKS. Clever little head you've got there. You could do better,
love.

A pause.

Takes years. Years. Ask your mothers and your fathers.

STANLEY. Get out a this area. Gracious. Rats big as cats.
(*To* KEN.) Tomorrow morning.

MR STANLEY *and* HICKS *go off. A pause.* BILLY *strikes
a nasty chord on his guitar.*

JANICE. What you show him the case for? What you do that
for?

KEN. Gesture?

ALF. My old Dad made a gesture, back in 1929. Drunk a whole
bottle a Dettol.

ALF *laughs.*

BILLY. Spose we could burn ourselves. Like them monks. But
I spose they'd just dial 999 and put the fire out.

LIZ. Oh let 'em close the place down. Crisps? Leaning over
stinking vats all day? Pushing bits a spuds through boiling oil?
Makes your skin all slime and your hair all seaweed.

A slight pause.

Think I'll go and get married.

STACKY *makes signals.*

JANICE. You're joking.

LIZ. No joke.

BILLY. What's he saying?

JANICE. Stacky says . . . We got a be happy.

BILLY. Highly profound, Stacky old son. Give him the Nobel

Prize.

KEN *sticks the knife into the briefcase several times.*

Better bury that. Give it to the rats . . . Big as cats.

BILLY *picks up a few of the papers, then looks at one.*

Don't seem right does it, your boss writing poems.

He reads.

'We live in an old con- (*he falters*) stituency of the sun
Or old de- (*he falters*) pendency of the day or night.'

He tears the paper up.

Let's get zonked.

JANICE. No . . .

BILLY. Sweet dreams.

KEN. Yeah. Bring out the little white powder Billy.

JANICE. No . . .

KEN. Sniff a fucking heaven.

BILLY. Rots your nose, you know.

KEN. Lovely.

BILLY. Dribbling snot in Nirvana.

JANICE. No . . .

ALF. Well you're all going a have drugs, I'll get on home for my Ovaltine.

BILLY. Actually I not got any stuff.

KEN. You what?

BILLY. Sold it. Payment on the bike came up.

KEN. It's up West then. Couple a dozen pints and a good sick on the tube.

LIZ. Ooh, am I getting took out?

ALF. See if I can get a 185. If they han't knifed the conductor.

JANICE (*to* FRANK). Why don't you help us? Why do you sit there like you were dead? You were a Communist, you said. Don't you care? We're in trouble. Tell us what a do.

JOSEF FRANK *turns his head away.*

LIZ. Get married Jan. Han't you seen 'em, the old women? Old tramp women? In the parks, on the tube. No home, living in a bottle a ruby wine? We could be like that, easy as . . . Nothing at all. Everything gone. Your body, your self-respect. Yeah, on the whole, I'm going a get married. (*To* KEN.) I warn you. I may leave you during the course a the evening with my new husband.

JANICE *looks at them. Then she runs to the motorcycle and gets on.*

BILLY. Oy Joey, that's my bike and that's my woman.

ALF. I used to be a like that. All that spunk gone a waste.

ALF *laughs.* JANICE *kicks the starter, the engine fails.*

BILLY. What you doing?

JANICE. Joey's taking me out.

LIZ. Jan his skin, it's horrible . . .

JANICE. You're going a have a good time, I'm going a have a good time. I'm going a bring this old man back from the dead.

FRANK. I . . .

KEN. We had a go, Jan! Hate and anger! Wan't enough, that's all!

JANICE *starts the motorcycle.*

That's all.

SCENE TEN

The London Planetarium.
A bare stage. But overhead and all round the spectacle of the galaxies, stars and planets, unfolds above the London skyline. A COMMENTATOR, *dressed in a suit with the mannerisms of a sentimental ballad singer, speaks into a hand microphone with a cancerous, cold American accent.* JOSEF FRANK *and* JANICE *stand, hand in hand, looking up.*
Space. Millions of stars.

COMMENTATOR. Look up from your city, see the aeons of space. Cold and infinite. We pass a galaxy.

With a whoosh the spiral nebula in Andromeda passes over the stage.

JANICE. London Planetarium!

COMMENTATOR. In such a cluster of a hundred thousand

million stars is our sun. A star is a sun.

JANICE. Come here as a kid. Sneak in the exit.

A comet zooms down from above.

COMMENTATOR. A comet. Lone ranger of the heavens.

JANICE. Put your hand up my skirt, if you want.

The comet goes down below the skyline.

COMMENTATOR. Trip now to the Solar System. Pluto. Ninth and furthest planet, most desolate of the Sun's family.

The dark form of Pluto looms.

JANICE. Nip in the ladies take my knickers off, if you want.

Pluto passes.

COMMENTATOR. We hurtle toward the sun.

JANICE. Undo your fly, if you want.

COMMENTATOR. Past the cold giants . . . Neptune, Uranus.

One after another, the huge dark forms of Neptune and Uranus loom and pass.

JANICE. I'll give your cock a blow, if you want.

COMMENTATOR. Dead worlds.

JANICE. I'll get a ice lolly a suck. Really make your balls zing.

COMMENTATOR. Deadly atmospheres of methane freeze there.

FRANK. Put me on a bus . . . I want to go home!

JANICE *gestures to an unseen usherette.*

JANICE. Oy miss, give us a rocket ice lolly.

FRANK. Let me alone!

JANICE. No!

FRANK. Please!

JANICE. I fancy you.

COMMENTATOR. Saturn.

Saturn with its rings looms, tilting slowly upon its axis.

The rings of ice and dust shine in the sunlight. The sun is eight hundred and eighty-six million miles away.

FRANK. I'm dead.

JANICE. Then get alive . . .

FRANK. It's not a personal matter . . .

JANICE. Least give me a cuddle!

Saturn passes.

Please?

COMMENTATOR. Jupiter.

JOSEF FRANK and JANICE embrace, awkwardly. They still look up at the spectacle, now over each other's shoulders.

JANICE. In't you stiff and knobbly.

COMMENTATOR. Giant of solar space. Here rage hydrogen and ammonia gales, the nightmare poison winds.

JANICE. Your spine's like cement. You need a massage.

Jupiter passes.

FRANK. I . . . Was broken.

JANICE. Here come the asteroids.

FRANK. Bone splintered. Marrow scraped. Brain beaten flat. Blood soiled with the rust of crumbling nails.

The asteroids, tumbling lumps of rock, hurtle forward and pass.

COMMENTATOR. Debris of space. A fistful of gravel thrown around our sun . . .

The COMMENTATOR continues to mouth his commentary in dumbshow.

FRANK. How cruel of the mindless stuff of which we're made to have nerves. To peel so easily. Lower the temperature a speck upon the scale. Put water and a few chemicals out of reach. And where's our humanism? Freud, Marx, Engels, our mighty systems? They are less than the yellow matter that blinds the eye of the sleepless prisoner. Ow.

JANICE. What's a matter?

FRANK. Boil on my elbow.

JANICE. Put a poultice on.

FRANK. Poultice? Poultice?

COMMENTATOR. Mars, red planet.

Mars looms.

JANICE. Or T.C.P. Got some in my handbag.

FRANK. T? T what?

COMMENTATOR. Mars.

JANICE. Or just give us a kiss.

JANICE *and* JOSEF FRANK *kiss.*

COMMENTATOR. World of red deserts. Fields of carbon dioxide snow. Thin, gentle winds.

JANICE *looks up.*

JANICE. Eh . . . If there's life on Mars, do you think it's communist? Even if it's only a bit a moss . . . Solid red. Serve the bloody Americans right when they get there.

JANICE *and* FRANK *kiss again. They go down on their knees. Meanwhile Mars passes, Earth and its Moon loom.*

COMMENTATOR. The sweet Earth and its milky bride.

FRANK *looks up.*

FRANK. I . . .

JANICE *kisses him again. They fumble.*

COMMENTATOR. We are ninety-two million, nine hundred and fifty-seven miles from the sun . . .

Suddenly the COMMENTATOR *lapses from American to London English. He waves his hand at* JANICE *and* FRANK.

Eh you, you down there. Get up off the floor. Sorry 'bout this, ladies and gents, get all kinds in here, don't care 'bout the universe. You in row . . .

The Sun rises over the horizon of the Earth. Beams of light strike across the stage. Music crashes in — quadraphonic, exultant. JANICE *and* JOSEF FRANK *stay kneeling in their embrace.*

SCENE ELEVEN

Factory yard. Morning. It is very cold. JOSEF FRANK *comes on to find* RALPH MAKEPEACE, SYLVIA MAKEPEACE *and* MR STANLEY *looking up. From high up offstage a sack of potatoes is thrown down on the stage.*

RALPH (*shouts*). Please!

STANLEY (*shouts*). You stupid hoodlums!

FRANK. Good morning. I . . .

KEN (*off*). Boo hoo Stanley.

Individual potatoes are thrown down on the stage. RALPH MAKEPEACE and MR STANLEY dodge them. SYLVIA MAKEPEACE stands still. JOSEF FRANK walks toward the side of the stage from where the potatoes were thrown.

STANLEY. Oy Joey! What do you think you're doing?

FRANK. Work . . .

KEN (*off*). Joey's down there. Oy Joey!

JANICE (*off*). Joey!

BILLY (*off*). Come in out the cold, Joey!

JANICE (*off*). Joey run!

KEN (*off*). You Ruskie!

JANICE (*off*). Put the ladder down for him.

JOSEF FRANK hesitates. HICKS comes on.

STANLEY. Stay where you are, Frank.

RALPH (*shouts*). Whatever you do, don't hurt the machines.

BILLY (*off*). Have a crisp Ralphy.

Three cardboard boxes full of loose crisps and open are thrown down on the stage. The crisps cascade out.

HICKS (*to* RALPH). Got your call, Ralph. What's up?

RALPH. They say they have occupied the factory or something . . .

STANLEY. Broke in last night. Barred the doors. Overturned the small van in the loading bay. Barricaded it.

HICKS. Out on a limb eh?

Two potatoes are thrown down on the stage near HICKS.

Spuds?

STANLEY. Got ten tons in there.

HICKS. Bloody hell.

SYLVIA (*to* RALPH). Call them.

RALPH. There must be . . .

SYLVIA. Call the police.

RALPH. Sweet reason . . .

SYLVIA. Now. If you don't I will.

JANICE (*off*). Joseph Frank!

FRANK (*aside*). What are the weapons of happiness?

KEN (*off*). Give him covering fire.

Potatoes and boxes rain down upon the stage.

JANICE (*off*). Joseph Frank!

STANLEY. Don't you . . .

FRANK *hesitates.*

Bastard commie . . .

FRANK *makes the first step of his dash toward the factory.*

Blackout.

Act Two

SCENE ONE

Out of the dark JOSEF FRANK, *blindfolded, barefoot and dressed in trousers and shirt sleeves, is rushed to the front of the stage by two* GUARDS.

FIRST GUARD. Stand.

SECOND GUARD. Keep your thumbs by the seams of your trousers.

The two GUARDS *go off. A pause.* JOSEF FRANK *turns his head this way and that way listening. Out of the dark* VICTOR CLEMENTIS, *also blindfolded, barefoot and dressed in trousers and shirt sleeves, is rushed to the front of the stage by the two* GUARDS. *They speak to* CLEMENTIS.

FIRST GUARD. Stand.

SECOND GUARD. Keep your thumbs by the seams of your trousers.

The GUARDS *take the blindfolds off* JOSEF FRANK *and* CLEMENTIS.

FIRST GUARD (*to* JOSEF FRANK). Talk to him. It is a privilege.

SECOND GUARD (*to* CLEMENTIS). Talk to him. It is a privilege.

The GUARDS *turn to go off.*

FRANK. What is the date?

The GUARDS *stop.*

Tell us the date.

FIRST GUARD. That's a privilege.

The GUARDS *go off. A silence.*

CLEMENTIS. Joseph?

FRANK. Victor?

A pause.

CLEMENTIS. How do I look?

FRANK. How . . . Do I look?

They do not look at each other. A pause.

CLEMENTIS. They gave me a lamb chop today. With carrots.

FRANK. They offered me meat. But . . . I cannot.

CLEMENTIS. I asked for the lamb to be pureed. They said they'd see what they could do.

A pause.

They told me you were dead.

FRANK. They told me you were dead.

CLEMENTIS. You accused me.

FRANK. Yes.

CLEMENTIS. So far from Moscow. We were government ministers then, riding high! Weren't we fine ones then.

He giggles, then weeps a little.

Moscow that winter, was so beautiful. The black cars in the snow.

FRANK. Please . . . No.

CLEMENTIS. Forgive me.

FRANK. Display. Any emotional . . . Disturbs me.

CLEMENTIS. Poor Joseph. You must be so tired.

FRANK. Not . . . So much now.

CLEMENTIS. No.

FRANK. Now . . .

CLEMENTIS. No.

FRANK. No.

CLEMENTIS. They gave me the date. It is the 20th of August, 1952.

FRANK. Summer?

CLEMENTIS. They gave me the date this morning. And a cigarette. Things are good.

FRANK. Now.

CLEMENTIS. What?

A pause.

How's your learning going?

FRANK. Very well.

CLEMENTIS. I've learnt all the answers I will give but they want me to learn the prosecutor's questions too.

FRANK. I slide a bit of card down the sentences to test myself.

CLEMENTIS. That's . . . I'll try that too, if you don't mind.

FRANK. It helps.

CLEMENTIS. So much better to have a transcript of a trial before the trial begins, don't you think?

FRANK. You know where you where.

CLEMENTIS. Absolutely. Was it orange juice?

A pause.

They gave you. First thing. When the confession was complete.

FRANK. Tea.

A pause.

Sweet. We aren't human, are we.

CLEMENTIS. No?

FRANK. They are feeding us now, they are telling us the day of the year now, but we aren't human.

CLEMENTIS. They offered me tea but I have . . . The oesophagus. Throat. Raw.

FRANK. So you took the orange juice?

CLEMENTIS. They told me the Third World War had begun.

A pause.

They told me the Americans bombed Peking at Christmas. Atom bombed.

A pause.

They told me Paris is a desert! And they are eating dogs in London!

A pause.

They said . . . Aren't you ashamed? The decisive struggle has begun! And you are in prison. Starving. Filth on your body. Your mind, my mind breaking.

A pause.

And I was ashamed. So very much, Joseph.

A pause.

Help the Party! Be the enemy we must root out! Yes, yes I said. Yes.

A pause.

Yes, I have difficulty with hot things. Rasp. The lining of the . . .

CLEMENTIS *touches his throat.*

FRANK. Yes.

CLEMENTIS. What torments me is . . . Did he know?

FRANK. Who?

CLEMENTIS. He can't have known. What they have done to us. What . . .

FRANK. Be silent!

CLEMENTIS. What they have done . . .

FRANK. Silent!

CLEMENTIS. To the Party. To socialism. To me. To my mind. He can't have known.

A pause.

Stalin.

A silence.

They are worried my voice will not carry. At the trial. They are giving me medicine. An anti-septic spray, every hour. I assure them I will speak loudly. I won't let them down.

FRANK. No.

CLEMENTIS. I am confident. Have they given you spinach?

FRANK. The Grand Inquisitor.

CLEMENTIS. I ate spinach once in Paris, with butter. And a little nutmeg.

FRANK. The story of the Grand Inquisitor. At the height of

the Spanish Inquisition, Christ appeared among the terrified people in a public place. A woman came to him with her dead son. Among the crowd, disguised as a poor monk, the Grand Inquisitor saw the miracle. He ordered Christ's arrest. That night the Grand Inquisitor went alone to Christ's cell. The Grand Inquisitor said to Christ . . . Why do you come? To give the people love and happiness now? Out of pity in a crowd restore that child's blindness, that woman's skin, that man's life? And the Grand Inquisitor argued . . . You left love. A few pure words of truth. But how can words of love become concrete, survive in the filth and tumult of earthy life? How often has truth been spoken on the earth only to be lost in war, riot, the massive movements of people? It is in the Church that your truth survives. The feared, cruel, impregnable Church. I am the Church. My dungeons, my racks and my tribunals endlessly purify the unbelievers so that the Church may survive. So that your truth may survive, through this dark age. But now you come with miracles. Sentimental gestures. Anarchy. Everything you taught will disappear in a morass of exultation and false hopes. My Lord, the Church is Christ on earth. I, the torturer, am Christ on earth. That is why, in the morning, I will hang you and burn you.

A pause.

Christ said nothing, but leant to the Grand Inquisitor and gave him his blessing and kissed him.

CLEMENTIS. Oh Joseph. Are you still a Communist?

The GUARDS come forward with a noose and blindfold.

FRANK. Victor Clementis. Hanged in Prague on the 3rd of December 1952.

The GUARDS blindfold CLEMENTIS.

CLEMENTIS. Last letter to Klement Gottwald, Chairman of the Communist Party of Czechoslovakia, President of the Czechoslovak Socialist Republic.

The GUARDS put the noose around CLEMENTIS'S neck and scuttle off into the dark.

A few hours before his death even the worst man speaks the truth. I declare that I have never been a traitor or a spy. I confessed only to fulfil my obligation to working people and the Communist Party. It was my duty. In order that the Party survive our days of lies and fear to lead the working people to full happiness. Long live the Communist Party of Czechoslovakia.

CAPITAL RADIO. Hello all you nightriders out there.

A snatch of music. Mina Ripperton sings 'Loving you'.
CLEMENTIS *begins to sink through the stage.*

JANICE (*off*). Joseph?

KEN (*off*). Oy Joey! Where you got to?

CLEMENTIS. I tried to keep my trousers up in court! I did not show my bum in disrespect!

CAPITAL RADIO. Insomniacs all, cold out there? Here comes Californian Sun.

The radio plays the Beach Boys singing 'Good Vibrations'.
CLEMENTIS *has sunk to his chest.* JOSEF FRANK *kneels beside him.*

CLEMENTIS. I've got a handful of raisins. In a matchbox. I'd give them to you if I were alive.

CLEMENTIS *disappears.* JOSEF FRANK *looks upstage as* STALIN *comes out of the dark smoking his pipe.* KEN *comes out of the dark carrying a transistor radio.*

KEN (*to* JOSEF FRANK). What you doing? Sleep walking about the factory?

STALIN *walks away into the dark.* JOSEF FRANK *watches him go.*

Oh go and tuck him up, Jan. Or whatever you get up to.

FRANK. He wanted to give me raisins.

KEN. What?

FRANK. Victor Clementis. In a matchbox. The last thing he said to me, before he died, in a corridor. You see . . . To keep raisins all those months, through the interrogation, the trial, the winter . . . That was an achievement.

A pause.

KEN. I don't know, old son. I just don't know what you're on about.

KEN *throws the transistor radio down the drain. A silence.*

JANICE. What you do that for?

KEN. Can't stand the Beach Boys, can I.

JANICE. Where's the grating to that drain gone, anyway?

KEN. Chucked it on the barricade didn't I. When I was pissed.

JANICE *about to say something.*

All right, all right! But the beer's run out. And I'm coming out all over in bleeding lumps, cos a eating bleeding crips all the time.

A pause.

The great idea, eh? I don't know. Zonked, weren't we. Night we went up West and had it. The great idea.

A pause.

Billy raving he could see the Milky Way, middle a Oxford Street. Liz making clucking noises at any man in a sharpish suit. Stacky with his dumbhead eyes going like a fruit machine. It was Piccadilly Circus the great idea came. I'd just had a very satisfying sick and was feeling wonderful. The adverts, all neon . . . Like you could put your hand out, pull 'em down off the buildings, put 'em on your coat like a badge. And suddenly we all got it. You only had to look at Stacky and you knew he had it too. Just like that. Out the air. Out the traffic. Bang. Occupy the place. Blew all our bread . . . Six crates a Guinness, three bottles a gin, piled in Stacky's van and straight down here. Broke in, built the barricade. Christ were we ill when dawn came round.

JANICE. Aren't you happy, Ken?

KEN. Course I'm happy. Taking over the world in't we? Workers' paradise in here, in't it?

A pause.

Floating away in a the sunset on a sea a crisps in't we?

A pause.

Yeah.

KEN *goes off.*

JANICE. And what you wandering off for?

FRANK. Nightmares, I . . . Figures. People I once knew.

JANICE. And that's another thing. Why you always go on about the dead? You go on for hours. Names with 'K' and 'Z' in 'em.

FRANK. They died.

JANICE. Good.

FRANK. Suffered.

JANICE. Don't care.

FRANK. They hold my hands when I eat. They tie my shoes when I dress. When I speak they hold my tongue. They turn my head to see a dead bird in a garden. They pull open the lids of my eyes when I wake.

JANICE. Oh what you carry around. Wads a rotting stuff. All in your pockets, all stuffed down your shirt, urrgh.

FRANK. History . . .

JANICE. Don't care about history.

FRANK. I thought the little girl was a Marxist . . .

JANICE. Don't you try and frighten me, Mr Dracula. Half in half out your grave . . . Or so you'd like me a think . . .

FRANK. Jan, I . . .

JANICE. No history. Right? Wipe it out.

FRANK. Wiped.

JANICE. And don't forget it. And don't forget what you are.

FRANK. Count Dracula?

JANICE. A dirty old man. What are you?

JOSEF FRANK *shrugs.*

FRANK. Dirty old man.

JANICE. Child fingerer.

FRANK. Child fingerer.

JANICE. Right.

FRANK. Right.

JANICE. And there in't no history. Never happened. And if it did, make it go away.

She claps her hands.

There, it went away. Goodbye history.

She claps her hands.

Now is what I want. Now . . . That's what I love. The now. My now. Lovely sexy here and now. Perhaps we just been made.

A second ago. The world came into existence . . . Pop! Last time you blinked. And here we are now. Think so?

JOSEF FRANK smiles.

FRANK. Not a chance.

A pause.

JANICE. You don't make me feel sick you know. I mean you don't physically revolt me.

FRANK. Ah.

JANICE. I like your body.

JANICE touches him.

Poor body.

He brushes JANICE'S hand away.

Give us a cuddle? Now? Middle a the night? Middle of a dirty old factory? Middle a London? England? Europe? World?

JANICE pauses, then touches JOSEF FRANK again.

SCENE TWO

Factory yard. Night. It is very cold. Powerful lights are rigged up shining into the wings at the factory. Two of the lights swivel and are manned by POLICE CONSTABLES — other CONSTABLES are on the edge of the scene.
Upstage, swathed in fur coats and scarves, RALPH MAKEPEACE and SYLVIA MAKEPEACE sit before a burning brazier in deck chairs, their backs to the audience. RALPH MAKEPEACE is asleep. A champagne bottle stands in a silver champagne bucket which is on an ornate tripod with wheels.
INSPECTOR MILLER and HICKS stand nearby.
JOSEF FRANK, barefoot his shoes hanging round his neck, is being led onto the stage by MR STANLEY.

FRANK. I do not wish to leave the factory . . .

INSPECTOR MILLER and HICKS turn.

MILLER. Light over there, lads.

The POLICE CONSTABLES swing the beams of the lights upon JOSEF FRANK and MR STANLEY. A pause, JOSEF FRANK blinking.

FRANK.   ⎫   I do not wish to leave the factory.

MILLER   ⎬ (*together*).   Got him.

HICKS.   ⎭   Very well done, Ted.

MILLER. Thank the Lord for that.

INSPECTOR MILLER *walks upstage to* RALPH MAKEPEACE.

STANLEY. Huddled up in filth in there! Gracious.

HICKS. Bad, is it?

STANLEY. Slime all over. Condensation from the vats. Ought a been hosed down days ago.

MILLER. Mr Makepeace?

STANLEY. And doing their business in corners. (*To* FRANK.) Barricades? Pissing on the floor a your place a work? Makes me sick a my bones.

HICKS. Mr Frank . . .

(HICKS *sees* JOSEF FRANK's *feet.*)

There's nothing on your feet.

FRANK. I was asleep.

MILLER. Mr Makepeace?

STANLEY (*to* FRANK). Known these kids from the cradle. And their Mums and Dads. Then of a sudden they are spitting at me. Who got at 'em? You?

FRANK. You dragged me out.

HICKS. I feel . . . The time is really ripe for sweet reason.

STANLEY. Or a smashed upper plate. (*To* FRANK.) Smell a bad news about you. Go home, foreigner.

FRANK. I know nothing. I am an exile.

MILLER. Mr Makepeace, please . . .

SYLVIA. Ralph. Wake up.

RALPH MAKEPEACE *wakes.*

RALPH. What? Oh. Where were we?

SYLVIA. Your mistress. The Jeye's cloth I found in the glove compartment of the car. Soggy with it.

RALPH. Ah, that's where we were.

RALPH MAKEPEACE *stands, lifting the champagne bucket, with its bottle, from the tripod.*

MILLER. Mr Makepeace . . .

HICKS. Ralph. Ted has got Mr Frank out. For a discussion.

SYLVIA. I would like you all back there to know he never liked me to touch my own breasts.

MILLER (*to* HICKS). Sacred Arthur, give me patience! People in charge living in a bottle! Not even physically fit!

HICKS. I know I know . . .

MILLER (*to* RALPH). Eight uniform men and two C.I.D. on roster round your . . . Little empire, sir. Meanwhile in the big world they are still parking on yellow lines and knocking over old ladies in the parks. Now are you or are you not going to press a high court order?

A pause.

RALPH. Frank you've come out of your hole. Ho . . . Ole.

HICKS. It has been seven days, Ralph. I feel compromised.

RALPH (*to* JOSEF FRANK). Out your burrow. Like a weasel. To gloat. (*To* HICKS.) Do weasels have burrows? Do weasels gloat?

HICKS. After seven days, at least . . . Weigh their grievances. We have Mr Frank from in there, as a maturer and an older man. Reasonable behaviour cannot be dying out. Can it?

STANLEY. Court order and bang. For their good, if not ours.

SYLVIA. I am taking the children to mother in the morning. You can come for Antonia's birthday. After that . . . I am told the tides off Brighton West Pier are blessedly strong.

RALPH. I asked you all a question about a common animal!

A silence.

Don't you know him? Little feet? Pitter patter?

A silence.

HICKS. I . . .

RALPH. Enemy of man. Little alien brain. Poking through little red a . . . alien eyes. In and out the ground. Nick nick, little teeth. Rabid with it too.

A silence.

(*To* HICKS.) Livid!

HICKS. ?

RALPH. The word I want.

HICKS. I . . .

RALPH. To describe how a weasel must see the world, livid meat.

HICKS. Ah.

RALPH. That's what we are to that animal, to our little enemy.
   Red going on to purplish stuff to bite. And his day's coming,
   oh. Hang ourselves up on butcher's hooks eh? Dripping a
   little eh? Waiting for the precise little teeth.

A pause.

STANLEY. Your father would drop down dead, if he were alive.

MILLER. You're tired, sir.

STANLEY (*to* HICKS). I had to say it.

HICKS. Yes Ralph, you're tired.

STANLEY. Would a killed that lovely old man.

RALPH. I am . . .

A pause. They hang on his next word.

Tired.

They sigh.

MILLER.		All a bit dyspeptic round here.
STANLEY.		Right now, Joey. Mr Hicks, Inspector Miller and I will not haggle.
FRANK	(*together*).	Hag . . . ?
HICKS		Perhaps if you lie down, Ralph, and try not to, eh . . .

RALPH. Haggle? (*A pause.*) I'll haggle.

MILLER. Oh my God.

HICKS. I think that's not the good idea we need right now.

RALPH. Haggle. Waggle. Woggle.

MILLER. Oh dear oh dear.

RALPH. Wiggle my life away! I will I do, my life away. So all you . . . Lackeys.

A slight pause.

Go away.

STANLEY (*to* RALPH). Your father, that saintly man . . . Even in his last years, in his wheelchair, still ruled with a rod a iron. He'd never have let it come to this. Dear oh dear! (*To the others.*) Sick a my bones! Human doo-dahs in the machines, goodness gracious! Thirty years at work. And what now? The little I hold dear gets murdered. Sneer if you like, but with me it's pigeons on my roof. I been getting a dream. One day they are all dead. (*To* JOSEF FRANK.) And whose fault will that be, eh? Whose fault will that be?

RALPH. Will you all get off my property?

STANLEY (*to* JOSEF FRANK). I was in the desert!

FRANK. I was in Ruzyn prison.

STANLEY. Never heard of it.

FRANK. Have the children in that factory, asleep, heard of your desert?

STANLEY. Don't you talk about our children! Fucking foreigner!

RALPH. It is my livelihood in ruins! My creditworthiness that's bacon rind for the birds!

A slight pause.

MILLER (*to* HICKS *and* MR STANLEY). There's a panda car round the corner with a bottle of scotch in the boot. Noggin?

HICKS. Came prepared?

MILLER. You do these days. (*To* RALPH MAKEPEACE.) Lackeys, eh? Well . . . You carry on running the country then, sir. Just let us heavies know when it really gets out of hand eh? Before it's too late and hoodlums rule the whole kerboodle, eh? Come on Bob, Ted.

INSPECTOR MILLER, HICKS *and* MR STANLEY *go off,* INSPECTOR MILLER *beckoning the* CONSTABLES *off with him.* JOSEF FRANK *and* RALPH MAKEPEACE *look at each other. A silence.* RALPH MAKEPEACE *puts his hand in his coat pocket.*

RALPH. Ping?

FRANK. I'm sorry?

RALPH. Sh.

RALPH MAKEPEACE *takes a champagne glass out of his pocket. He holds it up and pings it with a finger.*

Ping.

RALPH MAKEPEACE *walks sideways to* JOSEF FRANK, *glass in one hand, the other clutching the champagne bucket with its bottle.*

Take one.

FRANK. What?

RALPH. Pocket.

JOSEF FRANK *takes a champagne glass from* RALPH MAKEPEACE'S *other pocket.* JOSEF FRANK *looks at the glass.*

Are you a religious man?

FRANK. Why?

RALPH. The feet.

FRANK. No.

RALPH. Thought perhaps it was remorse.

FRANK. I do not think so.

RALPH. Self disgust?

FRANK. No.

RALPH. No.

A pause.

Do you mind putting your shoes and socks on? The colour of your feet is bothering me.

FRANK. What do you want of me?

RALPH. Pour the champagne, obviously.

FRANK. I don't drink alcohol.

RALPH. You know, old man, you really are something of a perpetual absence.

FRANK. If I am to put my shoes and socks on, I will have to hold your sleeve.

RALPH. Be my guest.

JOSEF FRANK holds RALPH MAKEPEACE'S sleeve. He raises a foot. He looks helplessly from his foot to his other hand, holding the champagne glass. RALPH MAKEPEACE and JOSEF FRANK sway.

FRANK. Balance . . .

RALPH. Give me the bloody thing.

RALPH MAKEPEACE takes the glass and throws it into the wings. He takes the champagne bottle out of the bucket and throws the bucket into the wings.

Come the dawn will we find ourselves . . . Returned to our senses? Wake up lying in a pool of liquid . . . On the floor of our garden shed? And will we look out of the window and say . . . Why are there red flags on our chimney pots? Why are there young men and women shouting from our windows? (*To* FRANK.) Is that what they want in there?

FRANK. They are sleeping.

RALPH MAKEPEACE struggles to open the champagne bottle.

RALPH. The young in one another's arms? I mean . . . Are you all writhing in the liberated area?

The champagne cork pops out.

A far country. Birds in the trees. I am utterly ruined. Do they know that? Your sweet youths? Your sweet limbed, snotty hoodlums? Have you noticed how the oil from the vats makes the girls . . . Glisten . . .

A pause.

Don't they know they are wrecking a wreck? Your shitty little change-the-worlders? I am a drowned man. Why hold my head down the toilet?

He hiccups.

Bloody hiccups now. Just know the night's going to end in physical indignity. Ruptured stomach wall?

He hiccups. He waves the champagne bottle.

Want some of this?

Nothing from JOSEF FRANK.

It was the pork chop flavour that finally did for me. The Makepeace crisp is, anyway, deeply obscure. The monoliths of the crunch world long wanted to bite me. Bite me . . .

He hiccups.

Out. The pork chop flavour was a last fling. But . . . Too much capital expenditure. Too little return. Sacks of pork chop powder piled up, going soggy in the rain. My accountant advised me to sell it fast, for cash, as fertiliser. Conducted a feasibility test. Tried it on my lawn. The lawn died.

He hiccups.

Frank, I plead with you!

SYLVIA. All I wanted was a family. A good life in a good house. A few trees in the garden. And to go south in the summer. Perhaps to Tuscany. And in my marriage, and with my friends, all I wanted was . . . Certain moments of ease. Silence and smiles. Not this endless grubbing around. Lunchtime drinking. Hysterical calls to accountants. My husband with his back to me in bed at night, sobbing. All because a few pubs are going over to sausage and mash and will no longer take a gross of packets of crisps oh god! I've got crisps in my knickers. Little bits of crisps under my eyelids. The debt. The bad temper. The nightmare audits. Life should be . . . Sun on the wall, children on a swing in the shade. Not this guilt.

RALPH (*to* JOSEF FRANK). Get them back to work in there. I'll take my heart out and give it to you. I'll lay my bowels upon the floor. I'll crawl . . .

He hiccups. A pause. He hiccups again. JOSEF FRANK *turns away.*

Where are you going? You've not had a drink. You've not put your shoes . . . Stop, let me help you . . . With your socks . . .

JOSEF FRANK *stops.*

FRANK. Reason. Reason. Reason. Violence!

A silence.

What are you people? All I wanted . . . Was nothing. My need was . . . A crack in the wall in this country. In which to vegetate, moulder away, so quietly to rack and ruin. Be . . . Tired. Burn a little self-pity in the grate. I would have drunk, if I had something of a liver left. When I came here they wanted me to teach at your Cambridge University. Modern History.

He laughs.

Teach the slow movement of corpses, sinking in a graveyard?

A pause.

For, if I told you what was done to me, you would say it is a miracle that I survived. But I did not survive. It is cruel! When the worst thing that can be done to a man has been done to you . . . To your body, to the valves of your heart, your skin, the molars of your jaw . . . Why do they want you to be a saint?

RALPH. God. If I'd known we'd have had you round to dinner.

A pause.

FRANK. I will tell the workers you employ what you said.

JOSEF FRANK *turns away.*

RALPH. I am not a bad man! I write poems!

FRANK. So?

SCENE THREE

The factory by the drain, night. JOSEF FRANK *alone.*

FRANK. So you're a fine human being? So there's a strip of carpet in Rasyn Gaol, blood and human hair in its pile. So, you wish no one harm? Love gardens? Autumn? The city of Venice, the music of Debussy? So, tonight the trains in Russia go for thousands of miles, each with a prison coach . . . the blacked out windows, seen on any station in that country . . . There are mothers alive, tonight, who have murdered babies rather than take them upon those trains . . . So. So. So what?

A pause.

The Soviet poet Mayakovsky, the last year of his life, before he blew out his brains . . . Took to carrying a little bit of soap about. To wash his hands, everywhere, even in the snow in the street. So? So I know how he felt.

He laughs. A pause.

And Rudolph Slansky in his cell in Prague, ran his head at the rim, rim of the lavatory in his cell . . . To beat his tortured mind into some kind of peace. And they took him to hospital to dress his wound . . . And three days later returned him to his cell . . . Where he found the lavatory padded, with steel strips and sacking. So, so he could not leave. So what?

Catalogues of horrors, fine feelings mangled, betrayal, generations lost, tyranny. So what?

JANICE (*off*). Joseph, where are you?

KEN (*off*). What you doing, Joey?

BILLY (*off*). Saw you out in the yard, Joey!

KEN (*off*) You creeping about in here Joey?

FRANK. I thought I could leave that bloodstained room. Be English. Anonymous, in a gentle climate?

KEN (*off*). Joey!

BILLY (*off*). Joey!

LIZ (*off*). Joey!

KEN (*off*). Where you at, Joey?

LIZ (*off*). Dirty old man!

FRANK. Right. If I am not to be left alone, all right. Right. I'll drag out all I once believed in.

STACKY *runs on, sees* JOSEF FRANK *and skids to a halt.*

(*Aside.*) Let the old melodrama hit the road again.

STACKY, *trying to call the others.*

STACKY. Huh! Huh!

JANICE, LIZ *and* BILLY *carrying* ALF *on an improvised stretcher and* KEN *come on. A silence.*

FRANK. Mr Makepeace wants you all to go back to work.

KEN. Oh great.

BILLY. News.

KEN. And what did you say to him?

FRANK. Nothing.

JANICE. Nothing?

BILLY. Never trust an old man.

ALF. I agree. I'm an old man and I don't trust me.

BILLY. What he offer you? Breakfast in a flash hotel? Silk underwear for your dirty old arse?

LIZ. Or just a wash. Wouldn't blame him. My blackheads are coming alive.

JANICE. Nothing, Joseph? Oh why? Why not tell 'em . . . We liberated the machines. The machines are free now. But you said nothing?

KEN. Course he said nothing! Cos he's a nothing man!

FRANK. Oh baby boy. You cannot even suck back your dribble.

A pause.

KEN. What you call me?

FRANK. A baby boy. Who has fouled his cradle a little and is proud of that. But really can do nothing for himself.

KEN *giggles.*

KEN. Think you rule do you Mister?

JANICE. Be careful, Joseph . . .

KEN *runs at* JOSEF FRANK.

BILLY. No don't . . .

BILLY *steps across* KEN's *path.* KEN *skids and falls.* FRANK *takes hold of* KEN's *ears from behind and puts his knee in his back.*

KEN. Let go my ears.

FRANK. Old lag's trick.

KEN. I said let go my ears.

FRANK. Hold a violent comrade for hours.

KEN. Get him a let go my ears!

FRANK. I am puffing out.

ALF. Puffed. Just puffed. That's English.

JANICE *and* LIZ *laugh.*

KEN. All right. All right.

A pause.

What do you want?

FRANK. No. What do you want?

KEN. Come all the way out the iron curtain, just a pull a bloke's earhole . . .

FRANK. Ken, the great idea.

KEN. Occupy the place.

FRANK. And?

KEN. No fucking 'and' about it ow!

LIZ. Steal, that's what we want a do in't it?

BILLY. Rip it all off!

JANICE. Run it ourselves.

BILLY. Liberate it. The lot! For us!

FRANK. And?

LIZ. And revenge. I don't mind saying it.

FRANK. Revenge and?

BILLY. Yeah! Sheds, machines yeah! Vats a oil!

FRANK. And?

BILLY. And chuck it at 'em!

FRANK. And?

BILLY. Yeah!

FRANK. And?

BILLY. Shut up saying 'and'!

FRANK. And how do you run the factory? And how do you buy the potatoes? And the cellophane, for the packets? And pay the printers, for the funny faces in pretty colours, upon the packets? And the oil in the vats?

JANICE. What you saying?

LIZ. 'Let go,' he's saying.

BILLY. Course he's saying 'let go'. They all say 'let go' in the end. Even Dylan, his last three LP's . . . He's said 'let go'.

FRANK (*to* KEN). You do not have the chance for revolt often. And, often, it is ridiculous. Fleeting. Difficult to think through. But it is rare. And not to be thrown away. It is the most precious thing on earth.

JOSEF FRANK *releases* KEN. *A pause.*

Revolt.

KEN. If we could take things all apart. Put 'em all agether again. There is a way, sometimes I do see it, like with words. And it goes blurred.

A pause.

Right. We go out the drain.

JANICE. What . . .

BILLY. What do you mean?

KEN. We chuck the factory.

A pause.

We get out.

A pause.

Only us we got, you see. (*To* JANICE.) Stacky's van. Parked out the back a Poppy Street, in't it?

JANICE. Yeah . . .

KEN. We go down the drain, out under the yard, out under the wall and . . . Away.

JANICE. Just walk out?

A pause.

ALF. In the war, last war, they walked out the cities. During the blitz. Thousands, just walked out. All over the countryside. 'Trekkers' they called 'em. Portsmouth, Coventry, Glasgow. You could see the camp fires for miles at night. Did it myself once. Visiting my sister in Pompey. One very bad night, just walked out on Portsdown. Out a that experience, I'll tell you what you need. Load a bog paper.

A pause. They look at the drain.

BILLY. Why not?

LIZ. Down there . . .

JANICE. Why not?

LIZ. Why not?

ALF gets up.

ALF. Don't know what I'm lying on this bleeding thing for, like a leper! Right, I'll go first.

ALF jumps down the drain and disappears.

BILLY. Fucking hell!

KEN. Oy, Alf!

KEN, BILLY and JANICE run to the drain. ALF shouts from down the drain.

ALF. Just hurt my leg a bit, that's all. Come on in, it's only muck

Blackout.

SCENE FOUR

In the blackout LIZ, KEN, BILLY, STACKY and ALF are heard passing along the drain.

BILLY. Lot a gunge down here!

LIZ. There's a smell, like seaweed.

ALF. Don't drop me in it, whatever you do don't do that. I got stiff knees.

LIZ. Didn't ought a jumped down the hole, ought you!

ALF. It was an impulse.

LIZ. Silly old man.

ALF. I'll be all right. I can look after myself. I been in brothels in Port Said. If you seen a woman going with a donkey you can put up with anything.

JANICE. Where's Joseph?

KEN. Don't know. Joey?

A silence.

Joey, keep behind us.

A silence.

JANICE. I'll find him.

KEN. Don't be stupid!

JANICE. Joseph?

Light appears at the mouth of the drain, revealing the same scene as the factory floor. JOSEF FRANK is sitting, shoulders rounded, legs dangling into the drain. JANICE climbs up holding a lamp.

JANICE. Joseph? They're waiting for us down there.

A pause.

Joseph?

FRANK. Excuse.

JANICE. What?

FRANK. You will have to excuse me.

JANICE. What's the matter? What is it?

FRANK. Something inside. A strange . . .

JANICE. Where?

FRANK. In. Inside.

JANICE. I'll get you to a hospital.

FRANK. No no, sh. Sh.

JANICE. I'll take you to the hospital.

FRANK. No be quiet.

JANICE. Don't be fucking stupid!

FRANK. No. Sh. Quiet. You will leave me here and go with the others.

JANICE. No.

FRANK. Look, 1968. I went back to Prague. Spring? Remember? The day I got back, tanks rolled down the Prague streets. Russian tanks?

He laughs.

I took a train to the Austrian border. I was lucky. Slipped back into the West, back into sweet nothing.

JANICE. Come on love.

FRANK. Do not ask me to move, I cannot move.

A pause.

After my trial, it was somewhen in the fifties, somewhere in the years, in the grey time . . . I met one of my interrogators. Kohoutek. A man who had told me that the Third World War had begun and that Paris was a radio-active desert. I was sitting at a cafe in a square and he walked up to me. He said . . . I too was arrested. And he offered to buy me a drink. I could not speak! And then he said . . . I'm sorry it was so bad for you. The old man.

JANICE. Alf?

FRANK. Put him in a doctor's waiting room. First opportunity.

JANICE. But . . .

FRANK. Elizabeth.

A slight pause.

JANICE. What about her?

FRANK. Put her on a bus back home.

JANICE. Why . . .

FRANK. Look they put me in a cellar. There were icicles on the bricks. I had to walk in mud. I suffered frostbite. They were trying to make a new human being.

JANICE. Don't tell me anymore . . .

FRANK. That young fool!

A slight pause.

JANICE. Who?

FRANK. Ken. Get him to read. And Billy. He has utopian tendencies. Squash them. Jan . . .

JANICE. What, love?

FRANK. Just that when I was on trial, injected with vitamins after the months of being starved . . . Glowing with a sunlamp tan . . . Parroting my confession, taught me by heart . . . I agreed.

JANICE. No.

FRANK. I agreed with what had been done to me!

JANICE. No.

FRANK. I was at peace.

He laughs.

JANICE. No.

FRANK. Plead a whole number of grave crimes!

JANICE. No don't . . .

FRANK. Only when my health returned, a little warmth creeping back . . . That the old pain began again. The old so, so what of the ugly world.

He laughs.

Don't stay in the countryside. Nothing revolutionary comes from agriculture, not in Western Europe. Make for another city.

JANICE. And what about me, eh Joseph?

A pause.

FRANK. Don't get pregnant.

JANICE. Now the old man says so.

FRANK. And don't . . .

A slight pause.

JANICE. What?

FRANK. Waste yourself.

JANICE. No.

FRANK. I cannot come with you, for you see the new human being, I do believe his liver is finally about to explode.

JANICE. Will you be . . . ?

FRANK. I will go to a hospital.

JANICE. You will.

FRANK. I will.

JANICE. Cos I . . . Got a go with the others.

FRANK. Yes.

> JANICE *kisses* JOSEF FRANK. *He runs a hand down her face.*

Go. My ignorant little English girl.

> *They smile.* JANICE *disappears down the drain. As the light of the lamp disappears he holds his forearms against his body in pain. The blackout is almost restored when brilliant light snaps on all over the stage. At the back stands a tank with Russian insignia.* STALIN *stands beside it.* JOSEF FRANK *stands and takes off his coat. He runs at the tank, leaps and flings his coat over the end of the barrel of the tank's gun. He sinks to his knees, exhausted.* STALIN *laughs.*

STALIN. Incurable romantic.

> *A blackout and, at once,* MR STANLEY, INSPECTOR MILLER *and* HICKS *come on with powerful torches.* JOSEF FRANK *lies where he fell. He is dead.*

MILLER. All right in here! Where you are, please!

STANLEY. Come on boys and girls.

A pause.

HICKS. Not here.

STANLEY. The bloody drain. Out in a Poppy Street. They got out the bloody drain.

HICKS. Sneaky buggers.

INSPECTOR MILLER *finds* JOSEF FRANK'S *body*.

MILLER. Mr Makepeace Sir! Over here, please.

RALPH MAKEPEACE *and* SYLVIA MAKEPEACE *come on. They gather around* JOSEF FRANK'S *body.* SYLVIA *looks, turns away and lights a cigarette.*

RALPH. Is . . . ?

MILLER. Yes, I do think so.

RALPH. Some sort of . . .

MILLER. Heart failure, or . . . Yes sir.

He calls off.

Oh Sergeant . . .

RALPH. He once was in the Government of his country, you know.

SYLVIA. Just gone have they? Your workers?

RALPH. It would look like that.

SYLVIA. And what does that leave you with?

RALPH. Oh I don't know. Potato cutters, heating system. Metal value in the machines. And a divorce? And a course of aversion therapy for the booze . . . And who knows what will happen?

SYLVIA. We do.

RALPH. Yes? Yes. God, the little shits! Children of the Revolution? I want them to . . . To bleed like pigs in a ditch.

SYLVIA. Wherever they are.

RALPH. Wherever they are.

Blackout.

SCENE FIVE

Wales. Snow. Brilliant light. A winter orchard. An envelope is nailed to a tree. JANICE *and* LIZ *come on.*

LIZ. It in't Wales. It's the middle a the moon.

JANICE. We got here.

LIZ. But nearly dead.

JANICE. Should a left you with Alf.

LIZ. Middle of a doctor's waiting room in Swindon? Thank you very much.

JANICE *turns away.*

I want a be in the warm. I want a be under a hair drier, a bit too warm, you know? Trickle a sweat between the shoulder blades. And everything fuggy and safe.

JANICE. Catch a bus then.

LIZ. You been trying a get rid of me, Jan, ever since we left London

JANICE. Just get on a bus. Out of here. Back home.

LIZ. See what I mean?

BILLY, KEN *and* STACKY *come on.*

KEN. No one in the house.

BILLY. Boarded up.

KEN. Not much in there. Empty deep freeze. Make a fire in there, though.

BILLY. Abandoned the place, looks like.

STACKY *has found the envelope pinned to the tree.*

What they grow here?

KEN. Be sheep wouldn't it? Yeah, baa baas.

BILLY. There's trees there. Apples eh? Or pears?

STACKY. Huh.

STACKY *gives* KEN *the envelope.*

KEN. What's this, then?

JANICE. Looks like a letter.

KEN. Read it, then.

JANICE. You read it.

KEN. Don't mess about.

JANICE. Least tell us what's the first word.

A pause. KEN *stares at the envelope.*

KEN. It's a 'T'. All right? All right?

JANICE *takes the envelope and reads.*

JANICE. 'To the Inspector of Taxes'.

JANICE *opens the envelope and reads the letter.*

It's from the farmer. 'Dear Sir. You do come from a town you do not know what the countryside is. It is a desert. The sheep die because we cannot buy winter foodstuff we are bankrupt. We cannot sell the animals. There is no life. Green things grow but it may as well be sand. Funny how you see cars on the road but it may as well be the middle ages or worse. So I and my Martha have left the land and Mr Taxes you will not find us, we are gone. We loved the land I and Martha but it drove us away. Edward Breckin, Farmer.'

A pause.

BILLY. The place is free.

JANICE. Let's go in the house and get warm.

LIZ. For godsake, yes.

JANICE. Is there wood?

KEN. Round the back.

JANICE. Maybe there're tins a something somewhere in the house.

KEN *and* STACKY *go off.*

BILLY. Live off the land eh? We could make a country of our own, eh? Declare independence? From the whole world eh?

LIZ. I'm going a rummage round that house. May find a hairdryer for all I know. And a bus timetable, eh Janice?

JANICE. Why not?

LIZ *goes off.* BILLY *puts his arm round* JANICE, *she puts her arm round him.*

JANICE. The farmer and his wife couldn't run the farm, Billy.

BILLY. No . . .

JANICE. So why can we?

BILLY. Don't know.

JANICE. Have to go back to the city.

BILLY. Not London . . .

JANICE. Manchester, I thought.

BILLY *shrugs.*

It's the city we know.

BILLY. Yeah? 'Ere Jan, that old man. Old Joey. You really got funny for him didn't you?

JANICE *shrugs. She and* BILLY *begin to walk off, their arms round each other.*

JANICE. So?

BILLY. What was he?

JANICE. He was a Communist.

Tom Stoppard

Tom Stoppard is one of the finest, funniest dramatists in the contemporary theatre. The sheer playfulness of his theatrical vision, his penchant for parody in language and stage metaphor keep audiences constantly on the edge of laughter. A comedian of ideas, he is also a scintillating wordsmith who writes trenchant satire, as this brief take-off of Switzerland shows:

> Oh, Switzerland! – unfurled like a white flag, pacific civilian Switzerland – the miraculous neutrality of it, the non-combatant impartiality of it, the non-aggression pacts of it, the international red cross of it –

Stoppard's view of the world, unlike the prevailingly dismal view of his doomsayer peers, is expansive, genial, undogmatic. Yet alongside a gusty good-humour is a compelling moral gravity rooted in traditional humanist values. Perhaps his truest peer, nearest comic kin, is the great classical conservative, Aristophanes.

Both playwrights use laughter to point to conditions in their respective worlds that need mending. Both imply moral absolutes that human beings turn from at peril. 'There is a sense of right and wrong that precedes utterance,' writes Stoppard in *Professional Foul*. Stoppard's linguistic virtuosity, like Aristophanes', ranges from running gags, puns, and epithets to lyrical eloquence. Both lampoon historical and literary figures to make audiences laugh, but also to subvert uncritical assumptions. They impishly pervert the subtleties of logical argument, in Stoppard's case to challenge ordinary presumptions about freedom, identity, the virtue of existence, the existence of God. Aristophanes has the edge in bawdiness, but nudity and sexual titillation are part of the fun in Stoppard, too. In *Dirty Linen*, for example, which takes off the British Parliament, garter-snapping MPs scramble for the furtive sexual favours of Maddie Gotobed, whose silk panties keep turning up in their briefcases.

Some Stoppard plays, like those of Aristophanes, blend the fantastic and the everyday in a clever theatre craft that breaks down the distinction between comedy and farce. Ordinary laws of probability are suspended to accommodate absurd situations, and then reapplied. Ideas and action, often zanily exuberant, overshadow characterization. Stoppard himself describes his characters as 'mouthpieces for points of view rather than explorations of individual psychology'. The results are often hilarious, showbiz at its trickiest best. Stoppard expresses what Aristophanes certainly understood: 'Drama that loses sight of showbiz is probably doomed and showbiz tends to have a lot to do with . . . bringing off effects . . . bluffing an audience.'

The madcap *Jumpers* is a case in point. It opens on a surrealist visual image: a woman swings high above the stage from a chandelier, discarding pieces of her clothing in a suspended striptease as she flies in and out of the spotlight warbling snatches of sentimental songs. Eight jumpers somersault onto the stage to form 'a short blunt human pyramid'. (The sprightly jumpers are academics recruited by their chairman, Archie Jumper, 'doctor of medicine, philosophy, literature and law, with diplomas in psychological medicine and P.T., including gym'.) A sudden gunshot blows one jumper out of the pyramid, which, after a frozen moment, slowly implodes. Meanwhile, a television screen tracks astronauts on the moon and a royal procession in London, while moral philosopher George Moore practises his upcoming lecture on the existence of God, moral absolutes, and the quirky unreliability of language, as understood by Wittgenstein, Stoppard's favourite philosopher:

> Putting aside the God of Goodness, to whom we will return, and taking first the God of creation – or to give him his chief philosophical *raison d'être*, the First Cause – we see that a supernatural or divine origin is the logical consequence of the assumption that one thing leads to another . . . that, if you like, though chickens and eggs may alternate back through the millenia, ultimately, we arrive at something which, while perhaps no longer resembling either a chicken or an egg, is nevertheless the first term of that series and can itself only be attributed to a First Cause – or to give it its theological soubriquet, God.

Moore maunders on through scenes in which his wife vainly tries to attract his attention by disrobing, or by upending a goldfish bowl on her head. Nothing, not even the commission and investigation of a murder on another part of the stage, can shake Moore out of his reflex intellectualizing:

Likewise to say that this is a good bacon sandwich is only to say that by the criteria applied by like-minded lovers of bacon sandwiches, this one is worthy of approbation.

Meanwhile Archie Jumper hypothesizes the murder victim is a suicide who, suffering from nervous strain, 'wandered into the park, where he crawled into a large plastic bag and shot himself, leaving [a] note which was found in the bag with his body by some gymnasts on an early morning run'.

Jumpers ends in a debate between Moore and Jumper that comically parodies the contradictions inherent in philosophical disquisition. Nevertheless, under the high-spirited comedy, like Aristophanes, Stoppard is serious about the issues debated. The lingering emotional effect of the play is a kind of bereavement for a lost moral universe that logic cannot console. So, too, in Aristophanes.

Stoppard was born in Zlin, Czechoslovakia, in 1938. Two years later, on the eve of the Nazi invasion, his father moved the family to Singapore. In 1942 Tom's mother moved again with her two sons, this time to India, while the father stayed behind to face the Japanese invasion, during which, apparently, he lost his life. After the war, Stoppard's widowed mother married a British army major, who took the family to England where Tom, born Straussler, adopted his stepfather's name and grew up to become 'one of the two or three most prosperous and ubiquitously adulated playwrights at present bearing a British passport'.

Stoppard is then an émigré writer. For Stoppard, as for Nabokov and Conrad, master-stylists in the English language to whom he is favourably compared, English is a second language. One of his early directors told Kenneth Tynan, 'You have to be foreign to write English with that kind of hypnotized brilliance.' It may be so. But his being an émigré is pertinent in a more fundamental way to Stoppard's singular qualities as a dramatist in contemporary Britain. His unusual childhood – the fear of loss of freedom, which sent his family twice into flight from totalitarian tyranny – disinclines him to the fierce attacks on the British system that are *de riguer* for many of his peers. He has not flirted with idealized communist theory like Bond, Brenton, and David Edgar, for example. He is often disparaged for his love affair with England, for failing to use drama to protest against social inequities in the British system.

Stoppard has been derogated as a political reactionary, a charge whose negative implications, the assumption that conservative values are ipso facto bad, are refuted by Stoppard's work, which shows an evolution from aesthetic detachment (or, to use Stoppard's own language 'withdrawal in style from chaos') to political and social commitment, though not necessarily of the variety in fashion. Jim Hunter defuses attacks on Stoppard by pointing out that the current orthodoxy of live theatre in Western society tends to be dogmatically leftist. It is the radicals among critics and editors who have sought to nudge Stoppard toward a party-line, all of which may simply show the insufficiency of labels. Stoppard describes himself as a supporter of 'Western liberal democracy, favouring an intellectual elite and a progressive middle class and based on a moral order derived from Christian absolutes'.

He confesses to his love affair with England. In a conversation with Kenneth Tynan, he was specific in defence of his 'conservatism', if that's what it is.

> I don't lose any sleep if a policeman in Durham beats somebody up, because I know it's an exceptional case. It's a sheer perversion of speech to describe the society I live in as one that inflicts violence on the underprivileged. What worries me is not the bourgeois exception but the totalitarian norm. Of all the systems that are on offer, the one I don't want is the one that denies freedom of expression – no matter what its allegedly redeeming virtues may be. The only thing that would make me leave England would be control over free speech.

Though he is often linked to the University wits, Stoppard abandoned formal education for journalism when he was only seventeen. He was the local drama critic on the *Bristol Evening Post* during the fifties when Osborne and the Royal Court were infusing the British theatre with new vitality. Peter O'Toole's blazing performances in *Hamlet* and as Jimmy Porter in *Look Back in Anger* drew Stoppard to the theatre. He eased from writing reviews and short stories into playwriting for radio, television, theatre and, later, films. The self-acquired erudition so notable in his plays suggests his acquaintance with the whole literary and intellectual tradition.

Obviously, *Rosencrantz and Guildenstern are Dead*, Stoppard's first major play, is based on *Hamlet*. The actor-manager who meets

Rosencrantz and Guildenstern on their way to Elsinore says that in life 'every exit is an extrance somewhere else'. In this play, as Tynan observed, 'every exit is an entrance somewhere else in *Hamlet*.' The plot traces what happened to the two attendant lords out of *Hamlet* on their passage to England, but its mainspring, according to Clive James, 'is the perception – surely a compassionate one – that the fact of their deaths mattering so little to Hamlet was something that ought to have mattered to Shakespeare.' While the play borrows situation, characters, lines, even whole scenes, from *Hamlet*, it owes debts also to others. Stoppard said of himself, 'Prufrock and Beckett are the twin syringes of my diet, my arterial system.' Rosencrantz and Guildenstern are dispatched on a Kafka-like mission that leads to their deaths – whether by fate or chance remains unclear. On the way, like the two Beckettian tramps of *Waiting for Godot*, they toss coins to pass the time. The coins always come up heads, which leads the characters to Wittgensteinian speculations about probability, chance, fate. 'Wheels have been set in motion,' Rosencrantz says, 'and they have their own pace, to which we are . . . condemned.' They are clowns who do pratfalls, but their barely masked pain mirrors the anguish of all sentient beings under the threat of mortality.

Most critics panned the Edinburgh Fringe premiere of the play in 1966. However, Ronald Bryden's reaction, 'It's the most brilliant debut of a young playwright since John Arden,' caught the eye of Tynan, literary manager of the National Theatre, who took the play to Olivier. It opened at the Old Vic in 1967 to rapturous reviews. Harold Hobson wrote that the play's opening was the most important event in the British professional theatre since the opening of Harold Pinter's *The Birthday Party*.

In their linguistic styles, however, Pinter and Stoppard are opposites. Stoppard is a maximalist, expansive, allusive, exuberant, while Pinter is a minimalist, his language spare, oblique, mysterious, interspersed with pauses. Both, however, are indebted to Beckett, after whom, as Mel Gussow wrote, 'theatre could be two men sitting in a basement-room with only a dumb waiter as conduit, or two men wandering blindly through the corridors of one of Shakespeare's greatest tragedies.'

Travesties, which won the *Evening Standard* Award in 1974 and the Tony in 1976, is a pastiche of political history, artistic debate, and intellectual high-jinks. In the frame of a travestied version of

The Importance of Being Earnest, Stoppard imagines a meeting that could have taken place among Joyce, Lenin, and the Dadaist Tristan Tzara during World War I, since they were all in Switzerland then. Unreliable history is refracted through the imperfect memory of an obscure British consular official, Henry Carr. Regarded by many critics as among Stoppard's finest work, the play reveals that its polemic purpose, as Tynan notes, is to argue that art must be independent of the world of politics, a position that gradually changed in Stoppard's later plays.

Dogg's Hamlet includes a breathless fifteen-minute version of *Hamlet*, followed by an encore mini-version that takes only two minutes. The hilarity of the speeded-up Shakespeare doesn't obscure the point of the piece – that human sensibility is in danger of being lost through the absurd speed and reductionism of modern life. *Cahoot's Macbeth*, usually coupled with *Dogg's Hamlet*, uses Shakespeare as the embodiment of the freedom that Eastern Europeans have lost to a repressive Communist regime.

Both *Night and Day*, which argues the case for freedom of the press, while at the same time cataloguing journalistic abuses of freedom, and *Every Good Boy Deserves Favour* mark an important transition in Stoppard's writing.

Stoppard had long been associated with the cool apolitical stylists like Pinter, Ayckbourn, Orton, and Simon Gray. Gradually, however, his focus shifted from witty disquisitions on art and philosophy to current issues, among them the repression of political dissidents. He became an activist as well, writing articles for the *New York Times*, addressing rallies against psychological abuse in the Soviet Union. He travelled to Moscow for Amnesty International. Then, in 1977, he flew to Prague to meet Vaclav Havel, a Czech playwright whose work has been proscribed since the Soviet Union invaded Czechoslovakia. Havel's plight (including his imprisonment), which could so easily have been Stoppard's had his family remained in Czechoslovakia, became a major impetus to Stoppard's political activism in and outside his plays. It may also explain why Stoppard abstains from the allegiance to socialism most of the politically committed British playwrights avow.

Cahoots Macbeth, the radio play *Professional Foul*, and *Every Good Boy Deserves Favour* deal directly with the inhumanity of bureaucratic repression behind the Iron Curtain. What is most remarkable in these plays is not that Stoppard finally confronts a major political issue, but that he does it with the familiar Stoppardian style and wit. The verbal pyrotechnics, the broad farce, the sure stage sense, and the good-humoured scrutiny of the human condition are all in evidence. But so too is the playwright's compassion for the victims of oppression.

Who but Stoppard could have written (albeit on invitation from André Previn) a play that calls for a full symphony orchestra to be visible on stage throughout the play? Such is the case in *EGBDF*, set in an assylum where Soviet political dissidents are incarcerated with mental patients. While the orchestra presumably exists only in the demented mind of one of the patients, it functions like a chameleon character playing a variety of roles through a pastiche of music, some derived from Russian composers, some written by Previn. Integrated into the action, the orchestra underscores the frightening rigidity of totalitarian bureaucracy swiftly crushing the feeblest gestures of individuality in anyone who dares to play out of tune. At times the music lyrically echoes the decent human longings of the hapless Alexander, pronounced insane for protesting against the unjust imprisonment of a friend. It is also part of the play's humour. Mocking strings accompany the entrances and exits of the examining physician, who is himself a member of an orchestra. A huge organ swell announces the arrival of the Colonel. Verbal passages alternate with musical passages as if the music were part of the dialogue.

The play begins with a surrealistic scene, one that mirrors what is all too real behind the Iron Curtain. Two men, the one genuinely lunatic who imagines he is conducting a symphony orchestra and the other a political dissident on a futile hunger strike, share a cell. They both happen to have the same name, a contrivance that makes a happy ending possible. For in the end both men are released, not by the triumph of virtue, truth, or justice, but by a typical bureaucratic confusion of their names. The political dissident's refusal to recant his protest celebrates the courage of all the artists and intellectuals behind the Iron Curtain who refuse to carry favour by being 'good boys'. The play makes the profoundly moral point that the difference between good and evil – *pace* Wittgenstein – is obvious to any reasonable person.

What Bernard Levin wrote in his London *Sunday Times* review of *EGBDF*'s premiere performance by the Royal Shakespeare Company sums up the effect of Stoppard's use of comedy to serious purpose:

Although this is a profoundly moral work, the argument still undergoes the full transmutation of art . . . I tell you this man could write a comedy about Auschwitz, at which we would sit laughing helplessly until we cried with inextinguishable anger.

The Real Thing, Stoppard's 1983 stage triumph, confounded another criticism levelled against the early Stoppard, namely that emotional experience lies outside his world and, in particular, that he can't create convincing women.

For what *The Real Thing* explores is the precise nature of love, a theme Stoppard interweaves with the larger issue of the difference between art and life. Which is the real thing? The play ruefully bares the emotional unreliability of people in love, inside and outside of marriage. As always in Stoppard, there is a trick, a *coup de théâtre*. The real-life love scenes between Henry and Annie (divorced from their former mates and married to each other) are juxtaposed with love scenes from plays, Henry's and others. Frequently the audience isn't sure which is the real thing. But the play is emotionally, as well as intellectually, moving; Henry suffers because of Annie's infidelity and Annie is as vulnerable to jealousy as he, which may or may not be symptoms of the real thing.

In sum, Stoppard brilliantly refutes the principal accusations against him: that he lacks political and social commitment and emotional power. By a series of plays in which his wit and inventiveness are not at all diminished by the increasing relevance of his serious themes, he has warned us not to assume we know what he can do.

Major Plays

Rosencrantz and Guildenstern are Dead, National Theatre at the Old Vic, 1967.
Jumpers, National Theatre at the Old Vic, 1972.
Travesties, Royal Shakespeare Company at the Aldwych, 1974.
Every Good Boy Deserves Favour, Royal Festival Hall, 1977.
Night and Day, Phoenix Theatre, 1978.
The Real Thing, Strand Theatre, 1983.

Selected Bibliography

C. W. E. Bigsby. *Tom Stoppard*. Harlow, Essex: Longman Group, Ltd., 1976.

Brustein, Robert. *The Third Theatre*. New York: Knopf, 1969.

Dean, Joan Fitzpatrick. *Tom Stoppard: Comedy as a Moral Matrix*. Columbia and Oxford: University of Missouri Press, 1981.

Durham, Weldon B. 'Symbolic Action in Tom Stoppard's *Jumpers*,' *Theatre Journal*, May 1980, pp. 169–79.

Egan, Robert. 'A Thin Beam of Light: The Purpose of Playing in *Rosencrantz and Guildenstern are Dead*,' *Theatre Journal*, March 1979, pp. 59–69.

Gussow, Mel. 'The Real Tom Stoppard,' *New York Times Magazine*, 11 January 1984, pp. 18–28.

Hunter, Jim. *Tom Stoppard's Plays*. London: Faber & Faber; New York: Grove Press, 1982.

James, Clive. 'Count Zero Splits the Infinite,' *Encounter*, November 1975.

Kroll, Jack, 'Stoppard at Play,' *Newsweek*, 24 September 1972, pp. 147–48.

Rothstein, Bobbi. 'The Reappearance of Public Man: Stoppard's *Jumpers* and *Professional Foul*.' *Kansas Quarterly*, Fall 1980, pp. 36–44.

Taylor, John Russell. *Anger and After*. London: Methuen, 2nd ed. 1969; Baltimore: Penguin, 1963. Published as *The Angry Theatre*. New York: Hill and Wang, 1969.

Tynan, Kenneth. 'Withdrawing with Style from Chaos: A Profile of Tom Stoppard.' *The New Yorker*, 19 December 1977, pp. 91–111.

Zeifman, Hersh. 'Comedy of Ambush: Tom Stoppard's *The Real Thing*,' *Modern Drama*, June 1983, pp. 139–148.

TOM STOPPARD

Every Good Boy
Deserves Favour

A Play for Actors and Orchestra

To Victor Fainberg and Vladimir Bukovsky

AUTHOR'S INTRODUCTION

Every Good Boy Deserves Favour is the title of a work of which the text is only a part. The sub-title, 'A Play for Actors and Orchestra', hardly indicates the extent to which the effectiveness of the whole depends on the music composed by André Previn. And it is to him that the work owes its existence.

As the principle conductor of the London Symphony Orchestra, Mr Previn invited me in 1974 to write something which had the need of a live full-size orchestra on stage. Invitations don't come much rarer than that, and I jumped at the chance. It turned out to be the fastest move I made on the project for the next eighteen months.

Usually, and preferably, a play originates in the author's wish to write about some particular thing. The form of the play then follows from the requirements of the subject. This time I found myself trying to make the subject follow from the requirements of the form. Mr Previn and I agreed early on that we would try to go beyond a mere recitation for the concert platform, and also that we were not writing a piece for singers. In short, it was going to be a real play, to be performed in conjunction with, and bound up with, a symphony orchestra. As far as we knew nobody had tried to do anything like that before; which, again, is not the preferred reason for starting a play, though I confess it weighed with me.

Having been given *carte blanche*, for a long time the only firm decision I was able to make was that the play would have to be in some way *about* an orchestra. For what play could escape *folie de grandeur* if it came with a hundred musicians in attendance but outside the action? And while it is next to impossible to 'justify' an orchestra, it is a simple matter to make it essential. Accordingly, I started off with a millionaire who owned one.

My difficulty in trying to make the cart pull the horse was aggravated by the fact that I knew nothing about orchestras and

very little about 'serious' music. I was in the position of a man
who, never having read anything but whodunnits, finds himself
writing a one-man show about Lord Byron on a *carte blanche*
from an actor with a club foot. My qualifications for writing
about an orchestra amounted to a spell as a triangle-player in a
kindergarten percussion band. I informed my collaborator that
the play was going to be about a millionaire triangle-player with
his own orchestra.

This basic implausibility bred others, and at the point where
the whimsical edifice was about to collapse I tried to save it by
making the orchestra a mere delusion of the millionaire's brain.
Once the orchestra became an imaginary orchestra, there was
no need for the millionaire to be a millionaire either. I changed
tack: the play would be about a lunatic triangle-player who
thought he had an orchestra.

By this time the first deadline had been missed and I was
making heavy weather. I had no genuine reason for writing about
an orchestra, or a lunatic, and thus had nothing to write. Music
and triangles led me into a punning diversion based on Euclid's
axioms, but it didn't belong anywhere, and I was ready to call
my own bluff.

This is where matters stood when in April 1976 I met Victor
Fainberg. For some months previously I had been reading books
and articles by and about the Russian dissidents, intending to
use the material for a television play, and so I knew that
Mr Fainberg had been one of a group of people arrested in Red
Square in August 1968 during a peaceful demonstration against
the Warsaw Pact invasion of Czechoslovakia. He had been
pronounced insane — a not unusual fate for perfectly sane
opponents of Soviet tyranny — and in 1974 he had emerged into
exile from five years in the Soviet prison-hospital system. He had
written about his experiences in the magazine *Index On
Censorship*, an invaluable, politically disinterested monitor of
political repression the world over. For Mr Fainberg freedom was,
and is, mainly the freedom to double his efforts on behalf of
colleagues left behind. His main concern when I met him was to
secure the release of Vladimir Bukovsky, himself a victim of the
abuse of psychiatry in the USSR, whose revelations about that
abuse had got him sentenced to consecutive terms of prison,

labour camp and internal exile amounting to twelve years.

Exceptional courage is a quality drawn from certain people in exceptional conditions. Although British society is not free of abuses, we are not used to meeting courage because conditions do not demand it (I am not thinking of the courage with which people face, say, an illness or a breavement). Mr Fainberg's single-mindedness, his energy (drawing more on anger than on pity) and his willingness to make a nuisance of himself outside and inside the walls of any institution, friend or foe, which bore upon his cause, prompted the thought that his captors must have been quite pleased to get rid of him. He was not a man to be broken or silenced; an insistent, discordant note, one might say, in an orchestrated society.

I don't recall that I consciously made the metaphor, but very soon I was able to tell Mr Previn, definitively, that the lunatic triangle-player who thought he had an orchestra was now sharing a cell with a political prisoner. I had something to write about, and in a few weeks the play was finished.

Not that the prisoner, Alexander, is Victor or anyone else. But the speech in which he describes the treatment he received in the Leningrad Special Psychiatric Hospital is taken from the article in *Index*,* and there are other borrowings from life, such as the doctor's comment, 'Your opinions are your symptoms.' Victor Fainberg in his own identity makes an appearance in the text as one of the group 'M to S' in the speech where Alexander identifies people by letters of the alphabet.

The off-stage hero of *Every Good Boy Deserves Favour*, referred to as 'my friend C', is Vladimir Bukovsky. The Bukovsky campaign, which was supported by many people in several countries, achieved its object in December 1976, when he was taken from prison and sent to the West. In June while we were rehearsing I met Mr Bukovsky in London and invited him to call round at the Royal Shakespeare Company's rehearsal rooms in Covent Garden. He came and stayed to watch for an hour or two. He was diffident, friendly, and helpful on points of detail in the production, but his presence was disturbing. For people

* Vol. 4, no. 2, *Index on Censorship*, published by a non-profit-making company, Writers and Scholars International, 21 Russell Street, London WC2.

working on a piece of theatre, terra firma is a self-contained world even while it mimics the real one. That is the necessary condition of making theatre, and it is also our luxury. There was a sense of worlds colliding. I began to feel embarrassed. One of the actors seized up in the middle of a speech touching on the experiences of our visitor, and found it impossible to continue. But the incident was not fatal. The effect wore off, and, on the night, *Every Good Boy Deserves Favour* had recovered its nerve and its own reality.

Every Good Boy Deserves Favour was first performed at the Festival Hall in July 1977, with the London Symphony Orchestra, conducted by André Previn. The cast was as follows:

ALEXANDER	Ian McKellen
IVANOV	John Wood
SACHA	Andrew Sheldon
DOCTOR	Patrick Stewart
TEACHER	Barbara Leigh-Hunt
COLONEL	Philip Locke

Directed by Trevor Nunn
Designed by Ralph Koltai

Although in this edition only the text is printed, *Every Good Boy Deserves Favour* is a work consisting of words and music, and is incomplete without the score composed by its co-author André Previn.

Three separate acting areas are needed.
  1. The CELL *needs two beds.*
  2. The OFFICE *needs a table and two chairs.*
  3. The SCHOOL *needs a school desk.*
  These areas can be as small as possible but each has to be approachable from each of the others, and the lighting on each ought to be at least partly controllable independently of the other two and of the orchestra itself, which needless to say occupies the platform.
  The CELL *is occupied by two men,* ALEXANDER *and* IVANOV. ALEXANDER *is a political prisoner and* IVANOV *is a genuine mental patient.*
  It will become clear in performance, but may well be stated now, that the orchestra for part of the time exists in the imagination of IVANOV. IVANOV *has with him an orchestral triangle.*
  The OFFICE *is empty.*
  In the SCHOOL *the* TEACHER *stands, and* SACHA *sits at the desk.*

Cell

The OFFICE *and* SCHOOL *are not 'lit'. In the* CELL, ALEXANDER *and* IVANOV *sit on their respective beds. The orchestra tunes-up. The tuning-up continues normally but after a minute or two the musicians lapse into miming the tuning-up.*
  Thus we have silence while the orchestra goes through the motions of tuning.
  IVANOV *stands up, with his triangle and rod. The orchestra becomes immobile.*
  Silence.
  IVANOV *strikes the triangle, once. The orchestra starts miming a performance. He stands concentrating, listening to music which*

*we cannot hear, and striking his triangle as and when the 'music'
requires it. We only hear the triangle occasionally.* ALEXANDER
*watches this — a man watching another man occasionally hitting
a triangle.*

*This probably lasts under a minute. Then, very quietly, we
begin to hear what* IVANOV *can hear, i.e. the orchestra becomes
audible. So now his striking of the triangle begins to fit into the
context which makes sense of it.*

*The music builds slowly, gently. And then on a single cue the
platform light level jumps up with the conductor in position and
the orchestra playing fully and loudly. The triangle is a prominent
part in the symphony.*

Now we are flying. ALEXANDER *just keeps watching*
IVANOV.

IVANOV (*furiously interrupts*). — No — no — no —

The orchestra drags to a halt.

(*Shouts.*) Go back to the timpani.

*The orchestra goes back, then relapses progressively, swiftly,
into mime, and when it is almost inaudible* ALEXANDER
coughs loudly. IVANOV *glances at him reproachfully. After
the cough there is only silence with* IVANOV *intermittently
striking his triangle, and the orchestra miming.*

IVANOV. Better — good — much better . . .

ALEXANDER *is trying not to cough.*

IVANOV *finishes with a final beat on the triangle.*

The orchestra finishes.

IVANOV *sits down.* ALEXANDER *coughs luxuriously.*

IVANOV (*apologetically*). I know what you're thinking.

ALEXANDER (*understandingly*). It's all right.

IVANOV. No, you can say it. The cellos are rubbish.

ALEXANDER (*cautiously*). I'm not really a judge of music.

IVANOV. I was scraping the bottom of the barrel, and that's how
they sound. And what about the horns? — should I persevere
with them?

ALEXANDER. The horns?

IVANOV. Brazen to a man but mealy-mouthed. Butter wouldn't melt. When I try to reason with them they purse their lips. Tell me, do you have an opinion on the fungoid log-rollers spreading wet rot through the woodwinds? Not to speak of the glockenspiel.

ALEXANDER. The glockenspiel?

IVANOV. I asked you not to speak of it. Give me a word for the harpist.

ALEXANDER. I don't really —

IVANOV. Plucky. A harpist who rushes in where a fool would fear to tread — with all my problems you'd think I'd be spared exquisite irony. I've got a blue-arsed bassoon, a blue-tongued contra-bassoon, an organ grinder's chimpani, and the bass drum is in urgent need of a dermatologist.

ALEXANDER. Your condition is interesting.

IVANOV. I've got a violin section which is to violin playing what Heifetz is to water-polo. I've got a tubercular great-nephew of John Philip Sousa who goes oom when he should be going pah. And the Jew's harp has applied for a visa. I'm seriously thinking of getting a new orchestra. Do you read music?

ALEXANDER. No.

IVANOV. Don't worry: crochets, minims, sharp, flat, every good boy deserves favour. You'll pick it up in no time. What is your instrument?

ALEXANDER. I do not play an instrument.

IVANOV. Percussion? Strings? Brass?

ALEXANDER. No.

IVANOV. Reed? Keyboard?

ALEXANDER. I'm afraid not.

IVANOV. I'm amazed. Not keyboard. Wait a minute — flute.

ALEXANDER. No. Really.

IVANOV. Extraordinary. Give me a clue. If I beat you to a pulp

would you try to protect your face or your hands? Which
would be the more serious — if you couldn't sit down for
a week or couldn't stand up? I'm trying to narrow it down,
you see. Can I take it you don't stick this instrument up your
arse in a kneeling position?

ALEXANDER. I do not play an instrument.

IVANOV. You can speak frankly. You will find I am without
prejudice. I have invited musicians *into my own house.* And
do you know why? — because we all have some musician in
us. Any man says he has no musician in him, I'll call that man
a *bigot.* Listen, I've had clarinet players eating *at my own
table.* I've had French whores and gigolos speak to me in the
public street, I mean horns, I mean piccolos, so don't worry
about *me,* maestro, I've sat down with them, *drummers* even,
sharing a plate of tagliatelle Verdi and stuffed Puccini — why,
I know people who make the orchestra eat in the kitchen, off
scraps, the way you'd throw a trombone to a dog, I mean a
second violinist, I mean to the lions; I love musicians, I respect
them, human beings to a man. Let me put it like this: if I
smashed this instrument of yours over your head, would you
need a carpenter, a welder, or a brain surgeon?

ALEXANDER. I do not play an instrument. If I played an
instrument I'd tell you what it was. But I do not play one. I
have never played one. I do not know how to play one. I am
not a musician.

IVANOV. What the hell are you doing here?

ALEXANDER. I was put here.

IVANOV. What for?

ALEXANDER. For slander.

IVANOV. Slander? What a fool! *Never speak ill of a musician!* —
those bastards won't rest. They're animals, to a man.

ALEXANDER. This was political.

IVANOV. Let me give you some advice. Number one — never
mix music with politics. Number two — never confide in
your psychiatrist. Number three — *practise*!

ALEXANDER. Thank you.

IVANOV *strikes his triangle once.*

The CELL *lighting fades.*

Percussion band. The music is that of a band of young children. It includes strings but they are only plucked.

Pretty soon the percussion performance goes wrong because there is a subversive triangle in it. The triangle is struck randomly and then rapidly, until finally it is the only instrument to be heard. And then the triangle stops.

School

The lights come up on the TEACHER *and* SACHA. *The* TEACHER *is holding a triangle.*

TEACHER. Well? Are you colour blind?

SACHA. No.

TEACHER. Let me see your music.

SACHA *has sheet music on his desk.*

Very well. What are the red notes?

SACHA. Strings.

TEACHER. Green?

SACHA. Tambourine.

TEACHER. Purple?

SACHA. Drum.

TEACHER. Yellow?

SACHA. Triangle.

TEACHER. Do you see forty yellow notes in a row?

SACHA. No.

TEACHER. What then? Detention is becoming a family tradition. Your name is notorious. Did you know that?

SACHA. Yes.

TEACHER. How did you know?

SACHA. Everybody tells me.

TEACHER. Open a book.

SACHA. What book?

TEACHER. Any book. *Fathers and Sons,* perhaps.

SACHA *takes a book out of the desk.*

Is it Turgenev?

SACHA. It's my geometry book.

TEACHER. Yes, your name goes round the world. By telegram. It is printed in the newspapers. It is spoken on the radio. With such a famous name why should you bother with different colours? We will change the music for you. It will look like a field of buttercups, and sound like dinnertime.

SACHA. I don't want to be in the orchestra.

TEACHER. Open the book. Pencil and paper. You see what happens to anti-social malcontents.

SACHA. Will I be sent to the lunatics' prison?

TEACHER. Certainly not. Read aloud.

SACHA. 'A point has position but no dimension.'

TEACHER. The asylum is for malcontents who don't know what they're doing.

SACHA. 'A line has length but no breadth.'

TEACHER. They know what they're doing but they don't know it's anti-social.

SACHA. 'A straight line is the shortest distance between two points.'

TEACHER. They know it's anti-social but they're fanatics.

SACHA. 'A circle is the path of a point moving equidistant to a given point.'

TEACHER. They're sick.

SACHA. 'A polygon is a plane area bounded by straight lines.'

TEACHER. And it's not a prison, it's a hospital.

Pause.

SACHA. 'A triangle is the polygon bounded by the fewest possible sides.'

TEACHER. Good. Perfect. Copy neatly ten times, and if you're a good boy I might find you a better instrument.

SACHA (*writing*). 'A triangle is the polygon bounded by the fewest possible sides.' Is this what they make papa do?

TEACHER. Yes. They make him copy, 'I am a member of the orchestra and we must play together.'

SACHA. How many times?

TEACHER. A million.

SACHA. A million.

Pause.

(*Cries*). Papa!

ALEXANDER (*cries*). Sacha!

This cry is ALEXANDER shouting in his sleep at the other end of the stage.

IVANOV sits watching ALEXANDER.

The orchestra plays chords between the following.

SACHA. Papa!

TEACHER. Hush!

ALEXANDER. Sacha!

The orchestra continues with percussion element for perhaps ten seconds and then is sabotaged by a triangle beaten rapidly, until the triangle is the only sound heard.

ALEXANDER sits up and the triangle stops.

Cell

IVANOV. Dinner time. (*Orchestra.*)

Office

IVANOV *goes to sit at the table in the* OFFICE, *which is now the lit area.*

In the orchestra one of the lowliest violinists leaves his place. The orchestra accompanies and parodies this man's actions as he leaves the platform and enters the OFFICE. IVANOV *is sitting at the table on one of the chairs. The man* (DOCTOR) *puts his violin on the table. The orchestra has been following him the whole time and the* DOCTOR's *movements fit precisely to the music.*

IVANOV *jumps up from his chair and shouts in the general direction of the orchestra.*

IVANOV. All right, all right!

The music cuts out. The DOCTOR *pauses looking at* IVANOV.

IVANOV (*to the* DOCTOR). I'm sorry about that.

IVANOV *sits down.*

The DOCTOR *sits down and all the strings accompany this movement into his chair.*

IVANOV *leaps up again.*

(*Shouts.*) I'll have your guts for garters!

DOCTOR. Sit down, please.

IVANOV (*sitting down*). It's the only kind of language they understand.

DOCTOR. Did the pills help at all?

IVANOV. I don't know. What pills did you give them?

DOCTOR. Now look, *there is no orchestra.* We cannot make progress until we agree that there is no orchestra.

IVANOV. Or until we agree that there is.

DOCTOR (*slapping his violin, which is on the table*). But there is *no orchestra.*

IVANOV *glances at the violin.*

I have an orchestra, but you do not.

IVANOV. Does that seem reasonable to you?

DOCTOR. It just happens to be so. I play in an orchestra occasionally. It is my hobby. It is a real orchestra. Yours is not. I am a doctor. You are a patient. If I tell you you do not have an orchestra, it follows that you do not have an orchestra. If you tell me you have an orchestra, it follows that you do not have an orchestra. Or rather it does not follow that you do not have an orchestra.

IVANOV. I am perfectly happy not to have an orchestra.

DOCTOR. Good.

IVANOV. I never asked to have an orchestra.

DOCTOR. Keep saying to yourself, 'I have no orchestra. I have never had an orchestra. I do not want an orchestra.'

IVANOV. Absolutely.

DOCTOR. 'There is no orchestra.'

IVANOV. All right.

DOCTOR. Good.

IVANOV. There is one thing you can do for me.

DOCTOR. Yes?

IVANOV. Stop them playing.

DOCTOR. They will stop playing when you understand that they do not exist.

IVANOV *gets up.*

IVANOV. I have no orchestra.

Music. 1 chord.

I have never had an orchestra.

Music. 2 chords.

I do not want an orchestra.

Music. 3 chords.

There is no orchestra.

The orchestra takes off in triumph.

Light fades on OFFICE, *comes up on* CELL.

Cell

ALEXANDER *has been asleep on his bed the whole time.*
IVANOV *returns to the* CELL. *He picks up his triangle rod. He stands by* ALEXANDER's *bed looking down on him. The music continues and becomes threatening. It becomes nightmare music.* ALEXANDER's *nightmare. The music seems to be approaching violent catharsis. But* ALEXANDER *jumps awake and the music cuts out in mid-bar.*
   Silence.

IVANOV. Sorry. I can't control them.

ALEXANDER. Please . . .

IVANOV. Don't worry, I know how to handle myself. Any trumpeter comes at me, I'll kick his teeth in. Violins get it under the chin to boot, this boot, and God help anyone who plays a cello. Do you play a musical instrument?

ALEXANDER. No.

IVANOV. Then you've got nothing to worry about. Tell me about yourself — your home, your childhood, your first piano-teacher . . . how did it all begin?

The next speech should be lit as a sort of solo. Musical annotation.

ALEXANDER. One day they arrested a friend of mine for possessing a controversial book, and they kept him in mental hospitals for a year and a half. I thought this was an odd thing to do. Soon after he got out, they arrested a couple of writers, A and B, who had published some stories abroad under different names. Under their own names they got five years' and seven years' hard labour. I thought this was most peculiar. My friend, C, demonstrated against the arrest of A and B. I told him he was crazy to do it, and they put him back into the mental hospital. D was a man who wrote to various people about the trial of A and B and held meetings with his friends, E, F, G and H, who were all arrested, so I, J, K, L and a fifth man demonstrated against the arrest of E, F, G and H, and were themselves arrested. D was arrested the next day. The fifth man was my friend C, who had just got out of the mental hospital where they put him for demonstrating against the arrest of A and B, and I told him he was crazy to demonstrate against the arrest of E, F, G and H, and he got three years in a labour camp. I thought this really wasn't fair. M compiled a book on the trials of C, I, J, K and L, and with his colleagues N, O, P, Q, R and S attended the trial of T who had written a book about his experiences in a labour camp, and who got a year in a labour camp. In the courtroom it was learned that the Russian army had gone to the aid of Czechoslovakia. M, N, O, P, W, R and S decided to demonstrate in Red Square the following Sunday, when they were all arrested and variously disposed of in labour camps, psychiatric hospitals and internal exile. Three years had passed since the arrest of A and B. C finished his sentence about the same time as A, and then he did something really crazy. He started telling everybody that sane people were being put in mental hospitals for their political opinions. By the time B finished his sentence, C was on trial for anti-Soviet agitation and slander, and he got seven years in prison and labour camps, and five years' exile.

You see all the trouble writers cause.

The children's percussion band re-enters as a discreet subtext.

They spoil things for ordinary people.

My childhood was uneventful. My adolescence was normal. I got an ordinary job, and married a conventional girl who died uncontroversially in childbirth. Until the child was seven the only faintly interesting thing about me was that I had a friend who kept getting arrested.

Then one day I did something really crazy.

The percussion is sabotaged exactly as before but this time by a snare drum being violently beaten. It stops suddenly and the light comes up on SACHA *sitting at the desk with a punctured drum on the desk, the* TEACHER *standing motionless in her position.*

Optional: On tape the sound of a children's playground at some distance.

School

TEACHER. So this is how I am repaid. Is this how it began with your father? First he smashes school property. Later he keeps bad company. Finally, slanderous letters. Lies. To his superiors. To the Party. To the newspapers. . . . To foreigners. . . .

SACHA. Papa doesn't lie. He beat me when I did it.

TEACHER. *Lies!* Bombarding *Pravda* with lies! What did he expect?

The light on the TEACHER *and* SACHA *fades just after the beginning of* ALEXANDER's *speech.*

Cell

ALEXANDER. They put me in the Leningrad Special Psychiatric Hospital on Arsenal'naya Street, where I was kept for thirty months, including two months on hunger strike.

They don't like you to die unless you can die anonymously. If your name is known in the West, it is an embarrassment.

The bad old days were over long ago. Things are different now. Russia is a civilized country, very good at Swan Lake and space technology, and it is confusing if people starve themselves to death.

So after a couple of weeks they brought my son to persuade me to eat. But although by this time he was nine years old he was uncertain what to say.

SACHA *speaks from the* SCHOOL, *not directly to* ALEXANDER.

SACHA. I got a letter from abroad, with our picture in the newspaper.

ALEXANDER. What did it say?

SACHA. I don't know. It was all in English.

ALEXANDER. How is school?

SACHA. All right. I've started geometry. It's horrible.

ALEXANDER. How is Babushka?

SACHA. All right. You smell like Olga when she does her nails.

ALEXANDER. Who is Olga?

SACHA. She has your room now. Till you come back.

ALEXANDER. Good.

SACHA. Do they make you paint your nails here?

End of duologue. Return to solo.

ALEXANDER. If you don't eat for a long time you start to smell of acetone, which is the stuff girls use for taking the paint off their finger-nails. When the body runs out of protein and carbohydrate it starts to metabolize its own fat, and acetone is the waste product. To put this another way, a girl removing her nail-varnish smells of starvation.

After two months you could have removed nail-varnish with my urine, so they brought Sacha back, but when he saw me he couldn't speak —

SACHA (*cries*). Papa!

ALEXANDER. — and then they gave in. And when I was well enough they brought me here.

This means they have decided to let me go. It is much harder to get from Arsenal'naya to a civil hospital than from a civil hospital to the street. But it has to be done right. They don't want to lose ground. They need a formula. It will take a little time but that's all right. I shall read *War and Peace*.

Everything is going to be all right.

Orchestra.

School

This scene is enclosed inside music which ends up as the
DOCTOR's violin solo into the following scene.

SACHA. A triangle is the shortest distance between three points.

TEACHER. Rubbish.

SACHA. A circle is the longest distance to the same point.

TEACHER. Sacha!

SACHA. A plane area bordered by high walls is a prison not a
    hospital.

TEACHER. Be quiet!

SACHA. I don't care! — he was never sick at home. Never!

    Music.

TEACHER. Stop crying.

    Music.

    Everything is going to be all right.

    Music to violin solo.

    Lights fade on SCHOOL.

Office

DOCTOR *in his* OFFICE *playing violin solo. Violin cuts out.*

DOCTOR. Come in.

    ALEXANDER *enters the* DOCTOR's *light.*

DOCTOR. Hello. Sit down please. Do you play a musical
    instrument?

ALEXANDER (*taken aback*). Are you a patient?

DOCTOR (*cheerfully*). No, I am a doctor. *You* are a patient. It's
    a distinction which we try to keep going here, though I'm told
    it's coming under scrutiny in more advanced circles of
    psychiatric medicine. (*He carefully puts his violin into its*
    case. Sententiously.) Yes, if everybody in the world played
    a violin, I'd be out of a job.

ALEXANDER. As a psychiatrist?

DOCTOR. No, as a violinist. The psychiatric hospitals would be packed to the doors. You obviously don't know much about musicians. Welcome to the Third Civil Mental Hospital. What can I do for you?

ALEXANDER. I have a complaint.

DOCTOR (*opening file*). Yes, I know — pathological development of the personality with paranoid delusions.

ALEXANDER. No, there's nothing the matter with me.

DOCTOR (*closing file*). There you are, you see.

ALEXANDER. My complaint is about the man in my cell.

DOCTOR. Ward.

ALEXANDER. He thinks he has an orchestra.

DOCTOR. Yes, he has an identity problem. I forget his name.

ALEXANDER. His behaviour is aggressive.

DOCTOR. He complains about you, too. Apparently you cough during the diminuendos.

ALEXANDER. Is there anything you can do?

DOCTOR. Certainly. (*Producing a red pill box from the drawer.*) Suck one of these every four hours.

ALEXANDER. But he's a raving lunatic.

DOCTOR. Of course. The idea that all the people locked up in mental hospitals are sane while the people walking about outside are all mad is merely a literary conceit, put about by people who should be locked up. I assure you there's not much in it. Taken as a whole, the sane are out there and the sick are in here. For example, *you* are here because you have delusions, that sane people are put in mental hospitals.

ALEXANDER. But I *am* in a mental hospital.

DOCTOR. That's what I said. If you're not prepared to discuss your case rationally, we're going to go round in circles. Did you say you *didn't* play a musical instrument, by the way?

ALEXANDER. No. Could I be put in a cell on my own?

DOCTOR. Look, let's get this clear. This is what is called an *Ordinary* Psychiatric Hospital, that is to say a civil mental hospital coming under the Ministry of Health, and we have *wards*. Cells is what they have in prisons, and also, possibly, in what are called *Special* Psychiatric Hospitals, which come under the Ministry of Internal Affairs and are for prisoners who represent a special danger to society. Or rather, patients. No, you didn't say, or no you don't play one?

ALEXANDER. Could I be put in a ward on my own?

DOCTOR. I'm afraid not. Colonel — or rather Doctor — Rozinsky, who has taken over your case, chose your cell- or rather ward-mate personally.

ALEXANDER. He might kill me.

DOCTOR. We have to assume that Rozinsky knows what's best for you; though in my opinion you need a psychiatrist.

ALEXANDER. You mean he's not really a doctor?

DOCTOR. Of course he's a doctor and he is proud to serve the State in any capacity, but he was not actually trained in psychiatry *as such*.

ALEXANDER. What is his speciality?

DOCTOR. Semantics. He's a Doctor of Philology, whatever that means. I'm told he's a genius.

ALEXANDER (*angrily*). I won't see him.

DOCTOR. It may not be necessary. It seems to me that the best answer is for you to go home. Would Thursday suit you?

ALEXANDER. Thursday?

DOCTOR. Why not? There is an Examining Commission on Wednesday. We shall aim at curing your schizophrenia by Tuesday night, if possible by seven o'clock because I have a concert. (*He produces a large blue pill box.*) Take one of these every four hours.

ALEXANDER. What are they?

DOCTOR. A mild laxative.

ALEXANDER. For schizophrenia?

DOCTOR. The layman often doesn't realize that medicine advances in a series of imaginative leaps.

ALEXANDER. I see. Well, I suppose I'll have to read *War and Peace* some other time.

DOCTOR. Yes. Incidentally, when you go before the Commission try not to make any remark which might confuse them. I shouldn't mention *War and Peace* unless they mention it first. The sort of thing I'd stick to is 'Yes', if they ask you whether you agree you were mad; 'No', if they ask you whether you intend to persist in your slanders; 'Definitely', if they ask you whether your treatment has been satisfatory, and 'Sorry', if they ask you how you feel about it all, or if you didn't catch the question.

ALEXANDER. I was never mad, and my treatment was barbaric.

DOCTOR. Stupidity is one thing I can't cure. I have to show that I have treated you. You have to recant and show gratitude for the treatment. We have to act together.

ALEXANDER. The KGB broke my door and frightened my son and my mother-in-law. My madness consisted of writing to various people about a friend of mine who is in prison. This friend was twice put in mental hospitals for political reasons, and then they arrested him for saying that sane people were put in mental hospitals, and then they put him in prison because he was sane when he said this; and I said so, and they put me in a mental hospital. And you are quite right — in the Arsenal'naya they have cells. There are bars on the windows, peepholes in the doors, and the lights burn all night. It is run just like a gaol, with warders and trusties, but the regime is more strict, and the male nurses are convicted criminals serving terms for theft and violent crimes, and they beat and humiliate the patients and steal their food, and are protected by the doctors, some of whom wear KGB uniforms under their white coats. For the politicals, punishment and medical treatment are intimately related. I was given injections of aminazin, sulfazin, triftazin, haloperidol and insulin, which caused swellings, cramps, headaches, trembling, fever and the loss of various abilities including the ability to read, write, sleep, sit, stand, and button my trousers. When all this failed to improve my condition, I was stripped and bound head to foot with lengths of wet canvas. As the canvas dried it became tighter and tighter until I lost consciousness. They did this to me for ten days in a row, and still my condition did not improve.

Then I went on hunger strike. And when they saw I intended to die they lost their nerve. And now you think I'm going to crawl out of here, thanking them for curing me of my delusions? Oh no. They lost. And they will have to see that it is so. They have forgotten their mortality. Losing might be their first touch of it for a long time.

DOCTOR *picks up his violin.*

DOCTOR. What about your son? He is turning into a delinquent.

DOCTOR *plucks the violin EGBDF.*

He is a good boy. He deserves a father.

DOCTOR *plucks the violin . . .*

School

TEACHER. Things have changed since the bad old days. When I was a girl there were terrible excesses. A man accused like your father might well have been blameless. Now things are different. The Constitution guarantees freedom of conscience, freedom of the press, freedom of speech, of assembly, of worship, and many other freedoms. The Soviet Constitution has always been the most liberal in the world, ever since the first Constitution was written after the Revolution.

SACHA. Who wrote it?

TEACHER (*hesitates*). His name was Nikolai Bukharin.

SACHA. Can we ask Nikolai Bukharin about papa?

TEACHER. Unfortunately he was shot soon after he wrote the Constitution. Everything was different in those days. Terrible things happened.

Cell

ALEXANDER *has just started to read 'War and Peace' and* IVANOV *looks over his shoulder.*

IVANOV. 'Well, prince, Genoa and Lucca are no more than the private estates of the Bonaparte family.'

ALEXANDER *is nervous, and* IVANOV *becomes hysterical but still reading.*

'If you dare deny that this means war —'

ALEXANDER *jumps up slamming the book shut and the orchestra jumps into a few bars of the '1812'.* IVANOV *holds* ALEXANDER *by the shoulders and there is a moment of suspense and imminent violence, then* IVANOV *kisses* ALEXANDER *on both cheeks.*

Courage, mon brave!

Every member of the orchestra carries a baton in his knapsack! Your turn will come.

Office

DOCTOR. Next!

ALEXANDER *goes into the* OFFICE.

Your behaviour is causing alarm. I'm beginning to think you're off your head. Quite apart from being a paranoid schizophrenic. I have to consider seriously whether an Ordinary Hospital can deal with your symptoms.

ALEXANDER. I have no symptoms, I have opinions.

DOCTOR. Your opinions are your symptoms. Your disease is dissent. Your kind of schizophrenia does not presuppose changes of personality noticeable to others. I might compare your case to that of Pyotr Grigorenko of whom it has been stated by our leading psychiatrists at the Serbsky Institute, that his outwardly well adjusted behaviour and formally coherent utterances were indicative of a pathological development of the personality. Are you getting the message? I can't help you. And furthermore your breath stinks of aeroplane glue or something — what have you been eating?

ALEXANDER. Nothing.

DOCTOR. And that's something else — we have never had a hunger strike here, except once and that was in protest against the food, which is psychologically coherent and it did wonders for the patients' morale, though not for the food. . . .

Pause.

You can choose your own drugs.

You don't even have to take them.

Just say you took them.

Pause.

Well, what do you *want*?

ALEXANDER (*flatly, not poetically*).
I want to get back to the bad old times
when a man got a sentence appropriate to his crimes —
ten years' hard for a word out of place,
twenty-five years if they didn't like your face,
and no one pretended that you were off your head.
In the good old Archipelago you're either well or dead —
And the —

DOCTOR. Stop it!

My God, how long can you go on like that?

ALEXANDER. In the Arsenal'naya I was not allowed writing materials, on medical grounds. If you want to remember things it helps if they rhyme.

DOCTOR. You gave me a dreadful shock. I thought I had discovered an entirely new form of mental disturbance. Immortality smiled upon me, one quick smile, and was gone.

ALEXANDER. Your name may not be entirely lost to history.

DOCTOR. What do you mean? — it's not *me*! I'm told what to do. Look, if you'll eat something I'll send for your son.

ALEXANDER. I don't want him to come here.

DOCTOR. If you don't eat something I'll send for your son.

Pause.

You mustn't be so rigid.

ALEXANDER *starts to leave.*

Pause.

Did the pills help at all?

ALEXANDER. I don't know.

DOCTOR. Do you believe that sane people are put in mental hospitals?

ALEXANDER. Yes.

DOCTOR. They didn't help.

ALEXANDER. I gave them to Ivanov. *His* name is also Ivanov.

DOCTOR. So it is. That's why Colonel or rather Doctor Rozinsky insisted you shared his cell, or rather ward.

ALEXANDER. Because we have the same name?

DOCTOR. The man is a genius. The layman often doesn't realize that medicine advances in —

ALEXANDER. I know. I have been giving Ivanov my rations. He needed a laxative. I gave him my pills.

ALEXANDER *leaves.*

DOCTOR. Next!

IVANOV *enters immediately, with his triangle, almost crossing* ALEXANDER.

IVANOV *is transformed, triumphant, awe-struck.*

Hello, Ivanov. Did the pills help at all?

IVANOV *strikes his triangle.*

IVANOV. I have no orchestra!

Silence.

IVANOV *indicates the silence with a raised finger. He strikes his triangle again.*

DOCTOR (*suddenly*). Wait a minute! — what day is it?

IVANOV. I have never *had* an orchestra!

Silence.

The DOCTOR, *however, has become preoccupied and misses the significance of this.*

DOCTOR. *What day is it*? Tuesday?

IVANOV *strikes the triangle.*

IVANOV. I do not want an orchestra!

Silence.

DOCTOR (*horrified*). What time is it? I'm going to be late for the orchestra!

The DOCTOR *grabs his violin case and starts to leave.* IVANOV *strikes his triangle.*

IVANOV. *There is no orchestra!*

DOCTOR (*leaving*). Of course there's a bloody orchestra!

Music — one chord. IVANOV *hears it and is mortified. More chords. The* DOCTOR *has left.*

IVANOV (*bewildered*). I have an orchestra.

Music.

I've *always* had an orchestra.

Music.

I always *knew* I had an orchestra.

Music.

ALEXANDER *has gone to sit on his bed.* IVANOV *sits in the* DOCTOR's *chair. The* DOCTOR *joins the violinists.* SACHA *moves across towards* IVANOV.

The music continues and ends.

IVANOV. Come in.

SACHA. Alexander Ivanov, sir.

IVANOV. Absolutely correct. Who are you?

SACHA. Alexander Ivanov, sir.

IVANOV. The boy's a fool.

SACHA. They said to come, sir. Is it about my father?

IVANOV. What's his name?

SACHA. Alexander Ivanov, sir.

IVANOV. This place is a madhouse.

SACHA. I know, sir.

Are you the doctor?

IVANOV. *Ivanov!* Of course. Sad case.

SACHA. What's the matter with him?

IVANOV. Tone deaf. Are you musical at all?

SACHA. No, sir.

IVANOV. What is your instrument?

SACHA. Triangle, sir.

Is it about *that* that I'm here?

IVANOV. Certainly, what else?

SACHA. Drum, sir.

IVANOV. What?

SACHA. Don't make me stay! I'll go back in the orchestra!

IVANOV. You can be in mine.

SACHA. I can't play anything, really.

IVANOV. Everyone is equal to the triangle. That is the first axiom of Euclid, the Greek musician.

SACHA. Yes, sir.

IVANOV. The second axiom! It is easier for a sick man to play the triangle than for a camel to play the triangle.

The third axiom! — even a camel can play the triangle!

The *pons asinorum* of Euclid! Anyone can play the triangle no matter how sick!

SACHA. Yes, sir — (*Crying.*) — please will you put me with Papa?

IVANOV (*raving*). The five postulates of Euclid!

    A triangle with a bass is a combo!

    Two triangles sharing the same bass is a trio!

SACHA. Are you the doctor?

IVANOV. A trombone is the longest distance between two
    points!

SACHA. You're not the doctor.

IVANOV. A string has length but no point.

SACHA (*cries*). Papa!

IVANOV. What is the Golden Rule?

SACHA. Papa!

IVANOV (*shouts*). A line *must be drawn*!

SACHA *runs out of* IVANOV*'s light and moves into the orchestra
among the players. The next four of* SACHA*'s speeches, which
are sung, come from different positions as he moves around the
orchestra platform.*
    There is music involved in the following scene.

SACHA (*sings*). Papa, where've they put you?

    ALEXANDER*'s 'poems' are uttered rapidly on a single
    rhythm.*

ALEXANDER. Dear Sacha, don't be sad,
    it would have been ten times as bad
    if we hadn't had the time we had,
    so think of that and please be glad.
    I kiss you now, your loving dad.
    Don't let them tell you I was mad.

SACHA (*sings*). Papa, don't be rigid!
    Everything can be all right!

ALEXANDER. Dear Sacha, try to see
    what they call their liberty
    is just freedom to agree
    that one and one is sometimes three.

I kiss you now, remember me.
Don't neglect your geometry.

SACHA (*sings*). Papa, don't be rigid!
Everything can be all right!

ALEXANDER. Dear Sacha, when I'm dead,
I'll be living in your head,
which is what your mama said,
keep her picture by your bed.
I kiss you now, and don't forget,
if you're brave the best is yet.

SACHA (*sings*). Papa, don't be rigid!
Be brave and tell them lies!

Cell

SACHA (*not singing*). Tell them lies. Tell them they've cured you.
Tell them you're grateful.

ALEXANDER. How can that be right?

SACHA. If they're wicked how can it be wrong?

ALEXANDER. It helps them to go on being wicked. It helps
people to think that perhaps they're not so wicked after all.

SACHA. It doesn't matter. I want you to come home.

ALEXANDER. And what about all the other fathers? And
mothers?

SACHA (*shouts*). It's wicked to let yourself die!

SACHA *leaves.*

The DOCTOR *moves from the orchestra to the* SCHOOL.

DOCTOR. Ivanov!

ALEXANDER. Dear Sacha —
be glad of —
kiss Mama's picture —
goodbye.

DOCTOR. Ivanov!

IVANOV *moves to* CELL.

Ivanov!

SACHA *moves towards the* SCHOOL.

ALEXANDER (*rapidly as before*).
Dear Sacha, I love you,
I hope you love me too.
To thine own self be true
one and one is always two.
I kiss you now, adieu.
There was nothing else to do.

School

SACHA *arrives at* SCHOOL. DOCTOR *is there.*
TEACHER *has remained near the desk.*

TEACHER. Sacha. Did you persuade him?

SACHA. He's going to die.

DOCTOR. I'm not allowed to let him die.

SACHA. Then let him go.

DOCTOR. I'm not allowed to let him go till he admits he's cured.

SACHA. Then he'll die.

DOCTOR. He'd rather die than admit he's cured? This is madness, and it's not allowed!

SACHA. Then you'll have to let him go.

DOCTOR. I'm not allowed to — it's a logical impasse. Did you tell him he mustn't be so rigid?

SACHA. If you want to get rid of Papa, *you* must not be rigid!

DOCTOR. What shall I tell the Colonel? He's a genius but he can't do the impossible.

Organ music. The COLONEL's *entrance is as impressive as possible. The organ accompanies his entrance.*

The DOCTOR *moves to meet him. The* COLONEL *ignores the* DOCTOR. *He stops in front of* ALEXANDER *and* IVANOV. *When the organ music stops the* COLONEL *speaks.*

Cell

COLONEL. Ivanov!

   ALEXANDER *and* IVANOV *stand up*.

   (*To* IVANOV.) Alexander Ivanov?

IVANOV. Yes.

COLONEL. Do you believe that sane people are put in mental hospitals?

DOCTOR. Excuse me, Doctor —

COLONEL. Shut up! —

   (*To* IVANOV.) Well? Would a Soviet doctor put a sane man into a lunatic asylum, in your opinion?

IVANOV (*baffled*). I shouldn't think so. Why?

COLONEL (*briskly*). Quite right! How do you feel?

IVANOV. Fit as a fiddle, thank you.

COLONEL. Quite right!

   The COLONEL *turns to* ALEXANDER.

   Alexander Ivanov?

ALEXANDER. Yes.

COLONEL. Do you have an orchestra?

   IVANOV *opens his mouth to speak*.

   (*To* IVANOV.) Shut up!

   (*To* ALEXANDER.) Well?

ALEXANDER. No.

COLONEL. Do you hear any music of any kind?

ALEXANDER. No.

COLONEL. How do you feel?

ALEXANDER. All right.

COLONEL. Manners!

ALEXANDER. Thank you.

COLONEL (*to* DOCTOR). There's absolutely nothing wrong with these men. Get them out of here.

DOCTOR. Yes, Colonel — Doctor.

The COLONEL's *exit is almost as impressive as his entrance, also with organ music. But this time the organ music blends into orchestral music — the finale.)*

The TEACHER *moves into the orchestra. The* DOCTOR *moves to the violins taking his instrument and joining in.* IVANOV *takes his triangle and joins the percussionists and beats the triangle.*

SACHA *comes across to the middle of the platform at the bottom. These directions assume a centre aisle going up the middle of the orchestra towards the organ.* ALEXANDER *and* SACHA *move up this aisle,* SACHA *running ahead. At the top he turns and sings to the same tune as before:*

SACHA (*sings*). Papa, don't be crazy!
Everything can be all right!

ALEXANDER. Sacha —

SACHA (*sings*). Everything can be all right!

Music. Music ends.

Peter Shaffer

'U.S. Playwrights Pale in Peter Shaffer's Light' was the headline of a *Philadelphia Inquirer* article by critic William Collins in 1980. 'For the last decade, the most successful serious playwright in the Broadway theatre has been an Englishman,' he continued. He had in mind *The Royal Hunt of the Sun*, *Equus*, and *Amadeus*, as hugely successful in New York as in London. Using Shaffer as a whip to flay American playwrights, he urged them to emulate Shaffer in craftsmanship, literacy, and simple clarity. Certainly Shaffer has deep respect for craft, 'hammering at it, working at it to get it right,' the very qualities that incline some critics to disparage him as middle-brow. Yet what attracts huge audiences are his grand metaphysical themes dramatized with the sweep and spectacle of opera, rich in aural and visual effects.

Peter Shaffer was born in 1926. During the war, he was a 'Bevin boy,' conscripted to work in the coal mines, as was his brother, Anthony, now famous as the author of *Sleuth*, one of the most successful stage thrillers of all time. After the war, Peter Shaffer took a history degree at Trinity College, Cambridge, sold books for a time, and worked at the Public Library in New York. He returned to London to work in a music publishing firm. During those years he also collaborated with his brother on three published mystery novels.

Between 1955 and 1957, two of Shaffer's television plays and a radio play were produced. Encouraged, he turned to writing for the stage. His first play, *Five Finger Exercise*, won the Evening Standard Award in London and the Drama Critics Circle Award in New York.

No reader of that first play could have guessed the sort of plays Shaffer would eventually write; it is conventional, modest in production demands, and conservative in style. It is more the theatre of Terence Rattigan than of Osborne, Pinter, or the other ground-breakers of the fifties. In a single interior locale, five members of a genteel household play out a domestic conflict that expresses itself almost totally in literate conversation. (What would recur in the big Shaffer plays to come is the frigid relationship between husband and wife and the painful inability of father and son to reach each other despite their desperate ache to do so.) Into the alienated family of *Five Finger Exercise* comes an emotionally vulnerable young German tutor who is soon a pawn in the family wars and so battered by them that he attempts suicide. While the aborted suicide may be criticized as an undermotivated plot device – the play needs a climax – Shaffer's theme rings very true: family psychosis is contagious, and sick people will devour healthy people who let themselves be vulnerable.

Shaffer next produced a double bill, *The Private Ear* and *The Public Eye*. The former is a rueful character study of a young man who fails to escape his loneliness because he reaches out to the wrong girl in the wrong way. The latter is a farce about a jealous middle-aged husband who hires a fantastical private detective to shadow his innocent young wife. As in all good farces, the husband's lack of trust earns him comic punishment. Though bills of one-act plays seldom score commercial success, this pair repeated Shaffer's earlier triumph, running over a year in the West End and moving on to Broadway.

In 1963, under the leadership of Sir Laurence Olivier, the fledgling National Theatre was preparing for its first productions. Shaffer's new script, *The Royal Hunt of the Sun*, as the story goes, was discovered on Olivier's desk by director John Dexter, quite by chance. The play had been rejected by a number of West End producers who found it too big, too expensive, too unstageable. What caught Dexter's interest, the story continues, was a single stage direction: 'They cross the Andes.' No wonder the commercial managers had backed off! The National scheduled the play almost at once, as the company's first premiere of a new English play, and Shaffer had another hit at the Chichester festival, then in London and New York.

The Royal Hunt of the Sun stakes out what is now considered to be Shaffer territory, what he himself called 'the nearly abandoned kingdom of epic theatre'. In the play several dozen characters recreate Spain's conquest of Peru. The vivid pageantry of war scenes and religious rituals is counterpointed by the psychological duelling in tautly-drawn scenes between Atahuallpa, god-king of the Incas, and Pizarro, the conquistador who conquers him, comes to love him, and, trapped in the net of political necessity, murders him.

The spectacular success of *Royal Hunt* began a long, productive relationship between Shaffer and the National Theatre. All his major plays since have premiered there. 'Largeness of resource was what I was looking for,' Shaffer has said. 'Because John Gielgud as Richard II was my archetypal image, I became a playwright finally to be part of the grandiloquent and showy world of imaginative realism.' Only a great subsidized theatre like the National could allow him such freedom.

In 1965, Kenneth Tynan, Literary Manager of the National, asked Shaffer for a one-act play which could share a bill with Strindberg's *Miss Julie*. Shaffer had seen a Peking Opera performance (in London) in which, by convention, bright light was used to represent darkness. Adopting the same convention, he devised *Black Comedy*, a lively one-act farce about modern art and a devious modern artist. At rise, the stage is pitch dark. The actors' voices are heard coming from the darkness. Suddenly full stage lights come on in a blinding flash, and the actors begin to grope as if they have been plunged into darkness by a power outage. The resulting dramatic irony has hilarious effect. The audience laughs at every close shave, near disaster, and mistaken identity that the characters are in the dark about. When an electrician repairs the lights, the stage goes pitchdark and the curtain falls. Shaffer had another hit, both in London and New York, where he added a slight three-character curtain raiser, *White Lies*.

Equus, which premiered in 1973, has been getting rave reviews every since. Like *Five Finger Exercise*, it garnered the major prizes on both sides of the Atlantic. Equal in theatrical invention to *Black Comedy*, and in its thematic exploration of the theme of worship to *Royal Hunt of the Sun*, *Equus* is at core a detective story in which psychiatrist Dysart must learn why a seventeen-year-old boy, Alan Strang, has blinded six horses with an iron spike. Dysart solves the mystery, and in the process learns as much about himself and the emptiness of his life as he does about the boy. He comes to question the accepted concepts of sanity that he and we live by. As Warren Smith explains, what happens to Dysart is not too different from what happens to Pizarro in his confrontation with the god-king. 'Uncivilized forces that we assume have been safely tamed by reason and by conformance to acceptable cultural patterns respond to the genuine primitive model with such violence as to shatter our conception of ourselves as civilized beings.'

In *Equus*, what might merely be highly effective melodrama is lifted to stirring theatre by Shaffer's stage imagery. On an almost bare stage, the key events are relived in flashback. The horses are incarnated by actors whose metal hooves, wire masks, and chestnut track suits provide just sufficient assistance to send the audience's imaginations soaring. *Equus* evokes the prelogical realm where theatre must have been born. The struggle between the psychiatrist and the boy is the universal struggle between the Apollonian and Dionysian impulses in human nature.

In the by now legendary *Amadeus*, Shaffer once again presents a story of two human beings locked in a terrible spiritual battle, this one of course between the immortal Mozart and his less gifted contemporary, court composer Salieri. Although the play was already a hit in London and a guaranteed New York success because of presale, Shaffer, a tireless craftsman, continued to work at polishing the play. Believing that Salieri had been too much the passive observer in the London version, Shaffer activated his protagonist in a number of ways. He added Salieri's tempting Mozart to betray the secrets of the Masonic order. He added Salieri's insinuating himself as substitute father to Mozart. And, for the melodramatic climax, he changed Mozart's masked visitor from Greybig, Salieri's servant, to Salieri himself. What had seemed to Clive Barnes already 'a near masterpiece,' became in the New York version 'far deeper, more complex.'

Still Shaffer had not finished with *Amadeus*. He approached scripting the film version as if he were telling a new story from scratch. Gone would be Salieri's elaborate attempt to seduce Constanze. Added would be the on-screen character of Leopold Mozart. But most daring would be the new scene in which Salieri and Mozart work on the Requiem Mass together, the dying Mozart pouring forth a flood of inspiration and the tortured Salieri, both loving and murderous, recording the composition in feverish wonder. Shaffer's Academy Award winning screenplay is not merely a stage script adjusted to the demands of film, but a rich new creation. Shaffer's scrupulous reworking represents his deep commitment to the classical vision of 'the better maker'. 'I have always entertained the profoundest respect for art,' he said, 'meaning "artifact," and for the suffix "wright" in the word "playwright."'

Music floods the stage in *Amadeus*. Its ceaseless sounding in Salieri's ears is one of the most moving conceits in the play. Music has been a key element in Shaffer's work since he borrowed the title for *Five Finger Exercise*, in which Brahms is a refuge for the sensitive tutor and a measure of the culture gap between father and son. Shaffer, who plays piano, wrote music criticism for *Time and Tide* in the early sixties. In a 1984 *New York Times* piece, 'Paying Homage to Mozart,' he wrote, 'My own apprehension of the divine is very largely aesthetic . . . the creation of the 'C Minor Mass' . . . seem[s] to me to give a point to evolution: most human activities do not.'

Shaffer's passion for music produces the moment of greatest irony in *Amadeus*. Salieri stands alone on stage, his arms full of Mozart's manuscripts. As he reads them, their music pours into his mind and fills the theatre. Salieri knows the music for what it is, the voice of the absolute and the proof of his own mediocrity. As the 'C Minor Mass' swells to its climax, Salieri falls senseless to the floor. The irony is perfect: of all the persons of the play, of all the people of Vienna, only he, Salieri, to whom it is reproof and rejection, who would destroy its maker if he could, only he can appreciate the music.

Shaffer's creative use of music is one more aspect of the richly inventive theatricality of his epic plays. He credits Peter Brook and John Dexter for setting important examples of theatricality, and he cites Japanese Noh theatre as an important inspiration, especially for his use of masks.

Shaffer uses masks ingeniously in each of the major plays. In *The Royal Hunt of the Sun* masked Indians join Pizarro to hold vigil over Atahuallpa's corpses. Both the Indians and Pizarro are praying for the miraculous resurrection of Atahuallpa that will confirm their connection to the eternal. The empty eyes of the funeral masks convey both the anxiety of waiting and the subsequent despair with a power no unadorned face could match. In *Equus*, of course, the horse masks, open frames leaving visible the faces of the actors, not only symbolize the horses, but compel attention to the mysterious intelligence within those frames, a potent natural spirit that lies just beyond ordinary human knowing. In *Amadeus*, Salieri's mask makes him all that Mozart fears and waits for, the messenger of God come for his final fee, and Mozart's dead Papa, every boy's God that fails and is still longed for.

Shaffer's gift for the aural and visual image is matched by his confident mastery of melodramatic technique. In each of the big plays, the action is simple and direct – to conquer a kingdom in *Royal Hunt*, to solve a mystery in *Equus*, to pull down a rival in *Amadeus*. Each protagonist pursues his goal passionately, beating aside one obstacle after another in tried and true melodramatic style. And Shaffer shares with every true melodramatist the nerve to use time-tested tricks. In a scene in *Amadeus*, he hides Salieri in a high-backed chair so that he may eavesdrop on Mozart and Constanze not once, but twice, and the second time he has Salieri taunt the audience: 'Believe it or not,' as if Shaffer were confidently saying, 'Sure, it's an old device, but I can make it stick – watch me.'

Two interlocking motifs dominate the big plays, *The Royal Hunt of the Sun, Equus* and *Amadeus*. One is the relationship between cynical age and young innocence; the other is the hopeless quest of man for God. In each play, the protagonist is an older man – Pizarro, Dysart, Salieri – brought face to face with an extraordinary young man – Atahuallpa, Alan Strang, Mozart. The older men possess some sort of temporal power and an unsatisfied hunger for meaning. Pizarro, the conquering general, quakes as he approaches life's end, unfortified by the healing faith of his age. Psychiatrist Dysart, the mender of other men's souls, feels his own withering within him. Salieri dictates the fates of other artists, but is tortured by the growing realization of his own mediocrity. The older men are also sexually dead – Pizarro has put women behind him; Dysart has not kissed his wife in six years; Salieri refers to his wife as *La Statua*.

The younger men are potent, natural, and, most important, in touch with God. Atahuallpa reigns over a kingdom of nature and a bevy of wives; he *is* God to his people and himself. Alan Strang, barely awake to the world of experience and charged with sex at the same time that he is tormented by it, has created his own god, Equus, and achieves union with him. Mozart, a wild child barely beyond the anal stage in social behaviour, takes his sex on every side and creates music that proclaims his close tie to God; his very name Amadeus betokens the blessedness that he enjoys and Salieri thirsts for.

Each younger man falls under the thrall of the older, Atahuallpa as Pizarro's prisoner, Alan as Dysart's patient, and Mozart as Salieri's seeming protégé. Each older man promises to become a sort of father-protector: Pizarro would save Atahuallpa's life; Dysart would cure Alan; Salieri offers to be second father indeed to Mozart. But each is tormented by the awareness that God favours the young innocent. Pizarro comes to half believe that Atahuallpa can overcome death – *be* a god. Dysart sees in Alan's madness the connection to primeval life that he, for all his pilgrimages to Greece, 'the womb of civilization,' cannot attain. Salieri envies Mozart, whom he sees as the usurper, the wrongful possessor of God's gift of music that he, Salieri, has honestly bargained for. Pizarro and Salieri conspire at the death of their young rivals. Dysart, on the other hand, cures Alan of his delusions, but he recognizes in that cure the killing of all that is special in Alan, who will now be doomed to the same mediocre existence that Dysart suffers. At the end, each older man is even emptier than before his encounter with the blessed innocent.

Each play subsumes these motifs within a large clear over-theme. In *Royal Hunt*, the theme may be taken to be sixteenth-century imperialism, the ravaging of innocent worlds by European power. In *Equus* it may be the emptiness of our definitions of sanity and insanity. In *Amadeus* it may be the pain felt by ordinariness when it faces genius.

But over all three plays one great theme seems to reign: the question of God, the search for God, and the failure to find Him. Peter Hall calls this Shaffer's obsession. If so, it is a fruitful obsession, the big theme that drives Peter Shaffer to write the biggest plays of our era.

Major Plays

Five Finger Exercise, Comedy Theatre, 1958.
The Private Ear and *The Public Eye*, Globe Theatre, 1962.
The Royal Hunt of the Sun, National Theatre at Chichester, 1964; then at the Old Vic.
Black Comedy, National Theatre of Chichester, 1965; then at the Old Vic.
Equus, National Theatre at the Old Vic, 1973.
Amadeus, Olivier Theatre (National Theatre), 1979.

Selected Bibliography

Barnes, Clive. 'Portrait of an Artist.' *Times*, 20 December 1980, p. 8c.

Hall, Peter. *Diaries*, ed. John Goodwin. London: Hamish Hamilton; New York: Harper and Row, 1983.

Klein, Dennis A. *Peter Shaffer*. Boston: Twayne, 1979.

Shaffer, Peter. Preface to *Collected Plays*. New York: Harmony Books, 1982.

—. 'Paying Homage to Mozart.' *New York Times*, 2 September 1984, pp. 22-38.

—. 'Psychic Energy,' interview with Colin Chambers. *Plays and Players*, February 1980, pp. 11-13.

Smith, Warren Sylvester. 'Peter Shaffer.' *Dictionary of Literary Biography*, Vol. 13, *British Dramatists Since World War II*, ed. Stanley Weintraub. Detroit: Gale Research Company, 1982, pp. 451-469.

Taylor, John Russell. *Peter Shaffer*, ed. Ian Scott-Kilvert, London: Longman, 1974.

PETER SHAFFER

Amadeus

For Robert with love

All applications regarding professional performing rights in this play should be made to Marc Berlin, London Management, 235-241 Regent Street, London W1A 2JT and regarding amateur performing rights to Samuel French Ltd, 52 Fitzroy Street, London W1P 6JR.

The Set: *Amadeus* can and should be played in a variety of settings. What is described in this text is to a large extent based on the exquisite formulation found for the play by the designer John Bury, conjured into being by the director, Peter Hall. I was of course in enthusiastic agreement with his formulation, and set it down here with their permission as a tribute to their exquisite work.

The set consisted basically of a handsome rectangle of patterned wood, its longest sides leading away from the viewer, set into a stage of ice-blue plastic. This surface shifted beguilingly under various lights played upon it, to show gunmetal grey, or azure, or emerald green, and reflected the actors standing upon it. The entire design was undeniably modern, yet it suggested without self-consciousness the age of the Rococo. Costumes and objects were sumptuously of the period, and should always be so wherever the play is produced.

The rectangle largely represented interiors: especially those of Salieri's salon; Mozart's last apartment; assorted reception rooms, and opera houses. At the back stood a grand proscenium sporting gilded cherubs blowing huge trumpets, and supporting grand curtains of sky blue, which could rise and part to reveal an enclosed space almost the width of the area downstage. Into this space superb backdrops were flown, and superb projections thrown, to show the scarlet boxes of theatres, the black shape of the guillotine, or a charming white Masonic Lodge copied from a china plate. In it the audience could see an eighteenth-century street at night (cunningly enlarged from the lid of Mozart's own curious snuff-box) or a vast wall of gold mirrors with an immense golden fireplace, representing the encrusted Palace of Schönbrunn. In it also appeared silhouettes of scandalmongering citizens of Vienna, or the formal figures of the Emperor Joseph II of Austria and his brocaded courtiers. This wonderful upstage space which was in effect an immense Rococo peepshow, will be referred to throughout this text as the Light Box.

On stage, before the lights are lowered in the theatre, four objects are to be seen by the audience. To the left, on the wooden rectangle, stands a small table, bearing an empty cake-stand and a small handbell. In the centre, further upstage and also on the wood, stands an empty wheelchair of the eighteenth century, with its back to us. To the right, on the reflecting plastic, stands a beautiful fortepiano in a marquetry case. Above the stage is suspended a large chandelier showing many globes of opaque glass.

All directions will be given from the viewpoint of the audience.

Changes of time and place are indicated throughout by changes of light.

In reading the text it must be remembered that the action is wholly continuous. Its fluidity is ensured by the use of servants played by actors in eighteenth-century livery, whose role it is to move the furniture and carry on props with ease and correctness, while the action proceeds around them. Through a pleasant paradox of theatre their constant coming and going, bearing tables, chairs or cloaks, should render them virtually invisible, and certainly unremarkable. This will aid the play to be acted throughout in its proper manner: with the sprung line, gracefulness and energy for which Mozart is so especially celebrated.

The asterisks which now and then divide the page indicate changes of scene: but there is to be no interruption. The scenes must flow into one another without pause from the beginning to the end of the play.

P.S.

Amadeus was first presented by the National Theatre in London on 2 November 1979, with the following cast:

THE 'VENTICELLI'	Dermot Crowley
	Donald Gee
VALET TO SALIERI	Philip Locke
ANTONIO SALIERI	Paul Scofield
JOHANN KILIAN VON STRACK	Basil Henson
COUNT ORSINI-ROSENBERG	Andrew Cruickshank
BARON VAN SWIETEN	Nicholas Selby
CONSTANZE WEBER	Felicity Kendal
WOLFGANG AMADEUS MOZART	Simon Callow
MAJOR-DOMO	William Sleigh
JOSEPH II, EMPEROR OF AUSTRIA	John Normington
SERVANTS	Nik Forster, David Morris, Louis Selwyn, Steven Slater,
CITIZENS OF VIENNA	Glyn Baker, Nigel Bellairs, Leo Dove, Jane Evers, Susan Gilmore, Robin McDonald, Peggy Marshall, Robin Meredith, Ann Sedgwick, Glenn Williams

Director: Peter Hall
Design and Lighting: John Bury
Assistant Designer: Sue Jenkinson
Music by Mozart and Salieri
Music Direction: Harrison Birtwistle
Fortepiano played by Christopher Kite

This is a revised version of *Amadeus* first produced at the Broadhurst Theater, New York City, on 17 December 1980. It starred Ian McKellen as Salieri, Tim Curry as Mozart, and Jane Seymour as Constanze. The Director was Peter Hall.

CHARACTERS

ANTONIO SALIERI
WOLFGANG AMADEUS MOZART
CONSTANZE WEBER, Wife of Mozart
JOSEPH II, Emperor of Austria
COUNT JOHANN KILIAN VON STRACK, Groom of the
    Imperial Chamber
COUNT FRANZ ORSINI-ROSENBERG, Director of the
    Imperial Opera
BARON GOTTFRIED VAN SWIETEN, Prefect of the Imperial
    Library
TWO 'VENTICELLI', 'Little Winds': purveyors of information,
    gossip and rumour
MAJOR-DOMO
SALIERI'S VALET (Silent part)
SALIERI'S COOK (Silent part)
TERESA SALIERI, Wife of Salieri (silent part)
KATHERINA CAVALIERI, Salieri's pupil (silent part)
KAPELLMEISTER BONNO (Silent part)
CITIZENS OF VIENNA

The CITIZENS OF VIENNA also play the SERVANTS who
move furniture and bring on props as required, and TERESA
SALIERI and KATHERINA CAVALIERI, neither of whom have
any lines to speak.

The action of the play takes place in Vienna in November 1823,
and, in recall, the decade 1781–1791.

ACT ONE

Vienna

Darkness.

Savage whispers fill the theatre. We can distinguish nothing at first from this snake-like hissing save the word Salieri! *repeated here, there and everywhere around the theatre.*

Also, the barely distinguishable word Assassin!

The whispers overlap and increase in volume, slashing the air with wicked intensity. Then the light grows upstage to reveal the silhouettes of men and women dressed in the top hats and skirts of the early nineteenth century — CITIZENS OF VIENNA, *all crowded together in the Light Box, and uttering their scandal.*

WHISPERERS. *Salieri!* . . . *Salieri!* . . . *Salieri!*

Downstage in the wheelchair, with his back to us, sits an old man. We can just see, as the light grows a little brighter, the top of his head encased in an old cap, and perhaps the shawl wrapped around his shoulders.

Salieri! . . . *Salieri!* . . . *Salieri!*

Two middle-aged gentlemen hurry in from either side, also wearing the long cloaks and tall hats of the period. These are the TWO VENTICELLI: *purveyors of fact, rumour and gossip throughout the play. They speak rapidly — in this first appearance extremely rapidly — so that the scene has the air of a fast and dreadful Overture. Sometimes they speak to each other; sometimes to us — but always with the urgency of men who have ever been first with the news.*

VENTICELLO 1. I don't believe it.

VENTICELLO 2. I don't believe it.

VENTICELLO 1. I don't believe it.

VENTICELLO 2. I don't believe it.

WHISPERERS. *Salieri!*

VENTICELLO 1. They say.

VENTICELLO 2. I hear.

VENTICELLO 1. I hear.

VENTICELLO 2. They say.

VENTICELLO 1 and VENTICELLO 2. *I don't believe it!*

WHISPERERS. *Salieri!*

VENTICELLO 1. The whole city is talking.

VENTICELLO 2. You hear it all over.

VENTICELLO 1. The cafés.

VENTICELLO 2. The Opera.

VENTICELLO 1. The Prater.

VENTICELLO 2. The gutter.

VENTICELLO 1. They say even Metternich repeats it.

VENTICELLO 2. They say even Beethoven, his old pupil.

VENTICELLO 1. But why now?

VENTICELLO 2. After so long?

VENTICELLO 1. Thirty-two years!

VENTICELLO 1 and VENTICELLO 2. *I don't believe it!*

WHISPERERS. SALIERI!

VENTICELLO 1. They say he shouts it out all day!

VENTICELLO 2. I hear he cries it out all night!

VENTICELLO 1. Stays in his apartments.

VENTICELLO 2. Never goes out.

VENTICELLO 1. Not for a year now.

VENTICELLO 2. Longer. Longer.

VENTICELLO 1. Must be seventy.

VENTICELLO 2. Older. Older.

VENTICELLO 1. Antonio Salieri —

VENTICELLO 2. The famous musician —

VENTICELLO 1. Shouting it aloud!

VENTICELLO 2. Crying it aloud!

VENTICELLO 1. Impossible.

VENTICELLO 2. Incredible.

VENTICELLO 1. I don't believe it!

VENTICELLO 2. I don't believe it!

WHISPERERS. SALIERI!

VENTICELLO 1. I know who *started* the tale!

VENTICELLO 2. *I* know who started the tale!

Two old men — one thin and dry, one very fat — detach themselves from the crowd at the back, and walk downstage, on either side: Salieri's VALET and PASTRY COOK.

VENTICELLO 1 (*indicating him*). The old man's valet!

VENTICELLO 2 (*indicating him*). The old man's cook!

VENTICELLO 1. The valet hears him shouting!

VENTICELLO 2. The cook hears him crying!

VENTICELLO 1. What a story!

VENTICELLO 2. What a scandal!

The VENTICELLI move quickly upstage, one on either side, and each collects a silent informant. VENTICELLO 1 walks down eagerly with the VALET; VENTICELLO 2 walks down eagerly with the COOK.

VENTICELLO 1 (*to VALET*). What does he say, your master?

VENTICELLO 2 (*to COOK*). What *exactly* does he cry, the Kapellmeister?

VENTICELLO 1. Alone in his house —

VENTICELLO 2. All day and all night —

VENTICELLO 1. What sins does he shout?

VENTICELLO 2. The old fellow —

VENTICELLO 1. The recluse —

VENTICELLO 2. What horrors have you heard?

VENTICELLO 1 and VENTICELLO 2. Tell us! Tell us! Tell us at once! What does he cry? What does he cry? *What does he cry?*

   VALET *and* COOK *gesture towards* SALIERI.

SALIERI (*in a great cry*). MOZART!!!

   Silence.

VENTICELLO 1 (*whispering*). Mozart!

VENTICELLO 2 (*whispering*). Mozart!

SALIERI. *Perdonami, Mozart! Il tuo assassino ti chiede perdono!*

VENTICELLO 1 (*in disbelief*). Pardon, Mozart!

VENTICELLO 2 (*in disbelief*). Pardon your assassin!

VENTICELLO 1 and VENTICELLO 2. *God preserve us!*

SALIERI. *Pietà, Mozart. Mozart, pietà!*

VENTICELLO 1. Mercy, Mozart!

VENTICELLO 2. Mozart, have mercy!

VENTICELLO 1. He speaks in Italian when excited!

VENTICELLO 2. German when not!

VENTICELLO 1. *Perdonami, Mozart!*

VENTICELLO 2. Pardon your assassin!

   The VALET *and the* COOK *walk to either side of the stage, and stand still. Pause. The* VENTICELLI *cross themselves, deeply shocked.*

VENTICELLO 1. There was talk once before, you know.

VENTICELLO 2. Thirty-two years ago.

VENTICELLO 1. When Mozart was dying.

VENTICELLO 2. He claimed he'd been poisoned.

VENTICELLO 1. Some said he accused a man.

VENTICELLO 2. Some said that man was Salieri.

VENTICELLO 1. But no one believed it.

VENTICELLO 2. They *knew* what he died of!

VENTICELLO 1. Syphilis, surely.

VENTICELLO 2. Like everybody else.

Pause.

VENTICELLO 1 (*slyly*). But what if Mozart was right?

VENTICELLO 2. If he really *was* murdered?

VENTICELLO 1. And by him. Our First Kapellmeister!

VENTICELLO 2. Antonio Salieri!

VENTICELLO 1. It can't possible be true.

VENTICELLO 2. It's not actually credible.

VENTICELLO 1. Because *why?*

VENTICELLO 2. Because why?

VENTICELLO 1 and VENTICELLO 2. *Why on earth would he do it?*

VENTICELLO 1. Our First Royal Kapellmeister —

VENTICELLO 2. Murder his inferior?

VENTICELLO 1. And why confess *now?*

VENTICELLO 2. After thirty-two years!

WHISPERERS. SALIERI!

SALIERI. *Mozart! Mozart! Perdonami! . . . Il tuo assassino ti chiede perdono!*

Pause. They look at him — then at each other.

VENTICELLO 1. What do you think?

VENTICELLO 2. What do you think?

VENTICELLO 1. I don't believe it!

VENTICELLO 2. *I* don't believe it!

VENTICELLO 1. All the same . . .

VENTICELLO 2. Is it just possible?

VENTICELLO 1 and VENTICELLO 2 (*whispering*). *Did he do it after all?!*

WHISPERERS. SALIERI!

The VENTICELLI *go off. The* VALET *and the* COOK *remain, on either side of the stage.* SALIERI *swivels his wheelchair around and stares at us. We see a man of seventy in an old stained dressing-robe, shawled. He rises and squints at the audience as if trying to see it.*

*   *   *

Salieri's Apartments
November 1823. The small hours

SALIERI (*calling to audience*). *Vi Saluto! Ombri del Futuro! Antonio Salieri — a vostro servizio!*

A clock outside in the street strikes three.

I can almost see you in your ranks — waiting for your turn to live. Ghosts of the Future! Be visible. I beg you. Be visible. Come to this dusty old room — this time, the smallest hours of dark November, eighteen hundred and twenty-three — and be my Confessors! Will you not enter this place and stay with me till dawn? Just till dawn — till six o'clock!

WHISPERERS. *Salieri! . . . Salieri! . . .*

The curtains slowly descend on the CITIZENS OF VIENNA. *Faint images of long windows are projected on the silk.*

SALIERI. Can you hear them? Vienna is a City of Slander. Everyone tells tales here: even my servants. I keep only two now — (*He indicates them*) — they've been with me ever since I came here, fifty years ago. The Keeper of the Razor: the Maker of the Cakes. One keeps me tidy, the other keeps me full. Tonight, I gave them instructions they never heard before. (*To them*) 'Leave me, both of you! Tonight I do not go to bed at all!'

They react in surprise.

'Return here tomorrow morning at six precisely — to shave, to feed your capricious master!' (*He smiles at them both and claps his hands in gentle dismissal.*) Via. Via, via, via! Grazie!

They bow, bewildered, and leave the stage.

How surprised they were! . . . They'll be even more surprised tomorrow: indeed they will! (*He peers hard at the audience, trying to see it.*) Oh, won't you appear? I need you — desperately! This is now the last hour of my life. Those about to die implore you! What must I do to make you visible? Raise you up in the flesh to be my last, last audience? . . . Does it take an Invocation? That's how it's always done in opera! Ah yes, of course: that's it. An *Invocation!* The only way (*He rises.*) Let me try to conjure you *now* — Ghosts of the distant Future — so that I can see you.

He gets out of the wheelchair and huddles over to the fortepiano. He stands at the instrument and begins to sing in a high cracked voice, interrupting himself at the end of each sentence with figurations on the keyboard in the manner of a recitativo secco. During this the house lights slowly come up to illuminate the audience.

(*Singing.*)

Ghosts of the Future!
Shades of Time to come!
So much more unavoidable than those of Time gone by!
Appear with what sympathy Incarnation may endow you!
Appear You —
The yet-to-be-born!
The yet-to-hate!
The yet-to-*kill!*
Appear — Posterity!

The light on the audience reaches its maximum. It stays like this during all of the following.

(*Speaking again.*) There. It worked. I can see you! That is the result of proper training. I was taught invocation by Chevalier Gluck, who was a true master at it. He had to be. In his day that is what people went to the opera for: the raising of Gods, and Ghosts . . . Nowadays, since Rossini became the rage, they prefer to watch the escapades of hairdressers.

Pause.

Scusate. Invocation is an exhausting business! I need refreshment. (*He goes to the cake-stand.*) It's a little repellent, I admit — but actually the first sin I have to confess to you is Gluttony. Sticky gluttony at that. Infantile — Italian gluttony! The truth is that all my life I have never been able to conquer a lust for the sweetmeats of northern Italy where I was born. From the ages of three to seventy-three my entire career has been conducted to the taste of almonds sprinkled with sifted sugar. (*Lustfully*). Veronese biscuits! Milanese macaroons! Snow dumplings with pistachio sauce! (*Pause*) Do not judge me too harshly for this. All men harbour patriotic feelings of some kind . . . Of course I was born in 1750, when no man of sophistication would have dreamed of talking about Love of Country, or Native Earth. We were men of Europe, and that was enough. My parents were provincial subjects of the Austrian Empire, and perfectly happy to be so. A Lombardy merchant and his Lombardy wife. Their notion of Place was the tiny town of Legnago — which I could not wait to leave. Their notion of God was a superior Hapsburg emperor inhabiting a heaven only slightly further off than Vienna. All they required of Him was to protect commerce and keep them forever unnoticed — preserved in mediocrity. My own requirements were very different.

Pause.

I wanted Fame. Not to deceive you. I wanted to *blaze,* like a comet, across the firmament of Europe. Yet only in one especial way. Music. Absolute music! A note of music is either right or wrong — *absolutely!* Not even Time can alter that: music is God's art. (*Excited by the recollection.*) Already when I was ten a spray of sounded notes would make me dizzy almost to falling! By twelve I was humming my arias and anthems to the Lord. My one desire was to join all the composers who had celebrated His glory through the long Italian past! . . . Every Sunday I saw Him in church, painted on the flaking wall. I don't mean Christ. The Christs of Lombardy are simpering sillies with lambkins on their sleeves. No: I mean an old candle-smoked God in a mulberry robe, staring at the world with dealer's eyes. Tradesmen had put him up there. Those eyes made bargains, real and irreversible. 'You give me so — I'll give you so! No more. No less!' (*He eats a sweet biscuit in his excitement.*) The night before I left Legnago for ever I went to see Him and made a bargain with Him myself! I was a sober sixteen, filled with a desperate sense of right. I knelt before the God of Bargains, and I prayed through the mouldering plaster with all my soul.

He kneels. The house lights go down.

'Signore, let me be a composer! Grant me sufficient fame to enjoy it. In return I will live with virtue. I will strive to better the lot of my fellows. And I will honour You with much music all the days of my life!' As I said Amen, I saw his eyes flare. (*As 'God'*) '*Bene.* Go forth Antonio. Serve Me and Mankind — and you will be blessed!' . . . '*Grazie!*' I called back. 'I am Your servant for life!'

He gets to his feet again.

The very next day, a family friend suddenly appeared — out of the blue — took me off to Vienna, and paid for me to study music!

Pause.

Shortly afterwards I met the Emperor, who favoured me — and was to advance my career beyond all expectations! *Clearly my bargain had been accepted!*

Pause.

The same year I left Italy, a young prodigy was touring Europe. A miraculous virtuoso aged ten years. Wolfgang Amadeus Mozart.

Pause. He smiles at the audience.

Pause.

And now — Gracious Ladies! Obliging Gentlemen! I present to you — for one performance only — my last composition, entitled *The Death of Mozart*, or *Did I Do It?* . . . dedicated to Posterity on this — the last night of my life!

He bows deeply, undoing as he does so the buttons of his old dressing-robe. When he straightens himself — divesting himself of this drab outer garment and his cap — he is a young man in the prime of life, wearing a sky-blue coat and the elegant decent clothes of a successful composer of the seventeen-eighties.

*   *   *

Transformation to the Eighteenth Century

Music sounds softly in the background: a serene piece for strings by Salieri. SERVANTS *enter. One takes away the dressing-robe and shawl; another places on the table a wig-stand bearing a powdered wig; a third brings on a chair and places it at the left, upstage.*

  At the back the blue curtains rise and part to show the EMPEROR JOSEPH II *and his Court bathed in golden light, against a golden background of mirrors and an immense golden fireplace. His Majesty is seated, holding a rolled paper, listening to the music. Also listening are* COUNT VON STRACK; COUNT ORSINI-ROSENBERG; BARON VAN SWIETEN; *and an anonymous* PRIEST *dressed in a soutane. An old wigged courtier enters and takes his place at the keyboard:* KAPELLMEISTER BONNO. SALIERI *takes his wig from the stand.*

SALIERI (*in a young man's voice: vigorous and confident*). The place throughout is Vienna. The year — to begin with — seventeen eighty-one. The age still that of the Enlightenment: that clear time before the guillotine fell in France and cut all our lives in half. I am thirty-one. Already a prolific composer to the Hapsburg Court. I own a respectable house and a respectable wife — Teresa.

Enter TERESA: *a padded placid lady who seats herself uprightly in the chair upstage.*

I do not mock her, I assure you. I required only one quality in a domestic companion — lack of fire. And in that omission Teresa was conspicuous. (*Ceremoniously he puts on his powdered wig.*) I also had a prize pupil: Katharina Cavalieri.

KATHERINA *swirls on from the opposite side: a beautiful girl of twenty. The music becomes vocal: faintly, we hear a soprano singing a concert aria. Like* TERESA's, KATHERINA's *part is mute — but as she enters she stands by the fortepiano, and energetically mimes her rapturous singing. At the keyboard old* BONNO *accompanies her appreciatively.*

SALIERI. She was later to become the best singer of her Age. But at that time she was mainly a bubbling student with merry eyes and a sweet, eatable mouth. I was very much in love with Katherina — or at least in lust. But because of my vow to God, I was entirely faithful to my wife. I had never laid a finger upon the girl — except occasionally to depress her diaphragm in the way of teaching her to sing. My ambition burned with an unquenchable flame. Its chief goal was the post of First Royal Kapellmeister, then held by Giuseppe Bonno — (*indicating him*) — seventy years old, and apparently immortal.

All on stage, save SALIERI, *suddenly freeze. He speaks very directly to the audience.*

You, when you come, will be told that we musicians of the eighteenth century were no better than servants: the willing slaves of the well-to-do. This is quite true. It is also quite false. Yes, we were servants. But we were learned servants! And we used our learning to celebrate men's average lives!

A grander music sounds. The EMPEROR *remains seated, but the other four men in the Light Box —* VON STRACK, ORSINI-ROSENBERG, VAN SWIETEN *and the* PRIEST — *come slowly out on to the main stage and process imposingly down it, and around it, and up it again to return to their places. Only the* PRIEST *goes off, as do* TERESA *on her side, and* KATHERINA *on hers.*

(*Over this.*) We took unremarkable men: usual bankers, run-of-the-mill priests, ordinary soldiers and statesmen and wives — and sacramentalized their mediocrity. We smoothed their noons with strings *divisi!* We pierced their nights with *chittarini!* We gave them processions for their strutting — serenades for their rutting — high horns for their hunting, and

drums for their wars! Trumpets sounded when they entered
the world, and trombones groaned when they left it! The
savour of their days remains behind because of *us*, our music
still remembered while their politics are long forgotten.

The EMPEROR *hands his rolled paper to* VON STRACK *and
goes off. In the Light Box are left standing, like three icons,*
ORSINI-ROSENBERG, *plump and supercilious, aged sixty;*
VON STRACK, *stiff and proper, aged fifty-five;* VAN
SWIETEN, *cultivated and serious, aged fifty. The lights go
down on them a little.*

Tell me, before you call us servants, who served whom? And
who I wonder, in your generations, will immortalize *you*?

The TWO VENTICELLI *come on quickly downstage, from
either side. They are now bewigged also, and are dressed well,
in the style of the late eighteenth century. Their manner is
more confidential than before.*

VENTICELLO 1 (*to* SALIERI). Sir!

VENTICELLO 2 (*to* SALIERI). Sir!

VENTICELLO 1. Sir. Sir.

VENTICELLO 2. Sir. Sir. Sir!

SALIERI *bids them wait for a second.*

SALIERI. I was the most successful young musician in the city of
musicians. And now suddenly, without warning —

They approach him eagerly, from either side.

VENTICELLO 1. Mozart!

VENTICELLO 2. Mozart!

VENTICELLO 1 and VENTICELLO 2. *Mozart has come!*

SALIERI. These are my *Venticelli.* My 'Little Winds', as I call
them. (*He gives each a coin from his pocket.*) The secret of
successful living in a large city is always to know to the minute
what is being done behind your back.

VENTICELLO 1. He's left Salzburg.

VENTICELLO 2. Means to give concerts.

VENTICELLO 1. Asking for subscribers.

SALIERI. I'd known of him for years, of course. Tales of his prowess were told all over Europe.

VENTICELLO 1. They say he wrote his first symphony at five.

VENTICELLO 2. I hear his first concerto at four.

VENTICELLO 1. A full opera at fourteen.

SALIERI (*to them*). How old is he now?

VENTICELLO 2. Twenty-five.

SALIERI (*carefully*). And how long is he remaining?

VENTICELLO 1. He's not departing.

VENTICELLO 2. He's here to stay.

The VENTICELLI *glide off.*

* * *

The Palace of Schönbrunn

Lights come up on the three stiff figures of ORSINI-ROSENBERG, VON STRACK *and* VAN SWIETEN, *standing upstage in the Light Box. The* CHAMBERLAIN *hands the paper he has received from the Emperor to the* DIRECTOR OF THE OPERA. SALIERI *remains downstage.*

VON STRACK (*to* ORSINI-ROSENBERG). You are required to commission a comic opera in German from Herr Mozart.

SALIERI (*to audience*). Johann von Strack. Royal Chamberlain. A Court official to his collar bone.

ROSENBERG (*loftily*). Why in German? Italian is the only possible language for opera!

SALIERI. Count Orsini-Rosenberg. Director of the Opera. Benevolent to all things Italian — especially myself.

VON STRACK (*stiffly*). The idea of a National Opera is dear to His Majesty's heart. He desires to hear pieces in good plain German.

VAN SWIETEN. Yes, but why comic? It is not the function of music to be funny.

SALIERI. Baron van Swieten. Prefect of the Imperial Library. Ardent Freemason. Yet to find anything funny. Known for his enthusiasm for old-fashioned music as 'Lord Fugue'.

VAN SWIETEN. I heard last week a remarkable *serious* opera from Mozart: *Idomeneo, King of Crete.*

ROSENBERG. I heard that too. A young fellow trying to impress beyond his abilities. Too much spice. Too many notes.

VON STRACK (*firmly, to* ORSINI-ROSENBERG). Nevertheless, kindly convey the commission to him today.

ROSENBERG (*taking the paper reluctantly*). I believe we are going to have trouble with this young man.

ORSINI-ROSENBERG *leaves the Light Box and strolls down the stage to* SALIERI.

ROSENBERG. He was a child prodigy. That always spells trouble. His father is Leopold Mozart, a bad-tempered Salzburg musician who dragged the boy endlessly round Europe making him play the keyboard blindfold, with one finger, and that sort of thing. (*To* SALIERI) All prodiges are hateful — *non è vero, Compositore?*

SALIEIRI. *Divengono sempre sterili con gli anni.*

ROSENBERG. *Precisamente. Precisamente.*

VON STRACK (*calling suspiciously*). What are you saying?

ROSENBERG (*airly*). Nothing, Herr Chamberlain! . . . *Niente,* Signor Pomposo! . . . (*He strolls on out.*)

VON STRACK *strides off irritated.* VAN SWIETEN *now comes downstage.*

VAN SWIETEN. We meet tomorrow, I believe, on your committee to devise pensions for old musicians.

SALIERI (*deferentially*). It's most gracious of you to attend, Baron.

VAN SWIETEN. You're a worthy man, Salieri. You should join our Brotherhood of Masons. We would welcome you warmly.

SALIERI. I would be honoured, Baron!

VAN SWIETEN. If you wished I could arrange initiation into my Lodge.

SALIERI. That would be more than my due.

VAN SWIETEN. Nonsense. We embrace men of talent of all conditions. I may invite young Mozart also: dependent on the impression he makes.

SALIERI (*bowing*). Of course, Baron.

VAN SWIETEN *goes out*.

(*To audience*:) Honour indeed. In those days almost every man of influence in Vienna was a Mason — and the Baron's Lodge by far the most fashionable. As for young Mozart, I confess I was alarmed by his coming. Not by the commission of a comic opera, even though I myself was then attempting one called *The Chimney Sweep*. No, what worried me were reports about the man himself. He was praised altogether too much.

The VENTICELLI *hurry in from either side*.

VENTICELLO 1. Such gaiety of spirit!

VENTICELLO 2. Such ease of manner!

VENTICELLO 1. Such natural charm!

SALIERI (*to the* VENTICELLI). Really? Where does he live?

VENTICELLO 1. Peter Platz.

VENTICELLO 2. Number eleven.

VENTICELLO 1. The landlady is Madame Weber.

VENTICELLO 2. A real bitch.

VENTICELLO 1. Takes in male lodgers, and has a tribe of daughters.

VENTICELLO 2. Mozart is after one of them.

VENTICELLO 1. Constanze.

VENTICELLO 2. Flighty little piece!

VENTICELLO 1. Her mother's pushing marriage.

VENTICELLO 2. His *father* isn't!

VENTICELLO 1. Daddy is worried sick!

VENTICELLO 2. Writes him every day from Salzburg!

SALIERI (*to them*). I want to meet him. What houses does he visit?

VENTICELLO 1. He'll be at the Baroness Waldstädten's tomorrow night.

SALIERI. *Grazie.*

VENTICELLO 2. Some of his music is to be played.

SALIERI (*to both*). *Restiamo in contatto.*

VENTICELLO 1 and VENTICELLO 2. *Certamente, Signore!*

> *They go off.*

SALIERI (*to audience*). So to the Baroness Waldstädten's I went. That night changed my life.

*   *   *

The Library of the Baroness Waldstädten

In the Light Box, two elegantly curtained windows surrounded by handsome subdued wallpaper.

Two SERVANTS *bring on a large table loaded with cakes and desserts. Two more carry on a grand high-backed wing-chair, which they place ceremoniously downstage at the left.*

SALIERI (*to audience*). I entered the library to take first a little refreshment. My generous hostess always put out the most delicious confections in that room whenever she knew I was coming. *Sorbetti — caramelli —* and most especially a miraculous *crema al mascarpone —* which is simply cream cheese mixed with granulated sugar and suffused with rum — which was totally irresistible!

> *He takes a little bowl of it from the cake-stand and sits in the wing-chair, facing out front. Thus seated, he is invisible to anyone entering from upstage.*

I had just sat down in a high-backed chair to consume this paradisal dish — unobservable as it happened to anyone who might come in.

Offstage, noises are heard.

CONSTANZE (*off*). Squeak! Squeak! Squeak!

CONSTANZE runs on from upstage: a pretty girl in her early twenties, full of high spirits. At this second she is pretending to be a mouse. She runs across the stage in her gay party dress, and hides under the fortepiano.

Suddenly a small, pallid, large-eyed man in a showy wig and a showy set of clothes runs in after her and freezes — centre — as a cat would freeze, hunting a mouse. This is WOLFGANG AMADEUS MOZART. As we get to know him through his next scenes, we discover several things about him: he is an extremely restless man, his hands and feet in almost continuous motion; his voice is light and high; and he is possessed of an unforgettable giggle — piercing and infantile.

MOZART. Miaouw!

CONSTANZE (*betraying where she is*). Squeak!

MOZART. Miaouw! Miaouw! Miaouw!

The composer drops on all fours and, wrinkling his face, begins spitting and stalking his prey. The mouse — giggling with excitement — breaks her cover and dashes across the floor. The cat pursues. Almost at the chair where SALIERI sits concealed, the mouse turns at bay. The cat stalks her — nearer and nearer — in its knee-breeches and elaborate coat.

I'm going to pounce-bounce! I'm going to scrunch-munch! I'm going to chew-poo my little mouse-wouse! I'm going to tear her to bits with my paws-claws!

CONSTANZE. No!

MOZART. Paws-claws! Paws-claws! . . . OHH!

He falls on her. She screams.

SALIERI (*to audience*). Before I could rise, it had become difficult to do so.

MOZART. I'm going to bite you in half with my fangs-wangs! My little Stanzerl-wanzerl-banzerl!

She giggles delightedly, lying prone beneath him.

You're trembling! . . . I think you're frightened of puss-wuss! . . . I think you're scared to death! (*Intimately*.) I think you're going to shit yourself!

She squeals, but is not really shocked.

MOZART. In a moment it's going to be on the floor!

CONSTANZE. Ssh! Someone'll hear you!

He imitates the noise of a fart.

Stop it, Wolferl! Ssh!

MOZART. Here it comes now! I can hear it *coming!* . . . Oh what a melancholy note! Something's dropping from your boat!

Another fart noise, slower. CONSTANZE *shrieks with amusement.*

CONSTANZE. Stop it now! It's stupid! Really *stupid!*

SALIERI *sits appalled.*

MOZART. Hey — Hey — what's Trazom!

CONSTANZE. What?

MOZART. T-R-A-Z-O-M. What's that mean?

CONSTANZE. How should *I* know?

MOZART. It's Mozart spelt backwards — shit-wit! If you ever married me, you'd be Constanze Trazom.

CONSTANZE. No, I wouldn't.

MOZART. Yes, you would. Because I'd want everything backwards once I was married. I'd want to lick my wife's arse instead of her face.

CONSTANZE. You're not going to lick anything at this rate. Your father's never going to give his consent to us.

The sense of fun deserts him instantly.

MOZART. And who cares about his consent?

CONSTANZE. *You* do. You care very much. You wouldn't do it without it.

MOZART. Wouldn't I?

CONSTANZE. No, you wouldn't. Because you're too scared of him. I know what he says about me. (*Solemn voice.*) 'If you marry that dreadful girl, you'll end up lying on straw with beggars for children.'

MOZART (*impulsively*). Marry me!

CONSTANZE. Don't be silly.

MOZART. Marry me!

CONSTANZE. Are you serious?

MOZART (*defiantly*). Yes! . . . Answer me this minute: yes or no! Say yes, then I can go home, climb into bed — shit over the mattress and shout 'I *did* it!'

He rolls on top of her delightedly, uttering his high whinnying giggle. The MAJOR-DOMO *of the house stalks in, upstage.*

MAJOR-DOMO (*imperviously*). Her Ladyship is ready to commence.

MOZART. Ah! . . . Yes! . . . Good! (*He picks himself up, embarrassed, and helps* CONSTANZE *to rise. With an attempt at dignity.*) Come, my dear. The music waits!

CONSTANZE (*suppressing giggles*). Oh, by all means — Herr Trazom! (*He takes her arm. They prance off together, followed by the disapproving* MAJOR-DOMO.)

SALIERI (*shaken: to audience*). And then, right away, the concert began. I heard it through the door — some Serenade: at first only vaguely — too horrified to attend. But presently the sound insisted — a solemn Adagio in E flat.

The Adagio from the Serenade for Thirteen Wind Instruments (K.361) begins to sound. Quietly and quite slowly, seated in the wing-chair, SALIERI *speaks over the music.*

It started simply enough: just a pulse in the lowest registers — bassoons and basset horns — like a rusty squeezebox. It would have been comic except for the slowness, which gave it instead a sort of serenity. And then suddenly, high above it, sounded a single note on the oboe.

We hear it.

It hung there unwavering — piercing me through — till breath could hold it no longer, and a clarinet withdrew it out of me, and sweetened it into a phrase of such delight it had me trembling. The light flickered in the room. My eyes clouded! (*With ever-increasing emotion and vigour.*) The squeezebox groaned louder, and over it the higher instruments wailed and warbled, throwing lines of sound around me — long lines of pain around and through me — Ah, the pain! Pain as I had never known it. I called up to my sharp old God '*What is this? . . . What?!*' But the squeezebox went on and on, and the pain cut deeper into my shaking head until suddenly I was running —

He bolts out of the chair and runs across the stage in a fever, to a corner, down right. Behind him in the Light Box the Library fades into a street scene at night: small houses under a rent sky. The music continues, fainter, underneath.

— dashing through the side-door, stumbling downstairs into the street, into the cold night, gasping for life. (*Calling up in agony.*) '*What?! What is this? Tell me, Signore!* What is this *pain?* What is this *need* in the sound? Forever unfulfillable yet fulfilling him who hears it, utterly. Is it *Your* need? Can it be Yours? . . .'

Pause.

Dimly the music sounded from the salon above. Dimly the stars shone on the empty street. I was suddenly frightened. It seemed to me I had heard a voice of God — and that it issued from a creature whose own voice I had also heard — and it was the voice of an obscene child!

Light change. The street scene fades.

* * *

Salieri's Apartments

It remains dark.

SALIERI. I ran home and buried my fear in work. More pupils — till there were thirty and forty. More committees to help musicians! More motets and anthems to God's glory. And at night I prayed for just one thing. (*He kneels desperately*.) 'Let your voice enter *me!* Let *me* conduct you! . . . *Let* me!' (*Pause. He rises.*) As for Mozart, I avoided meeting him — and sent out my Little Winds for whatever scores of his could be found.

The VENTICELLI *come in with manuscripts.* SALIERI *sits at the fortepiano, and they show him the music alternately, as* SERVANTS *unobtrusively remove the Waldstädten table and wing-chair.*

VENTICELLO 1. Six fortepiano sonatas composed in Munich.

VENTICELLO 2. Two in Mannheim.

VENTICELLO 1. A Parisian Symphony.

SALIERI (*to audience*). Clever. They were all clever. And yet they seemed to me completely empty!

VENTICELLO 1. A Divertimento in D.

VENTICELLO 2. A Cassazione in G.

VENTICELLO 1. A Grand Litany in E Flat.

SALIERI (*to audience*). The same. Conventional. Even boring. The productions of a precocious youngster — Leopold Mozart's swanky son — nothing more. That Serenade was obviously an exception in his work: the sort of accident which might visit any composer on a lucky day!

The VENTICELLI *go off with the music.*

Had I in fact been simply taken by surprise that the filthy creature could write music at all? . . . Suddenly I felt immensely cheered! I would seek him out and welcome him myself to Vienna!

*   *   *

The Palace of Schönbrunn

Quick light change. The EMPEROR JOSEPH *is revealed standing in bright light before the gilded mirrors and the fireplace, attended by* CHAMBERLAIN VON STRACK. *His Majesty is a dapper, cheerful figure, aged forty, largely pleased with himself and the world. Downstage, from opposite sides,* VAN SWIETEN *and* ORSINI-ROSENBERG *hurry on.*

JOSEPH. Fêtes and fireworks, gentlemen! Mozart is here! He's waiting below!

All bow.

ALL. Majesty!

JOSEPH. *Je suis follement impatient!*

SALIERI (*to audience*). The Emperor Joseph the Second of Austria. Son of Maria Theresa. Brother of Marie Antoinette. Adorer of music — provided that it made no demands upon the royal brain. (*To the* EMPEROR, *deferentially:*) Majesty, I have written a little march in Mozart's honour. May I play it as he comes in?

JOSEPH. By all means, Court Composer. What a delightful idea! Have you met him yet?

SALIERI. Not yet, Majesty.

JOSEPH. Fêtes and fireworks, what fun! Strack, bring him up at once.

VON STRACK *goes off. The* EMPEROR *comes on to the stage proper.*

Mon Dieu, I wish we could have a competition! Mozart against some other virtuoso. Two keyboards in contest. Wouldn't that be fun, Baron?

VAN SWIETEN (*stiffly*). Not to me, Majesty. In my view, musicians are not horses to be run against one another.

Slight pause.

JOSEPH. Ah. Well — there it is.

VON STRACK *returns.*

VON STRACK. Herr Mozart, Majesty.

JOSEPH. Ah! Splendid! . . . (*Conspiratorially he signs to* SALIERI, *who moves quickly to the fortepiano.*) Court Composer — *allons!* (*To* VON STRACK:) Admit him, please.

Instantly SALIERI *sits at the instrument and strikes up his*

March on the keyboard. At the same moment MOZART *struts in, wearing a highly ornate surcoat, with dress-sword.*

The EMPEROR *stands downstage, centre, his back to the audience, and as* MOZART *approaches he signs to him to halt and listen. Bewildered,* MOZART *does so — becoming aware of* SALIERI *playing his March of Welcome. It is an extremely banal piece, vaguely — but only vaguely — reminiscent of another march to become very famous later on. All stand frozen in attitudes of listening, until* SALIERI *comes to a finish. Applause.*

JOSEPH (*to* SALIERI). Charming . . . *Comme d'habitude!* (*He turns and extends his hand to be kissed.*) Mozart.

MOZART approaches and kneels extravagantly.

MOZART. Majesty! Your Majesty's humble slave! Let me kiss your royal hand a hundred thousand times!

He kisses it greedily, over and over again; until its owner withdraws it in embarrassment.

JOSEPH. *Non, non, s'il vous plaît!* A little less enthusiasm, I beg you. Come sir, *levez-vous!* (*He assists* MOZART *to rise.*) You will not recall it, but the last time we met you were also on the floor! My sister remembers it to this day. This young man — all of six years old, mind you — slipped on the floor at Schönbrunn — came a nasty purler on his little head . . . Have I told you this before?

ROSENBERG (*hastily*). No, Majesty!

VON STRACK (*hastily*). No, Majesty!

SALIERI (*hastily*). No, Majesty!

JOSEPH. Well, my sister Antoinette runs forward and picks him up herself. And do you know what he does? Jumps right into her arms — hoopla, just like that! — kisses her on both cheeks and says 'Will you marry me: yes or no?'

The COURTIERS *laugh politely.* MOZART *emits his high-pitched giggle. The* EMPEROR *is clearly startled by it.*

JOSEPH. I do not mean to embarrass you, Herr Mozart. You

know everyone here, surely?

MOZART. Yes, sire. (*Bowing elaborately to*
ORSINI-ROSENBERG.) Herr Director! (*To* VAN SWIETEN:)
Herr Prefect.

VAN SWIETEN (*warmly*). Delighted to see you again.

JOSEPH. But not, I think, our esteemed Court Composer! . . . A
most serious omission! No one who cares for art can afford
not to know Herr Salieri. He wrote that exquisite little March
of Welcome for you.

SALIERI. It was a trifle, Majesty.

JOSEPH. Nevertheless . . .

MOZART (*to* SALIERI). I'm overwhelmed, Signore!

JOSEPH. Ideas simply pour out of him — don't they, Strack?

STRACK. Endlessly, sire. (*As if tipping him.*) Well done, Salieri.

JOSEPH. Let it be my pleasure then to introduce you! Court
Composer Salieri — Herr Mozart of Salzburg!

SALIERI (*sleekly, to* MOZART). *Finalmente. Che gioia. Che
diletto straordinario.*

*He gives him a prim bow and presents the copy of his music to
the other composer, who accepts it with a flood of Italian.*

MOZART. *Grazie Signore! Mille milione di benvenuti! Sono
commosso! È un onore eccezionale incontrarla! Compositore
brillante e famosissimo!*

He makes an elaborate and showy bow in return.

SALIERI (*dryly*). Grazie.

JOSEPH. Tell me, Mozart, have you received our commission for
the opera?

MOZART. Indeed I have, Majesty! I am so grateful I can hardly
speak! . . . I swear to you that you will have the best — the
most perfect entertainment ever offered a monarch. I've
already found a libretto.

ROSENBERG (*startled*). Have you? I didn't hear of this!

MOZART. Forgive me, Herr Director, I entirely omitted to tell you.

ROSENBERG. May I ask why?

MOZART. It didn't seem very important.

ROSENBERG. Not important?

MOZART. Not really, no.

ROSENBERG (*irritated*). It is important to *me*, Herr Mozart.

MOZART (*embarrassed*). Yes, I see that. Of course.

ROSENBERG. And who, pray is it by?

MOZART. Stephanie.

ROSENBERG. A most unpleasant man.

MOZART. But a brilliant writer.

ROSENBERG. Do you think?

MOZART. The story is really amusing, Majesty. The whole plot is set in a — (*He giggles*) — in a . . .

JOSEPH (*eagerly*). Where? Where is it set?

MOZART. It's — it's — rather saucy, Majesty!

JOSEPH. Yes, yes! Where?

MOZART. Well it's actually set in a *seraglio*.

JOSEPH. A what?

MOZART. A pasha's harem. (*He giggles wildly*.)

ROSENBERG. And you imagine that is a suitable subject for performance at a National Theatre?

MOZART (*in a panic*). Yes! No! Yes, I mean yes, yes I do. Why not? It's very funny, it's amusing . . . on my honour — Majesty — there's nothing offensive in it. Nothing offensive in the world. It's full of proper German virtues, I swear it! . . .

SALIERI (*blandly*). *Scusate*, Signore, but what are those? Being a foreigner I'm not sure.

JOSEPH. You are being *cattivo*, Court Composer.

SALIERI. Not at all, Majesty.

JOSEPH. Come then, Mozart. Name us a proper German virtue!

MOZART. Love, Sire. I have yet to see that expressed in any opera.

VAN SWIETEN. Well answered, Mozart.

SALIERI (*smiling*). *Scusate.* I was under the impression one rarely saw anything *else* expressed in opera.

MOZART. I mean manly love, Signore. Not male sopranos screeching. Or stupid couples rolling their eyes. All that absurd Italian rubbish.

Pause. Tension. ORSINI-ROSENBERG *coughs.*

I mean the real thing.

JOSEPH. And do you know the real thing yourself, Herr Mozart?

MOZART. Under your pardon, I think I do, Majesty. (*He gives a short giggle.*)

JOSEPH. Bravo. When do you think it will be done?

MOZART. The first act is already finished.

JOSEPH. But it can't be more than two weeks since you started!

MOZART. Composing is not hard when you have the right audience to please, Sire.

VAN SWIETEN. A charming reply, Majesty.

JOSEPH. Indeed, Baron. Fêtes and fireworks! I see we are going to have fêtes and fireworks! *Au revoir, Monsieur Mozart. Soyez bienvenu à la cour.*

MOZART (*with expert rapidity*). *Majesté! — je suis comblé d'honneur d'être accepté dans la maison du Père de tous les musiciens! Servir un monarque aussi plein de discernement que votre Majesté, c'est un honneur qui dépasse le sommet de mes dûs!*

A pause. The EMPEROR *is taken aback by this flood of French.*

JOSEPH. Ah. Well — there it is. I'll leave you gentlemen to get better acquainted.

SALIERI. Good day, Majesty.

MOZART. *Votre Majesté.*

> *They both bow.* JOSEPH *goes out.*

ROSENBERG. Good day to you.

VON STRACK. Good day.

> *They follow the* EMPEROR.

VAN SWIETEN (*warmly shaking his hand*). Welcome, Mozart. I shall see much more of you. Depend on it!

MOZART. Thank you.

> *He bows. The* BARON *goes.* MOZART *and* SALIERI *are left alone.*

SALIERI. *Bene.*

MOZART. *Bene.*

SALIERI. I too wish you success with your opera.

MOZART. I'll have it. It's going to be superb. I must tell you I have already found the most excellent singer for the leading part.

SALIERI. Oh: who is that?

MOZART. Her name is Cavalieri. Katherina Cavalieri. She's really German, but she thinks it will advance her career if she sports an Italian name.

SALIERI. She's quite right. It was my idea. She is in fact my prize pupil. Actually she's a very innocent child. Silly in the way of young singers — but, you know, she's only twenty.

> *Without emphasis* MOZART *freezes his movements and* SALIERI *takes one easy step forward to make a fluent aside.*

(*To audience*:) I had kept my hands off Katherina. Yes! But, I could not bear to think of anyone else's upon her — least of all his!

MOZART (*unfreezing*). You're a good fellow, Salieri! And that's a jolly little thing you wrote for me.

SALIERI. It was my pleasure.

MOZART. Let's see if I can remember it. May I?

SALIERI. By all means. It's yours.

MOZART. *Grazie*, Signore.

MOZART tosses the manuscript on to the lid of the fortepiano where he cannot see it, sits at the instrument, and plays SALIERI's March of Welcome perfectly from memory — at first slowly, recalling it — but on the reprise of the tune, very much faster.

The rest is just the same, isn't it?

He finishes it with insolent speed.

SALIERI. You have a remarkable memory.

MOZART (*delighted with himself*). *Grazie ancora*, Signore!

He plays the opening seven bars again, but this time stops on the interval of the Fourth, and sounds it again with displeasure.

It doesn't really *work*, that Fourth — does it! . . . Let's try the Third above . . . (*He does so — and smiles happily.*) Ah yes! . . . Good! . . .

He repeats the new interval, leading up to it smartly with the well-known military-trumpet arpeggio which characterizes the celebrated March from The Marriage of Figaro, '*Non più andrai*'. *Then, using the interval — tentatively — delicately — one note at a time, in the treble — he steals into the famous tune itself.*

On and on he plays, improvising happily what is virtually the march we know now, laughing gleefully each time he comes to the amended interval of a Third. SALIERI watches him with an answering smile painted on his face.

MOZART's playing grows more and more exhibitionistic — revealing to the audience the formidable virtuoso he is. The whole time he himself remains totally oblivious to the offence he is giving. Finally he finishes the March with a series of triumphant flourishes and chords!

An ominous pause.

SALIERI. *Scusate.* I must go.

MOZART. Really? (*Springing up and indicating the keyboard.*) Why don't *you* try a Variation?

SALIERI. Thank you, but I must attend on the Emperor.

MOZART. Ah.

SALIERI. It has been delightful to meet you.

MOZART. For me too! . . . And thanks for the March!

> MOZART *picks up the manuscript from the top of the fortepiano and marches happily offstage.*
>
> *A slight pause.*
>
> SALIERI *moves towards the audience. The lights go down around him.*

SALIERI (*to audience*). Was it then — so early — that I began to have thoughts of murder? . . . Of course not: at least not in Life. In Art it was a different matter. I decided I would compose a huge tragic opera: something to astonish the world! — and I knew my theme. I would set the Legend of Danaius, who for a monstrous crime was chained to a rock for eternity — his head repeatedly struck by lightning! Wickedly in my head I saw Mozart in that position. In reality the man was in no danger at all . . . Not yet.

*   *   *

The First Performance of *The Abduction from the Seraglio*

The light changes, and the stage instantly turns into an eighteenth-century theatre. The backdrop projection shows a line of softly gleaming chandeliers.

> *The* SERVANTS *bring in chairs and benches. Upon them, facing the audience and regarding it as if watching an opera, sit the* EMPEROR JOSEPH, VON STRACK, ORSINI-ROSENBERG *and* VAN SWIETEN.
>
> *Next to them:* KAPELLMEISTER BONNO *and* TERESA SALIERI.
>
> *A little behind them:* CONSTANZE. *Behind her:* CITIZENS OF VIENNA.

SALIERI. The first performance of *The Abduction from the Seraglio*. The creature's expression of manly love.

MOZART *comes on briskly, wearing a gaudy new coat and a new powdered wig. He struts quickly to the fortepiano, sits at it and mimes conducting.* SALIERI *sits nearby, next to his wife, and watches* MOZART *intently.*

He himself contrived to wear for the occasion an even more vulgar coat than usual. As for the music, it matched the coat completely. For my dear pupil Katherina Cavalieri he had written quite simply the showiest aria I'd ever heard.

Faintly we hear the whizzing scale passages for SOPRANO *which end the aria 'Marten Aller Arten'.*

Ten minutes of scales and ornaments, amounting in sum to a vast emptiness. So ridiculous was the piece in fact — so much what might be demanded by a foolish young soprano — that I knew precisely what Mozart must have demanded in return for it.

The final orchestral chords of the aria. Silence. No one moves.

Although engaged to be married, *he'd had her!* I knew that beyond any doubt. (*Bluntly:*) The creature had had my darling girl.

Loudly we hear the brilliant Turkish Finale of Seraglio. *Great applause from those watching.* MOZART *jumps to his feet and acknowledges it. The* EMPEROR *rises — as do all — and gestures graciously to the 'stage' in invitation.* KATHERINA CAVALIERI *runs on in her costume, all plumes and flounces, to renewed cheering and clapping. She curtsies to the* EMPEROR — *is kissed by* SALIERI — *presented to his wife — curtsies again to* MOZART *and, flushed with triumph, moves to one side.*

In the ensuing brief silence CONSTANZE *rushes down from the back, wildly excited. She flings herself on* MOZART, *not even noticing the* EMPEROR.

CONSTANZE. Oh, well done, lovey! . . . Well done, pussy-wussy! . . .

MOZART *indicates the proximity of His Majesty.*

Oh! . . . 'Scuse *me!* (*She curtsies in embarrassment.*)

MOZART. Majesty, may I present my fiancée, Fraulein Weber.

JOSEPH. *Enchanté, Fraulein.*

CONSTANZE. Your Majesty!

MOZART. Constanze is a singer herself.

JOSEPH. Indeed?

CONSTANZE (*embarrassed*). I'm not at all, Majesty. Don't be silly, Wolfgang!

JOSEPH. So, Mozart — a good effort. Decidedly that. A good effort.

MOZART. Did you really like it, Sire?

JOSEPH. I thought it was most interesting. Yes, indeed. A trifle — how shall one say? (*To* ORSINI-ROSENBERG:) How shall one say, Director?

ROSENBERG (*subserviently*). Too many notes, Your Majesty?

JOSEPH. Very well put. Too many notes.

MOZART. I don't understand.

JOSEPH. My dear fellow, don't take it too hard. There are in fact only so many notes the ear can hear in the course of an evening. I think I'm right in saying that, aren't I, Court Composer?

SALIERI (*uncomfortably*). Well yes, I would say yes, on the whole, yes, Majesty.

JOSEPH. There you are. It's clever. It's German. It's quality work. And there are simply too many notes. Do you see?

MOZART. There are just as many notes, Majesty, neither more nor less, as are required.

Pause.

JOSEPH. Ah . . . Well, there it is. (*He goes off abruptly, followed by* ROSENBERG *and* VON STRACK.)

MOZART (*nervous*). Is he angry?

SALIERI. Not at all. He respects you for your views.

MOZART (*nervously*). I hope so . . . What did you think yourself, sir? Did you care for the piece at all?

SALIERI. Yes, of course, Mozart — at its best it is truly charming.

MOZART. And at other times?

SALIERI (*smoothly*). Well, just occasionally at other times — in Katherina's aria, for example — it was a little excessive.

MOZART. Katherina is an excessive girl. In fact she's insatiable.

SALIERI. All the same, as my revered teacher the Chevalier Gluck used to say to me — one must avoid music that smells of music.

MOZART. What does that mean?

SALIERI. Music which makes one aware too much of the virtuosity of the composer.

MOZART. Gluck is absurd.

SALIERI. What do you say?

MOZART. He's talked all his life about modernizing opera, but creates people so lofty they sound as though they shit marble.

CONSTANZE *gives a little scream of shock*.

CONSTANZE. Oh, 'scuse me! . . .

MOZART (*breaking out*). No, but it's too much! Gluck says! Gluck says! Chevalier Gluck! . . . What's Chevalier? I'm a Chevalier. The Pope made me a Chevalier when I was still wetting my bed.

CONSTANZE. Wolferl!

MOZART. Anyway it's ridiculous. Only stupid farts sport titles.

SALIERI (*blandly*). Such as Court Composer?

MOZART. What? . . . (*Realizing.*) Ah. Oh. Ha. Ha. Well! . . . My father's right again. He always tells me I should padlock my mouth . . . Actually, I shouldn't speak at all!

SALIERI (*soothingly*). Nonsense. I'm just being what the

Emperor would call *cattivo*. Won't you introduce me to your charming fiancée?

MOZART. Oh, of course! Constanze, this is Herr Salieri, the Court Composer. Fraulein Weber.

SALIERI (*bowing*). Delighted, *cara Fraulein*.

CONSTANZE (*bobbing*). How do you do, Excellency?

SALIERI. May I ask when you marry?

MOZART (*nervously*). We have to secure my father's consent. He's an excellent man — a wonderful man — but in some ways a little stubborn.

SALIERI. Excuse me, but how old are you?

MOZART. Twenty-six.

SALIERI. Then your father's consent is scarcely indispensable.

CONSTANZE (*to* MOZART). You see?

MOZART (*uncomfortably*). Well no, it's not *indispensable* — of course not! . . .

SALIERI. My advice to you is to marry and be happy. You have found — it's quite obvious — *un tesoro raro!*

CONSTANZE. Ta very much.

SALIERI *kisses* CONSTANZE's *hand. She is delighted.*

SALIERI. Good night to you both.

CONSTANZE. Good night, Excellency!

MOZART. Good night, sir. And thank you . . . Come, Stanzerl.

They depart delightedly. He watches them go.

SALIERI (*to audience*). As I watched her walk away on the arm of the Creature, I felt the lightning thought strike — 'Have her! Her for Katherina!' . . . Abomination! . . . Never in my life had I entertained a notion so sinful!

Light change: the eighteenth century fades.

The VENTICELLI *come on merrily, as if from some celebration. One holds a bottle; the other a glass.*

VENTICELLO 1. They're married.

SALIERI (*to them*). What?

VENTICELLO 2. Mozart and Weber — married!

SALIERI. Really?

VENTICELLO 1. His father will be furious!

VENTICELLO 2. They didn't even wait for his consent!

SALIERI. Have they set up house?

VENTICELLO 1. Wipplingerstrasse.

VENTICELLO 2. Number twelve.

VENTICELLO 1. Not bad.

VENTICELLO 2. Considering they've no money.

SALIERI. Is that really true?

VENTICELLO 1. He's wildly extravagant.

VENTICELLO 2. Lives way beyond his means.

SALIERI. But he has pupils.

VENTICELLO 1. Only three.

SALIERI (*to them*). Why so few?

VENTICELLO 1. He's embarrassing.

VENTICELLO 2. Makes scenes.

VENTICELLO 1. Makes enemies.

VENTICELLO 2. Even Strack, whom he cultivates.

SALIERI. Chamberlain Strack?

VENTICELLO 1. Only last night.

VENTICELLO 2. At Kapellmeister Bonno's.

*   *   *

Bonno's House

Instant light change. MOZART *comes in with* VON STRACK. *He is high on wine, and holding a glass. The* VENTICELLI *join the scene, but still talk out of it to* SALIERI. *One of them fills* MOZART's *glass.*

MOZART. Seven months in this city and not one job! I'm not to be tried again, is that it?

VON STRACK. Of course not.

MOZART. I know what goes on — and so do you. Germany is completely in the hands of foreigners. Worthless wops like *Kapellmeister Bonno!*

VON STRACK. Please! You're in the man's house!

MOZART. Court Composer *Salieri!*

VON STRACK. Hush!

MOZART. Did you see his last opera? — *The Chimney Sweep?* . . . Did you?

VON STRACK. Of course I did.

MOZART. Dogshit. Dried dogshit.

VON STRACK (*outraged*). I beg your pardon!

MOZART (*singing*). Pom-pom, pom-pom, pom-pom, pom-pom! Tonic and dominant, tonic and dominant from here to resurrection! Not one interesting modulation all night. Salieri is a musical idiot!

VON STRACK. Please!

VENTICELLO 1 (*to* SALIERI). He'd had too much to drink.

VENTICELLO 2. He often has.

MOZART. Why are Italians so terrified by the slightest complexity in music? Show them one chromatic passage and they *faint!* . . . 'Oh how sick!' 'How morbid!' (*Falsetto :*) *Morboso!* . . . *Nervoso!* . . . *Ohimè!* . . . No wonder the music at this court is so dreary.

VON STRACK. Lower your voice.

MOZART. Lower your breeches! . . . That's just a joke — just a joke!

Unobserved by him COUNT ORSINI-ROSENBERG *has entered upstage and is suddenly standing between the* VENTICELLI, *listening. He wears a waistcoat of bright green silk, and an expression of supercilious interest.* MOZART *sees him. A pause.*

(*Pleasantly, to* ORSINI-ROSENBERG:) You look like a toad . . . I mean you're goggling like a toad. (*He giggles.*)

ROSENBERG (*blandly*). You would do best to retire tonight, for your own sake.

MOZART. Salieri has fifty pupils. I have three. How am I to live? I'm a married man now! . . . Of course I realize you don't concern yourselves with *money* in these exalted circles. All the same, did you know behind his back His Majesty is known as Kaiser Keep It? (*He giggles wildly.*)

VON STRACK. *Mozart!*

He stops.

MOZART. I shouldn't have said that, should I? . . . Forgive me. It was just a joke. Another joke! . . . I can't help myself! . . . We're all friends here, aren't we?

VON STRACK *and* ORSINI-ROSENBERG *glare at him. Then* VON STRACK *leaves abruptly, much offended.*

MOZART. What's wrong with him?

ROSENBERG. Good night.

He turns to go.

MOZART. No, no, no — please! (*He grabs the* DIRECTOR's *arm.*) Your hand please, first!

Unwillingly ORSINI-ROSENBERG *gives him his hand.* MOZART *kisses it.*

(*Humbly:*) Give me a Post, sir.

ROSENBERG. That is not in my power, Mozart.

MOZART. The Princess Elizabeth is looking for an Instructor. One word from you could secure it for me.

ROSENBERG. I regret that is solely in the recommendation of Court Composer Salieri. (*He disengages himself.*)

MOZART. Do you know I am better than any musician in Vienna? . . . Do you?

ROSENBERG *leaves.* MOZART *calls after him.*

Foppy-wops — I'm *sick* of them! . . . (*Suddenly he giggles to himself, like a child.*) Foppy-wops! Foppy — poppy — snoppy — toppy — hoppy hoppy — wops! — wops!

And hops offstage.

SALIERI (*watching him go*). Barely one month later, that thought of revenge became more than thought.

*   *   *

The Waldstädten Library

Two simultaneous shouts bring up the lights. Against the handsome wallpaper stand three masked figures: CONSTANZE, flanked on either side by the VENTICELLI. All three are guests at a party, and are playing a game of forfeits.

Two SERVANTS stand frozen, holding the large wing-chair between them. Two more SERVANTS hold the big table of sweetmeats.

VENTICELLO 1. Forfeit! . . . Forfeit! . . .

VENTICELLO 2. Forfeit, Stanzerl! You've got to forfeit!

CONSTANZE. I won't.

VENTICELLO 1. You have to.

VENTICELLO 2. It's the game.

The SERVANTS unfreeze and set down the furniture. SALIERI moves to the wing-chair and sits.

SALIERI (*to audience*). Once again — believe it or not — I was in the same concealing chair in the Baroness's library — (*taking a cup from the little table*) — and consuming the same delicious dessert.

VENTICELLO 1. You lost — now there's the penalty!

SALIERI (*to audience*). A party celebrating the New Year's Eve. I was on my own — my dear spouse Teresa visiting her parents in Italy.

CONSTANZE. Well, *what?* . . . What is it?

VENTICELLO 1 snatches up an old-fashioned round ruler from the fortepiano.

VENTICELLO 1. I want to measure your calves.

CONSTANZE. Ooooo!

VENTICELLO 1. Well?

CONSTANZE. Definitely not. You cheeky bugger!

VENTICELLO 1. Now come on!

VENTICELLO 2. You've got to let him, Stanzerl. All's fair in love and forfeits.

CONSTANZE. No it isn't — so you can both buzz off!

VENTICELLO 1. If you don't let me, you won't be allowed to play again.

CONSTANZE. Well choose something else.

VENTICELLO 1. I've chosen that. Now get up on the table. Quick, quick! *Allez-oop!* (*Gleefully he shifts the plates of sweetmeats from the table.*)

CONSTANZE. Quick, then! . . . Before anyone sees!

The two masked men lift the shrieking masked girl up on to the table.

VENTICELLO 1. Hold her, Friedrich.

CONSTANZE. I don't have to be held, thank you!

VENTICELLO 2. Yes, you do: that's part of the penalty.

He holds her ankles firmly, while VENTICELLO 1 *thrusts the ruler under her skirts and measures her legs. Excitedly* SALIERI *reverses his position so that he can kneel in the wing-chair, and watch.* CONSTANZE *giggles delightedly, then becomes outraged — or pretends to be.*

CONSTANZE. Stop it! . . . Stop that! That's quite enough of that!

She bends down and tries to slap him.

VENTICELLO 1. Seventeen inches — knee to ankle!

VENTICELLO 2. Let me do it! You hold her!

CONSTANZE. That's not fair!

VENTICELLO 2. Yes, it is. You lost to me too.

CONSTANZE. It's been done now! Let me *down!*

VENTICELLO 2. Hold her, Karl.

CONSTANZE. No! . . .

>VENTICELLO 1 *holds her ankles.* VENTICELLO 2 *thrusts his head entirely under her skirts. She squeals.*

No — stop it! . . . *No!* . . .

>*In the middle of this undignified scene* MOZART *comes rushing on — also masked.*

MOZART (*outraged*). Constanze!

>*They freeze.* SALIERI *ducks back down and sits hidden in the chair.*

Gentlemen, if you please.

CONSTANZE. It's only a game, Wolferl! . . .

VENTICELLO 1. We meant no harm, 'pon my word.

MOZART (*stiffly*). Come down off that table please.

>*They hand her down.*

Thank you. We'll see you later.

VENTICELLO 2. Now look, Mozart, don't be pompous —

MOZART. Please excuse us now.

>*They go. The little man is very angry. He tears off his mask.*

(*To* CONSTANZE:) Do you realize what you've done?

CONSTANZE. No, what? . . . (*Flustered, she busies herself restoring the plates of sweetmeats to the table.*)

MOZART. Just lost your reputation, that's all! You're now a loose girl.

CONSTANZE. Don't be so stupid. (*She too removes her mask.*)

MOZART. You are a married woman, for God's sake!

CONSTANZE. And what of it?

MOZART. A young wife does not allow her legs to be handled in public. Couldn't you at least have measured your own ugly legs?

CONSTANZE. *What?*

MOZART (*raising his voice*). Do you know what you've done?! . . . You've shamed me — that's all! *Shamed* me!

CONSTANZE. Oh, don't be so ridiculous!

MOZART. Shamed me — in front of *them!*

CONSTANZE (*suddenly furious*). *You?* Shamed *you?* . . . That's a laugh! If there's any shame around, lovey, it's *mine!*

MOZART. What do you mean?

CONSTANZE. You've only had every pupil who ever came to you.

MOZART. That's not true.

CONSTANZE. Every single female pupil!

MOZART. Name them! *Name them!*

CONSTANZE. The Aurnhammer girl! The Rumbeck girl! Katherina Cavalieri — that sly little whore! *She* wasn't even your pupil — she was Salieri's. Which actually, my dear, may be why he has hundreds and you have none! He doesn't drag them into bed!

MOZART. Of course he doesn't! He can't get it up, that's why! . . . Have you heard his music? That's the sound of someone who *can't get it up!* At least *I* can do that!

CONSTANZE. I'm sick of you!

MOZART (*shouting*). No one ever said I couldn't do *that!*

CONSTANZE (*bursting into tears*). I don't give a fart! I hate you! I hate you for ever and ever — I hate you! (*A tiny pause. She weeps.*)

MOZART (*helplessly*). Oh Stanzerl, don't cry. Please don't cry . . . I can't bear it when you cry. I just didn't want you to look cheap in people's eyes, that's all. Here! (*He snatches up the ruler.*) Beat me . . . Beat me . . . I'm your slave. Stanzi marini. Stanzi marini bini gini. I'll just stand here like a little lamb and bear your strokes. Here. Do it . . . *Batti.*

CONSTANZE. No.

MOZART. *Batti, batti. Mio tesoro!*

CONSTANZE. No!

MOZART. Stanzerly wanzerly piggly poo!

CONSTANZE. Stop it.

MOZART. Stanzy wanzy had a fit! Shit her stays and made them split!

She giggles despite herself.

CONSTANZE. Stop it!

MOZART. When they took away her skirt, Stanzy wanzy ate the dirt!

CONSTANZE. Stop it now! (*She snatches the ruler and gives him a whack with it. He yowls playfully.*)

MOZART. Oooo! Oooo! Oooo! Do it again! Do it again! I cast myself at your stinking feet, Madonna!

He does so. She whacks him some more as he crouches, but always lightly, scarcely looking at him, divided between tears and laughter. MOZART *drums his feet with pleasure.*

MOZART. Ow! Ow! Ow!

And then suddenly SALIERI, *unable to bear another second, cries out involuntarily.*

SALIERI. *Ah!!!*

The young couple freeze. SALIERI — *discovered* — *hastily converts his noise of disgust into a yawn, and stretches as if waking up from a nap. He peers out of the wing-chair.*

SALIERI. Good evening.

CONSTANZE (*embarrassed*). Excellency . . .

MOZART. How long have you been there?

SALIERI. I was asleep until a second ago. Are you two quarrelling?

MOZART. No, of course not.

CONSTANZE. Yes, we are. He's being very irritating.

SALIERI (*rising*). *Caro Herr,* tonight is the time for New Year resolutions. Irritating lovely ladies cannot surely be one of yours. May I suggest you bring us each a *sorbetto* from the dining-room?

MOZART. But why don't we all go to the table?

CONSTANZE. Herr Salieri is quite right. Bring them here — it'll be your punishment.

MOZART. Stanzi!

SALIERI. Come now, I can keep your wife company. There cannot be a better peace offering than a *sorbetto* of aniseed.

CONSTANZE. I prefer tangerine.

SALIERI. Very well, tangerine. (*Greedily*:) But if you could possibly manage aniseed for me, I'd be deeply obliged . . . So the New Year can begin coolly for all three of us.

A pause. MOZART *hesitates — and then bows.*

MOZART. I'm honoured, Signore, of course. And then I'll play you at billiards. What do you say?

SALIERI. I'm afraid I don't play.

MOZART (*with surprise*). You don't?

CONSTANZE. Wolferl would rather play at billards than anything. He's very good at it.

MOZART. I'm the best! I may nod occasionally at composing, but at billiards — never!

SALIERI. A virtuoso of the cue.

MOZART. Exactly! It's a virtuoso's game! . . . (*He snatches up the ruler and treats it as if it were a cue.*) I think I shall write a Grand Fantasia for Billiard Balls! Trillos! Acciaccaturas! Whole arpeggios in ivory! Then I'll play it myself in public! . . . It'll have to be *me* because none of those Italian charlatans like Clementi will be able to get his fingers round the cue! *Scusate,* Signore!

He gives a swanky flourish of the hand and struts off.

CONSTANZE. He's a love, really.

SALIERI. And lucky, too, in you. You are, if I may say so, an astonishing creature.

CONSTANZE. Me? . . . Ta very much.

SALIERI. On the other hand, your husband does not appear to be so thriving.

CONSTANZE (*seizing her opportunity*). We're desperate, sir.

SALIERI. What?

CONSTANZE. We've no money and no prospects of any. That's the truth.

SALIERI. I don't understand. He gives many public concerts.

CONSTANZE. They don't pay enough. What he needs is pupils. Illustrious pupils. His father calls us spendthrifts, but that's unfair. I manage as well as anyone could. There's simply not enough. Don't tell him I talked to you, please.

SALIERI (*intimately*). This is solely between us. How can I help?

CONSTANZE. My husband needs security, sir. If only he could find regular employment, everything would be all right. Is there nothing at Court?

SALIERI. Not at the moment.

CONSTANZE (*harder*). The Princess Elizabeth needs a tutor.

SALIERI. Really? I hadn't heard.

CONSTANZE. One word from you and the post would be his. Other pupils would follow at once . . .

SALIERI (*looking off*). He's coming back.

CONSTANZE. Please . . . please, Excellency. You can't imagine what a difference it would make.

SALIERI. We can't speak of it now.

CONSTANZE. When then? Oh, please!

SALIERI. Can you come and see me tomorrow? Alone?

CONSTANZE. I can't do that.

SALIERI. I'm a married man.

CONSTANZE. All the same.

SALIERI. When does he work?

CONSTANZE. Afternoons.

SALIERI. Then come at three.

CONSTANZE. I can't possibly!

SALIERI. Yes or no? In his interests?

A pause. She hesitates — opens her mouth — then smiles and abruptly runs off.

SALIERI (*to audience*). So I'd done it! Spoken aloud. Invited her! What of that vow made in church? Fidelity — virtue — all of that? I couldn't think of that now! . . .

SERVANTS *remove the Waldstädten furniture. Others replace it with two small gilded chairs, centre, quite close together. Others again surreptitiously bring in the old dressing-gown and shawl which* SALIERI *discarded before Scene Three, placing them on the fortepiano.*

*   *   *

Salieri's Salon

On the curtains are thrown again projections of long windows.

SALIERI. Next afternoon I waited in a fever! Would she come? I had no idea. And if she did, how would I behave? I had no idea of that either. Was I actually going to seduce a young wife of two months' standing? . . . Part of me — much of me — wanted it, badly. *Badly.* Yes, badly was the word! . . .

The clock strikes three. On the first stroke the bell sounds. He rises excitedly.

There she was! On the stroke! She'd come . . . She *come!*

Enter from the right the COOK, *still as fat, but forty years younger. He proudly carries a plate piled with brandied chestnuts.* SALIERI *takes them from him nervously, nodding with approval, and sets them on the table.*

(To the COOK:) *Grazie. Grazie tanti . . . Via, via, via!*

The COOK *bows as* SALIERI *dismisses him, and goes out the same way, smirking suggestively. The* VALET *comes in from the left — he is also forty years younger — and behind him* CONSTANZE, *wearing a pretty hat and carrying a portfolio.*

SALIERI. Signora!

CONSTANZE (*curtseying*). Excellency.

SALIERI. *Benvenuta.* (*To* VALET *in dismissal:*) *Grazie.*

The VALET *goes.*

Well. You have come.

CONSTANZE. I should not have done. My husband would be frantic if he knew. He's a very jealous man.

SALIERI. Are you a jealous woman?

CONSTANZE. Why do you ask?

SALIERI. It's not a passion I understand . . . You're looking even prettier than you were last night, if I may say so.

CONSTANZE. Ta very much! . . . I brought you some manuscripts by Wolfgang. When you see them you'll understand how right he is for a royal appointment. Will you look at them, please, while I wait?

SALIERI. You mean now?

CONSTANZE. Yes, I have to take them back with me. He'll miss them otherwise. He doesn't make copies. These are all the originals.

SALIERI. Sit down. Let me offer you something special.

CONSTANZE (*sitting*). What's that?

SALIERI (*producing the box*). *Capezzoli di Venere.* Nipples of Venus. Roman chestnuts in brandied sugar.

CONSTANZE. No, thank you.

SALIERI. Do try. My cook made them especially for you.

CONSTANZE. Me?

SALIERI. Yes. They're quite rare.

CONSTANZE. Well then, I'd better, hadn't I? Just one . . . Ta very much. (*She takes one and puts it in her mouth. The taste amazes her.*) Oh! . . . Oh! . . . Oh! . . . They're *delish!*

SALIERI (*lustfully watching her eat*). Aren't they?

CONSTANZE. Mmmmm!

SALIERI. Have another.

CONSTANZE (*taking two more*). I couldn't possibly.

Carefully he moves round behind her, and seats himself on the chair next to her.

SALIERI. I think you're the most generous girl in the world.

CONSTANZE. Generous?

SALIERI. It's my word for you. I thought last night that Constanze is altogether too stiff a name for that girl. I shall rechristen her 'Generosa'. *La Generosa.* Then I'll write a glorious song for her under that title and she'll sing it, just for me.

CONSTANZE (*smiling*). I am much out of practice, sir.

SALIERI. *La Generosa.* (*He leans a little towards her.*) Don't tell me it's going to prove inaccurate, my name for you.

CONSTANZE (*coolly*). What name do you give your wife, Excellency?

SALIERI (*equally coolly*). I'm not an Excellency, and I call my wife Signora Salieri. If I named her anything else it would be *La Statua.* She's a very upright lady.

CONSTANZE. Is she here now? I'd like to meet her.

SALIERI. Alas, no. At the moment she's visiting her mother in Verona.

She starts very slightly out of her chair. SALIERI *gently restrains her.*

Constanze: tomorrow evening I dine with the Emperor. One word from me recommending your husband as Tutor to the Princess Elizabeth, and that invaluable post is his. Believe me, when I speak to His Majesty in matters musical, no one contradicts me.

CONSTANZE. I believe you.

SALIERI. *Bene.* (*Still sitting, he takes his mouchoir and delicately wipes her mouth with it.*) Surely service of that sort deserves a little recompense in return?

CONSTANZE. How little?

Slight pause.

SALIERI. The size of a kiss.

Slight pause.

CONSTANZE. Just one?

Slight pause.

SALIERI. If one seems fair to you.

She looks at him — then kisses him lightly on the mouth.

Longer pause.

Does it?

She gives him a longer kiss. He makes to touch her with his hand. She breaks off.

CONSTANZE. I fancy that's fairness enough.

Pause.

SALIERI (*carefully*). A pity . . . It's somewhat small pay, to secure a post every musician in Vienna is hoping for.

CONSTANZE. What do you mean?

SALIERI. Is it not clear?

CONSTANZE. No. Not at all.

SALIERI. Another pity . . . A thousand pities.

Pause.

CONSTANZE. I don't believe it . . . I just don't believe it!

SALIERI. What?

CONSTANZE. What you've just said.

SALIERI (*hastily*). I said nothing. What did I say?

CONSTANZE *gets up and* SALIERI *rises in panic.*

CONSTANZE. Oh, I'm going! . . . I'm getting out of this!

SALIERI. Constanze . . .

CONSTANZE. Let me pass, please.

SALIERI. Constanze, listen to me! I'm a clumsy man. You think me sophisticated — I'm not at all. Take a true look. I've no cunning. I live on ink and sweetmeats. I never see women at all . . . When I met you last night, I envied Mozart from the depths of my soul. Out of that envy came stupid thoughts. For one silly second I dared imagine that — out of the vast store you obviously possess — you might spare me one coin of tenderness your rich husband does not need — and inspire me also.

Pause. She laughs.

I amuse.

CONSTANZE. Mozart was right. You're wicked.

SALIERI. He said that?

CONSTANZE. 'All wops are performers,' he said. 'Be very careful with that one.' Meaning you. He was being comic of course.

SALIERI. Yes.

Abruptly he turns his back on her.

CONSTANZE. But not that comic, actually. I mean you're acting a pretty obvious role, aren't you, dear? A small town boy, and all the time as clever as cutlets! . . . (*Mock tender:*) Ah! — are you sulking? *Are* you? . . . When Mozart sulks I smack his botty. He rather likes it. Do you want me to scold you a bit and smack your botty too? (*She hits him lightly with the portfolio. He turns in a fury.*)

SALIERI. How dare you?! . . . *You silly, common girl!*

A dreadful silence.

(*Icy:*) Forgive me. Let us confine our talk to your husband. He is a brilliant keyboard player, no question. However, the

Princess Elizabeth also requires a tutor in vocal music. I am
not convinced he is the man for that. I would like to look at
the pieces you've brought, and decide if he is mature enough. I
will study them overnight — and you will study my proposal.
Not to be vague: that is the price. (*He extends his hand for the
portfolio, and she surrenders it.*) Good afternoon.

*He turns from her and places it on a chair. She lingers — tries
to speak — cannot — and goes out quickly.*

*   *   *

The Same

SALIERI *turns in a ferment to the audience.*

SALIERI. Fiasco! . . . Fiasco! . . . The sordidness of it! The sheer
sweating sordidness! . . . Worse than if I'd actually done it! . . .
To be that much in sin and feel so *ridiculous* as well! . . . I
didn't deserve any pity from the Old Bargainer above! There
was no excuse. If now my music was rejected by Him forever,
it was my fault, mine alone. Would she return tomorrow?
Never. And if she did, what then? What would I do? (*Brutally*:)
What would I actually *do*? . . . Apologize profoundly — or try
again? . . . (*Crying out*:) Nobile, nobile Salieri! . . . What had he
done to me — this Mozart! Before he came did I behave like
this? Did I? Toy with adultery? Blackmail women? It was all
going — slipping — growing rotten — because of *him!*

*He moves upstage in a fever — reaches out to take the
portfolio on the chair — but as if fearful of what he might find
inside it he withdraws his hand and sits instead. A pause. He
contemplates the music lying there as if it were a great
confection he is dying to eat, but dare not. Then suddenly he
snatches at it — tears the ribbon — opens the case and stares
greedily at the manuscripts within.*

*Music sounds instantly, faintly, in the theatre, as his eye falls
on the first page. It is the opening of the Twenty-ninth
Symphony, in A Major.*

(*Over the music, reading it*:) She had said that these were his
original scores. First and only drafts of the music. Yet they
looked like fair copies. They showed no corrections of any
kind.

He looks up from the manuscript at the audience: the music abruptly stops.

It was puzzling — then suddenly alarming. What was evident was that Mozart was simply transcribing music —

He resumes looking at the music. Immediately the Sinfonia Concertante for Violin and Viola sounds faintly.

— completely finished in his head. And finished as most music is never finished.

He looks up again: the music breaks off.

Displace one note and there would be diminishment. Displace one phrase and the structure would fall.

He resumes reading, and the music also resumes: a ravishing phrase from the slow movement of the Concerto for Flute and Harp.

Here again — only now in abundance — were the same sounds I'd heard in the library. The same crushed harmonies — glancing collisions — agonizing delights.

And he looks up: again the music stops.

The truth was clear. That Serenade had been no accident.

Very low, in the theatre, a faint thundery sound is heard accumulating, like a distant sea.

I was staring through the cage of those meticulous ink strokes at an Absolute Beauty!

And out of the thundery roar writhes and rises the clear sound of a soprano, singing the Kyrie from the C Minor Mass. The accretion of noise around her voice falls away — it is suddenly clear and bright — then clearer and brighter. The light also grows bright: too bright: burning white, then scalding white! SALIERI rises in the downpour of the music which is growing ever louder — filling the theatre — as the soprano yields to the full chorus, fortissimo, singing its massive counterpoint.

This is by far the loudest sound the audience has yet heard. SALIERI staggers towards us, holding the manuscripts in his hand, like a man caught in a tumbling and violent sea.

Finally the drums crash in below: SALIERI *drops the portfolio of manuscripts — and falls senseless to the ground. At the same second the music explodes into a long, echoing, distorted boom, signifying some dreadful annihilation.*

The sound remains suspended over the prone figure in a menacing continuum — no longer music at all. Then it dies away, and there is only silence.

The light fades again.

A long pause.

SALIERI *quite still, his head by the pile of manuscripts.*

Finally the clock sounds: nine times. SALIERI *stirs as it does. Slowly he raises his head and looks up. And now — quietly at first — he addresses his God.*

SALIERI. *Capisco!* I know my fate. Now for the first time I feel my emptiness as Adam felt his nakedness . . . (*Slowly he rises to his feet.*) Tonight at an inn somewhere in this city stands a giggling child who can put on paper, without actually setting down his billiard cue, casual notes which turn my most considered ones into lifeless scratches. *Grazie,* Signore! You gave me the desire to serve you — which most men do not have — then saw to it the service was shameful in the ears of the server. *Grazie!* You gave me the desire to praise you — which most do not feel — then made me mute. *Grazie tante!* You put into me perception of the Incomparable — which most men never know! — then ensured that I would know myself forever mediocre. (*His voice gains power.*) Why? . . . *What is my fault?* . . . Until this day I have pursued virtue with rigour. I have laboured long hours to relieve my fellow men. I have worked and worked the talent you allowed me. (*Calling up:*) *You know how hard I've worked!* — solely that in the end, in the practice of the art which alone makes the world comprehensible to me, I might hear Your Voice! And now I do hear it — and it says only one name: MOZART! . . . Spiteful, sniggering, conceited, infantine Mozart! — who has never worked one minute to help another man! — shit-talking Mozart with his botty-smacking wife! — *him* you have chosen to be your sole conduct! And *my* only reward — my sublime privilege — is to be the sole man alive in this time who shall clearly recognize your Incarnation! (*Savagely*:) *Grazie e grazie ancora!* (*Pause.*) So be it! From this time we are enemies, You and I! I'll not accept it from You — *Do you hear?* . . . They say God is not mocked. I tell you, *Man* is not mocked! *I* am not mocked! . . . They say the spirit bloweth where it listeth: I tell you NO! It must list to virtue or not blow at all! (*Yelling*:) *Dio Ingiusto!* — You are the Enemy! I name Thee now — *Nemico Eterno!* And this I swear. To my last breath I shall *block* you on earth, as far as I am able! (*He glares up at God. To audience*:) What use, after all, is Man, if not to teach God His lessons? (*Pause. Suddenly he speaks again to us in the voice of an old man.*) And now —

He slips off his powdered wig, crosses to the fortepiano and takes from its lid the old dressing-gown and shawl which he discarded when he conducted us back to the eighteenth century. These he slips on over his court coat. It is again 1823.

before I tell you what happened next — God's answer to me — and indeed Constanze's — and all the horrors that followed — let me stop. The bladder, being a human appendage, is not something you need concern yourselves with yet. I being alive, though barely, am at its constant call. It is now one hour before dawn — when I must dismiss us both. When I return I'll tell you about the war I fought with God through his preferred Creature — Mozart, named *Amadeus.* In the waging of which, of course, the Creature had to be destroyed.

He bows to the audience with malignant slyness — snatches a pastry from the stand — and leaves the stage, chewing at it voraciously. The manuscripts lie where he spilled them in his fall.

The lights in the theatre come up as he goes.

ACT TWO

Salieri's Salon

The lights go down in the theatre as SALIERI *returns.*

SALIERI. I have been listening to the cats in the courtyard. They are all singing Rossini. It is obvious that cats have declined as badly as composers. Domenico Scarlatti owned one which would actually stroll across the keyboard and pick out passable subjects for fugue. But that was a Spanish cat of the Enlightenment. It appreciated counterpoint. Nowadays all cats appreciate are High Cs. Like the rest of the public.

He comes downstage and addresses the audience directly.

This is now the very last hour of my life. You must understand me. Not forgive. I do not seek forgiveness. I was a good man, as the world calls good. What use was it to me? Goodness could not make a good composer. Was Mozart good? Goodness is nothing in the furnace of art.

Pause.

On that dreadful Night of the Manuscripts my life acquired a terrible and thrilling purpose. The blocking of God in one of his purest manifestations. I had the power. God needed Mozart to let himself into the world. And Mozart needed me to get him worldly advancement. So it would be a battle to the end — and Mozart was the battleground.

Pause.

One thing I knew of Him. He was a cunning Enemy. Witness the fact that in blocking Him in the world I was also given the satisfaction of obstructing a disliked human rival. I wonder which of you will refuse that chance if it is offered.

He regards the audience maliciously, taking off his dressing gown and shawl.

I felt the danger at once, as soon as I'd uttered my challenge. How would He answer? Would He strike me dead for my impiety? Don't laugh. I was not a sophisticate of the salons. I was a smalltown Catholic, full of dread!

He puts on his powdered wig, and speaks again in his younger voice. We are back in the eighteenth century.

The first thing that happened — barely one hour later —

The doorbell sounds. CONSTANZE *comes in followed by a helpless* VALET.

Suddenly Constanze was back. At ten o'clock at night! (*In* (*surprise*:) Signora!

CONSTANZE (*stiffly*). My husband is at a soirée of Baron van Swieten. A concert of Sebastian Bach. He didn't think I would enjoy it.

SALIERI. I see. (*Curtly, to the goggling* VALET:) I'll ring if we require anything. Thank you.

The VALET *goes out. Slight pause.*

CONSTANZE (*flatly*). Where do we go, then?

SALIERI. What?

CONSTANZE. Do we do it in here? . . . Why not?

She sits, still wearing her hat, in one of the little gilded upright chairs.

Deliberately she loosens the strings of her bodice, so that one can just see the tops of her breasts, hitches up her silk skirts above the knees, so that one can also just see the flesh above the tops of the stockings, spreads her legs and regards him with an open stare.

(*Speaking softly*:) Well? . . . Let's get on with it.

For a second SALIERI *returns the stare, then suddenly looks away.*

SALIERI (*stiffly*). Your manuscripts are there. Please take them and go. Now. At once.

Pause.

CONSTANZE. You shit.

She jumps up and snatches the portfolio.

SALIERI. *Via! Don't return!*

CONSTANZE. You rotten shit!

Suddenly she runs at him — trying furiously to hit at his face. He grabs her arms, shakes her violently, and hurls her on the floor.

SALIERI. *Via!*

She freezes, staring up at him in hate.

(*Calling to the audience*:) You see how it was! I would have liked her — oh yes, just then more than ever! But now I wanted nothing petty! . . . My quarrel wasn't with Mozart — it was *through* him! Through him to God who loved him so. (*Scornfully*:) Amadeus! . . . Amadeus! . . .

CONSTANZE *picks herself up and runs from the room.*

Pause. He calms himself, going to the table and selecting a 'Nipple of Venus' to eat.

The next day, when Katherina Cavalieri came for her lesson, I made the same halting speech about 'coins of tenderness' — and I dubbed the girl *La Generosa*. I regret that my invention in love, as in art, has always been limited. Fortunately Katherina found it sufficient. She consumed twenty 'Nipples of Venus' — kissed me with brandied breath — and slipped easily into my bed.

KATHERINA *comes in languidly, half-undressed, as if from his bedroom. He embraces her, and helps slyly to adjust her peignoir.*

She remained there as my mistress for many years behind my good wife's back — and I soon erased in sweat the sense of his little body, the Creature's, preceding me.

KATHERINA *gives him a radiant smile, and ambles off.*

So much for my vow of sexual virtue. (*Slight pause.*) The same evening I went to the Palace and resigned from all my committees to help the lot of poor musicians. So much for my vow of social virtue.

Light change.

Then I went to the Emperor and recommended a man of no talent whatever to instruct the Princess Elizabeth.

*   *   *

The Palace of Schönbrunn

The EMPEROR *stands before the vast fireplace, between the golden mirrors.*

JOSEPH. Herr Sommer. A dull man, surely? What of Mozart?

SALIERI. Majesty, I cannot with a clear conscience recommend Mozart to teach Royalty. One hears too many stories.

JOSEPH. They may be just gossip.

SALIERI. One of them I regret relates to a protégé of my own. A very young singer.

JOSEPH. *Charmant!*

SALIERI. Not pleasant, Majesty, but true.

JOSEPH. I see . . . Let it be Herr Sommer, then. (*He walks down on to the main stage.*) I daresay he can't do much harm. To be frank, no one can do much harm musically to the Princess Elizabeth. (*He strolls away.*)

SALIERI *goes.* MOZART *enters from the other side, downstage. He wears a more natural-looking wig from now on: one indeed intended to represent his own hair of light chestnut, full and gathered at the back with ribbon.*

SALIERI (*to audience*). Mozart certainly did not suspect me. The Emperor announced the appointment in his usual way —

JOSEPH (*pausing*). Well, there it is.

JOSEPH *goes off.*

SALIERI. — and I commiserated with the loser.

MOZART *turns and stares bleakly out front.* SALIERI *shakes his hand.*

MOZART (*bitterly*). It's my own fault. My father always writes I should be more obedient. *Know my place!* . . . He'll send me sixteen lectures when he hears of this!

MOZART *goes slowly up to the fortepiano. Lights lower.*

SALIERI (*to audience, watching him*). It was a most serious loss as far as Mozart was concerned.

*   *   *

Vienna, and Glimpses of Opera Houses

The VENTICELLI *glide on.*

VENTICELLO 1. His list of pupils hardly moves.

VENTICELLO 2. Six at most.

VENTICELLO 1. And now a child to keep!

VENTICELLO 2. A boy.

SALIERI. Poor fellow. (*To audience:*) I, by contrast, prospered. This is the extraordinary truth. If I had expected anger from God — none came. *None!* . . . Instead — incredibly — in eighty-four and eighty-five I came to be regarded as infinitely the superior composer. And this despite the fact that these were the two years in which Mozart wrote his best keyboard concerti and his string quartets.

The VENTICELLI *stand on either side of* SALIERI. MOZART *sits at the fortepiano.*

VENTICELLO 1. Haydn calls the quartets unsurpassed.

SALIERI. They were — but no one heard them.

VENTICELLO 2. Van Swieten calls the concerti sublime.

SALIERI. They were, but no one noticed.

MOZART *plays and conducts from the keyboard. Faintly we hear the Rondo from the Piano Concerto in A Major, K.488.*

(*Over this:*) The Viennese greeted each concerto with the squeals of pleasure they usually reserved for a new style of bonnet. Each was played once — then totally forgotten! I alone was empowered to recognize them for what they were: the finest things made by man in the whole of the eighteenth century . . . By contrast, my operas were played everywhere and saluted by everyone! I composed my *Semiramide* for Munich.

VENTICELLO 1. Rapturously received!

VENTICELLO 2. People *faint* with pleasure!

In the Light Box is seen the interior of a brilliantly coloured Opera House, and an audience standing up applauding vigorously. SALIERI, *flanked by the* VENTICELLI, *turns upstage and bows to it. The concerto can scarcely be heard through the din.*

SALIERI. I wrote a comic opera for Vienna. *La Grotta di Trofonio.*

VENTICELLO 1. The talk of the city!

VENTICELLO 2. The cafés are buzzing!

Another Opera House interior is lit up. Another audience claps vigorously. Again SALIERI *bows to it.*

SALIERI (*to audience*). I finally finished my tragic opera *Danaius*, and produced it in Paris.

VENTICELLO 1. Stupendous reception!

VENTICELLO 2. The plaudits shake the roof!

VENTICELLO 1. Your name sounds throughout the Empire!

VENTICELLO 2. Throughout all Europe!

Yet another Opera House and another excited audience. SALIERI *bows a third time. Even the* VENTICELLI *now applaud him. The concerto stops.* MOZART *rises from the keyboard and, while* SALIERI *speaks, crosses directly through the scene and leaves the stage.*

SALIERI (*to audience*). It was incomprehensible. Almost as if I were being pushed deliberately from triumph to triumph! . . . I filled my head with golden opinions — yes, and this house with golden furniture!

* * *

Salieri's Salon

The stage turns gold.

 SERVANTS *come on carrying golden chairs upholstered in golden brocade. They place these all over the wooden floor.*

 The VALET *appears, a little older, divests* SALIERI *of his sky-blue coat and clothes him instead in a frock-coat of gold satin.*

 The COOK — *also of course a little older* — *brings in a golden cake-stand piled with more elaborate cakes.*

SALIERI. My own taste was for plain things — but I *denied* it! . . . I grew confident. I grew resplendent. I gave salons and soirées, and worshipped the season round at the altar of Success!

 He sits at ease in his salon. The VENTICELLI *sit with him, one on either side.*

VENTICELLO 1. Mozart heard your comedy last night.

VENTICELLO 2. He spoke of it to the Princess Lichnowsky.

VENTICELLO 1. He said you should be made to clean up your own mess.

SALIERI (*taking snuff*). *Really?* What charmers these Salzburgers are!

VENTICELLO 2. People are outraged by him.

VENTICELLO 1. He empties drawing-rooms. Now Van Swieten is angry with him.

SALIERI. Lord Fugue? I thought he was the Baron's little pet.

VENTICELLO 2. Mozart has asked leave to write an Italian opera.

SALIERI (*briskly aside to audience*). *Italian opera! Threat! My kingdom!*

VENTICELLO 1. And the Baron is scandalized.

SALIERI. But why? What's the theme of it?

 VAN SWIETEN *comes on quickly from upstage.*

VAN SWIETEN. Figaro! . . . *The Marriage of Figaro!* That

disgraceful play of Beaumarchais!

At a discreet sign of dismissal from SALIERI, *the* VENTICELLI *slip away,* VAN SWIETEN *joins* SALIERI, *and sits on one of the gold chairs.*

(*To* SALIERI:) That's all he can find to waste his talent on: a vulgar farce! Noblemen lusting after chambermaids! Their wives dressing up in stupid disguises anyone could penetrate in a second! . . . When I reproved him, he said I reminded him of his father! . . . I simply cannot imagine why Mozart should want to set that rubbish!

MOZART *enters quickly from upstage, accompanied by* VON STRACK. *They join* SALIERI *and* VAN SWIETEN.

MOZART. Because I want to do a piece about real people, Baron! And I want to set it in a real place! A *boudoir!* — because that to me is the most exciting place on earth! Underclothes on the floor! Sheets still warm from a woman's body! Even a pisspot brimming under the bed!

VAN SWIETEN (*outraged*). Mozart!

MOZART. I want life, Baron. Not boring legends!

VON STRACK. Herr Salieri's recent *Danaius* was a legend and that did not bore the French.

MOZART. It is impossible to bore the French — except with real life!

VAN SWIETEN. I had assumed, now that you had joined our Brotherhood of Masons, you would choose more elevated themes.

MOZART (*impatiently*). Oh elevated! Elevated! . . . The only thing a man should elevate is his doodle.

VAN SWIETEN. You are provoking, sir! Has everything to be a joke with you?

MOZART (*desperate*). Excuse language, Baron, but really! . . . How can we go on forever with these gods and heroes?

VAN SWIETEN (*passionately*). Because they *go* on forever — that's why! They represent the eternal in us. Opera is here to ennoble us, Mozart — you and me just as well as the Emperor. It is an aggrandizing art! It celebrates the eternal in Man and ignores the ephemeral. The goddess in Woman and not the laundress.

VON STRACK. Well said, sir. Exactly!

MOZART (*imitating his drawl*). Oh well said, yes, well said! Exactly! (*To all of them:*) I don't understand you! You're all up on perches, but it doesn't hide your arseholes! You don't give a shit about gods and heroes! If you are honest — each one of you — which of you isn't more at home with his hairdresser than Hercules? Or Horatius? (*To* SALIERI:) Or your stupid *Danaius,* come to that! Or mine — *mine!* — *Idomeneo, King of Crete!* All those anguished antiques! They're all bores! Bores, bores, bores! (*Suddenly he springs up and jumps on to a chair, like an orator.* (*Declaring it :*) All serious operas written this century are boring!

They turn and look at him in shocked amazement. A pause. He gives his little giggle, and then jumps down again.

Look at us! Four gaping mouths. What a perfect quartet! I'd love to write it — just this second of time, this *now,* as you are! Herr Chamberlain thinking 'Impertinent Mozart: I must speak to the Emperor at once!' Herr Prefect thinking 'Ignorant Mozart: debasing opera with his vulgarity!' Herr Court Composer thinking 'German Mozart: what can he finally know about music?' And Herr Mozart himself, in the middle, thinking 'I'm just a good fellow. Why do they all disapprove of me?' (*Excitedly to* VAN SWIETEN:) That's why opera is important, Baron. Because it's realer than any play! A dramatic poet would have to put all those thoughts down one after another to represent this second of time. The composer can put them all down at once — and still make us hear each one of them. Astonishing device: a Vocal Quartet! (*More and more excited :*) . . . I tell you I want to write a finale lasting half an hour! A quartet becoming a quintet becoming a sextet. On and on, wider and wider — all sounds multiplying and rising together — and the together making a sound entirely new! . . . I bet you that's how God hears the world. Millions of sounds ascending at once and mixing in His ear to become an unending music, unimaginable to us! (*To* SALIERI:) That's our job! That's our job, we composers: to combine the inner minds of him and him and him, and her and her — the thoughts of chambermaids and Court Composers — and turn the audience into God.

Pause. SALIERI *stares at him fascinated. Embarrassed,* MOZART *blows a raspberry and giggles.*

I'm sorry. I talk nonsense all day: it's incurable — ask Stanzerl. (*To* VAN SWIETEN:) My tongue is stupid. My heart isn't.

VAN SWIETEN. No. You're a good fellow under all your nonsense: I know that. He'll make a fine new Brother, won't he, Salieri?

SALIERI. Better than I, Baron.

VAN SWIETEN. Just try, my friend, to be more serious with your gifts.

He smiles, presses MOZART's *hand, and goes.* SALIERI *rises.*

SALIERI. *Buona fortuna,* MOZART.

MOZART. *Grazie,* Signore. (*Rounding on* VON STRACK:) Stop frowning, Herr Chamberlain. I'm a jackass. It's easy to be friends with a jackass: just shake his 'hoof'.

He forms his hand into a 'hoof'. Warily VON STRACK *takes it — then springs back as* MOZART *brays loudly like a donkey.*

MOZART. *Hee-haw!* . . . Tell the Emperor the opera's finished.

VON STRACK. Finished?

MOZART. Right here in my noddle. The rest's just scribbling. Goodbye.

VON STRACK. Good-day to you.

MOZART. He's going to be proud of me. You'll see. (*He gives his flourish of the hand and goes out, delighted with himself.*)

VON STRACK. That young man really is . . .

SALIERI (*blandly*). Very lively.

VON STRACK (*exploding*). Intolerable . . . *Intolerable!*

VON STRACK *freezes in a posture of indignation.*

SALIERI (*to audience*). How could I stop it? . . . How could I block this opera of Figaro? . . . Incredible to hear, within six weeks the Creature had finished the entire score!

ORSINI-ROSENBERG *bustles in.*

ROSENBERG. Figaro is complete! The first performance will be on May the first!

SALIERI. So soon?

ROSENBERG. There's no way we can stop it!

A slight pause.

SALIERI (*slyly*). I have an idea. *Una piccola idea!*

ROSENBERG. What?

SALIERI. *Mi ha detto che c'è un balletto nel terzo atto?*

ROSENBERG (*puzzled*). *Sí.*

VON STRACK. What does he say?

SALIERI. *E dimmi — non è vero che l'Imperatore ha proibito il balletto nelle sue opere?*

ROSENBERG (*realizing*). *Un balletto* . . . Ah!

SALIERI. *Precisamente.*

ROSENBERG. *Oh, capisco! Ma che meraviglia! Perfetto!* (*He laughs in delight.*) *Veramente ingegnoso!*

VON STRACK (*irritated*). What is it? What is he suggesting?

SALIERI. See him at the theatre.

ROSENBERG. Of course. Immediately, I'd forgotten. You are brilliant, Court Composer.

SALIERI. I? . . . I have said nothing. (*He moves away upstage.*)

The light begins to change, dimming down.

VON STRACK (*very cross*). I must tell you that I resent this extremely. Mozart is right in some things. There is far too much Italian *chittero-chattero* at this Court! Now please to inform me at once, what was just said?

ROSENBERG (*lightly*). *Pazienza*, my dear Chamberlain. *Pazienza*. Just wait and see!

From upstage SALIERI *beckons to* VON STRACK. *Baffled and cross, the* CHAMBERLAIN *joins him. They watch together, unseen. The light dims further.*

*   *   *

An Unlit Theatre

In the background a projection of lamps glowing faintly in the darkened auditorium. ORSINI-ROSENBERG *sits on one of the gold chairs, centre.*

MOZART *comes in quickly from the left, wearing another bright coat, and carrying the score of* Figaro. *He crosses to the fortepiano.*

ROSENBERG. Mozart . . . *Mozart!*

MOZART. Yes, Herr Director.

ROSENBERG (*agreeably*). A word with you, please. Right away.

MOZART. Certainly. What is it?

ROSENBERG. I would like to see your score of *Figaro*.

MOZART. Oh yes. Why?

ROSENBERG. Just bring it here to me. (*Unmoving:*) Into my hand, please.

MOZART *hands it to him, puzzled.* ORSINI-ROSENBERG *turns the pages.*

Now tell me: did you not know that His Majesty has expressly forbidden ballet in his operas?

MOZART. Ballet?

ROSENBERG. Such as occurs in your third act.

MOZART. That is not a ballet, Herr Director. That is a dance at Figaro's wedding.

ROSENBERG. Exactly. A dance.

MOZART (*trying to control himself*). But, the Emperor doesn't mean to prohibit dancing when it's part of the story. He made that law to prevent insertions of stupid ballet like in French operas, and quite right too.

ROSENBERG (*raising his voice*). It is not for you, Herr Mozart, to interpret the Emperor's edicts. Merely to obey them. (*He seizes the offending pages between his fingers.*)

MOZART. What are you doing? . . . What are you doing, Excellency?

ROSENBERG. Taking out what should never have been put in.

In a terrible silence ROSENBERG *tears out the pages.* MOZART *watches in disbelief. Upstage* SALIERI *and* VON STRACK *look on together from the dimness.*

Now, sir, perhaps in future you will obey Imperial commands.

He tears out some more pages.

MOZART. But . . . But — if all that goes — there'll be a hole right at the climax of the story! . . . (*Crying out suddenly:*) Salieri! *This is Salieri's idea!*

ROSENBERG. Don't be absurd.

SALIERI (*to audience*). How did he think of that? Nothing I had ever done could possibly make him think of that on his own. Had God given him the idea?!

MOZART. It's a conspiracy. I can smell it. I can smell it!

ROSENBERG. Control yourself!

MOZART (*howling*). *But what do you expect me to do?* The first performance is two days off!

ROSENBERG. Write it over. That's your forte, is it not? — writing at speed.

MOZART. Not when the music's *perfect!* Not when it's absolutely perfect as it is! . . . (*Wildly:*) I shall appeal to the Emperor! I'll go to him myself! I'll hold a rehearsal especially for him.

ROSENBERG. The Emperor does not attend rehearsals.

MOZART. He'll attend this one. Make no mistake — he'll come to this one! Then he'll deal with *you!*

ROSENBERG. This issue is simple. Write your act again today — or withdraw the opera. That's final.

Pause. He hands back the mutilated score to its composer. MOZART *is shaking.*

MOZART. You shit-pot.

ORSINI-ROSENBERG *turns and walks imperturbably away from him.*

Woppy, foppy, wet-arsed, Italian-loving shit-pot!

Serenely, ORSINI-ROSENBERG *leaves the stage.*

(*Screeching after him:*) Count Orsini-Rosenshit! . . . Rosencunt! . . . Rosenbugger! . . . I'll hold a rehearsal! You'll see! The Emperor will come! You'll see! You'll see! . . . *You'll see!!* (*He throws down his score in a storm of hysterical rage.*)

Upstage in the dimness VON STRACK *goes out, and* SALIERI *ventures down towards the shrieking little man.* MOZART *suddenly becomes aware of him. He turns, his hand shooting out in an involuntary gesture of accusation.*

MOZART (*to* SALIERI). I am *forbidden!* . . . I am — forbidden! . . . But of course you know already!

SALIERI (*quietly*) Know what?

MOZART *flings away from him.*

MOZART (*bitterly*). No matter!

SALIERI (*always blandly*). Mozart, permit me. If you wish, I will speak to the Emperor myself. Ask him to attend a rehearsal.

MOZART (*amazed*). You wouldn't.

SALIERI. I cannot promise he will come — but I can try.

MOZART. Sir! —

SALIERI. Good-day. (*He puts up his hands, barring further intimacy.*)

MOZART *retreats to the fortepiano.*

(*To audience:*) Needless to say I did nothing whatever in the matter. Yet — to my total stupefaction —

VON STRACK *and* ORSINI-ROSENBERG *hurry on downstage.*

— in the middle of the last rehearsal of *Figaro* next day . . .

The EMPEROR JOSEPH *comes on from upstage.*

JOSEPH (*cheerfully*). Fêtes and fireworks! Fêtes and fireworks! Gentlemen, good afternoon!

*   *   *

The Theatre

SALIERI (*to audience*). Entirely against his usual practice, the Emperor appeared!

VON STRACK *and* ORSINI-ROSENBERG *look at each other in consternation.* JOSEPH *seats himself excitedly on one of the gold chairs, facing out front. As with the premiere of* Seraglio *seen in Act I, he watches the audience as if it were the opera.*

JOSEPH. I can't wait for this, Mozart, I assure you! *Je prévois des merveilles!*

MOZART (*bowing fervently*). Majesty!

The COURTIERS *sit also:* VON STRACK *on his right-hand side,* ORSINI-ROSENBERG *on his left.* SALIERI *also sits, near the keyboard.*

SALIERI (*to audience*). What did this mean? Was this proof God had finally decided to defend Mozart against me? Was He engaging with me at last?

MOZART *passes behind* SALIERI.

MOZART (*ernestly, sotto voice*). I am so grateful to you, I cannot express it!

SALIERI (*aside, to him*). Hush. Say nothing.

MOZART *goes on quickly to the fortepiano and sits at it.*

(*To audience:*) One thing about the event certainly seemed more than coincidence.

Music sounds faintly: the end of the third act of Figaro, *just before the dance music starts.*

Strangely, His Majesty had arrived at precisely the moment when the dancers would have begun, had not they and their music been entirely cut.

The music stops abruptly.

He and all of us watched the action proceed in total silence.

Flanked by his COURTIERS, *the* EMPEROR *stares out front, following with his eyes what is obviously a silent pantomime. His face expresses bewilderment.* ORSINI-ROSENBERG *watches his sovereign anxiously. Finally the monarch speaks.*

JOSEPH. I don't understand. Is it modern?

MOZART (*jumping up nervously from the keyboard*). No, Majesty.

JOSEPH. Then what?

MOZART. The Herr Director has removed a dance that would have occurred at this point.

JOSEPH (*to* ORSINI-ROSENBERG). Why was this done?

ROSENBERG. It's your own regulation, Sire. No ballet in your opera.

MOZART. Majesty, this is not a ballet. It is part of a wedding feast: entirely necessary for the story.

JOSEPH. Well, it certainly looks very odd the way it is. I can't say I like it.

MOZART. Nor do I, Majesty.

JOSEPH. Do you like it, Rosenberg?

ROSENBERG. It's not a question of liking, Majesty. Your own law decrees it.

JOSEPH. Yes. All the same, this is nonsense. Look at them: they're like waxworks up there.

ROSENBERG. Well, not exactly, Majesty.

JOSEPH. I don't like waxworks.

MOZART. Nor do I, Majesty.

JOSEPH. Well, who would? What do you say, Salieri?

SALIERI. Italians are fond of waxworks, Majesty. (*Pause.*) Our religion is largely based upon them.

JOSEPH. You are *cattivo* again, Court Composer.

VON STRACK (*intervening creamily*). Your Majesty, Count Rosenberg is very worried that if this music is put back it will create the most unfortunate precedent. One will have thereafter to endure hours of dancing in opera.

JOSEPH. I think we can guard against that, you know, Chamberlain. I really think we can guard against hours of dancing. (*To* ORSINI-ROSENBERG:) Please restore Herr Mozart's music.

ROSENBERG. But Majesty, I must insist —

JOSEPH (*with a touch of anger*). You will oblige me, Rosenberg! I wish to hear Mozart's music. Do you understand me?

ROSENBERG. Yes, Majesty.

MOZART *explodes with joy, jumps over a chair and throws himself at* JOSEPH's *feet.*

MOZART. Oh God, I thank your Majesty! (*He kisses the* EMPEROR's *hand extravagantly, as at their first meeting.*) Oh thank you — thank you — thank you Sire, forever!

JOSEPH (*withdrawing hand*). Yes, yes — very good. A little less enthusiasm, I beg you!

MOZART (*abashed*). Excuse me.

The EMPEROR *rises. All follow suit.*

JOSEPH. Well. *There it is!*

*   *   *

The First Performance of *Figaro*

The theatre glows with light for the first performance of Figaro. COURTIERS *and* CITIZENS *come in swiftly.*

The EMPEROR *and his Court resume their seats and the others quickly take theirs. In the front row we note* KATHERINA CAVALIERI, *all plumes and sequins, and* KAPELLMEISTER BONNO — *older than ever. Behind them sit*

CONSTANZE *and the* VENTICELLI. *All of them stare out at the audience as if it were the opera they have come to see: people of fashion down front; poorer people crowded into the Light Box upstage.*

SALIERI *crosses as he speaks to where two chairs have been placed side by side apart from the rest, on the left, to form his box. On the chair upstage sits his good wife* TERESA — *more statuesque than ever.*

SALIERI (*to audience*). And so *Figaro* was produced in spite of all my efforts. I sat in my box and watched it happen. A conspicuous defeat for me. And yet I was strangely excited.

Faintly we hear Figaro singing the tune of 'Non più andrai'. The stage audience is obviously delighted: they smile out front as they watch the (invisible) action.

My March! My poor March of Welcome — now set to enchant the world forever!

It fades. Applause. The EMPEROR *rises, and with him the audience, to denote an Intermission.* JOSEPH *greets* KATHERINA *and* BONNO. ORSINI-ROSENBERG *and* VON STRACK *go to* SALIERI's *box.*

ROSENBERG (*to* SALIERI). Almost in your style, that last bit. But more vulgar of course. Far more obvious than you would ever be.

VON STRACK (*drawling*). Exactly!

A bell rings for the end of the Intermission. The EMPEROR *returns quickly to his seat. The audience sits. A pause. All look out front, unmoving.*

SALIERI (*raptly and quietly: to audience*). Trembling, I heard the second act. (*Pause.*) The restored third act. (*Pause.*) The astounding fourth. What shall I say to you who will one day hear this last act for yourselves? You will — because whatever else shall pass away, this must remain.

Faintly we hear the solemn closing ensemble from Act IV of Figaro, *'Ah! Tutti contenti. Saremo così'.*

(*Over this:*) The scene was night in a summer garden. Pinprick stars gleaming down on shaking summerhouses. Plotters glided behind pasteboard hedges. I saw a woman, dressed in her maid's clothes, hear her husband utter the first tender words he has offered her in years only because he thinks she is someone else. Could one catch a realer moment? And how except in a net of pure artifice? The disguises of opera had been invented for Mozart. (*He can barely look out at the 'stage'.*) The final reconciliation melted sight. (*Pause.*) Through my tears I saw the Emperor yawn.

JOSEPH *yawns. The music fades. There is scant applause.* JOSEPH *rises and the* COURTIERS *follow suit.* MOZART *bows.*

JOSEPH (*coolly*). Most ingenious, Mozart. You are coming along nicely . . . I do think we must omit encores in future. It really makes things far too long. Make a note, Rosenberg.

ROSENBERG. Majesty.

MOZART *lowers his head, crushed.*

JOSEPH. Gentleman, good night to you. Strack, attend me.

JOSEPH *goes out, with* VON STRACK. *Director* ORSINI-ROSENBERG *gives* MOZART *one triumphant look and follows.* SALIERI *nods to his wife who leaves with the audience. Only* CONSTANZE *lingers for a second, then she too goes. A pause.* MOZART *and* SALIERI *are left alone:* SALIERI *deeply shaken by the opera,* MOZART *deeply upset by its reception. He crosses and sits next to* SALIERI.

MOZART (*low*). Herr Salieri.

SALIERI. Yes?

MOZART. What do you think? Do you think I am coming along nicely?

SALIERI (*moved*). I think the piece is . . . extraordinary, I think it is . . . *marvellous.* Yes.

Pause. MOZART *turns to him.*

MOZART. I'll tell you what it is. It's the best opera yet written. That's what it is. And only I could have done it. No one else living!

SALIERI *turns his head swiftly, as if he has been slapped.*
MOZART *rises and walks away. The light changes. The*
VENTICELLI *rush on.* SALIERI *and* MOZART *both freeze.*

VENTICELLO 1. Rosenberg is furious.

VENTICELLO 2. He'll never forgive Mozart.

VENTICELLO 1. He'll do anything to get back at him!

SALIERI (*rising: to audience*). So it wasn't hard to get the piece
cancelled. I saw to it through the person of the resentful
Director that in the entire year *Figaro* was played only *nine
times!* . . . My defeat finally turned into a victory. And God's
response to my challenge remained as inscrutable as ever . . .
Was He taking any notice of me *at all*? . . .

MOZART *breaks his freeze and comes downstage.*

MOZART. *Withdrawn!* Absolutely no plans for its revival!

SALIERI. I commiserate with you, my friend. But if the public
does not like one's work, one has to accept the fact gracefully.
(*Aside, to audience:*) And certainly they didn't.

VENTICELLO 1 (*complaining*). It's too complicated!

VENTICELLO 2 (*complaining*). Too tiresome!

VENTICELLO 1. All those morbid harmonies!

VENTICELLO 2. And never a good bang at the end of songs so
you know when to clap!

The VENTICELLI *go off.*

SALIERI (*to audience*). Obviously I would not need to plot too
hard against his operas in future. I must concentrate on the
man. I decided to see him as much as possible: to learn
everything I could of his weaknesses.

*   *   *

The Waldstädten Library

SERVANTS *again bring on the wing-chair.*

MOZART. I'll go to England. England loves music. That's the
answer!

SALIERI (*to audience*). We were yet again in the library of the Baroness Waldstädten: that room fated to be the scene of ghastly encounters between us. Again, too, the compensating *crema al mascarpone*.

He sits in the chair and eats greedily.

MOZART. I was there when I was a boy. They absolutely adored me. I had more kisses than you've had cakes! . . . When I was a child, people loved me.

SALIERI. Perhaps they will again. Why don't you go to London and try?

MOZART. Because I have a wife and child and no money. I wrote to Papa to take the boy off my hands just for a few months so I could go — and he refused! . . . He's a bitter man, of course. After he'd finished showing me off around Europe he never went anywhere himself. He just stayed up in Salzburg year after year, kissing the ring of the Fartsbishop and lecturing *me*! . . . (*Confidentially*:) The real thing is, you see, he's jealous. Under everything he's jealous of me! He'll never forgive me for being cleverer than he is.

He leans excitedly over SALIERI's *chair like a naughty child.*

I'll tell you a secret. Leopold Mozart is just a jealous, dried-up old turd . . . And I actually detest him.

He giggles guiltily. The VENTICELLI *appear quickly, and address* SALIERI, *as* MOZART *freezes.*

VENTICELLO 1 (*solemnly*). Leopold Mozart —

VENTICELLO 2 (*solemnly*). Leopold Mozart —

VENTICELLO 1 and VENTICELLO 2. Leopold Mozart is dead!

They go off. MOZART *recoils. A long pause.*

SALIERI. Do not despair. Death is inevitable, my friend.

MOZART (*desperately*). How will I go now?

SALIERI. What do you mean?

MOZART. In the world. There's no one else. No one who understands the wickedness around. *I can't see it!* . . . He watched for me all my life — and I betrayed him.

SALIERI. No!

MOZART. I talked against him.

SALIERI. No!

MOZART (*distressed*). I married where he begged me not. I left him alone. I danced and played billiards and fooled about, and he sat by himself night after night in an empty house, and no woman to care for him . . .

SALIERI *rises in concern.*

SALIERI. Wolfgang. My dear Wolfgang. Don't accuse yourself! . . . Lean upon me, if you care to . . . Lean upon me.

SALIERI *opens his arms in a wide gesture of paternal benevolence.* MOZART *approaches, and is almost tempted to surrender to the embrace. But at the last moment he avoids it, and breaks away down front, to fall on his knees.*

MOZART. *Papa!*

SALIERI (*to audience*). So rose the Ghost Father in *Don Giovanni!*

*   *   *

The two grim chords which open the Overture to Don Giovanni *sound through the theatre,* MOZART *seems to quail under them, as he stares out front. On the backdrop in the Light Box appears the silhouette of a giant black figure, in cloak and tricorne hat. It extends its arms, menacingly and engulfingly, towards its begetter.*

SALIERI. A Father more accusing than any in opera. So rose the figure of a Guilty Libertine, cast into Hell! . . . I looked on astounded as from his ordinary life he made his art. We were both ordinary men, he and I. Yet he from the ordinary created legends — and I from legends created only the ordinary.

The figure fades. SALIERI *stands over the kneeling* MOZART.

Could I not have stopped my war? Shown him some pity? Oh yes, my friends, at any time — if He above had shown me one drop of it! Every day I set to work I prayed — I still prayed, you understand — 'Make this one good in my ears! Just this one! *One!*' But would He ever? . . . I heard my music calmed in convention — not one breath of spirit to lift it off the shallows. And I heard *his* —

We hear the exquisite strains of the terzetto *'Soave sia il vento' from* Così Fan Tutte.

— the spirit singing through it unstoppable to my ears alone! (*To God, in anguish*:) 'Grant this to me! . . . *Grant this to me! . . .* (*As God*':) 'No, no, no: I do not need you, Salieri! I have Mozart! Better for you to be silent!' *Hahahahaha!*

The music cuts off as he giggles savagely.

The Creature's dreadful giggle was the laughter of God. I had to end it. But how? There was only one way. *Starvation.* Reduce the man to distitution. Starve out the God.

*   *   *

Vienna and the Palace of Schönbrunn

SALIERI (*to* MOZART). How do you fare today?

MOZART. Badly. I have no money, and no prospect of any.

SALIERI. It would not be too hard, surely.

Lights up on the Palace of Schönbrunn. The EMPEROR *stands in the Light Box, in his golden space.*

JOSEPH. We must find him a Post.

SALIERI (*to audience*). One danger! The Emperor.

SALIERI *goes upstage to* JOSEPH.

There's nothing available, Majesty.

JOSEPH. There's Chamber Composer now that Gluck is dead.

SALIERI (*shocked*). Mozart to follow Gluck?

JOSEPH. I won't have him say I drove him away. You know what a tongue he has.

SALIERI. Then grant him Gluck's post, Majesty, but not his salary. That would be wrong.

JOSEPH. Gluck got two thousand florins a year. What should Mozart get?

SALIERI. Two hundred. Light payment, yes, but for light duties.

JOSEPH. Perfectly fair. I'm obliged to you, Court Composer.

SALIERI (*bowing*). Majesty.

Lights down a little on JOSEPH *who still stands there.* SALIERI *returns to* MOZART.

(*To audience:*) Easily done. Like many men obsessed with being thought generous, the Emperor Joseph was quintessentially mean.

MOZART *kneels before the* EMPEROR.

JOSEPH. Herr Mozart. *Vous nous faites honneur! . . .*

Lights out on the Court. MOZART *turns and walks downstage.*

MOZART. It's a damned insult! Not enough to keep a mouse in cheese for a week!

SALIERI. Regard it as a token, *caro* Herr.

MOZART. When I was young they gave me snuff-boxes. Now it's tokens! And for what? Pom-pom, for fireworks! Twang-twang for contredanzes!

SALIERI. I'm sorry it's made you angry. I'd not have suggested it if I'd known you'd be distressed.

MOZART. You suggested it?

SALIERI. I regret I was not able to do more.

MOZART. Oh . . . forgive me! You're a good man! I see that now! You're a truly kind man — and I'm a monstrous fool!

He grasps SALIERI's *hand.*

SALIERI. No, please . . .

MOZART. You make me ashamed . . . You excellent man!

SALIERI. No, no, no, no, no, — *s'il vous plaît.* A little less enthusiasm I beg you!

MOZART *laughs delightedly at this imitation of the* EMPEROR. SALIERI *joins in.* MOZART *suddenly doubles over with stomach cramps. He groans.*

Wolfgang! What is it?

MOZART. I get cramps sometimes in my stomach.

SALIERI. I'm sorry.

MOZART. Excuse me . . . it's nothing really.

SALIERI. I will see you soon again?

MOZART. Of course.

SALIERI. Why not visit me?

MOZART. I will . . . I promise!

SALIERI. *Bene.*

MOZART. *Bene.*

SALIERI. My friend. My new friend.

> MOZART *giggles with pleasure and goes off. A pause.*

(*To audience*:) Now if ever was the moment for God to crush me. I waited — and do you know what happened? I had just ruined Mozart's career at Court: God rewarded me by granting my dearest wish!

The VENTICELLI *come on.*

VENTICELLO 1. Kapellmeister Bonno.

VENTICELLO 2. Kapellmeister Bonno.

VENTICELLO 1 and VENTICELLO 2. Kapellmeister Bonno is dead!

> SALIERI *opens his mouth in surprise.*

VENTICELLO 1. You are appointed —

VENTICELLO 2. By Royal Decree —

VENTICELLO 1. To fill his place.

> *Lights full up on the* EMPEROR *at the back. He is flanked by* VON STRACK *and* ORSINI-ROSENBERG, *standing like icons as at their first appearance.*

JOSEPH (*formally as* SALIERI *turns and bows to him*). First Royal and Imperial Kapellmeister to our Court.

The VENTICELLI *applaud.*

VENTICELLO 1. Bravo.

VENTICELLO 2. Bravo.

ROSENBERG. *Evviva*, Salieri!

VON STRACK. Well done, Salieri!

JOSEPH (*warmly*). Dear Salieri — There it is!

The lights go down on Schönbrunn. In the dark the EMPEROR *and his Court leave the stage for the last time.* SALIERI *turns round, alarmed.*

SALIERI (*to audience*). I was now truly alarmed. How long would I go unpunished?

VENTICELLO 1. Mozart looks appalling.

VENTICELLO 2. It must be galling of course.

VENTICELLO 1. I hear he's dosing himself constantly with medicine.

SALIERI. For what?

VENTICELLO 2. Envy, I imagine.

*   *   *

The Prater

Fresh green trees appear on the backdrop. The light changes to yellow, turning the blue surround into a rich verdant green.
    MOZART *and* CONSTANZE *enter arm-in-arm. She is palpably pregnant and wears a poor coat and bonnet; his clothes are poorer too.* SALIERI *promenades with the* VENTICELLI.

SALIERI. I met him next in the Prater.

MOZART (*to* SALIERI). Congratulations, sir!

SALIERI. I thank you. And to you both! (*To audience:*) Clearly there was a change for the worse. His eyes gleamed, oddly, like a dog's when the light catches. (*To* MOZART:) I hear you are not well, my friend.

He acknowledges CONSTANZE, *who curtsies to him.*

MOZART. I'm not. My pains stay with me.

SALIERI. How wretched. What can they be?

MOZART. Also, I sleep badly . . . I have . . . bad dreams.

CONSTANZE (*warningly*). Wolferl!

SALIERI. Dreams?

MOZART. Always the same one . . . A figure comes to me cloaked in grey — doing this. (*He beckons slowly.*) It has no face. Just grey — like a mask . . . (*He giggles nervously.*) What can it mean, do you think?

SALIERI. Surely you do not believe in dreams?

MOZART. No of course not — really!

SALIERI. Surely *you* do not, Madame?

CONSTANZE. I never dream, sir. Things are unpleasant enough to me, awake.

SALIERI *bows.*

MOZART. It's all fancy, of course!

CONSTANZE. If Wolfgang had proper work he might dream less, First Kapellmeister.

MOZART (*embarrassed, taking her arm*). Stanzi, please! . . . Excuse us, sir. Come, dearest. We are well enough, thank you!

Husband and wife go off.

VENTICELLO 1. He's growing freakish.

VENTICELLO 2. No question.

VENTICELLO 1. Grey figures with no faces!

SALIERI (*looking after him*). He broods on his father too much, I fancy. Also his circumstances make him anxious.

VENTICELLO 1. They've moved house again.

VENTICELLO 2. To the Rauhensteingasse. Number nine hundred and seventy.

VENTICELLO 1. They must be desperate.

VENTICELLO 2. It's a real slum.

SALIERI. Does he earn any money at all, apart from his Post?

VENTICELLO 1. Nothing whatever.

VENTICELLO 2. I hear he's starting to beg.

VENTICELLO 1. They say he's written letters to twenty Brother Masons.

SALIERI. Really?

VENTICELLO 2. And they're giving him money.

SALIERI (*to audience*). Of course! They *would!* . . . I had *forgotten* the Masons! *Naturally* they would relieve him — *how stupid of me!* . . . There could be no finally starving him with the Masons there to help! As long as he asked they would keep supplying his wants . . . How could I stop it? And quickly!

VENTICELLO 1. Lord Fugue is most displeased with him!

SALIERI. *Is* he?

*   *   *

A Masonic Lodge

A huge golden emblem descends, encrusted with Masonic symbols. Enter VAN SWIETEN. *He is wearing the ritual apron over his sober clothes. At the same time* MOZART *enters from the left. He too wears the apron. The two men clasp hands in fraternal greeting.*

VAN SWIETEN (*gravely*). This is not good, Brother. The Lodge was not created for you to beg from.

MOZART. What else can I do?

VAN SWIETEN. Give concerts, as you used to do.

MOZART. I have no subscribers left, Baron. I am no longer fashionable.

VAN SWIETEN. I am not surprised. You write tasteless comedies which give offence. I warned you, often enough.

MOZART (*humbly*). You did. I admit it. (*He holds his stomach in pain.*)

VAN SWIETEN. I will send you some fugues of Bach tomorrow. You can arrange those for my Sunday Concert. You shall have a small fee.

MOZART. Thank you, Baron.

> VAN SWIETEN *nods and goes out.* SALIERI *steps forward. He again wears the Masonic apron.*

(*Shouting after* VAN SWIETEN:) I cannot live by arranging Bach!

SALIERI (*sarcastically*). A generous fellow.

MOZART. All the same, I'll have to do it. If he were to turn the Lodge against me, I'd be finished. My Brother Masons virtually keep me now . . . Never mind. I'll manage: you'll see! Things are looking up already. I've had a marvellous proposal from Schikaneder. He's a new Member of this Lodge.

SALIERI. Schikaneder? The actor?

MOZART. Yes. He owns a theatre in the suburbs.

SALIERI. Well, more of a music-hall, surely?

MOZART. Yes . . . He wants me to write him a Vaudeville — something for ordinary German people. Isn't that a wonderful idea? . . . He's offered me half the receipts when we open.

SALIERI. Nothing in advance?

MOZART. He said he couldn't afford anything. I know it's not much of an offer. But a popular piece about Brotherly Love could celebrate everything we believe as Masons!

SALIERI. It certainly could! . . . Why don't you put the Masons *into* it?

MOZART. Into an opera? . . . I couldn't!

> SALIERI *laughs, to indicate that he was simply making a joke.*

All the same — what an idea!

SALIERI (*earnestly*). Our rituals are secret, Wolfgang.

MOZART. I needn't copy them exactly. I could adapt them a little.

SALIERI. Well . . . It would certainly be in a great cause.

MOZART. Brotherly love!

SALIERI. Brotherly Love!

They both turn and look solemnly at the great golden emblem hanging at their back.

(*Warmly*:) Take courage, Wolfgang. It's a glorious idea.

MOZART. It is, isn't it? It *really is!*

SALIERI. Of course say nothing till it's done.

MOZART. Not a word.

SALIERI (*making a sign: closed fist*). Secret!

MOZART (*making a similar sign*). Secret!

SALIERI. Good.

He steps out of the scene downstage.

(*To audience*:) And if that didn't finish him off with the Masons — nothing would!

The gold emblem withdraws. We hear the merry dance of Monostatos and the hypnotized slaves from The Magic Flute; *'Das Klinget so herrlich, Das Klinget so schön!' To the tinkling of the glockenspiel* SERVANTS *bring in a long plain table loaded with manuscripts and bottles. It also bears a plain upturned stool. They place this in the wooden area head-on to the audience. At the same time* CONSTANZE *appears wearily from the back, and enters this apartment: the Rauhensteingasse. She wears a stuffed apron, indicating the advanced state of her pregnancy. Simultaneously upstage left, two other* SERVANTS *have placed the gilded table bearing a loaded cakestand and three of the gilded chairs from* SALIERI's *resplendent Salon. We now have in view the two contrasting apartments.*

As soon as the emblem withdraws, the VENTICELLI *appear to* SALIERI.

*   *   *

Mozart's Apartment: Salieri's Apartment

VENTICELLO 1. Mozart is delighted with himself!

VENTICELLO 2. He's writing a secret opera!

VENTICELLO 1 (*crossly*). And won't tell anyone its theme.

VENTICELLO 2. It's really too tiresome.

The VENTICELLI *go off.*

SALIERI. He told *me*. He told me everything! . . . Initiation
ceremonies. Ceremonies with blindfolds. All rituals copied
from the Masons . . . He sat at home preparing his own
destruction. A home where life grew daily more grim.

*He goes upstage and sits on one of his gilded chairs, devouring
a cake.* MOZART *also sits at his table, wrapped in a blanket,
and starts to write music. Opposite him* CONSTANZE *sits on a
stool, wrapped in a shawl.*

CONSTANZE. I'm cold . . . I'm cold all day . . . Hardly surprising
since we have no firewood.

MOZART. Papa was right. We end exactly as he said. Beggars.

CONSTANZE. It's all his fault.

MOZART. What do you mean?

CONSTANZE. He kept you a baby all your life.

MOZART. I don't understand . . . You always loved Papa.

CONSTANZE. *I* did?

MOZART. You adored him. You told me so often.

Slight pause.

CONSTANZE (*flatly*). I hated him.

MOZART. What?

CONSTANZE. And he hated me.

MOZART. That's absurd. He loved us both very much. You're
being extremely silly now.

CONSTANZE. Am I?

MOZART (*airily*). Yes, you are, little-wife-of-my-heart!

CONSTANZE. Do you remember the fire we had last night, because it was so cold you couldn't even get the ink wet? You said 'What a blaze' — remember? 'What a blaze! All those old papers going up!' Well, my dear, those old papers were just all your father's letters, that's all — every one he wrote since the day we married.

MOZART. *What?*

CONSTANZE. Every one! All the letters about what a ninny I am — what a bad housekeeper I am! Every one!

MOZART (*crying out*). Stanzi!

CONSTANZE. *Shit on him! . . . Shit on him!*

MOZART. *You bitch!*

CONSTANZE (*savagely*). At least it kept us warm! What else will do that? Perhaps we should dance! You love to dance, Wolferl — let's dance! Dance to keep warm! (*Grandly:*) Write me a contredanze, Mozart! It's your job to write dances, isn't it?

Hysterical, she starts dancing roughly round the room like a demented peasant to the tune of 'Non più andrai'.

(*Singing wildly:*) *Non più andrai', farfallone amoroso —
Notte e giorno d'intorno girando!*

MOZART (*shrieking*). *Stop it! Stop it!* (*He seizes her.*) Stanzi-marini! Marini-bini! Don't please! Please, please, please I beg you . . . Look there's a kiss! Where's it coming from? Right out of that corner! There's another one — all wet, all sloppy wet coming straight to *you!* Kiss — kiss — kiss!

She pushes him away. CONSTANZE *dances.* MOZART *catches her. She pushes him away.*

CONSTANZE. Get off!

Pause.

MOZART. I'm frightened, Stanzi. Something awful's happening to me.

CONSTANZE. I can't bear it. I can't bear much more of this.

MOZART. And the Figure's like this now — (*Beckoning faster.*) 'Here! Come here! Here!' Its face still masked — invisible! It becomes realer and realer to me!

CONSTANZE. Stop it, for God's sake! . . . Stop! . . . It's me who's frightened . . . *Me!* . . . You frighten me . . . If you go on like this I'll leave you. I swear it.

MOZART (*shocked*). Stanzi!

CONSTANZE. I mean it . . . I do . . . (*She puts her hand to her stomach, as if in pain.*)

MOZART. I'm sorry . . . Oh God, I'm sorry . . . I'm sorry, I'm sorry, I'm sorry! . . . Come here to me, little wife of my heart! Come . . . Come . . .

He kneels and coaxes her to him. She comes half-reluctantly, half-willingly.

MOZART. Who am I? . . . Quick: tell me. Hold me and tell who I am.

CONSTANZE. Pussy-wussy.

MOZART. Who else?

CONSTANZE. Miaowy-powy.

MOZART. And you're squeeky-peeky. And Stanzi-manzi. And Bini-gini!

She surrenders.

CONSTANZE. Wolfi-polfi!

MOZART. Poopy-peepee!

They giggle.

CONSTANZE. Now don't be stupid.

MOZART (*insistent: like a child*). Come on — do it. Do it — Let's do it. Poppy.

They play a private game, gradually doing it faster, on their knees.

CONSTANZE. Poppy.

MOZART (*changing it*). Pappy.

CONSTANZE (*copying*). Pappy.

MOZART. Pappa.

CONSTANZE. Pappa.

MOZART. Pappa-pappa!

CONSTANZE. Pappa-pappa!

MOZART. Pappa-pappa-pappa-pappa!

CONSTANZE. Pappa-pappa-pappa-pappa!

>*They rub noses.*

TOGETHER. Pappa-pappa-pappa-pappa! Pappa-pappa-pappa-pappa!

CONSTANZE. *Ah!*

>*She suddenly cries out in distress, and clutches her stomach.*

MOZART. Stanzi! . . . Stanzi, what is it?

>*The* VENTICELLI *hurry in.*

VENTICELLO 1. News!

VENTICELLO 2. Suddenly!

VENTICELLO 1. She's been delivered.

VENTICELLO 2. Unexpectedly.

VENTICELLO 1. Of a boy.

VENTICELLO 2. Poor little imp.

VENTICELLO 1. To be born to that couple.

VENTICELLO 2. In that room.

VENTICELLO 1. With that money.

VENTICELLO 2. And the father a baby himself.

>*During the above,* CONSTANZE *has slowly risen and divested herself of her stuffed apron — thereby ceasing to be pregnant. Now she turns sorrowfully and walks slowly upstage and off it.* MOZART *follows her for a few steps, alarmed. He halts.*

VENTICELLO 1. And now I hear —

VENTICELLO 2. Now I hear —

VENTICELLO 1. Something more has happened.

VENTICELLO 2. Even stranger.

> MOZART *picks up a bottle — then moves swiftly into* SALIERI's *room.*

MOZART. *She's gone!*

SALIERI. What do you mean?

> *The* VENTICELLI *go off.* MOZART *moves up to* SALIERI's *apartment, holding his bottle, and sits on one of the gilded chairs.*

MOZART. Stanzerl's gone away. Just for a while, say says. She's taken the baby and gone to Baden. To the spa. It will cost us the last money we have!

SALIERI. But *why?*

MOZART. She's right to go . . . It's my fault . . . She thinks I'm mad.

SALIERI. Surely not?

MOZART. Perhaps I am . . . I think I am . . . Yes . . .

SALIERI. Wolfgang . . .

MOZART. Let me tell you! Last night I saw the Figure again — the figure in my dreams. (*Very disturbed* :) It stood before my table, all in grey, its face still grey, still masked. And this time it spoke to me! 'Wolfgang Mozart — you must write now a Requiem Mass. Take up your pen and begin!'

SALIERI. A Requiem? Who is this Requiem for?

MOZART. I asked 'Who has died?' It said, 'The work must be finished when you see me next!' Then it turned and left the room.

SALIERI. Oh, this is morbid fancy, my friend!

MOZART. It had the force of real things! . . . To tell the truth — I do not know whether it happened in my head or out of it . . . No wonder Stanzi has gone. I frightened her away . . . And now she'll miss the vaudeville.

SALIERI. You mean it's finished? So soon?

MOZART. Oh yes — music is easy: it's marriage that's hard!

SALIERI. I long to see it!

MOZART. Would you come, truly? The theatre isn't grand. No one from Court will be there.

SALIERI. Do you think that matters to me? I would travel anywhere for a work by you! . . . I am no substitute for your little wife — but I know someone who could be!

He gets up. MOZART *rises also.*

MOZART. Who?

SALIERI. I'll tell you what — I'll bring Katherina! She'll cheer you up!

MOZART. Katherina!

SALIERI. As I remember it, you quite enjoyed her company!

MOZART *laughs heartily.* CAVALIERI *enters, now fatter and wearing an elaborate plumed hat. She curtsies to* MOZART *and takes his arm.*

MOZART (*bowing*). Signora!

SALIERI (*to audience*). And so to the opera we went — a strange band of three!

The other two freeze.

The First Kapellmeister — sleek as a cat. His mistress — now fat and feathered like the great song-bird she'd become. And demented Mozart — drunk on the cheap wine which was now his constant habit.

They unfreeze and walk across the stage.

We went out into the suburbs — to a crowded music-hall — in a tenement!

*   *   *

The Theatre by the Weiden

Two benches are brought in and placed down front. Sudden noise. A crowd of working-class Germans swarm in from the back: a chattering mass of humanity through which the three have to push their way to the front. The long table is pushed horizontally, and the rowdy audience piles on top of it, smoking pipes and chewing sausages.

Unobserved, BARON VAN SWIETEN *comes in also and stands at the back.*

MOZART. You must be indulgent now! It's my first piece of this kind!

The three sit on the front bench: MOZART *sick and emaciated;* CAVALIERI *blowsy and bedizened;* SALIERI *as elegant as ever.*

SALIERI. We sat as he wished us to, among ordinary Germans! The smell of sweat and sausage was almost annihilating!

CAVALIERI *presses a mouchoir to her sensitive nose.*

(*To* MOZART:) This is so exciting!

MOZART (*happily*). Do you think so?

SALIERI (*looking about him*). Oh yes! This is exactly the audience we should be writing for! Not the dreary Court . . . As always — *you* show the way!

The audience freezes.

(*To us:*) As always, he did. My pungent neighbours *rolled* on their benches at the jokes —

They unfreeze — briefly to demonstate this mirth —

And I alone in their midst heard — *The Magic Flute!*

They freeze again. The great hymn at the end of Act II is heard: 'Heil sei euch Geweihten'.

He had put the Masons into it right enough. Oh yes — but how? He had turned them into an Order of Eternal Priests. I heard voices calling out of ancient temples. I saw a vast sun rise on a timeless land, where animals danced and children floated: and by its rays all the poisons we feed each other drawn up and burnt away!

A great sun does indeed rise inside the Light Box, and standing in it the gigantic silhouette of a priestly figure extending its arms to the world in universal greeting.

And in this sun — behold — I saw his father. No more an accusing figure, but forgiving! The Highest Priest of the Order — his hand extended to the world in love! Wolfgang feared Leopold no longer: a final Legend has been made! . . . Oh the sound — the sound of that new-found peace in him — mocking my undiminishing pain! *There* was the Magic Flute — *there beside me!*

He points to MOZART. *Applause from all.* MOZART *jumps up excitedly on to the bench and acknowledges the clapping with his arms flung out. He turns to us, a bottle in his hand — his eyes staring: all freeze again.*

SALIERI. Mozart the flute, and God the relentless player. How long could the Creature stand it — so frail, so palpably mortal? And what was this I was tasting suddenly? Could it be pity? . . . *Never!*

VAN SWIETEN (*calling out*). *Mozart!*

VAN SWIETEN *pushes his way to the front through the crowd of dispersing* CITIZENS. *He is outraged.*

MOZART (*turning joyfully to greet him*). Baron! You here! How wonderful of you to come!

SALIERI (*to audience*). I had of course suggested it.

VAN SWIETEN (*with cold fury*). What have you done?

MOZART. Excellency?

VAN SWIETEN. You have put our rituals into a vulgar show!

MOZART. No, sir —

VAN SWIETEN. They are plain for all to see! And to laugh at! You have betrayed the Order.

MOZART (*in horror*). *No!*

SALIERI. Baron, a word with you —

VAN SWIETEN. Don't speak for him, Salieri. (*To* MOZART, *with frozen contempt:*) You were ever a cruel vulgarian we hoped to mend. Stupid, hopeless task! Now you are a betrayer

as well. I shall never forgive you. And depend upon it — I shall
ensure that no Freemason or Person of Distinction will do so
in Vienna so long as I have life!

SALIERI. Baron, please, I must speak!

VAN SWIETEN. No, sir! Leave alone. (*To* MOZART:) I did not
look for this reward, Mozart. Never speak to me.

*He goes out. The crowd disperses. The lights change. The
benches are taken off.* SALIERI, *watching* MOZART
narrowly, dismisses KATHERINA. MOZART *stands as one
dead.*

SALIERI. Wolfgang?

*MOZART shakes his head sharply — and walks away from
him, upstage, desolate and stunned.*

Wolfgang — all is not lost.

MOZART enters his apartment and freezes.

(*To audience*:) But of course it was! Now he was ruined.
Broken and shunned by all men of influence. He did not even
get his half receipts from the opera.

*   *   *

The VENTICELLI *come in.*

VENTICELLO 1. Schikaneder pays him nothing.

VENTICELLO 2. Schikaneder cheats him.

VENTICELLO 1. Gives him enough for liquor.

VENTICELLO 2. And keeps all the rest.

SALIERI. I couldn't have managed it better myself.

*MOZART takes up a blanket and muffles himself in it. Then
he sits at his work-table, down front, staring out at the
audience, quite still, the blanket almost over his face.*

And then silence. No word came from him at all. Why? . . . I
waited each day. Nothing. Why? . . . (*To the* VENTICELLI,
brusquely:) What does he do?

MOZART writes.

VENTICELLO 1. He sits at his window.

VENTICELLO 2. All day and all night.

VENTICELLO 1. Writing —

VENTICELLO 2. Writing — like a man possessed.

MOZART *springs to his feet, and freezes.*

VENTICELLO 1. Springs up every moment!

VENTICELLO 2. Stares wildly at the street!

VENTICELLO 1. Expecting something —

VENTICELLO 2. Someone —

VENTICELLO 1 and VENTICELLO 2. We can't imagine what!

SALIERI (*to audience*). I could!

He also springs up excitedly, dismissing the VENTICELLI. MOZART *and* SALIERI *now both stand staring out front.*

Who did he look for? A Figure in grey, masked and sorrowing, come to take him away. I knew what he was doing, alone in that slum! He was writing his Requiem Mass — for himself! . . . And now I confess the wickedest thing I did to him.

His VALET *brings him the clothes which he describes, and he puts them on, turning his back to us to don the hat — to which is attached a mask.*

My friends — there is no blasphemy a man will not commit, compelled to such a war as mine! I got me a cloak of grey. Yes. And a mask of grey — Yes!

He turns round: he is masked.

and appeared myself to the demented Creature as — the *Messenger of God!* . . . I confess that in November seventeen ninety-one, I — Antonio Salieri, then as now First Kapellmeister to the Empire — walked empty Vienna in the freezing moonlight for seven nights on end! That precisely as the clocks of the city struck one I would halt beneath Mozart's window — and become his more terrible clock.

The clock strikes one. SALIERI, *without moving from the left side of the stage, raises his arms: his fingers show seven days.*

MOZART *rises — fascinated and appalled — and stands equally rigidly on the right side, looking out in horror.*

Every night I showed him one day less — then stalked away. Every night the face he showed me at the glass was more crazed. Finally — with no days left to him — *horror!* I arrived as usual. Halted. And instead of fingers, reached up beseechingly as the Figure of his dreams! 'Come! — Come! — Come! . . .'

He beckons to MOZART, *insidiously.*

He stood swaying, as if he would faint off into death. But suddenly — incredibly — he realized all his little strength, and in a clear voice called down to me the words of his opera *Don Giovanni,* inviting the statue to dinner.

MOZART (*pushing open the 'window'*). O statua gentilissima — venite a cena!

He beckons in his turn.

SALIERI. For a long moment one terrified man looked at another. Then — unbelievably — I found myself nodding, just as in the opera. Starting to move across the street!

The rising and falling scale passage from the Overture to Don Giovanni *sounds darkly, looped in sinister repetition. To this hollow music* SALIERI *marches slowly upstage.*

Pushing down the latch of his door — tramping up the stairs with stone feet. There was no stopping it. *I was in his dream!*

MOZART *stands terrified by his table.* SALIERI *throws open the door. An instant light change.*

SALIERI *stands still, staring impassively downstage.* MOZART *addresses him urgently, and in awe.*

MOZART. It's not finished! . . . Not nearly! . . . Forgive me. Time was I could write a Mass in a week! . . . Give me one month more, and it'll be done: I swear it! . . . He'll grant me that, surely? God can't want it unfinished! . . . Look — look, see what I've done.

He snatches up the pages from the table and brings them eagerly to the Figure.

Here's the Kyrie — that's finished! Take that to Him — He'll see it's not unworthy! . . .

Unwillingly SALIERI *moves across the room — takes the pages, and sits behind the table in* MOZART's *chair, staring out front.*

Grant me time, I beg you! If you do, I swear I'll write a real piece of music. I know I've boasted I've written hundreds, but it's not true. I've written nothing finally good!

SALIERI *looks at the pages. Immediately we hear the sombre opening of the Requiem Mass. Over this* MOZART *speaks.*

Oh it began so well, my life. Once the world was so full, so happy! . . . All the journeys — all the carriages — all the rooms of smiles! Everyone smiling at me once — the King at Schönbrunn; the Princess at Versailles. They lit my way with candles to the clavier! — my father bowing, bowing, bowing with such joy! 'Chevalier Mozart, my miraculous son!' . . . Why has it all gone? . . . Why? . . . Was I so bad? So wicked? . . . Answer for Him and tell me!

Deliberately SALIERI *tears the paper into pieces. The music stops instantly. Silence.*

(*Fearfully*:) Why? . . . Is it not good?

SALIERI (*stiffly*). It is good. Yes. It is good.

He tears off a corner of the music paper, elevates it in the manner of the Communion Service, places it on his tongue and eats it.

(*In pain*:) I eat what God gives me. Dose after dose. For all of life. His poison. We are both poisoned, Amadeus. I with you: you with me.

In horror MOZART *moves slowly behind him, placing his hand over* SALIERI's *mouth — then, still from behind, slowly removes the mask and hat.* SALIERI *stares at us.*

Eccomi. Antonio Salieri. Ten years of my hate have poisoned you to death.

MOZART *falls to his knees, by the table.*

MOZART. Oh God!

SALIERI (*contemptuously*). *God?!* . . . God will not help you! God *does* not help!

MOZART. Oh God! . . . Oh God! . . . Oh God!

SALIERI. God does not love you, Amadeus! God does not love! He can only *use!* . . . He cares nothing for who He uses: nothing for who He denies! . . . You are no use to Him any more — You're too weak — too sick! He has finished with you! All you can do now is *die!*

MOZART. *Ah!*

With a groan MOZART crawls quickly through the trestle of the table, like an animal finding a burrow — or a child a safe place of concealment. SALIERI kneels by the table, calling in at his victim in desperation.

SALIERI. Die, Amadeus! Die, I beg you, die! . . . Leave me alone, *ti imploro!* Leave me alone at last! Leave me alone!

He beats on the table in his despair.

Alone! Alone! Alone! Alone! Alone!

MOZART (*crying out at the top of his lungs*). PAPAAAAA!

He freezes — his mouth open in the act of screaming — his head staring out from under the table.

SALIERI *rises in horror. Silence. Then very slowly MOZART crawls out from under the table. He stares upwards. He sits. He smiles.*

(*In a childish voice:*) Papa!

Silence.

Papa . . . papa . . .

He extends his arms upwards, imploringly. He speaks now as a very young boy.

Take me, Papa. Take me. Put down your arms and I'll hop into them. Just as we used to do it! . . . Hop-hop-hop-hop-UP!

He jumps up on to the table. SALIERI watches in horror.

Hold me close to you, Papa. Let's sing our little Kissing Song together. Do you remember? . . .

He sings in an infantine voice.

Oragna figata fa! Marina gamina fa!

SALIERI. Reduce the man: reduce the God. Behold my vow fulfilled. The profoundest voice in the world reduced to a nursery tune.

He leaves the room, slowly, as MOZART resumes his singing.

MOZART. *Oragna figata fa! Marina gamina fa!*

As SALIERI withdraws, CONSTANZE appears from the back of the stage, her bonnet in her hand. She has returned from Baden. She comes downstage towards her husband, and finds him there on the table singing in an obviously childish treble.

Oragna figata fa! Marina gamina fa. Fa! Fa!

He kisses the air, several times. Finally he becomes aware of his wife standing beside him.

(*Uncertainly*:) Stanzi?

CONSTANZE. Wolfi? . . .

MOZART (*in relief*). Stanzi!

CONSTANZE (*with great tenderness*). Wolfi — my love! Little husband of my heart!

He virtually falls off the table into her arms.

MOZART. *Oh!*

He clings to her in overwhelming pleasure. She helps him gently to move around the table to the chair behind it, facing out front.

CONSTANZE. Oh, my dear one — come with me . . . Come on . . . Come on now. There . . . There . . .

MOZART *sits weakly.*

MOZART (*like a child still, and most earnestly*). Salieri . . . Salieri has killed me.

CONSTANZE. Yes, my dear.

Practically she busies herself clearing the table of its candle, its bottle and its inkwell.

MOZART. He has. He told me so.

CONSTANZE. Yes, yes: I'm sure.

She finds two pillows and places them at the left-hand head of the table.

MOZART (*petulantly*). He did . . . He did!

CONSTANZE. Hush now, lovey.

She helps her dying husband on to the table, now his bed. He lies down, and she covers him with her shawl.

I'm back to take care of you. I'm sorry I went away. I'm here now, for always!

MOZART. Salieri . . . Salieri . . . Salieri . . . Salieri!

He starts to weep.

CONSTANZE. Oh lovey, be silent now. No one has hurt you. You'll get better soon, I promise. Can you hear me?

Faintly the Lacrimosa of the Requiem Mass begins to sound. MOZART rises to hear it — leaning against his wife's shoulders. His hand begins feebly to beat out drum measures from the music. During the whole of the following it is evident that he is composing the Mass in his head, and does not hear his wife at all.

You've got to get well, Wolfi — because we need you. Karl and Baby Franz as well. There's only the three of us, lovey: we don't cost much. Just don't leave us — we wouldn't know what to do without you. And you wouldn't know much either, up in Heaven, without us. You soppy thing. You can't even cut up your own meat without help! . . . I'm not clever, lovey. It can't have been easy living with a goose. But I've looked after you, you must admit that. And I've given you fun too — quite a lot really! Are you listening!

The drum strokes get slower, and stop.

Know one thing. It was the best day of my life when you married me. And as long as I live I'll be the most honoured woman in the world . . . Can you hear me?

She becomes aware that MOZART *is dead. She opens her mouth in a silent scream, raising her arm in a rigid gesture of grief. The great chord of the 'Amen' does not resolve itself, but lingers on in intense reverberation.*

*   *   *

CITIZENS OF VIENNA *come in, dressed in black, from the right.* CONSTANZE *kneels and freezes in grief, as* SERVANTS *come in and stand at each of the four corners of the table on which the dead body lies.* VAN SWIETEN *also comes in.*

SALIERI (*hard*). The Death Certificate said kidney failure, hastened by exposure to cold. Generous Lord Fugue paid for a pauper's funeral. Twenty other corpses. An unmarked limepit.

VAN SWIETEN *approaches* CONSTANZE.

VAN SWIETEN. What little I can spare, you shall have for the children. There's no need to waste it on vain show.

The SERVANTS *lift the table and bear it, with its burden, upstage, centre. to the Light Box. The* CITIZENS *follow it.*

SALIERI. What did I feel? Relief, of course: I confess it. And pity too, for the man I helped to destroy. I felt the pity God can never feel. I weakened God's flute to thinness. God blew — as He must — without cease. The flute split in the mouth of His insatiable need.

The CITIZENS *kneel. In dead silence the* SERVANTS *throw* MOZART's *body off the table into the space at the back of the stage. All depart save* SALIERI *and* CONSTANZE. *She unfreezes and starts assiduously collecting the manuscripts scattered over the floor.*

SALIERI *now speaks with an increasingly ageing voice: a voice poisoned more and more by his own bitterness.*

As for Constanze, in the fullness of time she married again — a Danish diplomat as dull as a clock — and retired to Salzburg, birthplace of the Composer, to become the pious Keeper of his Shrine!

CONSTANZE *rises, wrapping her shawl about her, and clasping manuscripts to her bosom.*

CONSTANZE (*reverentially*). A sweeter-tongued man never lived! In ten years of blissful marriage I never heard him utter a single coarse or conceited word. The purity of his life is reflected absolutely in the purity of his music! . . . (*More briskly*:) In selling his manuscripts I charge by the ink. So many notes, so many schillings. That seems to me the simplest way.

She leaves the stage, a pillar of rectitude.

SALIERI. One amazing fact emerged. Mozart did not *imagine* that masked Figure who said 'Take up your pen and write a Requiem.' It was *real*! . . . A certain bizarre nobleman called Count Walsegg had a longing to be thought a composer. He actually sent his Steward in disguise to Mozart to commission the piece — secretly, so that he could pass it off as his own work. And this he even did! After Mozart's death it was actually performed as Count Walsegg's Requiem . . . And I conducted it.

He smiled at the audience.

Naturally I did. In those days I presided over all great musical occasions in Vienna.

He divests himself of his cloak.

SALIERI. I even conducted the salvos of cannon in Beethoven's dreadful Battle Symphony. The experience made me almost as deaf as *he* was!

* * *

The CITIZENS *bow and kiss their hands to him.*

SALIERI. So I remained in Vienna — City of Musicians — reverenced by all. And slowly I understood the nature of God's punishment! . . . What had I begged for in that church as a boy? Was it not fame? . . . Fame for excellence? . . . Well now I had fame! I was to become — quite simply — the most famous musician in Europe!

All the CITIZENS *fall on their knees before him, clapping their hands silently, and relentlessly extending their arms upwards and upwards, almost obliterating him.*

I was to be bricked up in fame! Embalmed in fame! Buried in fame — but for work I knew to be *absolutely worthless!* . . . This was my sentence: — I must endure thirty years of being called 'distinguished' by people incapable of distinguishing! . . . and finally — his Masterstroke! When my nose had been rubbed in fame to vomiting — it would all be taken away from me. Every scrap.

The CITIZENS *rise, and all walk away indifferently upstage, past him, on into the Light Box, and off the stage.*

I must survive to see myself become extinct!

A SERVANT *hands him his old stained dressing-gown and cap.*

When they trundled me out to a carriage to get my last Award, a man on the kerb said 'Isn't that one of the Generals from Waterloo?'

The last movement of the Jupiter Symphony begins to sound, growing ever louder.

Mozart's music sounded louder and louder through the world! And mine faded completely, till no one played it at all! (*Yelling upwards:*) Nemico dei Nemici! Dio Implacabile!

The Mozart symphony swells to a huge crescendo, seeming to drown SALIERI. *He sinks to his knees under the weight of it, and finally claps his hands to his aching ears to shut it out. The deafening music snaps off. The curtains descend in a rush. A clock strikes six.*

*   *   *

Salieri's Apartment November 1823

A SERVANT *comes in quickly with the wheelchair.* SALIERI *speaks again in the voice of an old man.*

SALIERI (*to audience*). Dawn has come. I must release you — and myself. One moment's violence and it's done. You see, I cannot accept this. I did not live on earth to be His joke for Eternity. I *will* be remembered! *I will be remembered!* — if not in fame, them infamy. One moment more and I win battle with Him. Watch and see! . . . All this month I've been shouting about murder. 'Have mercy, Mozart! Pardon your Assassin!' And now my last move. A false confession — short and convincing!

He pulls it out of his pocket.

How I really did murder Mozart — with arsenic — out of envy! And how I cannot live another day under the knowledge! By tonight they'll hear out there how I died — and they'll believe it's true! . . . Let them forget me then. For the rest of time whenever men say Mozart with love, they will say Salieri with loathing! . . . *I am going to be immortal after all!* And He is powerless to prevent it! So, Signore — see now if Man is mocked!

The VALET *comes in with a tray, bearing a bowl of hot shaving water, soap and a razor. He set this on the table.* SALIERI *hands him the Confession.*

(To VALET.*)* Good morning. Lay this on the desk in the Cabinet. Append your name to it in witness that this is my hand. *Via — subito!*

The man takes the paper and goes, bewildered, upstage right. SALIERI *picks up the razor and rises. He addresses the audience most simply and directly.*

Amici cari. I was born a pair of ears and nothing else. It is only through hearing music that I know God exists. Only through writing music that I could worship. All around me men seek liberty for Mankind. I sought only slavery for myself. To be owned — ordered — exhausted by an *Absolute.* This was denied me, and with it all meaning.

He opens the razor.

Now I go to become a ghost myself. I will stand in the shadows when you come here to this earth in your turn. And when you feel the dreadful bite of your failures — and hear the taunting of unachievable, uncaring God — I will whisper my name to you: 'Salieri: Patron Saint of Mediocrities!' And in the depth of your downcastness you can pray to me. And I will forgive you. *Vi saluto.*

He cuts his throat, and falls backwards into the wheelchair.

The COOK — *who has just come in, carrying a plate of fresh buns for breakfast — sees this and screams. The* VALET *rushes in at the same time from the other side. Together they pull the wheelchair, with its slumped body, backwards upstage, and anchor it in the centre.*

The VENTICELLI *appear again, in the costume of 1823.*

VENTICELLO 1. Beethoven's Conversation Book, eighteen twenty-three. Visitors write the news for the deaf man.

He hands a book to VENTICELLO 2.

VENTICELLO 2 (*reading*). 'Salieri has cut his throat — but is still alive!'

SALIERI *stirs and comes to life, looking about him bewilderedly. The* VALET *and the* COOK *depart. He stares out front like an astounded gargoyle.*

VENTICELLO 1. Beethoven's Conversation Book, eighteen twenty-four. Visitors write the news for the deaf man.

He hands another book to VENTICELLO 2.

VENTICELLO 2 (*reading*). 'Salieri is quite deranged. He keeps claiming that he is guilty of Mozart's death, and made away with him by poison.'

The light narrows into a bright cone, beating on SALIERI.

VENTICELLO 1. The *German Musical Times,* May the twenty-fifth, eighteen twenty-five.

He hands a newspaper to VENTICELLO 2.

VENTICELLO 2 (*reading*). 'Our worthy Salieri just cannot die. In the frenzy of his imagination he is even said to accuse himself of complicity in Mozart's early death. A rambling of the mind believed in truth by no one but the deluded old man himself.'

The music stops. SALIERI *lowers his head, conceding defeat.*

VENTICELLO 1. I don't believe it.

VENTICELLO 2. I don't believe it.

They look in turn at SALIERI.

VENTICELLO 1. I don't believe it.

VENTICELLO 2. I don't believe it.

VENTICELLO 1 and VENTICELLO 2. *No one believes it in the world!*

> *They go off. The light dims a little.* SALIERI *slowly rises and walks downstage: a lone figure in the darkness.*

SALIERI. Mediocrities everywhere — now and to come — I absolve you all. Amen!

> *He extends his arms upwards and outwards to embrace the assembled audience in a wide gesture of Benediction — finally folding his arms high across his own breast.*

> *The light fades completely. The last four chords of the Masonic Funeral Music of* AMADEUS MOZART *sound throughout the theatre.*

Peter Nichols

The plays of Peter Nichols are so varied that they defy summing up in terms of a single style or category. 'Do any damn thing you have to do to keep the heart and soul alive,' he is quoted as saying. It is the cry, as Richard Bryant suggests, that emanates, in different ways, from all of his plays. Nichols made his theatre name with *A Day in the Death of Joe Egg*, a tightly-knit, six-character, one-set drama, written in a quasi-Brechtian music hall style, in which the excruciating burden of a hopelessly spastic child shatters the marriage of its parents. Nichols next turned out *The National Health, or Nurse Norton's Affair*, in which more than two dozen characters are scrambled across the stage in a rambling fantasy-farce of hospital life and death interrupted by vaudeville comedy and scenes from a television soap opera about an operating room romance. His third full-length play, *Forget-Me-Not-Lane*, returns to the family and the dislocation between parent and child, but Nichols adds a nostalgic tour of the World War II home front and the music of a dozen pop and jazz recordings of the period. He also experimented with the device he would bring to full flower in *Passion Play*, the presentation of a character in simultaneous stage selves – in *Forget-Me-Not-Lane*, youthful and middle-aged versions of the same man.

In 1977 Nichols wrote a musical comedy, *Privates on Parade*, for which he composed the lyrics for thirteen songs, thereby winning the Ivor Novello Award for the best musical as well as his third Evening Standard Best Play Award. *Passion Play*, his next play, won him another Evening Standard Award. Then he wrote *Poppy*, a comic exposé of Victorian imperialism in the form of a Christmas panto. The panto is a genre familiar to every Englishman; for Americans it might be described as a pastiche of songs, fabulous costumes, and implausible fairy tale made even funnier by the traditional cross-casting of males and females.

Nichols, then, is an all-round 'man of the theatre': anything that can be done on stage he can write. For all the range and variety of his theatrical forms and themes, however, there are constants in his plays worth remarking: corrosive wit that evokes almost continuous laughter from audiences and a deeply compassionate concern about the effects of our turbulent culture on individual lives. 'Don't let the bastards get you down,' Nichols says. His list of bastards, Bryant notes, includes governments, institutions, professions, unions, and class structures. He also rails against acts of God, like terminal illness and brain-damaged children, and the dividedness in the human psyche that makes people hurt each other.

Laughter is a powerful suvival mechanism in the most tragic circumstances of Nichols' plays. Joe Egg is such cause for despair that her father, Bri, tries to kill her. The patients of *The National Health* suffer more pain and death than they enjoy cure. The soldiers in *Privates on Parade* are crippled and die in a nasty little anti-guerilla campaign in post-war Malaysia during a Communist insurrection. In *Poppy*, Dick Whittington's sister becomes a drug addict. Yet all these dreadful woes unfold amid jokes, stand-up comedy turns, and cheerful song and dance, in an atmosphere of constant good-humour. So unnerving is Nichols' mixture of comic and tragic moments that some critics have accused him of trivializing serious material for comic effect. Other critics laud Nichols for his ability to reach, as Victoria Glendinning put it, 'the unsayable truth' by way of shock comedy, distancing audiences from easy sentiment by the deep, true laughter of recognition.

Another constant in the work of Nichols is autobiography. Nichols candidly acknowledges that his life supplies the matter for his plays. *Joe Egg* reflects the anguish he and his wife experienced with their own spastic child, who died at ten. *The National Health* draws on his hospital stay for a collapsed lung. *Privates on Parade* is based on his own military experience that included touring British Asian bases in a show called 'At Your Service'.

Part of the great good-humour of plays with such sombre elements in them comes from Nichols' joyous exploitation of popular entertainment, especially the tricks of what the English call music hall and Americans call vaudeville. Both *Forget-Me-Not-Lane* and *Privates on Parade* nostalgically recreate the ritual of entertaining the troops in wartime. In *Forget-Me-Not-Lane*, amateurs do their bit by performing variety acts at an RAF station. In *Privates on Parade*, professional troupers in uniform trot out their music hall routines for soldiers in the jungle. Perhaps the most often noted of Nichols' music hall borrowings is the comic doctor routine in *Joe Egg*, when Bri and Sheila mimic an exchange with the Viennese specialist attending their spastic child:

> BRI: You vont a word for her? You can say she iss a spastic vis a damaged cerebral cortex, multiplegic, epileptic, but vis no organic malformation of ze brain.
> SHEILA: That IS a long word.
> BRI: Which is vy I prefer wegetable.

The information is communicated, the pain of the parents is revealed in the defence mechanism of their clowning, and audiences are reached through a theatrical tradition they know and cherish.

Like Bernard Shaw, Nichols came to playwriting late. Born in Bristol in 1927, he did RAF service from 1945 to 1948, after which he enrolled at the Bristol Old Vic Theatre School, where he studied acting 'because they had no courses in writing plays'. After five years of acting and two of teaching, Nichols turned to television writing. During 1959 to 1965 he turned out fourteen television plays. Then came *Joe Egg*, which he had conceived for television but converted to a stage play because he thought it unacceptable to the palates of broadcasters.

After achieving hit status in London, *Passion Play* reached Broadway in 1983 as *Passion*, the original title having been preempted in the United Sates by Jerzy Kosinski's novel. Under both titles and in both countries, the play divided the critical community. In New York, John Simon complained of an opaque ending and a too clever exploitation of the alter ego device. Robert Brustein declared the alter ego an already dead device and the play 'dramatic doodling'. But Frank Rich of the *New York Times* and Clive Barnes of the *Post* hailed the play as one of the season's best. In London, as John Russell Taylor put it, the play 'provoked the most varied reaction I can recall in a very long time, from total dismissal to ecstatic praise'.

The ultimate success of *Passion Play* outweighs the ephemera of reviewer debate, but the focus on Nichols' stunningly innovative use of the alter ego device to explore his theme is useful.

The play is dominated by the theme of adultery. As Harold Hobson wrote, it 'shows with almost unparalleled force the pain, the anguish, and the deceit that adultery involves, . . . in a hell more real than anything in Don Juan'. The play's middle-aged hero, James, commits what he expects to be a casual adultery with the shallow young Kate. But the act unleashes powerful destructive forces within James. He finds that he cannot do without the aphrodisiac of his illicit affair. Previously a decent honest man, he becomes a constant deceiver. Inevitably, his wife Eleanor discovers his secret, and she and James begin a fatal dance of mutual deceit and distrust. At the end of the play, though they continue to share a house, their marriage is dead.

Nichols deepens the conflict by introducing two alter egos, first Jim and then Nell, who speak the ordinarily unspeakable thoughts of James and Eleanor. They make the inner hell of adultery cruelly palpable.

But *Passion Play* is full of strong pointers toward a more complex theme, the relationship between our Christian heritage and sexual morality. The title, the sacred music that Eleanor's choir sings and James and Kate listen to as they lie in their adulterous bed, and the crystalline moment when James wraps up, that is, disposes of, a painting of Christ while his alter ego Jim proclaims his intention to fornicate away his consciousness of Christ's wounds – 'All that's holy' – combine to show the fierce combat in the human soul between the impulse to unleash the libido and the need to harness it to conventional Christian morality. This is an old conflict in Nichols' plays. Of his more conventional marital comedy, *Chez Nous*, Nichols said 'All my married men are like that – they feel trapped and want to be free . . .' At the final curtain of *Forget-Me-Not-Lane*, the middle-aged Frank follows his middle-aged, dispirited wife, Ursula, off to their unpromising bed as his trailing eye fixes on a vision of the remembered young Ursula, the nymphette who represents the liberated youth Frank never enjoyed, the freedom of the libido he never tasted. Frank envies his own son, whom he imagines lives a sexual romp unfettered by the inhibitions of Frank's generation: 'he'd claim the benefit of the new state I'd helped bring about – and it was so unfair!'

Frank in *Forget-Me-Not-Lane*, the husband in *Chez Nous*, and James/Jim are all torn between what a bio-sociologist would describe as the basic male drive to reproduce widely by impregnating every available female and the powerful cultural pressures toward monogamy, only one of which is the Christian morality that tracks James/Jim in *Passion Play*. In each play, the restless male eventually decides to resign his primitive desires and live within the bonds of the monogamous model. However, he does so with a lack of conviction that robs his choice of grace. James returns to domestic fidelity of the flesh, but Jim, his inner self, still pursues the fantasy of Kate and the total sexual licence she represents.

The alter-ego device, which has been used by numerous dramatists, from Eugene O'Neill to Brian Friel, is a perfect means to illumine the war between the primitive and civilized selves. Jim gives active, passionate flesh to the primeval hunger within James. It's hard to imagine a more powerful yet economical expression of James's inner sexual frenzy than the Act Two moment when Jim kneels before Kate as James mutters polite phrases from a discreet distance.

Nell expresses equally well the inner life of Eleanor, whose journey through discovery, pain, and growth is so great that an excellent case can be made, as James Fenton did in *The Times*, that Eleanor/Nell should be thought of as the motive character[s] of the play. Despite critic Simon's complaint about an opaque ending, Nell's final exit strikes us as a clear statement of Eleanor's permanent renunciation of inner marriage. In a cruel scene of empty Christmas festivity, James's secret self, Jim, opens the front door to embrace a Kate who exists there only in James's still lubricious imagination. Simultaneously, Eleanor's secret self, Nell, suitcase in hand, leaves the house. Eleanor and James will continue to live under the same roof, but their inner selves will never share the same house again.

Close examination shows that, however many dramatists may have used the alter-ego device before, Nichols uses it with such virtuosity and variety that he makes it indelibly his own. Jim is not introduced into the play casually as a merely colourful or amusing underside of James. Instead, Jim enters at the precise moment when James utters the first clear-cut lie of the play. Thus, the alter-ego frames a major motif of the play, the dishonesty in marital unfaithfulness. (That James lies before he commits adultery tells us that Nichols is more interested in the corrosion of the soul than in sins of the flesh.)

Later, as James approaches the first physical intercourse with Kate, Nichols gives the speeches to Jim, 'I could drop by your place . . .' The speeches immediately after the first sex with Kate are given to James. It is the perfect expression of *omnes triste post coitum est*. To the primitive Jim, Nichols gives the highest moment of lust; to the civilized James the tired moments after.

Nell's introduction is as effective as Jim's. The play is an hour old and the audience is settled into the comfortable assumption that James/Jim is all the trickery there is. Then Agnes hands the incriminating letter to Eleanor, forever blasting her innocence and trust. At that moment, Nell joins Eleanor, thereafter to stand at her shoulder, signifying a woman torn in two by the revelation of infidelity. Moments later, confronting James for the first time since learning the truth, Eleanor prowls restlessly about the stage, struggling so hard to control her emotions that she cannot speak. Instead, Nell speaks to Eleanor, filling the stage with the inner dialogue of a speechless woman.

Toward the end of Act Two, the conflict between James/Jim and Nell/Eleanor climaxes when all four selves confront each other for the first time. They speak honestly of Kate, love, and orgasms, 'not to mention paintings and Passions and plays'. They remain at odds, but their exchange suggests a new openness, an ability to speak of sensitive matters with unashamed frankness. Most ordinary people, however they may profess honesty, hold back things in their inner selves, but here the inner selves speak, there is no holding back. Again and again, Nichols uses the alter ego device to such subtle purposes, expanding the meaning and implications of *Passion Play*.

The device functions ironically, of course, all through the play. That irony is most powerful when audiences feel themselves omniscient, in possession of information denied to characters on stage. When Agnes protests her sisterly sympathy for Eleanor, and Nell says, unheard by Agnes, 'Come on, you're enjoying every minute,' audiences laugh because Agnes deserves the slur, but they shudder too at the ignorance, so like their own, that makes her vulnerable. At one time or another, every character in the play is the butt of such ironic laughter because he or she is ignorant of something being said or done within an arm's reach.

In 1983 Nichols announced his intention to retire from dramatic writing. Readers of *Passion Play* will hope for a change of heart. While Nichols has spoken of his work in the most self-effacing way – 'my aim is always to be an intelligent entertainer' – he combines both of those elements, intelligence and entertainment, so well that he ranks among the most valuable playwrights of our day.

Major Plays

A Day in the Death of Joe Egg, Citizens' Theatre, Glasgow, 1967.
The National Health, or Nurse Norton's Affair, National Theatre at the Old Vic, 1969.
Forget-Me-Not-Lane, Greenwich Theatre, then Apollo, 1971.
Chez Nous, Globe Theatre, 1974.
Privates on Parade, Royal Shakespeare Company at the Aldwych, 1977.
Passion Play, Royal Shakespeare Company at the Aldwych 1981.
Poppy, Royal Shakespeare Company at the Barbican Theatre, 1982.

Selected Bibliography

Bryant, Richard. 'Keeping the Heart and Soul Together,' *America's Arena*, 15 November 1984, pp. 6-8.
Brustein, Robert. Review of *Passion. New Republic*, 27 June 1983, p. 24.
Glendinning, Victoria. 'Only four can play.' *Times Literary Supplement*, 23 January 1981, p. 83a.
Hobson, Harold. 'Hobson's Choice.' *Drama: The Quarterly Theatre Review*, Autumn 1981, pp. 18-21.
Jones, Mervyn. 'Peter Nichols, the playwright who has had enough.' *Drama: The Quarterly Theatre Review*, Summer 1983, pp. 7-8.
Schleuter, June. 'Adultery Is Next to Godlessness: Dramatic Juxtaposition in Peter Nichols's *Passion Play*.' *Modern Drama*, December 1981, pp. 540-545.
Simon, John. Review of *Passion. New York*, 30 May 1983, pp. 74-5.

PETER NICHOLS

Passion Play

Passion Play was first performed by the Royal Shakespeare Company at the Aldwych Theatre, London, on 8th January 1981 (press night 13th January), with the following cast:

AGNES, *50*	Priscilla Morgan
ELEANOR, *45*	Billie Whitelaw
JAMES, *50*	Benjamin Whitrow
JIM, *50*	Anton Rodgers
KATE, *25*	Louise Jameson
NELL, *45*	Eileen Atkins

There are a number of other actors (at least six) who do not speak dialogue. They play waiters, assistants, a doctor, diners, guests at Private Views, etc.

Directed by Mike Ockrent

The set resembles (and at times represents) a fashionable art gallery. It includes a flight of stairs and is on two levels.

Retitled *Passion,* this play opened at the Longacre Theatre, New York, on 15 May 1983, with the following cast:

KATE	Roxanne Hart
JAMES	Bob Gunton
ELEANOR	Cathryn Damon
AGNES	Stephanie Gordon
JIM	Frank Langella
NELL	E. Katharine Kerr
OTHERS	Louis Beachner, Jonathan Bolt, Lisa Emery, Charles Harper, William Snovell, C.B. Toombes

Directed by Marshall W. Mason

Passion Play was revived at the Haymarket Theatre, Leicester, on 8 March 1984 and transferred to Wyndham's Theatre, London, on 18 April 1984.
The cast was as follows:

KATE	Heather Wright
JAMES	Leslie Phillips
ELEANOR	Judy Parfitt
AGNES	Patricia Heneghan
JIM	Barry Foster
NELL	Zena Walker
OTHERS	Thomas Armstrong, Kate Beswick, Angela Collins, Sarah Duncan, Peter McMichael, Tim Reynolds, Freda Rodgers, Anthony Shirvell

Directed by Mike Ockrent

In earlier versions of the play, the final scene, beginning on page 97, had ELEANOR doing what NELL does, and vice versa. In other words, NELL left while ELEANOR stayed. Differences in casting in various productions made me realise that their roles could be swapped, as in this version, and ELEANOR could leave while NELL stays, the point being that where the wives have learned from and been changed by the events in the play, the husbands have not. It may, in fact, be played either way.

P.N.
July 1985

ACT ONE

A living-room. ELEANOR, JAMES and KATE are seated, drinking from coffee cups and glasses. KATE is smoking. Someone has just finished speaking.

Silence. She puts out her cigarette. JAMES breathes in sharply, covers his mouth. ELEANOR drains her glass. A clock chimes the first half.

KATE. What's that? Midnight already?

JAMES. Half past.

KATE. No! My watch must have stopped. Christ. Sorry.

ELEANOR. Whatever for?

KATE. I'd no idea. No wonder James was yawning.

JAMES. Was I?

ELEANOR. He's always yawning.

KATE. I must go.

JAMES. At my age I nod off so easily.

ELEANOR. At your age? You've always been a yawner.

JAMES. A yawner possibly.

ELEANOR. All our married life.

JAMES. I've never been in the habit of nodding off before. Not like now, at the drop of a hat.

ELEANOR. You've always needed at least eight hours.

JAMES. There's no place like bed.

KATE. Right.

ELEANOR. We're all agreed on that.

KATE. And I must let you get to yours. I didn't mean to stay so long.

ELEANOR. You're mad. We love people dropping in.

KATE. In that case I'll come more often.

ELEANOR. We'd love that. Shouldn't we, James?

JAMES (*yawning*). Absolutely. Forgive me.

KATE. And thanks for offering to help with my book. It was your stories of the Arab sheikhs and their art collections gave me the idea in the first place.

JAMES. I'll be what use I can. Which isn't much, I'm afraid. Strictly Restoration.

ELEANOR. You've helped them buy the right pictures too.

JAMES. Only as a sideline.

KATE. Almost the last thing Albert did was get the publishers to commission this book.

ELEANOR. You must finish. You owe it to him.

KATE. Right. And I still haven't thanked you for helping me so much over his death and the funeral. Letting me cry on your shoulders.

ELEANOR. We all had a good cry. He was such an old friend.

KATE. You knew him even before his marriage.

JAMES. I knew him before you were born.

KATE. And yet, when he came to live with me, you accepted that too. That can't have been easy. Knowing Agnes as well as you did.

ELEANOR. Divided loyalties. Always tricky. But you were so obviously fond of him.

JAMES. And he of you. That's what Agnes couldn't forgive.

KATE. Still can't.

JAMES. No?

KATE. She seemed fine at the funeral but since then all the bad blood's gathered again.

JAMES *yawns. She stops.*

Why struggle, James? Just let it come.

JAMES. God. I'm sorry.

KATE (*kisses him*). Bye bye.

JAMES. I'll send you on a list of names.

KATE. Great. Really. And sometime soon an hour's chat with a tape recorder? Both of you?

ELEANOR. We're almost always here. You know our number.

KATE. Right.

ELEANOR *and* KATE *go to the hall.* JAMES *stays in the room, clearing glasses and putting* KATE*'s empty cigarette packet into the ashtray.*

ELEANOR *and* KATE *stay in the hall.* ELEANOR *helps* KATE *with her outdoor clothing. They talk but their dialogue is drowned by a sudden fortissimo burst of choral music. Mozart's Requiem: from 'Dies Irae' to 'Stricte Discussurus'.*

By the time it's over, KATE *has gone by the front door and* ELEANOR *has returned to* JAMES *in the living room. The music ends as suddenly as it began.*

JAMES. I thought she'd never go.

ELEANOR. That was obvious.

JAMES. Well, nearly quarter to one —

ELEANOR. I'd be in no hurry either. Back to an empty flat, a lonely bed. He died so suddenly. I don't know how she can stay on there, with so many memories of Albert.

JAMES. Could it be because *she's* not much more than a memory of Albert? She's got his phrases, gestures, points of view. Like a ghost!

ELEANOR. What chance has she had to be anything else? Five years with Albert *I'd* be a ghost.

JAMES. I doubt it. She was no-one to *start* with.

ELEANOR. I happen to like her.

JAMES. I don't *mind* her.

ELEANOR. You made her feel about this small.

JAMES. How d'you know what she felt?

ELEANOR. She told me.

JAMES. No.

ELEANOR. In the hall, just now. I think you might have made an effort.

JAMES. I *was* making an effort.

ELEANOR. It cost her a lot to ask that favour but you left her feeling about this small.

JAMES. As you said before.

ELEANOR. Why is it you never like my girl friends?

JAMES. Kate's one of your girl friends, is she?

ELEANOR. Why not?

JAMES. Isn't she a bit young?

ELEANOR. I enjoy young people's company.

JAMES. She's about the same age as our daughters.

ELEANOR. Same as Janet, older than Ruth.

JAMES. And you didn't crave *their* company.

ELEANOR. *I enjoyed it.* Anyway, Ruth and Janet have gone now, they've got their husbands to look to. And daughters are different. I'm not Kate's mother.

JAMES. You're old enough to be.

ELEANOR. I talk to her in a way I never could with the girls.

JAMES. Really? What about?

ELEANOR. Men. Sex. Love. She very much reminds me of myself when I was her age.

JAMES. Seriously?

ELEANOR. Can't you see the resemblance?

JAMES. You were a working-class drop-out on the run from a

provincial suburb. Kate's a stockbroker's daughter,
well-heeled, knows the score —

ELEANOR. That doesn't matter. We're both looking for a
brighter world, we go for the same kind of men —

JAMES. Albert?

ELEANOR. Not Albert. You. (*He looks at her.*) She told me
when we went to make the coffee. She finds you a very
attractive man. So there's your chance.

JAMES. If only I found her an attractive woman.

ELEANOR. You make it very obvious you don't. Which
must be quite a challenge to a girl like that.

JAMES. Then *you* don't think she *does* find me attractive?

ELEANOR. I'm sure she does. She means nothing by it, though.
Otherwise why tell *me*?

JAMES. She wants to flatter me into helping her with this
dreary book.

ELEANOR. But I was clearly meant to pass it on, so I have.

JAMES. Very generous.

ELEANOR. I like to see you happy.

JAMES. Knowing she doesn't interest me.

ELEANOR. Even if she did, an approach like that would only
send you pelting for cover.

*She leaves the room with the glasses, etc. She goes through
the kitchen and off, he following her, calling:*

JAMES. Don't be too sure! The right offer, on the right day,
from the right woman, I've already warned you, someone with
my lack of experience would be mad not to grab with both
hands.

*He bolts the front door. She returns and they move through
the hall together towards the stairs.*

ELEANOR. I'm sick of hearing this. You had as much as most
men. Certainly as many chances.

JAMES. In our day you could never be sure. Girls' behaviour then was criminal. There was so little action, it's a wonder the race survived.

ELEANOR. Quite a few girls tried the direct approach with you.

JAMES. *You* never tried the direct approach.

ELEANOR. I learnt from watching the other girls fail. They scared you off. I wanted you to come to me.

JAMES. You could afford to. (*He embraces and kisses her.*) You were the most attractive. Still are.

She avoids his advances and starts to climb the stairs.

No amount of coming out with it could ever be a match for you. Sitting there like a cat with cream. Smug's the word for that. (*He catches up and begins making love.*) Aren't you, eh, a cat with cream?

ELEANOR. What *are* you doing?

JAMES. Smug as hell. A girl like Kate can tell *you* I interest her because of course she knows she's safe. She knows I'm yawning for her to leave so that you and I can go upstairs.

ELEANOR. *Halfway* upstairs.

JAMES. Why not? Now the girls have gone? We're all alone. No-one's going to appear on the landing and ask us what we're doing. Why I'm hurting Mummy.

ELEANOR. It's many a year since they did that.

JAMES. And many a year since we did this.

ELEANOR. You *are* hurting Mummy. You'll put my back out.

JAMES. The top stair then. With the flat landing?

ELEANOR. James! I'm a grandmother. You're a grandfather. There's a place for that kind of thing. (*She frees herself.*) It's called the bedroom.

She climbs to the top, opens the door there and goes off by it. He follows, turns off all the lights and goes off too, closing the door.

The 'Dies Irae' burst out again.

A restaurant. KATE *sits alone, smoking with a drink. Behind
her, a table where two* WOMEN *sit talking and drinking coffee.*

A WAITER *replaces* KATE's *drink with another, smiles at her,
speaks. She thanks him, finishes the last and hands him the glass.
He leans over her and speaks. She listens, smiling. The* WAITER
*leads her to a vacated table and she sits. He lays a napkin in her
lap.* JAMES *arrives and the music ends.*

KATE. Hullo.

JAMES. God, I'm sorry.

KATE. Don't be.

> *He sits beside her. Mutter of conversation and sounds of knives
> and forks.*

JAMES. I thought you'd be gone. This Lebanese curator talks the
hind legs off a donkey.

KATE. It's all right.

JAMES. I thought —

KATE. You're here. That's all that matters. (*Offers her cheek to
be kissed, he does.*) I'd already scored with the waiter.

JAMES. You've got a drink.

KATE. My third.

> *The* WAITER *approaches, stands by.*

JAMES. I'm usually so punctual.

KATE. I'm not. I warn you. Just today. Serves me right for being
too eager.

JAMES. Cinzano Bianco, please.

> *The* WAITER *goes.* JAMES *looks at the menu.*

Have you ordered anything to eat?

KATE. I can't think about food. Too excited. Too many
butterflies. It's been like that ever since you called.

JAMES. That seems disproportionate. I only want to suggest
some other people you might interview for your book.

KATE. Is that all? I thought perhaps you'd received my message?

JAMES. Message?

KATE. I sent a message through your wife. She didn't pass it on?

JAMES. I don't think so.

KATE. Unexpected. (*She shrugs*.) She can't be as confident as she looks.

JAMES. Oh. If you mean about being *fond* of me — ?

KATE. Finding you attractive.

JAMES. That's it, yes, she told me that, yes, very flattering for a man of my age. Yes, she did. Thanks.

KATE. I like older men.

JAMES. Well, obviously. Albert was my age exactly.

KATE. D'you know he admired you more than anyone?

JAMES. That much? We were close friends certainly, over thirty years, but he had such a brilliant career, all get-up-and-go, by comparison I must have seemed a stick.

KATE. One of his strengths as an editor was he recognised the real stuff when he saw it. He made me watch you closely. Your modesty fascinated him. *The* man in his field, he used to say, no contenders.

JAMES. Well, restoring modern art is not that wide a field, you know. More like a kitchen garden.

KATE. Albert said: Watch my friend James. Never shows off. Doesn't need to. That's a man in total control of himself. Nobody's ever disturbed his equilibrium. Watch him closely. So I did.

The WAITER *returns with* JAMES's *drink, sets it before him, leaning over.* KATE *does not alter her voice.*

And that's how I came to realise you're one of the most desirable men I've ever met.

JAMES *looks up at the* WAITER.

JAMES. Thank you.

KATE. Almost painfully so. You must have noticed.

JAMES. Would you like some Vichyssoise? Gazpacho? A little salmon?

KATE. Anything light. I don't mind.

JAMES (*ordering*): Two Vichyssoise, fresh salmon for the lady, and for me escalopes provençales. (*To* KATE:) And to drink? Soave? Valpolicella? (*She shrugs.*) Soave.

The WAITER *writes and goes with the menus.*

KATE. I'm sorry if my interest was ever an embarrassment.

JAMES. Never. No. Except perhaps with that waiter —

KATE. It must have been so obvious at times. Though I tried not to let it show.

JAMES. I honestly didn't notice.

KATE. Come on —

JAMES. Never occurred to me.

KATE. Amazing.

JAMES. You were Albert's girl. Taboo.

KATE. Right. I didn't dare move while he was alive and as we never met without your wife I thought the best approach was through her.

JAMES. Eleanor assumed you only flattered me to use my connections. Luckily.

KATE. She was meant to.

JAMES. I did myself.

KATE. Ah. My cover-up was *too* effective.

JAMES. *Do* myself. I must admit.

KATE (*her hand on his*). Forget that now.

JAMES. The only time I thought of you like that was at his funeral.

KATE. I *chose* that dress for you.

JAMES. Dress?

KATE. Purple silk. Cost the earth.

JAMES. I didn't notice the dress. No, I meant that suddenly seeing you as Albert's what shall I call you — common-law widow?

KATE. Right.

JAMES. Among his middle-aged friends, I realised how young you were. And I couldn't help but see the way some of Albert's mates consoled you.

KATE. Right! The friends who'd been the last to accept me as his lover were the first to try to undress me as his widow.

JAMES. I remarked on that to Eleanor.

KATE. I didn't *mind*. Being suddenly available is quite arousing. The ultimate sexual threat. The other wives were very much aware. And I knew *you* were watching. Which was nice too.

JAMES. I wasn't watching. I *noticed*.

She smiles, finishes her gin. The WAITER *serves food.*

The lights fade slightly on the restaurant set and come up fully on the living room where ELEANOR *enters from the kitchen door with* AGNES. *They go into the living room. They bring mugs of coffee.*

AGNES. You noticed that, did you?

ELEANOR. Not till James remarked on it.

AGNES. Their hands were everywhere. God Almighty, I thought, you smutty little trollop.

ELEANOR. I'm not sure you can blame Kate for that.

AGNES. I can blame her for wearing a purple silk creation that must have cost my husband more than he ever spent on a dress for me. And scent you could have cut with a scythe. I blame her for rushing along that very morning to have an expensive hair-do.

ELEANOR. You don't *know* that, Agnes.

AGNES. I know how it looks without, my dear.

ELEANOR. She was only being the good hostess. Which is what she's chiefly known for.

AGNES. What she's chiefly known for is stealing other people's husbands.

ELEANOR. Only once.

AGNES. Once! You don't imagine that was the first time those old mates had felt her up?

ELEANOR. I thought so, yes.

AGNES. She might at least have fought off their drunken fingers till after the funeral. With our sons and daughters there and Albert's relatives —

ELEANOR. Kate's people didn't come?

AGNES. They've never approved. Her father didn't relish the thought of a son-in-law older than himself. Calling him 'dad'.

The lights favour JAMES *and* KATE.

KATE. I can't manage any more.

JAMES. You've eaten nothing.

KATE. My heart's in my mouth. I can hardly breathe. Can you?

JAMES. Shall I order coffee?

KATE. No. There's coffee at my place.

JAMES. That's out of the question, Kate. There's a painting I told Eleanor I must leave in Bond Street and as you know my home's half an hour's drive at least from there —

KATE. I can do it in fifteen minutes.

JAMES. I remember your driving, yes.

KATE. I didn't mean the drive. (*She takes his hand and kisses it.*)

JAMES. She'd wonder where I'd been.

KATE. So she doesn't know we're meeting?

JAMES. I told her I'd be eating with the Lebanese curator —

KATE. Two alibis? Not clever. It looks fishy. You get sussed out.

JAMES. But I could say I'd met you and given you a few more names.

He hands her an envelope.

KATE. Three alibis? And you didn't know I was interested? Well, it's all true so far.

JAMES. Would you rather she knew? You don't care?

KATE (*shrugs*). Why should I, if you can't come back for coffee?

JAMES. I'll probably tell her then.

KATE. Do.

JAMES. D'you want coffee here?

KATE. Mine's better.

JAMES. I'm sure.

KATE. I may have some alone, thinking of you. But it won't be the same.

JAMES *beckons to the* WAITER.

In the living-room, ELEANOR *is still moving and* AGNES *is still.*

ELEANOR. I hesitate to say this, Agnes, but if close friends can't, who can? I'm sorry to hear you still going on, that's all.

AGNES. Going on?

ELEANOR. About Albert and Kate. I'd hoped now he's dead, you'd find the generosity to forget what happened. Well, forgive anyway. Your new friend's such a pleasant man, your life's taken a fresh direction —

Pause. She looks straight at AGNES, *who pointedly waits as though for the end of a sermon.*

AGNES. My new friend and I have both been through the wars and without each other we might never have picked up the pieces again. But what makes you believe he could ever in a million years make up for the loss of my husband? And I don't mean his death. I mean the loss while he was alive! Haven't you even grasped that Albert was my life? We not only had four children, we made his career. Together. Coming from a semi-literate home, he rose to become a crusading editor, he influenced the finest minds of his generation. And finally threw all that away to satisfy an itching cock.

ELEANOR. Well, not entirely, Agnes —

AGNES. Then you tell me to forgive and forget?

ELEANOR. I mean, he did continue to function after he went to live with Kate —

AGNES. Forgive that bitch? What for?

ELEANOR. For *your* sake. Your peace of mind.

> JAMES *has paid the bill and he and* KATE *are leaving their table and making across the upper level to the stairs. The* WAITER *clears, light goes on him.*

AGNES. Don't waste your sympathy on me, dear. I've got a little man takes care of that.

ELEANOR. Then for the sake of your friends —

AGNES. What friends?

ELEANOR. *We're* still your friends.

AGNES. James never liked me.

ELEANOR. Not true. And we none of us like seeing you in this bitter state —

AGNES. Oh, don't you 'like' it? Oh, how sad!

ELEANOR. It's boring to listen to, frankly.

AGNES. It doesn't bore me. Christ, no! It keeps me alive. I'll see her in the poorhouse. Though perhaps the whorehouse would suit her better.

> JAMES *and* KATE *have come down the stairs and turn into the hall space.*

KATE. Thanks for lunch, if nothing else.

JAMES. Thank you for coming.

AGNES. I'll take back everything he gave her.

KATE. You must taste *my* coffee some time.

AGNES. Every lemon squeezer.

KATE. Some time soon.

AGNES. Everything she didn't buy.

JAMES. I'd like that, yes, but I can't often get away.

KATE. It's time you did.

AGNES (*smiling*). He never married her, did he?

JAMES. Perhaps it is.

KATE stands close, pressing her body against his.

ELEANOR. Kate wouldn't have him. She values her freedom.

AGNES. I'll fight her till I drop.

KATE. Please try, won't you?

ELEANOR. You'll lose your friends.

AGNES. I can manage without.

KATE. You know where I am. Just ring.

She kisses JAMES on the mouth, lingeringly.

AGNES. This is more important than pleasing friends. This is fighting evil, Eleanor, which Albert did too as long as he could spot it.

The kiss ends.

KATE. Next time we'll have the coffee first. Only eat when we've worked up an appetite.

She turns to go.

JAMES. I'll give your love to Eleanor.

He goes off the other way.

AGNES. You can only tell me to forgive because you haven't the vaguest idea how this experience *feels*.

ELEANOR. I suppose that's true. James and I have been unusually lucky. Our daughters used to complain we were getting dull.

AGNES. Well —

ELEANOR. Really?

AGNES. A bit.

ELEANOR. D'you think so?

AGNES. You never surprise us.

ELEANOR. Sometimes we'd have welcomed a dash of danger.

AGNES. It's how to stop it once you've started. I was tolerant to start with. I thought that was the best way to deal with it.

ELEANOR. Perhaps James and I are a naturally monogamous pair.

AGNES. Who isn't? Who doesn't believe it's made in Heaven?

ELEANOR. We don't think *that.* We're not romantic. My opinion is most couples come to grief through expecting too much of each other.

The front door opens and JAMES *enters.*

Oh, hullo love.

JAMES. Agnes! How good to see you! I was afraid you might have gone.

AGNES. I'm on my way.

They kiss. ELEANOR *stands by.*

You smell sexy. Nice after-shave.

JAMES. Why are you rushing off like this?

AGNES. I'm meeting my fellow at half-past three and isn't it getting on for that now?

JAMES. Ten past.

ELEANOR. Where on earth have you been till now?

JIM enters at the cupboard, dressed the same as JAMES. *No-one acknowledges him.*

JIM. The traffic. We agreed the traffic.

JAMES. The traffic.

AGNES. Oh, God, is it bad?

JAMES. Friday afternoon?

AGNES. Must dash. Bye-bye.

ELEANOR. Let's go shopping some time, shall we?

They kiss. The men watch.

JIM. Better *tell* her. I want to tell her.

AGNES. I don't get that much time.

JIM. After St. Agnes goes.

ELEANOR. Just an hour or two.

JIM. I *want* to tell her.

AGNES. I'll try.

JIM. Not everything.

AGNES. Good-bye James.

JAMES. Bye-bye.

> AGNES *goes.* ELEANOR *closes the door.*

JIM. Not about the kiss, for instance.

ELEANOR. Hullo, my love.

> *She embraces and kisses him.*

JIM. In the restaurant, the whole length of her body against mine —

ELEANOR. I've missed you.

JAMES. Have you?

JIM. — her tongue straight to the back of my mouth, circling like a snake inside —

ELEANOR. Haven't you missed me?

JAMES. I always miss you.

JIM. The almost forgotten feel of an unknown woman —

ELEANOR. Agnes was right. You reek of perfume —

JIM. Christ!

JAMES. Do I?

ELEANOR. *Is* it aftershave?

JIM. She *knows* your aftershave!

ELEANOR. I don't think so.

JAMES. I've no idea.

ELEANOR. Smells more like women's perfume.

JIM. The dealer. Magda.

JAMES. Oh, in the gallery, yes, this dragon was wearing some kind of knock-out drops, I remember.

ELEANOR. It *smells* like Bond Street.

JAMES. What does Bond Street smell like?

ELEANOR. Expensive tarts.

JAMES. What do you know about expensive tarts?

ELEANOR. Not a lot.

JAMES. They liked my work on the painting.

ELEANOR. Which was that?

JAMES. The Frank Stella.

ELEANOR. They must have kept you hanging about.

They have now returned to the living room.

JIM. No. She can easily catch you out there.

JAMES. Not long, no.

JIM. Talk more. You usually talk more, don't you? Simply say you had some lunch with Kate, gave her the list of names and —

ELEANOR. Did you have a drink at the gallery?

JAMES. No!

ELEANOR. Not white wine? You haven't drunk white wine?

JAMES. No.

ELEANOR. I thought I tasted it when you kissed me.

JIM. Lunch.

JAMES. That was lunch.

JIM. With Kate.

JAMES. With the Lebanese curator.

JIM. Kate!

JAMES. He wants me to buy more post-impressionists for his sheikhs.

JIM. And you met Kate for a drink nearby —

JAMES. It's a profitable sideline buying for The Gulf.

ELEANOR. Yes, indeed.

JIM. Why are you doing this? To hide the fact you've eaten lunch with an attractive girl who doesn't attract you?

ELEANOR. Arabs don't drink, do they?

JIM. Christ! Orange!

JAMES. Orange Juice. I had the wine.

JIM. Still not too late to say you met for a drink —

JAMES. Agnes looked rather well, I thought.

ELEANOR. We had a nasty scene.

JAMES. Oh, dear.

He is absently moving about. She is correcting a score.

JIM. But you're right, she wouldn't understand —

ELEANOR. If you'd been sooner, it wouldn't have happened.

JAMES. Sorry about that.

JIM. And anyway you don't *want* to tell her. Don't want it to finish there, do you?

JAMES. What was your disagreement about?

JIM. You feel alive.

ELEANOR. Oh, Kate, Kate, Kate, what else?

JIM (*to her*): I've just had lunch with Kate.

ELEANOR. She never talks of anything else.

JIM. Except that neither of us could eat.

ELEANOR. And I'm afraid I told her so.

JIM. Her tongue's been in my mouth.

ELEANOR. I told her it was boring.

JAMES. No wonder you had a disagreement.

JIM. She's not pretty, Eleanor.

ELEANOR. Well, she was so vindictive to Kate.

JIM. Not nearly as pretty as you.

JAMES. Even now that Albert's dead?

JIM. But different. More flagrant.

JAMES. What can she do?

JIM. Kate doesn't care who's watching.

ELEANOR. She wants everything back. Every single thing he bought her. I found myself defending Kate. I've decided I like her better.

JIM (*to her*): I love you, Eleanor. But she's exciting.

JAMES. Should we warn her, d'you think?

JIM. She's dangerous.

ELEANOR. She can look after herself.

JAMES. Absolutely.

JIM. Anyone could have seen that kiss.

ELEANOR. Intruders get caught in the crossfire.

JIM. Though I suppose it wouldn't *look* much to a passer-by.

JAMES. D'you feel like a little nap?

JIM. An affectionate goodbye at most.

JAMES (*embracing her*). An afternoon lie-down?

JIM. No more.

ELEANOR. I'm giving a lesson in fifteen minutes.

JIM. A passer-by couldn't have seen the tongue.

JAMES. How long for?

ELEANOR. An hour.

JAMES. And then?

ELEANOR. And then we're rehearsing Verdi's Requiem for the

Albert Hall and what you call a little nap requires a long nap afterwards.

She has her score and moves to the hall, JAMES *and* JIM *following.*

I don't want to repeat the occasion I was singled out from the other sopranos for yawning in the Sanctus. How about tonight?

JAMES. You know very well afternoons are best.

ELEANOR. Tomorrow afternoon then.

JAMES. All right. Tonight.

ELEANOR (*laughing*). Whatever's the matter with you suddenly? While I'm teaching have a cold bath. Or go for a run.

JAMES. I might do that.

She takes the score off to the music room upstage of the living-room. JAMES *stays in the hall.* JIM *goes to the cubicle representing the phone-booth; he dials, waits.* JAMES *calls off to* ELEANOR.

Are you sure you're free tomorrow afternoon?

Lights up on KATE's *room. Couch, chair, low lighting. A phone on the floor is ringing.* KATE *enters, wearing only a slip-on gown, smoking a cigarette. She kneels to answer.*

JIM *puts his money in. Sounds of the tone until he does.*

ELEANOR *comes from the music room.*

ELEANOR. What?

JAMES. Are you free tomorrow afternoon?

ELEANOR. One student in the morning. Afternoon quite free.

KATE. Yeah?

JIM. Hullo? Kate?

KATE. Yeah.

JIM. James Croxley here.

KATE. Hullo.

ELEANOR. Shall I book you in? (*She goes to the foot of the stairs.*)

KATE. How are you? (*She lies on the couch, resting the receiver on her stomach.*)

JAMES. And no choir rehearsal?

ELEANOR. Not till Saturday.

JIM. I was a bit late home and Eleanor wondered where I'd been.

JAMES. I'll keep you to that.

KATE. So you told her. What did she say?

JIM. I didn't, no —

KATE. I see —

JIM. Well, Agnes was there and I thought —

KATE. Agnes? She'd have suspected all kinds of wild things that I'm sad to say never happened.

ELEANOR (*to* JAMES, *who is following her up the stairs*): Where are you going now?

JIM. Yes.

JAMES. To put my running-shoes on.

JIM. And wasted no time suggesting them to Eleanor.

KATE. Right. A very heavy scene.

ELEANOR. Are you coming to Saturday's concert?

JAMES. Isn't it being broadcast live?

ELEANOR. Yes.

JIM. They both smelt your perfume on me.

KATE. Poor James.

JAMES. I'll listen at home. You won't mind?

She precedes him into the bedroom. He shuts the door behind them.

KATE. What did you say? About the perfume?

JIM. I said it was someone else's.

KATE. Someone else's?

JIM. The Bond Street dealers.

KATE. I suppose you're pretty nifty on your feet.

JIM. How d'you mean?

KATE. Used to dealing with narrow scrapes?

JIM. Not at all.

KATE. Did she believe you?

JIM. Yes, I think so. I was going to say I'd lunched with you but by the time Agnes had gone, the moment seemed to have passed. So can I ask you not to mention it?

KATE. I wasn't going to.

JIM. No, I'm sure.

KATE. You sound as breathless as I feel.

JIM. I've been jogging round the common. I've no more coins so I can't talk long. There's something you should be warned about. Would you care to come to dinner with us, here? Next week.

KATE. Warned about? What?

JIM. Otherwise on Saturday night, if you're not busy I could drop in at your place.

The 'Agnus Dei' from Mozart's Requiem, sudden and loud.

JIM *and* KATE *continue for some moments unheard, then lights fade on* JIM *as he replaces the telephone.* KATE *puts hers down too and continues lying on the settee, smoking.*

The lights change on her room to show more. JAMES *enters, wearing shirt, trousers, no shoes or socks, drinking coffee from a cup.*

JIM *walks over to join them, sits in the spare chair. For some time they listen to the music.*

JAMES. This is the 'Agnus Dei', I'll have to be going soon. There's only the 'Libera Me' to come.

KATE. How long does it take her from the Albert Hall?

JAMES. She gets a lift with one of the contraltos. A slow and careful driver who likes to hang about chatting afterwards.

KATE. You're all right then.

JAMES. But not for long.

> JAMES *sits on the settee. In moving to make room,* KATE *lets her gown slip and* JAMES *caresses her legs. Then he kisses her. Then he resumes drinking.*
>
> *She turns down the volume.*

KATE. Time to help yourself to another drop. It's simmering.

JIM. What does she want?

JAMES. No, really.

JIM. Not just me, surely?

KATE. You said you like the way I make it. Hot and strong. Well, now you know where to find it. If you want it.

JIM. You've had the list of names. The introductions.

KATE. I hope you think it was worth waiting for.

JAMES. Absolutely.

JIM. Well —

JAMES. I'm surprised you need to ask.

JIM. But since you did, it wasn't, no.

JAMES. And thank you —

JIM. Wasn't worth the lying and fear and risk of discovery, no.

KATE. Thank *you*. It's been quite a while for me.

JIM. Pull the other. It's got bells on.

KATE. I went a bit mad after Albert's death but I've calmed down since.

JAMES. Did anyone stay the night of the funeral?

KATE. I'm not giving names.

JIM. So someone did.

JAMES. I wasn't asking.

KATE. I told you I wore that dress for you. I wanted you so much I nearly creamed myself. I couldn't face bed alone that night. But I've been behaving myself for at least a month now. Which is why I was quick to come.

JAMES. I was afraid you found me slow.

KATE. Slow's best. Though quick's good too sometimes. Exciting and flattering.

JAMES. You didn't wear any scent.

KATE. No.

JAMES. Thoughtful.

JIM. I missed that scent.

JAMES. Nor any underclothes.

KATE. I know you like the wholesome approach.

JAMES. Who told you that?

KATE. Eleanor.

JIM. Christ.

KATE. I did my homework.

JAMES. You and Eleanor discussed underwear?

KATE. Women do, you know.

JIM. I didn't know.

KATE. We went shopping and I was buying the sort of lingerie Albert liked. Black lacy satin knickers, suspenders, and she said you hated all that.

JIM. On her, yes.

JAMES. I thought Albert did as well.

KATE. Is that what he said?

JAMES. I assumed it. Men don't discuss underwear.

KATE. Oh, yes, he loved all that. When we first met he bought me several sets. He found it very arousing, specially in the shop.

JIM. Dirty bugger.

KATE. He couldn't resist me in the changing cubicle. With all the assistants outside, we had it standing up.

JIM. There isn't anything she won't do.

KATE. Reflected in several mirrors.

JAMES. Talk about a dark horse.

JIM. He liked all that because your body's not attractive enough without.

KATE. He liked me to reek of scent.

JIM. That's the point, dear.

JAMES. I thought I knew him well.

JIM. Without the knocking-shop accountrements, you're far from irresistible.

JAMES. I always thought him puritanical.

KATE. No way. I was never exclusively his. If I fancied someone else — or if he did —

JIM. You're out of your depth here, go!

KATE. You didn't think we were totally loyal?

JAMES. I am.

KATE. No!

JAMES. Tonight's the first time.

KATE. Honestly?

JIM. And the last.

KATE. I'm very flattered.

JIM. Tell her it's the last time.

JAMES. Twenty-five years.

KATE. Staggering.

JAMES. Why? Millions live like that.

KATE. I've never thought of you as one of millions — owning and being owned. As I said, I hate ownership.

JAMES. It hasn't been like that.

KATE. No? Then what was to stop you?

JIM. Love. Affection.

KATE. You can't have lacked opportunities.

JIM. Habit.

JAMES. Almost totally, I'd say.

JIM. Cowardice.

JAMES. Picture my life.

JIM. The fear of failure.

JAMES. My respectable working life. I walk fifteen yards through the kitchen, from the back door, across the garden to the workshop. Few excuses to go outside. Now and then I've felt the need but I've suppressed it, sublimated it —

KATE. Taken yourself in hand?

Pause. JIM *laughs, then* JAMES.

JAMES. It wasn't difficult. I've enjoyed my work, the pleasure of my craft. You could say it was more a vocation than a craft. More like being an original creative artist.

KATE. Right.

JIM. This is shit. You're a second-rater.

JAMES. To work on a Matisse or a Picasso means I play my humble part in keeping the wolves at bay. Lighting the darkness.

JIM. She'll never swallow that? She must be bursting.

JAMES. Well, that's my life. Eleanor knows what I'm doing every hour of the day.

JIM. Till now.

KATE. Oh, God, why's life never simple? Why another married man?

JIM. You tell me. Will you?

KATE. The last thing I want is to mess with marriages.

JIM. No. You won't. So non-committal.

KATE. And Eleanor of all people!

JIM. A mystery. Like all the young.

KATE. Such a fantastic woman.

JAMES. By Christ, isn't she? Outspoken, tolerant, realistic. Sensual.

KATE. We're very much alike in that way.

JIM. You're not sensual. Just pretending.

JAMES. Wonderfully sane as well.

JIM. Those words you used when you were coming. That wasn't sensuality. That was to help me, wasn't it?

KATE. So unlike Agnes in every way.

JIM. It's so good, you said.

JAMES. She can't stand Agnes.

JIM. Christ, you said, don't stop now, please . . .

JAMES. All bitter and twisted.

JIM. Or did I really excite you?

KATE. Thanks for warning me, by the way.

JIM. Come on, man.

KATE. About Agnes.

JAMES. The Requiem's finished. I must go, dear.

KATE. Come and stir my cup again soon.

She and JAMES *kiss.* JIM *watches and feels.*

JIM. Far less alarming the tongue, now it's not in public. Also she smokes too much. Thank God it wasn't very good. It's better with Eleanor. Thank Christ. And what's more to the point, thank *you* for reminding me that I am naturally monogamous. I love my wife. So let's go home. Come on, man, it's up to you to finish. Now and forever.

JAMES. It might be as well if you came to dinner. Then I can give you those names I gave you at lunch.

KATE. And I can invite you to my private view.

JAMES. Absolutely.

KATE. I'll ring her and fix it.

They leave her and her room moves off.

JIM (*comes downstage and speaks to* JAMES). Home well before her and no suspicion. She was so full of the concert and how badly the soloist had sung the Recordare. Entirely trusting.

JAMES. I was aching to tell her where I'd been.

JIM. We'd always said we would.

JAMES. The fact remains I didn't. As it was a solitary episode, over as soon as started, I thought it was best forgotten.

JIM. So you'd enjoyed the broadcast —

JAMES. Nobody had telephoned —

JIM. Which I knew from the answering machine —

JAMES. And my love for the woman who shared my life was soon a tremendous physical desire.

JIM. That night and the next few days you were never off the nest.

JAMES. We hadn't made love like that for years.

JIM. Then Kate invited herself to dinner and both of us trod a minefield of lies all evening trying to remember what Eleanor was supposed to know and not know —

JAMES. I kept on yawning till she went.

They have brought on glasses and ELEANOR *opens the hall door and comes in.*

ELEANOR (*calls off*). Bye-bye, Kate. See you Tuesday. At the Gallery! (*She closes the door.*)

JAMES *waits for her to return to the living room. As she enters, he yawns.*

JAMES. Quarter past twelve. A slight improvement.

ELEANOR *doesn't answer but bustles about clearing up.*

I've done the ashtray. Ten cigarette-ends.

JIM. Why doesn't she answer?

JAMES. You must admit I'm right. She *is* a pale imitation of Albert.

Pause. ELEANOR *collects glasses.*

JIM (*urgently, to* JAMES). Has she got there? Christ.

JAMES. Well, we've done our duty for another month.

ELEANOR. Not quite.

She leaves the room for the hall, taking the glasses out.

JAMES. What d'you mean?

JIM. She means Kate's invited us to her —

ELEANOR. She's invited us to her Private View. (*She goes off to the kitchen.*)

JAMES. Her Private View of what?

JIM. If she's even slightly suspicious, say you'd rather not go.

ELEANOR (*returning*). What d'you think?

JAMES. Well, photographs, presumably. Isn't that what she is, a photographer.

ELEANOR. Her photos of the Far East, yes, taken when she and Albert were there together.

JAMES. Oh, no!

ELEANOR. Oh, yes! She asked me in the kitchen.

JAMES. Why didn't she ask us both together?

ELEANOR. She was afraid you'd say 'Oh, no', that's why. Afraid you'd bite her head off.

JIM. She's nowhere near!

JAMES. Me?

ELEANOR. You have been all the evening.

JAMES. *I* have?

ELEANOR. Ever since Albert's death, in fact.

JAMES. I wasn't aware of it.

ELEANOR. You're not a very aware person.

JIM (*sympathetically*). Oh, my darling!

ELEANOR. — or else you'd see your good opinion means a lot to her.

He has bolted the front door. She has put out the living room lights.

JIM (*to* JAMES). Like taking sweets from a baby.

ELEANOR. And yet when you're not biting her head off, you're yawning and looking at your watch.

JAMES. I sent her that list of names and addresses in the Middle East.

ELEANOR. She told me. But I should have thought you might have taken her out —

JIM. Taken her out?

ELEANOR. — and described all the people and how to approach them —

JAMES. Taken her out?

ELEANOR. Yes, to lunch.

JAMES. To lunch?

JIM. You should have told her.

ELEANOR. She sees you as a sort-of irascible uncle figure who has to be appeased.

JAMES. How d'you know?

ELEANOR. What?

JAMES. How d'you know she doesn't see me as a very attractive man?

JIM. Careful!

JAMES. She *said* she did.

ELEANOR. She probably does because you are. But as she can't expect any change in that department is it too much to ask you to go and see her Private View?

JAMES. Too much by far. All up to the West End to drink
Algerian Burgundy while a gang of bluffers shout at me
through a cloud of tobacco smoke —

*They have climbed the stairs and she turns at the bedroom
door, angrily.*

ELEANOR. It wouldn't hurt you to do something generous for
once! An act that didn't, in some way, contribute to
your own selfish pleasure! (*She goes into the bedroom.*)

JAMES (*following*). All right, all right, have it your own way.
We'll go. (*He slams the door behind them.*)

JIM *rushes up the stairs.*

JIM. Brilliant! Bravo!

A burst of joyful singing from the Ode in Beethoven's Ninth.

*The entire Company come on, moving screens to reveal
KATE's blown-up photographs: Japanese and Chinese faces,
city scenes, temples, squalor. They are clearly GUESTS at the
Private View, drinking, smoking, talking and laughing forcibly.
KATE, wearing a plain black cocktail dress, moves across
exchanging words, embraces with GUESTS. At the entrance
she greets ELEANOR and JAMES who are just arriving. JIM
has moved across from the bedroom door and follows KATE;
he watches as they greet one another. KATE hands them
glasses of red wine from a WAITER's tray.*

*The music ends. Now we hear the more subdued buzz of party
talk.*

KATE. Great to see you.

ELEANOR. We said we'd come.

KATE. Great, really.

ELEANOR. I see a few familiar faces.

JAMES. Several important critics.

KATE. Right.

ELEANOR. Are they the ones with pubic hair on their chins?

JAMES. Absolutely.

ELEANOR. That's the only way I remember.

She and JAMES *laugh.*

JIM (*to* KATE). This is not the kind of Private View I want of you. For example, I'd rather see that dress in a heap on the floor.

KATE *leads* ELEANOR *and* JAMES *to meet other* GUESTS *and leaves them talking while she meets others.* JIM *stays with her as she drifts away.*

Or hanging on a door the way it was yesterday afternoon. And you in that underwear! Are you wearing it now? And that was astounding the other night in our house, with Eleanor in the next room dealing with a music-student — forgotten already? Shall I say it then, in front of all these people?

Turns to them all.

She took my hand and placed it high on her thigh, raising her skirt and slightly opening her legs. She wasn't wearing anything above the stockings except the belt. And all the time we kept talking in loud voices about Cartier-Bresson and was photography an art, and sotto voce I told you how the nakedness excited me.

JAMES *is concentrating on his group but is in a good position to look across at* KATE. *She greets another* MAN, *kissing him on the mouth.*

Hullo, is he getting the tongue?

The kiss ends. JIM *shouts across to* JAMES.

No, not time enough!

No-one, of course, takes any notice.

But has he got the look of someone who's already had it? Have *all* these men? When they talk to her, their faces get so mawkish.

(*To one of the* MEN): You can't possibly think that's attractive? That alcoholic simper?

KATE *moves to another and* JIM *follows and speaks to him.*

That superior scowl . . . Do I do that? How can women find men bearable? But obviously they *do. She* does.

The MAN *puts his arm round* KATE.

How d'you find the thought they've been there? Above the stockings? Every one of them? I welcome it. I savour it. Reminds me how unimportant the whole thing is. Either or both of us could finish it whenever we liked and the other wouldn't care. But then again, what *is* essential? Man can't live by bread alone and once you've tasted honey . . .

JAMES *and* ELEANOR *move to look at the exhibits.* JIM *goes with* KATE *to another group and points to* JAMES.

Look at me. I'm over here with my wife, ostensibly studying your snaps but actually begging you to look in my direction and speak to me with your eyes.

KATE *laughs with some* GUESTS.

Yes, me, the well-known husband! Please!

ELEANOR *has left* JAMES, *goes to* KATE.

You looked! Our eyes met. I made you, with the force of my lust for you.

After a word or two, ELEANOR *leads* KATE *back to* JAMES. *They discuss one of the photographs.*

Thanks, my dear, for fetching the girl I sleep with. So that she can promise with her eyes to be there next time I telephone and prepare herself (*to* KATE:) like you did yesterday — by washing away all trace of perfume, dressing in black stockings and suspenders — (*Then to* ELEANOR:) — yes, I know I didn't, but people *change*, that's what it's all about — change — (*And to* KATE *again:*) — and you'll wait on the bed! you and Albert used to share while on the radio Eleanor and a hundred other choristers sing the Ode to Joy.

Again the music bursts out. The exhibition disappears as swiftly as possible by the GUESTS *turning the screens as they go out.*

JAMES *and* JIM *come forward and down and occupy the phone booth.* JAMES *takes coins from his pocket, sets them on the box in a pile, dials.*

KATE *enters by the door of her room as lights go up there. She's dressed as before, makes straight for the phone and lifts the receiver.*

The music ends.

KATE. Yes?

The pay tone is heard till JAMES *feeds in coins.*

JAMES. James here. James Croxley. Hello?

KATE. How are you?

JAMES. All the better for hearing you.

KATE. It's been ages.

JAMES. It *seems* ages. It's only two weeks. How've you been?

KATE. I've been pretty busy. Which is good.

JAMES. Good. That's good. When am I going to see you again?

KATE (*shrugs*). Name the day.

JAMES. It's not that easy. Eleanor's hardly ever out. Once or twice I rang from home while she was shopping but you weren't there.

KATE. Most days I'm out.

JAMES. I can sometimes get away to shop for turps or framing. Evenings are tricky. I've come for a jog on the Common but the first three phones had been vandalised. When can I see you?

KATE. Tonight's no good.

JAMES. No, not tonight.

JIM. What's she doing tonight, I wonder?

JAMES. But how about next Monday? Eleanor's rehearsing, the first time for weeks.

KATE. Oh, bloody hell, I can't.

JAMES. Never mind.

JIM. First jealousy. Then relief. Let off the hook.

KATE. I'm sorry. I really am.

JIM. No danger Monday.

JAMES. Two weeks is too long.

JIM. You can get your breath back.

KATE. Two weeks too long.

JIM. Your heart can slow down again.

JAMES. There's so much I want to say to you.

JIM. You can go back to sleep.

JAMES. But not on the phone. And anyway this has been a marathon jog.

KATE. Why don't you write?

JAMES. Write?

JIM. Better not.

KATE. If I can't see you.

JIM. There'd be proof. She could show people —

JAMES. I don't know.

JIM. Eleanor, for instance —

KATE. Darling —

JIM. But why should she show people?

KATE. Don't you trust me?

JAMES (*as* JIM *puts hand on mouth*). Of course I do. I'll write.

JIM (*breaking away*). Dear Kate -

KATE. Of course, you won't get any answer —

JAMES. No, of course not —

JIM. Dearest Kate —

KATE. Except I could reply to *both* of you with secret messages for *you* to find . . .

JIM. My darling —

KATE. Art postcards. Classical tits and bums.

JAMES. Be careful . . .

> KATE *laughs and lights go on her. She goes.*

> JAMES *comes to join* JIM, *writing the letter.*

JIM. Darling Kate, I suddenly realised this is the first love-letter
I've written for twenty-five years. So try to overlook the
stilted phraseology.

JAMES (*to* JIM). Is it a good idea to mention that? Does it make
me unattractive?

JIM (*to* JAMES). No. Anyway this isn't a love-letter, is it? That's
why I'm so grateful. Love's got nothing to do with it. We ask
nothing of each other except the occasional hour together and
the pleasure of our bodies.

> *Lights up on tea-room, similar to restaurant.* ELEANOR *and*
> AGNES *enter and take the free table.* WAITRESS *comes to
> take their order.*

JAMES (*to* JIM). I wish it could be longer though. How can it be
as good as with Eleanor when there's so little time to practise?

JIM (*writing*). I can't imagine why a nice young girl —

JAMES (*to* JIM). — a lovely girl —

JIM (*writing*). Why a *fantastic* girl like you should offer herself
without strings to an old man —

JAMES (*to* JIM). An older man —

JIM (*writing*). To a man like me.

JAMES (*musing*). It's the kind of thing men want and women
loathe, they always say.

JIM (*writing*). But whatever the reason, thanks.

> *The* WAITRESS *leaves the table.* ELEANOR *and* AGNES *talk.*

Because what you've brought me is not only marvellous fun
but pure. Unadulterated.

AGNES. Oh, yes, I'm much better, thanks. My new work's
exhausting but well worthwhile. We're really making progress
towards a better deal for battered wives.

ELEANOR. High time.

AGNES. And as a battered wife myself I feel —

ELEANOR (*laughing*). Oh, come on —

AGNES. No, I mean, it's partly a sublimation for my battered feelings but that's neither here nor there as long as I do some good. All do-gooders want to do themselves a bit of good as well.

ELEANOR. Absolutely.

  WAITRESS *brings their tray.*

JIM (*to* JAMES). Whereas, of course, marriage is anything but pure.

JAMES. It's ownership and children and duty and illness —

JIM. And joint accounts and property —

JAMES. And being an open book —

JIM. But I won't go into that —

JAMES. Heavy scene, man.

  They laugh as ELEANOR *pours tea.*

ELEANOR. I'm so relieved you're better. Tell the truth, I felt you were dwelling morbidly on Albert's memory.

AGNES (*taking tea*). *Did* you?

ELEANOR. You were so vindictive to Kate.

AGNES. You think so?

ELEANOR. And there was no way you could hurt her, so you'd be the one to suffer.

AGNES. Oh?

JIM (*to letter*). So not to get into that whole heavy scene —

JAMES. Yes, she'll like that —

JIM. — let me simply say I feel no guilt about having *you,* only a little in deceiving *her.*

AGNES. You underestimate me. We can make her suffer too.

ELEANOR. We?

AGNES. Oh, the children are with me. Some time ago, as part of a slimy attempt to win Susie over to his side, Albert gave her a key to the flat. The one where whatshername's still living. We've been using it to get in there and make an inventory of the contents.

ELEANOR. Oh, Agnes, no.

AGNES. Oh, Eleanor, yes. From the Oriental rugs to the Irish tea-towels.

ELEANOR. Agnes, I'm very fond of you, I can't let you destroy your own peace of mind like this.

AGNES. Peace of mind is ignorance.

ELEANOR. You know that isn't true.

AGNES. Oh, I've learnt it is. The only real peace of mind comes from punishing evil.

ELEANOR. She's not evil, she's a good-time girl.

AGNES. A star-fucker? That's what I thought. All the same she destroyed my marriage.

ELEANOR. There must have been something wrong already. With your marriage.

JIM. So few things in life are pure and harmless.

JAMES. This must be. There's nothing else in it for her. Pure. Unadulterated.

ELEANOR. I'm sorry that sounds unkind but if old friends can't be helpful, who can?

AGNES. What should we do without old friends?

ELEANOR. Why don't we talk about something else? It obviously upsets you —

AGNES. Oh, no, one good turn deserves another. I'd like to help *you* too.

JIM *has taken an official-looking envelope and writes an address.* JAMES *has got out a dictionary and is looking up a word.*

JAMES. Adult, adulter, adulterate —

AGNES. When Susie was in the flat one day, the star-fucker being fucked in Sweden at the time, the mail came bumping through the front door onto the welcome mat.

JAMES. Adulterate. To render corrupt, by base admixture.

JIM (*to* JAMES). The opposite of pure.

He puts a stamp on the envelope. AGNES *opens her bag and takes out an exactly similar envelope.*

AGNES. She opened all the official-looking letters to see if there was something we should be sharing.

ELEANOR. Honestly, Agnes, reading people's mail!

JAMES. Adultery. Violation of the marriage-bed. Image-worship.

AGNES. And as it turned out, there was.

JIM (*to* JAMES). Really? Image-worship.

JAMES. Enjoyment of a benefice during the translation of a bishop.

He and JIM *laugh.*

JIM. Trust the bloody clergy to get it wrong.

He scans the last part of the letter as JAMES *puts away the dictionary.*

ELEANOR *does not immediately take the letter but looks at it.*

AGNES. You'll recognise the handwriting?

JAMES. The dictionary's useless.

ELEANOR *takes the letter.*

What's pure *is* impure. Adulteration can clarify.

JIM. Purify.

During a pause, the sounds of the tea-room swell briefly while ELEANOR *reads and* AGNES *sips her tea.*

NELL, *dressed like* ELEANOR, *stands at the next table, where she's been sitting on her own with her back turned. She is between the two women.*

NELL. 'Of course I'm longing to be in your bed again but there aren't many chances to leave the house. Later this year there's the Matthew Passion and towards Christmas the Mozart Requiem and Messiah. Some — or all — of these I hope we shall be listening to together.'

JAMES. With half an ear.

JIM (*writing*). With — half — an — ear.

Reading again.

NELL. 'If I can come at a time you haven't any other callers, though I understand I have no claims on you. Any more than you on me. Which strikes me as a perfect arrangement. And sometimes when you come round here, we'll feel each other up while Eleanor's in the music-room. I like the way you whisper all that filth. And I liked it when you spilt wine from your mouth into mine. So — till the next rehearsal of a Passion, here's thinking of you, love, — all manner of kisses . . .'

ELEANOR *folds the letter and returns it to* AGNES. JIM *folds it too and the two letters are returned to the envelopes together.* JIM *seals his.*

AGNES. Join the club. I've poured some tea.

ELEANOR. Thank you.

AGNES. I never meant to show you that.

NELL. Hah!

ELEANOR. I'm glad you did.

AGNES. Glad — ?

NELL. How could he do this to me?

ELEANOR. Glad, certainly, you didn't keep it to yourself, as it obviously troubled you so much.

NELL. How could he risk humiliating me?

AGNES. Doesn't it trouble *you*?

NELL. In front of her?

ELEANOR *sips her tea.*

ELEANOR. It troubles me you and Susie have read this letter. Has anyone else?

AGNES. Of course not.

NELL. My cheeks are burning.

AGNES. D'you want to keep it?

NELL. She's bound to notice.

ELEANOR. That might be best.

NELL. My world's caved in but I'm sitting here.

Taking the letter.

ELEANOR. Thanks.

NELL. Come on, get away as quick as you —

AGNES. Eleanor love, I only wanted to put you on your guard by a couple of subtle hints — but when you started *defending* her and saying she was harmless, I knew it was time to show you the letter.

NELL. Come on, you're enjoying every minute.

ELEANOR. I didn't call her 'harmless'. I said she wasn't evil, that's all. I think the letter proves it. And, of course, I knew she fancied James. In fact, I told him.

NELL. That much is true, make do with that.

AGNES. But did you know they listened to your concerts in the bed she used to share with Albert?

NELL. Try not to imagine it.

ELEANOR. He wants a bit on the side, why not?

She shrugs and smiles, drinks tea.

AGNES. That's what Albert called it too.

NELL. Make your mind a blank.

AGNES. His very words.

NELL. She pities you.

AGNES. A bit on the side. It's nothing, he said when I found out, she's nothing to me.

NELL. Think of nothing or you'll cry.

AGNES. Be more tolerant, he used to say. More easy-going. He stood for tolerance. The permissive society. He did as much as anyone to advertise its virtues.

NELL. Why write a letter? Why take that risk?

AGNES. Well, now we see what that's led to — abortion, violence, the kids on drugs, apathy on one side and a neo-fascist law-and-order reaction on the other.

NELL. Shut up!

AGNES. It's not the first time liberalism's failed us. We should know better. Stop it now.

NELL. Shut up, I said!

AGNES. Don't try appeasement. You'll end at your own little Munich.

NELL (*to* ELEANOR). Come on.

JAMES *starts to use the phone.*

ELEANOR. Shan't be a minute, Agnes . . .

AGNES. Shall I come with you?

NELL. Haven't you had enough?

ELEANOR *goes, colliding with the* WAITRESS.

The dissonant fanfare from the Choral Symphony.

During this, the lights fade from the tea-shop as AGNES *beckons to the* WAITRESS, *who brings the bill. She pays and goes.*

At the same time, JAMES *is joined in the living-room by* JIM. *Lights up on* KATE's *room show that she is talking on the phone. She has a bottle of scent in the other hand.*

The music ends.

KATE. Well, it certainly hasn't arrived.

JAMES. I hope to God it doesn't come back here.

KATE. The last few weeks a lot of my mail's gone missing. Personal *and* official. Luckily my *work*'s arranged by phone.

JIM. Personal? That means from men.

JAMES. God save us from the British Post Office.

JIM (*behind him, into the receiver*). Yes, all right, you've made me jealous, made me wonder who the others are —

JAMES (*cutting over*). Used to be all right as the G.P.O. but since they started calling it 'Communications' —

KATE (*laughing*). Right.

JAMES. It's another example of the decline of Work.

JIM. I wish she wouldn't say 'Right' all the time.

JAMES. To someone like me raised on the idea that excellence was achieved by work, by application, these are confusing times.

JIM (*wagging a finger at him*). Careful, Dad, that's a heavy scene. Moralising.

KATE. Right. Well, am I going to see you?

JAMES. I can't today. She's expected back any minute.

KATE. No, not today. I've got to go out myself.

JIM (*into the receiver again*). Or some man's coming to have you —

JAMES. Next Tuesday afternoon I'm going to bid for the Arabs at Sotheby's Post-Impressionist sale. I could drop in on you afterwards for an hour or so —

KATE. Why don't we meet there?

JIM. You might be seen.

KATE. I'd love to see you bidding. Spending all those petro-dollars. Very sexy.

JAMES. Oh, it's not at all, believe me —

KATE. Then you could touch me up while I'm driving back here. With my hands on the wheel I'd be at your mercy.

JIM. Right.

ELEANOR *enters by the front door.* JAMES *reacts.* JIM *runs to the door to see, signals back to* JAMES.

It's Eleanor.

JAMES. Right you are then.

KATE. And I've got some soap the same as yours at home, so I can put on perfume this time and you can shower afterwards —

JAMES. Absolutely.

KATE. So she'll never know.

JAMES. Thank you very much.

ELEANOR listened for a moment and now hangs her coat. When she returns, it is with NELL.

KATE. I'm not just a pretty face and a pair of tits, you know —

JAMES. Goodbye. (JAMES *puts down phone*.)

NELL. Ting. D'you think that was her?

JIM returns to JAMES, who stands listening. KATE looks at the phone, sprays her neck and ears with scent and leaves the room as lights go.

JIM. That was Otto instructing you to buy Pissaros —

NELL. Is this what it's been then all the time?

JAMES (*going to meet her*). Hullo, love.

NELL. Is this what it's going to be like from now on?

JAMES. How are you?

NELL. So transparent! Christ, why did I never notice?

JAMES. How was your afternoon?

Tries to kiss ELEANOR but she evades him and goes into living room. JIM and NELL go with them.

JIM. What's this? What's up with her?

JAMES. I got on pretty well. The Douanier Rousseau's nearly finished. I ate my sandwiches — delicious, by the way — and got to feeling rather lonely. Randy.

NELL. So rang her for a horny chat?

He goes to ELEANOR and embraces her from behind. She pushes him off.

And now you want me for a wank?

JIM. Something's up.

JAMES. How was Agnes?

NELL (*to him*). How would you expect?

JAMES. More easy-going? Or still 'hard-done-by'?

NELL. Bastard!

JAMES. Still the Wronged Woman?

NELL. Bastard sod!

JIM. Don't talk too much. You don't usually talk this much!

ELEANOR *moves about, hiding her face from him. He shrugs. Silence.*

NELL (*to* ELEANOR). Don't let it drift. You can't.

ELEANOR. Who were you on the phone to?

JAMES. Just now, you mean?

ELEANOR. As I came in.

JIM. Otto.

JAMES. Otto.

JIM. The Black Widow has told her something.

JAMES. Instructing me to buy Pissaros and Signacs at the sale on Tuesday.

NELL. You can't lie to save your life.

JAMES. The sheikhs are interested, so those particular painters must have gone up a few points.

NELL (*over part of this*). Wouldn't deceive a cretin surely?

JIM (*as* ELEANOR *turns*). She's been crying.

NELL. He deceived *you*.

JAMES. Can I get you a drink?

NELL. A trusting wife must be easier than a cretin.

JAMES. Vodka and tonic?

ELEANOR's *taken the letter out and hands it to him.*

ELEANOR. Returned to sender.

He takes and looks at it. She gets herself a drink.

JAMES. How'd'you get this?

NELL. Does it matter?

JIM. Saint Agnes.

NELL. Not from Kate, if that's what you're thinking.

JAMES. Kate told me it hadn't arrived.

NELL. When you last went to fuck her? Or on the phone as I came in?

JAMES. She was on the phone as you came in.

JIM. Truth time. Good!

JAMES. I shouldn't have written, but now it's out I'm glad. You're the only one I wanted to tell and the only one I couldn't.

ELEANOR. You wanted to tell *me*? Tell me you were screwing a girl who's younger than our daughter?

JAMES. We always said we'd tell each other if and when —

ELEANOR. *You* did. My way was to keep it dark.

NELL. Which I did.

JAMES. Funny how things turn out.

ELEANOR. What?

JAMES. In the event, I've told the lies and you've been straight.

ELEANOR. You can't be serious.

NELL. Go on, tell him. Wipe that self-satisfied look off his face —

JAMES. What's that mean?

NELL. That 'I've been a naughty boy but ain't I clever' expression right off his —

ELEANOR. Nothing.

JAMES. I've lied to you and I'm sorry.

ELEANOR. How long have you been shagging Kate?

JIM (*insulted*). Shagging?

JAMES. I've been meeting her for a few weeks.

ELEANOR. A few weeks and I know already! God, you couldn't fool a cretin.

JAMES. My heart wasn't in it really.

NELL. Tell him how long you lied to *him*. How long you spared *his* feelings. Go on!

JAMES. As I said, I wanted to tell you. I'm glad you know.

NELL. I didn't want to know.

JAMES. I've always been very proud of the way we trusted each other. I totally trusted you and knew you'd have told me if any other man —

ELEANOR. No, no, that wasn't what *I* agreed. I said if it happened, spare the other's feelings.

NELL. As I did yours.

ELEANOR. Keep it dark.

JIM. She's cracked.

JAMES. I understood the opposite. If you had had a lover, you'd have told me.

NELL. You'd have been destroyed.

ELEANOR. I certainly would not have told you. You loved me then.

JAMES. I love you now.

NELL. I've read that letter! Four times. Once at the table of the tea-shop in front of the friend who gave it to me. Twice in the lavatory, once more in the train home. You called her 'darling'.

ELEANOR *shakes her head and goes for another drink.*

JAMES. Who gave you this? St. Agnes?

NELL. How could you humiliate me in front of her?

JIM. Who else could it be?

NELL. Don't you see that's the worst of it? The loss of dignity.

JAMES. She's an interfering bitch.

ELEANOR. She's a poor widow possessed by love.

JIM. Don't keep using that word.

JAMES. Love? She wanted to hurt you.

NELL. Who gave her the opportunity?

JIM. I must warn Kate.

ELEANOR. I thought that at first. And for some moments I
    considered hurting Agnes in return.

JAMES. *How* could you have hurt her?

NELL. Go on, tell him.

> *She waits.* ELEANOR *doesn't speak. To him, decisively.*

She still thinks —

ELEANOR. She still thinks Albert only had *one* other woman.
    The one you've taken over.

JAMES. I haven't taken her —

ELEANOR. Whereas I know of at least one other.

JAMES. Kate told me there were others, yes.

ELEANOR. This was before Kate.

JAMES. How d'you know?

NELL. He's hooked. Go on.

JAMES. You can't be sure.

ELEANOR. I know the only way you *can* be sure.

> *She sits and drinks.* NELL *studies* JAMES.

NELL. Are you getting there? How long can it possibly take —

JIM. Her?

JAMES. D'you mean — ?

JIM. Christ!

JAMES. You and Albert?

NELL. Talk about the Mills of God.

ELEANOR. Yes.

JAMES. Really?

NELL. Really, yes.

JIM. You never know anyone.

JAMES. When was this?

ELEANOR. In another century.

JAMES. Where? For how long?

NELL. How does it feel? Eh?

ELEANOR. I'm not going into details now —

JIM. Oh yes, you are —

ELEANOR. — because it wasn't important.

NELL. Even *that's* hurt him. Don't go further. Leave it there.

ELEANOR. An episode. A shoulder to cry on. After a few drinks.
    You were away.

JAMES. Where did you — ?

ELEANOR. Here. He brought me home.

JAMES. In our bed?

ELEANOR. In this room. Once. Nothing more.

    JAMES *recoils from the sofa then turns away to get a drink.*

JAMES. Was it alright?

ELEANOR. I'm not going into details.

    JIM *goes to* JAMES *and talks inaudibly.*

NELL. That's enough. He's had enough. Don't lose your
    advantage by saying it was hopeless, that you both felt
    ashamed of betraying James. Violating the taboo of best
    friends' wives or husbands. Leave it at that.

    JAMES *turns back smiling. They chuckle together.*

JAMES. I must say, he had some sauce.

JIM. In this room, eh?

JAMES. Crafty bugger.

NELL. He's smiling. He admires him even more.

JAMES. I always thought he was true to Agnes till he went for Kate. But now it seems he poked everything in sight. Including you.

JIM (*to heaven*). Well, can you hear me? You've had my wife, I've had your girl. Still am having her. Knock for knock.

JAMES. Tit for tat.

He and JIM *chuckle together.*

NELL. Christ, the camaraderie of cock. How they literally stand together! Whereas women never trust each other.

ELEANOR. You think it's funny?

NELL. Agnes can't trust me, I can't trust Kate —

JAMES. That you had Albert? Not that funny, no.

NELL. Though of course James can't trust *you* now. Perhaps his smile was only a bluff. He must feel hurt —

ELEANOR. The episode with Albert was more mess than ecstasy. A quick bang after a party with the kids asleep upstairs and Sarah Vaughan on the hi-fi. Not important.

JAMES. Like me and Kate.

NELL. But unlike the man I nearly left you for.

ELEANOR. If it's unimportant, why write a letter?

JIM (*to* JAMES). Exactly. What the hell did you write for?

NELL (*to* JAMES). Two years I had a sort of love affair and I never wrote a letter!

JAMES. I don't know.

NELL. Yes, he was in the choir. That's how we could meet once or twice a week without your finding out.

JAMES. So many years since I wrote that sort of letter. I wanted to see if I could remember how . . .

ELEANOR. You never wrote me that sort of letter.

NELL (*to* ELEANOR). Don't tell him, though. He'd discount it because you never went to bed.

ELEANOR. If it's as unimportant as you say, you won't mind giving her up? —

NELL. He'd call it romantic.

JAMES. Of course not.

JIM (*warning*). Steady!

NELL. I had the best of both worlds — him for flattery, you for bed and breakfast.

ELEANOR. So!

JAMES. So!

NELL. So you see I'm not a stranger in this house. Very much at home, in fact.

ELEANOR. There's not going to be any in-between. Either you go with her or stay with me.

JIM (*to* JAMES). Agree to anything.

JAMES. I never intended going anywhere with her. And she wouldn't want me to.

ELEANOR. Don't be simple, James.

NELL. It was your simplicity made me stay. I couldn't see how you'd manage without me.

JAMES. She doesn't want another married scene.

ELEANOR. She was after Albert and she's after you.

JIM (*excited*). D'you think that's possible?

JAMES. Absolutely not.

NELL. You'll be telling us next this is only a bit on the —

JAMES. Eleanor, for both of us this is only a bit on the side.

ELEANOR. Oh! (*Howling.*)

NELL. No!

JAMES (*angry*). What?

ELEANOR. That's what they *all* say. That's what Albert told Agnes.

NELL. About the same girl.

JIM (*to* ELEANOR). Can't you see this is doing us good?

ELEANOR. Perhaps she's funny for old men, loves her father, hates her mother, wants to hurt all women, I don't know.

JIM. This is enlarging us!

ELEANOR. Albert at least was celebrated. A star to fuck.

JAMES. You haven't stopped using off-colour language since you came in.

JIM. Fuck and bang and shagging and love.

JAMES. Albert's marriage was on its last legs. Ours is different. You're not Agnes.

JIM. So don't act like her.

JAMES. She treated Albert as property. But people aren't things.

ELEANOR. So nor is Kate. Not a bit on the side but a woman.

JIM. Both.

ELEANOR. She wants to take you away from me. I know her. I was like her once. Well, go with her if that's what you want.

NELL. And if you do, where does that leave *me*? A man of fifty's still all right but a grandmother is nobody's idea of —

JAMES. There's no question of leaving you.

Choral music, perhaps 'Quam Olim Abrahe' from Mozart's Requiem or a fugue from a Passion.

KATE *comes on wearing a gown and arrives downstage at the same time as* JIM. *Lights change.* JIM *and* KATE *face front.*

JIM. Hullo, Kate?

KATE. Hullo?

JIM. James speaking. James Croxley.

KATE. I know who it *is*. How *are* you?

JIM. Eleanor's found out.

KATE. Oh, no. How?

JIM. The letter I wrote got to her instead.

KATE. Through Agnes?

JIM. Yes.

KATE. I thought as much. They've got a key.

JIM. Of course I'll have to write an official letter.

KATE. Of course.

JIM. Ignore it.

KATE. Right.

JAMES *comes down too.*

KATE *continues to* JIM, *describing how she came to suspect* AGNES *was prying. The rest of the Act works like this — a fugue of voices, the written speeches predominating and improvised dialogue continuing behind.*

JAMES. Dear Kate, it doesn't matter how, but Eleanor's discovered we've been meeting. I suppose it's only natural she should be upset but I've tried to explain it was only a lark and there's no question of anything more.

ELEANOR (*joining them, while* JAMES, KATE *and* JIM *continue*). Dear Kate, I haven't read his letter but I hope James didn't give the impression I'm getting melodramatic. There's no need for any of us to get into a heavy scene, as he calls it.

KATE. Dearest Eleanor, thank you so much for writing. The worst thing about all this is the pain I've caused you —

NELL (*joining them*). Oh, yes, I'm sure —

KATE. — and the thought of losing your friendship.

NELL. You do seem to have your work cut out staying friendly with the wives.

ELEANOR. I've told him he's at liberty to go with you but if he does, it's for good. No using you as lover and me as safety-net.

NELL. You have him and the best of luck. Find out for yourself what fun it is to be the wife of a man who works at home.

JAMES. Eleanor and I both hope that, when this has spent itself, we'll all three pick up the pieces again and meet as friends . . .

NELL. No chance of a break or change of scene. Well, you've given him that. So take him, do his washing, his V.A.T. . . .

KATE. Let's please meet and talk as soon as I'm back from foreign parts.

JIM. I know that while you're — where is it? —

KATE. Kyoto, Tokio, Nagasaki, Los Angeles, San Francisco —

JIM. Yes, I know you'll have every man who takes your fancy —

KATE. Is it enough to say at the moment that my affection and respect for you have never diminished?

NELL. I'd rather be the mistress, with all the little mistressy excitements: will he come today, will *she* find out? I might suggest that — let him live with you and sneak away whenever he can for a crafty fuck with me.

JIM. And, though I long to be in their place, I don't resent you having those men. We don't love each other and you don't love them —

NELL. And I'll dress in frilly undies and wear exotic scent and enjoy the aphrodisiac of fooling you, the wife.

JAMES. And if by any chance Susie or Agnes is reading this, do let it through because it's written with Eleanor's approval and I've kept a carbon copy. (*To* ELEANOR:) Let's go for a lie-down, shall we?

ELEANOR. Why not? Two hours before my student comes.

JIM. All I ask is, while you're having them, spare a thought for me. On similar occasions I'll remember you . . .

JAMES *and* ELEANOR *move to the stairs.*

KATE. I'm so brought down and confused by all the trouble I've caused . . .

JIM. By Christ, Kate, I'll miss you . . .

KATE. . . . you'll survive . . .

JIM. Just about . . .

KATE. Till I get back . . .

JAMES and ELEANOR have climbed the stairs and near the top JAMES begins caressing her. She responds and they embrace on the top step.

NELL. Listen to his fifty-year-old moans about his failing health . . . his wasted life, the girls he never had . . .

JIM. Send a sexy card —

KATE. All right —

JIM. With a hidden message for me.

NELL. But why should you take him from me? He's mine! I love him!

They all continue.

JAMES and ELEANOR make love on the landing.

Music drowns all voices.

ACT TWO

*The Chorale: 'O Haupt von Blut und Wunden' from Bach's
St. Matthew Passion.*

    After some time, the lights show ELEANOR *in the living
room, a score on her knee, listening. Nearby is* NELL, *trying to
write a letter.*

    In the work-room JAMES *is restoring a Victorian head of
Christ crucified.* JIM *near him reading a book.*

    For awhile this tableau is almost still. First ELEANOR *puts
down her score and goes to refill her glass with vodka and tonic.*

    JAMES *throws down his brush and wipes his hands on a rag.*
JIM *looks up at him.* JAMES *studies the painting.*

    ELEANOR *returns to the sofa, drinking.* NELL *crumples the
page she's been writing, starts again.*

    JAMES *takes the painting off the easel and goes to the door
with it.* JIM *follows.*

    *The kitchen door at once opens and they enter the living
room. Neither of the women hear them.* JAMES *stands, listening
to the music till the chorus ends with 'So schändlich Zugericht'
Recitative continues quietly.*

JAMES. What does all that mean?

ELEANOR (*startled*). Hullo.

    NELL *hides the letter.*

JAMES. What's it all about?

ELEANOR (*translating*). Something like 'Head full of blood and
    wounds, full of sorrow and scoffing, mocked with a crown of
    thorns.'

JAMES. I thought so.

    *He goes to get himself a drink, putting down the painting
against a chair.*

NELL (*reads*). 'Dear James, it's funny writing a letter to someone you live with but there are things to say now that I suddenly find I can't say to your face.'

JAMES. Want a drink?

ELEANOR. Won't say no.

She finishes the one she's got.

Vodka and tonic.

NELL. 'While Kate's been away these last few weeks, I've learnt that I don't hate her. If anything, I'm grateful to her, for giving our marriage a shot in the arm.'

ELEANOR. That's not right . . .

JAMES (*turning from drinks cabinet*). What?

ELEANOR (*waking, faking*). It can't be a diminuendo.

JAMES *gives her the drink.*

I'm marking my score of The Matthew Passion and getting quietly sloshed.

JAMES. Ah. Well, cheers.

ELEANOR. Finished the painting?

JAMES. I couldn't face any more without a Scotch. Had more than enough of that insipid eunuch. (*Shows her the picture.*) The self-pity. Sickly. Sentimental.

ELEANOR. You're getting very well paid, aren't you — ?

JAMES. I asked more than I thought they'd give. And they said yes.

NELL. Thirty pieces of silver?

ELEANOR *laughs.*

JIM. It's not funny.

JAMES (*intensely*). We still live in the shadow of His death. And His birth, for that matter. A virgin birth. A conception and a birth without carnal love. It flies in the face of all we know and people like us don't believe it any more — but two thousand years of history are sitting on our backs.

JIM (*to* JAMES). She doesn't know what you're saying. (*To* ELEANOR:) This is all about *us*. What's been happening to you and me.

ELEANOR. The music's Christian and I like that.

JAMES. Of course. It's Bach. But what if it's this sickly Victoriana?

JIM. The holy oil that kept the wheels of industry turning?

JAMES. Propaganda for the Satanic mills. Putting a love of God in place of love for people. (*To the picture:*) 'Thou hast conquered, O pale Galilean —'

JIM (*reading*). 'The world has grown grey from Thy breath —'

JAMES. Poor old Swinburne must have had a bellyful of sanctity.

JIM. No wonder he spent his last years being flogged by whores!

JAMES. Even a healthy sexual passion was twisted into a craving for the infinite. The anti-lifers, the troubadours, the saints and martyrs. Saint Teresa caught by Bernini mid-orgasm, pierced by the lance of God. Anyone who's ever watched a partner in the act can see that's a statue of a woman coming.

JIM *goes, shows* ELEANOR *the book.*

NELL. He's worked himself into a lather, hasn't he? That usually means he's got some book.

ELEANOR. Have you been reading a book or what?

JIM (*resentfully*). Books are to help us understand.

JAMES. I do want to make some sense of my life, don't you?

ELEANOR. Of course.

JAMES. And not in terms of death.

NELL. He means her.

ELEANOR. Well, *we* don't see it like that, do we?

NELL. He means why can't he have her too?

ELEANOR. We're not Christians. I'm an atheist but I love church music and oratorio and hymns and Christmas carols. Hundreds of people singing together is the nearest we may ever come to heaven on earth. Communion.

JAMES. The Communion is a ceremony based on the pre-Christian orgy.

JIM. Dearest Kate, are you doing it now? At this moment are you saying to some other man what you said to me?

JAMES. The pagan fertility festivals? The Christians took them over.

ELEANOR. I meant 'communion' in the sense of people congregating.

JIM. Are you saying 'don't stop now, please' to some lucky Yank?

JAMES. People used to congregate to make love. Before the god-lovers and life-haters set down the couple as the largest legitimate sexual group.

ELEANOR. You've got sex in the head.

JIM. Where else can I have it?

NELL. She's in there, isn't she? In your head? With her frilly knickers and tricks with the wine?

ELEANOR. Has all this come from having a bit on the side?

JAMES. Either/or's not the answer. If it finishes with a new monogamy.

ELEANOR. It's hard to see an alternative.

JAMES. More than one.

ELEANOR. At a time?

    JIM *and* NELL *listen.*

JAMES. Why not?

ELEANOR. It's hard enough to find one person you fancy, leave alone two.

NELL. It took you twenty-five years to find Kate.

ELEANOR. I mean, I'm game. But where do we look?

NELL. And *she's* in California so —

ELEANOR. Shall we go through the phone-book or what?

JIM. You'd better take this seriously.

JAMES (*laughing*). We could go round the pub, see who we run into.

NELL. Anyone fancy a fertility festival?

> JAMES *and* ELEANOR *embrace.*

> Good clean house. Cold buffet to follow. (*She closes her eyes.*) Oh, my love, stop doing that with your tongue.

> *Doorbell rings.*

ELEANOR. That's my student. She wants me to run through her adjudication pieces. Sorry.

JAMES. Oh well. I'd better get back to Old Killjoy here.

> ELEANOR *goes towards the door.* JAMES *takes the picture to the kitchen.* JIM *talks after* ELEANOR.

JIM. I won't allow my life to close in again. I got my chance and opened the door. If I can change, then so can you —

> ELEANOR *opens the door to* KATE.

KATE. Hullo.

JIM. It's her. She's here!

ELEANOR. Good God!

KATE. Bad time?

ELEANOR. Not at all. Come in.

> KATE *does.* ELEANOR *shuts door.* JIM *runs back to* JAMES.

JIM. I made you come by thinking of you. By dwelling on your memory. Night and day.

KATE. You said to drop in if I was passing.

ELEANOR. Of course. Delighted.

NELL. Where would you be passing to?

ELEANOR. I thought you were still abroad.

KATE. Been back a few days.

ELEANOR takes KATE's outdoor coat and goes to hang it.

JIM. A few days. Why d'you leave it a few days?

ELEANOR. You're looking well. Wonderful colour.

KATE. That's California.

NELL. And dressed to kill. Kill *what*?

KATE. Won't last long in London.

NELL. Cost the earth, that little number.

ELEANOR. James is here.

NELL. The same perfume I smelt on James that day. That he said was from expensive tarts and now I know what he meant.

They go to the living room.

ELEANOR. We've got company.

JAMES (*turning, coming to greet* KATE). So I heard.

JIM. Kiss? No.

KATE *and* JAMES *shake hands.*

KATE. Oh, very formal. Surely we're allowed a friendly kiss?

They do. A social peck.

NELL. What's the game now? Can't be after him or she wouldn't have come here. Or would she?

ELEANOR. Lovely tan, hasn't she, James?

JAMES. Absolutely. As you told us in your card from — where was it?

KATE. Santa Monica?

JIM. Saucy as ever. A nude by Ingres —

KATE. You got that then?

JIM. — with an arse like a peach —

JAMES. Yes, indeed.

JIM. And a hope that both of us would see your tan before it faded away.

KATE. I'm brown all over.

JIM. Or as you said 'the tail-end of your tan'.

KATE. For the first time ever.

JIM. Tail-end!

JAMES. Can I get you a drink?

KATE. I thought you'd never ask.

JAMES. Gin and tonic?

KATE. Right.

NELL (*to* ELEANOR): Strange to watch the two of you together. First time since I found out . . .

JAMES. And you, love? Same again?

ELEANOR. Mmmm?

JAMES. Same again?

ELEANOR. Please.

NELL. Aren't you drinking rather a lot?

ELEANOR. I'm not driving.

JAMES. What?

JIM. What's she talking about?

NELL. You're pissed.

She moves off unsteadily.

JIM (*to* KATE). Find a way of saying if you got my letter.

JAMES. You had a good time, then?

KATE. Great, fantastic! In California anyway.

JIM. No, wait till the student comes.

ELEANOR. Get any work done?

KATE. In Japan I worked. In the States I played.

JIM. Then when Eleanor's in the music room you can say if it's yes to Zurich.

ELEANOR. Lucky girl.

NELL. Everything's instant, isn't it? Casual. Spur of the moment.

JIM. You'll like it. Three days. Nice hotel. The lake, the mountains.

KATE. Lucky . . . in some ways.

NELL. Arrivals, departures, eating, drinking, who you sleep with.

ELEANOR. Some ways?

JIM. And while I'm working you can shop. I'm being paid in francs.

ELEANOR. Why 'some ways'?

NELL. She even makes her pictures with a shutter. Instantly.

ELEANOR. No strings and no connections.

JAMES has given drinks.

JAMES. Cheers then.

KATE. Right.

NELL. I was like you once. At college. The fun-loving dolly.

JIM. I'd hoped you'd reply to my dealer — marking the envelope 'To be collected'.

KATE. So here we are again, all three of us. I've missed you both. I meant what I said in my letter. This thing James and I have had, we won't let that affect our relationship, will we?

ELEANOR. We're adult people.

NELL. What's she doing here — dressed to kill. What's her game?

KATE takes ELEANOR's hand.

KATE. If I'd been you I'd have scratched my eyes out.

ELEANOR. Really? No.

KATE. Yes, a very heavy scene. But it was only a 'lark'. Wasn't it, James?

JIM. I want you.

JAMES. I hope I've made that clear.

ELEANOR. He's tried.

KATE (*to* ELEANOR). I'd have felt far worse to lose *you*.

> *She kisses* ELEANOR's *hand, then her lips.*

NELL. Is she Lesbian, then?

JIM. This is either an elaborate cover or —

NELL. It would account for the string of married men.

ELEANOR. I felt the same about you.

NELL. Indirectly getting at the wives.

KATE. You may not believe this but I can't stand all that underhand business.

JIM. This is good but where's it leading?

KATE. I know you agree with me, Eleanor, that sex is terrific fun as long as it doesn't lose you friends. It should be open. Cards on the table.

> JIM *and* NELL *talk to* JAMES *and* ELEANOR *but we don't hear clearly and* KATE *continues:*

> If I like the look of a man or another woman — or both — I ought to say so and see what happens. I mean, I shouldn't be put down by conventional values and start a lot of lying that nearly led to losing *both*.

> *She reaches for* JAMES's *hand and he approaches. She holds both.*

> I'm putting this very badly —

JIM. I wouldn't say that.

NELL. Oh, I don't know —

KATE. — but d'you know what I mean, James?

JAMES. Yes, I believe so.

JIM. Just taking your hand has given me a hard-on.

NELL. She wants us both.

KATE. I know Eleanor does.

JIM. She's come for a sandwich!

KATE. I don't mean I wasn't attracted to you, James, of course I was, but not you only. It was both of you. Your life. Your whole relationship. You know?

She kisses him, as before.

JIM. You're doing beautifully.

NELL. I can feel his desire through her. I suppose that's how it works. A sort-of conductor.

JAMES *moves away.* KATE *breaks from* ELEANOR, *who sits.*

ELEANOR. I'm sure he understands. I do.

JAMES. We were talking about this before you arrived.

JIM (*behind her*). We know what you mean, both of us.

He runs his hands up and down her body, caressing her.

KATE. Well. I realised how I felt about you both when it all came out and it was in that mood I left for Japan. I tried to keep my head by working hard while I was there but on my last night I was taking some pictures of an American diplomat and his Japanese wife who finally made it clear they'd like me to stay the night.

ELEANOR. And did you?

JIM *runs his hand up her leg, kneeling now beside her. He raises her skirt, showing her thigh.*

KATE. I did, yes.

JIM. Wear this dress when you come to bed. Let Eleanor take it off.

JAMES. Japanese women seem too — I don't know — too much like porcelain — for a night of hanky-panky.

KATE. It's when the porcelain cracks, though.

NELL. The thought of another woman's never aroused me but a man as well —

ELEANOR. You enjoyed it then?

NELL. *That* man —

KATE. No.

She goes to sit, leaving JIM. *But he follows and kneels by her, caressing her leg.* NELL *goes to* JAMES *and embraces him.*

JAMES. Why not?

NELL. Maybe this is the best solution. I'm fond of her and you desire her and I love you.

KATE. The man was only interested in stimulating *her*. I felt left out in the end. Aroused but unsatisfied —

NELL. But can I watch you have her?

ELEANOR. Perhaps somebody's always left out.

JIM (*embracing her*). You won't be left out. I want you both.

JAMES. But there was nothing wrong in principle?

KATE. Oh, no.

JAMES. Especially in a non-Christian country. Before the Holy Ghost started haunting us, sex in crowds was the norm. Romantic passion for one beloved was to the Greeks and Romans an affliction you hoped wouldn't happen in your family.

KATE. I must say I've usually enjoyed it, Christian country or not. Another drink, James, please.

JAMES. And you, love?

ELEANOR. A little Dutch courage, yes.

JAMES *gets the drinks.*

NELL. Who begins and how?

KATE. Anyway. I left before either of them were up and hitched back into town on a truck, which was another unsatisfactory episode —

NELL. Are you making this up?

KATE. I had to pay my fare, so to speak, while we were crawling in the traffic.

JIM. She's anyone's.

KATE. Amusing with all the other drivers peering through the smog at me, on this truck driver's lap, but not very satisfying.

NELL. Pornography!

KATE. — so you can imagine that when I was finally sitting in the window-seat waiting for the airplane to start for the States, I was ready for anything.

NELL. Not a photographer — a pornographer!

JAMES (*giving her a drink*). There you are.

KATE (*tasting*). This is almost neat gin.

JAMES. We all need a stiff one.

They laugh at his unintended joke.

JIM. At this moment I'm the luckiest man in the history of civilisation. In a room with the two women I desire most in the world —

KATE. And now, at last, I've come to the point —

JIM. — and both of them desire me and there's nothing in art or science or religion to compare with this —

KATE. Well, to cut a long story short, I've fallen head-over-heels in love.

Pause.

JAMES. Well, well —

JIM. No, Kate, don't say that, please —

ELEANOR. How nice for you?

NELL. And even nicer for me!

KATE. Right.

JIM. And don't keep saying 'right'.

KATE. Suddenly there was this beautiful guy asking if he could move my gear from the seat next to mine —

NELL. Poor James!

She approaches him as he stands smiling and sipping his drink.

KATE. Then I realised bells were ringing.

JAMES. Was it a bomb-scare?

KATE. What?

JAMES. Hi-jackers?

ELEANOR *laughs*.

KATE. No, in my head. Or wherever they ring.

JAMES. I was going to say 'Bells on a jumbo'!

KATE. My heart was jumping. I could hardly speak. I thought to myself 'My God, it's love'.

JIM. You told me you didn't *want* love.

JAMES. I thought they always put on soothing strings.

NELL. I must say I'm relieved.

ELEANOR. That must be wonderful.

KATE. Yes, it is, but sad to say they were also warning-bells.

JIM. You didn't want another heavy scene.

NELL. Warning-bells?

KATE. They were saying 'Go no further'. But I didn't read them then, I'm glad to say. For two weeks it was knock-out.

JIM. *We* could be knock-out.

KATE. L.A., Vegas, San Francisco . . .

JIM. I've had no chance. The odd hour —

ELEANOR. Then why the warning-bells?

JIM. But in Zurich —

KATE (*shrugs*). Oh, problems, problems —

NELL. Aaaah.

JIM. Three days and nights —

JAMES. What problems exactly?

KATE. None on my side.

NELL (*to* ELEANOR). Another married man.

ELEANOR. American?

KATE. English. Lives not far from here. I'm on my way to see him now and thought, as it sort-of concerns us all, I'd break my journey to let you know. I told him, 'Let's take off, I'm yours'.

JIM. Be his, by all means, but mine as well.

ELEANOR. But he's not free?

KATE. He's got commitments.

ELEANOR. About your age?

KATE. No. Fortyish.

NELL. I thought so.

KATE. Forty-five-ish.

ELEANOR. And is he married?

KATE. Separated.

JAMES. Then what's the problem?

KATE. About to separate.

NELL. You mean you want to wreck *his* marriage?

KATE. Is that the end of the inquisition?

ELEANOR. Sorry. I was only asking.

> KATE *moves about, puts her glass on drinks shelf. The others wait.*

KATE. I didn't *choose* this to happen. I just fell in love.

JAMES. I never thought you were that romantic.

KATE. Eleanor doesn't think so either. She's cast me as a home-wrecker.

NELL. Oh, you can't stand disapproval, can you?

ELEANOR. *I* haven't cast you.

NELL. You want even the wives to love you.

KATE. You and Agnes both.

JIM. Don't compare my wife with Agnes.

ELEANOR. I'm not tolerant the way she was.

JAMES. You're tolerant in different ways.

He kisses her.

ELEANOR. I told James he could go with you or stay with me.

JAMES. And put like that I obviously stayed.

KATE. It was only a bit of fun. Now finished.

JIM (*going on his knees*). Please, Kate.

KATE. And we're the best of friends again.

She takes ELEANOR's *hand and reaches for* JAMES's. *He takes hers. She impulsively kisses* ELEANOR.

Aren't we?

She kisses JAMES *on the cheek.*

JIM (*getting to his feet*). Insulting bitch.

NELL. She's enjoying this.

ELEANOR. You look very happy.

KATE (*shrugs*). I suppose that's being in love.

ELEANOR. I can just remember.

JAMES. I wouldn't know.

ELEANOR. He says he's never been in love.

KATE. You love each other.

ELEANOR. Oh, yes, but that's like — our daily bread. Being *in* love is different.

KATE. It's coming to life after having been dead.

JIM. Well, thanks.

NELL (*sympathetically*). Oh, James, she can't be worth it.

ELEANOR. James won't fall in love. He's got too much self-esteem.

KATE (*pitying*). Aah.

She again kisses him on the cheek.

JIM. If you peck me again like that, I'll bite a piece from your ear.

Doorbell rings.

ELEANOR. There's my student. Why don't you keep James company a bit?

NELL (*to her*): Don't rub salt in the wound.

KATE. I should really go.

JAMES. One for the road?

KATE. No, really, I mustn't keep him waiting.

ELEANOR *opens front door.* KATE *finishes drink.* NELL *stays half-way between hall and room.*

JIM. She's only punctual when it's new.

JAMES. Remember our first time — in the restaurant?

JIM. When you wanted me?

JAMES. You were punctual then.

KATE (*with a smile and a shrug*). Right.

JAMES. D'you know you use that word too often?

ELEANOR *admits a young woman, takes her outer clothes and hangs them.*

KATE. Which word?

JAMES. 'Right.'

KATE. I do?

JAMES. Absolutely.

KATE. Same with you and 'absolutely'.

She goes to the hall. JAMES *and* JIM *follow.*

The WOMAN STUDENT's *gone into the music room. She starts limbering up her voice with scales.*

KATE *meets and kisses* ELEANOR.

KATE. Let's make a date to go shopping.

ELEANOR. Yes, lets.

KATE. I'm so sorry for any pain I caused you.

ELEANOR. All over now. Forgotten.

They embrace.

NELL. Should I be grateful? I don't know. He looks like death.

JIM. Love another man by all means but that doesn't mean I'm suddenly repulsive. How about my letter? Zurich?

KATE. I'll ring you.

ELEANOR. Do.

She goes to music room and almost at once the piano begins to assist the STUDENT *in her scales.*

JAMES. Did you have a coat?

KATE. Yes.

JAMES (*getting it*). There's quite a chill in the air tonight. *Winter* coming.

NELL. Poor James fell for your sex act. I almost did myself tonight.

JIM. My life's ending as abruptly as it began — how many weeks ago?

JAMES (*helping her on with the coat*). Here we are.

NELL. But, of course, you're really a romantic. Promiscuous people always are.

JIM. Kate, please . . .

He kisses her neck, goes on his knees before her.

JAMES. Did you get my letter?

KATE. It was nice of you to ask, but, well, you see how things are.

JIM. No, I don't.

JAMES. Absolutely.

KATE. We'll see each other soon. At Private Views.

JAMES. Why did you do it like this?

KATE. This was the best way.

She kisses him quickly and goes by the front door.

JIM (*following her, shouting*). I didn't know you wanted love.
I'll say I love you. I'll do anything!

JAMES *closes the front door.* NELL *goes to join* ELEANOR
in the music room.

Chorus: He trusted in God from 'Messiah'.

Lights on upper level.

*Private View begins, exactly as in Act One, but now the
photographs are of sexual acrobatics.*

JAMES *goes up the stairs and reveals a closer view of the
coupling.* GUESTS *loudly approve, clap, whistle, etc. He
reveals another, the face of Bernini's Saint Teresa. Laughter
and ribald comments. He gestures for the* GUESTS *to
follow him and leads them downstairs. They make themselves
at home in the living room while* JAMES *fetches the Christ
painting. At same time,* ELEANOR *comes from bedroom in
nightgown, wanders along balcony, looking over at the*
GUESTS, *trying not to be seen.*

JAMES *puts up the Christ and the reaction is as though this
were the most obscene picture of all. Among the crowd we
now distinguish* KATE, AGNES *and* A MAN *who might be
Albert. He caresses them in turn.*

As ELEANOR *sees this,* JAMES *notices her and points her
out to the crowd. She cowers but he calls her down and she
hesitantly descends. He introduces her and they all applaud.*

ELEANOR *now takes over the lecture as* JAMES *goes into the
crowd of onlookers, now waiting for* ELEANOR *to begin.
But she's only concerned with* JAMES *and tries to see who
he's with.*

There is A YOUNG WOMAN *behind the crowd and he stands
behind her, caressing her breasts, kissing her hair and neck as
she faces* ELEANOR, *listening.*

KATE, AGNES *and the* ALBERT MAN *begin catcalling for*
ELEANOR *to start. This is taken up by others. Someone
takes a flash photo, another plucks at the skirt of her
nightdress to lift it. She covers herself and tries to move*

towards JAMES *and the* GIRL *but they won't let her and*
KATE *and* AGNES *both embrace her, kiss her, restrain her.*
JAMES *has got some of the* GIRL's *clothing off and is pulling*
her down on to the floor.

The crowd gather to watch this and surround them.
ELEANOR *at last gets free and reaches this circle, pulling*
them away, fighting through. She reveals JIM *with the half-*
dressed girl, kissing her body. Flash of camera.

He is amused by ELEANOR's *appearance and points at her*
nightdress. The GIRL *is hidden by the crowd. They all exit*
through the various doors. JIM *is the last to go.*

The pictures upstairs go as they came, JAMES *comes from*
the bedroom in pyjamas and dressing gown.
Chorus ends and lights change.

ELEANOR *in living room,* JAMES *coming downstairs.*

ELEANOR. Then suddenly it was in this room and I was up there
trying to hide and you called me down in my nightdress to
talk about the Christ painting —

JAMES. It was a nightmare. We all have nightmares. We don't
have to spend the rest of the night going over —

ELEANOR. Meanwhile — at the back of the crowd you were
taking off her clothes.

JAMES. Whose clothes? Kate's?

ELEANOR. No, it's not Kate. I know that. Someone else.

JAMES. Listen, will you believe me? There isn't anyone else.
There never has been anyone else. Only her.

ELEANOR. How can I believe you? Ever again?

JAMES. Are you trying?

ELEANOR. You *lied* to me. You broke our trust.

JAMES. You lied to *me*! Over Albert.

ELEANOR *does not speak.*

By your own admission. How do I know that was the only
time? Shall I make you some tea?

ELEANOR. Just get me a glass of Perrier.

JAMES *goes off.*

ELEANOR. Albert was nothing, I told you. I didn't change because of that. You didn't even notice.

JIM *comes back with Perrier, wearing pyjamas.*

JIM. *I* haven't changed.

ELEANOR. Not changed, no. Become hidden. I hardly recognise you any more. Abstracted, irritable. All you want to do is sleep. You lie there snoring and when at last I drift off I dream I'm singing an aria in the wrong key while you and Albert and Kate and Agnes sit in the front row —

JIM. Of course all I want to do is sleep when every night is spent picking over the same old entrails —

ELEANOR. You nod off over a book, in front of the t.v., during concerts —

JIM (*over*). — looking for the same bad omens —

ELEANOR. — sleep is your way of getting through. Or is she so demanding you can't even keep awake?

JIM. Who? Who's 'she'? Kate?

ELEANOR. Not Kate, no. I know that's over —

JIM. There's no-one else.

ELEANOR. Then why does so much of your work these days take you away from home?

JIM. So much?

ELEANOR. Two days a week at least.

JIM. Most men are away for five —

ELEANOR. You're not most men.

JIM. Alright. I feel the need to get away. Nowadays, if there's a choice, I work at a gallery instead of here, yes —

ELEANOR. And when I ring you aren't there.

JIM. *Once* I wasn't there. I was running in the park. You won't even allow my jog on the common any more.

ELEANOR. I'm frightened alone.

She is crying. He embraces and holds her.

You never used to go away. We spent most of our lives together.

JIM. I've tried to persuade you that was wrong.

ELEANOR. You never wanted to go outside *then*.

JIM. How d'you know?

ELEANOR. You never *said*.

JIM. I should have. Variety is an aphrodisiac. Our married friends spend whole days apart. Without accounting. People need that freedom and privacy —

ELEANOR. *I* don't. You *didn't*.

JIM. Well, you were an untiring wife and mother. I worked hard to keep the family. Where many of our friends chanced their arms, took selfish risks with their children's futures, blew the lot on weekends away and sometimes tried a change of partner —

ELEANOR (*over this*). You didn't *want* that —

JIM (*not pausing*). — you and I made the long sure haul with no surprises. And one day we looked around to find our children gone. And you particularly were at the stage of life when every woman undergoes an inevitable change —

ELEANOR. Oh, no!

JIM (*angrily*). What?

ELEANOR. Not the change of life?

JIM. Whether you like the fact or not, my dear, you've reached the age when women suddenly . . .

ELEANOR. Go mad. Yes?

JIM. Can't feel the ground beneath their feet.

ELEANOR *shakes her head.*

ELEANOR. They go mad. *I'm* going mad. I feel it. What shall I do?

JIM. It isn't madness, love. It's an unwillingness to change.

ELEANOR. You keep on about change. But into what? A princess? A frog?

JIM. First you accept the need to. Then you find out. It's a question of bend or break at times. (*Leads her towards the stairs.*) Not only individuals but whole nations. Families are little countries. If they can't change they die. That last time Kate was here, for instance, you and I had accepted the thought of a sexual trio.

ELEANOR. It's always this. When you say 'change' you mean I must get used to the thought of —

JIM. Will you allow me to finish?

ELEANOR. Not if all you have to say is —

JIM. I am trying to help you.

ELEANOR. Then tell me what to do!

JIM. I hesitate to suggest this but I'm desperate —

ELEANOR. You're desperate?

JIM. I think we should get some outside help.

ELEANOR. Doctors?

JIM. I don't like it either but —

ELEANOR. Both of us.

JIM. Both of us, right. But first of all, you. Would you like me to arrange a check-up with Michael at the Middlesex? A physical first and if that's alright and you're still depressed, I dare say he'll be able to put you on to some other department.

ELEANOR. Us. Not me.

JIM (*gently*). It's you that's having the nightmares.

ELEANOR. It's you that brought them on.

JIM. The doctors may not agree. In fact, it may be best if you don't mention that business with Kate at all . . . They'd seize on that.

They've reached the upper landing now and go into the bedroom.

A slow chorus from the Matthew Passion.

A DOCTOR *enters, leading* NELL. *He speaks to her kindly, offers a chair on which she sits. He sits near her, opens a notebook, asks a question, she shakes her head, answers. We hear none of this, until the music ends.*

NELL. No, the nightmares started only recently. As long as we had one daughter left at home, I felt useful but James had begun to think he'd given up too much of his life to the family. When the last one left it seemed to mark the beginning of freedom for the two of us. So I looked around for him but found he was occupied elsewhere. Out to lunch. No-one home. I saw there was no-one home at all, except me. And half the time I was out to lunch myself. Dozing through a Passion. One day in rehearsal I found myself in tears when we sang 'Deliver me from the lion's mouth, call to me lest the bottomless pit shall swallow me . . .' Not tears for the dead or mankind in general but for myself — I'd sung them for years without thinking and now I realised that behind the noble Latin noise there was a meaning for me . . . my day of wrath was coming . . .

Music again. The DOCTOR *moves across behind her, reading the notes he's made. She turns to listen to him and, as he stands centre, lights come up slightly on the living room and* JIM *comes in with the* GIRL *from* ELEANOR's *nightmare, by the front door. She looks around as though she's never seen the house before. Music ends.*

It isn't fair to James, he spends hours of every day alone with a painting . . . when he comes back into the world he wants a sexy girl-friend, not a mental case, a woman whose true self is screaming with despair . . .

DOCTOR *has listened, now crosses to the side, making a note.* NELL *keeps her eyes on the living room, where* JIM *leads the* GIRL *to the stairs, caressing her as they climb.*

. . . if this is the change of life, I'd like some pills to regulate the chemistry . . . Help me sleep. Are there any pills to banish daydreams?

JIM *and the* GIRL *continue along the balcony into the bedroom. The* DOCTOR *nods, writes and gives* NELL *a prescription. Music resumes.* DOCTOR *asks her another question.*

ELEANOR *has come from the side to join* NELL.

ELEANOR. . . . not always in the same place, no. But always the same girl. A junior partner in this gallery . . . he finds any excuse to go there . . . I think he sometimes has her in our house . . . he leaves the windows open but enough of the scent still hangs about . . . know he's up to something, he's so remote . . .

NELL. He's always been a distant person. He was an only child, his parents spoilt him.

ELEANOR. They brought him up to believe in a life based on: take and it shall be given unto you.

NELL. So he finds love a mystery. He doesn't know what the word means. He says: why call affection, lust, belief in God, care for children, etcetera, by one word?

ELEANOR. We all recognise red, orange, yellow, blue, green and violet but we don't call them white just because they all become that when they're mixed together. He's trained himself to be precise about colours.

Music. Lights change. NELL *gets up and moves to the clothes cupboard by the front door. She takes out a coat.* JAMES *comes from the kitchen, doesn't see* NELL, *looks at his watch, looks upwards at the balcony as though guessing where she is.* ELEANOR *sits in the chair near the* DOCTOR. *She turns to the* DOCTOR *and speaks silently.* JAMES *moves towards* NELL, *sees her. Music ends.*

JAMES. Ah. You off now?

NELL. Yes.

JAMES. So am I. For a walk on the common. I did tell you. Possibly half an hour but it could be longer.

NELL. I didn't ask how long you'd be.

JAMES. If I undertake to be back within forty-five minutes, would that be acceptable?

NELL. Take as long as you like. I'll be out the whole afternoon, as you know. At the doctor's.

JAMES (*putting on a coat*). Tearing me apart?

NELL. He doesn't tear you apart.

ELEANOR (*to* DOCTOR). He resents it if I say we've talked about him.

JAMES (*shrugs*). He says I'm treating you badly.

NELL *looks in a glass, repairs her make-up, sits to do so.*
JAMES, *behind her, looks at his watch.*

ELEANOR. Doesn't like me seeing you at all, in fact.

NELL. He's only trying to help.

JAMES. By moralising about my behaviour? I thought shrinks weren't meant to allocate blame.

NELL. He's not a shrink. He's a clinical psychiatrist.

JAMES. Well, I hope he can be some help.

ELEANOR. It smacks of the church, he says, employing a professional to listen to our secrets. It means we've lost faith in human intercourse.

JAMES *moves towards the front door.*

NELL. Are you walking across the common towards the station? Let's stroll across together.

JAMES. I'm going the other way.

ELEANOR. I'm sure he doesn't mean to be cruel.

JAMES. If I came with you, I'd only have to walk all the way back before I could start my walk.

NELL. Yes, of course.

She has joined him at the front door, which he opens.

ELEANOR. We can't blame him for having a selfish nature.

JAMES (*kissing her*). See you later.

NELL. This incident as I left to come here gives you some idea what I mean. He set off positively enough, it's a chilly day, but I couldn't help seeing how soon he slowed down and seemed to be hovering. I didn't look back till I reached the main road near the station. Our house is easy to see from there and I took in something with half a mind that only really dawned when I was half way here in the train. Our car had gone.

KATE *and* ELEANOR *enter with* SHOP ASSISTANT *and go into the Dress Shop and start trying on the nightdresses.*

KATE. So you think he'd gone off in the car to see that girl?

ELEANOR. But the doctor suggested James had got into the car to give me a lift.

KATE. And hadn't found you?

ELEANOR. That was his suggestion.

KATE. Sounds reasonable.

ELEANOR. A belated kindness, yes it does. He's a belated kind of man. Except that when I got back two hours later the car still wasn't there and nor was he.

KATE. What did he say when he did come in?

ELEANOR. Showed me the paints and brushes he'd been to buy. Trouble is the supplier's only ten minutes away.

KATE. If I were you I'd turn a blind eye. He feels spied on, you can learn nothing, he can lie. It's useless. Somewhere I heard this great saying: Love isn't 'where've you been?', it's 'hello'.

ELEANOR. That's all right for a sexy affair. But what about afterwards?

KATE. Does there have to be any afterwards?

ELEANOR. Marriage, for instance.

KATE *has been changing into the underwear.* NELL *is climbing the stairs, but mostly hidden in half-light.*

KATE. Ah well, I wouldn't know.

ELEANOR. You lived with Albert five years.

KATE. Living with is different.

ELEANOR. Is it?

KATE (*displaying herself*). What d'you think?

ELEANOR. It's very you.

NELL (*appearing*). How could James have touched that repulsive flesh?

ELEANOR. Is that the kind of thing your lover likes? —

KATE. Right.

ELEANOR. I should buy it then.

> KATE *still considers herself in the glass.*
> ELEANOR's *trying on the negligee.*

NELL. You're an anthology of all James said he hated. Your smell, your complexion, the texture of your hair —

KATE. Trying on new clothes is life's greatest pick-me-up.

ELEANOR. Pick-me-up? I thought you were in love.

KATE (*shrugs*). Love's never easy. Unlike sex.

> ASSISTANT *shows in another* WOMAN *to try on clothes.*

NELL. Sex easy? You're talking like a man. *For* a man. Talk to *me*.

KATE. Don't misunderstand. It's not easy deceiving wives, for instance. Especially when they're friends, like you. Not pleasant either.

ELEANOR. Then why go for middle-aged husbands?

KATE. They're wittier, more interesting, they've done something with their lives . . .

NELL. And aren't so demanding sexually?

KATE. And as lovers they take their time.

NELL. There you are. (*She goes.*)

KATE. This does nothing for me.

ELEANOR. The fact I'm suspicious he's got another woman doesn't mean he has, it just means I'm suspicious.

KATE. Do what I did with Albert. Make him suspicious of you.

ELEANOR. Mistrusting each other hasn't been our way.

KATE. It seems to be now.

ELEANOR. And whose fault's that?

KATE. Good question. Does anything particularly make you doubt him?

ELEANOR. Oh no, a million signs. Either he talks too little or too much. I find cigarette ends in the ashtray of the car. He makes calls from public boxes, while he's supposed to be jogging.

KATE. Don't tell me you spy on him?

ELEANOR. I can hear the ten pence pieces clinking in his tracksuit pocket.

KATE. Now that looks more like a dirty weekend in Morocco, don't you think?

ELEANOR. Oh yes, and how about this for Florence?

KATE. For anywhere! I knew that was you somehow.

ELEANOR. But hell's bells, look at the price.

KATE. I'll take this one.

ELEANOR. Well I like it, but will my hubby?

KATE. I should think so.

ELEANOR. In that case I'll take it, because if she doesn't know, who does? How long will you be in Morocco?

KATE. Three days, just long enough to freshen up my fading tan.

ELEANOR. We're having a week in Florence, though not till after Christmas. He'll be working on a Crucifixion in Switzerland for a few days soon and I wanted to go with him. He said it would be all work and no play.

KATE. It doesn't sound like a load of laughs, I must say.

ELEANOR. And I said, Are you taking your floozie instead?

So, to allay my suspicions, perhaps, he's booked this week
by the Arno.

KATE. Well out of you and the floozie, I know who's got the
best of the bargain.

ELEANOR. It's where we spent our honeymoon, Florence.

KATE. Out of Florence and Zurich I know where I'd rather go.

NELL *and* AGNES *are found drinking in a bar. Men drink
behind them.*

NELL. In the ordinary way I might not have noticed.

AGNES. How do you mean, in the ordinary way?

NELL. Before suspicion became a way of life.

ELEANOR. Did I say Zurich?

KATE. What?

ELEANOR. I didn't mention Zurich.

KATE. I'll pay for that in cash.

ELEANOR. I didn't say he was going to Zurich. I said Switzerland.

KATE. So?

ELEANOR. How did you know it was Zurich? Who's told you if
it wasn't me? Don't think you can just walk off —

AGNES. I thought you knew it was still going on.

ELEANOR. Kate, did you hear what I said? Kate, wait for me.

AGNES. You must be the last person in London to find out.

NELL. She told me there was another man.

AGNES. One other?

NELL. One special man she met in America and fell in love with.

AGNES. Is that what she said? Well, it didn't last long. He was
the usual middle-aged man with the usual wife but with one
unusual feature — he preferred the wife to Kate. After a week
or two he wrote and told her so. Then she went back to yours.

NELL. Why didn't you tell me?

AGNES. They were at Private Views together, sales at Sotheby's.

NELL. I knew there was someone, I never suspected her.

AGNES. What did she say when you caught her out?

NELL. Walked straight from the shop and jumped into a cab, you were the only person I could turn to.

AGNES. Eleanor, my love, my poor love . . .

NELL. I was afraid it was only in here. They'd convinced me I was going mad.

AGNES. Who had?

NELL. The doctors.

AGNES. Were they all men?

NELL. Yes.

AGNES. The bastards are everywhere.

She looks round about at the MEN *drinking in the bar.*

NELL. They said it was the menopause.

AGNES. I'd heard he'd sent you to the shrink. The same one Albert sent me to.

NELL. Oh God!

AGNES. Their old chum Michael at the Middlesex sends all the psychologically battered wives to him.

NELL. James even pretended he didn't like me going there.

AGNES. One way or another we all get screwed. Eleanor, love, it's time you listened to the hooker's warning. Don't take it lying down.

NELL *and* AGNES *go off with the revolve.* JAMES *enters into the living room while the revolve is moving. He brings the Christ painting with him and speaks to it.*

JAMES. I've inspired love. I'm an unemotional man who's inspired a passion in my partner. And I needn't tell *you* what passion means. Suffering, self-inflicted torture, masochism, all that's holy. Like that exquisite depiction of a bleeding corpse that's waiting for me in Zurich. By day I'll patch it up, repair the blood and wounds where they've been knocked around over the years, but every night I'll fuck as though life depended on it. Which of course it does.

The doorbell rings. JAMES *answers it. A porter from the gallery delivers a new painting and collects the restored Christ.* JAMES *takes the new painting into the kitchen.*

The opening of the Lachrymosa from Mozart's Requiem, ELEANOR *enters at the front door with* NELL. *She sits sadly looking at the nightdress she's bought, while the music continues and fades.*

NELL. Alright, is it decided, do we tell him to go?

ELEANOR. And if he does?

NELL. We must learn to forget him.

ELEANOR. I can't forget him, he's half my life.

NELL. Imagine him dead, then you'd have to. Tell him he's free to go to Zurich but not come back, or stay with me and give her up, but no more lies.

ELEANOR. All right.

NELL. And don't let him dodge again, he'll fog the issue if he can. It's in his interest to keep you both.

ELEANOR. I said all right.

JAMES (*entering with the new painting, now unwrapped*). Hullo, love. How was your afternoon? You'll be glad to hear Old Killjoy's gone and look what they've bought instead. (*Shows her the painting — the canvas is uniformly yellow.*) It's going to be a swine matching this colour. That watermark there, you see. Swine. Been shopping?

ELEANOR. Yes, with Kate.

JAMES. How is she? Still head over heels in love?

ELEANOR. Oh yes.

JAMES. Is that what you've bought?

ELEANOR. A nightdress, yes, for the week in Florence.

JAMES. Must have cost the earth. Did Kate buy anything?

ELEANOR. A nightdress.

JAMES. Pretty tarty I'll bet.

ELEANOR. You'll be able to judge when you get to Zurich, only if you go don't bother coming back. I shan't be here. I know all about it from Kate. All I have to say is: if you go, you'll be leaving me.

JAMES. I've never wanted to.

ELEANOR. Is that because she isn't any good in bed? That's what you said last time you finished with her. Not sensual.

JAMES. Not sensual the way you are, no. Something a bit implausible. Sexy without sensuality.

ELEANOR. Sexy? I see.

JAMES. Automatic. The price of changing partners so often is that you have to become a soloist.

ELEANOR. You love her. You're describing her with love. Whenever you've had me lately you've talked about her immediately after. Oh Christ, that should have told me.

JAMES. I don't know what's meant by love. I never have. What I feel for her is sexual attraction. Pure and simple.

ELEANOR. That's what men want to hear. Pornography. No periods, no pregnancies, no growing fond. No consequences. Violence without bruises.

JAMES. It's a physical act. It can be at its best between two people who don't even know each other's names.

ELEANOR. You've known each other's names for years.

JAMES. We've tried not to let that matter. We enjoy it.

ELEANOR. She enjoys the power she has over you and indirectly over me.

JAMES. She hasn't any power over me.

ELEANOR. Then give her up. You can't. You went on seeing her after you swore you wouldn't.

JAMES. I had to swear.

NELL *comes from bedroom in nightdress, followed by* JIM *in pyjamas.*

JIM. I *had* to swear. You put a gun to my head.

NELL. I offered you a choice.

JIM. All or nothing.

NELL. Her or me.

JIM. You knew I wouldn't give you up.

NELL. You love *her,* why shouldn't you? She's young, available —

JIM. I don't know what's meant by love. Except pain and trouble and ownership. But you and I have been together twenty-five years — daughters, a string of flats and houses, annual holidays, narrow scrapes.

NELL. You make me sound like a family album. Whereas for her you feel desire, fascination . . .

JIM. I enjoyed the newness of her, yes. The flattery, the danger. At a time our life had grown secure and predictable, she brought back drama, looks across crowded rooms.

JAMES. Whenever I saw men touch her, I was elated because I'd been there.

ELEANOR. All the other ageing husbands?

NELL. Not to mention arms dealers, property speculators, drug-pushers and journalists.

JIM. Abusing her won't help —

ELEANOR (*to* JIM): That's not abuse. That's fact. She's essentially uncreative.

NELL. A parasite among parasites.

JAMES. So am I.

ELEANOR (*to* JIM). She'll never finish that book she's started.

NELL. She lacks the stamina.

JIM. There are too many books in the world already. Not to mention painting and Passions and plays.

JAMES. Too much of everything. Too many chairs and tables.

JIM. And curtains and carpets.

JAMES. Too much of all this clutter.

He goes about, throwing down books, cushions, magazines . . .

ELEANOR. He didn't throw anything fragile.

NELL. I noticed that.

JAMES. I can't. I'm too inhibited.

JIM. But she's got something I somehow never had — youth and independence.

NELL. I had that once before you turned me into a bourgeois wife, suffocated me with apparatus because it suited you.

JIM. Then throw it all off, be young again. She can help us. You must admit bed's been much better lately.

JAMES. The new flavour helped me relish the old.

ELEANOR. The old?

NELL. Get me a vodka.

JAMES. She belongs to another generation — free of convention, independent . . .

NELL. Hah!

JAMES. One of the people my generation wanted to create.

JIM. The freedom we championed is the air they breathe.

NELL. Her freedom's based on daddy's tax dodges.

JAMES. She parks on double yellow lines, she walks straight to the head of queues, she grabs what's going.

ELEANOR. In other words, disregards the morality you've always lived by.

JAMES. I've been very moral, yes.

ELEANOR. So go to her! What's keeping you here?

JIM. You.

NELL. An old flavour?

JIM. This!

NELL. A prison!

JIM. Eleanor, love, time is running out. You and I have twenty, twenty-five years if we're lucky, slowing down like a rusty old motor until one day we stop forever. So this is probably my last chance and where's the harm? It's marvellous, being a lover. More thrilling than war and warmer than sunshine. My only regret is hurting you so why can't you allow me this flash of happiness before the void?

NELL. You can't have both.

JIM. Why not? I mean that: why not?

NELL. Because I won't be second best. Why should you expect it? A housekeeper whose husband keeps his love and desire for another woman.

JIM. It's half past two in the morning. If you want me to get on with my moral working life tomorrow . . .

NELL. I don't —

JIM. You'll have to let me get some sleep.

He goes into bedroom.

NELL. It's over, James! We're finished.

NELL *takes pills from handbag and then goes to the stereo and puts on a rock record full blast. She goes off to the kitchen.*

JAMES. This is a game.

ELEANOR. A game?

JAMES. You must learn to play.

ELEANOR. You're a baby, James, you want to have your cake and eat it.

JAMES. When I was a young man cake was rationed.

JIM *comes from bedroom and down the stairs, running.*
JAMES *and* ELEANOR *watch. He gets to the player and takes off the record with a violent screech of skidding stylus.*

NELL *reappears from kitchen carrying a plastic bag full of laundry, which she tips in a heap on the floor.*

JIM. You surely don't want the neighbours to suffer because you and I — what's this?

NELL. Your lover's laundry.

JIM. What?

NELL. She had so much to do before her dirty weekend I offered to do it for her.

JIM. You what?

NELL. She put it in my car and I was going to drop it off next time I went to the doctor —

JIM. You should never have made such an offer.

NELL. But now you can give it to her when you catch the plane for Zurich.

ELEANOR. I thought she was a friend. And Agnes, too. You haven't even left me any girl-friends.

NELL throws articles of KATE's laundry at JIM, who tries to pick them up and return them to the bag.

NELL. These childish socks! This sequinned blouse! These frilly knickers! Hasn't she got filthy taste?

JIM. She's different, that's all.

NELL (*showing him her clothes*). You don't agree? You don't agree that's awful?

JAMES. Yours isn't the only way of dressing.

JAMES helps him clear up.

NELL (*to* JIM): A year ago you would have.

JIM. You shouldn't have done this —

NELL. Now you can only think of the times you took them off, I suppose — revealing that repulsive flesh of hers —

She attacks him with her fists, pounding at his chest and shoulders as he turns away to avoid her blows. He falls down and she kicks at him with her bare feet.

JAMES and ELEANOR watch in silence till she tires.

JIM. All right, you win. I'll go tomorrow. You won't be happy till I do. Tonight I'll sleep in another room and tomorrow I'll go. Later on we'll sort out what to do about the paintings in my workshop . . . and all the rest of it . . .

NELL. Yes.

Pause. They stand exhausted.

JIM. Is that all right?

NELL. It's what you want.

Pause.

JIM. If you say so.

She goes upstairs. He starts picking up KATE*'s clothes from about the room, stuffs them into the bag.*

NELL *goes to the small W.C. and pours a glass of water, takes out the bottle of pills.*

ELEANOR. Go and help.

JAMES. It had to come, some push from someone.

NELL *is swallowing the whole bottle of pills, one by one, with water.*

JIM. We can't go back to the old life now.

ELEANOR. Only thinking about yourself.

JAMES (*pointing upstairs*). You mean you're not?

JIM. I don't want to leave her but life's so short.

JAMES (*to* ELEANOR). Look how suddenly Albert died.

JIM. What's kindness and decency and loyalty going to matter then?

JAMES. In the endless night when no-one screws!

ELEANOR (*to* JAMES): Why didn't you guess what was happening?

JAMES. Because I'd never do that. Not for you or Kate or the children.

ELEANOR. Help us, someone.

JAMES (*in the hall, looking up*). I lack the passion.

JIM *takes the bag of clothes to the kitchen.*

NELL *finishes the pills and comes to upper landing, drowsily. She sits on the top step.*

Pause.

JIM *returns to hall, looks up to see* NELL *sitting there.*

JIM. Ah, listen, why don't you stay in our bed? I'll have Ruth's old room. That will give us a night's sleep, or what's left of it. We'll need clear heads tomorrow to discuss the question of our joint account and the credit cards and how to divide the spoils. You'll need the car, I'll use the train. Or perhaps I can take one of the girls' old bikes. You'll have to pass on messages from the answering machine.

ELEANOR. You looked free at last.

JAMES. I was frightened.

JIM. See how we've become an institution? The house, the girls, the pension fund —

JAMES. A whole political structure.

ELEANOR. Blow it up. Thousands do.

JAMES. I tried. You saved it all.

NELL. I should have thought of this sooner. So much simpler for everyone. You could keep this place, she could move in with you . . .

JIM. What? You're rambling rather —

NELL. And I'd be free of both of you. All of it . . .

JIM. Well, when I go you will be, yes . . .

He is at the bottom of the stairs.

NELL. I love my children . . . tell them I love them.

She stands, loses balance and falls down several stairs till JIM *saves her.*

JIM. What's the matter with you?

NELL. The sleeping tablets.

JIM. No. Oh, no.

He holds her face and looks at it. Her eyes are closed.

How many?

NELL. Mmm?

JIM. How many did you take?

NELL. The whole lot.

JIM. How many's that?

NELL. I don't know.

JIM. Think.

NELL. I stopped counting at thirty.

JIM. Stand up. Come on, stand.

He pulls her to her feet and unsteadily helps her up the stairs and into the W.C. He lets her collapse on her knees in front of the lavatory and then sticks two fingers into her mouth. She makes retching sounds and he holds her head over the pedestal but she does not vomit. He tries again. She protests and tries to push his hand away.

JIM. You've got to. Come on.

ELEANOR *and* JAMES *are standing downstage looking up at* NELL *and* JIM *as* NELL *again makes retching noises.*

ELEANOR. What did you feel for me?

JAMES. At this moment? Let me think . . .

ELEANOR. Love?

JAMES. Christ, no! Hadn't we had enough of love? It was love that brought us to that!

He points to the scene above.

ELEANOR. What then?

JAMES. Amazement, I think.

ELEANOR. Why?

JAMES. That you could have tried to take the only life you'll ever have.

NELL *retches.*

JIM. That's a good try . . . but I don't think you've brought up anything . . . come on now . . . up on your feet . . .

NELL. Leave me alone . . .

He helps her as they leave the lavatory for the stairs.

ELEANOR. Why amazed? I'd lost your love. I'd nothing to live for.

JIM. We're going downstairs to the doctor . . . try to concentrate on walking . . .

JAMES. I thought we agreed we'd never loved.

ELEANOR. But now I realised we had.

NELL *tries to sit on stairs but* JIM *keeps her walking.*

JIM. Don't depend on me.

ELEANOR. All the time. Without knowing it.

JIM. That's a good girl.

ELEANOR. In this game, as you call it, I had no cards left to play.

JIM (*as they reach the lower level and the sofa*). Now where's the telephone? Tell me where it is.

ELEANOR. Except my life.

JIM. What's the doctor's number? Try to remember, head up, tell me the doctor's number.

ELEANOR *goes.* JAMES *moves after her some paces, speaking to her.*

JAMES. More than amazement, I felt anger. That you'd yet again held a gun to my head.

NELL. . . . the front of the book.

JIM. I know but try to remember it. Concentrate.

He finds the number and dials while NELL *mumbles.*

JAMES (*returning to look down at* NELL). 'I'll show you how much I love you . . . I'll die for you. Which may well ruin the rest of *your* life too . . .'

JIM. Doctor? Sorry. James Croxley here . . .

JAMES. Of course I prayed to the god I don't believe in that you
wouldn't die.

JIM. Very urgent, yes, I'm afraid my wife's taken an overdose . . .

JAMES. Or survive with a damaged brain.

JIM. Over thirty. We're not really sure.

JAMES. I imagined you dead and as a hopeless cripple and none
of that made me love you either.

JIM. What can I do until you get here?

JAMES. You'll never know this, Eleanor, but as I saw you lying
there I hated you. For the first and last time.

JIM. All right, doctor, thank you.

Puts down phone. Pulls NELL *to her feet.*

Come on, my dear —

JAMES. No pangs of guilt. Why should I? It wasn't my fault.

JIM. Now make an effort to stand upright.

JAMES. I don't want anyone to die for love of me.

He goes. Lights on JIM *and* NELL. *He has moved her to the
stairs.*

JIM. We're going to climb the stairs again now. Then we may
come down them again because you mustn't fall asleep before
the doctor gets here.

Gets her to stairs and up they go again.

He says you'll be all right. It takes half an hour for
barbiturates to get into the bloodstream. So, though it was a
stupid thing to do, you weren't in any danger as long as you
let me know in time. Which you did.

On upper level he walks her along, back and forth.

Someone told me most women who try to kill themselves
don't succeed. Whereas most men do. Did you know that?

NELL. Who?

JIM. What?

NELL. Who told you that? Was it Michael at the Middlesex?

They go as the lights go.

Christmas music. A choir singing 'In the Bleak Midwinter'.

*Lights come up slowly on living room. Outside snowy scenes.
A YOUNG WOMAN (JAMES and ELEANOR's daughter) is
decorating with tinsel and paper chains. NELL comes from
bedroom doing the same on the upper level. A YOUNG MAN
(their son-in-law) brings a Christmas tree in a tub from the
kitchen and stands it in the living room. Begins to add bells,
tinsel etc.*

*NELL has come down and her daughter goes to the kitchen.
JAMES comes from there with the finished yellow canvas.
JIM follows. The women come back with trays of drinks and
glasses. They all make welcoming and cheerful sounds as the
music continues behind. JAMES leans the picture against
a sofa and they all take glasses of wine. They raise their
glasses as the music ends.*

NELL. Happy Christmas.

THREE OTHERS. Happy Christmas.

*They drink. ELEANOR comes on upstairs and watches from
the balcony.*

JAMES. And the painting's finished.

NELL. Oh, well done.

JAMES. As near as I can get. That yellow was a swine to match.
Acrylics are always tricky.

They look at the canvas.

NELL. It looks exactly the same to me but I couldn't even *see*
a stain.

They laugh.

How did you know it was there?

JAMES. It was there all right. Stood out a mile if you're used to
looking at paintings.

ELEANOR. You mean, like her?

NELL. It may be philistine, but I always say I could do those paintings with a roller.

JAMES. I know you do.

NELL. Now that you've done, you can give a hand here.

JAMES. Absolutely.

NELL. We're a bit behind so hang some mistletoe and holly.

JAMES. Right.

NELL. You and Robert can go and dress now. Your father and I can finish here.

The other two go upstairs and off to another room.

JIM. Dearest Kate, I picked up your latest letter from the gallery.

ELEANOR. This isn't any good, is it? Nothing's settled, nothing's changed.

JIM. Eleanor's still got a way to go before I've nursed her back to health.

ELEANOR. I offered you all I had but you couldn't respond.

JIM. She won't go back to the shrink. Several nights a week we're up all night . . .

ELEANOR. Poor baby . . .

JIM. Obviously I can't risk hurting her so till she's well again we'll have to make do with letters.

ELEANOR. You can't grow. You dream of change but when the chance comes you flirt with both.

JIM. And while yours are as hot as the last, I shan't grumble . . .

Takes out air letter and reads it over.

ELEANOR. You're not even promiscuous . . . it's always the same dream-girl over and over . . .

NELL. How are you getting on with the mistletoe?

JAMES. What do you think?

NELL. Well, it's sparing, isn't it?

JAMES. Is it?

NELL. Minimal. Like the painting.

ELEANOR. Like you. Minimal man.

JAMES. Another bit of paganism swallowed up by Christianity. Let's try it, shall we?

They kiss. JIM *finishes reading* KATE's *letter, goes back to his room.*

JIM. Getting your letter home nearly burnt a hole in my pocket.

ELEANOR. But where are you? Out to lunch as usual.

JAMES. It seems to work.

NELL. Yes?

ELEANOR. No-one home.

JAMES. I think we can make a go of it, don't you?

ELEANOR. No.

NELL. We can try.

JIM. I want you both but she wants all or nothing.

ELEANOR. I want a lover, not an old friend.

NELL. Now you've ruined my face and guests are due.

ELEANOR. You can't do without all this. But I can. Change doesn't frighten me . . . Once I'd lost your love there was nothing to keep me here. So goodbye.

JIM. Love's a terrible thing. It means whatever you want it to. So let's not either of us ever mention the word again.

ELEANOR *goes off to the bedroom as* JAMES *comes back and puts on a record of 'In Dolci Jubilo', very joyous, and now there is no more dialogue.*

JIM *folds and seals his letter in the envelope.*

The doorbell rings as ELEANOR *goes.* NELL *comes from the music room and opens the door to* AGNES *and a* MALE FRIEND. *They embrace and warmly greet one another, talking above the music but unintelligibly.* JAMES *too greets them and gives them drinks. The* YOUNG COUPLE *come from the bedroom, dressed for a party, and join in.* AGNES *and her* FRIEND *go through a routine of removing outer clothes, which* NELL *hangs in the cupboard.*

Again the doorbell rings. They all gesture to each other to answer the door. The YOUNG WOMAN *goes to admit two more* FRIENDS, *who take off coats, etc., embrace their hosts, accept drinks, look at Christmas tree.* JIM *has crossed to a place near the kitchen. He stands staring out at the audience while* JAMES *politely deals with his* GUESTS. *Again the bell rings and this time* JAMES *goes to admit a single* FRIEND.

ELEANOR *appears from the bedroom, wearing her outer clothes and carrying a suitcase. She stares down at the party from there. As many* GUESTS *as possible have arrived and filled the stage before* JIM *closes his eyes and smiles. The doorbell rings but no-one hears it. It rings on continuously till* JIM *crosses the room to the door.* ELEANOR *comes downstairs and passes* NELL, *who looks at her before returning to her* GUESTS. JIM *opens the door to* KATE, *who enters in a fur coat and high-heeled shoes. He leads her through the party, leaving the door open.* ELEANOR *goes by it, closing the door behind her.*

JIM *embraces* KATE, *unbuttons her coat, opens it and stares at her naked body beneath. He kneels before her and kisses her body.* JAMES *absently stares at the audience as* NELL *chats to her* GUESTS. *The party goes on, the singing swells.*

Curtain.

Simon Gray

The word Chekhovian arises immediately in any discussion of *Quartermaine's Terms*, a play that openly invites critics to measure it against the Chekhov standard for painful comedy. Champions of the play, like John Glore, literary manager of Washington's Arena Stage, which mounted the play in 1984, find Gray 'the playwright who comes closest to being Chekhov's heir in the contemporary theatre'. In the *New York Times*, Frank Rich said Gray was 'in full possession of that Chekhovian territory where the tragedies and absurdities of life become one and the same'.

In Act I, Scene Two, of *Quartermaine's Terms*, Gray introduces Chekhov directly into the play. St. John Quartermaine, who hopes one of his fellow-teachers will join him for the evening, has theatre tickets for what he thinks is a play by Strindberg. Eddie Loomis, his principal, corrects him: '. . . it's an Ibsen, *Hedda Gabler*, I believe.' Later, fellow teacher Melanie corrects him again. She remembers the play is by Chekhov, *The Cherry Orchard*, she thinks. 'All that Russian gloom and doom and people shooting themselves from loneliness and depression and that sort of thing.' Finally, Windscape, the most collected member of the faculty, states flat out that the play is Chekhov's *Uncle Vanya*.

It's fair to say that most realistic modern dramas may be called either Ibsenesque or Chekhovian, and *Quartermaine's Terms*, as the theatre ticket business hints, is certainly Chekhovian. Instead of opening his story, as Ibsen would have done, at a penultimate moment of high tension and arriving at a catastrophe through a sequence of increasingly serious incidents inexorably leading to a painful climax, Gray uses indirect action leading to an anticlimactic ending and develops a gradually darkening mood through the subtle undertones of trivial incidents.

The sin or arrogance that propels an Ibsen character like Hedda Gabler towards an at least partly deserved tragic end appears nowhere in St. John Quartermaine. Like most Chekhov characters, Quartermaine stumbles innocently toward his sad fate. Like Chekhov's Vanya, he is a bit of a bumbler and clown, a gentle man without personal force, whose life slips through his fingers while he immerses himself in meaningless activity.

Although Gray has disclaimed any conscious intention to write a Chekhovian play or to prompt a Chekhovian comparison, artists are often deeply influenced by admired predecessors. And Gray openly expressed his admiration for Chekhov, saying, 'Chekhov, apart from Shakespeare, seems to me the greatest writer for the theatre in the English language, even in translation.'

Born in Hampshire in 1936, Gray was sent to spend the war years with his grandparents in Canada. After an English public school education, he returned to Canada to take a BA from Dalhousie College. He earned a second BA from Cambridge and began a career as a college teacher, a profession he would pursue long after he had become a famous playwright, composing his major plays while lecturing in English at London University. Though he finally gave up his permanent teaching post in 1984, he said that he expects to go on teaching part-time.

First a writer of novels and short stories, Gray claims to have been converted to the drama when he discovered he could make more money adapting one of his stories for television than he had earned from its original publication. A series of produced television scripts led in 1967 to *Wise Child*, which Gray originally conceived for television, but diverted to the stage because of its Ortonesque sexual oddities: a middle-aged male crook disguised in women's clothes uses his seventeen-year-old accomplice as sexual barter to cover their expenses while they are on the run. Neither that play nor a subsequent farce about a wife murderer, *Dutch Uncle* (1969), give a sense of Gray's typical style, however.

That style declared itself in the witty dialogue and careful characterization of *Butley*, the play that established Gray in the West End and on Broadway as a major playwright. The original production was directed by Harold Pinter, who has directed all of Gray's major plays since. Gray offhandedly explains this unusual collaboration with England's most celebrated playwright by saying that Pinter simply enjoys directing plays so different from his own. And they are different. Where Pinter tends to the oblique and mysterious, Gray is straightforward and explicit. Nevertheless, there is at least one important commonality. Both playwrights create central characters who are islands of despair, permanently alienated from those around them. Pinter conveys this alienation primarily through the way his characters talk past each other, their wary words never trustworthy or clear. Gray, by contrast, shows his characters alienating themselves from one another by a process of gradual psychic withdrawal. Their words may make sense, they may speak honestly to each other, but they build walls between themselves and others, impenetrable psychological barriers. Finally, by choice or by chance, they live in a world as lonely as Pinter's.

In a review of *Quartermaine's Terms*, Walter Kerr wrote that 'almost any [Gray] play could legitimately be construed as a withdrawal symptom'. His assessment is applicable not only to *Quartermaine's Terms*, but to many of Gray's plays. In *Butley* the title character drives off all hope of normal friendly relationships by barrages of withering scorn. In the end of the play he crouches behind the locked door of his lonely academic office, inaccessible even to his students. Simon Hench in *Otherwise Engaged* throws up a sound barrier of Wagnerian records between himself and the encroaching world of demanding friends and uncomfortable feelings. As Hench's wife finally tells him, 'You're one of those men who only give permission to little bits of life to get through to you.'

In later plays, Gray depicted other sorts of withdrawal. In *The Rear Column*, singular among Gray plays in that it is set not in contemporary England but in nineteenth-century Africa, a tiny cadre of Englishmen stand guard over H.M. Stanley's supply depot while (off-stage) Stanley leads his 1887 expedition against the Mahdi. As the group's morale deteriorates in a welter of jungle heat and cruelty, the patina of civilization drops away. Only Jameson somehow preserves his optimism and decency. As he staunchly tries to keep his comrades sane and up to the mark, Jameson seems an ideal Victorian hero, sharing dwindling supplies and medicines, settling conflicts, comforting the sick. He seems humanely immune from the weaknesses of his fellow Englishmen. An enthusiastic naturalist and artist, he uses their hellish situation constructively as an unparalleled opportunity to study and record jungle life. However, in a stunning climax to this powerful play, it turns out that Jameson's equanimity is really another insidious form of withdrawal. In Jameson's case, withdrawal into the cool detachment of the scientific observer allows him to become an accomplice to an act of cannibalism. In a horrifying lapse of decent humaneness, he sketches the ritualistic murder of a native girl and the feasting upon her body that follows as if he were observing a laboratory rat.

In *Close of Play*, Gray dramatizes the ultimate passive withdrawal. Throughout the play, stroke victim Jasper sits helplessly silent and immobile while his middle-aged sons, daughters-in-law, and wife pour over him oceanic plaints about their appalling lives, speeches which, considering Jasper's inability to respond, might be called soliloquies. In the play's last moments, the hitherto speechless Jasper rallies to utter twice a phrase that seems to welcome the final withdrawal, his approaching death: 'The door is open! . . . The door is open!' *Close of Play* may be properly compared to another play in this volume, Ayckbourn's *Just Between Ourselves*. Not only do the plays share a key image extraordinarily dark for the world of social comedy – the chairbound human vegetable – but *Close of Play*, Gray's most domestic piece by far, demonstrates his knack for the sort of family comedy – the rueful celebration of familial inanity – at which Ayckbourn also excels. Gray's Marianne, a baby-making machine who tires one and all with nattering about her children, complains: 'What is it about Nindy's pottie that brings out the worst in Nanty . . . all that fuss over the soup tureen last week . . . though what could be less offensive than a toddler's wee. . . .'

Quartermaine's isolation has a poignant quality that sets it apart from the isolation of other Gray characters. He doesn't fend off friendly overtures by being obnoxious or defensive. On the contrary, he wishes nothing more than intimacy and communion with his colleagues at the school. Exuding genuine good feeling, ever ready to help when called upon, he spends the entire play reaching hopefuly for companionship and human warmth. But except on those occasions when he is useful to his fellow-teachers – as a baby sitter for the Windscapes, as an emergency therapist for Sackling, as a buffer between the warring factions of Anita's dinner party – Quartermaine is always thrust back upon himself. Whenever there's no profit for them, his colleages reject Quartermaine's overtures, a pattern that culminates in his dismissal from their ranks, leaving him cruelly alone, his entire community having withdrawn from him. Full as he is of the desire for human contact, however, Quartermaine contributes to his own alienation by an inability to grasp the realities around him. He functions myopically, in a foggy preoccupation with himself. He alienates his students and the new teacher, Derek, by forgetting their names. (Other teachers miscall Derek Dennis, but they learn faster than

Quartermaine.) And for all his warm sociability, Quartermaine is oblivious to the real pain and trauma in the lives of his colleagues. As Sackling tells him, 'You have an amazing ability not to let the world impinge on you.' Finally, of course, Quartermaine does not contribute to the academic community. He isn't a good teacher; he seems to lack both the teaching gift and the discipline. The only testimonial he gets is in a badly written letter from one of his foreign students whose feeble grasp of English is comment enough on Quartermaine's ability as a teacher: 'I must written to thanking you for all excellent times in your most glorified classes, your true Ferdinand Muller.'

So, although he is good in that he is warm, gentle, and affectionate, Quartermaine is inadequate to hold his place in his community. Gray does not explain Quartermaine's inadequacy; he merely portrays it. The audience may guess that Quartermaine is organically flawed – the chemical flow of thought and energy within him is simply too feeble to support effective life. Such a hypothesis, of course, implying as it does the inevitability of defeat, makes of the play a small tragedy compounded of comic mishaps. No matter how he tries, Quartermaine is fated to end defeated and alone, a clown protagonist created by sadistic gods whose only purpose in making him is to knock him down.

Several critics have noted that most of the important events in *Quartermaine's Terms* occur off-stage, leaving to the play on stage the melancholy aftermath, again an effect that suggests Chekhov. Gray explains it by saying that dramatic reality for him includes making the point that his characters have ongoing off-stage lives. Thus Gray takes his audience deep into the stories of Susan Windscape's 'O' level exams, Nigel's quarterly journal, and Sackling's novel, through narration. And in telling these stories, Gray achieves a clever musical effect. Each major off-stage story has its own climax – each climax a kind of death, actual or metaphorical – and the climaxes come in an ascending order, producing a sort of musical crescendo to precede the on-stage climax, which is Quartermaine's dismissal from his post.

The first off-stage death, that of Derek's aunt, is the least significant because the audience knows nothing of her. And it is less a climax than a turning point because it brings together Derek and his bride-to-be. Next comes the death of Melanie's mother, its impact greater because the audience sympathizes with Melanie's pain and because her demise comes as the climax to a long mother-daughter struggle. Next comes the double death of Nigel's magazine and Sackling's novel – two stories climaxing together – followed immediately by Anita's revelation that her love for Nigel has died, a death more poignant than the preceding physical deaths because it is a blow to life's hopes rather than an inevitable end. Then, in the final scene of the play, two last off-stage death-climaxes complete the ascending scale. First comes the death of Susan – the cruel death of a young life that hits harder than anything before. Immediately thereafter the audience learns that Thomas – the heart of the school – has died, a death that clearly sounds a tragic coda to the comic opera of off- stage lives and loves. Now, the off-stage stories all told, Windscape delivers the final on-stage coup, the firing of Quartermaine, a climax that is the death of all that is Quartermaine's life. After a cruelly swift flurry of meaningless politeness, Quartermaine is left alone to sound twice Chekhov's breaking string, 'Oh Lord! Well – I say – Oh, Lord!'

'I suppose it's the play of mine that I am most attached to,' said Gray of *Quartermaine's Terms*. An artist who composes with such elegant precision has good reason to be fond.

Major Plays

Butley, Criterion Theatre, 1971.
Otherwise Engaged, Queen's Theatre, 1975.
The Rear Column, Globe Theatre, 1978.
Close of Play, Lyttleton Theatre (National Theatre), 1979.
Quartermaine's Terms, Queen's Theatre, 1981.
The Common Pursuit, Lyric Theatre, Hammersmith, 1984.

Selected Bibliography

Billington, Michael. Review of *Quartermaine's Terms*, *Guardian*, 31 July 1981, p. 11.

Hobson, Harold. 'Hobson's Choice.' *Drama: The Quarterly Theatre Review*. No. 142 (Winter 1981), pp. 29-34.

Kerr, Walter. 'Stage View.' *New York Times*, 25 February 1983, p. 17.

Oliver, Edith. Review of *Quartermaine's Terms*. *New Yorker*, 7 March 1983, p. 110.

SIMON GRAY

Quartermaine's Terms

For Beryl

Quartermaine's Terms was first presented by Michael Codron at the Queen's Theatre, London, on 30 July 1981, with the following cast:

ST. JOHN QUARTERMAINE	Edward Fox
ANITA MANCHIP	Jenny Quayle
MARK SACKLING	Peter Birch
EDDIE LOOMIS	Robin Bailey
DEREK MEADLE	Glyn Grain
HENRY WINDSCAPE	James Grout
MELANIE GARTH	Prunella Scales

Directed by Harold Pinter
Designed by Eileen Diss
Lighting by Leonard Tucker

The Set: The staff-room of the Cull-Loomis School of English for foreigners, Cambridge, or rather a section of the staff-room — the last quarter of it. On stage are French windows, a long table, lockers for members of the staff, pegs for coats etc. and a number of armchairs; on the table a telephone, newspapers and magazines. This is the basic set, to which, between scenes and between the two Acts, additions can be made to suggest the varying fortunes of the school. Off stage, left, a suggestion of hard-backed chairs, and off left, a door to the main corridor of the school, where the class-rooms are.

The period: early 1960s.

ACT ONE

Scene One

Monday morning, Spring term. The French windows are open. It is about 9.30. Sunny.

 QUARTERMAINE is sitting with his feet up, hands folded on his lap, staring ahead. From off, outside the French windows, in the garden, the sound of foreign voices excited, talking, laughing etc; passing by. As these recede:

 ANITA comes through the French windows carrying a briefcase.

QUARTERMAINE. Hello, Anita.

ANITA. 'Morning, St. John.

QUARTERMAINE. But I say, you know, you look different, don't you?

ANITA. Do I? Oh — my hair probably. I've put it up.

QUARTERMAINE. Oh yes. Well, it looks — looks really terrific!

ANITA. Thank you.

QUARTERMAINE. Of course I liked it the other way too, tumbling down your shoulders.

ANITA. It hasn't tumbled down my shoulders for three years St. John.

QUARTERMAINE. Oh. How was it then before you changed it?

ANITA. Back in a pony tail. (*She indicates.*)

QUARTERMAINE. That's it. Yes. Well, I liked it like that, too.

ANITA. Oh by the way, Nigel asked me to apologise again for having to cancel dinner. He was afraid he was a little abrupt on the 'phone.

QUARTERMAINE. Oh Lord, not at all, it was lucky he was, you know how my landlady hates me using the 'phone, but I understood exactly what he was getting at, um — something to do with his new magazine, wasn't it?

ANITA. He still hasn't got enough material for the first issue even. He was up until four, going through all the unsolicited poems and essays and short stories and bits of plays and God knows what. Without much luck, too. He's in despair, poor darling. Anyway, he felt really rotten about messing up *your* evening.

QUARTERMAINE. Oh, do tell him, no need to worry about that. Because as it happened, a few minutes after he 'phoned to cancel, old Henry 'phoned to invite me round there. So that was all right.

ANITA. How smashing! For dinner, you mean?

QUARTERMAINE. Well no, to baby-sit actually.

ANITA. Oh.

QUARTERMAINE. They suddenly remembered there was a film at The Arts, some old um, um German classic that they seem very fond of, about — about a child-murderer as far as I could make out from what Henry said.

ANITA. Still St. John, how boring for you!

QUARTERMAINE. No, no, I enjoyed it enormously, I used to baby-sit for them all the time. It was lovely seeing them again. Children are such . . . And they were as good as gold really, no trouble at all, except that Susan would keep screaming at the little ones. She's working for her 'O' levels you see. The least little bit of noise seems to upset her concentration. But the one they call little Fanny — very charming, very charming. . . . once she'd got used to me again. As for Ben — my word, what a little devil, full of mischief, he told me little Fanny had drowned in the bath and when I ran in, there she was . . . lying face down — hair floating around — and I stood there thinking, you know, (*He laughs.*) Lord, what am I going to say to Henry and Fanny when they get back. Especially after seeing a film like that — but it turned out it was only one of those enormous dolls, you know. (*They both laugh.*)

ANITA. Still St. John, I hope at least you had a bit of an evening with Henry and Fanny when they got back.

QUARTERMAINE. Oh yes. Rather well, except poor old Fanny had a bit of a headache from straining to read the subtitles — a very poor print apparently — and Henry got into a tussle with Susan about going to bed, so I felt you know — that they rather wanted me out of the way —

The sound of the door opening, during the above. Footsteps.

Oh hello Mark, top of the morning to you, have a good weekend?

SACKLING *appears on stage. He is carrying a briefcase, is unshaven, looks ghastly.*

ANITA (*looking at him in concern*). Are you all right?

SACKLING. Yes, yes, fine, fine. (*He drops the briefcase, slumps into chair.*)

ANITA. Are you growing a beard?

SACKLING. What? Oh Christ! (*Feeling his chin.*) I forgot! Haven't been to bed you see. All weekend.

QUARTERMAINE. Ah, been hard at it, eh?

SACKLING. What?

QUARTERMAINE. Hard at it. The old writing.

SACKLING. Oh yes — hard at it.

QUARTERMAINE. Terrific!

ANITA. Oh, I've got a message from Nigel, by the way, he asked me to ask you to hurry up with the extract from your novel, they're desperate to get it into the first issue, he says don't worry about whether it's not quite ready, they can always shove it in as 'Work in Progress' or something.

SACKLING. Right.

ANITA. You look to me as if you've over-done it — are you sure you're all right?

QUARTERMAINE. I say, how's old Camelia?

SACKLING (*barks out a laugh*). Oh fine! just — fine!

QUARTERMAINE. Terrific, and little Tom too?

SACKLING. Tom too, oh yes, Tom too.

QUARTERMAINE. The last time I saw him he was teething, standing there in his high chair dribbling away like anything, while Camelia was sitting on old Mark's lap making faces at him with orange peel in her mouth —

SACKLING *bursts into tears.* ANITA *goes to* SACKLING, *puts her hand on his shoulder.*

QUARTERMAINE. What? Oh — oh Lord!

ANITA. Mark — what is it?

SACKLING. Sorry — sorry — I'll be all right — still digesting.

QUARTERMAINE. Something you had for breakfast, is it?

ANITA *shakes her head at him.*

Mmmm?

ANITA. Do you want to talk about it?

SACKLING. I don't want anyone — anyone else to know — not Thomas or Eddie — don't want them dripping their — their filthy compassion all over me.

ANITA. We're to keep it to ourselves, St. John.

QUARTERMAINE. Oh Lord yes. Of course. (*A pause.*) What though?

SACKLING. She's left me.

QUARTERMAINE. Who?

ANITA. Camelia, of course.

QUARTERMAINE. What! Old Camelia! Oh no!

SACKLING. Taking Tom — taking Tom with her.

QUARTERMAINE. Oh, not little Tom too!

SACKLING. Tom too.

ANITA. Well, did she — say why?

SACKLING (*makes an effort, pulls himself together*). She — (*He takes an envelope out of his pocket.*) I was upstairs in the attic — writing away — as far as I knew she was downstairs where she usually is — in the kitchen or — ironing — with the television on. And Tom in bed, of course. So I wrote on and on — I felt inspired, quite inspired, a passage about — about what I'd felt when I saw Tom coming out of her womb — so shiny and whole and beautiful — a wonderful passage — full of — full of my love for her and him — and when I finished I went downstairs to her — to read it to her — as I always do when it's something I'm burning with — and this was on the pillow. (*He opens the letter.*) 'I'm sorry darling, but it seems after all that I wasn't cut out to be a writer's wife. I can't stand the strain of it, the lonely evenings, your remoteness, and most of all the feeling that your novel means more to you than Tom and I do. Perhaps that's what being an artist is. Not caring about those who love you. I'm going back to mother's, I'll take the car' — yes, taken the car — she'd take that all right, wouldn't she! — 'until you've passed your driving test' and begin proceedings as soon as I've got a lawyer. Take care, my love, look after yourself, I wish you such success and I know that one day I'll be proud to have been your first wife, just as Tom will be proud to be your father.'

There is a pause.

QUARTERMAINE. Um, son, surely.

SACKLING. What?

QUARTERMAINE. Um, Tom's your son. Not your father. You read out that he was your father. Not your son.

SACKLING. Oh, if only I'd been able to read her that passage — she would have understood my feelings, she'd have known — but what do I do, I can't give up my novel now, not when I'm so close to finishing — my fourth draft — my penultimate draft — I *know* it's the penultimate — then one final one — and — and — so what do I do —

LOOMIS *enters through the French windows. He walks awkwardly, has thick glasses, is carrying a file.*

LOOMIS. Good morning, good morning, Anita my dear, Mark,
   St. John. I trust you all had a good weekend?

QUARTERMAINE. ⎫
ANITA.   ⎬   Yes, thank you Eddie.
SACKLING.   ⎭

LOOMIS. I'm just on my way through to do my little welcome
   speech to the new students, with a small dilation this time on
   the problems of our Cambridge landladies, we've just heard
   that our faithful Mrs Cornley is refusing to take any of our
   students except what she calls traditional foreigners, all over
   some dreadful misunderstanding she's had with those three
   really delightful Turks we sent her, over the proper function
   of the bathroom — such a nuisance, Thomas has been on the
   'phone to her for hours — but still, I suppose the problems
   of a flourishing school — nine Japanese have turned up, by
   the way, instead of the anticipated six, and as it was three last
   time we can hope for a round dozen next — Mark, is it these
   fast-fading old eyes of mine, or did you forget to shave this
   morning, and yesterday morning, even?

SACKLING. No, no — I'm thinking of growing a beard, Eddie.

LOOMIS. Alas! And what saith the fair Camelia to that?

SACKLING (*mutters*). I don't think she'll mind, Eddie.

LOOMIS. Good, good — Anita, my dear, may I pay you a
   compliment?

ANITA. Yes please, Eddie.

LOOMIS. I like your hair even more *that* way.

ANITA. Well, thank you Eddie, actually I had it cut for a dinner
   party we had last night — so I suppose I'm stuck with it for a
   bit — it was a sort of editorial dinner, you see — (*Realising.*)

LOOMIS. Ah! And the magazine's progressing well, or so we
   gathered from Nigel. We bumped into him on the Backs, on
   Saturday afternoon, did he tell you?

ANITA. No. No he didn't.

LOOMIS. He was having a conference with one of his co-editors,
   I suppose it was.

ANITA. Oh. Jeffrey Pine.

LOOMIS. No no, I don't think Jeffrey Pine, my dear, but co-editress I should have said, shouldn't I, one can't be too precise these days.

ANITA. Oh. Was she — blonde and — rather pretty?

LOOMIS. Oh, very pretty — at least Thomas was much smitten, you know what an eye he's got.

ANITA. Ah, then that would be Amanda Southgate, yes, I expect he was trying to persuade her to take on all the dog-bodying — you know, hounding contributors, keeping the printers at bay — she's terrifically efficient. She's an old friend of mine. We were at school together. (*Little pause.*) She's smashing, actually.

LOOMIS. Good good — now St. John, what was it Thomas asked me to tell you — or was it Henry and Melanie I'm to tell what to? Oh yes, this postcard of course, from one of your old students. (*He hands him a post-card from the file.*) We couldn't resist having a look, post-cards being somehow in the public domain, one always thinks. At least when they're other people's. (*He laughs.*) Do read it out to Mark and Anita, don't be modest St. John.

QUARTERMAINE. Um, I must writing to thanking you for all excellent times in your most glorified classes, your true Ferdinand Muller. Lord! (*He laughs.*)

LOOMIS. And which one was he, can you recall?

QUARTERMAINE. Oh. Well, you know a — a German —

LOOMIS. Post-marked Zurich, I believe, so more likely a Swiss.

QUARTERMAINE. Oh yes, that's right, a Swiss, a — a well, rather large, Eddie, and with a round face — in his forties or so, with his hair cut en brosse.

LOOMIS. — and wearing lederhosen, perhaps, and good at yodelling, no no, St. John, I don't think I quite believe in your rather caricature Swiss, I suspect you must have made rather more of an impression on Herr Ferdinand Muller than he managed to make on you, still, I suppose that's better than the other way round, and his sentiments are certainly quite a tribute — would that his English were, too eh? But do try to remember them St. John, match names to faces. (*He laughs.*) And on that subject, you haven't forgotten Mr Middleton begins this morning, have you?

QUARTERMAINE. Who, Eddie?

LOOMIS. Middleton. Dennis Middleton, St. John. Our new part timer. Thomas told you all about him at the last staff meeting. He should be here any minute — so whilst I'm making the students welcome, perhaps you'd do the same for him, and tell him that either Thomas or I will be along before the bell. Mark?

SACKLING. Mmm?

LOOMIS. Middleton, Mark.

SACKLING (*blankly*). Yes. Yes. Right Eddie.

LOOMIS. Good good. See you all at the bell then — (*He walks off, stage left. Sound of him stopping. Slight pause.*) Oh Mark, there is one other thing — If I could just have a quick private word — May I put in my personal plea against the beard, I do think they make even the handsomest chaps red-eyed and snively looking, I don't want to end up begging Camelia to be Delilah to your Samson, eh, and think of poor little Tom too, having to endure Daddy's whiskers against his chubby young cheeks at cuddle-time —

SACKLING *rushes past him, out of the door.*

But — but — what did I say? It was only about about the beard, I couldn't have been more playful.

QUARTERMAINE. Oh, it's not your fault, Eddie, is it Anita, the poor chap's had a — a horrible weekend — you see —

ANITA (*warningly, cutting in*). Yes, up all night, working at his novel. I'll go and see if he's all right. (*She goes off, left.*)

LOOMIS. I see. Well that's all very well, after all nobody could respect Mark's literary ambitions more than Thomas and myself, but we really can't have him running about in this sort of state, what on earth would the students make of it if he were to gallop emotionally off in the middle of a dictation —

MEADLE *appears at the French windows.*

MEADLE. Um, is this the staff room, please?

He is hot and flustered, wearing bicycle clips, carrying a briefcase.

LOOMIS. Yes, what do you want?

MEADLE. I'm the new member of staff.

LOOMIS. Oh, of course, it's Mr Middleton, isn't it?

MEADLE. Well, yes — well, Meadle, actually, Derek Meadle.

LOOMIS. Yes, yes, Derek Meadle, well, I'm Eddie Loomis, the Principal. One of two Principals, as you know, as you've met Mr Cull of course, and this is St. John Quartermaine who's been with us since our school started, and you've come down to join us from Huddersfield, isn't it.

MEADLE. Yes sir, well Hull actually.

LOOMIS. Hull, good good — and when did you arrive?

MEADLE. Yesterday afternoon.

LOOMIS. And found yourself a room?

MEADLE. Yes, yes thank you, sir.

LOOMIS. Good good, and found yourself a bicycle too, I see.

MEADLE (*who throughout all this has been standing rather awkwardly keeping face on to* LOOMIS). Yes, sir. My landlady — I happened to ask her where could be a good place to buy a second-hand one, not being familiar with the shops, and she happened to mention that her son had left one behind in the basement and I could have it for two pounds, but unfortunately —

LOOMIS (*interrupting*). Good good, most enterprising — at least of your landlady. (*He laughs.*) But Mr Meadle I've got to have a little talk with the students, and Mr Cull is still looking after enrolment, but one of us will be back at the bell to introduce you to your first class — intermediary comprehension isn't it —

MEADLE. Dictation sir.

LOOMIS. Quite. So I'll leave you in St. John's capable hands —

MEADLE. Yes sir. Thank you.

LOOMIS. Oh, one thing, though, Mr Meadle — sir us no sirs, we're very informal here — I'm Eddie, Mr Cull is Thomas and you're Dennis.

MEADLE. Oh, well thank you very much —

LOOMIS *goes off left.*

Derek actually —

QUARTERMAINE. Well, I must say — jolly glad to have you with us — I think you'll enjoy it here — the staff is — well, they're terrific — and the students are — well, they've very interesting, coming as they do from all quarters of the globe, so to speak — but look here, why don't you sit down and make yourself at home.

MEADLE. Yes, thanks, but — well, you see the trouble is I've had a bit of an accident.

QUARTERMAINE. Oh really? Oh Lord.

MEADLE. Yes, well — you'd better see for yourself.

He turns. His trousers are rent at the seat.

How bad is it actually?

QUARTERMAINE. Well — they're a bit of a write off, I'm afraid. How did it happen?

MEADLE. Some bloody Japanese! I rode into a little pack of them coming up the school drive. They were laughing and chattering so much among themselves they didn't hear my bell until I was almost on top of them, and then a big, bald one stepped right out in front of me and of course I lost control on the gravel and skidded.

QUARTERMAINE. Oh dear.

MEADLE. And as there was the minutest bit of spring sticking out of the seat — I suppose it must have worked its way into my trousers on the way here — the worm in the apple, eh?

But anyway — what do you think I should do about it?

QUARTERMAINE. Well you know, old chap, I think the best thing would be to go back and change.

MEADLE. Ah yes, but into what is the question.

QUARTERMAINE. Well — into another pair of trousers, I — I suppose.

MEADLE. Yes, but you see, I haven't got another pair is the problem. An elderly gentleman on the train yesterday spilt hot chocolate out of his thermos right over the pair I happened to have on, so the first thing I did when I got in — irony of ironies — was to take them to the cleaners. And my trunk, which I'd sent on from Hull and which contained my suit and my other two pairs, hasn't arrived yet. So there it is. What do I do? Any suggestions? I mean if I pull them really high — like this — and leave my clips on — well how do I look?

QUARTERMAINE. Well, well, jolly formidable, actually.

MEADLE (*takes a few more steps*). No, no, I can't go round like this! I'm meant to be teaching — people will think I'm sort of — some sort of — my first day of my new job — oh, this is the sheerest, the sheerest — !

WINDSCAPE (*enters through the French windows. He is carrying a brief-case, wears bicycle clips, smokes a pipe. Seeing MEADLE*). Ah —

QUARTERMAINE. Hello Henry — um, come and meet our new chap —

WINDSCAPE. Oh yes, of course. Merton, isn't it?

QUARTERMAINE. Middleton, actually.

MEADLE. Meadle, as a matter of fact.

QUARTERMAINE. Meadle. That's right. So sorry. Dennis Meadle.

WINDSCAPE (*comes over*). Well, whatever yours happens to be — mine's Windscape. Henry Windscape. How do you do.

MEADLE. How do you do.

WINDSCAPE. Very glad to have you with us.

MEADLE. Thank you.

QUARTERMAINE. Henry's our academic tutor — syllabus and all that.

MEADLE. Oh.

WINDSCAPE. Oh, St. John, I didn't thank you properly last night for baby-sitting. It was most kind.

QUARTERMAINE. Oh, not at all — I enjoyed it. I say, how were they in the end — Susan, little Fanny and old Ben?

WINDSCAPE. Oh fine thank you, St. John, fine. I didn't get Susan to bed until midnight of course. (*To* MEADLE:) She's studying for her 'O' levels — a couple of years in advance.

QUARTERMAINE. And what about Fanny's headache?

WINDSCAPE. Oh fine thank you, fine. Though she did have rather a bad moment actually, when she went to have her bath and thought little Fanny was lying in it — drowned.

QUARTERMAINE. Oh yes — that blessed doll.

WINDSCAPE. Yes, Ben told me you'd put it there. St. John was good enough to come over and sit with our three last night — we went to see *M* you know — such a fine film — so delicate and human in its treatment of a — a sexual freak, and Peter Lorre — unfortunately the print was a trifle worn — but still — memorable — memorable — but isn't it interesting — on another subject — this English thing about names, how we forget them the second we hear them. Just now, for instance, when St. John was introducing you. Unlike Americans for instance. (*He puffs and pulls on his pipe throughout this speech.* MEADLE *nods and chuckles tensely.*) I suppose because we — the English that is — are so busy looking at the person the name represents — or *not* looking, being English (*He laughs.*) that we don't take in the name itself — whereas the Americans, you see, make a point of beginning with the name — when one's introduced they repeat it endlessly. 'This is Dennis Meadle. Dennis Meadle, why hello Dennis, and how long have you been in this country Dennis, this is Dennis Meadle dear, Dennis was just telling me how much he liked our fair city, weren't you Dennis . . . ' (*All this is an execrable imitation of an American accent.*) And — and so forth.

MEADLE (*tacit*). Derek actually.

WINDSCAPE. And in no time at all they've learnt what you're called by even if not who you are (*He laughs.*) while we, the English, being more empirical, don't learn your name until you yourself have taken on a complicated reality — you and your name grow, so to speak, in associated stages in our memories, until what you are as Dennis Meadle and the sounds Dennis Meadle are inseparable which is actually — when you think about it, a radical division in ways of perceiving that goes back to the Middle Ages in the Nominalists — the name callers — calling the name preceeding the object, so to speak, and the realists —

During this, MELANIE *has entered through the French windows. She puts her briefcase on the table.*

— who believed the object preceeded the name — but one could go on and on; and, there's Melanie, come and meet (*A pause.*) our new chap —

MELANIE. You're in top form for a Monday morning Henry, how do you do, I'm Melanie Garth.

MEADLE. Meadle. Derek Meadle.

MELANIE. And you've come to reinforce us, well we certainly could do with you, Thomas was just telling me about the enrolment chaos, you'll be getting a lot of overspill from my groups, I can tell you.

WINDSCAPE. Melanie's our Elementary Conversation specialist, by the way.

MELANIE. Oh, I don't know about specialist, Henry, Henry's our only real specialist here, he specialises in — well, everything, doesn't he, St. John, from pronounciation to British Life and Institutions, but what I enjoyed most about the sight of you two philosophising away here was that you both still had your bicycle clips on — as if you'd met on a street corner —

WINDSCAPE (*laughing*). Good heavens, so they are. Thank you for reminding me, my dear, whenever I forget to take them off I spend hours after school hunting for them — (*He bends, to take them off.*)

MEADLE *grinning and distraught, makes a gesture towards taking his off.*

QUARTERMAINE (*taking this in*). I say — I say, Melanie, how's — um, how's mother?

MELANIE. Top form, thanks, St. John, her left leg's still giving her bother, and the stairs are a dreadful strain, you know, because of this sudden vertigo, but yesterday she managed to hobble down to the corner-shop all by herself, and was halfway back by the time I got there to pick her up.

QUARTERMAINE. Oh, that's terrific! Melanie's mother's just recovering from a thingemebob.

MELANIE. Stroke, if you please, St. John. She insists on the proper term, she hates euphemisms.

WINDSCAPE. Not surprisingly, as Melanie's mother was Cambridge's first lady of philology — I had the honour of being supervised by her in my second year as an undergraduate. A remarkable woman who seems to be coming to terms with her little upset in a characteristically — characteristically indomitable — fashion.

MEADLE. I have an aunt who had a stroke a year ago. She was the active sort too.

MELANIE. And how is *she* coping?

MEADLE. Well, she was doing splendidly until she had the next. Now she's pretty well out of it altogether, my uncle has to do virtually everything for her. But then that's one of the usual patterns, they said at the hospital. First a mild stroke, followed by a worse stroke, and then, if that doesn't do the job — (*He gestures.*)

MELANIE. Yes, well, Mr Meadle, I'm sorry for your aunt — and for your uncle — but sufficient unto the day, sufficient unto the day. (*She picks up her briefcase and goes to a locker.*)

WINDSCAPE. Of course that's only *one* of the possible patterns —

there are many cases of complete — or — or more than merely partial recovery — Dennis, if I might — might just — Melanie puts on a remarkably brave front, but don't be led astray, she's an intensely feeling person who knows very well the likely outcome of her mother's — her mother's - she's deeply attached to her, as you probably gathered.

I hope you don't mind my er —

MEADLE. No, no. Thank you. Thank you.

WINDSCAPE. Good man! (*He puts his hand on* MEADLE's *shoulder.*) Well, I'd better unpack my own — (*He goes over to a locker, looking towards* MELANIE, *who is still standing still by hers.*)

MELANIE (*whispered*). Well naught out of ten for tact, I thought!

WINDSCAPE (*whispered*). Yes well, it is his first day, Melanie my dear — he didn't really understand.

MEADLE (*crossing to* QUARTERMAINE). I don't think I can stand much more of this. I hardly know what I'm saying. Look, what I need is some safety pins and a few minutes in the toilet.

QUARTERMAINE. Yes, of course, you come along with me.

LOOMIS (*comes through the French windows*). Good morning, Melanie, my dear. Good morning Henry — good weekend, I trust?

MELANIE.
WINDSCAPE. } Yes thanks, Eddie.

QUARTERMAINE (*to* MEADLE). Better hang on a tick.

LOOMIS. All well with mother, I trust?

MELANIE. Yes thanks Eddie. Top form.

LOOMIS. Good, good — and Fanny and the children?

WINDSCAPE. Yes, thanks Eddie — all splendid.

LOOMIS. Good good —

As ANITA *and* SACKLING *enter from right.*

Ah, and here you are, you two, and quite composed again
Mark, I trust —

ANITA. Well Eddie, actually I'm not sure that Mark's quite up
to it.

SACKLING *feebly gestures silence to* ANITA.

LOOMIS. And Mr Meadle, I don't know which of you had
the chance to meet him yet, but those who haven't can make
their separate introductions, in the meanwhile I'll say a welcome
on all our behalves, we're delighted to have you with us — I
see you've still got your clips on, by the way.

MEADLE. Oh yes.

LOOMIS. Perhaps you'd better remove them or you'll create the
impression that you're just pedalling through — (*He laughs.*)

MEADLE *bends, to take them off.*

Good — now as we're all here and there are a few minutes
before the bell, I'd like to say a few words, if I may. So,
gather ye round — gather ye round. (*They all do so.*) As you've
no doubt realised, we have an exceptionally high enrolment
for the month, the highest in the school's career, as a matter
of fact. (*Little murmurs.*)

QUARTERMAINE. I say, terrific!

LOOMIS. Yes, very gratifying. You all know how hard Thomas
has worked for this. Though he'd loathe to hear me say it.
But what he wouldn't mind hearing me say is that in his turn
he knows how hard you've worked. I think we all have a right
to be proud of our growing reputation as one of the best
schools of English — not one of the biggest but one of the
best — in Cambridge. Which, when it comes down to it, means
in the country.

ALL. Murmur.

MELANIE (*murmurs*). Solemn thought.

LOOMIS. Well and good. Well and good. But success will
bring — has already begun to bring — its own problems. (*He
gestures to* MEADLE.) As Mr Meadle's presence here testifies.
But even with Mr Meadle — or Dennis, as I've already told

him I intend to call him — with Dennis to help us, there is going to be a considerable strain on our resources. Perhaps a few too many students to a classroom, more work to take home and correct, more difficulties in developing personal contact — that so crucial personal contact —

QUARTERMAINE. Absolutely crucial.

LOOMIS. Many of whom are only here for a short time — well, as I say, you've already become familiar with the problems, the problems, as Thomas remarked 'midst the chaos this morning, of a flourishing school —

SACKLING *faints.*

ANITA. Oh my God!

ANITA *cries out.*
WINDSCAPE *gets to him.*

WINDSCAPE. The thing is to — (*He puts his hand on* SACKLING's *heart.*) His heart — I can't feel his heart —

A pause.

QUARTERMAINE (*also looking down*). Oh Lord!

The bell rings.

Lights.

Scene Two

QUARTERMAINE. Oh Lord! Hello Eddie.

LOOMIS. You're in sprightly mood, St. John.

QUARTERMAINE. Friday evening you know — and I'm off to the theatre tonight with old Mark and Anita.

LOOMIS. And what are you going to see?

QUARTERMAINE. Oh that — that Strinberg, I think it is. At The Arts.

LOOMIS. I believe it's an Ibsen, Hedda Gabler — I believe.

QUARTERMAINE. Oh, is it really?

LOOMIS. But tell me, the bell's gone then, has it, I didn't hear it — but then these old ears of mine —

QUARTERMAINE. Ah yes, well I let them out a little early, you see Eddie.

LOOMIS. Why?

QUARTERMAINE. Well, it was my turn to give the advance British Life and Institutions Lecture, and I chose Oxford Colleges — to give them the other point of view, for once — illustrated with slides, but I'd only just got going, and blow me tight — the old projector broke.

LOOMIS. Broke? But we've only just bought it. It's the newest model.

QUARTERMAINE. Yes, I think that's part of the problem, all those extra bits to master — anyway, one of the colleges went in upside down and wouldn't come out so I had to — to abandon technology and do it all off my own bat — you know, reminiscences of my time at the House and — and anedotes — and — you know — that sort of thing. The personal touch. But of course I ran out of steam a little, towards the end, I'm afraid.

LOOMIS. And how many turned up?

QUARTERMAINE. Oh well — about a handful.

LOOMIS. A handful!

QUARTERMAINE. A good handful.

LOOMIS. But there are meant to be twenty-three in the group that that special lecture's designed for.

QUARTERMAINE. Yes, well I think you know — it's being Friday and — and the sun shining and the Backs so lovely and the Cam jam-packed with punts and — but the ones who did come were jolly interested — especially that little Italian girl — you know um — um — almost midget sized, the one with the wart —

LOOMIS. If you mean Angelina, she happens to be Greek. Her father's an exceptionally distinguished army officer. Thomas will be very disappointed to hear about all this, St. John, he devised that lecture series himself, you know, it's quite an

innovation, and if you can't keep attendances up — and you
know very well how important it is to keep classes going until
at least the bell — ah, hello my dear, you've finished a trifle
on the early side too, then?

ANITA. Oh, isn't it past five?

LOOMIS. Well, the bell hasn't gone yet, even in your part of the
corridor — intermediary dictation, wasn't it, and how was
your attendance?

ANITA. Oh, nearly a full complement, Eddie, they're a very keen
lot, mostly Germans, in fact that's why I thought the bell had
gone, one of them said he'd heard it.

LOOMIS. Which one?

ANITA. I think it was Kurt.

LOOMIS. I see.

ANITA *makes to go to her locker.*

LOOMIS. My dear, have I told you what I think about your
sandals?

ANITA. No, Eddie.

QUARTERMAINE. I think they're smashing.

LOOMIS. Well, when I first saw you in them I wondered if they
were quite *comme il fault,* Thomas and I had quite a thing
about them — but I've been quite won around, I've come to
the view that they're most fetching. Or that your feet are. Or
both. (*He laughs.*)

ANITA. Thank you, Eddie.

LOOMIS. And Nigel's still in London, is he, with his co-editress?

ANITA. Yes, he comes back on Saturday or Sunday.

LOOMIS. Quite a coincidence Thomas seeing them on the train
like that, he's scarcely been out of his office this many a
month, as you know — and it's all working out all right, is it?

ANITA. Yes, Amanda's been absolutely wonderful, quite a
surprise really, because when I first met her at a party a few
months ago, I thought she was — well, absolutely charming,

of course, but rather — rather feckless, if anything. But it turns out she's got a really good tough brain. Her boyfriend's being a great help too. He's invaluable.

LOOMIS. But you met her at a party. How odd, I had an idea you went to school with her?

ANITA (*slight hesitation*). No no — with her sister, Seraphina.

LOOMIS. Ah yes — but I was really asking about the magazine itself, how that was coming?

ANITA. Oh, they've finally settled on a title. It's going to be called *Reports*.

QUARTERMAINE. Terrific!

LOOMIS. *Reports.*

The bell rings.

Reports, mmm, well, tell Nigel when he gets back that Thomas has decided to take out *two* subscriptions, one for ourselves and one for the student common room, so we'll be showing a great personal interest —

ANITA. Oh thank you, Eddie, Nigel will be so pleased —

From the garden, the sound of WINDSCAPE, *off.*

WINDSCAPE (*off*). I can't stay too long, I'm afraid, just to start you off and explain the rules — but first let's get the mallets and balls —

The voices recede.

LOOMIS (*going to the window*). Ah, the croquet's under way again, good, good, — and who's playing — ah, Piccolo and Jean-Pierre, Gisela — Teresa — Okona — Liv and Gerta — you know, I always feel that if ever our little school had to justify itself, we could do it by showing the world the spectacle of an Italian, a Frenchman, a German, a Japanese, a Swedish girl and a Belgian girl, all gathered together on an English lawn, under an English sky to play a game of croquet —

ANITA *through this has gone to her locker.*

QUARTERMAINE. Absolutely, Eddie, absolutely — croquet —

I must try my hand again — haven't for years — not since my
aunt's when I was a child — she had such a lawn, you know, and
I remember, oh Lord, (*Shaking his head, laughing.*) Oh Lord,
I say, I forgot, Thomas told me to tell you he was looking
for you.

LOOMIS. Thomas? When?

QUARTERMAINE. Oh, just at the end of my lecture — he
popped his head in.

LOOMIS. Really, St. John, I wish you'd mentioned it straight
away, it would have to be something urgent for Thomas to
interrupt a class — was he going back to the office?

SACKLING *enters, during this. Carrying books, etc. He sports
a moustache.*

QUARTERMAINE. He didn't say, Eddie.

LOOMIS. Mark, have you happened to glimpse Thomas —

SACKLING. Yes. I think he and Melanie were going up to your
flat —

LOOMIS. Oh. Well, if he should come down here looking for me,
tell him I've gone upstairs to the flat — and that I'll stay there
so that we don't do one of our famous boxes and coxes —
(*He goes out left.*)

SACKLING. Right Eddie. (*Going to his locker.*)

ANITA, *during the above, has finished packing, is leaving.
There is an air of desperate rush about her.*

QUARTERMAINE. Wasn't he in a dodgy mood — but I say, where
shall we meet, Anita, shall Mark and I come and pick you
up at your place, or shall we go to Mark's place, or the foyer,
or — or we could go to The Eagle — or you two could come
to my place —

ANITA. Oh, I'm sorry, St. John, I completely forgot — you see
I'm going to London. It suddenly occurred to me that as Nigel
can't get back until tomorrow or Sunday, why not pop down
and spend the weekend with him.

QUARTERMAINE. What a good idea. Much more fun than some

old Ibsen thing.

SACKLING. Does he know you're coming?

ANITA. No, it's a surprise.

SACKLING. Shouldn't you 'phone him first? I mean he may be going out or — you know.

ANITA. I haven't got time. Look, I've got to dash if I'm going to make the five-thirty — damn Eddie! (*Rushing off.*)

SACKLING. Oh Christ! Poor old Nigel.

QUARTERMAINE. Mmmm?

SACKLING. Well, surely you know?

QUARTERMAINE. What?

SACKLING. About Nigel and Amanda Southgate. They're having a passionate affair. He only started the magazine because of her — she's got literary ambitions.

QUARTERMAINE. Oh — oh, Lord, poor old Anita! But they always seemed so happy —

SACKLING. You know, St. John, you have an amazing ability not to let the world impinge on you. Anita's the unhappiest woman I know, at the moment. And has been, ever since she met Nigel. Amanda's his fifth affair in the last two years, even if the most serious. But Anita covers up for him, pretends it isn't happening, or tries to protect a reputation he hasn't got and probably doesn't want anyway, he's made her have three abortions although she's desperate for children — haven't you had the slightest inkling of any of that?

QUARTERMAINE. No.

SACKLING. But what I don't understand is why she's suddenly gone down to confront him. She's only survived so far by not daring to have anything out with him — she's never once mentioned even the most blatant of his infidelities, actually that's one of the things about her that drives him mad. Anyway, there's nothing we can do about it, is there? I haven't even got his number, so I can't warn him.

QUARTERMAINE. Don't you like Anita?

SACKLING. Of course I do. Far more than I like Nigel, as a matter of fact.

QUARTERMAINE. Oh. Oh well it all seems — all seems — I mean these things between people — people one cares for — it's hard to bear them — but, but I say, what about this evening then, how would you like to play it? Eagle or — shall we meet at the theatre?

SACKLING. As a matter of fact, St. John, I'm going to have to bow out of the theatre, too.

QUARTERMAINE. Oh. Oh well —

SACKLING. You see, last night I went back to it again. My novel. The first time since Camelia left. And there was the old flame aflickering as strongly as ever. So I've got to get back to it this evening. Look, you haven't actually bought the tickets, have you?

QUARTERMAINE (*makes to say yes, changes his mind*). No, no, never any need to at the Arts, so don't worry about that but — but it's terrific that you've starting writing again, that's far more important than going to see some — some old Ibsen thing.

SACKLING. Thanks. And St. John, thanks also for your companionship these last weeks. It must have been bloody boring for you, having me grind on and on in my misery.

QUARTERMAINE. Lord no, I've enjoyed it enormously. Not your misery I don't mean but your (*He laughs.*) — your — but I say, have you heard from Camelia?

SACKLING. Yes, this morning. She's allowing me a few hours tomorrow afternoon. With my son.

QUARTERMAINE. But that's wonderful, Mark. Look, when will you be back?

SACKLING. Tomorrow evening, I suppose.

QUARTERMAINE. Well, perhaps we could have lunch on Sunday or dinner or meet for a drink — and you could tell me how things went with little Tom — I'd really love to know.

During this, the sound of the door opening, closing, followed by a yelp.

MEADLE (*off*). Blast!

QUARTERMAINE. You all right, old man?

MEADLE (*he is wearing a suit, has a bump on his forehead, covered by a piece of sticking plaster*). Yes, yes — (*Rubbing his hand.*) It's that door-knob, a bit too close to the door-jamb — at least for my taste — (*He laughs.*) I'm always scraping my knuckles on it — hello, Mark, haven't seen you around for a bit, I suppose because you're usually gone before I finish.

SACKLING. Don't worry, I do my time. Right to the bell.

MEADLE. Oh, I didn't mean any reflection — (*He laughs.*) Good God, I only meant that I always seem to get caught by students who want to practise their English after hours too — of course it doesn't help to be carrying a conversation piece around on your forehead — What 'appen 'ead, Mr Mittle, whasa matter weet de het, Meester Meetle, Mister Mittle vat goes mit der hed b- (*Laughing.*) up the corridor, down, in the classroom, in the garden — by the time I'd gone through all the details, with pantomime, landlady calling to the telephone, toe stubbing in cracked linoleum, body pitching down the stairs and bonce cracking down on tile I'd have settled for serious internal injuries instead.

SACKLING (*smiles*). Goodnight. (*He goes out through the French windows.*)

QUARTERMAINE (*who has been laughing with MEADLE*). Oh, night old man, but oh, just a minute, we haven't fixed our meeting — (*He goes to the French windows, stares out.*)

MEADLE (*who has registered SACKLING's manner*). He's a hard chap to get to know, isn't he?

QUARTERMAINE. Who? Old Mark? Lord no — oh, well perhaps to begin with but once you do know him you can't imagine a — a better friend.

MEADLE. Oh. Well, I'll keep working on it then. (*Going to his locker.*)

QUARTERMAINE. I say, I've managed to get hold of some tickets for the theatre tonight. They're doing an Ibsen! Would you like to come?

MEADLE. To tell you the truth, Ibsen's not quite my cup of tea, thanks, but anyway as a matter of fact Oko-Ri's taking me out to dinner tonight with the rest of the boys.

QUARTERMAINE. Oko — what?

MEADLE. Ri. Oko-Ri. My Japanese chum.

QUARTERMAINE. Oh, old baldy, you mean? Taking you out to dinner — well, that's — that's — I didn't know you'd hit it off so well with them, after your trouser —

MEADLE. Well, I never thought they'd made me skid deliberately — and we've had lots of good laughs about it since — now that I'm on their wave-length — Oko-Ri's got a splendid sense of humour. Loves a drink too, I gather, from some of their jokes.

QUARTERMAINE. Oh, well, you'll have a good evening then —

MEADLE. It's really just to say thank you for all the extra hours I've put in with them. They left it to me to decide where we'd go, and I've chosen that French place that's just opened opposite Trinity, Eddie and Thomas were saying it's very good.

QUARTERMAINE. So I hear.

MEADLE. Anyway, I'd better get back. I'd ask you to come along too, but it's not really my invitation —

QUARTERMAINE. No, no — I quite understand.

The sound of the door opening and closing, feet.

MEADLE. Oh. Here. Let me give you a hand with those, Melanie —

MELANIE (*off*). No, it's quite all right, I've got them —

MEADLE (*off*). Well, let me just take this one —

MELANIE. No, no, really — there's no need —

The sound of books dropping on the floor.

MEADLE (*off*). Oh, sorry, Melanie —

MELANIE (*irritably*). Oh — really! I had them perfectly well — and Thomas has just lent me that one with great warnings to be careful, it's a rare edition —

MEADLE *coming on stage, carrying a distinguished volume.*

(*Coming on stage, carrying a briefcase, exercise books and further books.*) If you could just put it on the table — Have either of you seen Eddie, Thomas has been looking for him.

QUARTERMAINE. Now what did Eddie say — oh yes, that he was going to wait for Thomas in the — in the office, it must have been.

MELANIE. Oh, good, well that's where Thomas has gone — so you're the last two then, are you?

QUARTERMAINE. Yes, well apart from old Henry, that is, he's playing croquet —

MELANIE. Is he, jolly good! (*She goes to her locker.*)

MEADLE (*who has been looking through the book*). No, no damage done, Melanie. (*He looks at his watch.*) So Thomas is in the office, is he?

MELANIE. Yes, why, what do you want him for?

MEADLE. Oh — well — well actually he said something about seeing if he could get me some extra pronunciation classes — as I'm part-time, I need all the hours I can get, you see. (*He laughs.*)

MELANIE. I wouldn't go disturbing him now, if I were you, he's had a particularly fraught day. He's got a dreadful headache. The only person he'll want to see is Eddie.

MEADLE. Oh. Well, in that case, goodnight, Melanie.

MELANIE. Goodnight — oh, that reminds me, I'd be very grateful if you'd stop putting your bicycle against the wall where I park my car — there's not enough room for both.

MEADLE. Oh, sorry about that — right Melanie — well, see you Monday then.

QUARTERMAINE. See you Monday, old man. (*As* MEADLE *goes out through the French windows.*)

MELANIE. I really think I'd get on much better with Mr Meadle if he didn't try so hard to get on with me.

MEADLE (*meanwhile, off*). 'Night Henry, see you Monday.

WINDSCAPE (*off*). Oh. 'Night Derek. Have a good weekend.

MEADLE (*off*). Thanks, Henry — same to you.

MELANIE. Still, apparently he works very hard at his teaching, from all accounts. Thomas and Eddie are both rather thrilled with him. And really I had no right to stop him from seeing Thomas — not my business at all. But Thomas really is in a terrible state. He's spent the whole afternoon on the telephone because of that wretched Jap — the big, bald one, you know — apparently he got drunk and ran amok in that new French restaurant last night, and the owners are demanding damages and threatening to call the police, if he shows up again, and then one of the other Japanese turned up at lunch-time to book a table for tonight — Goodness knows what's going to happen if the bald one appears too. Well, St. John, and what are your plans for the weekend, something on the boil, I'll bet!

QUARTERMAINE. Oh, well I thought I might take in a show tonight — that Ibsen thing at the Arts —

MELANIE. Isn't it *The Cherry Orchard*?

QUARTERMAINE. Oh, is it? Well — something terrific like that. And then a bit of supper, I suppose. I might try that French place in fact. Might be rather — rather amusing. (*He laughs.*)

MELANIE. It must be jolly nice being a bachelor and having the weekend before you. Especially in Cambridge.

QUARTERMAINE. Yes, terrific fun.

MELANIE. Well, I'd better get on with this. I don't think Thomas really wants me to take it off the premises. (*She pulls the book towards her.*)

QUARTERMAINE. Oh. Righto. (*He begins to wander up and down, gaze out of the French windows etc.*)

MELANIE *writing, glancing occasionally at him. She is, in fact, anxious for him to be gone. There are occasional cries and sounds of* WINDSCAPE's *voice from the garden, 'Oh yes,*

yes, right to the very beginning,' to which MELANIE
responds by lifting her head, or stopping writing.

QUARTERMAINE. I say, Melanie — do you like *The Cherry
Orchard*?

MELANIE. Loathe it.

QUARTERMAINE. Oh. Why?

MELANIE. All that Russian gloom and doom and people
shooting themselves from loneliness and depression and that
sort of thing. But then mother says I don't understand
comedy. I expect she's right.

QUARTERMAINE. How is mother?

MELANIE. Oh, top hole, thanks. (*Automatically*.)

QUARTERMAINE. Well, if there's ever anything I can do —
you know — if she wants company when you want to go
out —

MELANIE. That's very thoughtful of you, St. John, thank you.

QUARTERMAINE. No, no — I'd enjoy it — I say, that is an
impressive tome old Thomas has lent you, what are you
copying out exactly?

MELANIE. Recipes. This one's for roasted swan.

QUARTERMAINE. Oh. For a dinner party?

MELANIE. No, no, St. John, it's for my British Life and
Institutions lot, to give them some idea of a Medieval
banquet. Swans are protected birds, you know, these days.

QUARTERMAINE. Oh yes, of course they are. (*He laughs*.)
Fancy thinking you'd give them for a — a — oh Lord! But
aren't they the most — most beautiful creatures. I was
looking at one — oh, just the other day, you know — on the
Cam — drifting behind a punt — and they were all shouting
and drinking champagne and — and it was just drifting
behind them — so calm — and I remember there used to be
oh! a dozen or so — they came every year to a pond near my
aunt's — when I was — was and I could hear their wings —
great wings beating — in the evenings when I was lying in bed

— it could be quite — quite frightening even after I knew
what was making the noise — and then the next morning
there they'd be — a dozen of them or so — drifting — drifting
around — and it was hard to imagine — their long necks
twining and their way of drifting — all that — that power —
those wings beating — I wonder where they went to. I'd like
to know more about them really. Where they go, what they —

MELANIE. St. John, please don't think me fearfully rude, but
I must try and finish this and I can't write and talk at the
same time, you see.

QUARTERMAINE. What? Oh — oh sorry, Melanie, no, you're
quite right, I can't either. Anyway, I ought to be getting
on —

MELANIE. Yes, with such a full evening. I do hope you enjoy it.

QUARTERMAINE. Well — well 'night Melanie, see you Monday.
And don't forget about your mother — any time —

MELANIE. I won't, St. John, goodnight.

QUARTERMAINE *goes.*

MELANIE *sits, not writing, as:*

QUARTERMAINE (*off*). I say, Henry, any chance of a game?

WINDSCAPE (*off*). Actually, I've just finished, I'm afraid —
perhaps next week.

QUARTERMAINE (*off*). Right, I'll hold you to that. 'Night.

WINDSCAPE (*off*). 'Night.

QUARTERMAINE (*off*). Oh, by the way, if you want any
baby-sitting done during the weekend, I'll try and make myself
available —

WINDSCAPE (*off*). Righto, I'll put it to Fanny — I know she's
quite keen to see the *Uncle Vanya* at the Arts — perhaps
tomorrow night —

QUARTERMAINE (*off*). *A votre disposition*. 'Night.

WINDSCAPE (*off*). 'Night.

MELANIE, *during this, has got up, gone to the French windows and during the latter part hurries back to the table, sits down, pretends to continue transcribing.*

WINDSCAPE *enters through the French windows. He stops on seeing* MELANIE, *braces himself, then enters properly, jovially.*

WINDSCAPE. Hello Melanie, my dear, I thought everyone had gone.

MELANIE. How are they taking to the croquet?

WINDSCAPE. At the moment they find it a bit sedate, I think, but another time or two around and they'll discover just how much — how much incivility is possible on our tranquil English lawns. (*He laughs, embarrassed.*) Now I must sort myself out — I promised Fanny I'd be home by six — now where's my briefcase — ah, yes — and a pile of unseens I seem to remember — (*Going to his locker.*) to be marked by Monday —

MELANIE. How is Fanny?

WINDSCAPE. Oh, very well, thanks, very well — a bit tired in the evenings, what with the children on the one hand and her two hours voluntary with the O.A.P's — but she's enjoying every minute of her day —

MELANIE. Good! — And the children — are all well?

WINDSCAPE. Oh yes — they're fine! Susan's a little tense at the moment, actually, with her 'O' levels — a pity she's taking them so early, I think, but she insists — she's in with a particularly bright lot and doesn't want to fall behind or let herself down so she works away until all hours. Quite often after Fanny and I have gone to bed. But she's developing quite an interest in — in — well, philosophical speculation, I suppose it is, really — the other evening — (*Bending down during this to put on his clips.*) she suddenly insisted — in the middle of supper — she'd been very quiet until then — she suddenly insisted that we couldn't prove that other people existed — and that perhaps when we thought about them or remembered them or saw and heard them even — we were actually just making them up — and of course I took her up on this and attempted to explain how it is we do know that other people exist including people we don't know exist, if you follow — (*Laughing*.) and she kept saying 'But you can't prove it, Daddy, you can't actually prove it!' And she was right. I found myself getting quite tangled in my own arguments.

MELANIE. I've always thought she was the one who takes most after you.

WINDSCAPE. Yes, yes — perhaps she does, perhaps she does — I'm afraid I rather like to think so anyway — but you haven't seen them for ages have you, you really must come over sometime soon — Fanny would love to see you again. We all would.

MELANIE. That would be lovely.

WINDSCAPE. I'll get Fanny to give you a ring over the weekend or —

MELANIE. Good.

WINDSCAPE. Right — well, oh, by the way, I've been meaning to ask — how is your mother's day-nurse working out, with the name out of Dickens?

MELANIE. Nurse Grimes. Well enough so far — she seems a very efficient, cheerful little soul — a little too cheerful for my taste perhaps, as apparently she belongs to one of those peculiar revivalist sects that seem to be springing up all over the place now — you know, meeting in each other's homes and chanting prayers and dancing about in their love of God.

WINDSCAPE. Oh Lord.

MELANIE. At least that's how she describes it — but Mother seems to like her.

WINDSCAPE. Well, that's the main thing, isn't it?

MELANIE. Yes. Yes it is.

WINDSCAPE. Well do give her my — my very best — see you Monday, Melanie, my dear.

MELANIE. See you Monday, Henry.

> WINDSCAPE, *carrying papers, books, etc., goes off left. The sound of the door closing.*

> MELANIE *sits. She lets out a sudden wail, and then in a sort of frenzy, tears at the page of the book from which she's been copying, sobbing. She checks herself as: the sound of the door opening.*

WINDSCAPE (*laughing*). What on earth can I be thinking of — going off with all these in my arms and leaving my briefcase behind — I do that sort of thing more and more now — perhaps it's premature senility — (*Entering, going to the briefcase, shovelling the papers and books in.*) or did I get switched on to the wrong track and think I was going off to teach a class — I must have as I went out that way — (*He looks at her smiling. Little pause.*) Melanie — Melanie — (*He hesitates, then goes to her, leaving the briefcase on the desk.*) Is something the matter?

MELANIE. She hates me, you see.

WINDSCAPE. Who?

MELANIE. Mother.

WINDSCAPE. Oh Melanie, I'm sure she doesn't.

MELANIE. When I get home in the evenings — do you know what she does? She sits there for hours refusing to speak — then when I get her supper on the table — she refuses to eat. I know she can only work one side of her face now, but she can eat perfectly well. And when I try to feed her — she lets the food fall out of her mouth, and — and stares at me with such malevolence, until suddenly she'll say something — something utterly — Last night she said 'It's not my fault you've spent your life in my home. I've never wanted you here, but as you're too stupid and too unattractive to make any reasonable man a wife, I accepted the responsibility for you. And now I need you at last, you refuse to pay your debt.' And coming out of the side of her mouth like a — like a gangster in one of those films you used to take me to. And she wets herself. She wets herself all the time.

WINDSCAPE. Oh Melanie, I'm so sorry. Of course I realised
that last attack must have left her more — more incapacitated
— and — possibly even a little incontinent —

MELANIE. She's not incontinent, Henry. She does it on
purpose. Out of spite. She never does it with Grimes. Only
with me. She says that as I'm behaving like a neglectful
parent, she'll behave like a neglected child. The only child
I'll ever have. Of course, she adores Grimes — or at least she
pretends to. And she's started giving her things — things
that belong to me she knows I love. The buttons from
Daddy's uniform or, the other day, a silly lithograph of a
donkey that's hung in my room all my life almost — of
course Grimes gives them back but — but — the worst thing is
I'm beginning to hate her. To hate going home or when I'm
there have such dreadful feelings. Because the thought of
years — it could be years apparently — years of this — and so
wishing she would have another attack and die now —
dreadful — too dreadful — almost imagining myself doing
something to — get her out of the way.

WINDSCAPE. She must love you really, mustn't she, or she
wouldn't — wouldn't resent your being away from her so
much —

MELANIE. But I can't give up my teaching, Henry, I can't.
Your getting me this job was the best thing that ever
happened to me. Of course she always despised it. Even
before she was ill she used to say teaching foreigners was a
job for failures — but I love it and I'm not going to give it up.

A pause.

WINDSCAPE. I only wish I could give you some comfort, my
dear.

MEALNIE. You do, Henry. Your just being here and knowing
that you — that you care about me makes all the difference.
All the difference. It always has. (*She begins to cry.*) What a
fool I was not to — not to marry you when you gave me the
chance — I keep thinking of it now — and what she said
about your being too young and not knowing what you were
doing — and blighting your career — even then she was my

enemy — my real enemy. Of course I'm happy that you're so
happy — I wouldn't have been able to make you so happy, I
know — (*Sobbing.*) I'm sorry, sorry —

WINDSCAPE (*hesitates, then with reluctance puts his arms around
her*). There there, my dear, there there — mustn't think of the
past — it's the — the future — the future — there there —

The telephone rings.

(*After a moment.*) Perhaps I'd better — perhaps I'd better —
um — (*Releasing himself, he picks up the telephone.*) Hello.
Oh Hello Nigel, yes it is! No Anita's gone I'm afraid — at
least I think she has — have you seen Anita in the last half
hour —

MELANIE, *now handkerchiefing her tears, shakes her head.*

Melanie hasn't seen her either so I'm fairly sure — yes of course
I will. (*He listens.*) You're 'phoning from Liverpool Street
and you're about to catch the 6.13 so you'll be home before
eight, right, got that — but if Melanie or I do see her by any
unlikely — yes, right, goodbye — and oh, Nigel, good luck with
your first issue. We're all looking forward to it enormously —
yes — goodbye. (*He hangs up.*) That was Nigel — for Anita — as
you probably realised and — and anyway she's certainly left,
hasn't she — Look Melanie, you must come around, and have a
real — a real talk with Fanny — take you out of yourself —
away from your problems —

MELANIE. Thank you, Henry.

WINDSCAPE. No, we'd love to see you, I'll get her to ring you.
All right? And now I must — I really must —

MELANIE. Yes, you must get back.

WINDSCAPE. Yes. See you Monday, my dear.

MELANIE. Monday, Henry.

WINDSCAPE *looks around vaguely for a moment, then goes
out through the French windows.*

MELANIE *stands for a moment, then sees the briefcase,
registers it, takes it to* WINDSCAPE's *locker, puts it in, goes*

back to the book, looks down at it, tries futiley to sort it out, pressing the page flat with her hand, as she does so.

The sound of the door opening, footsteps.

MELANIE (*closes the book quickly, gathers herself together*). Oh, hello Eddie! (*Brightly.*)

LOOMIS. Thomas is not here then — I can't make out — I've been everywhere, everywhere, up to the flat, all the class-rooms and in the office — and the 'phone going all the time about some of our Japanese and that French restaurant, and they're not even French. It turns out they're from Wiltshire — and I don't know what Thomas has said to them, I didn't even know about it — he knows I can't deal with that sort of thing — and he's booked a table for the two of us tonight at their request, forcing us to take responsibility, I don't see what it's got to do with the school if a few Japanese can't hold their drink, I don't know why he agreed — it really is too all too —

MELANIE. Now Eddie. Now. (*Going to him.*) You mustn't worry. You'll make yourself ill, and it's not worth it. Why don't you go upstairs to the flat and have a rest, I'm sure it'll all sort itself out, you know Thomas, he'll get it completely under control, he always does, in the end.

LOOMIS. Yes, yes, of course you're right, my dear, thank you, thank you. And a little rest — and I'll try and make Thomas have one, too —

MELANIE. That's right, Eddie, you both need it — oh, and would you give this back to him when you see him, and tell him I'm terribly sorry (*As she collects her briefcase and hands* LOOMIS *the book.*) a page of it seems to have got torn — our Mr Meadle insisted on snatching it out of my hands and then dropped it — he was only trying to be helpful of course — but you know how clumsy he is —

LOOMIS. Oh — oh dear, Cussons' — one of our favourite books, Thomas will find it difficult to forgive Meadle. Oh, by the way, how's mother?

MELANIE. Oh, top hole, thanks Eddie.

LOOMIS. Good, good.

MELANIE. See you Monday.

LOOMIS. See you Monday. (MELANIE *goes off, left*. LOOMIS *looks at Cussons' and turns to see* QUARTERMAINE *standing at the French windows.*

QUARTERMAINE. Hello Eddie.

LOOMIS. Hello St. John. I thought you'd left.

QUARTERMAINE. No — I just thought I'd see if there was anyone still about.

LOOMIS. No, they've all gone.

QUARTERMAINE. Ah.

LOOMIS. Goodnight then, St. John.

QUARTERMAINE. Goodnight, Eddie. See you Monday.

LOOMIS. See you Monday.

> LOOMIS *goes off, left.* QUARTERMAINE *stands for a moment. A distant spire chimes.* QUARTERMAINE *goes to his chair, sits, crosses his legs and lies back.*

Lights.

Curtain.

ACT TWO

Scene One

The following year, towards summer. It is a Monday morning, about nine-thirty.

There have been a few improvements, different pictures perhaps; a record player, with a record rack consisting of poetry readings and Shakespeare plays. There is also a large new tape-recorder, sophisticated for the period.

QUARTERMAINE is seated, staring ahead.

WINDSCAPE enters through the French windows, carrying a briefcase, smoking a pipe, wearing bicycle clips.

WINDSCAPE. Hello St. John. (*He goes to his locker.*)

QUARTERMAINE (*doesn't respond at first, then takes in WINDSCAPE*). Oh, hello — um (*He thinks.*) Henry.

WINDSCAPE (*turns, looks at him*). Deep in thought?

QUARTERMAINE. Mmmm? Oh. No, no — just — just — you know.

WINDSCAPE. Ah. Did you have a good half term?

QUARTERMAINE. Oh. Yes thanks. Yes.

WINDSCAPE. What did you do? Did you go away? (*Going to his locker.*)

QUARTERMAINE. Well, I — I — no, I stayed here.

WINDSCAPE. Here!

QUARTERMAINE. Yes.

WINDSCAPE. Oh, in Cambridge, you mean? Just for a moment I thought you meant actually *here* — in this room — I think, perhaps because the last time I saw you, you were sitting in exactly the same place in very much that position — as if you haven't moved all week.

QUARTERMAINE. Oh. (*He laughs.*) But I say — good to be back, isn't it?

WINDSCAPE. Well, I could have done with a little longer myself.

QUARTERMAINE (*watches* WINDSCAPE *at the locker*). I say, Henry, what did you do for the half?

WINDSCAPE. Mmmm? Oh nothing very exciting really, we packed ourselves into the caravan and took ourselves off to a spot we'd heard about in Norfolk —

QUARTERMAINE. That sounds terrific!

WINDSCAPE. Yes — yes — well, the trouble was that it rained fairly steadily — all week, in fact — so we didn't get out as much as we would have liked — a shame really as among other things we were hoping that a few jaunts would cheer Susan up.

QUARTERMAINE. Oh — is she a bit low then?

WINDSCAPE. Yes yes — well she's still brooding over her 'O' level results — we keep telling her that at her age six positive passes — I mean threes and fours — is jolly good — but she seems to feel she's let herself down — but I'll tell you what we did see — it really was most — extraordinary — one morning at about six it was, I was up trying to plug the leak — it was right over little Fanny's bunk — and so she was awake and so was Ben — and Susan hadn't slept at all — so it was all rather — rather fraught, with tempers fraying — but Fanny she'd gone outside to the loo, as a matter of fact — and suddenly she called us — all of us — told us to put on our wellies and macs and come out and look — and we did — and there — silhouetted against the sky was the most — the most —

MEADLE *enters through the French windows in bicycle clips, carrying a briefcase.*

MEADLE. Greetings, Henry, St. John.

QUARTERMAINE. Hello, old chap.

WINDSCAPE. Hello, Derek. Have a good holiday?

MEADLE. Yes, thanks, Henry, very, very good indeed. What

about you? (*He goes to his locker, taking off clips, etc.*)

WINDSCAPE. Yes, I was just telling St. John, we went to Norfolk, a little wet, but there really was one very remarkable — well, moment is all it amounted to really. In temporal terms.

MEADLE. Sounds marvellous. Thomas isn't around yet, is he?

WINDSCAPE. He wasn't in the office when I came through, have you seen him, St. John?

QUARTERMAINE. Mmmm?

WINDSCAPE. Thomas. Have you seen him?

QUARTERMAINE. No no — but I expect he's here somewhere. I say — I say, Dennis, did you have a good holiday?

MEADLE. Who's Dennis, St. John? (*He laughs.*)

QUARTERMAINE. Mmmm?

WINDSCAPE. You said Dennis, instead of Derek. And he's already said he had a very good holiday.

QUARTERMAINE. Oh. What did you do?

MEADLE. I went to Sheffield, as a matter of fact.

WINDSCAPE. Sheffield, I know it well, Fanny and I went there the year before Susan was born, we were doing a tour of out-of-the-way urban domestic architecture, I've got great affection for Sheffield, what were *you* doing there?

MEADLE. Um — oh. Attending my aunt's funeral, as a matter of fact.

QUARTERMAINE. What?

WINDSCAPE. Oh Derek, I'm so sorry. How upsetting for you.

MEADLE. Yes, it was. Very. Very.

WINDSCAPE. But when I asked you just now you did say — I suppose it was merely social reflex — that you'd had a good half-term —

MEADLE. Yes, well actually I met someone there I used to know. And I managed to see quite a lot of her. That was the good part of it. Not my aunt's death, I need hardly say. (*He laughs.*)

WINDSCAPE. Ah.

QUARTERMAINE. Who was she?

MEADLE. Oh, just a girl St. John — we were at Hull University
together, as a matter of fact, she was doing the library
course but we — we lost contact, for various reasons. Although
I hadn't forgotten her. And when I had to take back all my
poor aunt's books — there she was. Behind the counter.

QUARTERMAINE. What was she doing there?

MEADLE. Well, stamping the books in and out of course. What
do you think she was doing? (*With a mitigating laugh*.)

WINDSCAPE. Oh don't worry about St. John, one of his absent
days, eh St. John?

QUARTERMAINE. What Henry?

WINDSCAPE. But how nice for you to bump into her like that,
especially under those circumstances, eh?

MEADLE. Yes, I can't tell you what a — a blessing it turned out
to be. As soon as she was off work she'd come over and sit
with me and my uncle, and on a couple of evenings when I
had to go out and console some of my aunt's friends, she came
and sat with him anyway, by herself. He's very keen on football,
but he can't follow it in the newspapers as his eyesight's nearly
gone and they're too quick for him on the radio. So she'd read
out all the teams and their scores. Which was very tiring for her,
as she's got a bit of a speech impediment actually.

WINDSCAPE. What a nice girl she sounds, eh, St. John?

QUARTERMAINE. What, Henry?

WINDSCAPE. What a nice girl Derek's friend sounds.

QUARTERMAINE. Oh — oh yes, smashing, smashing. Um, tell me
— tell me — what — what are her legs like?

MEADLE. What!

WINDSCAPE. Good heavens, St. John, what an extraordinary
question!

QUARTERMAINE. Oh yes, — oh — I'm sorry — I was just trying
to imagine — I have a sort of thing about girls' legs, you see.

(*He laughs apologetically*.) I can't stand them if they're dumpy or stumpy.

MEADLE. Well, let's just say, shall we, St. John, (*Manifestly exercising smiling control*.) that Daphne's legs happen to be my sort of legs.

A pause.

QUARTERMAINE. Your sort of legs. (*He looks at MEADLE's legs.*)

MEADLE. The sort of legs I happen to like. But I don't want to dilate on the subject of Daphne's legs (*He laughs*.) at least just at the moment — look, St. John, I wonder if you'd mind, there's a matter I was very much hoping to have a conversation with Henry about. As a matter of fact, it's rather urgent.

QUARTERMAINE. Oh. No. Sorry. Go ahead.

MEADLE. Well the thing is, St. John, it's — it's of a confidential nature.

QUARTERMAINE. Oh — oh well, I'll go and have a little stroll then, in the garden. (*Getting up*.) To tell you the truth my head feels a little — a little — as if it could do with some air.

MEADLE. Thanks very much, St. John, very decent of you.

QUARTERMAINE (*going off*). Oh, not at all — but I say — I say — (*Exiting*.) what a beautiful morning! (*He goes out*.)

MEADLE (*smiling*). You know, I can't help wondering sometimes about old Quartermaine. I can't imagine a more charming fellow but from the students' point of view — do you know what one of the advanced Swedes was telling me just before half-term —

WINDSCAPE (*interrupting*). I think it would be better really — really much better — if we didn't find ourselves talking about a colleague and a friend — I know that your concern is entirely — entirely disinterested, but — but — these little conflabs can do unintended harm. I hope you don't mind my — er —

MEADLE. Not at all, Henry, you're quite right, one can't be too careful, needless to say I meant no — no slur on St. John —

WINDSCAPE. I know you didn't, I know you didn't. But now. You said you had something urgent —

MEADLE. Yes, well, the thing is — well look, Henry, I've been here a year now and Thomas said when I started that it wouldn't be long before I'd be made a Permanent — and yet here I am, you see, still on part-time. The only one of the staff on part-time, as it happens.

WINDSCAPE. And part-time isn't really very satisfactory for you, then?

MEADLE. Well, no, it isn't, Henry, frankly. I get paid one pound two and sixpence for every hour I teach.

WINDSCAPE. But surely, Derek, one pound two and sixpence an hour isn't such a bad rate, is it?

MEADLE. Ah yes, Henry, but you see I don't get paid during the vacations, you see. I only get paid by the hour for the hours I'm allowed to do, while the rest of the staff get paid an annual salary. So even though I'm currently doing twice as many hours again as — well, St. John for example, I in fact get slightly less than half of what St. John gets, over the year. I mean, take this half-term we've just had, Henry, a week of paid holiday for everybody else but a week of no money at all for me, it was just luck that my aunt died in it, or I might have had to miss an earning week to go to her funeral and sort out my uncle you see. — And last Christmas, well, I've kept this very quiet, Henry, but last Christmas I had to be a post-man. (*He laughs*.)

WINDSCAPE. Oh dear!

MEADLE. Yes, and let me tell you it wasn't simply the work, Henry — being up at six, and trudging through the snow and sleet we had the whole of those three weeks — it was also the sheer embarrassment. Twice during my second round I nearly bumped into some students. I only got away with it because I kept my head lowered and once Thomas himself went right past me in the car — it was a miracle he didn't see me, especially as I'd slipped on some ice and I was actually lying on the pavement with the letters scattered everywhere — and now the summer holiday's looming ahead — I simply don't know how I'm going to get through that. Or at least I do. I've already sent in my application to be an Entertainments Officer at a holiday camp in Cleethorpes.

WINDSCAPE. Oh, have you?

MEADLE. Yes. And now that Daphne's back in the picture — well you probably gathered from what I said that we're pretty serious about each other — and I don't want to keep her waiting around with a long engagement — there's been a lot of tragedy in that family, Henry.

WINDSCAPE. Oh dear!

MEADLE. Yes, I won't go into it, if you don't mind. Not that Daphne tries to conceal it. She's too straightforward for that.

WINDSCAPE. Well, she really does sound a most — a most remarkable —

MEADLE. Yes, I consider myself a very very lucky man. So what do you think, Henry — I know how much Eddie and Thomas respect you — I'm going to try and nab Thomas for a few minutes this morning — how should I go about it, with him?

WINDSCAPE. Well, Derek, I think there's no doubt that you have a very strong case. Very strong. And as we all know, Thomas and Eddie are very fair, always. I know they'd respond most sympathetically — to all that you've told me about yourself and Daphne — but you see Derek, the thing is —

The sound of the door opening, footsteps.

SACKLING (*off*). 'Morning. (*He enters somewhat jauntily, his moustache now accompanied by a beard.*) Henry — Derek —

WINDSCAPE. Oh hello, Mark, good holiday?

MEADLE. You didn't notice if Thomas was in his office as you went by, did you?

SACKLING. Yes, he was. Just come down. I like the chin. A comparatively unexplored area, isn't it? How did you come by it, not shaving, I trust.

MEADLE (*who has been getting up*). No, not shaving, don't
worry — (*Attempting a chuckle.*) I'll tell you all about it
later — and thanks, Henry, for your advice. It was most
helpful —

WINDSCAPE. Oh, not at all, I'm glad if — if —

MEADLE *goes out during this, and as the door closes:*

WINDSCAPE. Oh — no — Derek! Oh — blast!

SACKLING. What's the matter?

WINDSCAPE. I think we had a slight misunderstanding — he's
under the impression that I was advising him to go and see
Thomas about being put on a more — a more permanent basis,
and the truth is I was going on to explain to him that in
spite of the — the strong claim he has — he should — well, in
my view anyway — hold his horses for the moment — Of
course — I do sometimes feel, strictly between ourselves, that
it *is* hard on Meadle as the only part-time teacher — and we
must be careful in the staff-room not to show any — any —
well, make fun of him more than is absolutely necessary —
if you see, Mark.

SACKLING. Oh, I shouldn't worry about Meadle. (*He's been at
the locker during all the above.*) even St. John's observed that
he's one of those people who always lands on his feet — even
if he damages a toe in the process. The thing is to make sure
it's his and not yours. Well, Henry, peace-maker, apostle
and saint, what sort of half did you have?

WINDSCAPE. Oh, we did the usual sort of thing, took the
caravan to a spot near the Broads. The weather wasn't too
splendid but as I was telling — St. John, I think it was — there
was one rather exceptional experience. To tell you the truth
I've never seen anything quite like it. Fanny actually wrote a
small sort of prose poem about it.

SACKLING. Really? I didn't know Fanny wrote!

WINDSCAPE. Oh yes, you see —

SACKLING. But on that subject — listen — I must tell you. I've
finished.

WINDSCAPE. Finished?

SACKLING. My novel, old cheese.

WINDSCAPE. Oh Mark — well, congratulations, congratulations!

SACKLING. Thanks Henry. Of course, it's still only the first
draft. But the point is I feel — in my guts — that it's the first
draft of the final version and damned near the thing itself,
actually. Because of the way it happened, you see. What I did
was — I put everything I'd previously written — round about
three thousand pages — into a box and lugged it into the
cellar and started again. Completely from scratch. Just me,
the typewriter and a carton of paper. I was actually quite —
quite frightened. But it was all perfectly simple. No strain.
No effort. Almost no thought. Just a steady untaxing
continuous flow of creation. For a whole week. It was the
nearest I've come, will probably ever come, to a mystical
experience.

WINDSCAPE. I envy you. I once tried to write a novel — but as
Fanny said my forte — if I have a forte — (*He laughs.*)

SACKLING. The thing is, though — the thing is — it proves to
me that I'm a novelist. The doubts I've had since Camelia
left — and worst of all, the envy! I'd read the reviews and
seen the photographs of other novelists — the real ones,
who'd been published — some of them people I knew, had
been up with — God, there's a man at Trinity — an absolute
imbecile — his *second* novel came out last month, well
received too — and when I saw his face in the middle of some
interview he'd given — the same imbecile face, with a smirk
added — that I used to see opposite me in Hall I — I — well,
I'd better not go into what I wanted to do to him. And all
those women that are getting published everywhere —
everyone, everyone but me, that's what I began to think —
as if they'd got something, through some genetic accident —
like an extra gland or double joints — that I hadn't. And so
they could do it, again and again while I was working away
like some — some drudge — some lunatic drudge who'd given
up his wife and child and hours and hours of his life — and
would go on and on drudging, through thousands and

thousands of pages, not one of them publishable, to the end of my life — so I suppose that what I've discovered at last is my — well, let's use the word. My talent. Perhaps it's been growing down there, in the dark, all this time — until finally it's strong enough to take over, eh? Anyway, now all I've got to do is a bit of pruning, no doubt some tightening up — correct the spelling and the typing mistakes, and float an extract or two in Nigel's currently fashionable little magazine — I've been promising him for years — (*He laughs.*)

QUARTERMAINE *enters through the French windows.*

QUARTERMAINE. All clear, then?

WINDSCAPE. What — oh good Heavens, St. John — yes, yes, I forgot that you were still out there.

QUARTERMAINE. Oh no — I enjoyed it — to tell the truth it seems to have cleared my head.

WINDSCAPE. Oh good.

QUARTERMAINE. Hello Mark.

SACKLING. Hello St. John. Have a good holiday?

QUARTERMAINE. Yes — yes — terrific thanks. Terrific. And how were they?

SACKLING. Who?

QUARTERMAINE. Camelia. And little Tom too. Weren't you going to see them over the half term?

SACKLING. St. John, I'd be grateful if you'd stop referring to him as little Tom, and little Tom too — it makes him sound like something out of the workhouse.

QUARTERMAINE. Oh right — right.

WINDSCAPE *during this goes to his briefcase, takes out books, puts the briefcase and other books into his locker.*

SACKLING. Actually, they were unavailable. He was getting over mumps, or so at least Camelia claimed, so she took him to a friends' to convalesce. They have a cottage by the sea, and of course I couldn't offer him that, could I?

QUARTERMAINE. Um — but what a pity I didn't know you were stuck in Cambridge over the half, we could have got together.

ANITA *enters through the French windows.*

SACKLING. Hi, Anita!

QUARTERMAINE. Hello, Anita!

WINDSCAPE. Anita, my dear —

ANITA *takes off her coat.*
She is pregnant.

SACKLING. — you're swelling along pleasantly. Rapidly too.

ANITA *laughs.*

QUARTERMAINE. But you look — you look — (*Gazing at her in a sort of reverence.*) I mean (*He gestures.*) in just a week, good Lord!

ANITA. Well, it's taken a bit longer than a week, St. John.

QUARTERMAINE. No, no, but I mean —

WINDSCAPE. Just like Fanny, nothing shows for ages and then one day there it is — for the world to see —

SACKLING. And how's Nigel getting on in New York?

ANITA. Oh, he decided not to go. He suddenly became convinced — he had a dream, or something — that I'd spawn prematurely, so he stayed at home and mugged up on all the texts — Spock for practicals, and Blake and D.H. Lawrence and some Indian writer he's discovered and is going to publish, for significance — which was lovely for me as I didn't have to go to my parents, I spent most of the time in the bath reading thrillers. It was lovely.

QUARTERMAINE. Oh, I wish I'd known you were here, so was Mark, as it turned out, weren't you Mark, we could have got together — but I say, I say, it's good to be back in a way, isn't it — I mean, after a good holiday of course —

SACKLING. Tell him I'm going to give him a ring, will you — (*To* ANITA.)

The sound of the door opening, closing, during this.

— there's something I've got for him. At last.

QUARTERMAINE. You don't mean you've finished your novel?

SACKLING. Yes!

QUARTERMAINE. Oh wonderful!

ANITA. Oh Mark, really! He'll be so thrilled — he keeps refusing to 'phone you because he says it's like soliciting —

QUARTERMAINE. Hello, Derek, have you had a good half —

MEADLE *enters.*

(*Laughing.*) But of course I've seen you already, I'm sorry if I was a bit — off-colour, don't know what was the matter with me — but oh Lord, what have you done to your chin, you do get in the wars, though, don't you, old man. Was it shaving?

ANITA. Derek, are you all right?

MEADLE. Yes, yes thanks — well — (*He laughs.*) apart from finding out that I won't be joining you as a full-time member of the staff. In fact, my hours are going to be cut. By over a quarter. Which won't give me enough money to survive on. Furthermore, I may not have any hours at all next month. So I'll — I'll probably be leaving you then.

QUARTERMAINE. Leave! Oh no! That's rotten!

WINDSCAPE. I'm very sorry. I blame myself. I should have explained more fully. But you were out of the room so quickly —

SACKLING. Look, we must have a word with Thomas, with Eddie — we can't allow him just to be chucked out — Henry, perhaps you could speak to them on behalf of us all —

ANITA. Yes. Henry, you will, won't you?

WINDSCAPE. Of course I'll — I'll do my best. But whatever happens, Dennis — it's no reflection on your teaching. None at all.

MEADLE. Oh, I know that. It's Derek, by the way, Henry. (*Laughing.*) But that's life, isn't it? That's the joke. How hard

I've worked. I mean, old Quartermaine here — well, according to one of the Swedes I'm not allowed to mention because it's a fraction on the unethical side to speak ill of a colleague — well, he sometimes sits for a whole hour not speaking. Even in dictation classes or if he does condescend to speak, goes off into little stories about himself they can't make head or tail of.

There is a pause.

QUARTERMAINE. What, a Swede, did you say? What does he look like?

MEADLE. Oh, what does it matter? Everybody knows that for you one Swede is like another German, one Greek is like another Italian, you can't tell them apart and you don't know what they're called — unlike me, you see — because do you know what I do? I memorise their names before their first class, and then study their faces during it, and then when I go home I close my eyes and practise putting the two together so that by the second class I know every one of my students *personally*, and do you know what else I do, I keep a look-out not only in term-time but also in my holidays — my *unpaid* holidays — for any item that might interest them for British Life and Institutions and actually make a note of them — here — in my notebook, which I always keep especially in my pocket (*Wrestling with it with increasing violence, jerking it out of his pocket, tearing his pocket as he does so.*) along with any of the out-of-the-way idioms and interesting usages I might happen across — and do you know what *else* I do — I — but what does it matter what else I do, that's what I mean by joke or life or whatever it is, because I'm the one that's facing the push, and you're the one that's on Permanent. (*During this speech* MEADLE's *accent has become increasingly North Country.*) Not that I begrudge you — it's just that I reckon that I've earned it. Look — look, I don't mean — I don't mean — the last thing I mean is — (*He turns away, possibly in tears.*)

There is silence, into which MELANIE *enters, through the French windows.*

WINDSCAPE. Hello Melanie, my dear.

QUARTERMAINE. Hello Melanie, have a good half?

SACKLING. Melanie.

ANITA. Hello Melanie.

MELANIE goes to the table, puts down the briefcase, takes off her coat.

QUARTERMAINE. Um — um — how's your mother?

WINDSCAPE. Yes, how — how is she?

MELANIE. She's dead. She died last Tuesday.

There is silence.

WINDSCAPE. Oh Melanie — I'm so sorry — so sorry —

Murmurings from the others.

Was it another attack, my dear?

MELANIE. No, she fell down the stairs and broke her neck. We don't quite know how it happened as it was after I'd gone to bed. Nurse Grimes found her there in the morning, I still hadn't got up, the first I knew of it was Nurse Grimes calling me — and — and — that's really all there is to tell. I'd be grateful if we could dispense with condolences and that sort of thing, because what I really want most of all is to get on in the usual fashion, without any — any fuss.

The sound of the door opening. The sound of footsteps, rather odd, though.

LOOMIS. Hello everybody, hello, all rested up I trust, welcome back, welcome back — but first, is Melanie here?

MELANIE. Yes.

LOOMIS. Ah there you are, Melanie my dear (*Appearing on stage He has a stick, his glasses are tinted, and his voice and manner are frailer.*) there are a couple of policemen in the office with Thomas, who want a word with you. They refuse to say what about, but not to worry, not to worry, because I asked whether it was illness or accident, and they assured me it wasn't so your mother's perfectly all right, my dear, which is the main thing, isn't it, it's probably some nonsense to do with your car, anyway if you'd go along to the office and flirt with them — and whatever you do, don't let Thomas lose his temper. (*He laughs.*) Mmmm?

MELANIE. Right Eddie.

> MELANIE *stands for a moment, then braces herself, walks off, left as:*

LOOMIS. Really! Our Cambridge bobbies, they always have to make such a solemn meal out of the most trivial business — Anita, my dear, how blooming you look, how blooming — and how did Nigel find New York?

ANITA. Oh fine, thank you Eddie, fine —

LOOMIS. Good good good, well tell Nigel how much we're looking forward to the first Anglo-American edition, and how sorry we are we've had to cut back to just the one subscription but *semper fidelis*. Henry, what sort of half term did you · have — one of your adventurous caravan treks, where to this time?

WINDSCAPE. Yes Eddie — to Norfolk.

LOOMIS. Weather all right, I trust?

WINDSCAPE. Oh yes, Eddie, yes, lovely thank you, except when it rained and — and even then we had one — one amazing moment at sunrise —

LOOMIS. Good, good, especially for Fanny, little Fanny, Ben and Susan eh — and how did Susan get on with her 'O' levels, results as expected?

WINDSCAPE. Yes, Eddie, thanks, lots of 'threes' and 'fours' — and so forth.

LOOMIS. I'm not surprised, with you and Fanny behind her, give her our congratulations do, and Mark — if that is Mark I see behind a week's further fuzzy-wuzzy, lots of tap, tap, tapping?

SACKLING. Oh, well, as a matter of fact Eddie, as I was just telling —

LOOMIS. Well keep at it, we know that one day — ah, there's our Derek, but I've already said my welcomes to him, haven't I Derek, in the corridor — I gather you found Thomas?

MEADLE. Yes thank you, Eddie, yes yes.

LOOMIS. And that you got whatever it was you were so anxious to get sorted out, sorted out, at least Thomas seemed very pleased with the fruits of your deliberations.

MEADLE. Well — well yes, thank you, Eddie, all sorted out, yes.

LOOMIS. Good, good — and St. John — yes well — gather ye round — gather ye round. (*They all do so.*) I'd like to take the opportunity of saying to you, just between ourselves, and a little behind Thomas's back, so to speak, I expect you've all noticed the very distinct drop in student enrolment these last few months. This business of the Japanese suddenly deserting us has really hit us very hard — and what with all the recent renovation expenses — anyway — Thomas is slightly more worried than perhaps he's let any of you realise. We all know how dedicated he is to the future of the school — and to the future of the staff —

QUARTERMAINE. Hear, hear!

LOOMIS. — we've long thought of you as part of a family, I think you all know that we do our best to care for you in that spirit —

QUARTERMAINE. Absolutely!

LOOMIS. — and I'm sure you're all wondering what you can do to help us through this little rough patch — and the answer is, to go on giving of your very best to your teaching, and to show what students we've got that while we may not be as grand as some schools in Cambridge, we yield to no school in the country in the thing that matters most, our devotion to their devotion to their learning of our language. That's how —

QUARTERMAINE (*amid murmurs*). Hear, hear!

LOOMIS. That's how we can best serve our school at this time of slight crisis, and as I say, this strictly *entre nous,* without reference to Thomas — thank you everybody and bless you all — the bell will ring in a minute or so I believe, so — (*He gestures.*)

And as all except QUARTERMAINE *move to lockers, etc.*

QUARTERMAINE. Eddie that was — that was terrific!

LOOMIS. St. John a word of warning, I'm afraid there have been a number of complaints about your teaching — Thomas, I regret to say, received a round robin before half-term.

QUARTERMAINE. Oh Lord, that Swede, you mean?

LOOMIS. What Swede?

During this, the sound of door opening, footsteps.

Ah — Melanie, my dear, you've cleared it up, have you, what was it all about?

MELANIE. Oh yes, Eddie. All too preposterous. Apparently a group of French girls — from my intermediary Life and Institutions got hold of the wrong end of the stick. They didn't realise my recipe for roasting swan was for a medieval banquet, and actually tried to kill one on the Cam, can you believe it! Club one to death from a punt, with the intention of taking it back to their rooms and cooking and eating it! And then when they were reported to the police, blamed me. I'm glad to say that the swan, being a swan, survived. And gave one of them a badly bruised arm. Typically French.

Towards the end of this speech, MELANIE *begins to laugh. All remain still. The laugh — now almost hysterical — builds.* ANITA *half moves towards* MELANIE.

The bell rings.

Lights.

Scene Two

A Friday evening, some months later. The French windows are open. QUARTERMAINE *is asleep in an armchair, papers and books on his lap, in which he is visible to the audience, but not to anyone on stage who doesn't look specifically in it.*

QUARTERMAINE *suddenly groans.*

There is a pause.

QUARTERMAINE (*in sleep*). Oh Lord! (*Pause.*) I say! (*Pause, laughs. Sleeps.*)

The sound of the door opening. Footsteps.

MELANIE *enters from left. She goes to her locker, puts her books in.*

QUARTERMAINE, *not heard, or perhaps half heard, by* MELANIE, *lets out a groan.*

MELANIE *takes out of her locker an over-night bag.*

QUARTERMAINE (*lets out another groan*). Oh, Lord!

MELANIE (*starts, turns, sees* QUARTERMAINE). St. John! (*She goes towards him.*) Are you all right?

QUARTERMAINE (*blinks at her*). Oh — oh yes thanks — um — Melanie — next class, is it?

MELANIE. Heavens no, we've finished for the day. For the week, in fact.

QUARTERMAINE (*clearly confused*). Oh, I — I didn't hear the bell.

MELANIE. It hasn't gone yet. Don't worry, Eddie's having one of his very out-of-sorts days, poor lamb, and Thomas is in the office. We're safe.

QUARTERMAINE. Oh. Oh yes — I suppose I must have let them go early — always restless on a Friday, aren't they, and then sat down and — and —

MELANIE. St. John, what are you doing tonight?

QUARTERMAINE. Oh — usual — nothing very —

MELANIE. Then I'd like to introduce you to some very special friends of mine. Would you like that?

QUARTERMAINE. Well yes — yes — thank you, Melanie.

MELANIE. I'm sure you'll enjoy it — we always end up with singing and dancing, the food's delicious and the people are — well you'll see for yourself.

QUARTERMAINE. Well, it sounds — sounds terrific!

The sound of the door, footsteps.

MELANIE. Right, you wait for me here, and I'll come and collect you when I'm ready —

QUARTERMAINE. Right oh.

MELANIE. Oh hello Derek, you too — what a bunch of skyvers we're all turning out to be, eh?

MEADLE. Yes, well, it's only a few minutes off — besides Daphne's coming down for the weekend, I don't want to miss her train —

MELANIE (*exiting*). Jolly good — give her my love —

MEADLE. Right, Melanie, right — but I had a bloody near one in the corridor I can tell you. I was sloping past the office — terrible din coming from it, sounded like a gang of Germans, all bellowing away and Thomas trying to calm them down — anyway I'd just got past the door when Eddie came round the corner.

QUARTERMAINE. Phew!

MEADLE. Yes. I began to mumble some nonsense about wanting to check up on a student — but he didn't see me — went right on past — I mean, we were like that! (*Showing.*)

QUARTERMAINE. He didn't even see you, you say? Well, I hope he's all right —

MEADLE. Oh, by the way, Daphne and I have got an invitation for you — to celebrate our engagement. Now that I've got my Permanency, we've decided to make it official.

QUARTERMAINE. Oh congratulations!

MEADLE. We're getting married on the first day of the summer vac', and I'm going to ask Thomas and Eddie to be the best man. I mean, let them decide which — I don't want to upset one by choosing the other.

QUARTERMAINE. Oh terrific! And then off on your honeymoon, eh?

MEADLE. Yes. We've settled for Cleethorpes. Not very exciting, I know, but there may be a way to pick up a little money as well as have a good holiday ourselves. Daphne's keen to start saving for a house — you know how it is, there's a very practical head on those little shoulders of hers. There's a good

chance she might even come and do a bit of teaching here
— to replace me as the part-time, you see. I've already
dropped a little hint to Thomas — I think he was worried by
her speech impediment, but I pointed out that in some
respects that could be an asset.

QUARTERMAINE. Absolutely — and she'd be — a great asset
here, wouldn't she, in the staff room, I mean — she's a
wonderful girl, Derek.

MEADLE. Yes, well, I think you'll like her even more when you
meet her. Because frankly she's — she's — (*He shakes his head.*)
And I'll tell you something — I don't know whether you've
noticed but since she came back into my life I've stopped
having all those ridiculous accidents. They were the bane of
my life, even though I was always trying to make light of
them. I suppose it's — it's something to do with needing —
well, well, the right person, eh? Love. Let's face it. Love. Oh,
I'd better get going. So see you at seven for supper. It'll be
nothing special.

QUARTERMAINE. Derek, I'm very — I'm very honoured —

MEADLE. Actually, you'd better make it 6.30, as it'll be more
on the lines of a high tea. And if you could bring along a
couple of bottles of wine —

QUARTERMAINE. My dear chap, I'll bring — I'll bring *champagne*
— and — and — oh Lord, I'd forgotten! Oh no! I've already
accepted an invitation for this evening.

MEADLE. Oh. What to?

QUARTERMAINE. Well, I can't make out, quite — I was in a bit
of a haze when Melanie asked me, but she said something
about friends and singing and dancing —

MEADLE. And you accepted?

QUARTERMAINE. Well yes.

MEADLE. But it's — it's — one of those evenings. What they sing
is hymns and the dancing up and down and around and about
and then that Nurse Grimes declares for Jesus — and then the
rest of them follow suit, and then they all stand around and
wait for you to do it.

QUARTERMAINE. Oh Lord!

MEADLE. At least, that's how it went the night she got me along. She's trying to convert you.

QUARTERMAINE. Oh Lord!

The bell rings.

MEADLE. But I told you all about it —

QUARTERMAINE. Yes, but I'd forgotten — I mean she didn't mention Jesus —

MEADLE. Well, she won't let you get out of it now. (*During this, he has been getting ready to go, putting on bicycle clips, etc.*)

SACKLING *enters.*

Well, I'll get you and Daphne together very soon — don't worry — (*Making to go.*) Here, Mark, guess what St. John's got himself into — one of Melanie's evening.

SACKLING (*in a hurry, with books etc.*). Christ, you haven't, have you? (*He is clean-shaven, by the way.*) You *are* a chump, St. John, you must have heard her going on about Nurse Grimes and her dark night of the soul, after her mother died. Don't you take anything in!

QUARTERMAINE. Yes, yes I did, but —

SACKLING. But you didn't know how to say no. Which, if I may say so, is both your charm and your major weakness.

QUARTERMAINE. Well, you never know — it may be — may be quite interesting — one has to — has to have a go at anything really — and I wasn't doing anything else this evening.

SACKLING (*who is now ready to go*). This evening! Yes, you bloody *are* doing something else this evening. You're going out to dinner.

QUARTERMAINE. What — where?

SACKLING. At my place — oh Christ! Don't say I forgot to invite you. Well you're invited. So there you are, saved from salvation. All you have to do is to tell Melanie that you'd forgotten —

QUARTERMAINE. Oh, this is terrible. You mean I'd be having dinner with you.

SACKLING. You *are* having dinner with us. It's obligatory. For one thing, I told Camelia I'd asked you — she's counting on you — we all are — even Tom, I promised him he could stay up an extra half an hour especially to see you again.

QUARTERMAINE. But what about Melanie? I promised her —

SACKLING. Oh, to Hell with Melanie! It's all a load of pathetic nonsense — and probably blasphemous, too, if one believed in God. Look, speaking as one of your best and oldest and dearest, etc., — it's *crucial* that you come. Of the greatest importance. To me. You see. O.K.? Look, I've got to dash, I'm picking Tom up from school —

The sound of the door opening, sound of footsteps.

Make sure (*To off.*) that he turns up tonight, won't you? He's got himself into one of his usual messes — see you both at eight. (*Going out as:*)

ANITA *enters. She has a look of weariness about her, is subtly less well-turned out than in previous scenes.*

QUARTERMAINE. Oh don't say you and Nigel are going to be there too — oh dear.

ANITA. Why can't you come?

QUARTERMAINE. Well I fell into one of those dozes again — you know how they keep coming over me suddenly — for a minute or so — and — and when I came out of it, there I was, right in the middle of this — this Melanie business.

ANITA. Poor St. John.

QUARTERMAINE. Well, I can't just turn around to her now and say — 'Sorry Melanie, something much more amusing's turned up'. She was so — well — her eyes — I can't explain — oh, if only Mark hadn't forgotten! — but then I suppose he knows I'm usually free and thought — but what do I do, Anita, what do I do?

ANITA. Oh do come if you can. It's meant to be a reconciliation

dinner, and you know how they usually turn out. So you'd
be a great help, as the perfect outsider.

QUARTERMAINE. Well, you know I'd do anything — anything —
to make sure that old Mark and his Camelia stay together.

ANITA. Oh, it's not them that need reconciling. They already
are. It's Mark and Nigel.

QUARTERMAINE. Mark and Nigel — but they're such friends,
what happened?

ANITA. Oh, it was all a couple of months ago. They had the
most appalling row, because Nigel turned down an extract
from Mark's novel. About seven extracts, actually.

QUARTERMAINE. Oh no. Oh, poor Mark!

ANITA. Of course, Nigel made everything worse by deciding
to be completely honest for once. I suppose he thought Mark,
being an old friend, had it coming to him. He said that
everything Mark had sent him was imitative and laboured, and
anyway who really cared any more about the mysteries of
sex, the wonders of childbirth, the delicacies of personal
relationships — it had all been done and done and done to
death, there were far bigger issues. And then of course when
the magazine folded, and Nigel was going through his rough
patch, with the printers threatening to sue and various other
things, Mark wrote him a gloating letter — and added a P.S.
about the old Amanda Southgate affair, claiming to be
indignant on my account. I must say, I rather wish he'd
resisted that.

QUARTERMAINE. But still — but still — he has asked Nigel to
dinner —

ANITA. Oh, that was probably Camelia. She never took literature
seriously. I loathe the thought of it — for one thing we haven't
been able to find a baby-sitter, so we'll have to bring Ophelia
in her carry-cot — she's still got six weeks cholic, after
four months — so it would be nice if you came, St. John,
you'd make the whole thing more bearable.

QUARTERMAINE. Oh, I'd love to — and to see Ophelia — I've
only seen her the once, in hospital — what hair she had!

ANITA *laughs. In fact crying slightly.*

Oh Anita — what is it — oh, I hate to see you unhappy —
more than anyone else — (*He makes to make a move towards
her. Checks himself. Makes a move again.*) Oh Lord! (*He
stands before her, helplessly.*)

ANITA. I'm all right, St. John, honestly — it's just that — oh,
the way things go, I mean. Or don't go. Nothing seems to
come out right. All the years I adored him and he couldn't
bear me. And now he adores me and I can't bear him. You
see. (*She looks at him.*) What a — what a nice man you are.
(*She begins to cry again.*) I'm sorry — I'm tired, I expect, I'm
just tired — (*Turning away, blowing nose, wiping eyes, etc.,
as:*)

The sound of the door opening, footsteps.

QUARTERMAINE (*turning*). Oh — oh hello Henry, you've
finished late — um —

WINDSCAPE (*appearing rather heavily*). Yes, I got into a bit of
a tangle with my Intermediary British Life and Institutions,
over our parliamentary system. Usually it's perfectly clear to
me but this time it all came out rather oddly. Or it must
have done, as I had the whole lot of them dismissing it with
contempt — the three or four from the Eastern bloc, all the
ones from Fascist countries — the French were the loudest,
as always — but even the Japanese — normally such a polite,
reticent man — and I don't see quite how it happened or
what I said, but it was rather hard being lectured at on — on
political decencies — and shouted at by — by — still, I
suppose it's better they should all join up for a wrangle with
me than with each other — although to tell you the truth I
found it rather hard to keep my temper (*Sitting down.*) but
I think I managed to — with the result that I've got a — a
slight heachache. After all, I was only *explaining* our
constitution, not boasting about it. I've got my own — own
distinct reservations — no system's perfect, as I kept having
to say to Santos. His father's a Bolivian cabinet minister.

ANITA (*who has been discreetly composing herself during the
above*). It's awful when they get like that, isn't it? I always

make them explain our politics to me, and then just correct their English, whatever they say — one of the advantages of being female, I suppose — (*She attempts a little laugh*.) well, goodnight, Henry, see you Monday —

WINDSCAPE. 'Night, Anita, my dear. Best to Nigel, and little Ophelia —

ANITA. And St. John, see you later I hope. Do come if you can.

QUARTERMAINE. Yes, well — I'll — I'll — right, Anita. Right. If I can.

ANITA *goes out through the French windows.*

There is a pause. WINDSCAPE *is sitting in the chair, stroking his forehead.*

QUARTERMAINE (*is staring in a state of desperation*). I say, Henry — I say — I wonder if you could give me some advice.

WINDSCAPE. Mmmm?

QUARTERMAINE. I'm in a bit of a pickle, you see.

WINDSCAPE. Oh, St. John, is there any chance you could come over tonight?

QUARTERMAINE. What?

WINDSCAPE. I'm sorry it's such short notice, it wouldn't have been if I'd remembered. The thing is that Fanny's really very down in the dumps, very down, she really does need a — So do I, come to that. It's Susan, you see. She's taken a turn for the worse.

QUARTERMAINE. Oh, I am sorry.

WINDSCAPE. Oh, it's probably just withdrawal from all the tranquilising drugs they put her on in hospital, and then her friends will keep coming over in the evenings and talking about their plans and their blasted 'A' Levels and of course there's no possibility that Susan — at least for a few years — anyway. You see — last night — we heard her shrieking with laughter at something on television. A good sign, Fanny and I thought. The first time she's laughed since her breakdown.

So we went into the living-room and laughed with her — until we realised that what we were laughing at was a news flash to do with some particularly hideous atrocity in — in — (*He gestures.*) and what followed was a bit of a nightmare, especially for Ben and little Fanny — it ended with the doctor having to sedate her — almost forcibly, I'm afraid — so — so I noticed *La Regle du Jeu* was on at the Arts, one of our favourite films, so decent and — and humane — and then a quiet dinner afterwards at the French place — just the two of us — if you can manage it. You're the only person Susan will allow to baby-sit, you see. She seems to feel some — some reassurance from you. And of course little Fanny and Benjamin love it too, when you come.

QUARTERMAINE. I'd love to, Henry — love to — but could it be tomorrow?

WINDSCAPE. No, Saturday's no good — we have our family therapy session in the afternoon and we all feel so exhausted afterwards. Demoralised, really. I've still to be persuaded that they serve a — a useful — though of course one mustn't prejudge —

QUARTERMAINE. Sunday, then?

WINDSCAPE. Unfortunately Fanny's mother's coming on Sunday. Rather against our inclinations as — as she's rather insensitive with Susan — advises her to pull her socks up — that sort of thing — you can't manage this evening then.

QUARTERMAINE. Well — I — I — you see the problem is — Henry the problem is —

The sound of the door opening. Footsteps.
MELANIE appears. She has changed her dress, is wearing high-heeled shoes, some make-up, and has taken much trouble with her hair.

MELANIE. Well, there we are then, St. John — sorry to have been so long — oh, hello, Henry, I didn't know you were still here.

WINDSCAPE. Hello Melanie (*Slightly awkward.*) Oh, I've meant to say all day how much I like that dress.

MELANIE (*smiles*). Thank you. I'm taking St. John to one of my evenings —

WINDSCAPE. Oh. Oh I see. I'm so sorry that Fanny and I have been unable to come so far —

MELANIE. Oh, I know how difficult things are for you at the moment — as long as you both realise that any time you want to come along, I've been thinking that perhaps Susan might —

WINDSCAPE. Yes, yes, thank you, Melanie. (*Cutting her slightly.*)

MELANIE. Are you all right, you look a little fraught.

WINDSCAPE. Oh just tired, Friday eveningish, that's all.

QUARTERMAINE. And a bit of a headache — eh Henry?

MELANIE. Oh? Where?

WINDSCAPE. Well — in my head.

MELANIE. Yes, but which part?

WINDSCAPE. Well, it seems to be — just here — (*Rubbing his brow.*)

MELANIE. Ah, well then it's a tension headache, Nurse Grimes showed me a marvellous trick for dealing with that, let me have a go at it. (*She comes over to* WINDSCAPE, *behind the chair.*) Now put your head back — right back —

WINDSCAPE *does so, with perceptible lack of enthusiasm.*

MELANIE. There. Now. (*She proceeds to knead her fingers into the back of* WINDSCAPE's *neck.*)

QUARTERMAINE. So that's how they do it — looks jolly relaxing, Henry.

WINDSCAPE *endures for a few seconds, then suddenly lets out a cry, leaps up.*

WINDSCAPE. No!

There is a pause.

I'm — Melanie, I'm sorry — I — don't know quite what —

MELANIE. I expect I hurt you, pressed the wrong nerve or — I still haven't quite got the trick of it, with my clumsy —

WINDSCAPE. Well — well actually it feels a little better. (*He tries a laugh*.) Thank you.

MELANIE (*smiles*). Well, St. John, we'd better be on our way. It's quite a drive. Goodnight, Henry, and rest yourself during the weekend, won't you?

WINDSCAPE. Yes, yes — the same to you (*A slight hesitation*.) my dear. Goodnight, St. John, see you Monday.

QUARTERMAINE. See you Monday Henry and — oh, if it turns out that Saturday or Sunday — well, I'm sure I'll be free —

WINDSCAPE *smiles, nods*.

MELANIE. Off we go, St. John.

QUARTERMAINE. Right.

As they go out through the French windows there is the sound of the door opening and feet, a stick.

WINDSCAPE. Oh hello Eddie, I didn't know you were about today.

LOOMIS (*enters. He is much frailer than when last seen*). Well, there was a frightful schmozzle in the office — and Thomas asked me to come down — but was that St. John's voice I heard just now?

WINDSCAPE. Yes. His and Melanie's —

LOOMIS. Ah. Well, I would have quite liked a word with our St. John. He's caused us quite an afternoon. He appears to have missed his last class entirely. His students waited doggedly through the whole hour for him to turn up, and then went to the office and berated poor Thomas — they were mostly Germans, and you know what they're like if they think they're not getting their money's worth of syllabus.

WINDSCAPE. Oh dear.

LOOMIS. Though I doubt whether they'd get much more

sensible English from St. John present than from St. John
absent — as far as I know that Swiss Ferdinand Müller was
the only student who ever felt he got value for money from
St. John, thank goodness he's stopped sending those
postcards at last, they made Thomas quite upset — but I
wonder what it was he enjoyed so much about St. John's
classes — perhaps the lack of — of — I don't know what
we're going to do about him in the end, though, if we turned
him out where would he go, who else would have him, one
does look after one's own, I suppose, when it comes to it. I
agree with Thomas on that, after all the school's our — our
family, the only family Thomas and I have between us, so
one has a responsibility for them — but a responsibility for
the students too —

*There should be a slightly rambling quality in the delivery of
this speech.*

it's so difficult to get the balance right — so difficult —
St. John's forgetting to teach them, and now Melanie's
starting up her missionary work amongst them — Thomas is
going to have a word with her too — the Catholic countries
won't stand for it, and why should they, and now our
Meadle, taking to slipping away before the bell now he's got
his Permanency, trying to bluff his way past me in the hall
as if I couldn't see him — ha — well, at least Mark's pulling
his weight now he's got his Camelia back, I never thought for
a moment there was a writer in that lad, did you? — and
Anita — really I don't know how these modern young
couples cope — but I gather Nigel's taken to fatherhood quite
wonderfully, Thomas and I saw the three of them on the
Backs the other day, a very pretty sight it was too — so — so
— good, good, — just the problems of a flourishing school,
eh? (*He laughs.*)

WINDSCAPE. Yes. Yes indeed, Eddie.

LOOMIS. Well, I'd best get back up to bed, or Thomas will have
a fit, goodnight Henry, see you Monday, bless you, bless you.

WINDSCAPE. Yes, see you Monday Eddie.

LOOMIS (*goes off, stops*). Oh, I haven't asked for a while — how's
our Susan?

WINDSCAPE. oh, responding I think — slowly — slowly responding.

LOOMIS. Good, good. (*The sound of the door closing.*)

During this, the sound of students' voices, young, distant, in the garden. They get closer as the scene concludes.

WINDSCAPE *stands for a moment, touches his forehead.*

Students' voices, probably two girls, two boys, now laughing, calling out to each other in some sort of game.

WINDSCAPE *gets out bicycle clips, bends to put them on, as he does so looks towards the French windows. He smiles slightly, continues putting on the clips, as sounds of voices, still raised in laughter.*

Lights.

Scene Three

Eighteen months later. It is around Christmas. Not yet dark, but darkening slightly. The French windows are closed, but the curtains are opened. There is an atmosphere of chill. One table-light is on.
      SACKLING, QUARTERMAINE, MELANIE, ANITA, WINDSCAPE, MEADLE *are variously sitting and standing.*
      SACKLING *is smoking a pipe, has a beard.*
      WINDSCAPE *is also smoking a pipe.*
      ANITA *is pregnant.*
      MEADLE *has a plaster neck-brace.*
      QUARTERMAINE *is in a dinner-jacket.*
      MELANIE *is sitting, rather hunched, nervously smoking a cigarette. It is the first time in the play that she smokes, of course. She smokes throughout the scene, lighting one after another.*
      After a pause.

SACKLING. It's always at Christmas, somehow, isn't it?

WINDSCAPE. Yes.

SACKLING. Oh Henry, I'm sorry —

WINDSCAPE. No, you're right. I was thinking much the same thing. Both my parents too, but — but of course in Susan's case I don't think the season was — was relevant. At least to her. The blinds were always down, you see. Because any brightness hurt her mind. Natural brightness, that is. She could tolerate artificial light. Until the last — last bit.

ANITA (*there is a faint touch of querulousness in her voice*). Look, I'm sorry, but I'll have to go soon, I'm afraid. I promised the *au pair* she could have the night off, and Nigel's probably not coming back from London until tomorrow —

MEADLE. Yes, I've got to get back pretty soon. Daphne's not too grand, what with her morning sickness and all the redecorating — she's been over-doing it and I promised — I don't want to leave her alone too long.

WINDSCAPE. Of course — of course — there's really no need for all of us when it comes to it — it's just that — that — as soon as I heard I had some idea that you would want — well — without perhaps enough consideration — it was a bad idea, perhaps —

QUARTERMAINE. Oh, I say Henry — well, I'm jolly glad you got in touch with me — though of course I wasn't doing anything in particular —

SACKLING. Well, I must say it St. John, (*Smiling.*) you do look as if you might have been about to be up to something —

QUARTERMAINE. What? Oh — (*He laughs.*) well, no, no, not really — it was just — just —

During this, the sound of the door opening.

They all look towards it, as footsteps, dragging feet, a stick.

LOOMIS (*in an over-coat, with his stick, and with a deaf-aid attached to his glasses*). I saw the lights on so I guessed that some of you — one or two perhaps — had come. But I didn't expect all of you. Not at this time of year, with your families and responsibilities. Thomas would have been so touched. So touched. My thanks on his behalf. My thanks. (*Little pause.*) He died an hour ago. They did everything they could, right to the end, but of course, as we've all known for some time, there was nothing to be done. (*Little pause.*) You know how much you all meant to him. He talked of every one of you, every evening, until — (*He gestures.*) But you'll also want to know what its future is to be, this school's that he loved so much. I know what his wishes are, we discussed them quite openly once we both knew that he was bound to leave us. I've also talked to Henry. I'm sure it will be no surprise to all of you that I asked Henry some time ago to take over the school as its sole Principal. I've no desire to take an active part in it, now that Thomas is no longer here. I loved it for his sake, you see. I'll make no secret of that. Not this evening. (*Pause, he nearly breaks down, pulls himself together.*) Not this evening. I shall be leaving the flat as soon as possible — it has too many memories — and settle somewhere by the sea. As we'd always planned to do. I hope that some of you will come and see me — (*Little pause.*) Bless you. Bless you. (*He turns. Goes. The sound of his feet dragging slowly. The sound of the door shutting.*)

There is a pause.

WINDSCAPE. I — I really don't want to speak at such a moment about plans or changes. We'll have a meeting at the beginning of term to go into those, but I should just say that I've already talked to Mark about his following me as the academic tutor. I am happy to say that he has accepted.

There are murmurs.

So until next term — which has a very reasonable enrolement, I am glad to report, let me merely assure you that I intend to do my best, as I know you will, to maintain our reputation as a flourishing school. I know — I know — Thomas and Eddie wouldn't want me to let you part without wishing you all a Happy Christmas.

Murmurs of 'Happy Christmas'.

Well, see you all next term!

They rise to go, putting on coats, etc.

QUARTERMAINE. Henry — I say, well you and Mark — that's quite a team, you know.

WINDSCAPE. Thank you, St. John.

SACKLING (*coated*). Well, night Henry — we'll speak. And St. John — over the Christmas, eh? You must come round. (*Gesturing with his pipe.*)

QUARTERMAINE. Oh, I'd love that — thanks Mark. See you then. Love to Camelia and Tom and little Mark too.

ANITA. Sorry if I was a little edgy earlier Henry, (*Also coated.*) put it down to my current condition and Yugoslav *au pairs*! (*She laughs.*)

WINDSCAPE. You get home to your Ophelia, my dear, and make Nigel look after you.

ANITA. Oh, I will, Henry — see you over Christmas, St. John, I hope.

QUARTERMAINE. Oh Lord yes — lovely — lovely — 'night, Anita and love to little Ophelia and Nigel too.

MEADLE (*coated*). Sorry Daphne couldn't make it, Henry. She wanted to, of course. But I'll fill her in, don't worry, she's very much looking forward to her courses next term —

WINDSCAPE. And I'm looking forward to having her join us. Goodnight, Derek.

MEADLE. Drop around when you feel in the mood, St. John. Lots of paint-brushes for you to wield — (*He laughs.*)

QUARTERMAINE. Terrific! I love the smell of paint — love to Daphne —

MELANIE (*comes up, hunched, smoking*). 'Night Henry. 'Night.

WINDSCAPE. Night Melanie my dear. And perhaps we can all get together after Christmas — Fanny was saying how much she'd like to see you, after all this time.

MELANIE. Love to, love to, and St. John, if you're free pop around and have a drink. (*She laughs.*)

QUARTERMAINE. Oh yes please Melanie — I'd like that.

WINDSCAPE. Well St. John where were you off to tonight by the way?

QUARTERMAINE. Oh Lord, nowhere Henry. (*He laughs.*) You

see, there was a suitcase I still hadn't unpacked — it's been down in Mrs Harris' cellar all these years. But suddenly she wanted the space, so she made me take it upstairs, and of course I opened it and there was this. (*Indicating the dinner-jacket.*) So I decided to try it on, to see if it still fits. And then you 'phoned, so — so I came straight over here, forgetting I had it on. Stinks of moth-balls, I'm afraid, but not a bad fit, eh? Might come in useful sometime. But I say, poor old Eddie, poor old Eddie. Wasn't he — wasn't he terrific!

WINDSCAPE. Yes. Indeed. (*A slight pause.*) St. John. St. John. I've been worrying about this for — oh, ever since I realised I was to take over from Eddie and Thomas. If I'm to be Principal, I have to run the school in my own way, you see.

QUARTERMAINE. Oh, I know that, Henry. We all do.

WINDSCAPE. And — and — I don't see, you see — however fond of you I happen to be — we all happen to be — that there's any room for you any more. You see?

A pause.

I thought it only right to tell you at the first — the very first possible moment. So that you can — well, look around —

QUARTERMAINE. No, that's — right, thank you Henry. I — oh Lord, I know that I haven't got much to offer — never had, I suppose — and recently it's got even worse — it's a wonder — a wonder people have put up with me so long, eh? (*He attempts a laugh.*)

WINDSCAPE. If I could see any way —

QUARTERMAINE. No, no — I mean it's no good being all right in the staff room if you're no good in the classroom, is it? They're different things.

WINDSCAPE. I can't tell you how much I'll miss you. We all will.

QUARTERMAINE. And I — I'll miss it. All of you.

WINDSCAPE. Yes, I know. Would you like a quick drink — or — or — come back and see Fanny.

QUARTERMAINE. Oh, no — no thank you Henry, I'll stay here

for a while — if I may — you know — and get myself used to — and — I'll go in a minute.

WINDSCAPE (*hesitates, looks at* QUARTERMAINE). Well, goodnight, St. John.

QUARTERMAINE. Goodnight, Henry, see you next — (*He gestures.*)

WINDSCAPE *goes off. The sound of feet, door opening and closing.*

Oh Lord!

Well — I say —

Oh Lord!

Lights.

Curtain.

Caryl Churchill

'Something's changing. Suddenly women are writing plays in great numbers,' Benedict Nightingale reported in a 1982 issue of *New Statesman*. Naming more than a dozen women playwrights, Nightingale saluted Caryl Churchill as the most talented of all for her 'genuine audacity and wit' and her riveting dramatic style. She is the most often produced British woman playwright on both sides of the Atlantic. At one point in 1983 three of Churchill's plays were running simultaneously in New York: *Cloud Nine*, *Top Girls*, and *Fen*. *Fen*, nominated by the Arena Stage in Washington, won the 1984 Susan Blackburn Prize, an international award for the best new play by a woman.

Churchill's plays are feminist in sensibility without being simplistically anti-men; they all link sexual repression with the authoritarian oppressiveness of the capitalist system. They all shatter stage conventions and gender stereotypes and they confound the conventional wisdom by proving that social and political issues can be seriously addressed in the theatre without polemic or harangue. In Churchill's plays such issues are lightened by an antic sense of humour expressed not only in funny lines, but in playful and eccentric dramaturgy. Churchill mixes genders and reverses chronology.

The title of an article by Judith Thurman in a recent issue of *Ms*. catches the playwright's style and the range of her themes: 'Caryl Churchill: The Playwright Who Makes You Laugh about Orgasm, Racism, Class Struggle, Homophobia, Woman-Hating, the British Empire, and the Irrepressible Strangeness of the Human Heart.' According to Thurman, what Churchill wants to do is 'redistribute the usual things – the wealth and power – but also the emotional responsibility.'

Born in 1938 the daughter of a political cartoonist father and an actress/model mother, Churchill spent the war years in London. From 1949 to 1956 she lived in Montreal. On her return to London, she began to feel abhorrence for the English class system. Enrolled at Oxford, where she studied English, her antipathy for capitalism grew and she developed a 'wobbly attraction' to

Marxism. In her vision of a non-authoritarian, non-sexist society, she joins a growing band of British playwrights who insist more and more explicitly in their plays on the connection between politics and the quality of daily life, between 'people's internal state of being and the external political structures which affect them, which make them insane,' as Churchill herself explained.

Like many of her contemporaries, Churchill insists on consonance between the politics she espouses in her plays and what she does about them in her life. In *Stages in the Revolution* Itzin cites the example of Churchill's challenge in 1978 to BBC censorship of her television play *The Legion Hall Bombing*, based on the trial of a convicted North Ireland terrorist. The BBC 'toned down' the political stance of her prologue and omitted the epilogue, which included objections to the court's accepting uncorroborated statements from the police as evidence against the accused in the trial. When her challenge failed, Churchill withdrew her name from the credits.

Like Virginia Woolf, Churchill sees her life as a writer inseparable from her life as a woman. 'What politicized me,' she explains, 'was being discontent with my own way of life – of being a barrister's wife and just being at home with small children.' The mother of three sons, she came to feel that 'women's true liberation on the domestic front must involve the education of men to share fully in the raising of children even at the expense of their own careers.' Her barrister husband, himself an activist who left his law practice to work for a legal aid group, took a six months leave from his job to allow his wife more time for her work.

Churchill had already written a series of radio plays using middle-class life as a way of getting at the problems of war, ecology, and the self-destructiveness of the capitalist system before she turned to writing for the stage. In *Owners*, her first major stage play, the central character is a female property speculator with an insatiable acquisitiveness. She is the archetypal feminist rebel: 'Every one of you thinks I'll give in. Because I'm a woman, is it? I'm meant to be kind. I won't. I can be as terrible as any one else . . . I can massacre too.' Her husband is the typical chauvinist: 'She's legally mine.'

Owners was first staged in the Theatre Upstairs at the Royal Court, where Churchill became the theatre's first resident woman playwright. Since 1972 six of Churchill's plays have been staged at the Court and one – *Cloud Nine* – has been revived there.

A new phase of Churchill's writing career began when she encountered the theatre collective, Joint Stock Theatre Group. Before the actual writing of *Light Shining in Buckinghamshire*, a play about sexual and political oppression in 17th-century England, she took part in a workshop with the actors exploring the subject matter. 'It is hard to explain exactly the relationship between the workshop and the text', she writes in a note on the play. 'The play is not improvised: it is a written text and the actors did not make up its lines. But many of the characters and scenes were based on ideas that came from improvisation at the workshop and during rehearsal'. *Cloud Nine*, her second play for the group, and the one that made her internationally famous, was born of the same process. The cast was hired, according to their sexual preferences as well as their professional experience, before the play was even written. Churchill spent weeks with them in group readings of appropriate texts and conscious-raising exercises to explore conventional assumptions about sexual identity. Through their role-playing, they discovered that assigned gender roles outweigh real-life gender. The play that emerged was a devastating attack on sexual stereotypes, hilariously high-lighted by cross-casting, men playing women's roles, women men's. The zany first act with its daft characters behaving with wild improbability as their improper sexual urges burst the seams of their Victorian propriety is vintage Churchill.

In Act One, a typical English family – authoritarian father, submissive wife, their two well-bred children – copes genteelly with the white man's burden in darkest Africa in 1880. They are, it quickly turns out, not what they seem. They sip their ritual tea on languorous afternoons and picnic stiffly on the veldt in their rustling petticoats and starched collars, familiar images of British colonial life. Minutes later they are scrambling lecherously in the bushes in a variety of unseemly couplings. The daring theatrical coup of mixing the genders undermines all certainty about them. The wife is played by a man, the son by a woman, the native servant by a white man, who then plays a small girl in Act Two, set a hundred years later in a London park. In Act Two, moreover, the characters have aged only twenty-five years between acts and, despite the sexual liberation of the new times, they are still scrambling outside the conventions for their sexual pleasure. Without the restraints of proprieties, their lives seem somehow bleaker. Lesbian and homosexual preferences seem like promising alternatives, yet they are no more fulfilling than straight ways. Perhaps less so. Everything is permissible, so nothing seems interesting. Nothing is at stake. There are no more rituals to add texture to life, no hunting, no picnicking, no natives to add colour. The Betty of Act One, played by a man, and the Betty of Act Two, played by a woman, embrace as if to signal some new partnership for the next stage in the muddled human march.

What Virginia Woolf wrote of her own work describes Churchill's feminism: 'A woman's writing is always feminine; it cannot help being feminine . . .' Churchill's plays imply the wry qualification Woolf added: 'The only difficulty lies in defining what we mean by being feminine.' In *Cloud Nine* Churchill experiments with circumstances that expose the indefiniteness of sexual boundaries, the uncertainties about whether social conditioning or biology determines sexual roles.

The semi-documentary *Fen*, transferred from London to Joseph Papp's Public Theatre as part of Britain's 1983 *Salute to New York*, is a far bleaker play than *Cloud Nine*. Based on a study of women living in isolated communities, the play developed out of a group experiment in communal living. Members of Joint Stock lived and worked among farm women in the gloomy mists and dank marshes of the East Anglian potato fields. The actors asked questions, listened to stories and dreams, absorbed attitudes and actions, and reported back to Churchill, who recorded what they said in a big black book, the source for the finished play, which she went off to compose alone.

At the centre of the play, which has a more coherent plot than is usual in Churchill's work, is the doomed, illicit love affair of Frank and Val, trapped in helpless misery, resourceless, aching with frustrated yearnings. Val convinces Frank to kill her when she can no longer bear being torn between her children and her lover. Their emotional misery is deepened by the appalling poverty of their circumscribed lives. That interpenetration of economic deprivation and the most poignant personal dilemmas is manifested with utter simplicity. The result is a moving theatre piece, built on a series of haunting vignettes, stark in themselves, yet implying human lives that are complex, lives to which attention should be paid. While women are explored more fully than men in the play, Churchill's compassion extends to men who are equally victimized by the dreary landscape, the unyielding land, religious superstition, and the greed of landowners and business conglomerates.

Top Girls focuses on the women who get what the feminists say they want: liberation from domesticity and child-bearing, the chance for success in the male enclave, the world of work. Like *Cloud Nine* the play bends rules of time and sexual role. In a dazzling first scene, Marlene, recently promoted managing director of the Top Girls Employment Agency, throws a party to celebrate. She has invited a witty quintet of historical and fictional women achievers: Pope Joan, thought to have been a woman disguised as a man who actually bore a child during her brief tenure as pope in the ninth century; Chaucer's patient Griselda; Lady Nijo, a medieval courtesan-turned nun; Isabella Bird, a Victorian world-traveller; and Dull Gret, who leads a female charge through hell in a Breughel painting. They chatter on about their lives, their dialogue overlapping, their words often indecipherable since they rarely listen to each other. Marlene toasts them, 'Well, we've all come a long way. To our courage and the way we changed our lives and our extraordinary achievements.' The trouble is their stories tell more of personal sacrifice and suffering than success.

Act Two describes Marlene's rise to power. The anachronistic ladies of Act One are transformed into interviewers and interviewees in Marlene's Top Girl agency. As staff, they counsel female clients to be tough, ruthless, and competitively aggressive like the men whose success they want to emulate. Marlene herself is rude to her inferiors and contemptuous of women beneath her who haven't made it by male success standards. They could make it if they wanted to. She has abandoned her own illegitimate daughter to be reared by her unliberated sister, Joyce. She treats both of them coldly. Yet in the final scene, on a visit she makes to her sister and child, Marlene weeps. And Joyce, shushing her, says matter-of-factly, 'Everyone's always crying in this house. Nobody takes any notice.' The barriers between them drop for a moment as they trade confidences about their lives, especially their relations with men. Joyce's unfaithful husband doesn't support her; Marlene's suitors 'like to be seen with a high-flying lady. Shows them they've got something really good in their pants. But they can't take the day to day. They're waiting for me to turn into the little woman.' She adds, with some pathos, 'Or maybe I'm just horrible of course.' As in the first scene the dialogue begins to overlap, each sister intent on making her own case. Marlene admires Thatcher, whom Joyce calls Hitlerina. She hates the working class, the way they talk, their 'beer guts and football vomit and saucy tits.' Joyce spits when she sees a Rolls-Royce and hates the cows she works for 'and their dirty dishes with blanquette of fucking veau.' Suddenly, the inspiriting humour of the play's opening tour de force seems anachronistic. Suddenly the bright gabbiness of those ladies from history and legend, and Marlene's stylish success seem insubstantial cover for desperately sad lives. All the women in the play are trapped and forlorn. The ones who stay on the farm are made callous by their emotional and economic deprivations. The city ladies fare no better, given the price – childlessness and loneliness – that success exacts.

In sum, Churchill's work, infused as it is with a feminist sensibility, does not celeberate feminism. Women, like men, are silly, weak, foolish, cruel, arrogant. They are complicit as well as victimized. Like men, they are conditioned more by their social roles than by their biology.

Churchill's plays are arresting for their inventive theatricality and the profound human questions they raise without sacrifice of wit or compassion. They offer a good night in the theatre and send audiences home to rethink fundamental human issues they thought they'd decided about. Some critics complain that Churchill's juggling of chronology results in plays that seem to break into two unintegrated parts, the historical fantasy of *Top Girls'* first act, followed by the contemporary realism of the second act, for example. Such a division certainly frustrates conventional expectations. The plot of *Top Girls* does not really begin until Act One, Scene Two, when Marlene begins to deal with the problems of her everyday world. But the earlier scene prepares audiences to see Marlene as a comrade-in-arms of the top girls who battled the confines of traditional roles before she did. If Marlene abandons her child to rise in a man's world, she is no more extreme than Pope Joan, who abandoned her sexual identity to rise. If Marlene decides she must travel alone, she is no more perverse than Isabella Bird, who preferred solitude in a rat-infested ship's cabin to a shared berth on land.

Scene One, then, is not a mere curtain-raiser, but a consciousness-raiser that prepares audiences to judge Marlene in the context of a centuries-old system of gender politics. That rootedness in political and social history enriches the play's dramatic texture significantly.

Major Plays

Owners, Royal Court Theatre Upstairs, 1972.

Objections to Sex and Violence, Royal Court Theatre, 1975.

Light Shining in Buckinghamshire, Traverse Theatre, Edinburgh, 1976; then on tour including Royal Court Theatre.

Traps, Royal Court Theatre Upstairs, 1977.

Cloud Nine, Royal Court Theatre, 1979.

Top Girls, Royal Court Theatre, 1982.

Fen, Joint Stock Theatre Group at University of Essex, 1983; then Almeida Theatre.

Softcops, Royal Shakespeare Company at the Barbican Pit, 1984.

Selected Bibliography

Nightingale, Benedict. 'Top Girls,' *New Statesman*, 10 September 1982, p. 27.

Thurman, Judith, 'Caryl Churchill: The Playwright Who Makes You Laugh About Orgasm, Racism, Class Struggle, Homophobia, Woman-Hating, the British Empire, and the Irrepressible Strangeness of the Human Heart,' *Ms*. May 1972, pp. 51–54, 57.

Weintraub, Erica Beth. 'Caryl Churchill,' *Dictionary of Literary Biography*, Vol. 13, Part I, *British Dramatists Since World War II*, ed. Stanley Weintraub. Detroit: Gale Research Co., 1982, pp. 118-124.

CARYL CHURCHILL

Top Girls

The author gratefully acknowledges use of the following books:

The Confessions of Lady Nijo, translated from the Japanese by Karen Brazell, and published by Peter Owen Ltd, London
A Curious Life for a Lady. (about Isabella Bird) by Pat Barr, originally published by Macmillan, London

Top Girls was first performed at the Royal Court Theatre, London on 28 August 1982 with the following cast:

MARLENE	Gwen Taylor
ISABELLA BIRD JOYCE MRS KIDD	Deborah Findlay
LADY NIJO WIN	Lindsay Duncan
DULL GRET ANGIE	Carole Hayman
POPE JOAN LOUISE	Selina Cadell
PATIENT GRISELDA NELL JEANINE	Lesley Manville
WAITRESS KIT SHONA	Lou Wakefield

Directed by Max Stafford Clark
Designed by Peter Hartwell

This production transferred to Joe Papp's Public Theatre, New York, later the same year, and returned to the Royal Court early in 1983.

ACT ONE

Scene One: Restaurant. Saturday night.
Scene Two: 'Top Girls' Employment agency. Monday morning.
Scene Three: Joyce's back yard. Sunday afternoon.

ACT TWO

Scene One: Employment agency. Monday morning.
Scene Two: Joyce's kitchen. Sunday evening, a year earlier.

Note on characters

ISABELLA BIRD (1831-1904) lived in Edinburgh, travelled extensively between the ages of 40 and 70.

LADY NIJO (b.1258) Japanese, was an Emperor's courtesan and later a Buddhist nun who travelled on foot through Japan.

DULL GRET is the subject of the Brueghel painting, Dulle Griet, in which a woman in an apron and armour leads a crowd of women charging through hell and fighting the devils.

POPE JOAN, disguised as a man, is thought to have been Pope between 854-856.

PATIENT GRISELDA is the obedient wife whose story is told by Chaucer in The Clerk's Tale of *The Canterbury Tales*.

Note on layout

A speech usually follows the one immediately before it BUT:
1: when one character starts speaking before the other has finished, the point of interruption is marked / .

eg. ISABELLA:	This is the Emperor of Japan? / I once met the Emperor of Morocco.
NIJO:	In fact he was the ex-Emperor.

2: a character sometimes continues speaking right through another's speech:

eg. ISABELLA:	When I was forty I thought my life was over. / Oh I was pitiful. I was
NIJO:	I didn't say I felt it for twenty years. Not every minute.
ISABELLA:	sent on a cruise for my health and I felt even worse. Pains in my bones, pins and needles ... etc.

3: sometimes a speech follows on from a speech earlier than the one immediately before it, and continuity is marked*.

eg. GRISELDA:	I'd seen him riding by, we all had. And he'd seen me in the fields with the sheep*.
ISABELLA:	I would have been well suited to minding sheep.
NIJO:	And Mr Nugent riding by.
ISABELLA:	Of course not, Nijo, I mean a healthy life in the open air.
JOAN:	*He just rode up while you were minding the sheep and asked you to marry him?

where 'in the fields with the sheep' is the cue to both 'I would have been' and 'He just rode up'.

ACT ONE

Scene One

Restaurant. Table set for dinner with white tablecloth. Six places.
   MARLENE *and* WAITRESS.

MARLENE. Excellent, yes, table for six. One of them's going to
   be late but we won't wait. I'd like a bottle of Frascati straight
   away if you've got one really cold.

The WAITRESS *goes.*

ISABELLA BIRD *arrives.*

Here we are. Isabella.

ISABELLA. Congratulations, my dear.

MARLENE. Well, it's a step. It makes for a party. I haven't time
   for a holiday. I'd like to go somewhere exotic like you but I
   can't get away. I don't know how you could bear to leave
   Hawaii. / I'd like to lie in the sun forever, except of course I

ISABELLA. I did think of settling.

MARLENE. can't bear sitting still.

ISABELLA. I sent for my sister Hennie to come and join me. I
   said, Hennie we'll live here forever and help the natives. You
   can buy two sirloins of beef for what a pound of chops costs
   in Edinburgh. And Hennie wrote back, the dear, that yes, she
   would come to Hawaii if I wished, but I said she had far better
   stay where she was. Hennie was suited to life in Tobermory.

MARLENE. Poor Hennie.

ISABELLA. Do you have a sister?

MARLENE. Yes in fact.

ISABELLA. Hennie was happy. She was good. I did miss its face, my own pet. But I couldn't stay in Scotland. I loathed the constant murk.

MARLENE. Ah! Nijo!

She sees LADY NIJO *arrive.*

The WAITRESS *enters with wine.*

NIJO. Marlene!

MARLENE. I think a drink while we wait for the others. I think a drink anyway. What a week.

The WAITRESS *pours wine.*

NIJO. It was always the men who used to get so drunk. I'd be one of the maidens, passing the sake.

ISABELLA. I've had sake. Small hot drink. Quite fortifying after a day in the wet.

NIJO. One night my father proposed three rounds of three cups, which was normal, and then the Emperor should have said three rounds of three cups, but he said three rounds of nine cups, so you can imagine. Then the Emperor passed his sake cup to my father and said, 'Let the wild goose come to me this spring.'

MARLENE. Let the what?

NIJO. It's a literary allusion to a tenth-century epic, / His Majesty was very cultured.

ISABELLA: This is the Emperor of Japan? / I once met the Emperor of Morocco.

NIJO. In fact he was the ex-Emperor.

MARLENE. But he wasn't old? / Did you, Isabella?

NIJO. Twenty-nine.

ISABELLA. Oh it's a long story.

MARLENE. Twenty-nine's an excellent age.

NIJO. Well I was only fourteen and I knew he meant something but I didn't know what. He sent me an eight-layered gown and I sent it back. So when the time came I did nothing but cry. My thin gowns were badly ripped. But even that morning when he left / — he'd a green robe with a scarlet lining and

MARLENE. Are you saying he raped you?

NIJO. very heavily embroidered trousers, I already felt different about him. It made me uneasy. No, of course not, Marlene, I belonged to him, it was what I was brought up for from a baby. I soon found I was sad if he stayed away. It was depressing day after day not knowing when he would come. I never enjoyed taking other women to him.

ISABELLA. I certainly never saw my father drunk. He was a clergyman. / And I didn't get married till I was fifty.

The WAITRESS *brings menus.*

NIJO. Oh, my father was a very religious man. Just before he died he said to me, 'Serve His Majesty, be respectful, if you lose his favour enter holy orders.'

MARLENE. But he meant stay in a convent, not go wandering round the country.

NIJO. Priests were often vagrants, so why not a nun? You think I shouldn't? /I still did what my father wanted.

MARLENE. No no, I think you should. / I think it was wonderful.

DULL GRET *arrives.*

ISABELLA. I tried to do what my father wanted.

MARLENE. Gret, good. Nijo. Gret. / I know Griselda's going to be late, but should we wait for Joan? / Let's get you a drink.

ISABELLA. Hello Gret! (*Continues to* NIJO:) I tried to be a clergyman's daughter. Needlework, music, charitable schemes. I had a tumour removed from my spine and spent a great deal of time on the sofa. I studied the metaphysical poets and hymnology. / I thought I enjoyed intellectual pursuits.

NIJO. Ah, you like poetry. I come of a line of eight generations of poets. Father had a poem / in the anthology.

ISABELLA. My father taught me Latin although I was a girl. / But

MARLENE. They didn't have Latin at my school.

ISABELLA. really I was more suited to manual work. Cooking, washing, mending, riding horses. / Better than reading books,

NIJO. Oh but I'm sure you're very clever.

ISABELLA. eh Gret? A rough life in the open air.

NIJO. I can't say I enjoyed my rough life. What I enjoyed most was being the Emperor's favourite / and wearing thin silk.

ISABELLA: Did you have any horses, Gret?

GRET. Pig.

POPE JOAN *arrives.*

MARLENE. Oh Joan, thank God, we can order. Do you know everyone? We were just talking about learning Latin and being clever girls. Joan was by way of an infant prodigy. Of course you were. What excited you when you were ten?

JOAN. Because angels are without matter they are not individuals. Every angel is a species.

MARLENE. There you are.

They laugh. They look at menus.

ISABELLA. Yes, I forgot all my Latin. But my father was the mainspring of my life and when he died I was so grieved. I'll have the chicken, please, / and the soup.

NIJO. Of course you were grieved. My father was saying his prayers and he dozed off in the sun. So I touched his knee to rouse him. 'I wonder what will happen,' he said, and then he was dead before he finished the sentence. / If he'd died saying

MARLENE. What a shock.

NIJO. his prayers he would have gone straight to heaven. / Waldorf salad.

JOAN. Death is the return of all creatures to God.

NIJO. I shouldn't have woken him.

JOAN. Damnation only means ignorance of the truth. I was always attracted by the teachings of John the Scot, though he was inclined to confuse / God and the world.

ISABELLA. Grief always overwhelmed me at the time.

MARLENE. What I fancy is a rare steak. Gret?

ISABELLA. I am of course a member of the / Church of England.*

GRET. Potatoes.

MARLENE. *I haven't been to church for years. / I like Christmas carols.

ISABELLA. Good works matter more than church attendance.

MARLENE. Make that two steaks and a lot of potatoes. Rare. But I don't do good works either.

JOAN. Canelloni, please, / and a salad.

ISABELLA. Well, I tried, but oh dear. Hennie did good works.

NIJO. The first half of my life was all sin and the second / all repentance.*

MARLENE. Oh what about starters?

GRET. Soup.

JOAN. *And which did you like best?

MARLENE. Were your travels just a penance? Avocado vinaigrette. Didn't you / enjoy yourself?

JOAN. Nothing to start with for me, thank you.

NIJO. Yes, but I was very unhappy. / It hurt to remember

MARLENE. And the wine list.

NIJO. the past. I think that was repentance.

MARLENE. Well I wonder.

NIJO. I might have just been homesick.

MARLENE. Or angry.

NIJO. Not angry, no, / why angry?

GRET. Can we have some more bread?

MARLENE. Don't you get angry? I get angry.

NIJO. But what about?

MARLENE. Yes let's have two more Frascati. And some more bread, please.

The WAITRESS *exits.*

ISABELLA. I tried to understand Buddhism when I was in Japan but all this birth and death succeeding each other through eternities just filled me with the most profound melancholy. I do like something more active.

NIJO. You couldn't say I was inactive. I walked every day for twenty years.

ISABELLA. I don't mean walking. / I mean in the head.

NIJO. I vowed to copy five Mahayana sutras. / Do you know how

MARLENE. I don't think religious beliefs are something we have in common. Activity yes.

NIJO. long they are? My head was active. / My head ached.

JOAN. It's no good being active in heresy.

ISABELLA. What heresy? She's calling the Church of England / a heresy.

JOAN. There are some very attractive / heresies.

NIJO. I had never heard of Christianity. Never / heard of it. Barbarians.

MARLENE. Well I'm not a Christian. / And I'm not a Buddhist.

ISABELLA. You have heard of it?

MARLENE. We don't all have to believe the same.

ISABELLA. I knew coming to dinner with a pope we should keep off religion.

JOAN. I always enjoy a theological argument. But I won't try to convert you, I'm not a missionary. Anyway I'm a heresy myself.

ISABELLA. There are some barbaric practices in the east.

NIJO. Barbaric?

ISABELLA. Among the lower classes.

NIJO. I wouldn't know.

ISABELLA. Well theology always made my head ache.

MARLENE. Oh good, some food.

WAITRESS *is bringing the first course.*

NIJO. How else could I have left the court if I wasn't a nun? When father died I had only His Majesty. So when I fell out of favour I had nothing. Religion is a kind of nothing / and I dedicated what was left of me to nothing.

ISABELLA. That's what I mean about Buddhism. It doesn't brace.

MARLENE. Come on, Nijo, have some wine.

NIJO. Haven't you ever felt like that? Nothing will ever happen again. I am dead already. You've all felt / like that.

ISABELLA. You thought your life was over but it wasn't.

JOAN. You wish it was over.

GRET. Sad.

MARLENE. Yes, when I first came to London I sometimes . . . and when I got back from America I did. But only for a few hours. Not twenty years.

ISABELLA. When I was forty I thought my life was over. / Oh I

NIJO. I didn't say I felt it for twenty years. Not every minute.

ISABELLA. was pitiful. I was sent on a cruise for my health and I felt even worse. Pains in my bones, pins and needles in my hands, swelling behind the ears, and — oh, stupidity. I shook all over, indefinable terror. And Australia seemed to me a hideous country, the acacias stank like drains. / I had a

NIJO. You were homesick.

ISABELLA. photograph for Hennie but I told her I wouldn't send it, my hair had fallen out and my clothes were crooked, I looked completely insane and suicidal.

NIJO. So did I, exactly, dressed as a nun. I was wearing walking shoes for the first time.

ISABELLA. I longed to go home, / but home to what? Houses

NIJO. I longed to go back ten years.

ISABELLA. are so perfectly dismal.

MARLENE. I thought travelling cheered you both up.

ISABELLA. Oh it did / of course. It was on the trip from

NIJO. I'm not a cheerful person, Marlene. I just laugh a lot.

ISABELLA. Australia to the Sandwich Isles, I fell in love with the sea. There were rats in the cabin and ants in the food but suddenly it was like a new world. I woke up every morning happy, knowing there would be nothing to annoy me. No nervousness. No dressing.

NIJO. Don't you like getting dressed? I adored my clothes. / When I was chosen to give sake to His Majesty's brother,

MARLENE. You had prettier colours than Isabella.

NIJO. the Emperor Kameyana, on his formal visit, I wore raw silk pleated trousers and a seven-layered gown in shades of red, and two outer garments, / yellow lined with green and a light

MARLENE. Yes, all that silk must have been very . . .

The WAITRESS *starts to clear the first course.*

JOAN. I dressed as a boy when I left home.*

NIJO. green jacket. Lady Betto had a five-layered gown in shades of green and purple.

ISABELLA. *You dressed as a boy?

MARLENE. Of course, / for safety.

JOAN. It was easy, I was only twelve. / Also women weren't allowed in the library. We wanted to study in Athens.

MARLENE. You ran away alone?

JOAN. No, not alone, I went with my friend. / He was sixteen

NIJO. Ah, an elopement.

JOAN. but I thought I knew more science than he did and almost as much philosophy.

ISABELLA. Well I always travelled as a lady and I repudiated strongly any suggestion in the press that I was other than feminine.

MARLENE. I don't wear trousers in the office. / I could but I don't.

ISABELLA. There was no great danger to a woman of my age and appearance.

MARLENE. And you got away with it, Joan?

JOAN. I did then.

The WAITRESS *starts to bring the main course.*

MARLENE. And nobody noticed anything?

JOAN. They noticed I was a very clever boy. / And when I

MARLENE. I couldn't have kept pretending for so long.

JOAN. shared a bed with my friend, that was ordinary — two poor students in a lodging house. I think I forgot I was pretending.

ISABELLA. Rocky Mountain Jim, Mr Nugent, showed me no disrespect. He found it interesting, I think, that I could make scones and also lasso cattle. Indeed he declared his love for me, which was most distressing.

NIJO. What did he say? / We always sent poems first.

MARLENE. What did you say?

ISABELLA. I urged him to give up whisky, / but he said it was too late.

MARLENE. Oh Isabella.

ISABELLA. He had lived alone in the mountains for many years.

MARLENE. But did you — ?

The WAITRESS *goes.*

ISABELLA. Mr Nugent was a man that any woman might love but none could marry. I came back to England.

NIJO. Did you write him a poem when you left? / Snow on the

MARLENE. Did you never see him again?

ISABELLA. No, never.

NIJO. mountains. My sleeves are wet with tears. In England no tears, no snow.

ISABELLA. Well, I say never. One morning very early in Switzerland, it was a year later, I had a vision of him as I last saw him / in his trapper's clothes with his hair round his face,

NIJO. A ghost!

ISABELLA. and that was the day, / I learnt later, he died with a

NIJO. Ah!

ISABELLA. bullet in his brain. / He just bowed to me and vanished.

MARLENE. Oh Isabella.

NIJO. When your lover dies — One of my lovers died. / The priest Ariake.

JOAN. My friend died. Have we all got dead lovers?

MARLENE. Not me, sorry.

NIJO (to ISABELLA). I wasn't a nun, I was still at court, but he was a priest, and when he came to me he dedicated his whole life to hell. / He knew that when he died he would fall into one of the three lower realms. And he died, he did die.

JOAN (to MARLENE). I'd quarrelled with him over the teachings of John the Scot, who held that our ignorance of God is the same as his ignorance of himself. He only knows what he creates because he creates everything he knows but he himself is above being — do you follow?

MARLENE. No, but go on.

NIJO. I couldn't bear to think / in what shape would he be reborn.*

JOAN. St. Augustine maintained that the Neo-Platonic Ideas are indivisible from God, but I agreed with John that the created

ISABELLA. *Buddhism is really most uncomfortable.

JOAN. world is essences derived from Ideas which derived from God. As Denys the Areopagite said — the pseudo-Denys — first we give God a name, then deny it / then reconcile the

NIJO. In what shape would he return?

JOAN contradiction by looking beyond / those terms —

MARLENE. Sorry, what? Denys said what?

JOAN. Well we disagreed about it, we quarrelled. And next day he was ill, /I was so annoyed with him, all the time I was

NIJO. Misery in this life and worse in the next, all because of me.

JOAN. nursing him I kept going over the arguments in my mind. Matter is not a means of knowing the essence. The source of the species is the Idea. But then I realised he'd never understand my arguments again, and that night he died. John the Scot held that the individual disintegrates / and there is no personal immortality.

ISABELLA. I wouldn't have you think I was in love with Jim Nugent. It was yearning to save him that I felt.

MARLENE (*to* JOAN). So what did you do?

JOAN. First I decided to stay a man. I was used to it. And I wanted to devote my life to learning. Do you know why I went to Rome? Italian men didn't have beards.

ISABELLA. The loves of my life were Hennie, my own pet, and my dear husband the doctor, who nursed Hennie in her last illness. I knew it would be terrible when Hennie died but I didn't know how terrible. I felt half of myself had gone. How could I go on my travels without that sweet soul waiting at home for my letters? It was Doctor Bishop's devotion to her in her last illness that made me decide to marry him. He and Hennie had the same sweet character. I had not.

NIJO. I thought his majesty had sweet character because when he found out about Ariake he was so kind. But really it was because he no longer cared for me. One night he even sent me out to a man who had been pursuing me. /He lay awake on the other side of the screens and listened.

ISABELLA. I did wish marriage had seemed more of a step. I tried very hard to cope with the ordinary drudgery of life. I was ill again with carbuncles on the spine and nervous prostration. I ordered a tricycle, that was my idea of adventure then. And John himself fell ill, with erysipelas and anaemia. I began to love him with my whole heart but it was too late. He was a skeleton with transparent white hands. I wheeled him on various seafronts in a bathchair. And he faded and left me. There was nothing in my life. The doctors said I had gout /

and my heart was much affected.

NIJO. There was nothing in my life, nothing, without the
Emperor's favour. The Empress had always been my enemy,
Marlene, she said I had no right to wear three-layered gowns. /
But I was the adopted daughter of my grandfather the Prime
Minister. I had been publicly granted permission to wear thin
silk.

JOAN. There was nothing in my life except my studies. I was
obsessed with pursuit of the truth. I taught at the Greek
School in Rome, which St Augustine had made famous. I was
poor, I worked hard. I spoke apparently brilliantly, I was still
very young, I was a stranger; suddenly I was quite famous,
I was everyone's favourite. Huge crowds came to hear me. The
day after they made me cardinal I fell ill and lay two weeks
without speaking, full of terror and regret. / But then I got up

MARLENE. Yes, success is very . . .

JOAN. determined to go on. I was seized again / with a desperate
longing for the absolute.

ISABELLA. Yes, yes, to go on. I sat in Tobermory among
Hennie's flowers and sewed a complete outfit in Jaeger
flannel. / I was fifty-six years old.

NIJO. Out of favour but I didn't die. I left on foot, nobody saw
me go. For the next twenty years I walked through Japan.

GRET. Walking is good.

The WAITRESS *enters.*

JOAN. Pope Leo died and I was chosen. All right then. I would
be Pope. I would know God. I would know everything.

ISABELLA. I determined to leave my grief behind and set off for
Tibet.

MARLENE. Magnificent all of you. We need some more wine,
please, two bottles I think, Griselda isn't even here yet, and
I want to drink a toast to you all.

ISABELLA. To yourself surely, / we're here to celebrate your
success.

NIJO. Yes, Marlene.

JOAN. Yes, what is it exactly, Marlene?

MARLENE. Well it's not Pope but it is managing director.*

JOAN. And you find work for people.

MARLENE. Yes, an employment agency.

NIJO. *Over all the women you work with. And the men.

ISABELLA. And very well deserved too. I'm sure it's just the beginning of something extraordinary.

MARLENE. Well it's worth a party.

ISABELLA. To Marlene.*

MARLENE. And all of us.

JOAN. *Marlene.

NIJO. Marlene.

GRET. Marlene.

MARLENE. We've all come a long way. To our courage and the way we changed our lives and our extraordinary achievements.

They laugh and drink a toast.

ISABELLA. Such adventures. We were crossing a mountain pass at seven thousand feet, the cook was all to pieces, the muleteers suffered fever and snow blindness. But even though my spine was agony I managed very well.

MARLENE. Wonderful.

NIJO. Once I was ill for four months lying alone at an inn. Nobody to offer a horse to Buddha. I had to live for myself, and I did live.

ISABELLA. Of course you did. It was far worse returning to Tobermory. I always felt dull when I was stationary. / That's why I could never stay anywhere.

NIJO. Yes, that's it exactly. New sights. The shrine by the beach, the moon shining on the sea. The goddess had vowed to save all living things. /She would even save the fishes. I was full of hope.

JOAN. I had thought the Pope would know everything. I thought God would speak to me directly. But of course he knew I was a woman.

MARLENE. But nobody else even suspected?

The WAITRESS *brings more wine.*

JOAN. In the end I did take a lover again.*

ISABELLA. In the Vatican?

GRET. *Keep you warm.

NIJO. *Ah, lover.

MARLENE. *Good for you.

JOAN. He was one of my chamberlains. There are such a lot of servants when you're a Pope. The food's very good. And I realised I did know the truth. Because whatever the Pope says, that's true.

NIJO. What was he like, the chamberlain?*

GRET. Big cock.

ISABELLA. Oh Gret.

MARLENE. *Did he fancy you when he thought you were a fella?

NIJO. What was he like?

JOAN. He could keep a secret.

MARLENE. So you did know everything.

JOAN. Yes, I enjoyed being Pope. I consecrated bishops and let people kiss my feet. I received the King of England when he came to submit to the church. Unfortunately there were earthquakes, and some village reported it had rained blood, and in France there was a plague of giant grasshoppers, but I don't think that can have been my fault, do you?*

Laughter.

The grasshoppers fell on the English Channel / and were

NIJO. I once went to sea. It was very lonely. I realised it made very little difference where I went.

JOAN. washed up on shore and their bodies rotted and poisoned the air and everyone in those parts died.

Laughter.

ISABELLA. *Such superstition! I was nearly murdered in China by a howling mob. They thought the barbarians ate babies and put them under railway sleepers to make the tracks steady, and ground up their eyes to make the lenses of cameras. / So

MARLENE. And you had a camera!

ISABELLA. they were shouting, 'child-eater, child-eater.' Some people tried to sell girl babies to Europeans for cameras or stew!

Laughter.

MARLENE. So apart from the grasshoppers it was a great success.

JOAN. Yes, if it hadn't been for the baby I expect I'd have lived to an old age like Theodora of Alexandria, who lived as a monk. She was accused by a girl / who fell in love with her of being the father of her child and —

NIJO. But tell us what happened to your baby. I had some babies.

MARLENE. Didn't you think of getting rid of it?

JOAN. Wouldn't that be a worse sin than having it? / But a Pope with a child was about as bad as possible.

MARLENE. I don't know, you're the Pope.

JOAN. But I wouldn't have known how to get rid of it.

MARLENE. Other Popes had children, surely.

JOAN. They didn't give birth to them.

NIJO. Well you were a woman.

JOAN. Exactly and I shouldn't have been a woman. Women, children and lunatics can't be Pope.

MARLENE. So the only thing to do / was to get rid of it somehow.

NIJO. You had to have it adopted secretly.

JOAN. But I didn't know what was happening. I thought I was getting fatter, but then I was eating more and sitting about, the life of a Pope is quite luxurious. I don't think I'd spoken to a woman since I was twelve. The chamberlain was the one who realised.

MARLENE. And by then it was too late.

JOAN. Oh I didn't want to pay attention. It was easier to do nothing.

NIJO. But you had to plan for having it. You had to say you were ill and go away.

JOAN' That's what I should have done I suppose.

MARLENE. Did you want them to find out?

NIJO. I too was often in embarrassing situations, there's no need for a scandal. My first child was His Majesty's, which unfortunately died, but my second was Akebono's. I was seventeen. He was in love with me when I was thirteen, he was very upset when I had to go to the Emperor, it was very romantic, a lot of poems. Now His Majesty hadn't been near me for two months so he thought I was four months pregnant when I was really six, so when I reached the ninth month / I

JOAN. I never knew what month it was.

NIJO. announced I was seriously ill, and Akebono announced he had gone on a religious retreat. He held me round the waist and lifted me up as the baby was born. He cut the cord with a short sword, wrapped the baby in white and took it away. It was only a girl but I was sorry to lose it. Then I told the Emperor that the baby had miscarried because of my illness, and there you are. The danger was past.

JOAN. But Nijo, I wasn't used to having a woman's body.

ISABELLA. So what happened?

JOAN. I didn't know of course that it was near the time. It was Rogation Day, there was always a procession. I was on the horse dressed in my robes and a cross was carried in front of me, and all the cardinals were following, and all the clergy of Rome, and a huge crowd of people. / We set off from

MARLENE. Total Pope.

JOAN. St Peter's to go to St John's. I had felt a slight pain earlier,
I thought it was something I'd eaten, and then it came back,
and came back more often. I thought when this is over I'll go
to bed. There were still long gaps when I felt perfectly all right
and I didn't want to attract attention to myself and spoil the
ceremony. Then I suddenly realised what it must be. I had to
last out till I could get home and hide. Then something
changed, my breath started to catch, I couldn't plan things
properly any more. We were in a little street that goes between
St Clement's and the Colosseum, and I just had to get off the
horse and sit down for a minute. Great waves of pressure were
going through my body, I heard sounds like a cow lowing,
they came out of my mouth. Far away I heard people
screaming, 'The Pope is ill, the Pope is dying.' And the baby
just slid out onto the road.*

MARLENE. The cardinals / won't have known where to put
themselves.

NIJO. Oh dear, Joan, what a thing to do! In the street!

ISABELLA. *How embarrassing.

GRET. In a field, yah.

They are laughing.

JOAN. One of the cardinals said, 'The Antichrist!' and fell over
in a faint.

They all laugh.

MARLENE. So what did they do? They weren't best pleased.

JOAN. They took me by the feet and dragged me out of town
and stoned me to death.

They stop laughing.

MARLENE. Joan, how horrible.

JOAN. I don't really remember.

NIJO. And the child died too?

JOAN. Oh yes, I think so, yes.

Pause.

The WAITRESS *enters to clear the plates. They start talking quietly.*

ISABELLA (*to* JOAN). I never had any children. I was very fond of horses.

NIJO (*to* MARLENE). I saw my daughter once. She was three years old. She wore a plum-red / small-sleeved gown. Akebono's

ISABELLA. Birdie was my favourite. A little Indian bay mare I rode in the Rocky Mountains.

NIJO. wife had taken the child because her own died. Everyone thought I was just a visitor. She was being brought up carefully so she could be sent to the palace like I was.

ISABELLA. Legs of iron and always cheerful, and such a pretty face. If a stranger led her she reared up like a bronco.

NIJO. I never saw my third child after he was born, the son of Ariake the priest. Ariake held him on his lap the day he was born and talked to him as if he could understand, and cried. My fourth child was Ariake's too. Ariake died before he was born. I didn't want to see anyone, I stayed alone in the hills. It was a boy again, my third son. But oddly enough I felt nothing for him.

MARLENE. How many children did you have, Gret?

GRET. Ten.

ISABELLA. Whenever I came back to England I felt I had so much to atone for. Hennie and John were so good. I did no good in my life. I spent years in self-gratification. So I hurled myself into committees, I nursed the people of Tobermory in the epidemic of influenza, I lectured the Young Women's Christian Association on Thrift. I talked and talked explaining how the East was corrupt and vicious. My travels must do good to someone beside myself. I wore myself out with good causes.

MARLENE. Oh God, why are we all so miserable?

JOAN. The procession never went down that street again.

MARLENE. They rerouted it specially?

JOAN. Yes they had to go all round to avoid it. And they introduced a pierced chair.

MARLENE. A pierced chair?

JOAN. Yes, a chair made out of solid marble with a hole in the seat / and it was in the Chapel of the Saviour, and after he was

MARLENE. You're not serious.

JOAN. elected the Pope had to sit in it.

MARLENE. And someone looked up his skirts? / Not really?

ISABELLA. What an extraordinary thing.

JOAN. Two of the clergy / made sure he was a man.

NIJO. On their hands and knees!

MARLENE. A pierced chair!

GRET. Balls!

    GRISELDA *arrives unnoticed.*

NIJO. Why couldn't he just pull up his robe?

JOAN. He had to sit there and look dignified.

MARLENE. You could have made all your chamberlains sit in it.*

GRET. Big one, small one.

NIJO. Very useful chair at court.

ISABELLA. *Or the laird of Tobermory in his kilt.

    They are quite drunk. They get the giggles.

    MARLENE *notices* GRISELDA.

MARLENE. Griselda! / There you are. Do you want to eat?

GRISELDA. I'm sorry I'm so late. No, no, don't bother.

MARLENE. Of course it's no bother. / Have you eaten?

GRISELDA. No really, I'm not hungry.

MARLENE. Well have some pudding.

GRISELDA. I never eat pudding.

MARLENE. Griselda, I hope you're not anorexic. We're having pudding, I am, and getting nice and fat.

GRISELDA. Oh if everyone is. I don't mind.

MARLENE. Now who do you know? This is Joan who was Pope in the ninth century, and Isabella Bird, the Victorian traveller, and Lady Nijo from Japan, Emperor's concubine and Buddhist nun, thirteenth century, nearer your own time, and Gret who was painted by Brueghel. Griselda's in Boccaccio and Petrarch and Chaucer because of her extraordinary marriage. I'd like profiteroles because they're disgusting.

JOAN. Zabaglione, please.

ISABELLA. Apple pie / and cream.

NIJO. What's this?

MARLENE. Zabaglione, it's Italian, it's what Joan's having, / it's delicious.

NIJO. A Roman Catholic / dessert? Yes please.

MARLENE. Gret?

GRET. Cake.

GRISELDA. Just cheese and biscuits, thank you.

MARLENE. Yes, Griselda's life is like a fairy-story, except it starts with marrying the prince.

GRISELDA. He's only a marquis, Marlene.

MARLENE. Well everyone for miles around is his liege and he's absolute lord of life and death and you were the poor but beautiful peasant girl and he whisked you off. / Near enough a prince.

NIJO. How old were you?

GRISELDA. Fifteen.

NIJO. I was brought up in court circles and it was still a shock. Had you ever seen him before?

GRISELDA. I'd seen him riding by, we all had. And he'd seen me in the fields with the sheep.*

ISABELLA. I would have been well suited to minding sheep.

NIJO. And Mr Nugent riding by.

ISABELLA. Of course not, Nijo, I mean a healthy life in the open air.

JOAN. *He just rode up while you were minding the sheep and asked you to marry him?

GRISELDA. No, no, it was on the wedding day. I was waiting outside the door to see the procession. Everyone wanted him to get married so there'd be an heir to look after us when he died, / and at last he announced a day for the wedding but

MARLENE. I don't think Walter wanted to get married. It is Walter? Yes.

GRISELDA. nobody knew who the bride was, we thought it must be a foreign princess, we were longing to see her. Then the carriage stopped outside our cottage and we couldn't see the bride anywhere. And he came and spoke to my father.

NIJO. And your father told you to serve the Prince.

GRISELDA. My father could hardly speak. The Marquis said it wasn't an order, I could say no, but if I said yes I must always obey him in everything.

MARLENE. That's when you should have suspected.

GRISELDA. But of course a wife must obey her husband. / And of course I must obey the Marquis.*

ISABELLA. I swore to obey dear John, of course, but it didn't seem to arise. Naturally I wouldn't have wanted to go abroad while I was married.

MARLENE. *Then why bother to mention it at all? He'd got a thing about it, that's why.

GRISELDA. I'd rather obey the Marquis than a boy from the village.

MARLENE. Yes, that's a point.

JOAN. I never obeyed anyone. They all obeyed me.

NIJO. And what did you wear? He didn't make you get married in your own clothes? That would be perverse.*

MARLENE. Oh, you wait.

GRISELDA. *He had ladies with him who undressed me and they had a white silk dress and jewels for my hair.

MARLENE. And at first he seemed perfectly normal?

GRISELDA. Marlene, you're always so critical of him. / Of course he was normal, he was very kind.

MARLENE. But Griselda, come on, he took your baby.

GRISELDA. Walter found it hard to believe I loved him. He couldn't believe I would always obey him. He had to prove it.

MARLENE. I don't think Walter likes women.

GRISELDA. I'm sure he loved me, Marlene, all the time.

MARLENE. He just had a funny way / of showing it.

GRISELDA. It was hard for him too.

JOAN. How do you mean he took away your baby?

NIJO. Was it a boy?

GRISELDA. No, the first one was a girl.

NIJO. Even so it's hard when they take it away. Did you see it at all?

GRISELDA. Oh yes, she was six weeks old.

NIJO. Much better to do it straight away.

ISABELLA. But why did your husband take the child?

GRISELDA. He said all the people hated me because I was just one of them. And now I had a child they were restless. So he had to get rid of the child to keep them quiet. But he said he wouldn't snatch her, I had to agree and obey and give her up. So when I was feeding her a man came in and took her away. I thought he was going to kill her even before he was out of the room.

MARLENE. But you let him take her? You didn't struggle?

GRISELDA. I asked him to give her back so I could kiss her. And I asked him to bury her where no animals could dig her up. / It

ISABELLA. Oh my dear.

GRISELDA. was Walter's child to do what he liked with.*

MARLENE. Walter was bonkers.

GRET. Bastard.

ISABELLA. *But surely, murder.

GRISELDA. I had promised.

MARLENE. I can't stand this. I'm going for a pee.

MARLENE *goes out.*

The WAITRESS *brings dessert.*

NIJO. No, I understand. Of course you had to, he was your life. And were you in favour after that?

GRISELDA. Oh yes, we were very happy together. We never spoke about what had happened.

ISABELLA. I can see you were doing what you thought was your duty. But didn't it make you ill?

GRISELDA. No, I was very well, thank you.

NIJO. And you had another child?

GRISELDA. Not for four years, but then I did, yes, a boy.

NIJO. Ah a boy. / So it all ended happily.

GRISELDA. Yes he was pleased. I kept my son till he was two years old. A peasant's grandson. It made the people angry. Walter explained.

ISABELLA. But surely he wouldn't kill his children / just because —

GRISELDA. Oh it wasn't true. Walter would never give in to the people. He wanted to see if I loved him enough.

JOAN. He killed his children / to see if you loved him enough?

NIJO. Was it easier the second time or harder?

GRISELDA. It was always easy because I always knew I would do what he said.

Pause. They start to eat.

ISABELLA. I hope you didn't have any more children.

GRISELDA. Oh no, no more. It was twelve years till he tested me again.

ISABELLA. So whatever did he do this time ? / My poor John, I never loved him enough, and he would never have dreamt . . .

GRISELDA. He sent me away. He said the people wanted him to marry someone else who'd give him an heir and he'd got special permission from the Pope. So I said I'd go home to my father. I came with nothing / so I went with nothing. I

NIJO. Better to leave if your master doesn't want you.

GRISELDA. took off my clothes. He let me keep a slip so he wouldn't be shamed. And I walked home barefoot. My father came out in tears. Everyone was crying except me.

NIJO. At least your father wasn't dead. / I had nobody.

ISABELLA. Well it can be a relief to come home. I loved to see Hennie's sweet face again.

GRISELDA. Oh yes, I was perfectly content. And quite soon he sent for me again.

JOAN. I don't think I would have gone.

GRISELDA. But he told me to come. I had to obey him. He wanted me to help prepare his wedding. He was getting married to a young girl from France / and nobody except me knew how to arrange things the way he liked them.

NIJO. It's always hard taking him another woman.

MARLENE *comes back.*

JOAN. I didn't live a woman's life. I don't understand it.

GRISELDA. The girl was sixteen and far more beautiful than me. I could see why he loved her. / She had her younger brother with her as a page.

The WAITRESS *enters.*

MARLENE. Oh God, I can't bear it. I want some coffee. Six coffees. Six brandies. / Double brandies. Straightaway.

GRISELDA. They all went in to the feast I'd prepared. And he stayed behind and put his arms round me and kissed me. / I felt half asleep with the shock.

NIJO. Oh, like a dream.

MARLENE. And he said, 'This is your daughter and your son.'

GRISELDA. Yes.

JOAN. What?

NIJO. Oh. Oh I see. You got them back.

ISABELLA. I did think it was remarkably barbaric to kill them but you learn not to say anything. / So he had them brought up secretly I suppose.

MARLENE. Walter's a monster. Weren't you angry? What did you do?

GRISELDA. Well I fainted. Then I cried and kissed the children. / Everyone was making a fuss of me.

NIJO. But did you feel anything for them?

GRISELDA. What?

NIJO. Did you feel anything for the children?

GRISELDA. Of course, I loved them.

JOAN. So you forgave him and lived with him?

GRISELDA. He suffered so much all those years.

ISABELLA. Hennie had the same sweet nature.

NIJO. So they dressed you again?

GRISELDA. Cloth of gold.

JOAN. I can't forgive anything.

MARLENE. You really are exceptional, Griselda.

NIJO. Nobody gave me back my children.

NIJO *cries. The* WAITRESS *brings brandies.*

ISABELLA. I can never be like Hennie. I was always so busy in England, a kind of business I detested. The very presence of people exhausted my emotional reserves. I could not be like

Hennie however I tried. I tried and was as ill as could be. The doctor suggested a steel net to support my head, the weight of my own head was too much for my diseased spine. / It is dangerous to put oneself in depressing circumstances. Why should I do it?

JOAN. Don't cry.

NIJO. My father and the Emperor both died in the autumn. So much pain.

JOAN. Yes, but don't cry.

NIJO. They wouldn't let me into the palace when he was dying. I hid in the room with his coffin, then I couldn't find where I'd left my shoes, I ran after the funeral procession in bare feet, I couldn't keep up. When I got there it was over, a few wisps of smoke in the sky, that's all that was left of him. What I want to know is, if I'd still been at court, would I have been allowed to wear full mourning?

MARLENE. I'm sure you would.

NIJO. Why do you say that? You don't know anything about it. Would I have been allowed to wear full mourning?

ISABELLA. How can people live in this dim pale island and wear our hideous clothes? I cannot and will not live the life of a lady.

NIJO. I'll tell you something that made me angry. I was eighteen, at the Full Moon Ceremony. They make a special rice gruel and stir it with their sticks, and then they beat their women across the loins so they'll have sons and not daughters. So the Emperor beat us all / very hard as usual — that's not it,

MARLENE. What a sod.

NIJO. Marlene, that's normal, what made us angry, he told his attendants they could beat us too. Well they had a wonderful time. / So Lady Genki and I made a plan, and the ladies all hid

The WAITRESS *has entered with coffees.*

MARLENE. I'd like another brandy please. Better make it six.

NIJO. in his rooms, and Lady Mashimizu stood guard with a stick at the door, and when His Majesty came in Genki seized him and I beat him till he cried out and promised he would never order anyone to hit us again. Afterwards there was a terrible fuss. The nobles were horrified. 'We wouldn't even dream of stepping on your Majesty's shadow.' And I had hit him with a stick. Yes, I hit him with a stick.

JOAN. Suave, mari magno turbantibus aequora ventis,
e terra magnum alterius spectare laborem;
non quia vexari quemquamst iucunda voluptas,
sed quibus ipse malis careas quia cernere suave est.
Suave etiam belli certamina magna tueri
per campos instructa tua sine parte pericli.
Sed nil dulcius est, bene quam munita tenere
edita doctrina sapientum templa serena, /
despicere unde queas alios passimque videre
errare atque viam palantis quaerere vitae,

GRISELDA. I do think — I do wonder — it would have been nicer if Walter hadn't had to.

ISABELLA. Why should I? Why should I?

MARLENE. Of course not.

NIJO. I hit him with a stick.

JOAN. certare ingenio, contendere nobilitate,
noctes atque dies niti praestante labore
ad summas emergere opes retumque potiri.
O miseras / hominum mentis, o pectora caeca!*

ISABELLA. Oh miseras!

NIJO. *Pectora caeca.

JOAN. qualibus in tenebris vitae quantisque periclis
degitur hoc aevi quodcumquest! / nonne videre
nil aliud sibi naturam latrare, nisi utqui
corpore seiunctus dolor absit, mente fruatur

JOAN *subsides.*

GRET. We come into hell through a big mouth. Hell's black and red. / It's like the village where I come from. There's a river and

MARLENE (*to* JOAN). Shut up, pet.

ISABELLA. Listen, she's been to hell.

GRET. a bridge and houses. There's places on fire like when the soldiers come. There's a big devil sat on a roof with a big hole in his arse and he's scooping stuff out of it with a big ladle and it's falling down on us, and it's money, so a lot of the women stop and get some. But most of us is fighting the devils. There's lots of little devils, our size, and we get them down all right and give them a beating. There's lots of funny creatures round your feet, you don't like to look, like rats and lizards, and nasty things, a bum with a face, and fish with legs, and faces on things that don't have faces on. But they don't hurt, you just keep going. Well we'd had worse, you see, we'd had the Spanish. We'd all had family killed. My big son die on a wheel. Birds eat him. My baby, a soldier run her through with a sword. I'd had enough, I was mad, I hate the bastards. I come out my front door that morning and shout till my neighbours come out and I said, 'Come on, we're going where the evil come from and pay the bastards out.' And they all come out just as they was / from baking or washing in their

NIJO. All the ladies come.

GRET. aprons, and we push down the street and the ground opens up and we go through a big mouth into a street just like ours but in hell. I've got a sword in my hand from somewhere and I fill a basket with gold cups they drink out of down there. You just keep running on and fighting / you didn't stop for nothing. Oh we give them devils such a beating.

NIJO. Take that, take that.

JOAN. Something something something mortisque timores
tum vacuum pectus — damn.
Quod si ridicula —
something something on and on and on and something
splendorem purpureai.

ISABELLA. I thought I would have a last jaunt up the west river in China. Why not? But the doctors were so very grave. I just went to Morocco. The sea was so wild I had to be landed by ship's crane in a coal bucket. / My horse was a terror to me a

GRET. Coal bucket, good.

JOAN. nos in luce timemus
something
terrorem.

ISABELLA. powerful black charger.

> NIJO *is laughing and crying.*
> JOAN *gets up and is sick in a corner.*
> MARLENE *is drinking* ISABELLA's *brandy.*

So off I went to visit the Berber sheikhs in full blue trousers
and great brass spurs. I was the only European woman ever
to have seen the Emperor of Morocco. I was seventy years old.
What lengths to go to for a last chance of joy. I knew my
return of vigour was only temporary, but how marvellous
while it lasted.

Scene Two

Employment Agency. MARLENE *and* JEANINE.

MARLENE. Right Jeanine, you are Jeanine aren't you? Let's
have a look. Os and As. / No As, all those Os you probably

JEANINE. Six Os.

MARLENE. could have got an A. / Speeds, not brilliant, not too
bad.

JEANINE. I wanted to go to work.

MARLENE. Well, Jeanine, what's your present job like?

JEANINE. I'm a secretary.

MARLENE. Secretary or typist?

JEANINE. I did start as a typist but the last six months I've been
a secretary.

MARLENE. To?

JEANINE. To three of them, really, they share me. There's

Mr Ashford, he's the office manager, and Mr Philby / is sales, and —

MARLENE. Quite a small place?

JEANINE. A bit small.

MARLENE. Friendly?

JEANINE. Oh it's friendly enough.

MARLENE. Prospects?

JEANINE. I don't think so, that's the trouble. Miss Lewis is secretary to the managing director and she's been there forever, and Mrs Bradford/ is —

MARLENE. So you want a job with better prospects?

JEANINE. I want a change.

MARLENE. So you'll take anything comparable?

JEANINE. No, I do want prospects. I want more money.

MARLENE. You're getting — ?

JEANINE. Hundred.

MARLENE. It's not bad you know. You're what? Twenty?

JEANINE. I'm saving to get married.

MARLENE. Does that mean you don't want a long-term job, Jeanine?

JEANINE. I might do.

MARLENE. Because where do the prospects come in? No kids for a bit?

JEANINE. Oh no, not kids, not yet.

MARLENE. So you won't tell them you're getting married?

JEANINE. Had I better not?

MARLENE. It would probably help.

JEANINE. I'm not wearing a ring. We thought we wouldn't spend on a ring.

MARLENE. Saves taking it off.

JEANINE. I wouldn't take it off.

MARLENE. There's no need to mention it when you go for an interview. / Now Jeanine do you have a feel for any particular

JEANINE. But what if they ask?

MARLENE. kind of company?

JEANINE. I thought advertising.

MARLENE. People often do think advertising. I have got a few vacancies but I think they're looking for something glossier.

JEANINE. You mean how I dress? / I can dress different. I

MARLENE. I mean experience.

JEANINE. dress like this on purpose for where I am now.

MARLENE. I have a marketing department here of a knitwear manufacturer. / Marketing is near enough advertising. Secretary

JEANINE. Knitwear?

MARLENE. to the marketing manager, he's thirty-five, married, I've sent him a girl before and she was happy, left to have a baby, you won't want to mention marriage there. He's very fair I think, good at his job, you won't have to nurse him along. Hundred and ten, so that's better than you're doing now.

JEANINE. I don't know.

MARLENE. I've a fairly small concern here, father and two sons, you'd have more say potentially, secretarial and reception duties, only a hundred but the job's going to grow with the concern and then you'll be in at the top with new girls coming in underneath you.

JEANINE. What is it they do?

MARLENE. Lampshades. / This would be my first choice for you.

JEANINE. Just lampshades?

MARLENE. There's plenty of different kinds of lampshade. So we'll send you there, shall we, and the knitwear second choice. Are you free to go for an interview any day they call you?

JEANINE. I'd like to travel.

MARLENE. We don't have any foreign clients. You'd have to go elsewhere.

JEANINE. Yes I know. I don't really . . . I just mean . . .

MARLENE. Does your fiancé want to travel?

JEANINE. I'd like a job where I was here in London and with him and everything but now and then — I expect it's silly. Are there jobs like that?

MARLENE. There's personal assistant to a top executive in a multinational. If that's the idea you need to be planning ahead. Is that where you want to be in ten years?

JEANINE. I might not be alive in ten years.

MARLENE. Yes but you will be. You'll have children.

JEANINE. I can't think about ten years.

MARLENE. You haven't got the speeds anyway. So I'll send you to these two shall I? You haven't been to any other agency? Just so we don't get crossed wires. Now Jeanine I want you to get one of these jobs, all right? If I send you that means I'm putting myself on the line for you. Your presentation's OK, you look fine, just be confident and go in there convinced that this is the best job for you and you're the best person for the job. If you don't believe it they won't believe it.

JEANINE. Do you believe it?

MARLENE. I think you could make me believe it if you put your mind to it.

JEANINE. Yes, all right.

Scene Three

JOYCE's *back yard. The house with back door is upstage. Downstage a shelter made of junk, made by children. Two girls, ANGIE and KIT, are in it, squashed together. ANGIE is 16, KIT is 12. They cannot be seen from the house. JOYCE calls from the house.*

JOYCE. Angie. Angie are you out there?

Silence. They keep still and wait. When nothing else happens they relax.

ANGIE. Wish she was dead.

KIT. Wanna watch *The Exterminator?*

ANGIE. You're sitting on my leg.

KIT. There's nothing on telly. We can have an ice cream. Angie?

ANGIE. Shall I tell you something?

KIT. Do you wanna watch *The Extermintor?*

ANGIE. It's X, innit.

KIT. I can get into Xs.

ANGIE. Shall I tell you something?

KIT. We'll go to something else. We'll go to Ipswich. What's on the Odeon?

ANGIE. She won't let me, will she?

KIT. Don't tell her.

ANGIE. I've no money.

KIT. I'll pay.

ANGIE. She'll moan though, won't she?

KIT. I'll ask her for you if you like.

ANGIE. I've no money, I don't want you to pay.

KIT. I'll ask her.

ANGIE. She don't like you.

KIT. I still got three pounds birthday money. Did she say she don't like me? I'll go by myself then.

ANGIE. Your mum don't let you. I got to take you.

KIT. She won't know.

ANGIE. You'd be scared who'd sit next to you.

KIT. No I wouldn't.
She does like me anyway.
Tell me then.

ANGIE. Tell you what?

KIT. It's you she doesn't like.

ANGIE. Well I don't like her so tough shit.

JOYCE (off). Angie. Angie. Angie. I know you're out there. I'm
not coming out after you. You come in here.

Silence. Nothing happens.

ANGIE. Last night when I was in bed. I been thinking yesterday
could I make things move. You know, make things move
by thinking about them without touching them. Last night
I was in bed and suddenly a picture fell down off the wall.

KIT. What picture?

ANGIE. My gran, that picture. Not the poster. The photograph
in the frame.

KIT. Had you done something to make it fall down?

ANGIE. I must have done.

KIT. But were you thinking about it?

ANGIE. Not about it, but about something.

KIT. I don't think that's very good.

ANGIE. You know the kitten?

KIT. Which one?

ANGIE. There only is one. The dead one.

KIT. What about it?

ANGIE. I heard it last night.

KIT. Where?

ANGIE. Out here. In the dark. What if I left you here in the dark all night?

KIT. You couldn't. I'd go home.

ANGIE. You couldn't.

KIT. I'd / go home.

ANGIE' No you couldn't, not if I said.

KIT. I could.

ANGIE. Then you wouldn't see anything. You'd just be ignorant.

KIT. I can see in the daytime.

ANGIE. No you can't. You can't hear it in the daytime.

KIT. I don't want to hear it.

ANGIE. You're scared that's all.

KIT. I'm not scared of anything.

ANGIE. You're scared of blood.

KIT. It's not the same kitten anyway. You just heard an old cat, / you just heard some old cat.

ANGIE. You don't know what I heard. Or what I saw. You don't know nothing because you're a baby.

KIT. You're sitting on me.

ANGIE. Mind my hair / you silly cunt.

KIT. Stupid fucking cow, I hate you.

ANGIE. I don't care if you do.

KIT. You're horrible.

ANGIE. I'm going to kill my mother and you're going to watch.

KIT. I'm not playing.

ANGIE. You're scared of blood.

   KIT *puts her hand under her dress, brings it out with blood on her finger.*

KIT. There, see, I got my own blood, so.

ANGIE *takes* KIT's *hand and licks her finger.*

ANGIE. Now I'm a cannibal. I might turn into a vampire now.

KIT. That picture wasn't nailed up right.

ANGIE. You'll have to do that when I get mine.

KIT. I don't have to.

ANGIE. You're scared.

KIT. I'll do it, I might do it. I don't have to just because you say. I'll be sick on you.

ANGIE. I don't care if you are sick on me, I don't mind sick. I don't mind blood. If I don't get away from here I'm going to die.

KIT. I'm going home.

ANGIE. You can't go through the house. She'll see you.

KIT. I won't tell her.

ANGIE. Oh great, fine.

KIT. I'll say I was by myself. I'll tell her you're at my house and I'm going there to get you.

ANGIE. She knows I'm here, stupid.

KIT. Then why can't I go through the house?

ANGIE. Because I said not.

KIT. My mum don't like you anyway.

ANGIE. I don't want her to like me. She's a slag.

KIT. She is not.

ANGIE. She does it with everyone.

KIT. She does not.

ANGIE. You don't even know what it is.

KIT. Yes I do.

ANGIE. Tell me then.

KIT. We get it all at school, cleverclogs. It's on television. You haven't done it.

ANGIE. How do you know?

KIT. Because I know you haven't.

ANGIE. You know wrong then because I have.

KIT. Who with?

ANGIE. I'm not telling you / who with.

KIT. You haven't anyway.

ANGIE. How do you know?

KIT. Who with?

ANGIE. I'm not telling you.

KIT. You said you told me everything.

ANGIE. I was lying wasn't I?

KIT. Who with? You can't tell me who with because / you never —

ANGIE. Sh.

JOYCE has come out of the house. She stops half way across the yard and listens. They listen.

JOYCE. You there Angie? Kit? You there Kitty? Want a cup of tea? I've got some chocolate biscuits. Come on now I'll put the kettle on. Want a choccy biccy, Angie?

They all listen and wait.

Fucking rotten little cunt. You can stay there and die. I'll lock the back door.

They all wait.

JOYCE goes back to the house.

ANGIE and KIT sit in silence for a while.

KIT. When there's a war, where's the safest place?

ANGIE. Nowhere.

KIT. New Zealand is, my mum said. Your skin's burned right off. Shall we go to New Zealand?

ANGIE. I'm not staying here.

KIT. Shall we go to New Zealand?

ANGIE. You're not old enough.

KIT. You're not old enough.

ANGIE. I'm old enough to get married.

KIT. You don't want to get married.

ANGIE. No but I'm old enough.

KIT. I'd find out where they were going to drop it and stand right in the place.

ANGIE. You couldn't find out.

KIT. Better than walking round with your skin dragging on the ground. Eugh. / Would you like walking round with your skin dragging on the ground?

ANGIE. You couldn't find out, stupid, it's a secret.

KIT. Where are you going?

ANGIE. I'm not telling you.

KIT. Why?

ANGIE. It's a secret.

KIT. But you tell me all your secrets.

ANGIE. Not the true secrets.

KIT. Yes you do.

ANGIE. No I don't.

KIT. I want to go somewhere away from the war.

ANGIE. Just forget the war.

KIT. I can't.

ANGIE. You have to. It's so boring.

KIT. I'll remember it at night.

ANGIE. I'm going to do something else anyway.

KIT. What? Angie come on. Angie.

ANGIE. It's a true secret.

KIT. It can't be worse than the kitten. And killing your mother. And the war.

ANGIE. Well I'm not telling you so you can die for all I care.

KIT. My mother says there's something wrong with you playing with someone my age. She says why haven't you got friends your own age. People your own age know there's something funny about you. She says you're a bad influence. She says she's going to speak to your mother.

ANGIE *twists* KIT's *arm till she cries out.*

ANGIE. Say you're a liar.

KIT. She said it not me.

ANGIE. Say you eat shit.

KIT. You can't make me.

ANGIE *lets go.*

ANGIE. I don't care anyway. I'm leaving.

KIT. Go on then.

ANGIE. You'll all wake up one morning and find I've gone.

KIT. Good.

ANGIE. I'm not telling you when.

KIT' Go on then.

ANGIE. I'm sorry I hurt you.

KIT. I'm tired.

ANGIE. Do you like me?

KIT. I don't know.

ANGIE. You do like me.

KIT. I'm going home.

KIT *gets up.*

ANGIE. No you're not.

KIT. I'm tired.

ANGIE. She'll see you.

KIT. She'll give me a chocolate biscuit.

ANGIE. Kitty.

KIT. Tell me where you're going.

ANGIE. Sit down.

KIT *sits in the hut again.*

KIT. Go on then.

ANGIE. Swear?

KIT. Swear.

ANGIE. I'm going to London. To see my aunt.

KIT. And what?

ANGIE. That's it.

KIT. I see my aunt all the time.

ANGIE. I don't see my aunt.

KIT. What's so special?

ANGIE. It is special. She's special.

KIT. Why?

ANGIE. She is.

KIT. Why?

ANGIE. She is.

KIT. Why?

ANGIE. My mother hates her.

KIT. Why?

ANGIE. Because she does.

KIT. Perhaps she's not very nice.

ANGIE. She is nice.

KIT. How do you know?

ANGIE. Because I know her.

KIT. You said you never see her.

ANGIE. I saw her last year. You saw her.

KIT. Did I?

ANGIE. Never mind.

KIT. I remember her. That aunt. What's so special?

ANGIE. She gets people jobs.

KIT. What's so special?

ANGIE. I think I'm my aunt's child. I think my mother's really my aunt.

KIT. Why?

ANGIE. Because she goes to America, now shut up.

KIT. I've been to London.

ANGIE. Now give us a cuddle and shut up because I'm sick.

KIT. You're sitting on my arm.

   Silence.

   JOYCE *comes out and comes up to them quietly.*

JOYCE. Come on.

KIT. Oh hello.

JOYCE. Time you went home.

KIT. We want to go to the Odeon.

JOYCE. What time?

KIT. Don't know.

JOYCE. What's on?

KIT. Don't know.

JOYCE. Don't know much do you?

KIT. That all right then?

JOYCE. Angie's got to clean her room first.

ANGIE. No I don't.

JOYCE. Yes you do, it's a pigsty.

ANGIE. Well I'm not.

JOYCE. Then you're not going. I don't care.

ANGIE. Well I am going.

JOYCE. You've no money, have you?

ANGIE. Kit's paying anyway.

JOYCE. No she's not.

KIT. I'll help you with your room.

JOYCE. That's nice.

ANGIE. No you won't. You wait here.

KIT. Hurry then.

ANGIE. I'm not hurrying. You just wait.

ANGIE *goes into the house. Silence.*

JOYCE. I don't know.

Silence.

How's school then?

KIT. All right.

JOYCE. What are you now? Third year?

KIT. Second year.

JOYCE. Your mum says you're good at English.

Silence.

Maybe Angie should've stayed on.

KIT. She didn't like it.

JOYCE. I didn't like it. And look at me. If your face fits at school it's going to fit other places too. It wouldn't make no difference to Angie. She's not going to get a job when jobs are hard to get. I'd be sorry for anyone in charge of her. She'd better get married. I don't know who'd have her, mind. She's one of those girls might never leave home. What do you want to be when you grow up, Kit?

KIT. Physicist.

JOYCE. What?

KIT. Nuclear physicist.

JOYCE. Whatever for?

KIT. I could, I'm clever.

JOYCE. I know you're clever, pet.

Silence.

I'll make a cup of tea.

Silence.

Looks like it's going to rain.

Silence.

Don't you have friends your own age?

KIT. Yes.

JOYCE. Well then.

KIT. I'm old for my age.

JOYCE. And Angie's simple is she? She's not simple.

KIT. I love Angie.

JOYCE. She's clever in her own way.

KIT. You can't stop me.

JOYCE. I don't want to.

KIT. You can't, so.

JOYCE. Don't be cheeky, Kitty. She's always kind to little children.

KIT. She's coming so you better leave me alone.

ANGIE *comes out. She has changed into an old best dress, slightly small for her.*

JOYCE. What you put that on for? Have you done your room? You can't clean your room in that.

ANGIE. I looked in the cupboard and it was there.

JOYCE. Of course it was there, it's meant to be there. Is that why it was a surprise, finding something in the right place? I should think she's surprised, wouldn't you Kit, to find something in her room in the right place.

ANGIE. I decided to wear it.

JOYCE. Not today, why? To clean your room? You're not going

to the pictures till you've done your room. You can put your dress on after if you like.

ANGIE *picks up a brick.*

Have you done your room? You're not getting out of it, you know.

KIT. Angie, let's go.

JOYCE. She's not going till she's done her room.

KIT. It's starting to rain.

JOYCE. Come on, come on then. Hurry and do your room, Angie, and then you can go to the cinema with Kit. Oh it's wet, come on. We'll look up the time in the paper. Does your mother know, Kit, it's going to be a late night for you, isn't it? Hurry up, Angie. You'll spoil your dress. You make me sick.

JOYCE *and* KIT *run in.*

ANGIE *stays where she is. Sound of rain.*

KIT *comes out of the house and shouts.*

KIT. Angie. Angie, come on, you'll get wet.

KIT *comes back to* ANGIE.

ANGIE. I put on this dress to kill my mother.

KIT. I suppose you thought you'd do it with a brick.

ANGIE. You can kill people with a brick.

KIT. Well you didn't, so.

ACT TWO

Scene One

Office of 'Top Girls' Employment Agency. Three desks and a small interviewing area. Monday morning. WIN and NELL have just arrived for work.

NELL. Coffee coffee coffee coffee / coffee.

WIN. The roses were smashing. / Mermaid.

NELL. Ohhh.

WIN. Iceberg. He taught me all their names.

    NELL *has some coffee now.*

NELL. Ah. Now then.

WIN. He has one of the finest rose gardens in West Sussex. He exhibits.

NELL. He what?

WIN. His wife was visiting her mother. It was like living together.

NELL. Crafty, you never said.

WIN. He rang on Saturday morning.

NELL. Lucky you were free.

WIN. That's what I told him.

NELL. Did you hell.

WIN. Have you ever seen a really beautiful rose garden?

NELL. I don't like flowers. / I like swimming pools.

WIN. Marilyn. Esther's Baby. They're all called after birds.

NELL. Our friend's late. Celebrating all weekend I bet you.

WIN. I'd call a rose Elvis. Or John Conteh.

NELL. Is Howard in yet?

WIN. If he is he'll be bleeping us with a problem.

NELL. Howard can just hang onto himself.

WIN. Howard's really cut up.

NELL. Howard thinks because he's a fella the job was his as of
right. Our Marlene's got far more balls than Howard and that's
that.

WIN. Poor little bugger.

NELL. He'll live.

WIN. He'll move on.

NELL. I wouldn't mind a change of air myself.

WIN. Serious?

NELL. I've never been a staying put lady. Pastures new.

WIN. So who's the pirate?

NELL. There's nothing definite.

WIN. Inquiries?

NELL. There's always inquiries. I'd think I'd got bad breath if
there stopped being inquiries. Most of them can't afford me.
Or you.

WIN. I'm all right for the time being. Unless I go to Australia.

NELL. There's not a lot of room upward.

WIN. Marlene's filled it up.

NELL. Good luck to her. Unless there's some prospects
moneywise.

WIN. You can but ask.

NELL. Can always but ask.

WIN. So what have we got? I've got a Mr Holden I saw last week.

NELL. Any use?

WIN. Pushy. Bit of a cowboy.

NELL. Good-looker?

WIN. Good dresser.

NELL. High flyer?

WIN. That's his general idea certainly but I'm not sure he's got it up there.

NELL. Prestel wants six high flyers and I've only seen two and a half.

WIN. He's making a bomb on the road but he thinks it's time for an office. I sent him to IBM but he didn't get it.

NELL. Prestel's on the road.

WIN. He's not overbright.

NELL. Can he handle an office?

WIN. Provided his secretary can punctuate he should go far.

NELL. Bear Prestel in mind then, I might put my head round the door. I've got that poor little nerd I should never have said I could help. Tender heart me.

WIN. Tender like old boots. How old?

NELL. Yes well forty-five.

WIN. Say no more.

NELL. He knows his place, he's not after calling himself a manager, he's just a poor little bod wants a better commission and a bit of sunshine.

WIN. Don't we all.

NELL. He's just got to relocate. He's got a bungalow in Dymchurch.

WIN. And his wife says.

NELL. The lady wife wouldn't care to relocate. She's going through the change.

WIN. It's his funeral, don't waste your time.

NELL. I don't waste a lot.

WIN. Good weekend you?

NELL. You could say.

WIN. Which one?

NELL. One Friday, one Saturday.

WIN. Aye — aye.

NELL. Sunday night I watched telly.

WIN. Which of them do you like best really?

NELL. Sunday was best, I liked the Ovaltine.

WIN. Holden, Barker, Gardner, Duke.

NELL. I've a lady here thinks she can sell.

WIN. Taking her on?

NELL. She's had some jobs.

WIN. Services?

NELL. No, quite heavy stuff, electric.

WIN. Tough bird like us.

NELL. We could do with a few more here.

WIN. There's nothing going here.

NELL. No but I always want the tough ones when I see them. Hang onto them.

WIN. I think we're plenty.

NELL. Derek asked me to marry him again.

WIN. He doesn't know when he's beaten.

NELL. I told him I'm not going to play house, not even in Ascot.

WIN. Mind you, you could play house.

NELL. If I chose to play house I would play house ace.

WIN. You could marry him and go on working.

NELL. I could go on working and not marry him.

    MARLENE *arrives*.

MARLENE. Morning ladies.

WIN *and* NELL *cheer and whistle.*

Mind my head.

NELL. Coffee coffee coffee.

WIN. We're tactfully not mentioning you're late.

MARLENE. Fucking tube.

WIN. We've heard that one.

NELL. We've used that one.

WIN. It's the top executive doesn't come in as early as the poor working girl.

MARLENE. Pass the sugar and shut your face, pet.

WIN. Well I'm delighted.

NELL. Howard's looking sick.

WIN. Howard is sick. He's got ulcers and heart. He told me.

NELL. He'll have to stop then won't he?

WIN. Stop what?

NELL. Smoking, drinking, shouting. Working.

WIN. Well, working.

NELL. We're just looking through the day.

MARLENE. I'm doing some of Pam's ladies. They've been piling up while she's away.

NELL. Half a dozen little girls and an arts graduate who can't type.

WIN. I spent the whole weekend at his place in Sussex.

NELL. She fancies his rose garden.

WIN. I had to lie down in the back of the car so the neighbours wouldn't see me go in.

NELL. You're kidding.

WIN. It was funny.

NELL. Fuck that for a joke.

WIN. It was funny.

MARLENE. Anyway they'd see you in the garden.

WIN. The garden has extremely high walls.

NELL. I think I'll tell the wife.

WIN. Like hell.

NELL. She might leave him and you could have the rose garden.

WIN. The minute it's not a secret I'm out on my ear.

NELL. Don't know why you bother.

WIN. Bit of fun.

NELL. I think it's time you went to Australia.

WIN. I think it's pushy Mr Holden time.

NELL. If you've any really pretty bastards, Marlene, I want some for Prestel.

MARLENE. I might have one this afternoon. This morning it's all Pam's secretarial.

NELL. Not long now and you'll be upstairs watching over us all.

MARLENE. Do you feel bad about it?

NELL. I don't like coming second.

MARLENE. Who does?

WIN. We'd rather it was you than Howard. We're glad for you, aren't we Nell.

NELL. Oh yes. Aces.

Interview
WIN *and* LOUISE.

WIN. Now Louise, hello, I have your details here. You've been very loyal to the one job I see.

LOUISE. Yes I have.

WIN. Twenty-one years is a long time in one place.

LOUISE. I feel it is. I feel it's time to move on.

WIN. And you are what age now?

LOUISE. I'm in my early forties.

WIN. Exactly?

LOUISE. Forty-six.

WIN. It's not necessarily a handicap, well it is of course we have to face that, but it's not necessarily a disabling handicap, experience does count for something.

LOUISE. I hope so.

WIN. Now between ourselves is there any trouble, any reason why you're leaving that wouldn't appear on the form?

LOUISE. Nothing like that.

WIN. Like what?

LOUISE. Nothing at all.

WIN. No long term understandings come to a sudden end, making for an insupportable atmosphere?

LOUISE. I've always completely avoided anything like that at all.

WIN. No personality clashes with your immediate superiors or inferiors?

LOUISE. I've always taken care to get on very well with everyone.

WIN. I only ask because it can affect the reference and it also affects your motivation, I want to be quite clear why you're moving on. So I take it the job itself no longer satisfies you. Is it the money?

LOUISE. It's partly the money. It's not so much the money.

WIN. Nine thousand is very respectable. Have you dependants?

LOUISE. No, no dependants. My mother died.

WIN. So why are you making a change?

LOUISE. Other people make changes.

WIN. But why are you, now, after spending most of your life in the one place?

LOUISE. There you are, I've lived for that company, I've given my life really you could say because I haven't had a great

deal of social life, I've worked in the evenings. I haven't had
office entanglements for the very reason you just mentioned
and if you are committed to your work you don't move in
many other circles. I had management status from the age of
twenty-seven and you'll appreciate what that means. I've built
up a department. And there it is, it works extremely well, and
I feel I'm stuck there. I've spent twenty years in middle
management. I've seen young men who I trained go on, in my
own company or elsewhere, to higher things. Nobody notices
me, I don't expect it, I don't attract attention by making
mistakes, everybody takes it for granted that my work is
perfect. They will notice me when I go, they will be sorry I
think to lose me, they will offer me more money of course, I
will refuse. They will see when I've gone what I was doing for
them.

WIN. If they offer you more money you won't stay?

LOUISE. No I won't.

WIN. Are you the only woman?

LOUISE. Apart from the girls of course, yes. There was one,
she was my assistant, it was the only time I took on a young
woman assistant, I always had my doubts. I don't care greatly
for working with women, I think I pass as a man at work. But
I did take on this young woman, her qualifications were
excellent, and she did well, she got a department of her own,
and left the company for a competitor where she's now on the
board and good luck to her. She has a different style, she's
a new kind of attractive well-dressed — I don't mean I don't
dress properly. But there is a kind of woman who is thirty now
who grew up in a different climate. They are not so careful.
They take themselves for granted. I have had to justify my
existence every minute, and I have done so, I have proved —
well.

WIN. Let's face it, vacancies are going to be ones where you'll
be in competition with younger men. And there are
companies that will value your experience enough you'll be
in with a chance. There are also fields that are easier for a
woman, there is a cosmetic company here where your

experience might be relevant. It's eight and a half, I don't know if that appeals.

LOUISE. I've proved I can earn money. It's more important to get away. I feel it's now or never. I sometimes / think —

WIN. You shouldn't talk too much at an interview.

LOUISE. I don't. I don't normally talk about myself. I know very well how to handle myself in an office situation. I only talk to you because it seems to me this is different, it's your job to understand me, surely. You asked the questions.

WIN. I think I understand you sufficiently.

LOUISE. Well good, that's good.

WIN. Do you drink?

LOUISE. Certainly not. I'm not a teetotaller, I think that's very suspect, it's seen as being an alcoholic if you're teetotal. What do you mean? I don't drink. Why?

WIN. I drink.

LOUISE. I don't.

WIN. Good for you.

Main office
MARLENE *and* ANGIE.
ANGIE *arrives.*

ANGIE. Hello.

MARLENE. Have you an appointment?

ANGIE. It's me. I've come.

MARLENE. What? It's not Angie?

ANGIE. It was hard to find this place. I got lost.

MARLENE. How did you get past the receptionist? The girl on the desk, didn't she try to stop you?

ANGIE. What desk?

MARLENE. Never mind.

ANGIE. I just walked in. I was looking for you.

MARLENE. Well you found me.

ANGIE. Yes.

MARLENE. So where's your mum? Are you up in town for the day?

ANGIE. Not really.

MARLENE. Sit down. Do you feel all right?

ANGIE. Yes thank you.

MARLENE. So where's Joyce?

ANGIE. She's at home.

MARLENE. Did you come up on a school trip then?

ANGIE. I've left school.

MARLENE. Did you come up with a friend?

ANGIE. No. There's just me.

MARLENE. You came up by yourself, that's fun. What have you been doing? Shopping? Tower of London?

ANGIE. No, I just come here. I come to you.

MARLENE. That's very nice of you to think of paying your aunty a visit. There's not many nieces make that the first port of call. Would you like a cup of coffee?

ANGIE. No thank you.

MARLENE. Tea, orange?

ANGIE. No thank you.

MARLENE. Do you feel all right?

ANGIE. Yes thank you.

MARLENE. Are you tired from the journey?

ANGIE. Yes, I'm tired from the journey.

MARLENE. You sit there for a bit then. How's Joyce?

ANGIE. She's all right.

MARLENE. Same as ever.

ANGIE. Oh yes.

MARLENE. Unfortunately you've picked a day when I'm rather busy, if there's ever a day when I'm not, or I'd take you out to lunch and we'd go to Madame Tussaud's. We could go shopping. What time do you have to be back? Have you got a day return?

ANGIE. No.

MARLENE. So what train are you going back on?

ANGIE. I came on the bus.

MARLENE. So what bus are you going back on? Are you staying the night?

ANGIE. Yes.

MARLENE. Who are you staying with? Do you want me to put you up for the night, is that it?

ANGIE. Yes please.

MARLENE. I haven't got a spare bed.

ANGIE. I can sleep on the floor.

MARLENE. You can sleep on the sofa.

ANGIE. Yes please.

MARLENE. I do think Joyce might have phoned me. It's like her.

ANGIE. This is where you work is it?

MARLENE. It's where I have been working the last two years but I'm going to move into another office.

ANGIE. It's lovely.

MARLENE. My new office is nicer than this. There's just the one big desk in it for me.

ANGIE. Can I see it?

MARLENE. Not now, no, there's someone else in it now. But he's leaving at the end of next week and I'm going to do his job.

ANGIE. Is that good?

MARLENE. Yes, it's very good.

ANGIE. Are you going to be in charge?

MARLENE. Yes I am.

ANGIE. I knew you would be.

MARLENE. How did you know?

ANGIE. I knew you'd be in charge of everything.

MARLENE. Not quite everything.

ANGIE. You will be.

MARLENE. Well we'll see.

ANGIE. Can I see it next week then?

MARLENE. Will you still be here next week?

ANGIE. Yes.

MARLENE. Don't you have to go home?

ANGIE. No.

MARLENE. Why not?

ANGIE. It's all right.

MARLENE. Is it all right?

ANGIE. Yes, don't worry about it.

MARLENE. Does Joyce know where you are?

ANGIE. Yes of course she does.

MARLENE. Well does she?

ANGIE. Don't worry about it.

MARLENE. How long are you planning to stay with me then?

ANGIE. You know when you came to see us last year?

MARLENE. Yes, that was nice wasn't it?

ANGIE. That was the best day of my whole life.

MARLENE. So how long are you planning to stay?

ANGIE. Don't you want me?

MARLENE. Yes yes, I just wondered.

ANGIE. I won't stay if you don't want me.

MARLENE. No, of course you can stay.

ANGIE. I'll sleep on the floor. I won't be any bother.

MARLENE. Don't get upset.

ANGIE. I'm not, I'm not. Don't worry about it.

MRS KIDD *comes in.*

MRS KIDD. Excuse me.

MARLENE. Yes.

MRS KIDD. Excuse me.

MARLENE. Can I help you?

MRS KIDD. Excuse me bursting in on you like this but I have to talk to you.

MARLENE. I am engaged at the moment. / If you could go to reception —

MRS KIDD. I'm Rosemary Kidd, Howard's wife, you don't recognise me but we did meet, I remember you of course / but you wouldn't —

MARLENE. Yes of course, Mrs Kidd, I'm sorry, we did meet. Howard's about somewhere I expect, have you looked in his office?

MRS KIDD. Howard's not about, no. I'm afraid it's you I've come to see if I could have a minute or two.

MARLENE. I do have an appointment in five minutes.

MRS KIDD. This won't take five minutes. I'm very sorry. It is a matter of some urgency.

MARLENE. Well of course. What can I do for you?

MRS KIDD. I just wanted a chat, an informal chat. It's not something I can simply — I'm sorry if I'm interrupting your work. I know office work isn't like housework / which is all interruptions.

MARLENE. No no, this is my niece. Angie. Mrs Kidd.

MRS KIDD. Very pleased to meet you.

ANGIE. Very well thank you.

MRS KIDD. Howard's not in today.

MARLENE. Isn't he?

MRS KIDD. He's feeling poorly.

MARLENE. I didn't know. I'm sorry to hear that.

MRS KIDD. The fact is he's in a state of shock. About what's happened.

MARLENE. What has happened?

MRS KIDD. You should know if anyone. I'm referring to you being appointed managing director instead of Howard. He hasn't been at all well all weekend. He hasn't slept for three nights. I haven't slept.

MARLENE. I'm sorry to hear that, Mrs Kidd. Has he thought of taking sleeping pills?

MRS KIDD. It's very hard when someone has worked all these years.

MARLENE. Business life is full of little setbacks. I'm sure Howard knows that. He'll bounce back in a day or two. We all bounce back.

MRS KIDD. If you could see him you'd know what I'm talking about. What's it going to do to him working for a woman? I think if it was a man he'd get over it as something normal.

MARLENE. I think he's going to have to get over it.

MRS KIDD. It's me that bears the brunt. I'm not the one that's been promoted. I put him first every inch of the way. And now what do I get? You women this, you women that. It's not my fault. You're going to have to be very careful how you handle him. He's very hurt.

MARLENE. Naturally I'll be tactful and pleasant to him, you don't start pushing someone round. I'll consult him over any decisions affecting his department. But that's no different, Mrs Kidd, from any of my other colleagues.

MRS KIDD. I think it is different, because he's a man.

MARLENE. I'm not quite sure why you came to see me.

MRS KIDD. I had to do something.

MARLENE. Well you've done it, you've seen me. I think that's probably all we've time for. I'm sorry he's been taking it out on you. He really is a shit, Howard.

MRS KIDD. But he's got a family to support. He's got three children. It's only fair.

MARLENE. Are you suggesting I give up the job to him then?

MRS KIDD. It had crossed my mind if you were unavailable after all for some reason, he would be the natural second choice I think, don't you? I'm not asking.

MARLENE. Good.

MRS KIDD. You mustn't tell him I came. He's very proud.

MARLENE. If he doesn't like what's happening here he can go and work somewhere else.

MRS KIDD. Is that a threat?

MARLENE. I'm sorry but I do have some work to do.

MRS KIDD. It's not that easy, a man of Howard's age. You don't care. I thought he was going too far but he's right. You're one of these ballbreakers / that's what you are. You'll end up

MARLENE. I'm sorry but I do have some work to do.

MRS KIDD. miserable and lonely. You're not natural.

MARLENE. Could you please piss off?

MRS KIDD. I thought if I saw you at least I'd be doing something.

    MRS KIDD *goes*.

MARLENE. I've got to go and do some work now. Will you come back later?

ANGIE. I think you were wonderful.

MARLENE. I've got to go and do some work now.

ANGIE. You told her to piss off.

MARLENE. Will you come back later?

ANGIE. Can't I stay here?

MARLENE. Don't you want to go sightseeing?

ANGIE. I'd rather stay here.

MARLENE. You can stay here I suppose, if it's not boring.

ANGIE. It's where I most want to be in the world.

MARLENE. I'll see you later then.

> MARLENE *goes.*
>
> ANGIE *sits at* WIN's *desk.*

Interview
NELL *and* SHONA.

NELL. Is this right? You are Shona?

SHONA. Yeh.

NELL. It says here you're twenty-nine.

SHONA. Yeh.

NELL. Too many late nights, me. So you've been where you are
for four years, Shona, you're earning six basic and three
commission. So what's the problem?

SHONA. No problem.

NELL. Why do you want a change?

SHONA. Just a change.

NELL. Change of product, change of area?

SHONA. Both.

NELL. But you're happy on the road?

SHONA. I like driving.

NELL. You're not after management status?

SHONA. I would like management status.

NELL. You'd be interested in titular management status but
not come off the road?

SHONA. I want to be on the road, yeh.

NELL. So how many calls have you been making a day?

SHONA. Six.

NELL. And what proportion of those are successful?

SHONA. Six.

NELL. That's hard to believe.

SHONA. Four.

NELL. You find it easy to get the initial interest do you?

SHONA. Oh yeh, I get plenty of initial interest.

NELL. And what about closing?

SHONA. I close, don't I?

NELL. Because that's what an employer is going to have doubts about with you a lady as I needn't tell you, whether she's got the guts to push through to a closing situation. They think we're too nice. They think we listen to the buyer's doubts. They think we consider his needs and his feelings.

SHONA. I never consider people's feelings.

NELL. I was selling for six years, I can sell anything, I've sold in three continents, and I'm jolly as they come but I'm not very nice.

SHONA. I'm not very nice.

NELL. What sort of time do you have on the road with the other reps? Get on all right? Handle the chat?

SHONA. I get on. Keep myself to myself.

NELL. Fairly much of a loner are you?

SHONA. Sometimes.

NELL. So what field are you interested in?

SHONA. Computers.

NELL. That's a top field as you know and you'll be up against some very slick fellas there, there's some very pretty boys in computers, it's an American-style field.

SHONA. That's why I want to do it.

NELL. Video systems appeal? That's a high-flying situation.

SHONA. Video systems appeal OK.

NELL. Because Prestel have half a dozen vacancies I'm looking to fill at the moment. We're talking in the area of ten to fifteen thousand here and upwards.

SHONA. Sounds OK.

NELL. I've half a mind to go for it myself. But it's good money here if you've got the top clients. Could you fancy it do you think?

SHONA. Work here?

NELL. I'm not in a position to offer, there's nothing officially going just now, but we're always on the lookout. There's not that many of us. We could keep in touch.

SHONA. I like driving.

NELL. So the Prestel appeals?

SHONA. Yeh.

NELL. What about ties?

SHONA. No ties.

NELL. So relocation wouldn't be a problem.

SHONA. No problem.

NELL. So just fill me in a bit more could you about what you've been doing.

SHONA. What I've been doing. It's all down there.

NELL. The bare facts are down here but I've got to present you to an employer.

SHONA. I'm twenty-nine years old.

NELL. So it says here.

SHONA. We look young. Youngness runs in the family in our family.

NELL. So just describe your present job for me.

SHONA. My present job at present. I have a car. I have a Porsche. I go up the M1 a lot. Burn up the M1 a lot. Straight up the M1 in the fast lane to where the clients are, Staffordshire, Yorkshire, I do a lot in Yorkshire. I'm selling electric things. Like dishwashers, washing machines, stainless steel tubs are a feature and the reliability of the programme. After sales service, we offer a very good after sales service, spare parts, plenty of spare parts. And fridges, I sell a lot of fridges specially in the summer. People want to buy fridges in the summer because of the heat melting the butter and you get fed up standing the milk in a basin of cold water with a cloth over, stands to reason people don't want to do that in this day and age. So I sell a lot of them. Big ones with big freezers. Big freezers. And I stay in hotels at night when I'm away from home. On my expense account. I stay in various hotels. They know me, the ones I go to. I check in, have a bath, have a shower. Then I go down to the bar, have a gin and tonic, have a chat. Then I go into the dining room and have dinner. I usually have fillet steak and mushrooms, I like mushrooms. I like smoked salmon very much. I like having a salad on the side. Green salad. I don't like tomatoes.

NELL. Christ what a waste of time.

SHONA. Beg your pardon?

NELL. Not a word of this is true is it?

SHONA. How do you mean?

NELL. You just filled in the form with a pack of lies.

SHONA. Not exactly.

NELL. How old are you?

SHONA. Twenty-nine.

NELL. Nineteen?

SHONA. Twenty-one.

NELL. And what jobs have you done? Have you done any?

SHONA. I could though, I bet you.

Main office
ANGIE *sitting as before.*
WIN *comes in.*

WIN. Who's sitting in my chair?

ANGIE. What? Sorry.

WIN. Who's been eating my porridge?

ANGIE. What?

WIN. It's all right, I saw Marlene. Angie isn't it? I'm Win. And I'm not going out for lunch because I'm knackered. I'm going to set me down here and have a yoghurt. Do you like yoghurt?

ANGIE. No.

WIN. That's good because I've only got one. Are you hungry?

ANGIE. No.

WIN. There's a cafe on the corner.

ANGIE. No thank you. Do you work here?

WIN. How did you guess?

ANGIE. Because you look as if you might work here and you're sitting at the desk. Have you always worked here?

WIN. No I was headhunted. That means I was working for another outfit like this and this lot came and offered me more money. I broke my contract, there was a hell of a stink. There's not many top ladies about. Your aunty's a smashing bird.

ANGIE. Yes I know.

MARLENE. Fan are you? Fan of your aunty's?

ANGIE. Do you think I could work here?

WIN. Not at the moment.

ANGIE. How do I start?

WIN. What can you do?

ANGIE. I don't know. Nothing.

WIN. Type?

ANGIE. Not very well. The letters jump up when I do capitals. I was going to do a CSE in commerce but I didn't.

WIN. What have you got?

ANGIE. What?

WIN. CSE's, O's.

ANGIE. Nothing, none of that. Did you do all that?

WIN. Oh yes, all that, and a science degree funnily enough. I started out doing medical research but there's no money in it. I thought I'd go abroad. Did you know they sell Coca-Cola in Russia and Pepsi-cola in China? You don't have to be qualified as much as you might think. Men are awful bullshitters, they like to make out jobs are harder than they are. Any job I ever did I started doing it better than the rest of the crowd and they didn't like it. So I'd get unpopular and I'd have a drink to cheer myself up. I lived with a fella and supported him for four years, he couldn't get work. After that I went to California. I like the sunshine. Americans know how to live. This country's too slow. Then I went to Mexico, still in sales, but it's no country for a single lady. I came home, went bonkers for a bit, thought I was five different people, got over that all right, the psychiatrist said I was perfectly sane and highly intelligent. Got married in a moment of weakness and he's inside now, he's been inside four years, and I've not been to see him too much this last year. I like this better than sales, I'm not really that aggressive. I started thinking sales was a good job if you want to meet people, but you're meeting people that don't want to meet you. It's no good if you like being liked. Here your clients want to meet you because you're the one doing them some good. They hope.

ANGIE *has fallen asleep.* NELL *comes in.*

NELL. You're talking to yourself, sunshine.

WIN. So what's new?

NELL. Who is this?

WIN. Marlene's little niece.

NELL. What's she got, brother, sister? She never talks about her family.

WIN. I was telling her my life story.

NELL. Violins?

WIN. No, success story.

NELL. You've heard Howard's had a heart attack?

WIN. No, when?

NELL. I heard just now. He hadn't come in, he was at home, he's gone to hospital. He's not dead. His wife was here, she rushed off in a cab.

WIN. Too much butter, too much smoke. We must send him some flowers.

MARLENE *comes in.*

You've heard about Howard?

MARLENE. Poor sod.

NELL. Lucky he didn't get the job if that's what his health's like.

MARLENE. Is she asleep?

WIN. She wants to work here.

MARLENE. Packer in Tesco more like.

WIN. She's a nice kid. Isn't she?

MARLENE. She's a bit thick. She's a bit funny.

WIN. She thinks you're wonderful.

MARLENE. She's not going to make it.

Scene Two

A year earlier. Sunday evening. JOYCE'*s kitchen.* JOYCE, ANGIE, MARLENE. MARLENE *is taking presents out of a bright carrier bag.* ANGIE *has already opened a box of chocolates.*

MARLENE. Just a few little things. / I've no memory for

JOYCE. There's no need.

MARLENE. birthdays have I, and Christmas seems to slip by. So I think I owe Angie a few presents.

JOYCE. What do you say?

ANGIE. Thank you very much. Thank you very much, Aunty Marlene.

She opens a present. It is the dress from Act One, new.

ANGIE. Oh look, Mum, isn't it lovely?

MARLENE. I don't know if it's the right size. She's grown up since I saw her. / I knew she was always tall for her age.

ANGIE. Isn't it lovely?

JOYCE. She's a big lump.

MARLENE. Hold it up, Angie, let's see.

ANGIE. I'll put it on, shall I?

MARLENE. Yes, try it on.

JOYCE. Go on to your room then, we don't want / a strip show thank you.

ANGIE. Of course I'm going to my room, what do you think? Look Mum, here's something for you. Open it, go on. What is it? Can I open it for you?

JOYCE. Yes, you open it, pet.

ANGIE. Don't you want to open it yourself? / Go on.

JOYCE. I don't mind, you can do it.

ANGIE. It's something hard. It's — what is it? A bottle. Drink is it? No, it's what? Perfume, look. What a lot. Open it, look, let's smell it. Oh it's strong. It's lovely. Put it on me. How do you do it? Put it on me.

JOYCE. You're too young.

ANGIE. I can play wearing it like dressing up.

JOYCE. And you're too old for that. Here, give it here, I'll do it, you'll tip the whole bottle over yourself / and we'll have you smelling all summer.

ANGIE. Put it on you. Do I smell? Put it on Aunty too. Put it on Aunty too. Let's all smell.

MARLENE. I didn't know what you'd like.

JOYCE. There's no danger I'd have it already, / that's one thing.

ANGIE. Now we all smell the same.

MARLENE. It's a bit of nonsense.

JOYCE. It's very kind of you Marlene, you shouldn't.

ANGIE. Now I'll put on the dress and then we'll see.

    ANGIE *goes*.

JOYCE. You've caught me on the hop with the place in a mess. / If you'd let me know you was coming I'd have got

MARLENE. That doesn't matter.

JOYCE. something in to eat. We had our dinner dinnertime. We're just going to have a cup of tea. You could have an egg.

MARLENE. No, I'm not hungry. Tea's fine.

JOYCE. I don't expect you take sugar.

MARLENE. Why not?

JOYCE. You take care of yourself.

MARLENE. How do you mean you didn't know I was coming?

JOYCE. You could have written. I know we're not on the phone but we're not completely in the dark ages, / we do have a postman.

MARLENE. But you asked me to come.

JOYCE. How did I ask you to come?

MARLENE. Angie said when she phoned up.

JOYCE. Angie phoned up, did she?

MARLENE. Was it just Angie's idea?

JOYCE. What did she say?

MARLENE. She said you wanted me to come and see you. /

It was a couple of weeks ago. How was I to know that's a

JOYCE. Ha.

MARLENE. ridiculous idea? My diary's always full a couple of weeks ahead so we fixed it for this weekend. I was meant to get here earlier but I was held up. She gave me messages from you.

JOYCE. Didn't you wonder why I didn't phone you myself?

MARLENE. She said you didn't like using the phone. You're shy on the phone and can't use it. I don't know what you're like, do I.

JOYCE. Are there people who can't use the phone?

MARLENE. I expect so.

JOYCE. I haven't met any.

MARLENE. Why should I think she was lying?

JOYCE. Because she's like what she's like.

MARLENE. How do I know / what she's like?

JOYCE. It's not my fault you don't know what she's like. You never come and see her.

MARLENE. Well I have now / and you don't seem over the moon.*

JOYCE. Good.
   *Well I'd have got a cake if she'd told me.

   Pause.

MARLENE. I did wonder why you wanted to see me.

JOYCE. I didn't want to see you.

MARLENE. Yes, I know. Shall I go?

JOYCE. I don't mind seeing you.

MARLENE. Great, I feel really welcome.

JOYCE. You can come and see Angie any time you like, I'm not stopping you. / You know where we are. You're the

MARLENE. Ta ever so.

JOYCE. one went away, not me. I'm right here where I was.

And will be a few years yet I shouldn't wonder.

MARLENE. All right. All right.

JOYCE *gives* MARLENE *a cup of tea.*

JOYCE. Tea.

MARLENE. Sugar?

JOYCE *passes* MARLENE *the sugar.*

It's very quiet down here.

JOYCE. I expect you'd notice it.

MARLENE. The air smells different too.

JOYCE. That's the scent.

MARLENE. No, I mean walking down the lane.

JOYCE. What sort of air you get in London then?

ANGIE *comes in, wearing the dress. It fits.*

MARLENE. Oh, very pretty. / You do look pretty, Angie.

JOYCE. That fits all right.

MARLENE. Do you like the colour?

ANGIE. Beautiful. Beautiful.

JOYCE. You better take it off, / you'll get it dirty.

ANGIE. I want to wear it. I want to wear it.

MARLENE. It is for wearing after all. You can't just hang it up
and look at it.

ANGIE. I love it.

JOYCE. Well if you must you must.

ANGIE. If someone asks me what's my favourite colour I'll
tell them it's this. Thank you very much, Aunty Marlene.

MARLENE. You didn't tell your mum you asked me down.

ANGIE. I wanted it to be a surprise.

JOYCE. I'll give you a surprise / one of these days.

ANGIE. I thought you'd like to see her. She hasn't been here since I was nine. People do see their aunts.

MARLENE. Is it that long? Doesn't time fly?

ANGIE. I wanted to.

JOYCE. I'm not cross.

ANGIE. Are you glad?

JOYCE. I smell nicer anyhow, don't I?

KIT *comes in without saying anything, as if she lived there.*

MARLENE. I think it was a good idea, Angie, about time. We are sisters after all. It's a pity to let that go.

JOYCE. This is Kitty, / who lives up the road. This is Angie's Aunty Marlene.

KIT. What's that?

ANGIE. It's a present. Do you like it?

KIT. It's all right. / Are you coming out?*

MARLENE. Hello, Kitty.

ANGIE. *No.

KIT. What's that smell?

ANGIE. It's a present.

KIT. It's horrible. Come on.*

MARLENE. Have a chocolate.

ANGIE. *No, I'm busy.

KIT. Coming out later?

ANGIE. No.

KIT (*to* MARLENE). Hello.

KIT *goes without a chocolate.*

JOYCE. She's a little girl Angie sometimes plays with because she's the only child lives really close. She's like a little sister to her really. Angie's good with little children.

MARLENE. Do you want to work with children, Angie? / Be a teacher or a nursery nurse?

JOYCE. I don't think she's ever thought of it.

MARLENE. What do you want to do?

JOYCE. She hasn't an idea in her head what she wants to do. /
Lucky to get anything.

MARLENE. Angie?

JOYCE. She's not clever like you.

Pause.

MARLENE. I'm not clever, just pushy.

JOYCE. True enough.

MARLENE takes a bottle of whisky out of the bag.

I don't drink spirits.

ANGIE. You do at Christmas.

JOYCE. It's not Christmas, is it?

ANGIE. It's better than Christmas.

MARLENE. Glasses?

JOYCE. Just a small one then.

MARLENE. Do you want some, Angie?

ANGIE. I can't, can I?

JOYCE. Taste it if you want. You won't like it.

MARLENE. We got drunk together the night your grandfather
died.

JOYCE. We did not get drunk.

MARLENE. I got drunk. You were just overcome with grief.

JOYCE. I still keep up the grave with flowers.

MARLENE. Do you really?

JOYCE. Why wouldn't I?

MARLENE. Have you seen Mother?

JOYCE. Of course I've seen Mother.

MARLENE. I mean lately.

JOYCE. Of course I've seen her lately, I go every Thursday.

MARLENE (*to* ANGIE). Do you remember your grandfather?

ANGIE. He got me out of the bath one night in a towel.

MARLENE. Did he? I don't think he ever gave me a bath. Did he give you a bath, Joyce? He probably got soft in his old age. Did you like him?

ANGIE. Yes of course.

MARLENE. Why?

ANGIE. What?

MARLENE. So what's the news? How's Mrs Paisley? Still going crazily? / And Dorothy. What happened to Dorothy?*

ANGIE. Who's Mrs Paisley?

JOYCE. *She went to Canada.

MARLENE. Did she? What to do?

JOYCE. I don't know. She just went to Canada.

MARLENE. Well / good for her.

ANGIE. Mr Connolly killed his wife.

MARLENE. What, Connolly at Whitegates?

ANGIE. They found her body in the garden. / Under the cabbages.

MARLENE. He was always so proper.

JOYCE. Stuck up git. Connolly. Best lawyer money could buy but he couldn't get out of it. She was carrying on with Matthew.

MARLENE. How old's Matthew then?

JOYCE. Twenty-one. / He's got a motorbike.

MARLENE. I think he's about six.

ANGIE. How can he be six? He's six years older than me. / If he was six I'd be nothing, I'd be just born this minute.

JOYCE. Your aunty knows that, she's just being silly. She means it's so long since she's been here she's forgotten about Matthew.

ANGIE. You were here for my birthday when I was nine. I had a pink cake. Kit was only five then, she was four, she hadn't started school yet. She could read already when she went to school. You remember my birthday? / You remember me?

MARLENE. Yes, I remember the cake.

ANGIE. You remember me?

MARLENE. Yes, I remember you.

ANGIE. And Mum and Dad was there, and Kit was.

MARLENE. Yes, how is your dad? Where is he tonight? Up the pub?

JOYCE. No, he's not here.

MARLENE. I can see he's not here.

JOYCE. He moved out.

MARLENE. What? When did he? / Just recently?*

ANGIE. Didn't you know that? You don't know much.

JOYCE. *No, it must be three years ago. Don't be rude, Angie.

ANGIE. I'm not, am I Aunty? What else don't you know?

JOYCE. You was in America or somewhere. You sent a postcard.

ANGIE. I've got that in my room. It's the Grand Canyon. Do you want to see it? Shall I get it? I can get it for you.

MARLENE. Yes, all right.

ANGIE *goes.*

JOYCE. You could be married with twins for all I know. You must have affairs and break up and I don't need to know about any of that so I don't see what the fuss is about.

MARLENE. What fuss?

ANGIE *comes back with the postcard.*

ANGIE. 'Driving across the states for a new job in L.A. It's a long way but the car goes very fast. It's very hot. Wish you were here. Love from Aunty Marlene.'

JOYCE. Did you make a lot of money?

MARLENE. I spent a lot.

ANGIE. I want to go to America. Will you take me?

JOYCE. She's not going to America, she's been to America, stupid.

ANGIE. She might go again, stupid. It's not something you do once. People who go keep going all the time, back and forth on jets. They go on Concorde and Laker and get jet lag. Will you take me?

MARLENE. I'm not planning a trip.

ANGIE. Will you let me know?

JOYCE. Angie, / you're getting silly.

ANGIE. I want to be American.

JOYCE. It's time you were in bed.

ANGIE. No it's not. / I don't have to go to bed at all tonight.

JOYCE. School in the morning.

ANGIE. I'll wake up.

JOYCE. Come on now, you know how you get.

ANGIE. How do I get? / I don't get anyhow.

JOYCE. Angie.
       Are you staying the night?

MARLENE. Yes, if that's all right. / I'll see you in the morning.

ANGIE. You can have my bed. I'll sleep on the sofa.

JOYCE. You will not, you'll sleep in your bed. / Think I can't

ANGIE. Mum.

JOYCE. see through that? I can just see you going to sleep / with us talking.

ANGIE. I would, I would go to sleep, I'd love that.

JOYCE. I'm going to get cross, Angie.

ANGIE. I want to show her something.

JOYCE. Then bed.

ANGIE. It's a secret.

JOYCE. Then I expect it's in your room so off you go. Give us a shout when you're ready for bed and your aunty'll be up and see you.

ANGIE. Will you?

MARLENE. Yes of course.

> ANGIE *goes.*
> Silence.

It's cold tonight.

JOYCE. Will you be all right on the sofa? You can / have my bed.

MARLENE. The sofa's fine.

JOYCE. Yes the forecast said rain tonight but it's held off.

MARLENE. I was going to walk down to the estuary but I've left it a bit late. Is it just the same?

JOYCE. They cut down the hedges a few years back. Is that since you were here?

MARLENE. But it's not changed down the end, all the mud? And the reeds? We used to pick them when they were bigger than us. Are there still lapwings?

JOYCE. You get strangers walking there on a Sunday. I expect they're looking at the mud and the lapwings, yes.

MARLENE. You could have left.

JOYCE. Who says I wanted to leave?

MARLENE. Stop getting at me then, you're really boring.

JOYCE. How could I have left?

MARLENE. Did you want to?

JOYCE. I said how, / how could I?

MARLENE. If you'd wanted to you'd have done it.

JOYCE. Christ.

MARLENE. Are we getting drunk?

JOYCE. Do you want something to eat?

MARLENE. No, I'm getting drunk.

JOYCE. Funny time to visit, Sunday evening.

MARLENE. I came this morning. I spent the day.

ANGIE (*off*). Aunty! Aunty Marlene!

MARLENE. I'd better go.

JOYCE. Go on then.

MARLENE. All right.

ANGIE (*off*). Aunty! Can you hear me? I'm ready.

MARLENE *goes*.

JOYCE *goes on sitting*.

MARLENE *comes back*.

JOYCE. So what's the secret?

MARLENE. It's a secret.

JOYCE. I know what it is anyway.

MARLENE. I bet you don't. You always said that.

JOYCE. It's her exercise book.

MARLENE. Yes, but you don't know what's in it.

JOYCE. It's some game, some secret society she has with Kit.

MARLENE. You don't know the password. You don't know the code.

JOYCE. You're really in it, aren't you. Can you do the handshake?

MARLENE. She didn't mention a handshake.

JOYCE. I thought they'd have a special handshake. She spends hours writing that but she's useless at school. She copies things out of books about black magic, and politicians out of the paper. It's a bit childish.

MARLENE. I think it's a plot to take over the world.

JOYCE. She's been in the remedial class the last two years.

MARLENE. I came up this morning and spent the day in Ipswich.

I went to see mother.

JOYCE. Did she recognise you?

MARLENE. Are you trying to be funny?

JOYCE. No, she does wander.

MARLENE. She wasn't wandering at all, she was very lucid thank you.

JOYCE. You were very lucky then.

MARLENE. Fucking awful life she's had.

JOYCE. Don't tell me.

MARLENE. Fucking waste.

JOYCE. Don't talk to me.

MARLENE. Why shouldn't I talk? Why shouldn't I talk to you? / Isn't she my mother too?

JOYCE. Look, you've left, you've gone away, / we can do without you.

MARLENE. I left home, so what, I left home. People do leave home / it is normal.

JOYCE. We understand that, we can do without you.

MARLENE. We weren't happy. Were you happy?

JOYCE. Don't come back.

MARLENE. So it's just your mother is it, your child, you never wanted me round, / you were jealous of me because I was the

JOYCE. Here we go.

MARLENE. little one and I was clever.

JOYCE. I'm not clever enough for all this psychology / if that's what it is.

MARLENE. Why can't I visit my own family / without all this?*

JOYCE. Aah.
     Just don't go on about Mum's life when you have'nt been to see her for how many years. / I go and see her every week.

MARLENE. It's up to me.
     *Then don't go and see her every week.

JOYCE. Somebody has to.

MARLENE. No they don't. / Why do they?

JOYCE. How would I feel if I didn't go?

MARLENE. A lot better.

JOYCE. I hope you feel better.

MARLENE. It's up to me.

JOYCE. You couldn't get out of here fast enough.

MARLENE. Of course I couldn't get out of here fast enough.
    What was I going to do? Marry a dairyman who'd come home
    pissed? / Don't you fucking this fucking that fucking bitch

JOYCE. Christ.

MARLENE. fucking tell me what to fucking do fucking.

JOYCE. I don't know how you could leave your own child.

MARLENE. You were quick enough to take her.

JOYCE. What does that mean?

MARLENE. You were quick enough to take her.

JOYCE. Or what? Have her put in a home? Have some stranger /
    take her would you rather?

MARLENE. You couldn't have one so you took mine.

JOYCE. I didn't know that then.

MARLENE. Like hell, / married three years.

JOYCE. I didn't know that. Plenty of people / take that long.

MARLENE. Well it turned out lucky for you, didn't it?

JOYCE. Turned out all right for you by the look of you. You'd
    be getting a few less thousand a year.

MARLENE. Not necessarily.

JOYCE. You'd be stuck here / like you said.

MARLENE. I could have taken her with me.

JOYCE. You didn't want to take her with you. It's no good
    coming back now, Marlene, / and saying —

MARLENE. I know a managing director who's got two children, she breast feeds in the board room, she pays a hundred pounds a week on domestic help alone and she can afford that because she's an extremely high-powered lady earning a great deal of money.

JOYCE. So what's that got to do with you at the age of seventeen?

MARLENE. Just because you were married and had somewhere to live —

JOYCE. You could have lived at home. / Or live with me

MARLENE. Don't be stupid.

JOYCE. and Frank. / You said you weren't keeping it. You

MARLENE. You never suggested.

JOYCE. shouldn't have had it / if you wasn't going to keep it.

MARLENE. Here we go.

JOYCE. You was the most stupid, / for someone so clever you was the most stupid, get yourself pregnant, not go to the doctor, not tell.

MARLENE. You wanted it, you said you were glad, I remember the day, you said I'm glad you never got rid of it, I'll look after it, you said that down by the river. So what are you saying, sunshine, you don't want her?

JOYCE. Course I'm not saying that.

MARLENE. Because I'll take her, / wake her up and pack now.

JOYCE. You wouldn't know how to begin to look after her.

MARLENE. Don't you want her?

JOYCE. Course I do, she's my child.

MARLENE. Then what are you going on about / why did I have her?

JOYCE. You said I got her off you / when you didn't —

MARLENE. I said you were lucky / the way it —

JOYCE. Have a child now if you want one. You're not old.

MARLENE. I might do.

JOYCE. Good.

Pause.

MARLENE. I've been on the pill so long / I'm probably sterile.

JOYCE. Listen when Angie was six months I did get pregnant and I lost it because I was so tired looking after your fucking baby / because she cried so much — yes I did tell

MARLENE. You never told me.

JOYCE. you — / and the doctor said if I'd sat down all day with

MARLENE. Well I forgot.

JOYCE. my feet up I'd've kept it / and that's the only chance I ever had because after that —

MARLENE. I've had two abortions, are you interested? Shall I tell you about them? Well I won't, it's boring, it wasn't a problem. I don't like messy talk about blood / and what a bad

JOYCE. If I hadn't had your baby. The doctor said.

MARLENE. time we all had. I don't want a baby. I don't want to talk about gynaecology.

JOYCE. Then stop trying to get Angie off of me.

MARLENE. I come down here after six years. All night you've been saying I don't come often enough. If I don't come for another six years she'll be twenty-one, will that be OK?

JOYCE. That'll be fine, yes, six years would suit me fine.

Pause.

MARLENE. I was afraid of this.
I only came because I thought you wanted . . .
I just want . . .

MARLENE *cries.*

JOYCE. Don't grizzle, Marlene, for God's sake.
Marly? Come on, pet. Love you really.
Fucking stop it, will you?

MARLENE. No, let me cry. I like it.

They laugh, MARLENE *begins to stop crying.*

I knew I'd cry if I wasn't careful.

JOYCE. Everyone's always crying in this house. Nobody takes any notice.

MARLENE. You've been wonderful looking after Angie.

JOYCE. Don't get carried away.

MARLENE. I can't write letters but I do think of you.

JOYCE. You're getting drunk. I'm going to make some tea.

MARLENE. Love you.

JOYCE *gets up to make tea.*

JOYCE. I can see why you'd want to leave. It's a dump here.

MARLENE. So what's this about you and Frank?

JOYCE. He was always carrying on, wasn't he? And if I wanted to go out in the evening he'd go mad, even if it was nothing, a class, I was going to go to an evening class. So he had this girlfriend, only twenty-two poor cow, and I said go on, off you go, hoppit. I don't think he even likes her.

MARLENE. So what about money?

JOYCE. I've always said I don't want your money.

MARLENE. No, does he send you money?

JOYCE. I've got four different cleaning jobs. Adds up. There's not a lot round here.

MARLENE. Does Angie miss him?

JOYCE. She doesn't say.

MARLENE. Does she see him?

JOYCE. He was never that fond of her to be honest.

MARLENE. He tried to kiss me once. When you were engaged.

JOYCE. Did you fancy him?

MARLENE. No, he looked like a fish.

JOYCE. He was lovely then.

MARLENE. Ugh.

JOYCE. Well I fancied him. For about three years.

MARLENE. Have you got someone else?

JOYCE. There's not a lot round here. Mind you, the minute you're on your own, you'd be amazed how your friends' husbands drop by. I'd sooner do without.

MARLENE. I don't see why you couldn't take my money.

JOYCE. I do, so don't bother about it.

MARLENE. Only got to ask.

JOYCE. So what about you? Good job?

MARLENE. Good for a laugh. / Got back from the US of A a bit

JOYCE. Good for more than a laugh I should think.

MARLENE. wiped out and slotted into this speedy employment agency and still there.

JOYCE. You can always find yourself work then.

MARLENE. That's right.

JOYCE. And men?

MARLENE. Oh there's always men.

JOYCE. No one special?

MARLENE. There's fellas who like to be seen with a high-flying lady. Shows they've got something really good in their pants. But they can't take the day to day. They're waiting for me to turn into the little woman. Or maybe I'm just horrible of course.

JOYCE. Who needs them?

MARLENE. Who needs them? Well I do. But I need adventures more. So on on into the sunset. I think the eighties are going to be stupendous.

JOYCE. Who for?

MARLENE. For me. / I think I'm going up up up.

JOYCE. Oh for you. Yes, I'm sure they will.

MARLENE. And for the country, come to that. Get the economy

back on its feet and whoosh. She's a tough lady, Maggie. I'd give her a job. / She just needs to hang in there. This country

JOYCE. You voted for them, did you?

MARLENE. needs to stop whining. / Monetarism is not stupid.

JOYCE. Drink your tea and shut up, pet.

MARLENE. It takes time, determination. No more slop. / And

JOYCE. Well I think they're filthy bastards.

MARLENE. who's got to drive it on? First woman prime minister. Terrifico. Aces. Right on. / You must admit. Certainly gets my vote.

JOYCE. What good's first woman if it's her? I suppose you'd have liked Hitler if he was a woman. Ms Hitler. Got a lot done, Hitlerina. / Great adventures.

MARLENE. Bosses still walking on the workers' faces? Still Dadda's little parrot? Haven't you learned to think for yourself? I believe in the individual. Look at me.

JOYCE. I am looking at you.

MARLENE. Come on, Joyce, we're not going to quarrel over politics.

JOYCE. We are though.

MARLENE. Forget I mentioned it. Not a word about the slimy unions will cross my lips.

Pause.

JOYCE. You say Mother had a wasted life.

MARLENE. Yes I do. Married to that bastard.

JOYCE. What sort of life did he have? / Working in the fields like

MARLENE. Violent life?

JOYCE. an animal. / Why wouldn't he want a drink?

MARLENE. Come off it.

JOYCE. You want a drink. He couldn't afford whisky.

MARLENE. I don't want to talk about him.

JOYCE. You started, I was talking about her. She had a rotten life because she had nothing. She went hungry.

MARLENE. She was hungry because he drank the money. / He used to hit her.

JOYCE. It's not all down to him. / Their lives were rubbish. They

MARLENE. She didn't hit him.

JOYCE. were treated like rubbish. He's dead and she'll die soon and what sort of life / did they have?

MARLENE. I saw him one night. I came down.

JOYCE. Do you think I didn't? / They didn't get to America and

MARLENE. I still have dreams.

JOYCE. drive across it in a fast car. / Bad nights, they had bad days.

MARLENE. America, America, you're jealous. / I had to get out,

JOYCE. Jealous?

MARLENE. I knew when I was thirteen, out of their house, out of them, never let that happen to me, / never let him, make my own way, out.

JOYCE. Jealous of what you've done, you're ashamed of me if I came to your office, your smart friends, wouldn't you, I'm ashamed of you, think of nothing but yourself, you've got on, nothing's changed for most people / has it?

MARLENE. I hate the working class / which is what you're going

JOYCE. Yes you do.

MARLENE. to go on about now, it doesn't exist any more, it means lazy and stupid. / I don't like the way they talk. I don't

JOYCE. Come on, now we're getting it.

MARLENE. like beer guts and football vomit and saucy tits / and brothers and sisters —

JOYCE. I spit when I see a Rolls Royce, scratch it with my ring / Mercedes it was.

MARLENE. Oh very mature —

JOYCE. I hate the cows I work for / and their dirty dishes with blanquette of fucking veau.

MARLENE. and I will not be pulled down to their level by a flying picket and I won't be sent to Siberia / or a loony bin

JOYCE. No, you'll be on a yacht, you'll be head of Coca-Cola and you wait, the eighties is going to be stupendous all right because we'll get you lot off our backs —

MARLENE. just because I'm original. And I support Reagan even if he is a lousy movie star because the reds are swarming up his map and I want to be free in a free world —

JOYCE. What? / What?

MARLENE. I know what I mean / by that — not shut up here.

JOYCE. So don't be round here when it happens because if someone's kicking you I'll just laugh.

Silence.

MARLENE. I don't mean anything personal. I don't believe in class. Anyone can do anything if they've got what it takes.

JOYCE. And if they haven't?

MARLENE. If they're stupid or lazy or frightened, I'm not going to help them get a job, why should I?

JOYCE. What about Angie?

MARLENE. What about Angie?

JOYCE. She's stupid, lazy and frightened, so what about her?

MARLENE. You run her down too much. She'll be all right.

JOYCE. I don't expect so, no. I expect her children will say what a wasted life she had. If she has children. Because nothing's changed and it won't with them in.

MARLENE. Them, them. / Us and them?

JOYCE. And you're one of them.

MARLENE. And you're us, wonderful us, and Angie's us / and Mum and Dad's us.

JOYCE. Yes, that's right, and you're them.

MARLENE. Come on, Joyce, what a night. You've got what it takes.

JOYCE. I know I have.

MARLENE. I didn't really mean all that.

JOYCE. I did.

MARLENE. But we're friends anyway.

JOYCE. I don't think so, no.

MARLENE. Well it's lovely to be out in the country. I really must make the effort to come more often.
I want to go to sleep.
I want to go to sleep.

JOYCE *gets blankets for the sofa.*

JOYCE. Goodnight then. I hope you'll be warm enough.

MARLENE. Goodnight. Joyce —

JOYCE. No, pet. Sorry.

JOYCE *goes.*

MARLENE *sits wrapped in a blanket and has another drink.*

ANGIE *comes in.*

ANGIE. Mum?

MARLENE. Angie? What's the matter?

ANGIE. Mum?

MARLENE. No, she's gone to bed. It's Aunty Marlene.

ANGIE. Frightening.

MARLENE. Did you have a bad dream? What happened in it?
Well you're awake now, aren't you pet?

ANGIE. Frightening.

Methuen Modern Plays

include work by

Jean Anouilh
John Arden
Margaretta D'Arcy
Brendan Behan
Edward Bond
Bertolt Brecht
Howard Brenton
Mikhail Bulgakov
Noel Coward
Shelagh Delaney
David Edgar
Michael Frayn
Max Frisch
Jean Giraudoux
Simon Gray
Peter Handke
Vaclav Havel
Kaufman & Hart
Barrie Keeffe
Arthur Kopit
John McGrath
David Mercer
Arthur Miller
Mtwa, Ngema & Simon
Peter Nichols
Joe Orton
Harold Pinter
Luigi Pirandello
Stephen Poliakoff
David Rudkin
Jean-Paul Sartre
Wole Soyinka
C.P. Taylor
Peter Whelan
Nigel Williams